Fedora Linux
System Administration

Install, manage, and secure your Fedora Linux environments

Alex Callejas

‹packt›

BIRMINGHAM—MUMBAI

Fedora Linux System Administration

Group Product Manager: Pavan Ramchandani
Publishing Product Manager: Neha Sharma
Senior Editor: Sayali Pingale
Technical Editor: Arjun Varma
Copy Editor: Safis Editing
Project Manager: Ashwin Kharwa
Proofreader: Safis Editing
Indexer: Manju Arasan
Production Designer: Vijay Kamble
Marketing Coordinators: Marylou De Mello and Shruthi Shetty

First published: November 2023

Production reference: 1271023

Published by Packt Publishing Ltd.
Grosvenor House
11 St Paul's Square
Birmingham
B3 1RB, UK

ISBN 978-1-80461-840-0

www.packtpub.com

To Mayra, my beloved sidekick and wife –

thank you for being there and being the right spark.

To Angel and Gael – never stop dreaming.

To Mom, Dad, and my brothers forever.

– Alex Callejas

Contributors

About the author

Alex Callejas is a services content architect at Red Hat, the world's leading provider of enterprise open source solutions, including Linux, the cloud, containers, and Kubernetes. He is based in Mexico City and is a free and open source software contributor. With more than 20 years of experience as a system administrator, he has strong expertise in infrastructure hardening and automation. An enthusiast of open source solutions, he supports the community by sharing his knowledge at different public-access and university events.

Geek by nature, Linux by choice, and Fedora of course.

About the reviewers

Ben Cotton has been active in Fedora and other open source communities for over a decade. His career has taken him through the public and private sector in roles that include desktop support, high-performance computing administration, marketing, and program management. Ben is the author of *Program Management for Open Source Projects*, and he has contributed to the book *Human at a Distance* and to articles for *The Next Platform*, Opensource.com, *Scientific Computing*, and others.

Jose "Kaz" Casimiro Rios has been working with Linux since 1994. He has been a jack-of-all-trades in the IT industry, covering roles as diverse as system administrator, DBA, developer, support engineer, and instructor. Kaz currently works for Red Hat as a systems design engineer for the Certification team, helping them with the building, development, and support for the certification exams.

I want to thank my wife for always bringing her support and understanding into my life. I'd also like to thank my cats for making my life fun every day.

Iván Chavero

Table of Contents

3

Tuning the Desktop Environment 73

4

Optimizing Storage Usage 109

5

Network and Connectivity 139

Part 3: Productivity Tools

6

Sandbox Applications   183

7

Text Editors   219

8

LibreOffice Suite   271

9

Mail Clients and Browsers   301

Part 4: System Administration Tools

10

System Administration   369

11

Performance Tuning Best Practices   429

12

Untangling Security with SELinux   475

13

Virtualization and Containers   491

Index   529

Other Books You May Enjoy   538

Preface

Linux system administration is a job that requires you to always be on the cutting edge. That is why you need to have the right tools to perform properly.

Fedora Linux, being a distribution based on the development of Red Hat Enterprise Linux, provides the tools that can help us with this task.

In this book, I will share with you how to use Fedora Linux as a workstation operating system to manage Linux systems.

Through advice, best practices, tips, and even some tricks based on my 20 years of experience as a system administrator, I will help you set up a workstation that allows you to optimize a system administrator's tasks.

Who this book is for

This book is for all those who want to start using Fedora Linux as a workstation to perform daily tasks as a system administrator. It will also help you learn how to optimize the distribution's tools for administration tasks.

You need to understand the basics of Linux and system administration, but extensive knowledge is not required.

This book provides a real-world context to use workstations for the most common system administration tasks.

What this book covers

Chapter 1, *Linux and Open Source Projects*, introduces the most popular open source projects and Linux distributions in use today, highlighting their main uses and differences.

Chapter 2, *Best Practices for Installation*, examines the best practices for installing Fedora Linux and optimizing its use as a workstation.

Chapter 3, *Tuning the Desktop Environment*, provides an overview of the different applets and plug-ins that enhance the usability of the working environment.

Chapter 4, *Optimizing Sorage Usage*, offers an analysis of the different types of local storage as well as their configurations to optimize performance.

Chapter 5, *Network and Connectivity*, provides an overview of network connectivity management as well as performance monitoring tools.

Chapter 6, *Sandbox Applications*, explores the use and configuration of desktop sandbox applications.

Chapter 7, *Text Editors*, summarizes the features of the most popular and widely used text editors included in Fedora Linux.

Chapter 8, *LibreOffice Suite*, offers an overview of the office tools of the LibreOffice suite and summarizes the main options for each application in the suite – Writer for word processing , Calc for spreadsheets, Impress for slides, and Draw for images.

Chapter 9, *Mail Clients and Browsers*, explores the internet productivity tools, mail clients, and browsers included in Fedora Linux, such as Evolution, Thunderbird, Firefox, and Google Chrome.

Chapter 10, *System Administration*, provides the basics of system administration, plus some useful tricks and shortcuts. It also looks at the basics of applying best practices.

Chapter 11, *Performance Tuning Best Practices*, explores the best practices for operating system tuning as a method of improving system administration performance.

Chapter 12, *SELinux*, introduces the basics of policy-based access control as a security enforcement module in Fedora Linux.

Chapter 13, *Virtualization and Containers*, offers an overview of the different Fedora Linux virtualization resources. It provides the basics of virtualization and the methods available in Fedora Linux – virtualization based on KVM/libvirt or containers with Podman.

To get the most out of this book

Although basic knowledge of Linux is required to administer systems, no in-depth knowledge is needed to follow the installation and configuration guides shown in each chapter.

Operating system	Download link
Fedora Linux workstation	`https://fedoraproject.org/workstation/download/`

If you are using the digital version of this book, we advise you to type the code yourself or access the code from the book's GitHub repository (a link is available in the next section). Doing so will help you avoid any potential errors related to the copying and pasting of code.

Download the example code files

You can download the example code files for this book from GitHub at `https://github.com/PacktPublishing/Fedora-Linux-System-Administration`. If there's an update to the code, it will be updated in the GitHub repository.

We also have other code bundles from our rich catalog of books and videos available at `https://github.com/PacktPublishing/`. Check them out!

Conventions used

There are a number of text conventions used throughout this book.

`Code in text`: Indicates code words in text, database table names, folder names, filenames, file extensions, pathnames, dummy URLs, user input, and Twitter handles. Here is an example: "Mount the downloaded `WebStorm-10*.dmg` disk image file as another disk in your system."

A block of code is set as follows:

```
for <variable> in <list>
do
command <variable>
done
```

When we wish to draw your attention to a particular part of a code block, the relevant lines or items are set in bold:

```
if <condition>;
then

<statement 1>
...
<statement n>
else
<statement alternative>
fi
```

Any command-line input or output is written as follows:

```
$ sudo grep -E 'svm|vmx' /proc/cpuinfo
$ sudo dnf install qemu-kvm virt-manager virt-viewer guestfstools
virt-install genisoimage
```

Bold: Indicates a new term, an important word, or words that you see on screen. For instance, words in menus or dialog boxes appear in **bold**. Here is an example: "Select **System info** from the **Administration** panel."

> **Tips or important notes**
> Appear like this.

Get in touch

Feedback from our readers is always welcome.

General feedback: If you have questions about any aspect of this book, email us at `customercare@packtpub.com` and mention the book title in the subject of your message.

Errata: Although we have taken every care to ensure the accuracy of our content, mistakes do happen. If you have found a mistake in this book, we would be grateful if you would report this to us. Please visit `www.packtpub.com/support/errata` and fill in the form.

Piracy: If you come across any illegal copies of our works in any form on the internet, we would be grateful if you would provide us with the location address or website name. Please contact us at `copyright@packtpub.com` with a link to the material.

If you are interested in becoming an author: If there is a topic that you have expertise in and you are interested in either writing or contributing to a book, please visit `authors.packtpub.com`.

Share Your Thoughts

Once you've read *Fedora Linux System Administration*, we'd love to hear your thoughts! Scan the QR code below to go straight to the Amazon review page for this book and share your feedback.

`https://packt.link/r/1804618403`

Your review is important to us and the tech community and will help us make sure we're delivering excellent quality content.

Download a free PDF copy of this book

Thanks for purchasing this book!

Do you like to read on the go but are unable to carry your print books everywhere? Is your eBook purchase not compatible with the device of your choice?

Don't worry, now with every Packt book you get a DRM-free PDF version of that book at no cost.

Read anywhere, any place, on any device. Search, copy, and paste code from your favorite technical books directly into your application.

The perks don't stop there, you can get exclusive access to discounts, newsletters, and great free content in your inbox daily

Follow these simple steps to get the benefits:

1. Scan the QR code or visit the link below

https://packt.link/free-ebook/978-1-80461-840-0

2. Submit your proof of purchase
3. That's it! We'll send your free PDF and other benefits to your email directly

Part 1:
The Fedora Project

This part introduces you to today's most popular open source projects and Linux distributions, highlighting their main uses and differences. It focuses on the benefits of the Fedora Project and how you can collaborate with it.

This part contains the following chapter:

- *Chapter 1, Linux and Open Source Projects*

1

Linux and Open Source Projects

System administration is a job that requires the right tools to achieve the required process optimization. To administrate GNU/Linux-based systems, you must have a workstation that facilitates this aforementioned optimization. A Linux workstation provides many advantages in this regard. In my experience, **Fedora Linux**, a *community-developed* distribution sponsored by **Red Hat**, has a recommended set of tools for Linux-based system administration.

Before learning how to configure a workstation for system administration, we'll review the history of this operating system so that we have a better context and, above all, know how we can help develop the distribution so that we can improve it.

In this chapter, we will learn a little more about the following:

- A brief history of Linux
- Understanding Linux distributions
- The Fedora Project
- The command-line interface
- Desktop environments

Let's get started!

A brief history of Linux

Before getting into the subject, I would like to provide a little background on the history of the operating system. As we know, the history of personal computing is somewhat short – only about 50 years, and, speaking of **GNU/Linux** in particular, a little less than that.

It was dark times at the end of the 1960s when *Ken Thompson* wrote the first version of **Unix** on a PDP-7 minicomputer based on Multics, composed of a kernel, a shell, an editor, and an assembler.

In 1970, the development of the operating system continued at AT&T Bell Labs. Now on a PDP-11 machine, *Brian Kernighan* suggested the name **Uniplexed Information & Computing Service (UNICS)**.

However, the BCPL and B languages that were used presented several implementation problems on the new platform. In 1972, *Denis Ritchie*, using both languages, developed a new high-level language, now known as the **C language**, adding data typing and other powerful functions. With that, the **Unix** system was born.

Software development for this platform continues, with important additions to the operating system. In 1976, *Richard Stallman*, a student at MIT, while working in a group that used free software exclusively, wrote the first version of **Emacs** in **Text Editor & Corrector** (**TECO**).

In the early 1980s, almost all software was proprietary because technology companies focused their efforts individually, without thinking about collaborative development. This led *Stallman* to create the **GNU Project** (meaning *GNU is not Unix*) in 1983, which pursued the creation of a free operating system that was based on Unix. This was because the general design was already proven and portable, bringing back the spirit of cooperativity that had prevailed in the computer community in earlier days.

Stallman started **GNU Emacs** by distributing the code for 150 USD. He then used this money to fund the creation of the **Free Software Foundation** in 1985. Emacs was distributed under the *Emacs General Public License*, which allowed it to be distributed and used freely while preserving its copyright and restricting him to preserve it even through modifications or additions to the code that could be made later.

Under this same concept, in 1989, the first version of the **GNU General Public License** (**GPL**) was released, extending the use and distribution of free software to all programming developments that adopted it as part of the GNU Project.

The second version of the license was published in 1991, with the main difference being that the license's obligations couldn't be separated due to conflicting obligations. This provision was intended to discourage any party from using a claim of patent infringement or other litigation to prejudice the freedom of users to use the earlier version.

In the same year, *Linus Torvalds*, a Finnish student, used Tanenbaum's 1987 book [Operating Systems: Design and Implementation], Bach's 1986 book [Design of the UNIX Operating System. Bach, Maurice J. Pearson Education. 1986], and the Jolitz articles [Porting UNIX to the 386: A Practical Approach. William Jolitz. Dr. Dobb's Journal, Volume 16, Issue 1, Jan. 1991. pp 16–46.], to port some basic tools to create a *(free) operating system … for 386(486) AT clones* as a hobby and asked for help on the Usenet group `comp.os.minix` (`https://groups.google.com/g/comp.os.minix/c/dlNtH7RRrGA/m/SwRavCzVE7gJ`), which became what we know today as **Linux**:

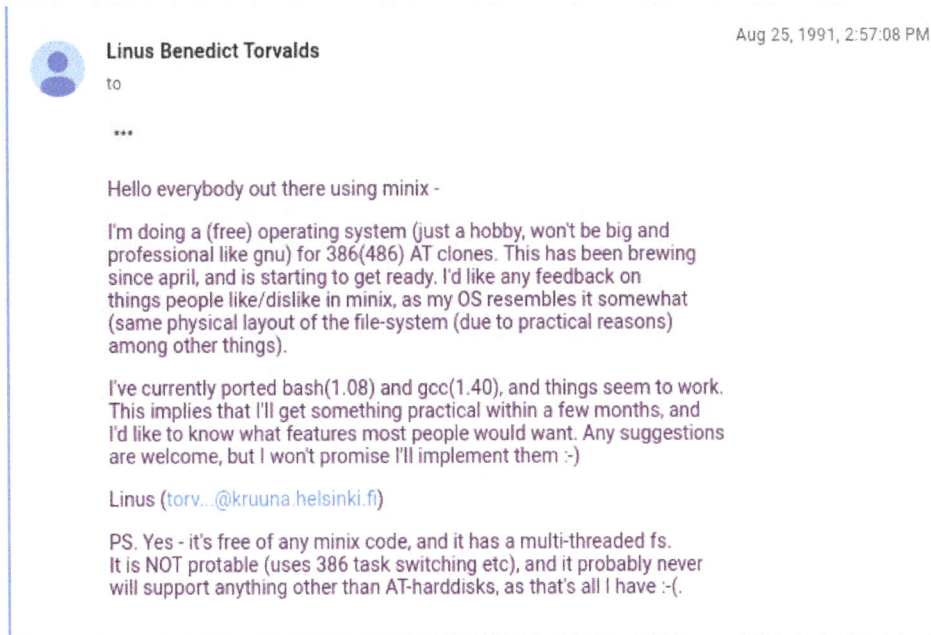

Figure 1.1 – Original post by Linus Torvalds in the Usenet group comp.os.minix

Linux was not always open source. The first Linux licenses prohibited commercial redistribution. It was with version **0.12**, released in early 1992, that the Linux kernel was released under the GPL. According to Linus Torvalds, open sourcing Linux was the best thing he ever did.

Inspired by the success of this effort, various new software development projects emerged to boost the newly created operating system. These developments provided new functionalities and tools that complemented and facilitated the use of Linux, besides expanding the use of the platform to different areas such as business and personal use.

The use of the GPL was the driving force behind the development based on the cooperative nature of the computing community.

This spirit of collaboration founded the basis of what we know today as Linux, but it took a push to make the fruits of these efforts reach everyone. This came with Linux distributions, known as distros.

Understanding Linux distributions

The **GNU Project** experienced some problems implementing the kernel it had officially developed. Known as **Hurd**, this kernel is a collection of protocols that formalizes how different components should interact with each other (`https://www.gnu.org/software/hurd/index.html`). The tools worked well but did not have the right cohesion to integrate with the operating system.

When Linus Torvalds released the Linux kernel, many enthusiastic developers ported the GNU code, including the compiler to run on it. These efforts filled in the remaining gaps to get a completely free operating system.

In 1992, Linux and the GNU Project joined forces (`http://laurel.datsi.fi.upm.es/~ssoo/IG/download/timeline.html`), and *Richard Stallman* urged to call it GNU/Linux since many of its tools were integrated from the GNU project. This led to the creation of new projects that integrated these GNU tools and the Linux kernel into what we know today as **Linux distributions**.

Distributions consist of the Linux kernel, the GNU tools, and a lot of other packages; many distributions also provide an installation system like that of other modern operating systems. Distributions are usually segmented into packages, some of which provide only the kernel binary, compilation tools, and an installer. Packages come as compiled code, with the installation and removal of packages handled by a **package management system** (**PMS**) rather than a simple file archiver.

Some distributions are even delivered as *embedded operating systems* on some devices, except for mobile distributions, which are based on **Android**. These distributions are created separately for mobile phones.

Throughout the years, there have been different GNU/Linux distribution projects, with the ones that have lasted over time being the most important. Besides that, they have led to the birth of new distributions, including the following:

- **Slackware**: Released in 1993, it was originally named **Softlanding Linux System** (**SLS**) and included the X Window System. It was the most complete distribution for a short period (1992). With the newest tools of the time, Slackware Linux offered both new and experienced users a full-featured system, suited for use for any need, as a desktop workstation or as a server. Web, FTP, and email services were ready to go out of the box, as was a wide selection of popular desktop environments. A full range of development tools, editors, and libraries was included for users wishing to develop or compile additional software. It was the first distribution to benefit from the work of millions of developers around the world.

- **Debian**: In 1993, *Ian Murdock*, disappointed with the poor maintenance and the prevalence of bugs in SLS (later known as *Slackware*), released what he initially called the *Debian Linux Release*. Debian is a *portmanteau* (a blend of words in which parts of several words are combined into a new word) of his then-girlfriend Debra Lynn's first name and his name. The stable branch of Debian is the most used in personal computers and servers. The release included the *Debian Linux Manifesto*, with Murdock's vision for his operating system, in which he called to keep it *"open in the spirit of Linux and GNU."* Debian releases are codenamed based on characters from the **Toy Story** movies. Debian is also the basis for many other distributions, with **Ubuntu** being the most notable of them. Debian uses dpkg (**Debian Package**) as a package management system, as well as its numerous derivations.

- **Red Hat**: Also in 1993, *Marc Ewing* was creating, debugging, and circulating his own Linux distribution on CD from his home in Raleigh, North Carolina. The name Red Hat came from his computer lab days in college; he always wore a red hat and users would say. "*If you need help, look for the guy in the red hat.*" Bob Young met him at a tech conference and started buying his CDs for resale due to the growing interest in Linux. In 1995, they joined forces to create Red Hat Software. Red Hat uses `rpm` (named **Red Hat Package Manager** initially; as it became popular among various Linux distributions, it changed to **RPM Package Manager**) as a package management system, as well as its numerous derivations.

Now, it is time to learn about the distribution we use, which has several interesting precepts.

The Fedora Project

Red Hat Linux was released every 6 months and was even available at Best Buy. After several releases, it began to have large enterprise customers, partly thanks to the monopoly lawsuit suffered by Microsoft around 2000, but it did not have a defined support cycle to meet these customers' needs. The company realized that they were trying to develop their product on two different fronts – on the one hand, looking for the stability required by the industry, while on the other hand, looking for innovation using the latest open source developments.

Thus, they opted to split their efforts into two fundamentally separate entities – **Red Hat Enterprise Linux** (**RHEL**) and the **Fedora Project** – each of which addressed its own problems as best it could.

For **RHEL**, the job was to make it a solid, stable platform that its customers and partners could count on for 5 to 7-year support cycles. Red Hat first offered an enterprise Linux support subscription for **Red Hat Linux 6.1**. This was not a standalone product; rather, the subscription offering was called **Red Hat 6.2E**. Subsequently, Red Hat began building a standalone product with commercial service-level agreements and a longer life cycle based on Red Hat Linux.

Fedora Linux is developed by the **Fedora Project** (originally named **Fedora.us**) and sponsored by Red Hat. It follows its own release schedule, with a new version every 6 months (in April and October). Fedora provides a modern Linux operating system that uses many of the latest technologies.

To create a new version of RHEL, most development happens in *upstream projects*. This new version is then integrated into Fedora Linux, with additional "productization" happening in CentOS Stream, which becomes RHEL.

This process, known as Red Hat's contribution path, is important to delve into to understand the distribution's development flow. It will also help us understand the importance of the distribution in that flow.

The Red Hat contribution path

In December 2020, Red Hat announced the discontinuation of the development of the **CentOS Project**, a project it had sponsored since 2014 and which, in its version 2 of 2004, was forked from **RHEL 2.1 AS**, which from that moment on was integrated as **CentOS Stream**, to the RHEL development contribution path.

The development of RHEL starts in community projects, where the latest and most innovative technologies in the industry are developed. Fedora's role is to take these technologies and adapt them in each new release of the distribution.

Every 3 years, a new major version of RHEL is released. When the next major release of RHEL is about 1 year away, these innovations reach an optimal level of development, fueled by feedback between **Fedora Project** developers and integrators and independent software and hardware vendors, providing the stability required by the industry. **CentOS Stream** then branches from **Fedora Linux**. The CentOS Stream code becomes the next release of RHEL, meaning that users can contribute to the product and test their workloads before it is released. This becomes a continuous integration of RHEL development, thus shortening the feedback loop that should be considered in future RHEL releases.

The following figure shows this flow:

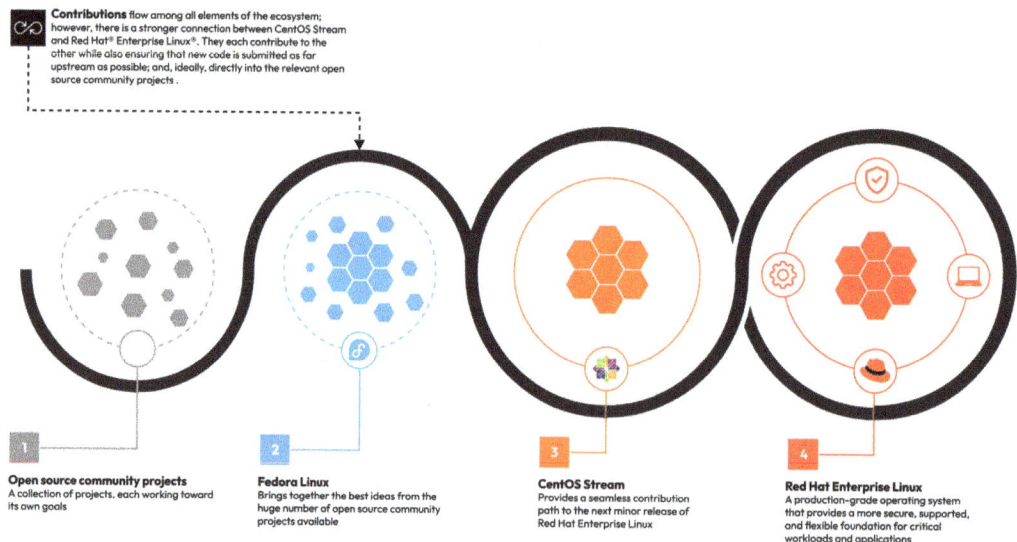

Figure 1.2 – The Red Hat contribution path

The role of **Fedora Linux** is essential in the development of RHEL, as described previously, but **Fedora Linux** is a usable operating system in its own right, with the most modern and innovative tools in the industry. As a side result, it is also widely used in enterprise environments to manage RHEL-based systems. This is due to the facilities provided by the Red Hat contribution path, described above.

Fedora's mission and foundations

The Fedora Project works to build a free and open source software platform that collaborates and shares end user-focused solutions.

Since the **Fedora community** includes thousands of individuals with different views and approaches, they base their cooperativeness on what they call the **four foundations**:

Figure 1.3 – The four foundations of Fedora

Let's look at them in detail:

- **Freedom**

  "We are dedicated to free software and content."

  (https://docs.fedoraproject.org/en-US/project/)

  The goal is to produce a usable operating system that includes only free software. Avoid proprietary or patented content and use free alternatives that allow you to provide a distribution that can bring the most innovative software to everyone so that anyone can use it, legally.

- **Friends**

  "We are a strong, caring community."

  (https://docs.fedoraproject.org/en-US/project/)

  The Fedora community is multidisciplinary and diverse with a common goal: pushing free software forward. Anyone who wants to help, regardless of their skills, can have a place in the community, a friendly and collaborative environment, so long as they believe in its core values.

- **Features**

  "We care about excellent software."

  (https://docs.fedoraproject.org/en-US/project/)

Many of the features that have empowered Linux come from the Fedora community, making it flexible and useful for many people around the world. The Fedora community is a fervent believer in free software development, whether it's used or not in the distribution. It allows features to be developed clearly and transparently, making them available to anyone who wants to take part in the distribution.

- **First**

  "*We are committed to innovation.*"

  (https://docs.fedoraproject.org/en-US/project/)

The Fedora Project offers the latest in stable and robust free software and is a platform that showcases the future of operating system usage. It advances such software to demonstrate collaborative technical progress. Fedora always thinks about providing for the future before anything else.

Besides these four foundations, the Fedora Project has a very clear vision and mission.

Vision

> "*The Fedora Project envisions a world where everyone benefits from free and open source software built by inclusive, welcoming, and open-minded communities.*"

(https://docs.fedoraproject.org/en-US/project/#_our_vision)

Fedora's vision follows the precepts of the GNU Project, where the benefit of using free and open source software extends to all those who need to use it, in a way that is inclusive of all communities and open to all possibilities.

Mission

> "*Fedora creates an innovative platform for hardware, clouds, and containers that enables software developers and community members to build tailored solutions for their users.*"

(https://docs.fedoraproject.org/en-US/project/#_our_mission)

Fedora's mission focuses on innovating and adapting technology on existing and future platforms for solutions that enhance the end user experience.

Contributing to the project

The Fedora community contributes to building and developing free and open source software and making advances of importance to the community in general. It quickly and regularly incorporates these advances into the distribution or even into other GNU/Linux distributions. Fedora integrates the free and open source approach and ease of use in the short term.

Software development not only involves programmers – it also requires designers, artists, writers, speakers, translators, system administrators, and others. Coordinating all this effort requires leadership throughout the community, which allows for decision-making without excessive dragging.

> **Important**
>
> You don't have to be a contributor to use **Fedora Linux**. In the following chapters, you will learn *how to use Fedora Linux for system administration*. But, if you want to contribute to the project, here's how!

The leadership of the project is provided by the **Fedora Council**, which is made up of eight positions, two of which are held by elected community contributors. Besides the council, there are several leadership groups:

- **Fedora Engineering Steering Committee** (**FESCo**): Manages the technical features of the Fedora distribution and specific implementations of the policy in the Fedora Project.
- **Fedora Mindshare Committee**: Represents leadership for user and contributor community growth and support.

Besides working groups, where various editions of the distribution are developed, such as **Workstation**, **Server**, **IoT**, **Cloud**, and **CoreOS**, some subprojects develop opportunity areas under the *Fedora model*. There are also other interest groups (**SIGs**) that are more informal, where they adopt a framework or lightweight desktop for the distribution.

Code of Conduct

Fedora aims for the best interaction between its collaborators and members of its community through a set of guidelines contained in a document known as the **Code of Conduct**, whose decisions are applied using all the information and context available in pursuit of having the best environment for its members. It does not intend to restrict expressions or penalize any member of the community; it only details the type of behavior that is considered acceptable or unacceptable.

> **Note**
>
> For the full Code of Conduct, refer to the Fedora Docs at `https://docs.fedoraproject.org/en-US/project/code-of-conduct/`.

Getting started with Fedora

To contribute to the Fedora Project, follow these steps:

1. The first step is to create a user account at `https://accounts.fedoraproject.org/`:

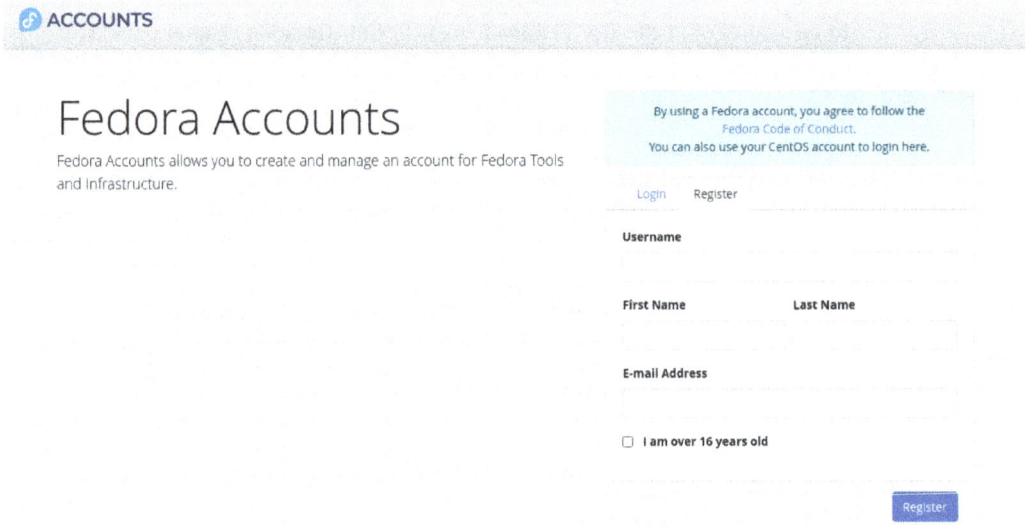

Figure 1.4 – Fedora Accounts

2. After filling out the registration form, the system will ask you to verify the registered email address:

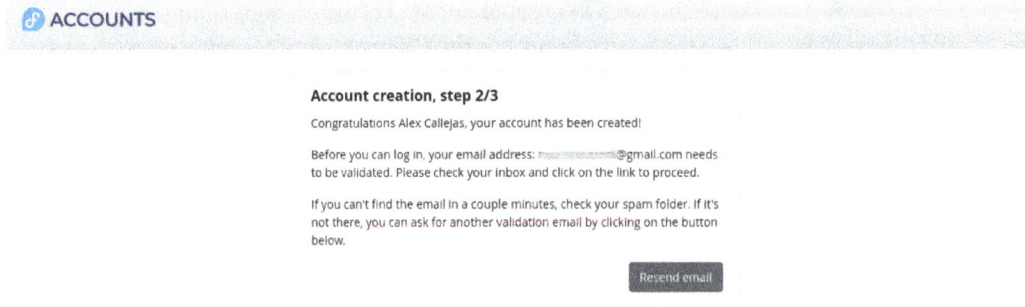

Figure 1.5 – Fedora Accounts – Account creation

3. Upon clicking on the link you received via mail, the system will ask you to create a password:

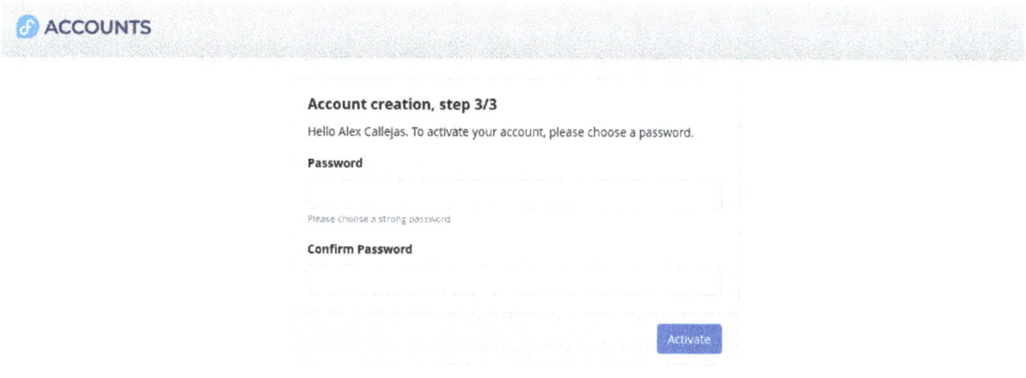

Figure 1.6 – Fedora Accounts – set password

4. Once you've accessed your profile, click on the **Agreements** tab to sign the **Fedora Project Contributor Agreement** document:

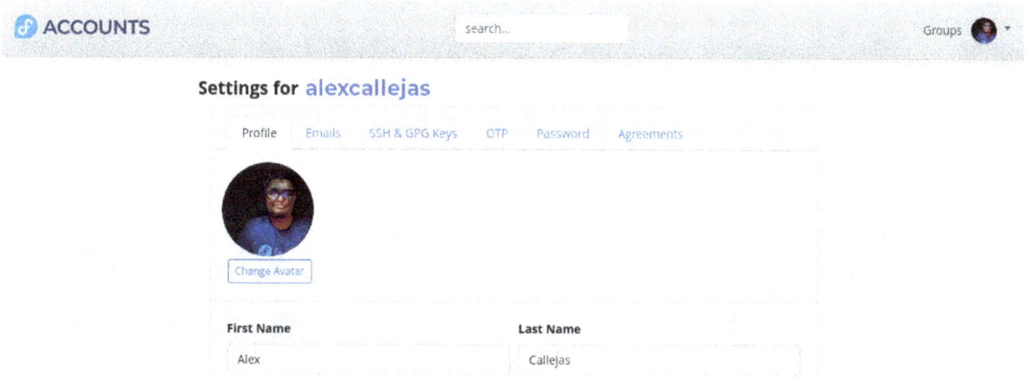

Figure 1.7 – Fedora Accounts – profile settings

5.　Click on the **Sign** button to sign the agreement:

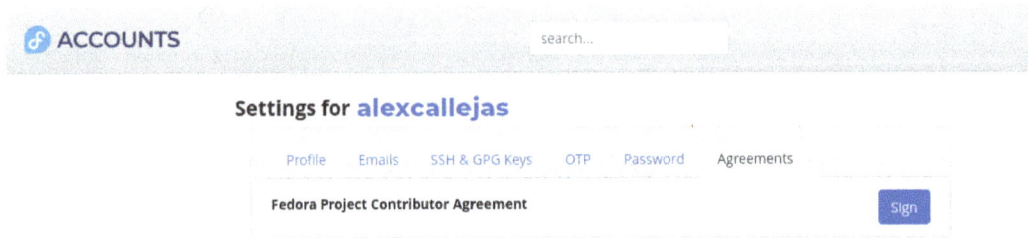

Figure 1.8 – Fedora Accounts – Fedora Project Contributor Agreement

After signing the agreement, continue to the profile configuration area and join a development or collaboration group of interest.

If needed, Fedora provides an online tool at `https://whatcanidoforfedora.org/` that guides you to the appropriate group(s) that match your interests, based on the questions you ask:

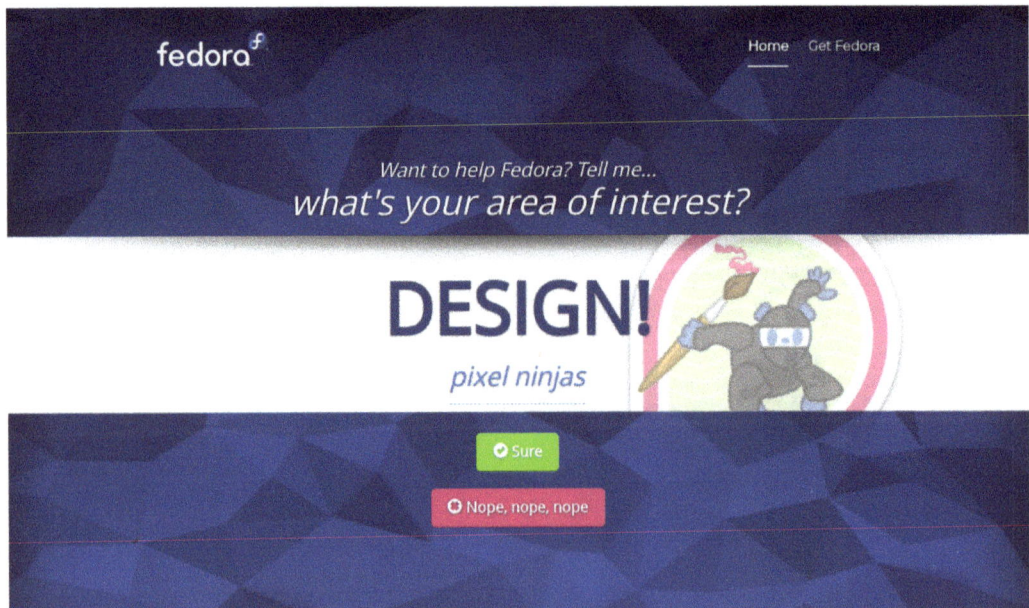

Figure 1.9 – What can I do for Fedora?

> **Note**
>
> This page, although very useful for a first approach, is already deprecated by the documentation of the project. For further reference, please refer to a group of interest (SIG) at `https://docs.fedoraproject.org/en-US/project/join/`.

Now that we know how to contribute to the Fedora project, let's learn how to use the distribution to administrate Linux-based systems.

Fedora as a system administration tool

Using **Fedora Linux** as the main distribution, in work or study, also supports the development of the Fedora Project, as an end user. You can contribute with feedback on the use of the tools and services included in the distribution, and also take advantage of these innovations to become more productive and efficient in day-to-day activities.

One of the most important activities in the IT industry is system administration, where the main responsibility is to maintain, configure, and ensure the reliable operation of computer systems, especially multi-user computers such as servers. The system administrator tries to ensure that the uptime, performance, resources, and security of the computers that are managed meet the needs of the users, without exceeding a set target budget during this process.

Managing Linux systems using a Linux workstation provides many advantages that lead to a high level of efficiency and productivity since, from the host operating system, you can automate tasks or perform functional tests based on an operating system, such as the one being managed.

Fedora, given its privileged position within the contributory development of RHEL, becomes a highly profitable tool in the administration of similar platforms, such as its variants (**CentOS Stream**, **Rocky**, and **AlmaLinux**), as well as any distribution that uses `rpm` packages.

At the same time, when using this approach for Linux system administration, it is possible to contribute to the development of the distribution since continuously testing the platform and its various packages and projects within it takes place here.

So, if you wish to use **Fedora Linux** to manage Linux-based systems, you could support the **Fedora Project** by reporting unexpected behaviors or contributing to the improvement of system performance. This includes making suggestions for new features. Before reporting a bug, it is recommended to consult the **Ask Fedora** website at `https://ask.fedoraproject.org/`, the community support forum, in case this unexpected behavior has occurred before:

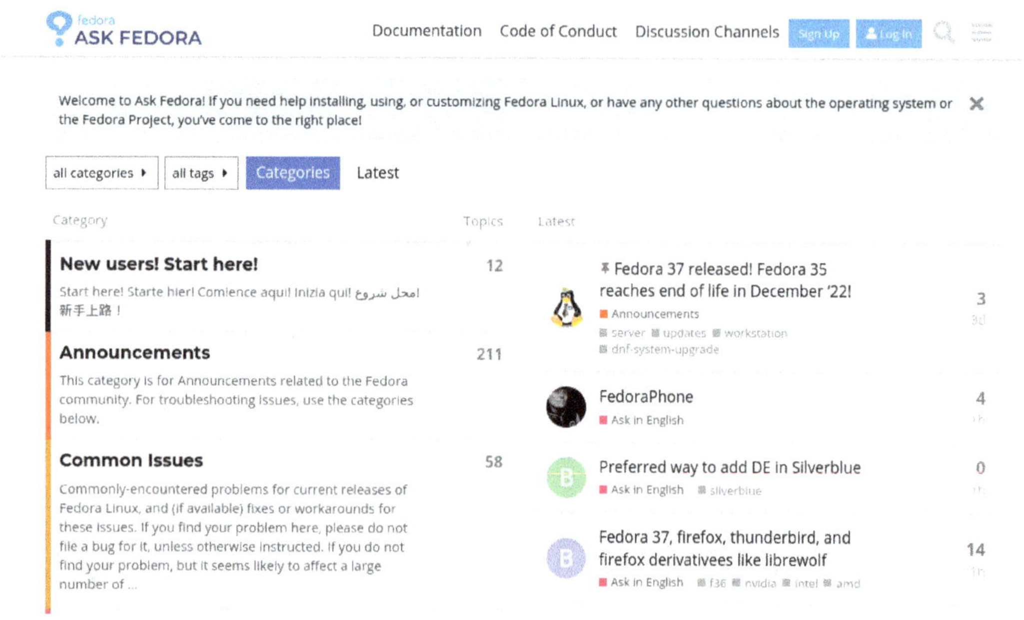

Figure 1.10 – Ask Fedora

> **Note**
>
> For more information on how to file a bug, refer to the Fedora Docs at `https://docs.fedoraproject.org/en-US/quick-docs/howto-file-a-bug/`.

Before we customize the distribution as our system administration workstation, let's review how to use our main tool.

The command-line interface

As the development of graphical user interfaces progressed, the use of the command line was often discarded. However, it is the main tool for operating system administration in general, whether it's for *system administrators* or *Advanced and Power users*. Apart from Linux-based systems, the CLI is also used on Windows or Mac systems. The use of the command line extends system management and administration capabilities.

Achieving the fluency necessary for maximum efficiency requires practice at every opportunity. Using Linux as a workstation allows us to practice this skill so that we can improve our productivity and efficiency when performing daily tasks.

The default command-line interpreter (shell) in **Fedora Linux** is **Bourne Again Shell** (**Bash**) and can be accessed through different Terminal emulators available with the distribution:

- `xterm`: This is the original terminal emulator program for the X Window System.
- `Konsole`: The terminal emulator program for the **Konsole Desktop Environment** (**KDE**).
- `gnome-terminal`: The terminal emulator program for the GNOME desktop environment.
- `Alacritty`: This is a lightweight, OpenGL-based terminal emulator program that focuses on performance.
- `yakuake` (`guake`): This is a drop-down terminal emulator program that can easily be accessed via a keyboard shortcut. `guake` is the version that's used for the GNOME desktop environment.
- `Terminator`: This is based on `gnome-terminal`. It provides multiple instances of the terminal emulator in a single window, generating a terminal console that fills the size of the screen area and divides it into a resizable grid.

Now that we know about the different terminal emulator options, let's dive into the topics that will help us get into system administration.

The basics

Practice is the only way to develop our console skills, but there is a path that can help with such improvement. This path consists of four sections with three levels each; following it as a guide while practicing should help you develop fluency in the console.

1. Ask the one who knows

Upon encountering an unexpected behavior or requiring a tool to make a task more efficient, it is a very common mistake to first look it up on the internet; it has even become a common term: *Google it*. But open source projects offer us reference material (that is, man and info pages) explaining the options, and, in most cases, the use of the packages, commands, processes, and services that follow it. The flow of information search is the first paradigm we have to break to develop efficiency as a system administrator.

Basic level

Use the built-in `help` command. If you do not know or remember how to use a command, use the built-in `help` module. To do so, add the `--help` or `-h` parameter or even run the command without parameters. The command may have one of these basic *help* options.

> **Note**
> Not all commands have a built-in help option. In some cases, they may offer one or two. Just test which one comes with the command. If not, use the next level.

Let's look at an example of each of them:

- A command run with the built-in `help` module:

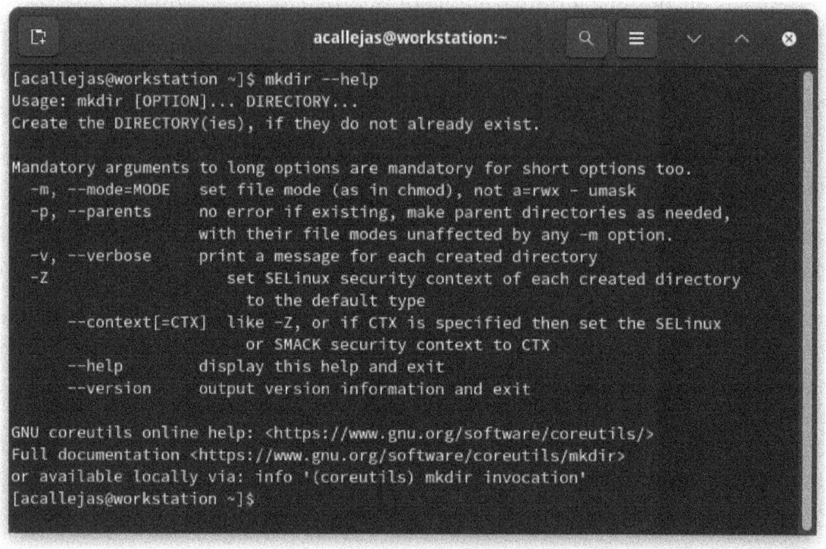

Figure 1.11 – Built-in help module

- A command run with the `-h` parameter:

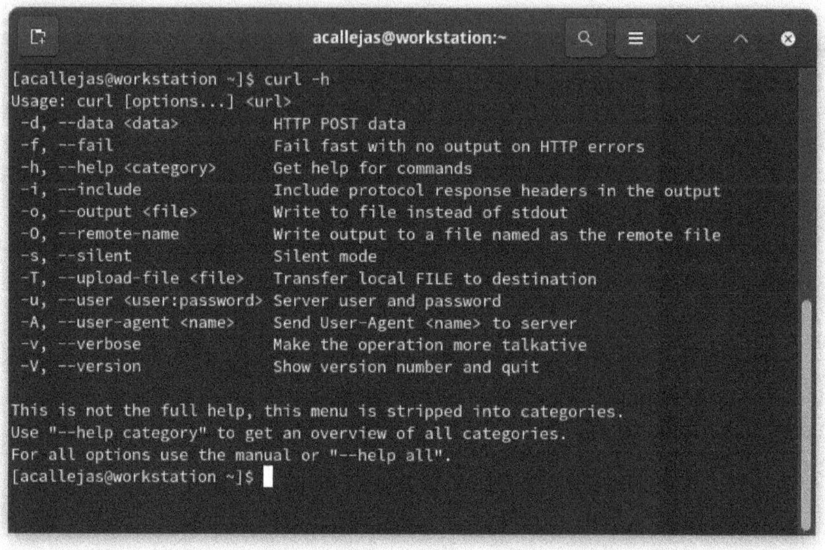

Figure 1.12 – Command run with the -h parameter

- A command run without parameters:

```
[acallejas@workstation ~]$ ssh
usage: ssh [-46AaCfGgKkMNnqsTtVvXxYy] [-B bind_interface]
           [-b bind_address] [-c cipher_spec] [-D [bind_address:]port]
           [-E log_file] [-e escape_char] [-F configfile] [-I pkcs11]
           [-i identity_file] [-J [user@]host[:port]] [-L address]
           [-l login_name] [-m mac_spec] [-O ctl_cmd] [-o option] [-p port]
           [-Q query_option] [-R address] [-S ctl_path] [-W host:port]
           [-w local_tun[:remote_tun]] destination [command [argument ...]]
[acallejas@workstation ~]$
```

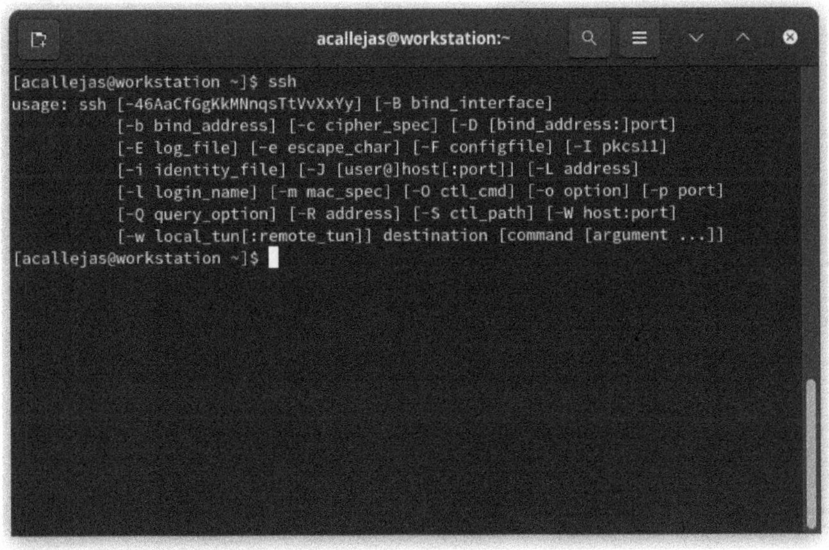

Figure 1.13 – Command run without parameters

These are the basic recommended options included in most of the commands. Now let's look at a more elaborate type of help. Unfortunately, sometimes it is not included as part of the package or requires a separate package to be installed to get this help. In each case, there is mention of it.

Intermediate level

man is your *friend*. Most of the commands, besides the built-in `help` command, come with a user manual, which details the use of each of the options and parameters that are available with it. To consult the manual, run the `man  <command>` command:

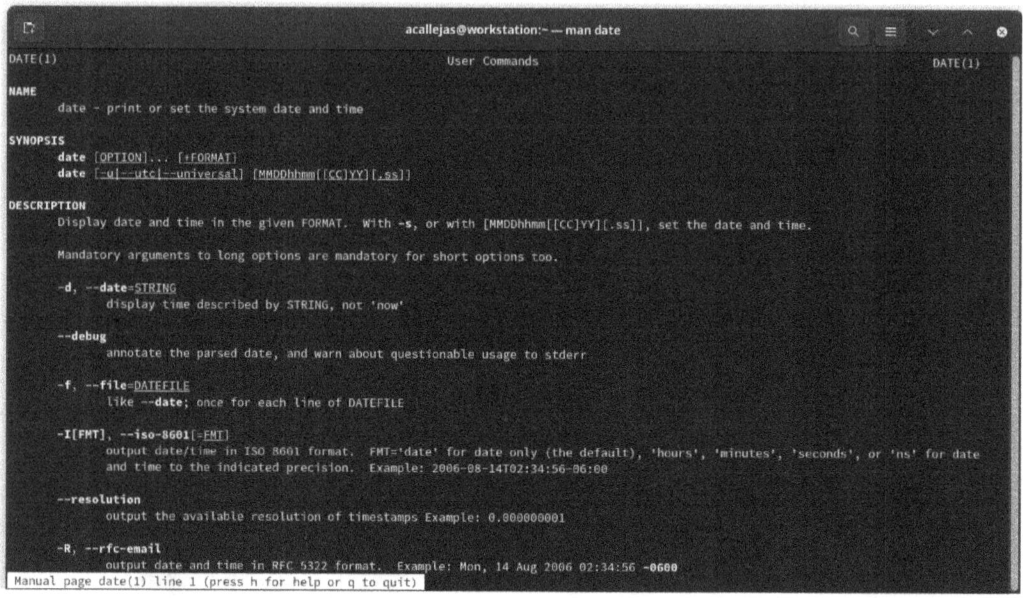

Figure 1.14 – Command user manual

In some cases, the commands may include *info pages*. These may reference the same man pages or, in some cases, have more detailed information on the usage and options of the command. To consult the info pages, run the info <command> command.

Advanced level

The operating system provides a directory where the documentation for packages and services resides – for example, in /usr/share/doc. You should consider installing the kernel documentation, which includes documentation for the drivers shipped with the kernel, and references to various configuration options. The kernel-doc package contains the kernel documentation for installing and running several tasks as a root user:

```
[root@workstation ~]# dnf -y install kernel-doc
...output omitted...


[root@workstation ~]# ls /usr/share/doc/kernel-doc-6.0.9-300/
Documentation/
ABI atomic_t.txt crypto  features  ia64  kernel-hacking memory-
barriers.txt
...output omitted...


[root@workstation ~]# cat \
> /usr/share/doc/kernel-doc-6.0.9-300/Documentation/networking/
bonding.rst
```

```
...output omitted...
Introduction
============

The Linux bonding driver provides a method for aggregating
multiple network interfaces into a single logical "bonded" interface.
The behavior of the bonded interfaces depends upon the mode; generally
speaking, modes provide either hot standby or load balancing services.
Additionally, link integrity monitoring may be performed.
...output omitted...
```

After exhausting the options that the operating system contains, you can access the different *online options*. The **community** is very helpful if you haven't found a suitable solution. To do so, you can access *mailing lists*, *telegram channels*, and *IRC* sites such as *Reddit*, *Stack Overflow*, or the ones provided by the **Fedora Project** itself, such as **Ask Fedora**. Using these options, you can get in touch with the community, which will always offer a helping hand.

2. Use the console

Having a Linux-based workstation brings with it the ability to use the console in all circumstances, even in your free time. The idea is to take advantage of any opportunity to use it to launch applications or tasks and reduce the use of the mouse and graphic solutions as much as possible.

The use of the console depends on the *privileges* of the users who use it. A privileged account is a user account that has more privileges than regular users. Privileged accounts can, for example, install or remove software, update the operating system, or change system or application settings. They might also have access to files that non-privileged users can't access.

The *command prompt* provides information on the privileges of the user using it.

If, upon opening the console, the prompt shows $, this means that the user is logged on to this system as a *non-privileged* user. The $ prompt is the default for normal users:

```
[user@workstation ~]$
```

The root user's prompt is #. Logging in as a root user can be done in two ways:

- By logging in with the root user's username and password

- By switching to the root user

This last point could involve the same username and password of the privileged user. Use the su – command to become the root user:

```
[user@workstation ~]$ su -
Password: [root password]
[root@workstation ~]#
```

Alternatively, we can use the sudo (*Super User DO*) command, which is a program that helps us provide privileges to normal users.

Most Linux distributions have sudo installed by default. In some cases, even root access is turned off. When this happens, we can only access it through the sudo command.

While installing the operating system, when creating the user, we can choose to add them as part of the *system administration group*. This will allow them to switch to the root user by using the sudo command and their *own* password.

To find out if your user has access to different privileges with sudo, run the following code:

```
[user@workstation ~]$ sudo -l
Password: [user password]
Matching Defaults entries for user on workstation:
...output omitted...

User user may run the following commands on workstation:
    (ALL) PASSWD: ALL
...output omitted...
```

(ALL) PASSWD: ALL indicates that the user can gain access to any command of the operating system by using the sudo command and their password. To switch to the root user, run the following code:

```
[user@workstation ~]$ sudo -i
Password: [user password]
[root@workstation ~]#
```

So, now that we know how to use the console, depending on our activities and privileges, let's learn how to improve our console skills.

Basic level

Just use it. Type as much as you can to list, search for, and open applications.

Intermediate level

Chain, redirect, and concatenate. After typing commands and understanding the result of their output, we can start playing with them and put them together in such a way that they simplify tasks. By using pipes (|) and redirecting the output and input with > and <, we can generate a string of commands that we know as *one-liners*. **Bash-one-liners** are famous in the computer world, and it is even considered an art to be able to chain commands for certain tasks. There are many internet sites and even social networks where we can find them. Some of them use such redirection to interpret pattern processing written in the *AWK programming language* as output.

Example: Send the output of the following command to a new file:

```
[user@workstation ~]$ ip link show > link.txt
[user@workstation ~]$ cat link.txt
1: lo: <LOOPBACK,UP,LOWER_UP> mtu 65536 qdisc noqueue state UNKNOWN
mode DEFAULT group default qlen 1000
    link/loopback 00:00:00:00:00:00 brd 00:00:00:00:00:00
2: enp1s0: <BROADCAST,MULTICAST,UP,LOWER_UP> mtu 1500 qdisc fq_codel
state UP mode DEFAULT group default qlen 1000
    link/ether 52:54:00:f9:69:14 brd ff:ff:ff:ff:ff:ff
```

Example: Get the open and listening TCP ports and the processes related to them, separated by commas:

```
[root@workstation ~]# ss -tulpn | grep tcp | awk '{ print
$1","$2","$5","$7 }'
tcp,LISTEN,0.0.0.0:22,users:(("sshd",pid=844,fd=3))
tcp,LISTEN,127.0.0.54:53,users:(("systemd-resolve",pid=707,fd=19))
tcp,LISTEN,0.0.0.0:5355,users:(("systemd-resolve",pid=707,fd=11))
tcp,LISTEN,127.0.0.1:6010,users:(("sshd",pid=1514,fd=9))
tcp,LISTEN,127.0.0.53%lo:53,users:(("systemd-resolve",pid=707,fd=17))
tcp,LISTEN,127.0.0.1:631,users:(("cupsd",pid=842,fd=7))
tcp,LISTEN,[::]:22,users:(("sshd",pid=844,fd=4))
tcp,LISTEN,[::]:5355,users:(("systemd-resolve",pid=707,fd=13))
tcp,LISTEN,[::1]:6010,users:(("sshd",pid=1514,fd=8))
tcp,LISTEN,[::1]:631,users:(("cupsd",pid=842,fd=6))
```

Advanced level

If you typed it twice, you should have scripted it once.

In system administration, it is very common for tasks to become repetitive. The first step in automating them, and with this, reducing the time taken to perform them, is to put them together and turn them into a series of instructions, known as a **shell script**. This script or series of instructions can contain the commands to run complex tasks, such as using outputs as variable settings and reusing them in the same execution.

There is a lot of documentation on how to create shell scripts. They should have a structure similar to the following:

```
#!/bin/bash ← [1]
#
# IDENTITY ← [2]
#

# VARIABLES ← [3]

# COMMANDS ← [4]
```

Let's look at what the highlighted text indicates in each section:

- [1]: *Shebang*. This indicates the command-line interpreter that uses the instructions; the functional tests of the script must confirm its use.
- [2]: The script must contain identification information – what it works for, who the author is, what version is being used, and even the date of creation and the changes it has undergone. This documentation will help you use it and identify its scope.
- [3]: In this section, the variables used to execute the instructions are set.
- [4]: In this section, you will find the instructions that will be executed.

3. Edit text files

On Linux, *everything is a file*. Thus, we must use a text editor to help us perform configuration or administration tasks. Knowing about the editor of choice in more depth helps make this activity more efficient, especially if some of them have specialized add-ons or plugins for cases such as identifying or validating syntax in files written in diverse programming languages or formats.

Basic level

GNU Nano is a simple, lightweight, open source command-line text editor written in C. Developed as part of the GNU Project, it emulates the Pico text editor, part of the Pine mail client:

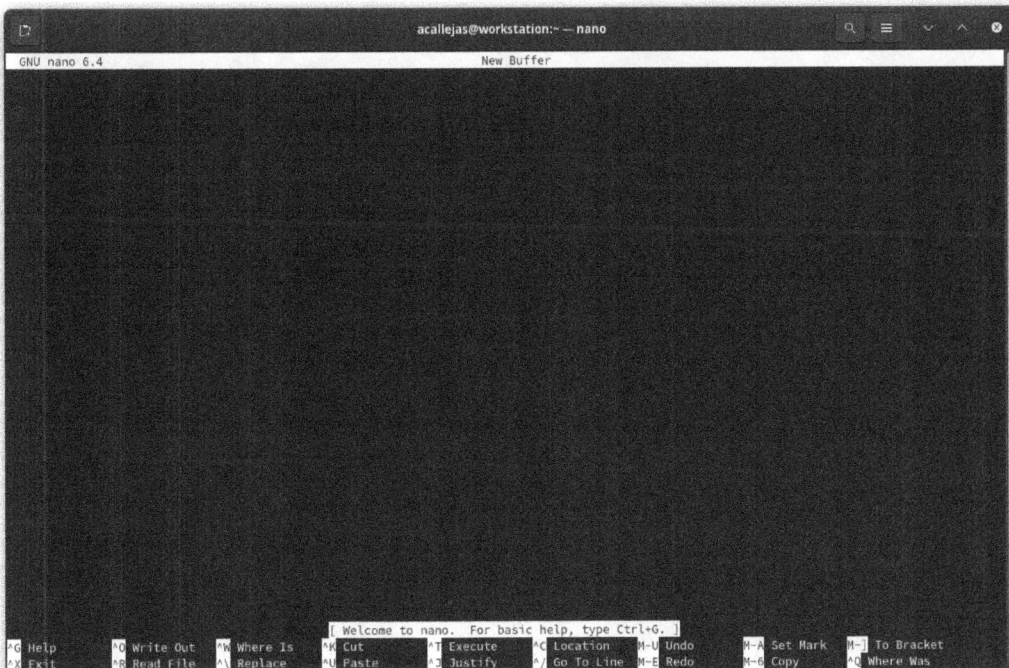

Figure 1.15 – The Nano editor

GNU Nano does not have many add-ons, but it does have built-in features, such as one to highlight different programming languages.

Intermediate level

Vim is an open source command-line text editor (licensed under its *charityware* license), written in C and with a scripting language called Vim (or VimL). It was developed in the 1970s as the *visual mode* (vi, its base) of the ex line editor. The original vi was a modal text editor that had no syntax highlighting, was written in C, and had only a command-line interface. Later, in the 1980s, vim was released as a clone of the vi text editor for personal computers, ported as **Vi IMproved (Vim)**. Eventually, Vim got a graphical user interface (along with a CLI) called gVim, syntax highlighting, a scripting language (to customize and extend it), and support for many more computer platforms:

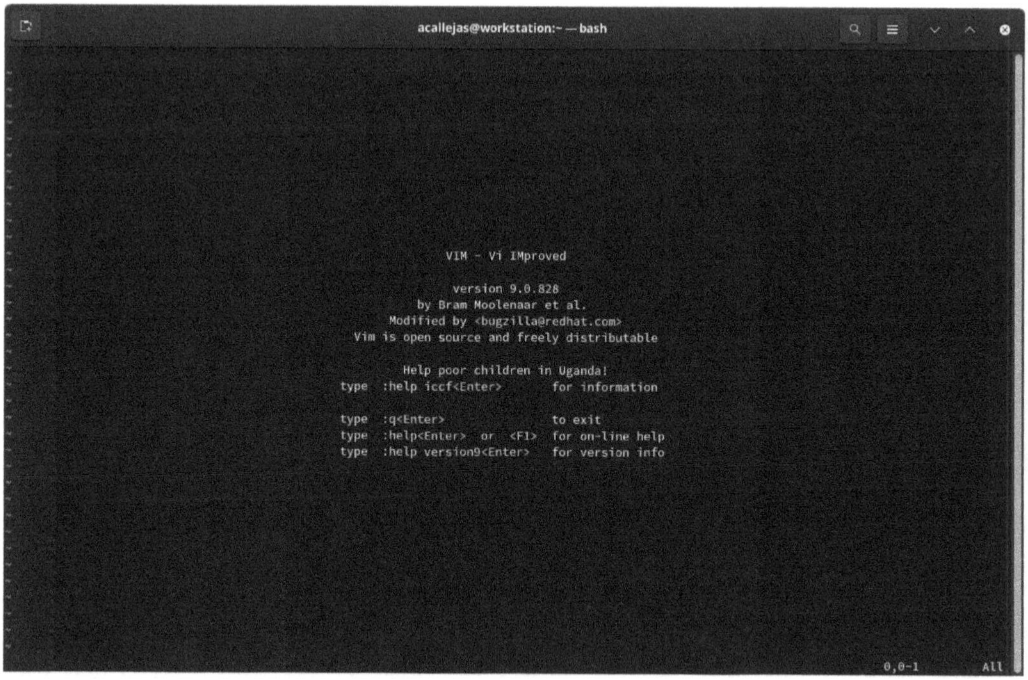

Figure 1.16 – The Vim editor

`vim` has many add-ons and plugins to enhance its use. It is even possible to create special add-ons for specific or special needs.

Advanced level

GNU Emacs is a free, open source, extensible, self-documenting text editor written in `C` and its own `Lisp` programming language (`Emacs Lisp`). It was developed by *Richard Stallman* and *Guy L. Steele Jr.*. Its initial release was in 1985 and it has been ported to all major operating systems. Developed as part of the GNU Project, its use is extended through plugins written in `Emacs Lisp`, which are available in the official Fedora repositories. It also runs on Fedora via an **AppImage** package (sandboxed application):

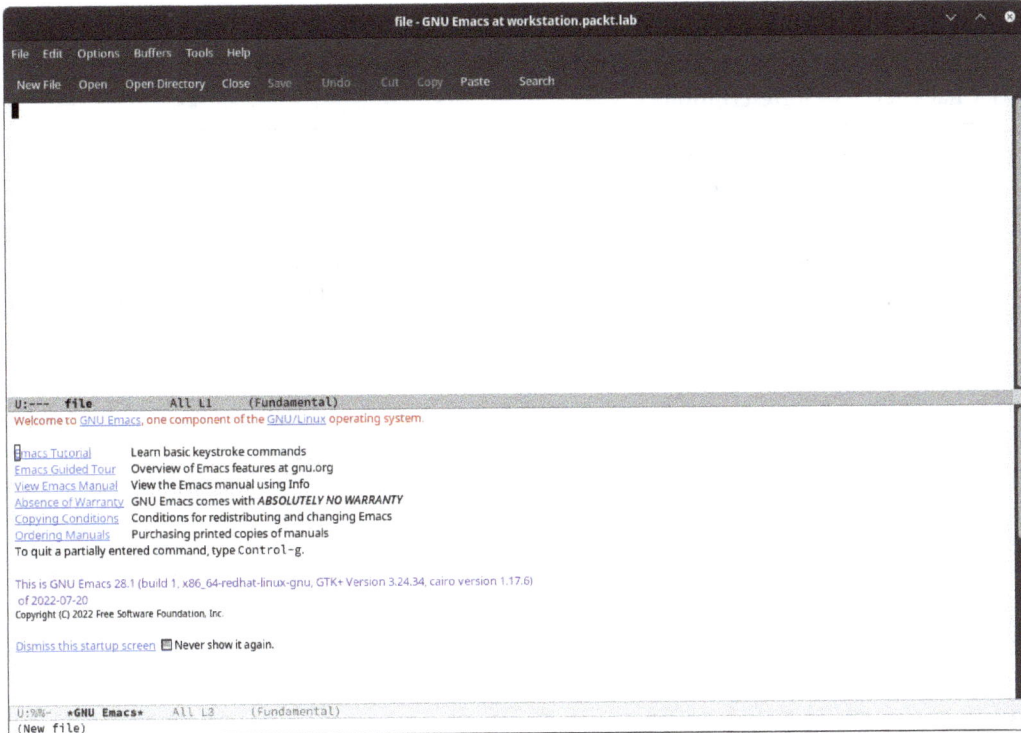

Figure 1.17 – The GNU Emacs editor

4. Handle regular expressions

The bash command interpreter has many ways to handle regular expressions, which it does by expanding the power of the command line.

Basic level

At a basic level, it is important to use pattern matching (wildcards), loops, and exit codes. With **wildcards**, it is easier to handle many files. By using metacharacters as wildcards that expand to match the filenames and paths searched for, commands act on one set of files at a time.

The following table shows the characters that are used as wildcards in terms of basic usage:

Character	Description
*	Matches any number of characters – for example, list all `.txt` files in a directory: `$ ls *.txt`

?	Matches any single character – for example, list the `.sh` files that start with the `compar` string:
	
	`$ ls compar*.sh`
	
	`compare.sh`

[ ]	Matches one of the characters between the brackets – for example, list files in a directory and filter out files starting with letters:
	
	`$ ls | grep ^[a-z]`
	
	`compare.sh`
	
	`conkyrc`
	
	`labkey`
	
	`labkey.pub`

{ }	Contains a comma-separated list of strings or a sequence. If so, use double-dot syntax. An example is to create five empty files and list them:
	
	`$ touch file{1..5}`
	`$ ls file?`
	`file1   file2   file3   file4   file5`

~	Match the current user's home directory – for example, list the `Downloads` directory in the user's home directory: `$ ls ~/Downloads/`

$	Denotes a string as a variable – for example, print the user's `PATH` variable on the screen:
	
	`$ echo $PATH`
	`/home/user/.local/bin:/home/user/bin::/usr/local/bin:/usr/local/sbin:/usr/bin:/usr/sbin`

Loops help us perform repetitive tasks simply. In Bash, a `for` loop is built from the following syntax:

```
for <variable> in <list>
do
command <variable>
done
```

You could add a condition to these loops so that they run different actions, depending on the situation:

```
if <condition>;
    then
        <statement 1>
        ...
        <statement n>
    else
        <statement alternative>
fi
```

Running a script provides an output and passes control to the calling process. The script may exit before finishing if it encounters an error condition, for example. The `exit` command shown in the following code, with an optional argument between 0 and 255, represents an **exit code**:

```
[user@workstation ~]$ cat test.sh
#!/bin/bash
echo "Hello, I'm a test"
exit 0
[user@workstation ~]$ ./test.sh
Hello, I'm a test
[user@workstation ~]$ echo $?
0
```

In the output, the exit code's value of 0 indicates that the script ran successfully with no errors; any other value indicates an error output.

Intermediate level

Regular expressions provide a *pattern-matching* mechanism that helps you search for specific content. The `grep`, `less`, and `vim` commands support regular expressions in their use. Most programming languages also support them, although the syntax in each may differ. As mentioned previously, these commands can be chained and converted into a search for more complex structures.

At the end of this section, you will find a guided example that better illustrates this level.

Advanced level

Write scripts with regular expressions and patterns in an optimized way.

Be careful when handling regular expressions within scripts since chained commands use a certain amount of memory and CPU processing that should not be underestimated. The battery and functional testing phase should be planned carefully and never on a productive server; at this point, it is highly profitable to have a Linux workstation to manage our servers. We can recreate the production environment in an instance based on a local virtual machine and perform the first functional tests of our *super-script*.

"*This is the way.*"

"*Patience, young Padawan.*"

It may seem a very laborious journey, but it is not. A lot of it depends on practice, incorporating the characteristics mentioned, and thus, developing the necessary skills. It is not a matter of 1 day of practice – it requires effort and dedication, so you must go one step at a time.

Next, we will perform a guided exercise where I will show, step by step, how to go from a simple command to a chained command with a defined purpose. This will show you how the tools shown below can be incorporated as the need arises.

Guided example – releasing space in the filesystem

Description: A ticket gets assigned to us because a managed server shows the root filesystem at 92% disk use. It is necessary to determine various responsibilities and provide evidence so that we can document the issue and resolve it so that we can close it.

Analysis: Since the server has no separate directories in the filesystems, it is necessary to determine which directory or directories have used the most disk space and identify which application or service it is relative to.

Solution:

1. As root, switch to the `root` directory (`/`) and list the available directories:

    ```
    [root@workstation ~]# cd /
    [root@workstation /]# ls
    afs  bin  boot  dev  etc  home  lib  lib64  lost+found  media
    mnt  opt  proc  root  run  sbin  srv  sys  tmp  usr  var
    ```

2. Run the following command to list the directories. Use the `-l` parameter to run a long list and identify the directories only:

    ```
    [root@workstation /]# ls -l | grep ^d
    dr-xr-xr-x.   1 root root     0 Aug  9 08:27 afs
    ```

```
dr-xr-xr-x.    6 root root 4096 Nov 22 13:12 boot
drwxr-xr-x.   21 root root 4000 Nov 22 13:12 dev
drwxr-xr-x.    1 root root 5186 Nov 22 13:12 etc
drwxr-xr-x.    1 root root   18 Nov 21 21:41 home
drwx------.    1 root root    0 Nov  5 02:18 lost+found
drwxr-xr-x.    1 root root    0 Aug  9 08:27 media
drwxr-xr-x.    1 root root    0 Aug  9 08:27 mnt
drwxr-xr-x.    1 root root    0 Aug  9 08:27 opt
dr-xr-xr-x. 329 root root    0 Nov 22 13:12 proc
dr-xr-x---.    1 root root  188 Nov 22 01:45 root
drwxr-xr-x.   58 root root 1580 Nov 22 13:14 run
drwxr-xr-x.    1 root root    0 Aug  9 08:27 srv
dr-xr-xr-x.   13 root root    0 Nov 22 13:12 sys
drwxrwxrwt.   20 root root  460 Nov 23 00:06 tmp
drwxr-xr-x.    1 root root  168 Nov  5 02:4.0 usr
drwxr-xr-x.    1 root root  200 Nov  5 03:15 var
```

3. Use awk to select only the names of the directories (column 9):

```
[root@workstation /]# ls -l | grep ^d | awk '{ print $9 }'
afs
boot
dev
etc
home
lost+found
media
mnt
opt
proc
root
run
srv
sys
tmp
usr
var
```

4. Determine the disk space used by each directory with the xargs and du commands:

```
[root@workstation /]# ls -l | grep ^d | awk '{ print $9 }' |
xargs du -sk
0       afs
293680      boot
0       dev
```

```
33212      etc
176728       home
0     lost+found
0     media
0     mnt
0     opt
du: cannot read directory 'proc/3945/task/3945/net': Invalid
argument
du: cannot read directory 'proc/3945/net': Invalid argument
du: cannot read directory 'proc/3946/task/3946/net': Invalid
argument
du: cannot read directory 'proc/3946/net': Invalid argument
du: cannot access 'proc/7762/task/7762/fd/3': No such file or
directory
du: cannot access 'proc/7762/task/7762/fdinfo/3': No such file
or directory
du: cannot access 'proc/7762/fd/3': No such file or directory
du: cannot access 'proc/7762/fdinfo/3': No such file or
directory
0     proc
32    root
du: cannot access 'run/user/1000/doc': Permission denied
1632  run
0     srv
0     sys
8     tmp
8371056      usr
6576996      var
```

5. To avoid confusion, send the standard error output (stderr) to /dev/null:

```
[root@workstation /]# ls -l | grep ^d | awk '{ print $9 }' | \
> xargs du -sk 2> /dev/null
0     afs
293680       boot
0     dev
33212      etc
176728       home
0     lost+found
0     media
0     mnt
0     opt
0     proc
32    root
1632      run
```

```
0        srv
0        sys
8        tmp
8371056      usr
6576996      var
```

6. Sort the results:

```
[root@workstation /]# ls -l | grep ^d | awk '{ print $9 }' | \
> xargs du -sk 2> /dev/null   | sort -n
0        afs
0        dev
0        lost+found
0        media
0        mnt
0        opt
0        proc
0        srv
0        sys
8        tmp
32       root
1632        run
33212        etc
176728        home
293680        boot
6576996       var
8371056       usr
```

7. Discard the directories with the lowest disk space usage and keep only the *Top 5*:

```
[root@workstation /]# ls -l | grep ^d | awk '{ print $9 }' | \
> xargs du -sk 2> /dev/null   | sort -n | tail -5
33212        etc
176728        home
293680        boot
6576996       var
8371056       usr
```

8. Now that we have found the *Top 5* directories with the highest disk usage, we will only deal with this order so that we can use it as evidence:

```
[root@workstation /]# ls -l | grep ^d | awk '{ print $9 }' | \
> xargs du -sk 2> /dev/null   | sort -n | tail -5 \
> awk '{ print $2 }' | xargs du -sh
33M          etc
```

```
173M    home
287M    boot
6.3G    var
8.0G    usr
```

The same steps should be executed for each of the *Top 5* directories so that we can find the subdirectory that occupies the most disk space and is the one causing the issue. Finding out which service determines who handles releasing the issue depends on the directory.

Now that these concepts are clear, we can start thinking about how to install our workstation for system administration purposes. However, before that, we should take a moment to select the desktop environment we want to use.

Desktop environments

Fedora's default desktop environment is **GNOME**, but it provides us with the alternative of using other desktop environments, either lightweight ones or those with special features, such as those that use different graphic engines and specialized libraries or are focused on performance. These alternatives are offered by the Fedora Project as *Spin distributions*. You can download a *Spin* with a preconfigured desktop environment based on Fedora:

> **Note**
>
> For more information about alternative desktops for Fedora, refer to *Fedora Spins* at `https://spins.fedoraproject.org/`.

With this, we have come to the end of *Chapter 1*. Let's quickly recap what we learned.

Summary

In this chapter, we briefly walked through the history of the Unix operating system, which taught us about the beginning and development of Linux and its distributions. Apart from teaching us how the project that develops the distribution that we will use as a workstation for system administration operates, it helped us learn how we can be part of it and improve the distribution while we perform our day-to-day tasks.

In the next chapter, we will learn about some best practices and tips that will help ensure we have a good installation that will help us develop our work.

Further reading

To learn more about the topics that were covered in the chapter, please visit the following links:

- *Timeline of GNU/Linux and Unix*: `http://laurel.datsi.fi.upm.es/~ssoo/IG/download/timeline.html`

- *Overview of the GNU System, GNU Operating System*: `https://www.gnu.org/gnu/gnu-history.html`

- *Linux and GNU – GNU Project – Free Software Foundation*: `https://www.gnu.org/gnu/linux-and-gnu.html`

- *Red Hat brand standards – Our history*: `https://www.redhat.com/en/about/brand/standards/history`

- *A Short History of Fedora Linux (Video), YouTube*: `https://www.youtube.com/watch?v=NlNlcLD2zRM`

- *CentOS Stream: A contribution path to Red Hat Enterprise Linux*: `https://www.redhat.com/en/resources/centos-stream-datasheet`

Part 2:
Workstation Configuration

In this part, you will learn how to set up a computer as a workstation for the tasks of a system administrator – from the best practices for the installation of an operating system and tools to configuring and optimizing resources, such as storage and networks.

This part contains the following chapters:

- *Chapter 2, Best Practices for Installation*
- *Chapter 3, Tuning the Desktop Environment*
- *Chapter 4, Optimizing Storage Usage*
- *Chapter 5, Network and Connectivity*

2
Best Practices for Installation

Now that we have a very complete context of the history and development of the Linux distribution, let's see what the recommendations and best practices for the installation of an **operating system (OS)** are on the computer that will be our workstation. The most advisable thing, in this case, is that our OS is a portable computer with good resources of memory and CPU, since if we can virtualize with it, it will help us a lot with functional tests.

The topics that will be covered in this chapter are as follows:

- Creating the boot media
- Partitioning local storage
- The first startup
- Package management

Let's get started!

Technical requirements

According to the **Fedora documentation** (`https://getfedora.org/en/workstation/download/`), a **Fedora Linux** image requires a USB flash drive of 2 GB for the creation of the boot media. To install Fedora Linux, it requires at least 20 GB of local storage and 2 GB of RAM; the recommended amount is double the amount of both.

Visit `https://getfedora.org` to get the image of the **Fedora Edition** to be installed. Fedora images are hybrid ISOs, so you can test them in *live mode* before installing them.

In this chapter, we will cover the best practices to install our workstation, in terms of performance and flexibility for the applications that help us to administer Linux systems.

To create the bootable media, we will use Fedora Linux. However, the creation of the bootable media is possible from any Linux distribution, preferably *rpm-based*, as well as on Windows or Mac systems.

For our installation, we will select the **Fedora Workstation** image as the best edition to use, as it is an OS that is refined and simple to use on laptops and desktops, with a full set of tools for developers and all kinds of users. After downloading the corresponding image, we will create a boot media, of which there are different methods.

Creating the boot media

There are many methods to create the boot media, from the dd command to applications such as **Unetbootin** or **balenaEtcher** that work on different platforms. However, these applications extract files from the image and write the syslinux bootloader to the device. This process builds a bootloader based on Fedora Linux, but it's different from the one contained in the image, so the boot media build is inconsistent with the image, which results in boot errors.

Fedora Media Writer is the official supported application to create Fedora bootable media. It works on different platforms. It is built with *Qt* (https://www.qt.io/). According to the official Fedora Project documentation, this is the recommended option to create bootable media. To install the tool, on an rpm-based Linux distribution, run the dnf or yum command as a root user:

```
[root@host ~]# dnf install mediawriter
```

> **Note**
> You can download Fedora Media Writer for other platforms at https://github.com/
> FedoraQt/MediaWriter.

Let's see how the process of creating the boot media works.

Fedora Media Writer

This method involves erasing the existing data on the USB flash drive, so back up your data if necessary.

> **Note**
> For more information on alternative methods of boot media creation, visit *Creating and using a live installation image* from **Fedora Docs** at https://docs.fedoraproject.
> org/en-US/quick-docs/creating-and-using-a-live-installation-
> image/#proc_creating-and-using-live-usb.

Follow these steps to create the boot media with Fedora Media Writer:

1. Select **Fedora Media Writer** from the **Applications** menu. If you have not downloaded the image, the tool offers the option to do it:

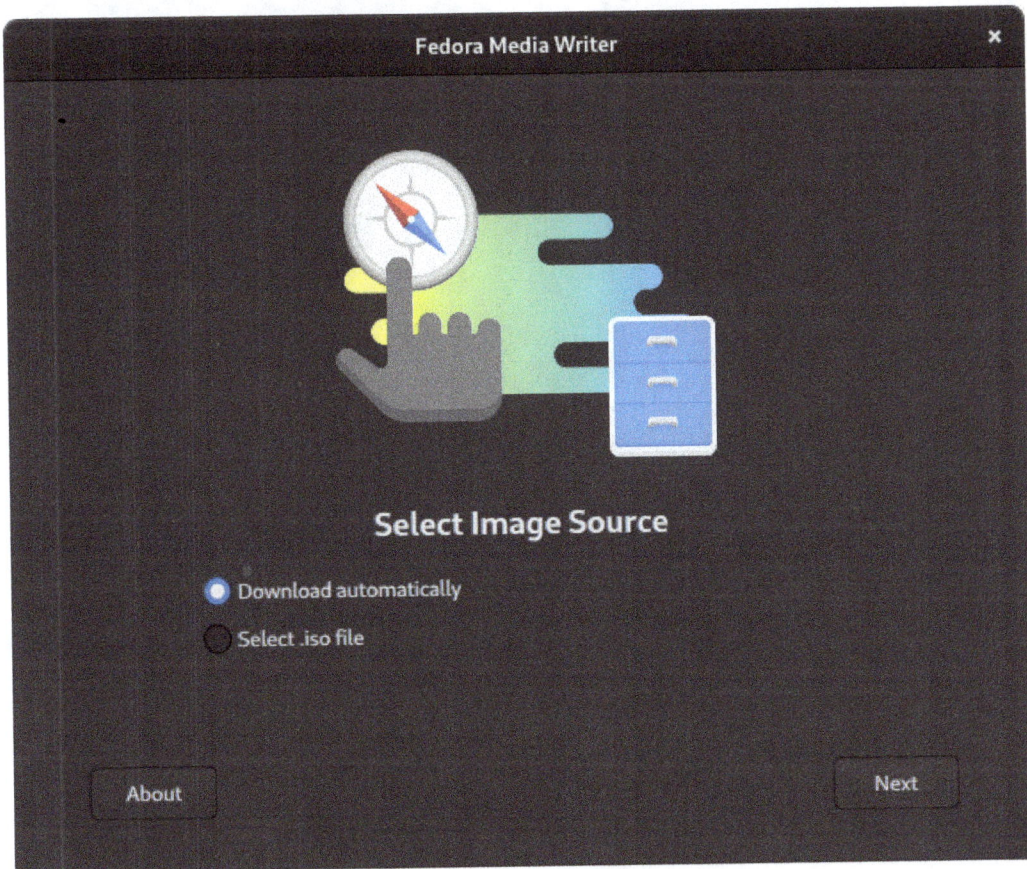

Figure 2.1 – Fedora Media Writer

2. Click the **Next** button to select the version to install:

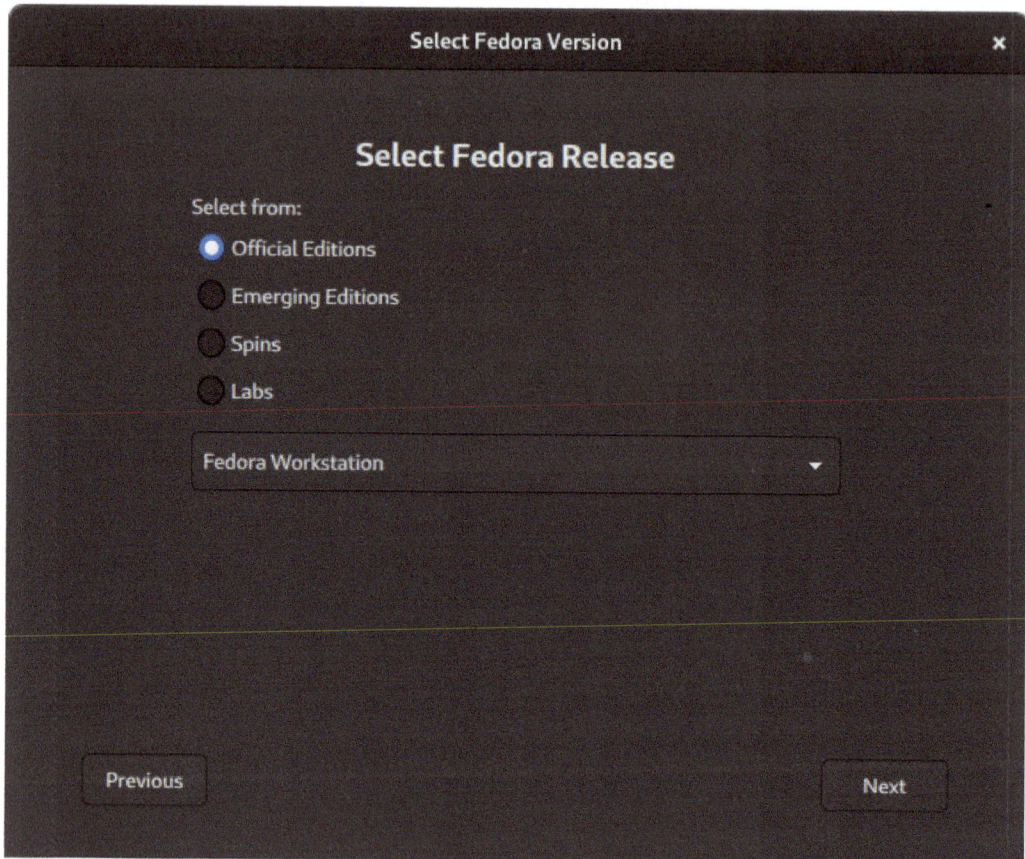

Figure 2.2 – Fedora Media Writer – Select Fedora Release

If you choose to download the image, enable the **Official Editions** radio button and select **Fedora Workstation** from the drop-down menu.

3. Click the **Next** button, and on the next screen, select the options to write the release/version, the hardware architecture, and the device to install. You have the option to delete the downloaded image after writing the device:

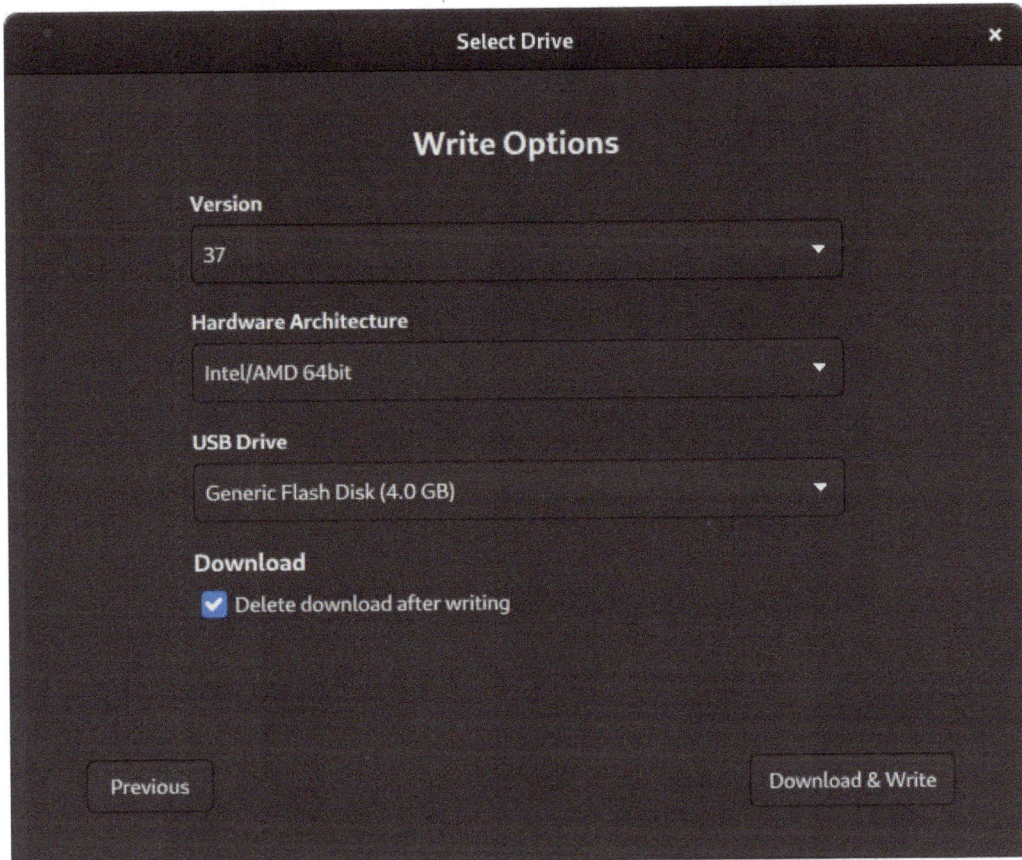

Figure 2.3 – Fedora Media Writer – Write Options

4. Click the **Download & Write** button, and wait for it to download the image and write it to the device.

When the image download completes, it will start writing the image to the device:

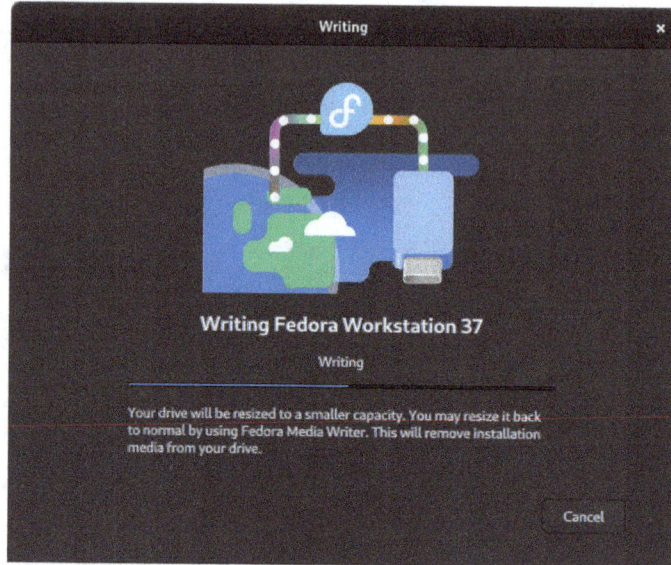

Figure 2.4 – Fedora Media Writer – writing the image

Once the image writing finishes, it starts with the review of the data written to the device:

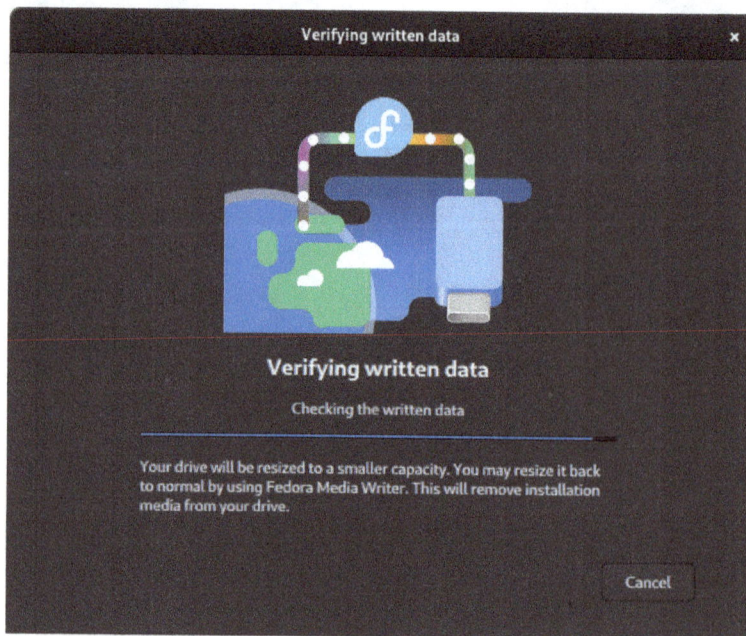

Figure 2.5 – Fedora Media Writer – Verifying written data

5.   When data verification finishes, click the **Finish** button, and remove the bootable media device:

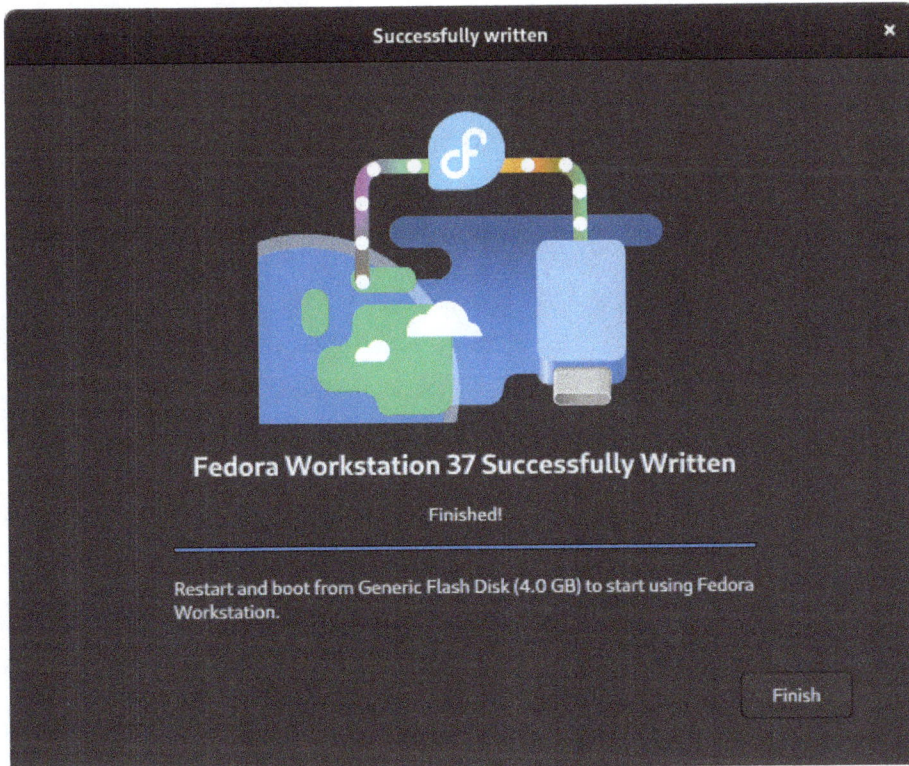

Figure 2.6 – Fedora Media Writer – writing completed

With the image written on the boot media, it's now time to install it on the computer and start the installation.

Booting

As mentioned in a previous section, Fedora Linux images are hybrid, which means that the OS can boot from boot media to perform functional tests and, from there, perform the complete installation of the distribution. To do this, follow the following steps:

1. Restart the computer and insert the boot media created to start the installation of the Fedora Linux image. The boot screen appears:

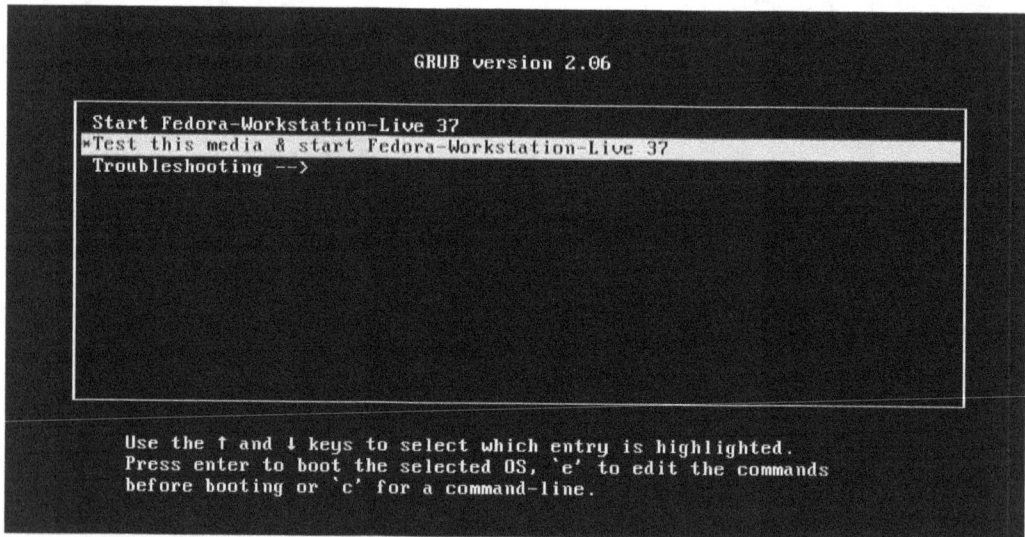

```
                        GRUB version 2.06


   Start Fedora-Workstation-Live 37
  *Test this media & start Fedora-Workstation-Live 37
   Troubleshooting -->








      Use the ↑ and ↓ keys to select which entry is highlighted.
      Press enter to boot the selected OS, `e' to edit the commands
      before booting or `c' for a command-line.
```

Figure 2.7 – The boot media screen

2. Select the **Test this media & start Fedora-Workstation-Live 37** option; this is important to determine whether the bootable media has inconsistency problems when installing the workstation.

3. At the end of the tests, the desktop displays the **Welcome to Fedora** screen, where we can choose to test the *Fedora Live* distribution or install it on the hard disk device:

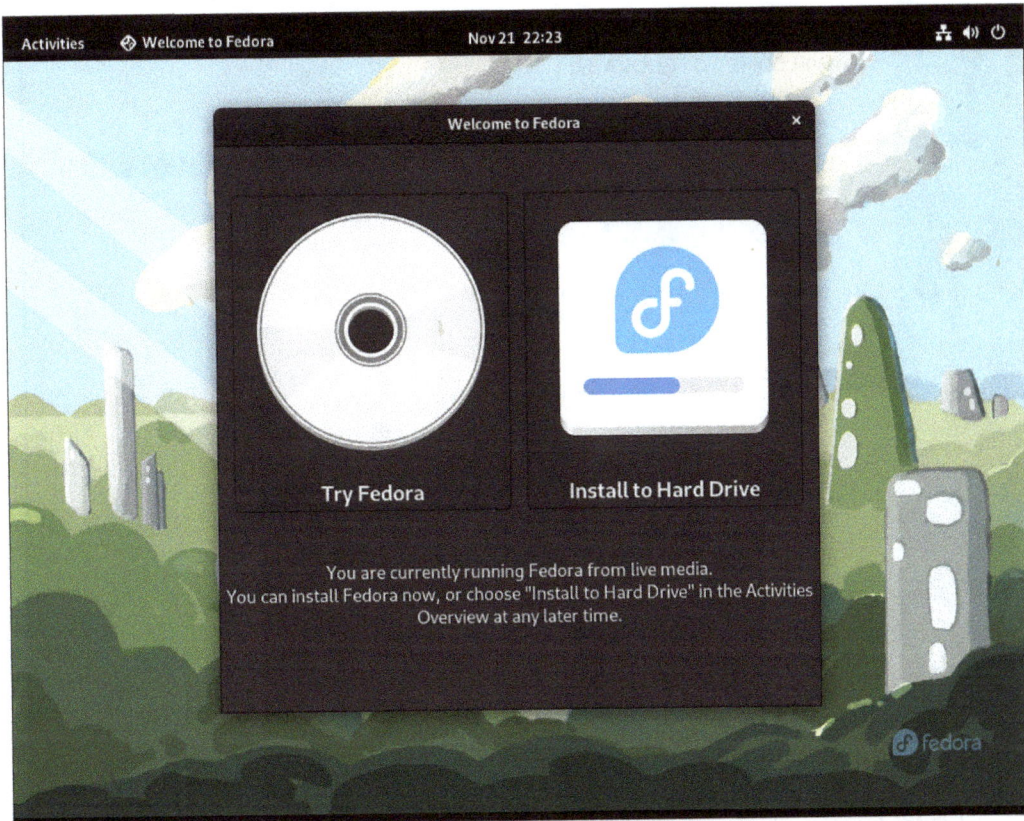

Figure 2.8 – Fedora Live – the welcome screen

4. Select the **Install to Hard Drive** option. On the next screen, select the *language* to be used during installation, according to your preference:

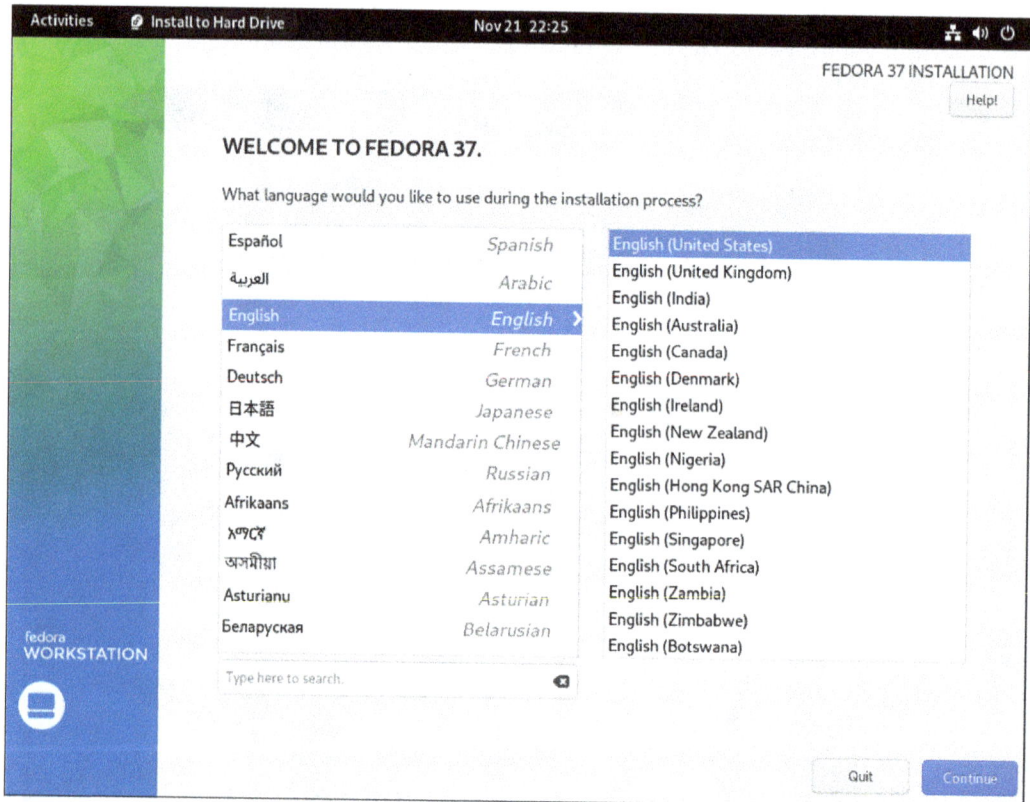

Figure 2.9 – Fedora Install – selecting a language

Click the **Continue** button.

5. The **INSTALLATION SUMMARY** screen appears. Select the keyboard mapping, and set the date and time and your current location.

    Click the **Installation Destination** button to select the device where the system should be installed:

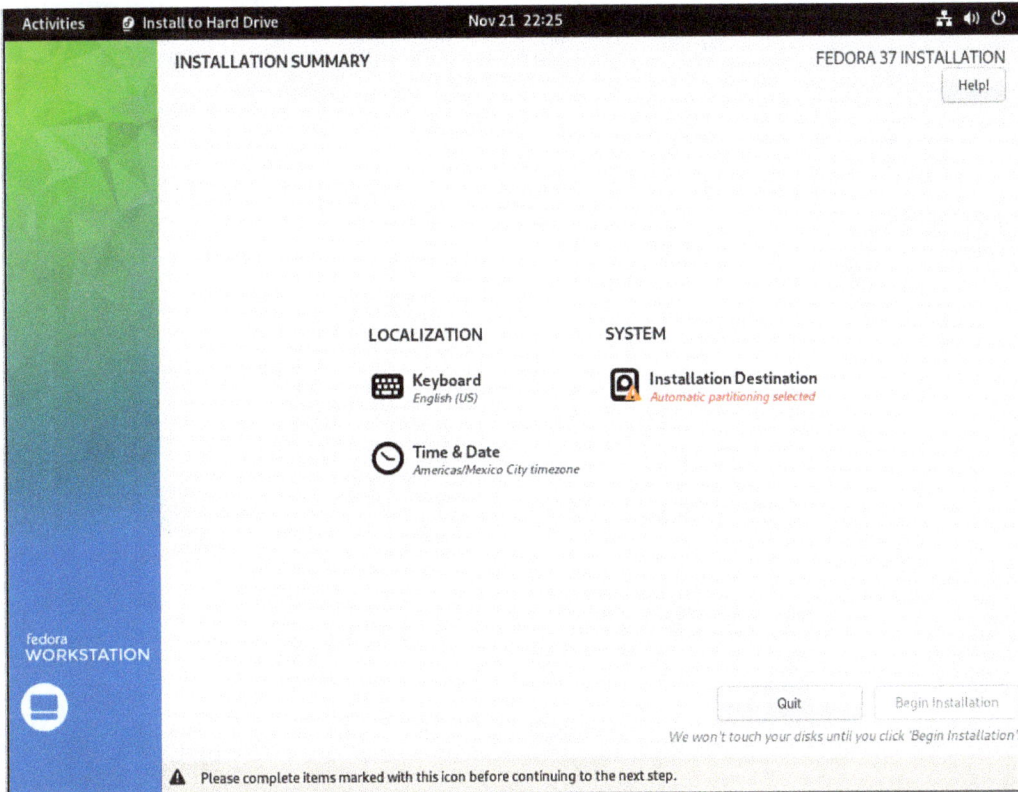

Figure 2.10 – Fedora Installation Summary

6.   Set the **Storage Configuration** option to **Custom**:

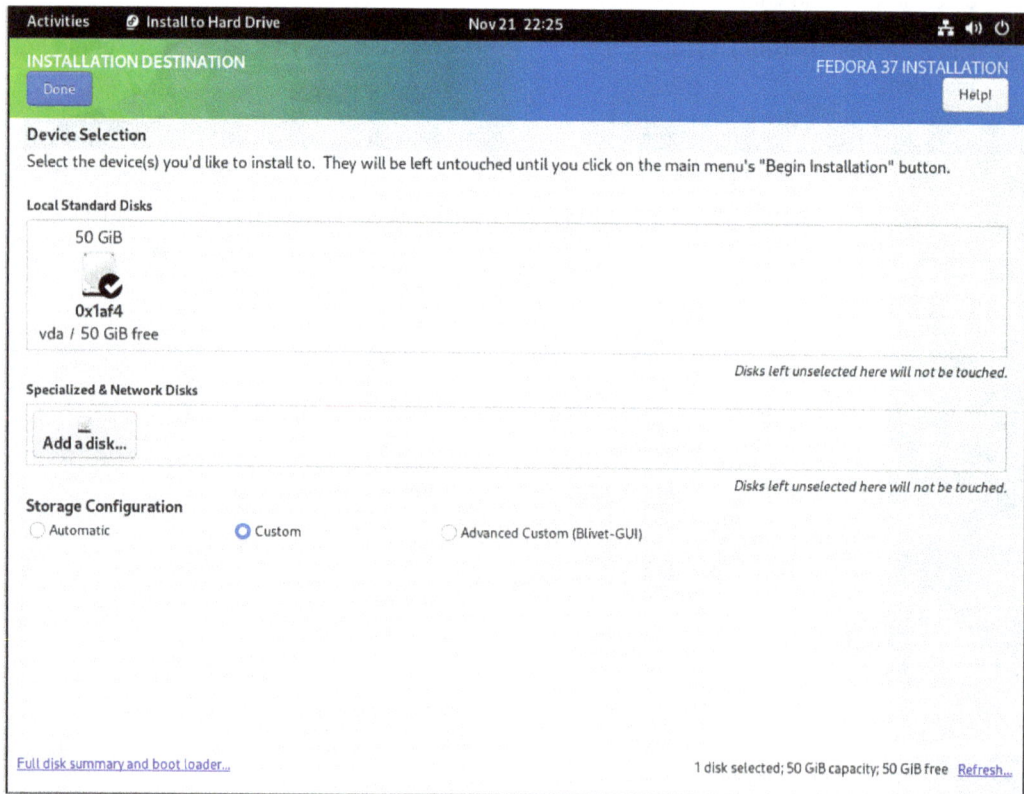

Figure 2.11 – Fedora INSTALLATION DESTINATION

7.   Click the **Done** button when finished.

Partitioning is one of the basic best practices of storage management. It means dividing the local storage into small units, as you decide, to separate the data stored in each section, and with this, apart from a better organization, you avoid the possible collapse of the entire OS. In an extreme case where there were no divisions, the storage would not have enough free space to continue operating.

Since it is best to perform this organization during the installation of the OS, let's take advantage of this step to analyze it in depth. Let's get to it.

Partitioning local storage

The installation wizard includes a shortcut to create partitioning as standard. This is very useful for cases such as this, installing a workstation, but not in other cases such as specific use servers. We will discuss these cases and expand on several basic storage management concepts in a later chapter.

Let's start with the standard partitioning provided by the wizard and add some extra mount points that will help with our system administration task.

Follow these steps to partition the local storage:

1. The **MANUAL PARTITIONING** screen enables you to select the format scheme, leave it as **Btrfs**, and create the base mount points by clicking the **Click here to create them automatically** link.

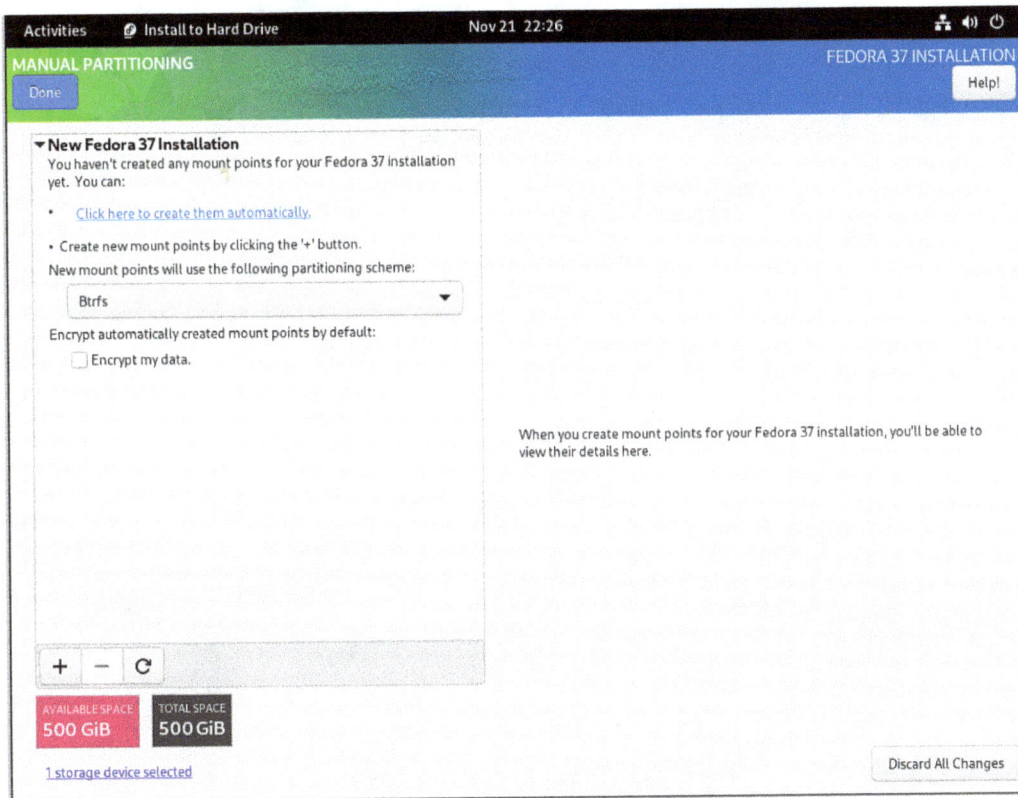

Figure 2.12 – Fedora Manual Partitioning

A mount point base should be created, with the filesystems of the /home and / directories, plus the /boot directory and BIOS boot, mounted on the first two physical partitions of the hard drive device.

2. Click the plus sign [+] button to add another filesystem mounted on the `/var/lib/libvirt/images` directory; this directory should become the location of the guest **virtual machines (VMs)** that will be configured in a later chapter.

3. Change the disk space assigned so that the `/home` and `/` directories are about 50 GiB. The remaining storage space on the hard disk device should assign them to the `/var/lib/libvirt/images` directory.

   For example, with a 500 GiB hard disk device, after allocating 100 GiB to the `/home` and `/` directories, there is 400 GiB of storage space left that is allocated to the `/var/lib/libvirt/images` directory.

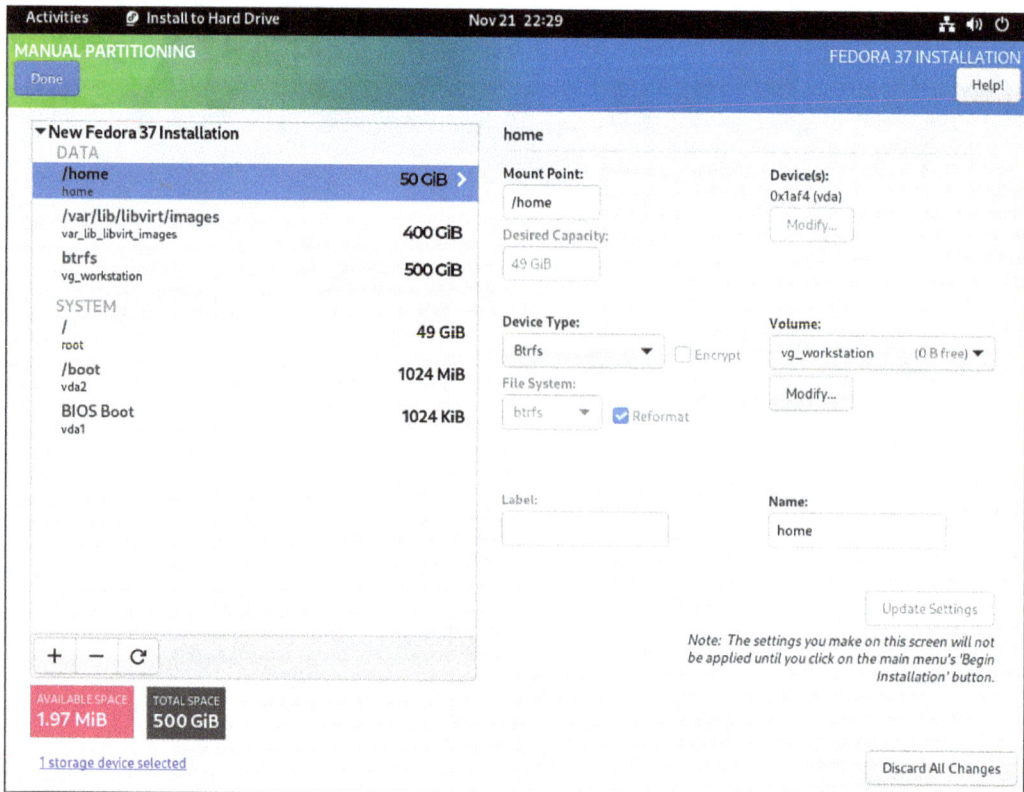

Figure 2.13 – Fedora Manual Partitioning

Click the **Done** button.

4. The **INSTALLATION SUMMARY** screen displays that there are no missing items to configure and enables the **Begin Installation** button:

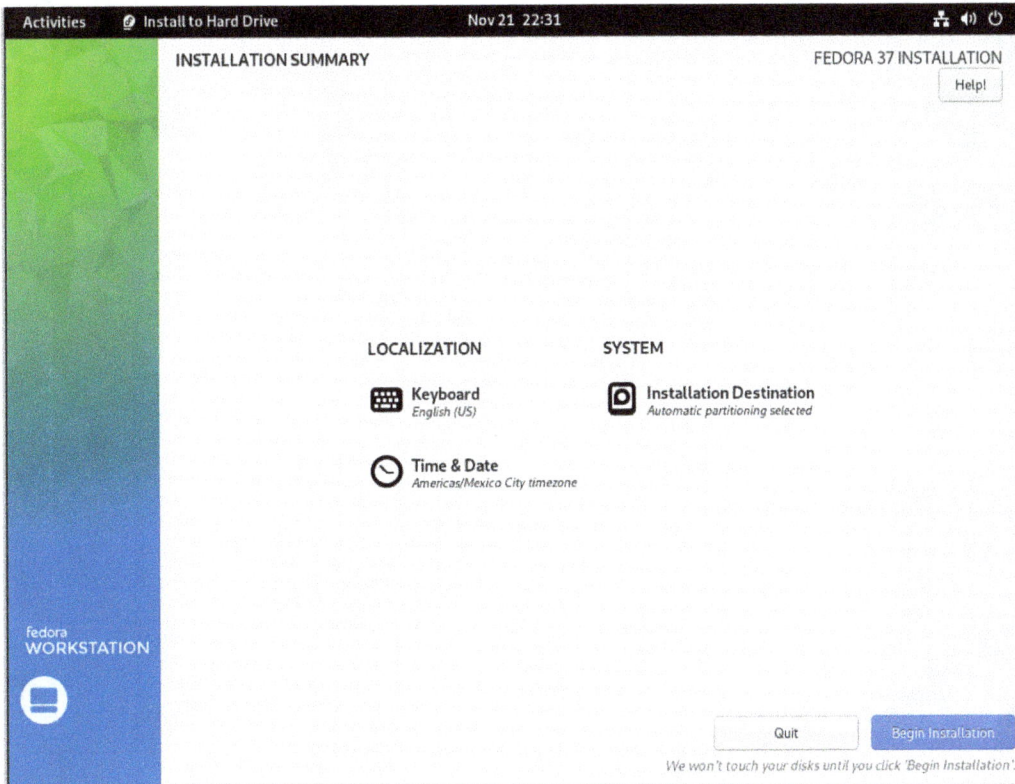

Figure 2.14 – Fedora Installation Summary

Click the **Begin Installation** button and wait for the installation to finish.

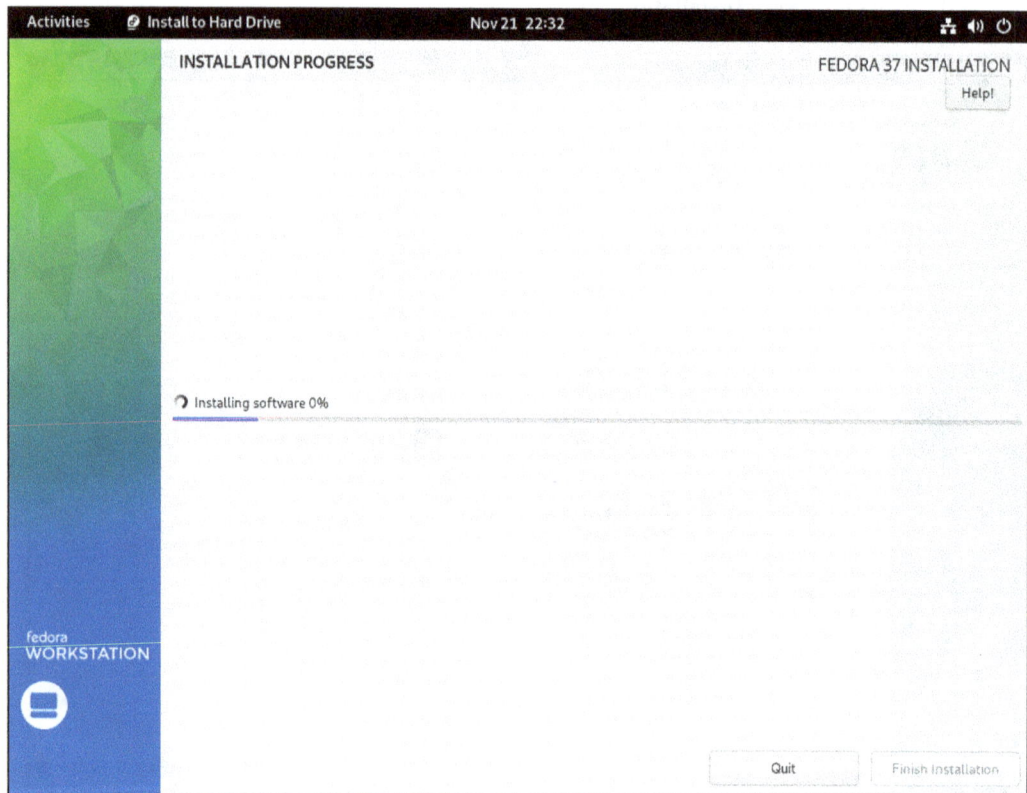

Figure 2.15 – Fedora INSTALLATION PROGRESS

5.   Click the **Finish Installation** button.

6.   Restart the live media and remove the bootable media device.

Now that we have the OS installed on our computer, let's finish the configuration on the first boot.

The first startup

The OS installs on the computer, but the user configuration for access is still missing, as well as some customization that could perform from the first start. Let's add some customization to conclude the installation of the distribution.

Follow these steps to finish the configuration:

1.   On restarting the system, the **Setup** screen displays:

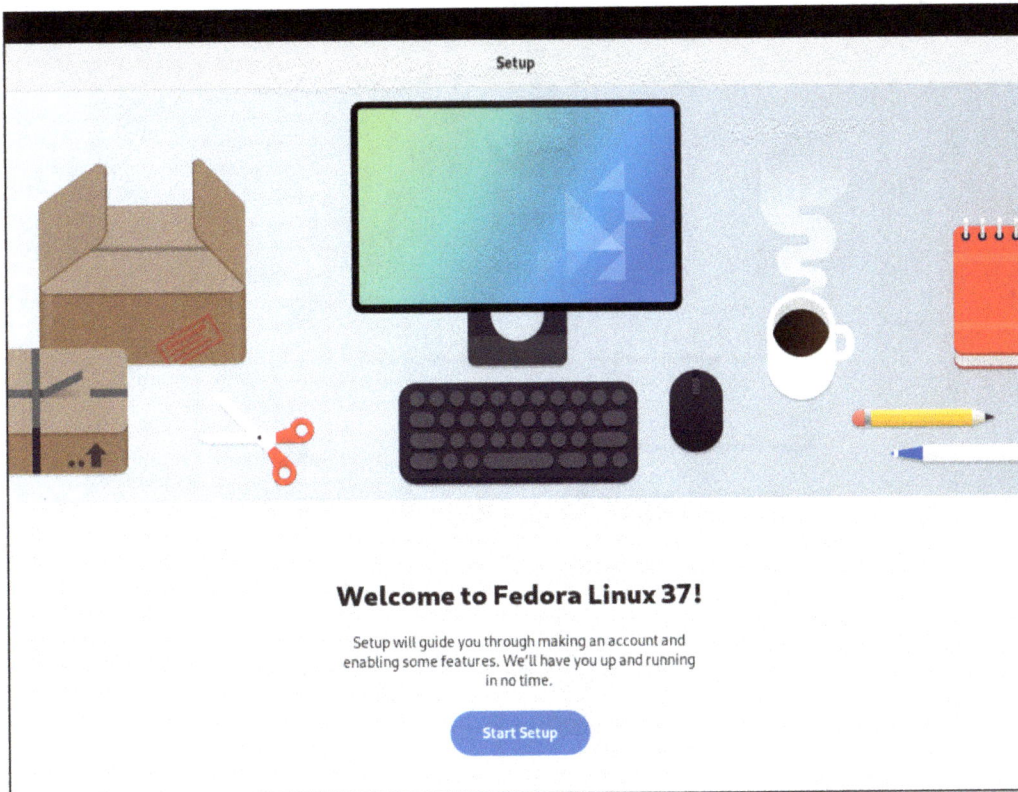

Figure 2.16 – The Fedora welcome screen

Click the **Start Setup** button.

2. On the **Privacy** settings screen, if you agree, activate the **Location Services** and **Automatic Problem Reporting** switches.

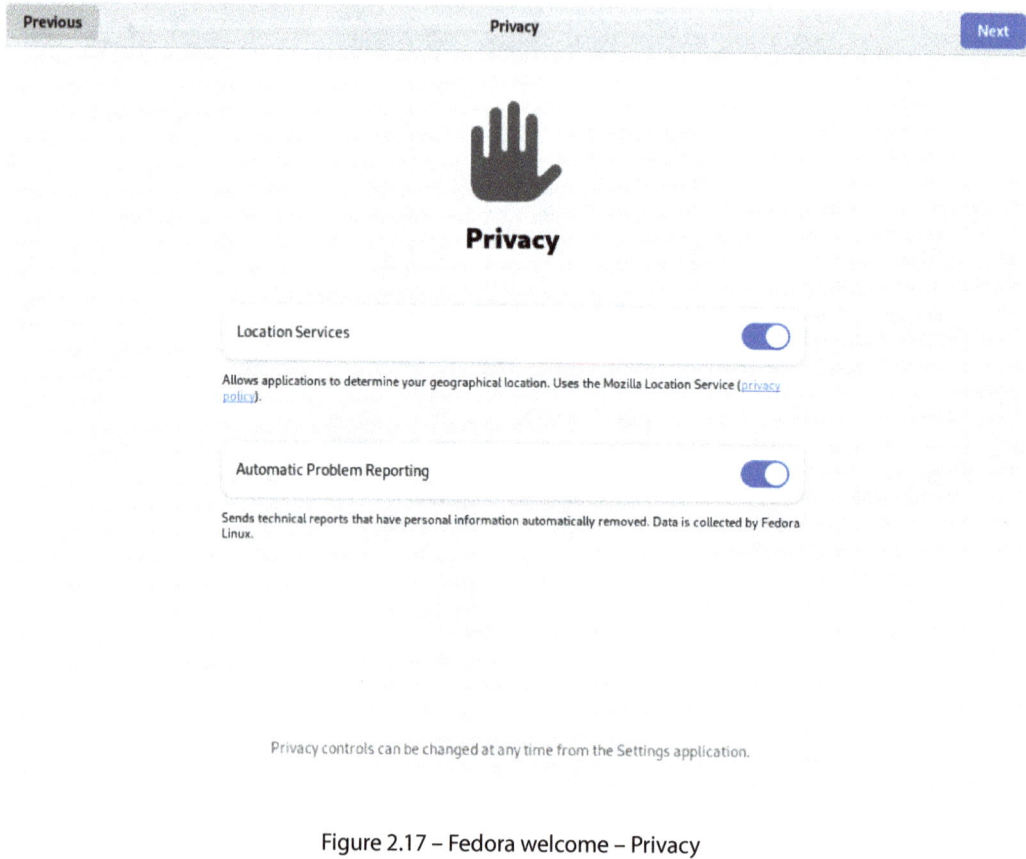

Figure 2.17 – Fedora welcome – Privacy

Enabling **Location Services** allows some applications, such as *maps* or *weather*, to provide you with local information based on your current location. Please read the privacy policy before considering activating the switch.

Enabling **Automatic Problem Reporting** sends technical reports of failures to the **Fedora Project**. Personal information is removed before sending. The OS collects this information.

Click the **Next** button.

3. On the next screen, enable third-party repositories by clicking the **Enable Third-Party Repositories** button.

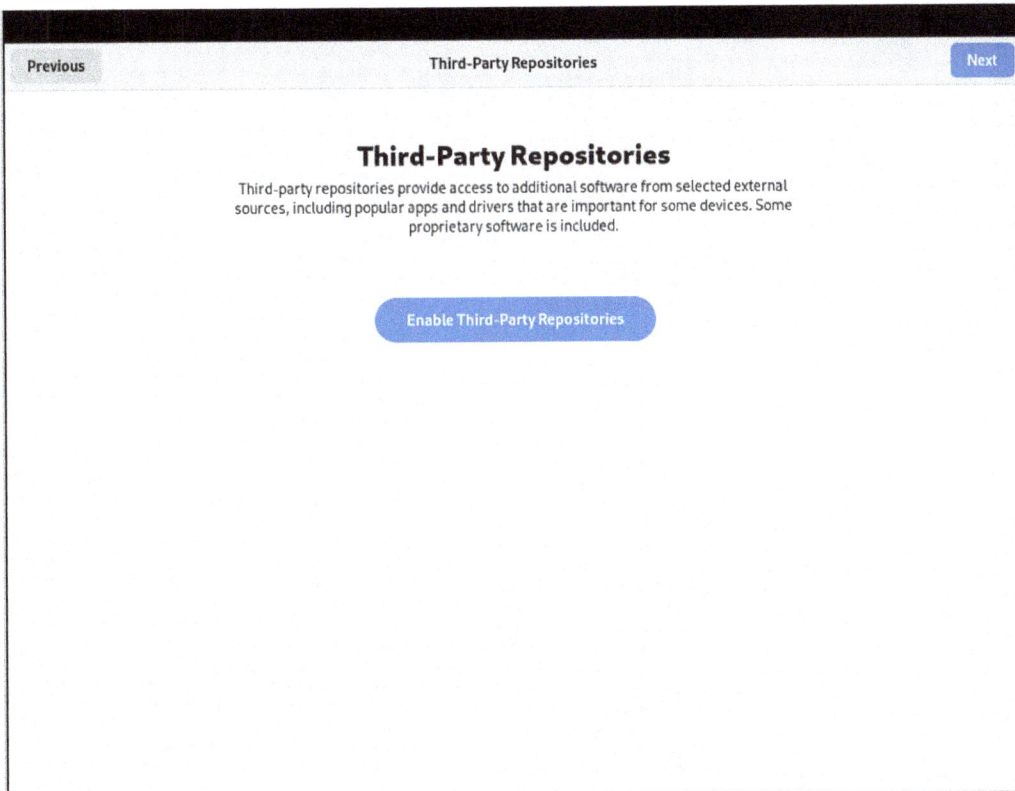

Figure 2.18 – Fedora welcome – Third-Party Repositories

Third-party repositories provide access to extra software from selected external sources, such as popular applications or some drivers, including proprietary software.

Click the **Next** button.

4. The next screen enables you to connect your **Google**, **Nextcloud**, or **Microsoft** online service accounts by selecting the service and logging in to your account.

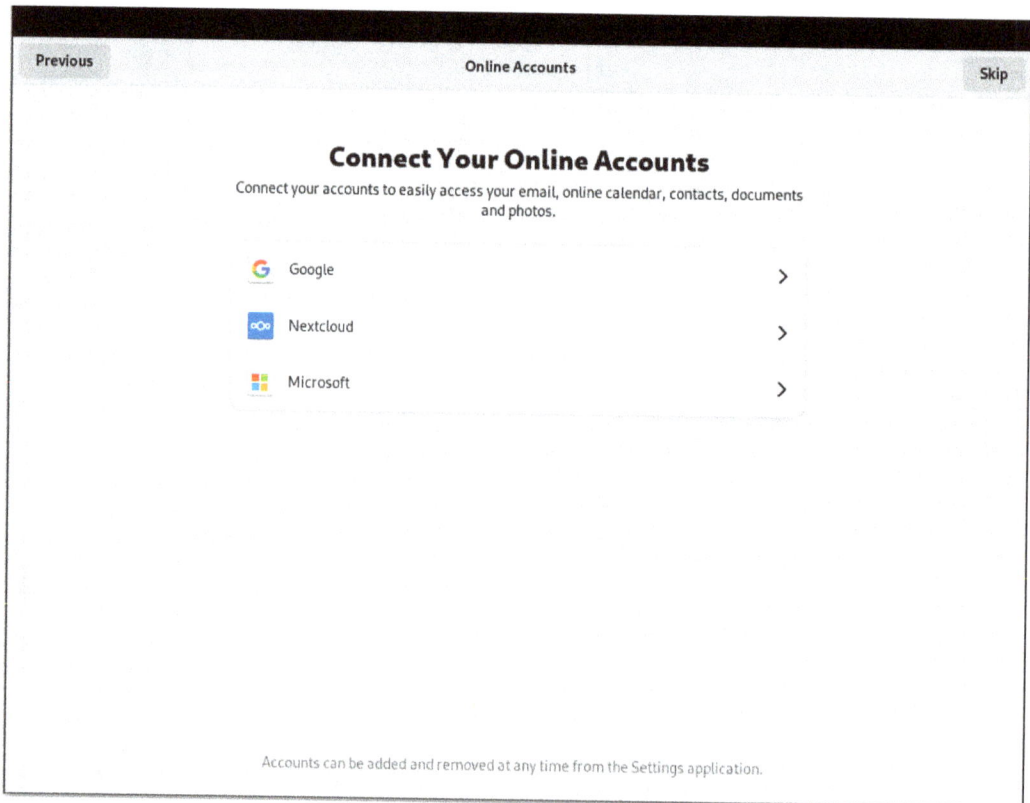

Figure 2.19 – Fedora welcome – Online Accounts

Note

This step is optional and won't interfere with the OS activities.

To skip this step, click the **Skip** button.

5.   Create your login account on the next screen:

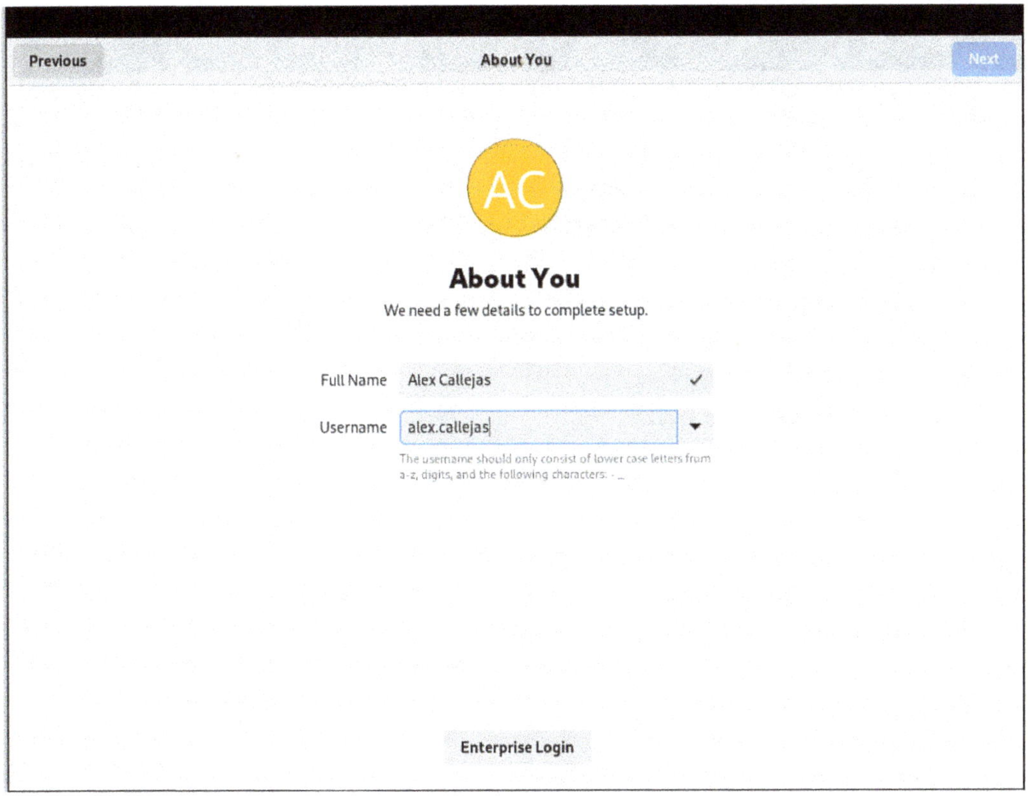

Figure 2.20 – Fedora welcome – About You

When complete, click the **Next** button.

6. Then, create a strong password for your login account; the system indicates the *minimum acceptable password strength.*

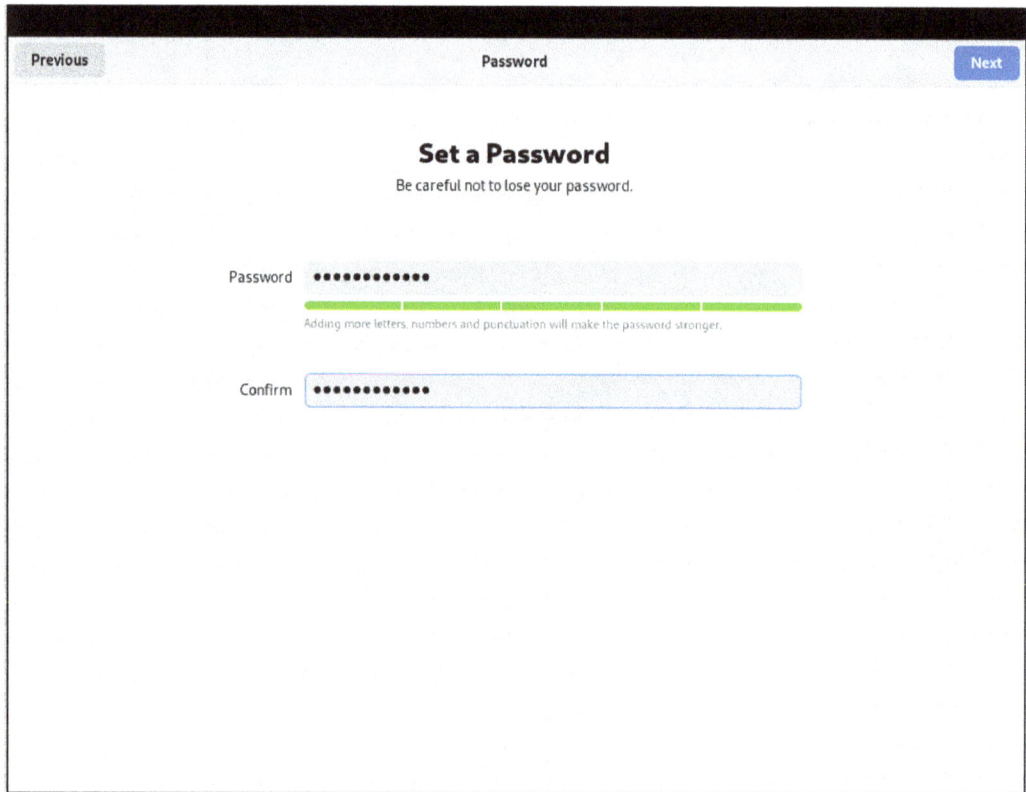

Figure 2.21 – Fedora welcome – Password

7. When complete, click the **Next** button. The setup is now complete.

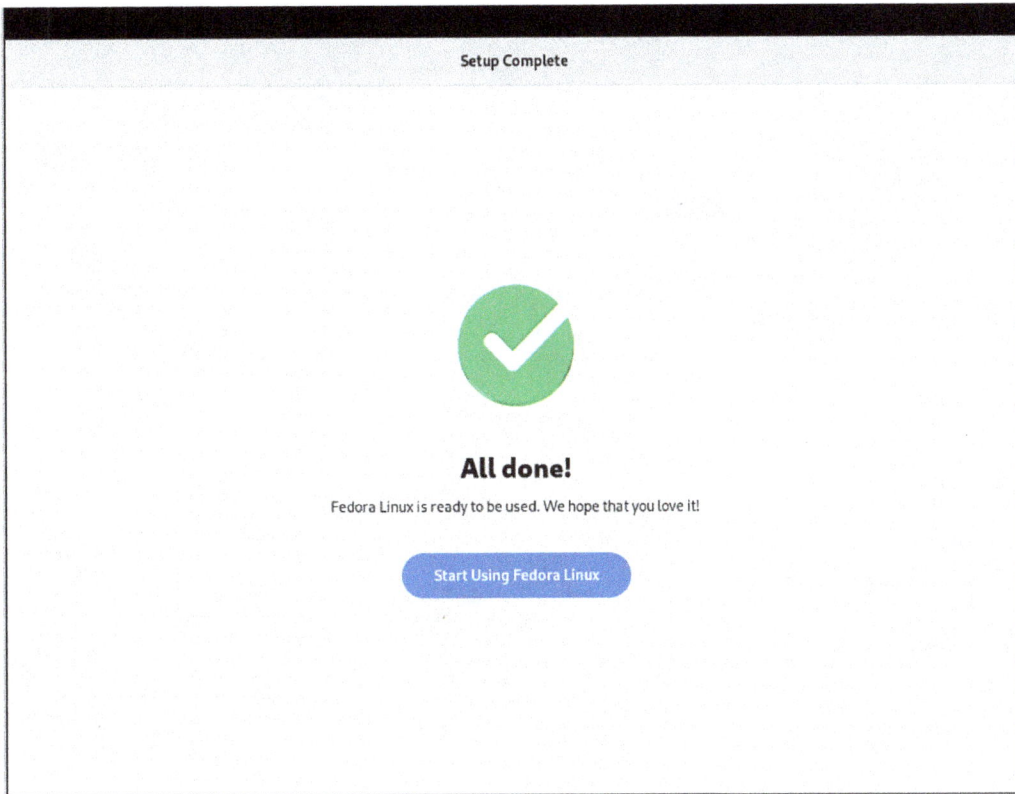

Figure 2.22 – Fedora welcome – Setup Complete

8.   Click the **Start Using Fedora Linux** button. The workspace desktop displays.

Figure 2.23 –Fedora Linux 37 Workstation GNOME desktop

When working for a long time at the console, it is vital to take care of our vision, preventing permanent damage as much as possible. One of the options that GNOME offers us is to configure a *dark mode* that can help to avoid these visual effects.

Click the button in the upper-right corner and select dark mode by clicking the **Dark Mode** button.

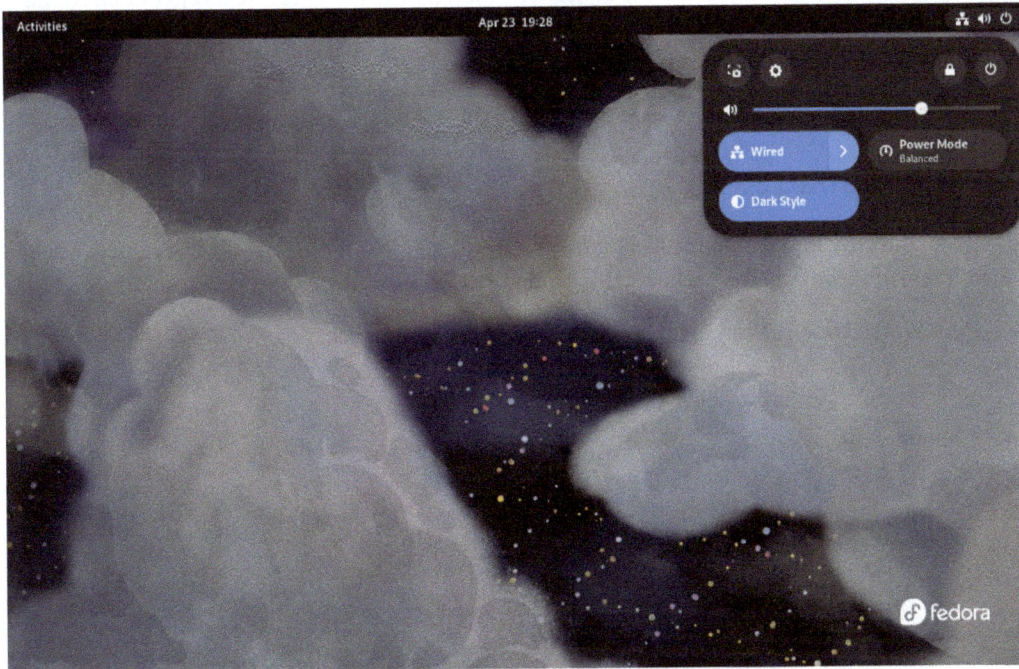

Figure 2.24 – Fedora desktop – Dark Mode

> **Important note**
>
> **Give your eyes a rest**. If you spend a lot of time at the computer or focusing on any one thing, you sometimes forget to blink, and your eyes can get fatigued. Try the 20-20-20 rule – every 20 minutes, look away about 20 feet in front of you for 20 seconds. This short exercise can help reduce eyestrain.
>
> For more tips on how to prevent vision loss, refer to the **Vision Health Initiative** (**VHI**) at `https://www.cdc.gov/visionhealth/risk/tips.htm/`.

With the installation and basic configuration finished, we can start with the installation of the software that will help us to have the most useful tools for our day-to-day tasks.

For this, it is indispensable to have our computer connected to the internet. As with storage, in a later chapter, we will review the basic concepts of network configuration to optimize its operation. At this point, it is only necessary to know that the system network is available, either in wired or wireless form, to download and install packages and updates of the OS.

Let's now learn how to update the OS and download extra packages that provide the tools needed.

Package management

The Fedora Linux live installation media build is based on a `kickstart` (text) file where, depending on the version of the image, the packages that compose it are included.

The Fedora Workstation version includes the following groups of packages:

- Common Network Manager Submodules
- Container management
- Core
- Fedora Workstation product core
- Firefox web browser
- Fonts
- GNOME
- Guest desktop agents
- Hardware support
- LibreOffice
- Multimedia
- Printing support
- base-x

> **Note**
>
> For more information about **Fedora Composes**, refer to `fedora-kickstarts` at `https://pagure.io/fedora-kickstarts/`.

To review the installed packages, perform the following steps:

1. Open the **Activities** overview window and select **Software** from the bottom icon bar:

Figure 2.25 – Activities overview

2.   Click the **Installed** tab:

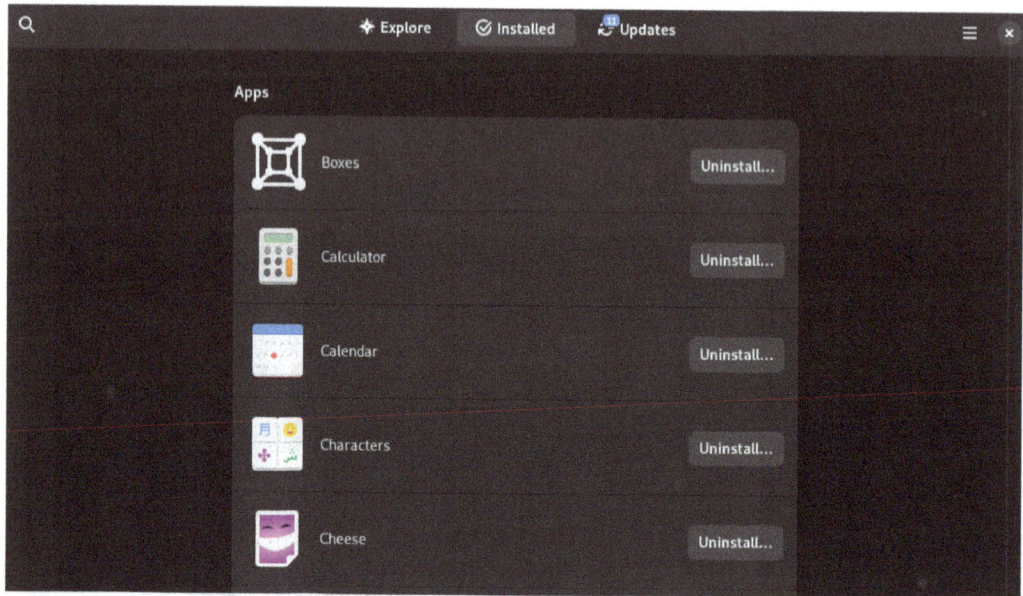

Figure 2.26 – Software installed

> **Note**
>
> Get the detailed list of packages contained in the distribution from our *GitHub repository* at `https://github.com/PacktPublishing/Fedora-Linux-System-Administration/blob/main/chapter2/fedora-37-packages.txt`.

3. The **Updates** tab indicates that packages need to update. Click the **Updates** tab:

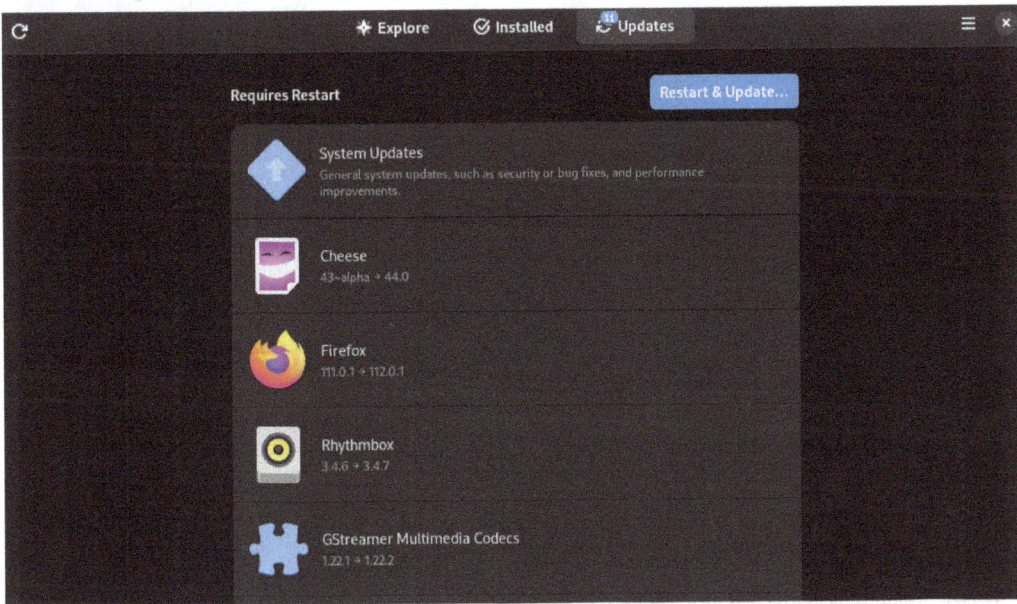

Figure 2.27 – Software updates

> **Important**
>
> *As this is the first boot, it is important to update all OS packages.*
>
> For detailed information on the content of the package updates, refer to *Fedora Updates System* at `https://bodhi.fedoraproject.org/releases/F38`.

4. Click the **Restart & Update** button.

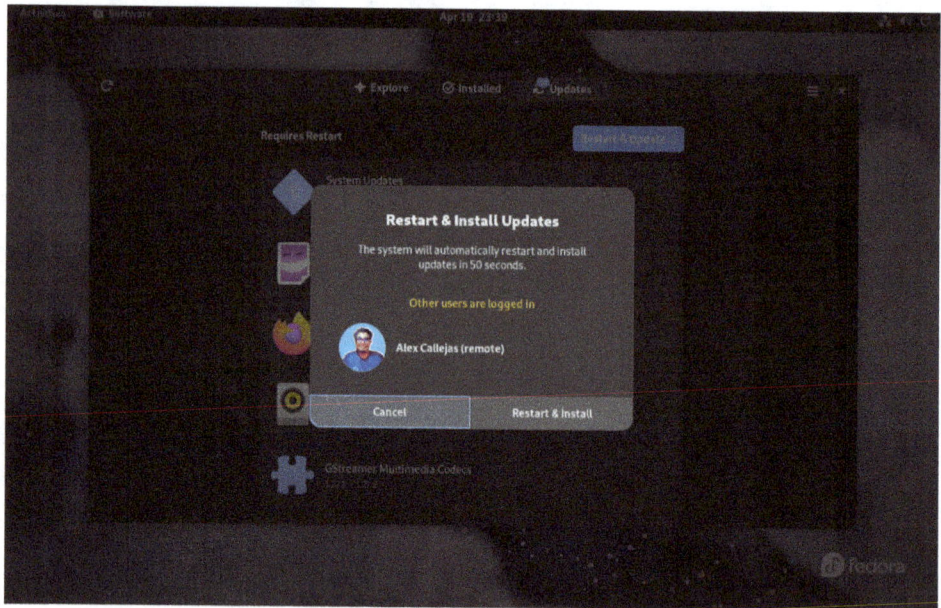

Figure 2.28 – Restart & Install Updates

5. Click the **Restart & Install** button.

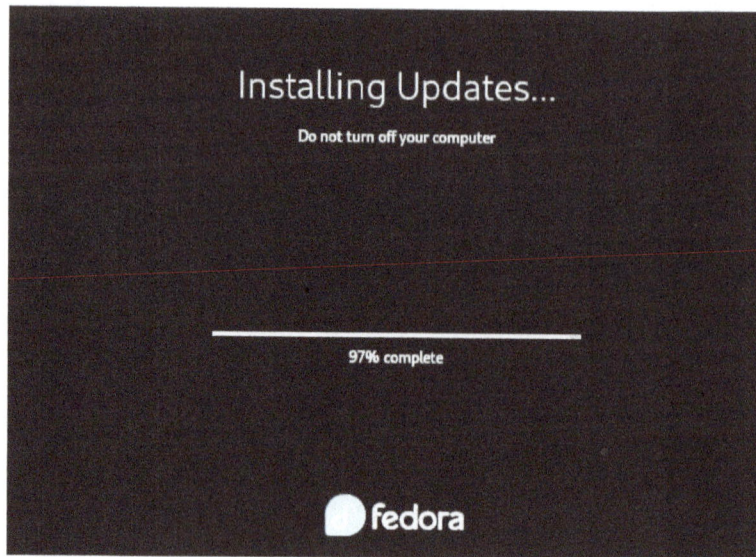

Figure 2.29 – Installing Updates…

Wait for the installation updates, and when the computer restarts, log in and verify, under **Software | Updates**, that the updates are up to date.

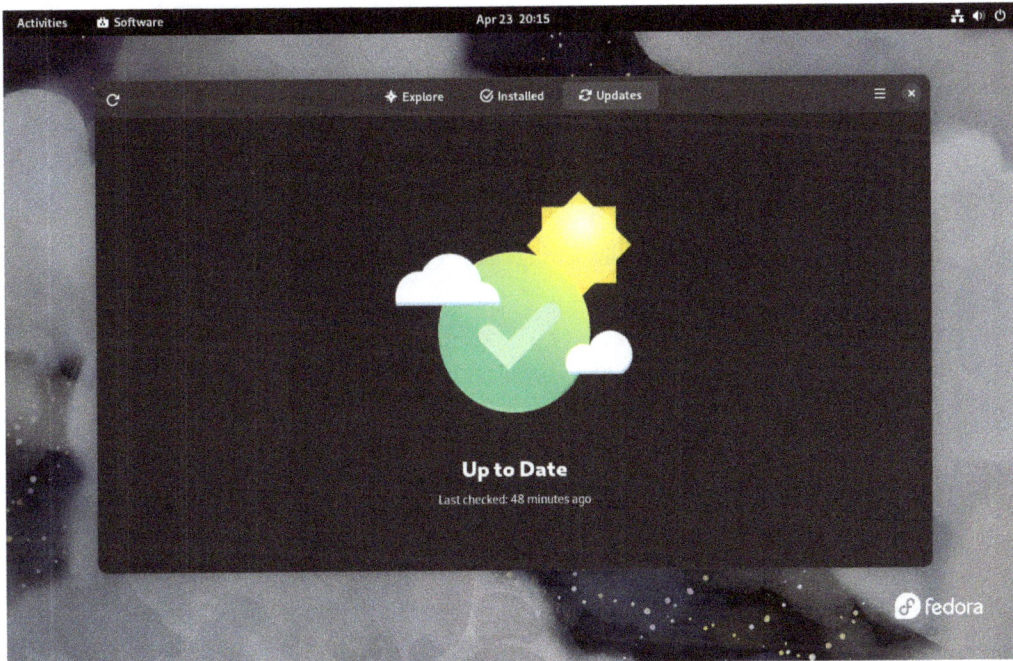

Figure 2.30 – Software updates

Close this window to continue with the installation of extra packages.

Extra package selection

Fedora Linux includes in its repositories many tools that can make day-to-day tasks in system administration easier, but some of them are not included in the system installation, so it is necessary to install them. To install packages on Fedora Linux, which has a package manager based on *rpm packages* (**RPM Package Manager**), use the **PackageKit GUI** and the dnf command in the Terminal.

> **Note**
>
> For more information about **installing packages** in Fedora Linux, refer to *Package Management System* at https://docs.fedoraproject.org/en-US/quick-docs/package-management/.

Some of these recommended tools are as follows:

- **Development**:

  - `gcc`: A GNU project C and C++ compiler

  - `git`: A distributed revision control system

  - `make`: A GNU Make utility to maintain groups of programs

- **Laptop battery power**:

  - `tlp`: A tool to apply power-saving settings and control battery care features

- **Network scanner**:

  - `nmap`: A network exploration tool and security/port scanner

- **Terminal emulator**:

  - `terminator`: Stores and runs multiple GNOME Terminals in one window

- **Virtualization**:

  - `genisoimage`: A program to generate ISO 9660/Joliet/HFS hybrid filesystems

  - `libguestfs`: A tool to access and modify VM disk images

  - `qemu-kvm`: A QEMU PC system emulator

  - `virt-install`: A tool to create new KVM, Xen, or *Linux container guests* using the `libvirt` hypervisor management library

  - `virt-manager`: A graphical tool to manage `libvirt` VMs

  - `virt-viewer`: A tool to display the graphical console of a virtual machine

Open the GNOME Terminal to install extra packages. Then, open the **Activities Overview** window and select **Terminal**:

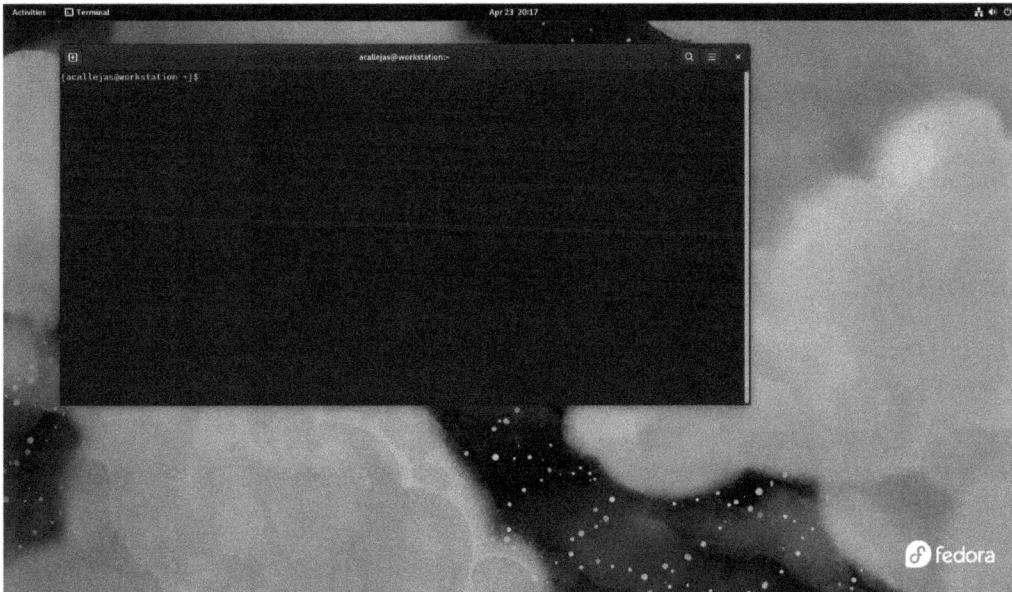

Figure 2.31 – The GNOME Terminal

Switch to the root user using the sudo command and clean all the repository metadata:

```
[user@workstation ~]$ sudo -i
[sudo] password for user: [password]
[root@workstation ~]# dnf clean all
68 files removed
```

> **Note**
> Clearing the metadata to force the package manager to refresh it is optional. I have always considered it a good practice.

Install the extra packages using the dnf command:

```
[root@workstation ~]# dnf install gcc make libgcc git \
> qemu-kvm virt-manager virt-viewer libguestfs \
> virt-install genisoimage terminator nmap tlp
```

In later chapters, we will install more tools for some specific tasks.

Once the system is upgraded and the extra packages are installed, everyone gets to enjoy the experience of using the tools. However, you may find that a tool or package could be enhanced with some added function or feature. You should take your proposal to the Fedora Project for evaluation of the enhancement.

The installation and basic configuration of our workstation are now complete, so let's summarize what we have learned.

Summary

In this chapter, we reviewed the best practices and tips to install Fedora on our computer, including the basic partitioning of the internal storage, as well as the first steps of a basic configuration of our workstation.

In the next chapter, we will learn how to customize our workstation with the proper tools to perform Linux system administration.

Further reading

To learn more about the topics that were covered in this chapter, take a look at the following resources:

- *Fedora*: https://getfedora.org
- *Preparing Boot Media*: https://docs.fedoraproject.org/en-US/fedora/ f35/install-guide/install/Preparing_for_Installation/#sect- preparing-boot-media
- *Fedora Media Writer*: https://github.com/FedoraQt/MediaWriter/
- *Fedora 37 – DistroWatch*: https://distrowatch.com/?newsid=11673
- *fedora-kickstarts*: https://pagure.io/fedora-kickstarts
- *fedora build system*: https://koji.fedoraproject.org/koji/
- *Fedora Updates System*: https://bodhi.fedoraproject.org/
- *Fedora Workstation Working Group*: https://pagure.io/fedora-workstation
- *Fedora Pagure – Issues*: https://pagure.io/fedora-workstation/issues

3

Tuning the Desktop Environment

With the operating system installed on our computer and the least necessary configuration completed, we can continue with the customization of our workstation, looking to optimize the processes. But at this point, it is very important to feel comfortable with the experience as users of our desktop environment. In this chapter, we will look, step by step, at how to have a customized desktop environment; you can omit or add any component to your liking, based on your personal taste. The desktop environment we are going to use is **GNOME**, but most of the customizations, except the GNOME plugins, could be done in any desktop environment.

The following customization components are covered in the chapter:

- Initial system tuning
- Customizing the panel and taskbar
- Making tasks easy with widgets
- Handy applications with docks

Technical requirements

For the exercises in this chapter, you need to have a personal computer with **Fedora Workstation** installed, with release 37, the release this book is based on. If you do not have the operating system installed on the computer, you can refer to the previous chapter where I provided the best practices for its installation.

Let's start the desktop tuning with resource optimization.

Initial system tuning

Tuning a Linux system involves many of its components. For this reason, we will start by going through desktop tuning step by step so that we have a workstation optimized as best as possible. As always, in these cases, the main thing to take care of is the memory and CPU usage of our computer.

According to Fedora's official documentation (https://docs.fedoraproject.org/en-US/fedora/latest/release-notes/welcome/Hardware_Overview/), the minimum system requirements that we must have in our hardware are as follows:

- 2 GHz dual-core processor or faster
- 2 GB system memory

According to several resource usage benchmark websites, such as diffen.com (https://www.diffen.com/difference/GNOME_vs_KDE), webdock.io (https://webdock.io/en/docs/how-guides/desktop-environments/overview-of-desktop-environments), and pcgamebenchmark.com (https://www.pcgamebenchmark.com/find-the-gnome-system-requirements), the GNOME desktop has the following specifications:

- 800 MHz CPU power (1 GHz for optimal performance)
- 512 MB of **Random Access Memory** (**RAM**) (1 GB for optimal performance)

A tuning that can help us, if we have limited system memory, is adjusting the **swappiness** value.

Swappiness is a property of the **Linux kernel** that allows adjusting the balance between the use of *swap space* and RAM. Swap space gets used when the amount of physical memory (RAM) is full. Swap space is a physical storage space on the system. Swappiness values range from 0 to 100, a ratio between *anonymous pages* and *file pages*.

Tuning the swappiness value

The swappiness value determines the amount of data written to the virtual memory of the hard disk drive (swap space), which can slow down the system.

By default, this value is 60, which you can verify by running the following command from Terminal:

```
[root@workstation ~]# cat /proc/sys/vm/swappiness
60
```

This value could change through the /etc/sysctl.conf file by adding a lower value to this parameter. As a recommendation, add a comment of the change made as a backup:

```
[root@workstation ~]# cat /etc/sysctl.conf
...output omitted...
```

```
# The default value is 60, decrementing the value of parameter
vm.swappiness=10
```

After saving the file, reboot the computer and confirm the changed value. With this, less information should write to the virtual drive.

With this basic tuning done, let's get a better experience with the use of our desktop resources. So now, let's go ahead and customize it to have the tools at hand and perform better day-to-day activities.

Tuning the desktop experience

In the GNOME desktop, in the upper-left corner, you will find the **Activities** menu button. By clicking it, access to the programs and system settings is available. Pressing the *Super* key also opens the **Activities** menu.

From the **Activities** menu, we can search for any program, but GNOME can not only search for software but also for any item that is available, such as locations, contacts, calendar appointments, notes, and so on.

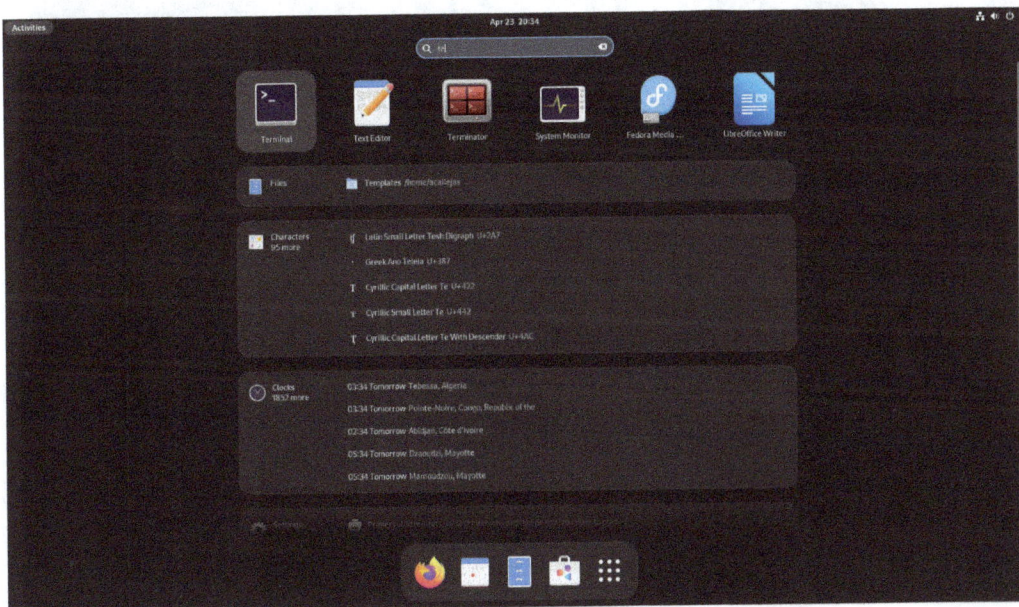

Figure 3.1 – Searching from the Activities menu

This is very useful, but it can also mean a resource drain on the performance of the desktop environment. To limit GNOME's search, click on the icons at the top right and click on the gear to open the configuration window. In the **Search** section, select only the source of the items to search for.

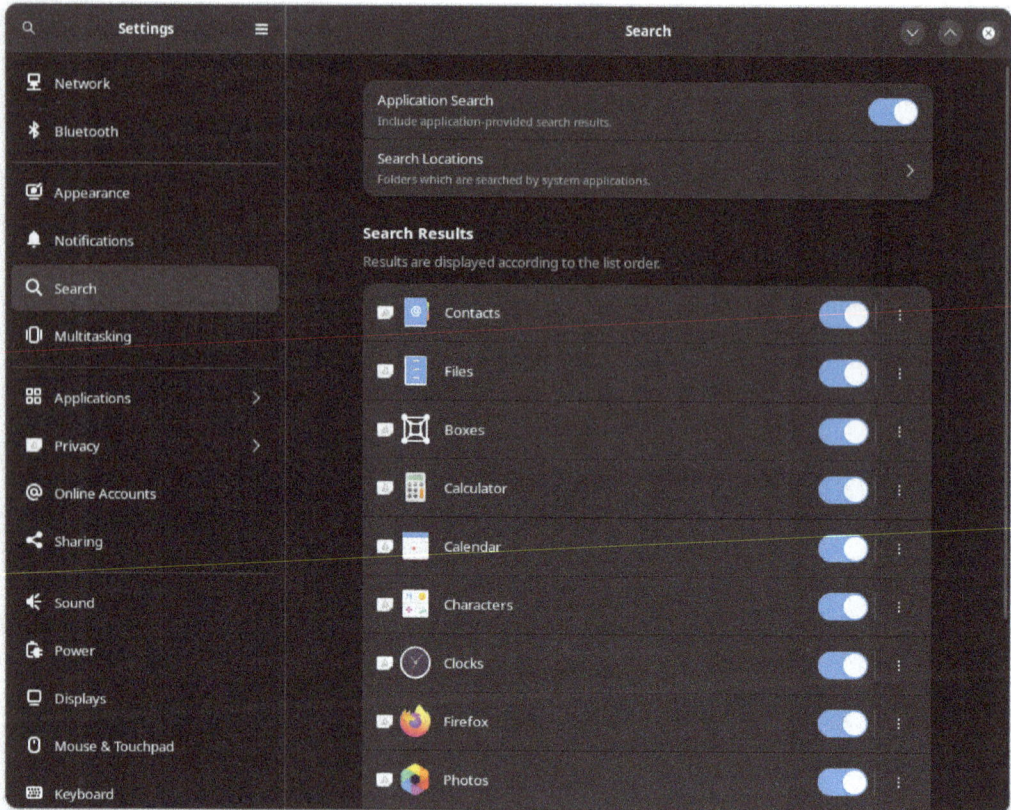

Figure 3.2 – Settings – Search

When a file search is enabled, a background program runs to read filenames and generate an index of them. This service runs often to detect new files as they are created. So, disabling file indexing can free up resources.

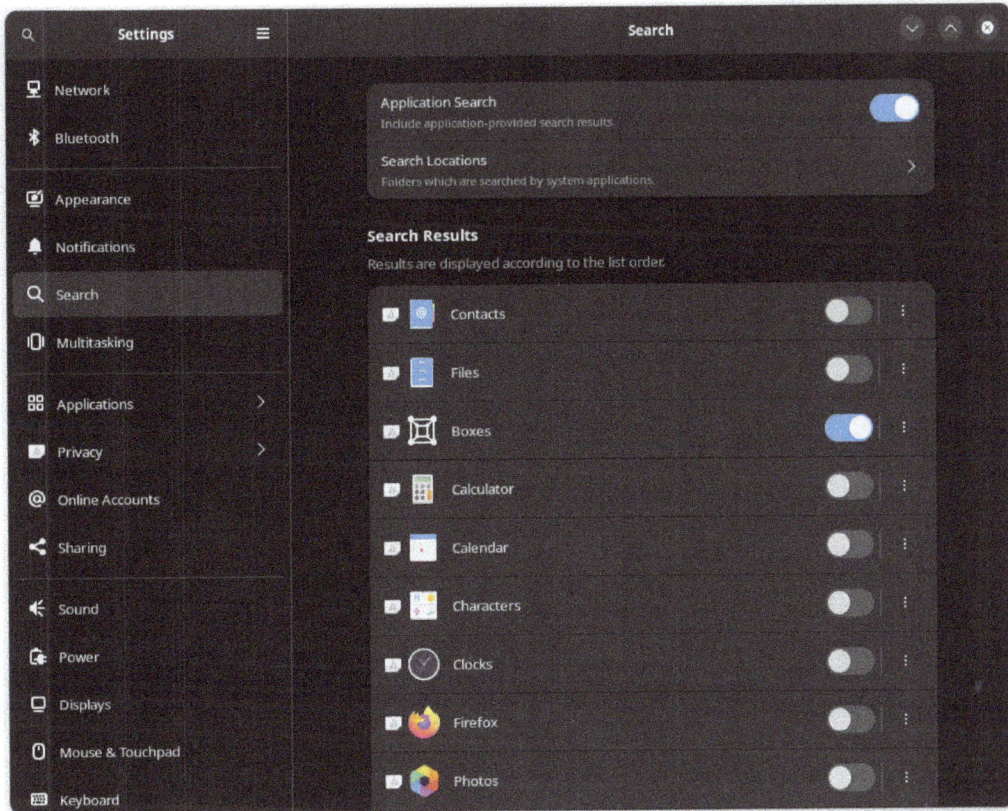

Figure 3.3 – Settings – Files disabled

Note

File indexing in GNOME comes from a service called `tracker`, which can be completely uninstalled to ensure that it does not run in the background. To uninstall it, run the `dnf remove` command:

```
[root@workstation ~]# dnf remove tracker
```

More tuning exists under GNOME, but the **tweak tool** should do the job. Install the tweak tool using the following `dnf` command:

```
[root@workstation ~]# dnf install gnome-tweaks
```

Let's now take a look at some of the tunings available with the tool.

GNOME Tweak Tool

GNOME Tweak Tool is a new application that contains a variety of customization options beyond what's available in the system settings (`https://wiki.gnome.org/Gnome3CheatSheet`).

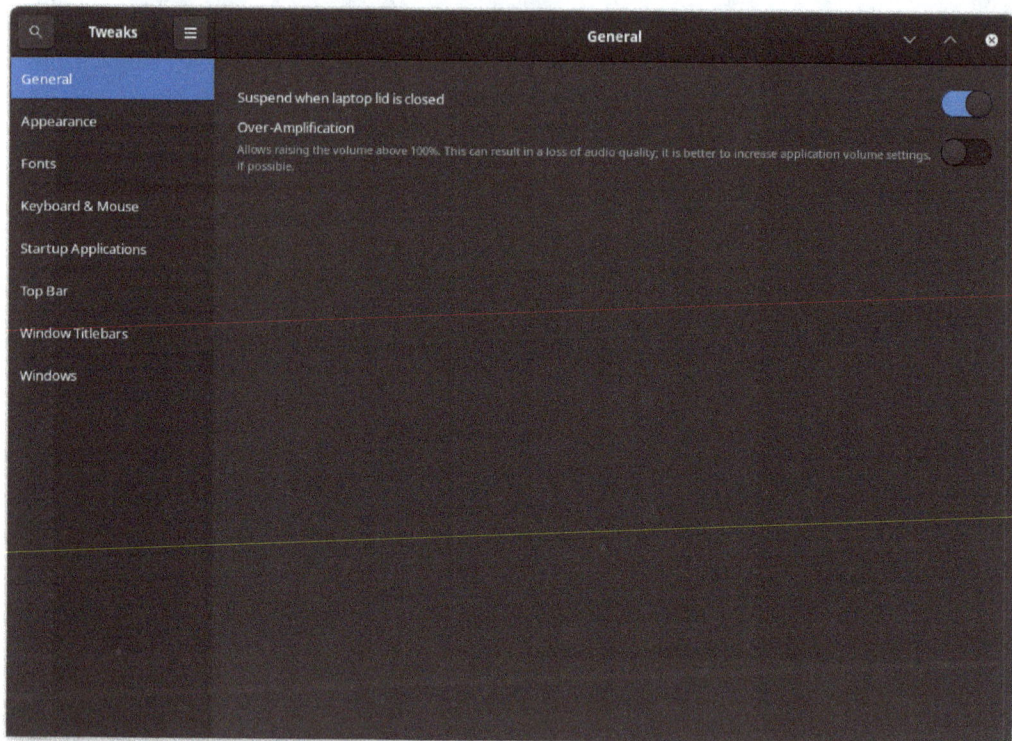

Figure 3.4 – GNOME Tweaks

These tunings change the behavior or use of different desktop elements, such as the following:

- **Appearance**
- **Fonts**
- **Keyboard & Mouse**
- **Startup Applications**
- **Top Bar**
- **Window Titlebars**
- **Windows**

A very useful tuning when our workstation is not portable is to disable the **suspension** of the computer when the lid closes. To disable this behavior, turn off the **Suspend when laptop lid is closed** switch in the **General** section of **Tweaks**.

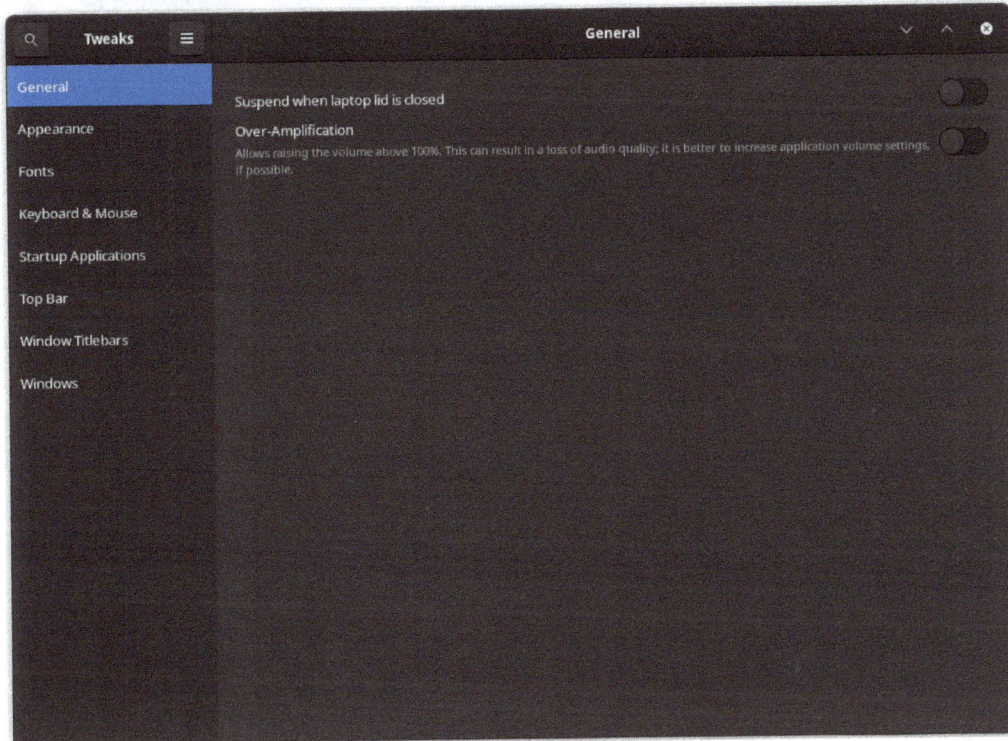

Figure 3.5 – GNOME Tweaks – General

Note

Suspension is useful when moving around because it *saves* battery power. Please consider whether this option is useful for your day-to-day tasks.

Another tuning we should keep an eye on is the **system startup** applications, which are set in the **Startup Applications** section of **Tweaks**.

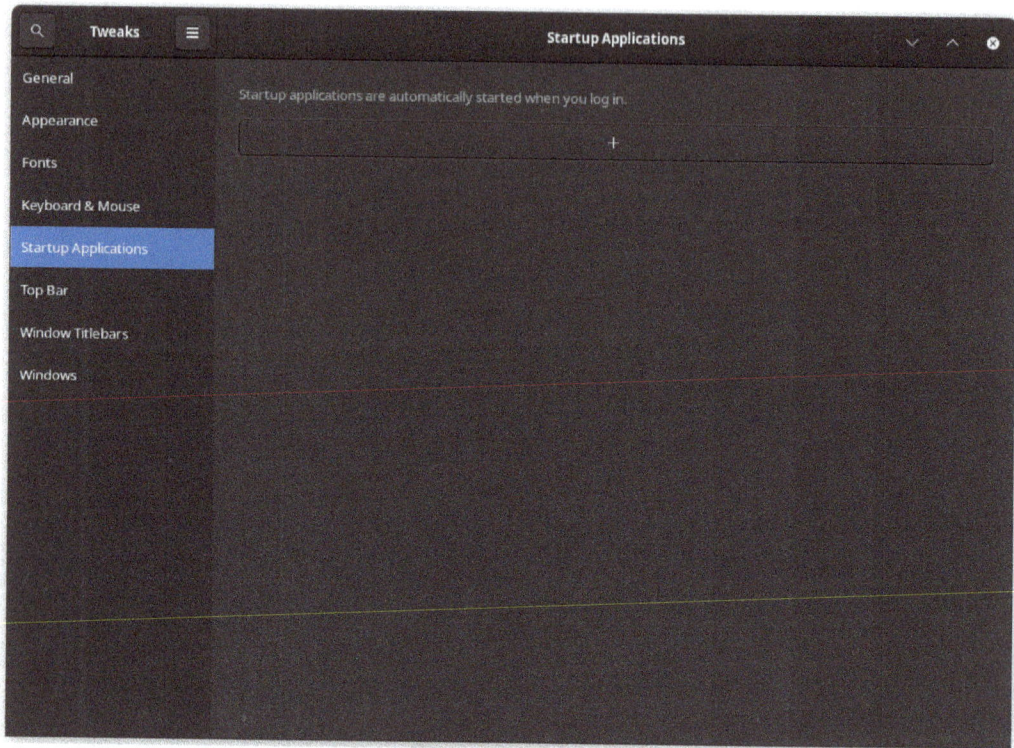

Figure 3.6 – GNOME Tweaks – Startup Applications

To add a startup application, click on the plus sign (+) and add the program.

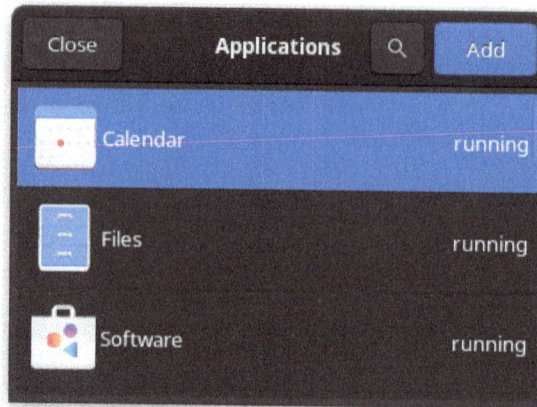

Figure 3.7 – GNOME Tweaks – Adding Startup Applications

These tunings are the basic ones to optimize the performance of the desktop environment in our workstation. Now, let's see some customizations to improve the user experience.

GNOME Shell extensions

These customizations come through the available GNOME desktop extensions. In the same way as with Chrome and Firefox browser extensions, **GNOME Shell extensions** enable small changes and modify the way GNOME works.

GNOME shell extensions can be installed with the `dnf install` command, and also from the browser, as follows:

1. Open the URL `https://extensions.gnome.org/` in the Firefox web browser.

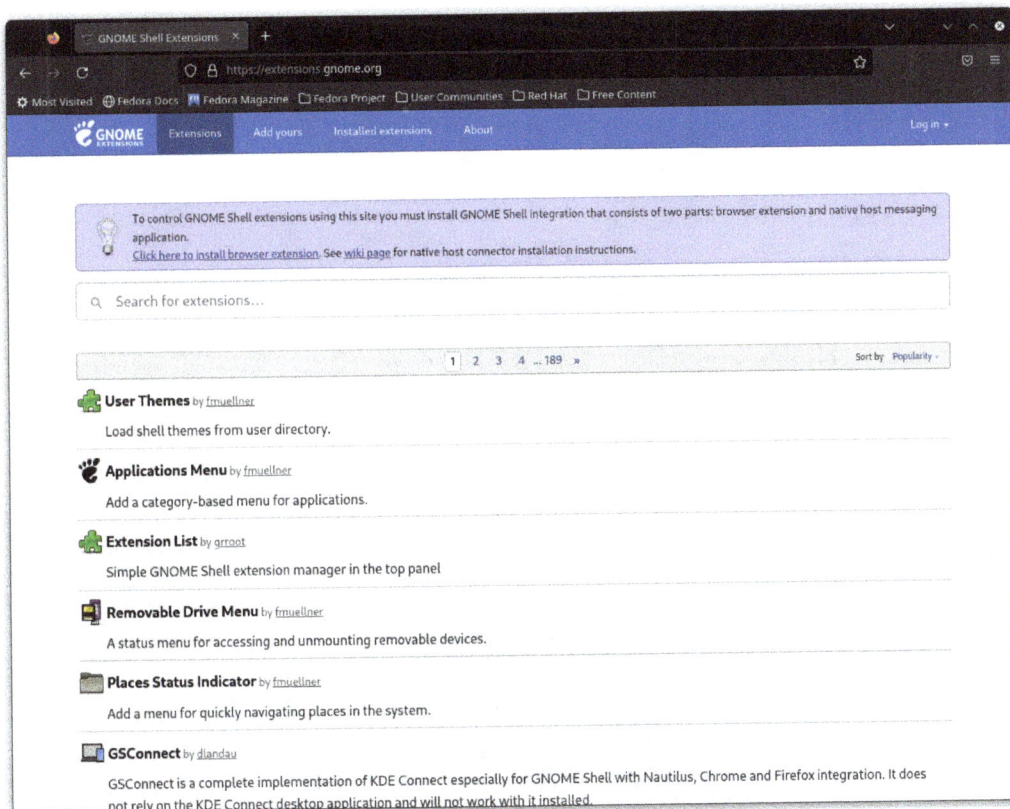

Figure 3.8 – GNOME Shell extensions

2. Click on the **Click here to install browser extension** link to install the browser extension, add the **GNOME Shell integration** extension, and accept the installation.

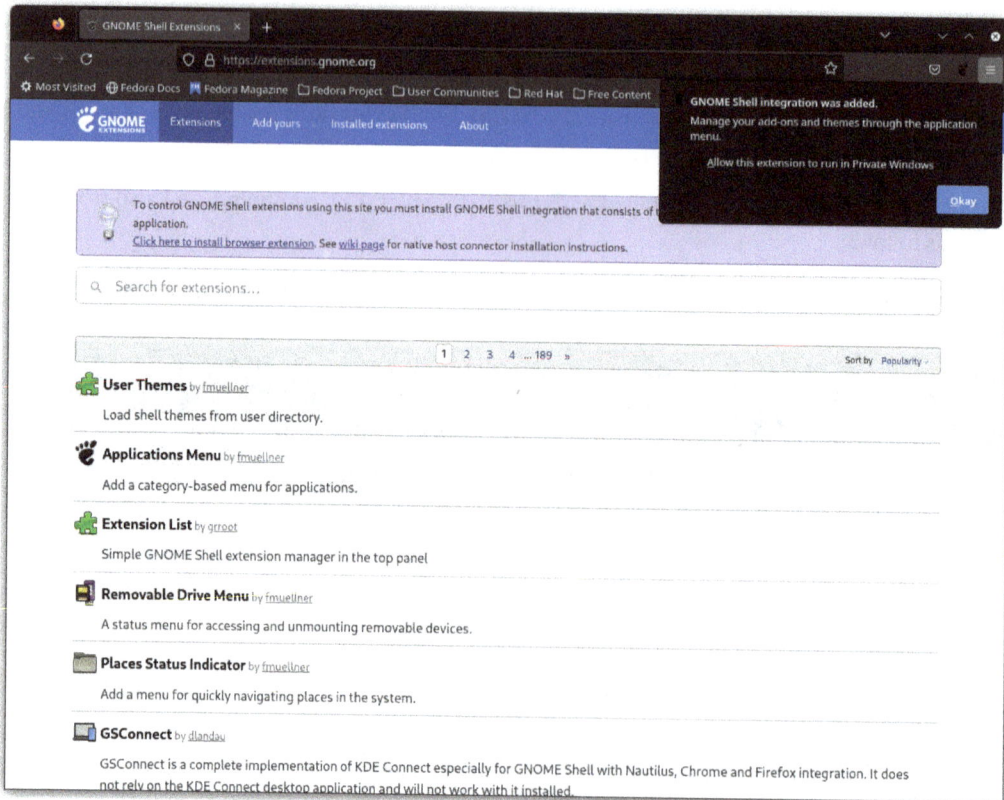

Figure 3.9 – GNOME Shell integration extension installed

3. Once the installation is complete, the GNOME icon appears in the browser bar.

Figure 3.10 – GNOME icon in the browser bar

4. Press the *F5* key to refresh the page and install the extensions.

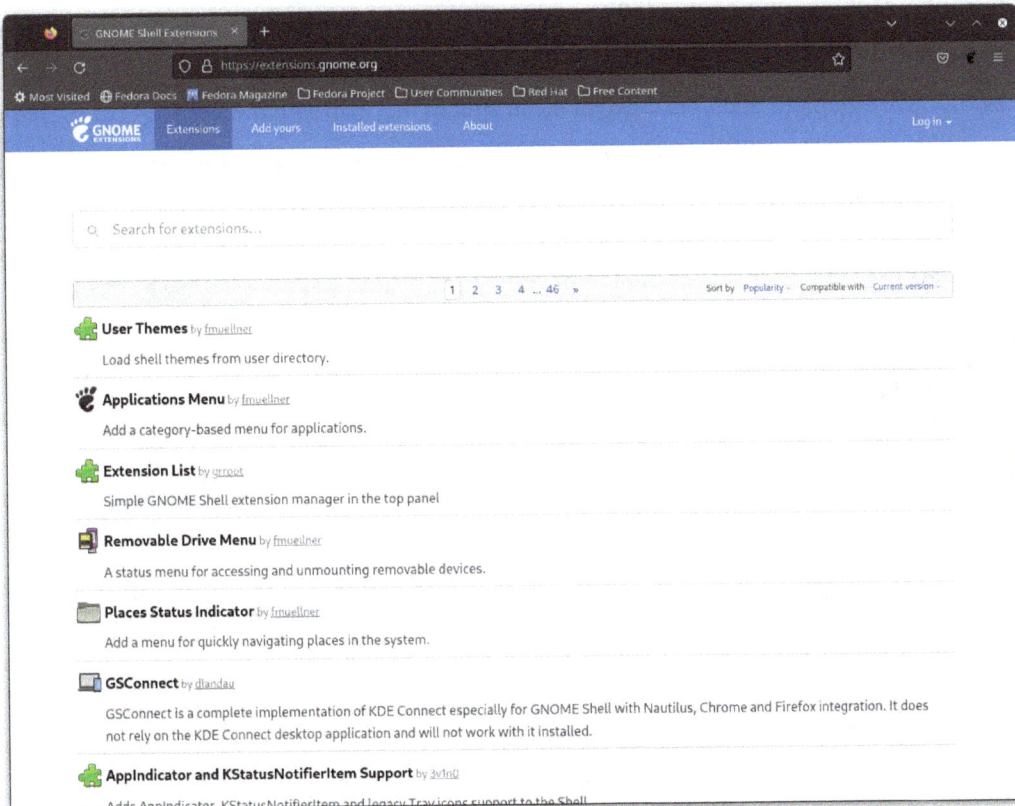

Figure 3.11 – GNOME Extensions page

Now, let's go over how to customize each component of our desktop environment, starting with the panel and the taskbar.

Customizing the panel and the taskbar

One of the functionalities that everybody misses in the desktop environment is having a menu that allows organized access to applications.

In the GNOME extensions, there are different menu options that help with this need.

In my case, I like to use the **ArcMenu extension**, as it provides a clean and clear organization of applications, and it adds some shortcuts to directories and system settings.

In the search bar, type ArcMenu, then click on the extension name, and toggle the switch to **ON** on the extension page (`https://extensions.gnome.org/extension/3628/arcmenu/`). Click on the **Install** button.

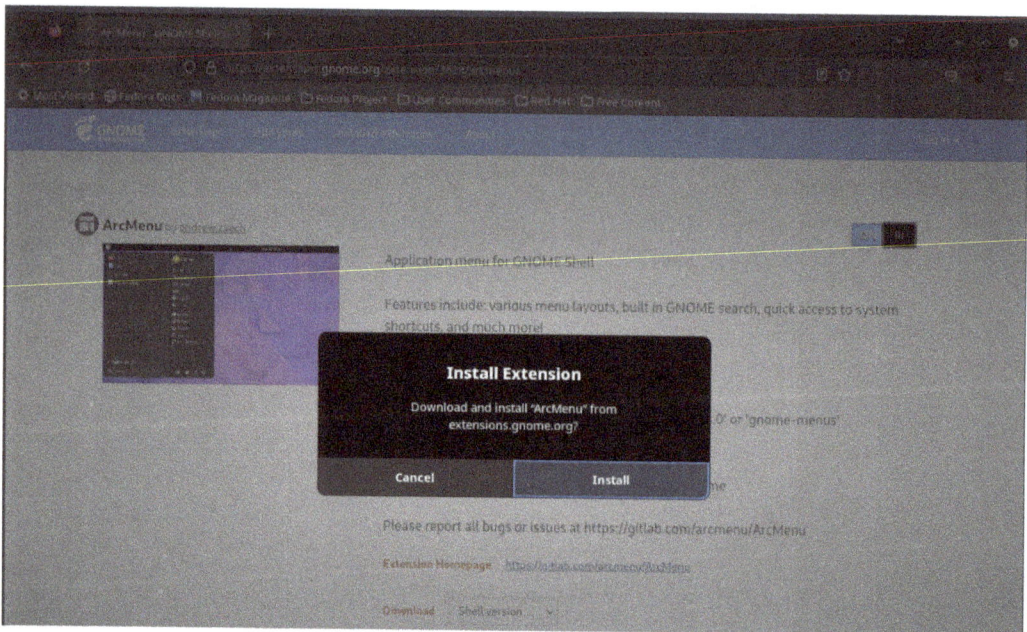

Figure 3.12 – ArcMenu extension installation

The **ArcMenu** icon appears in the upper-left corner instead of the **Activities** menu. Click on it, and the menu opens.

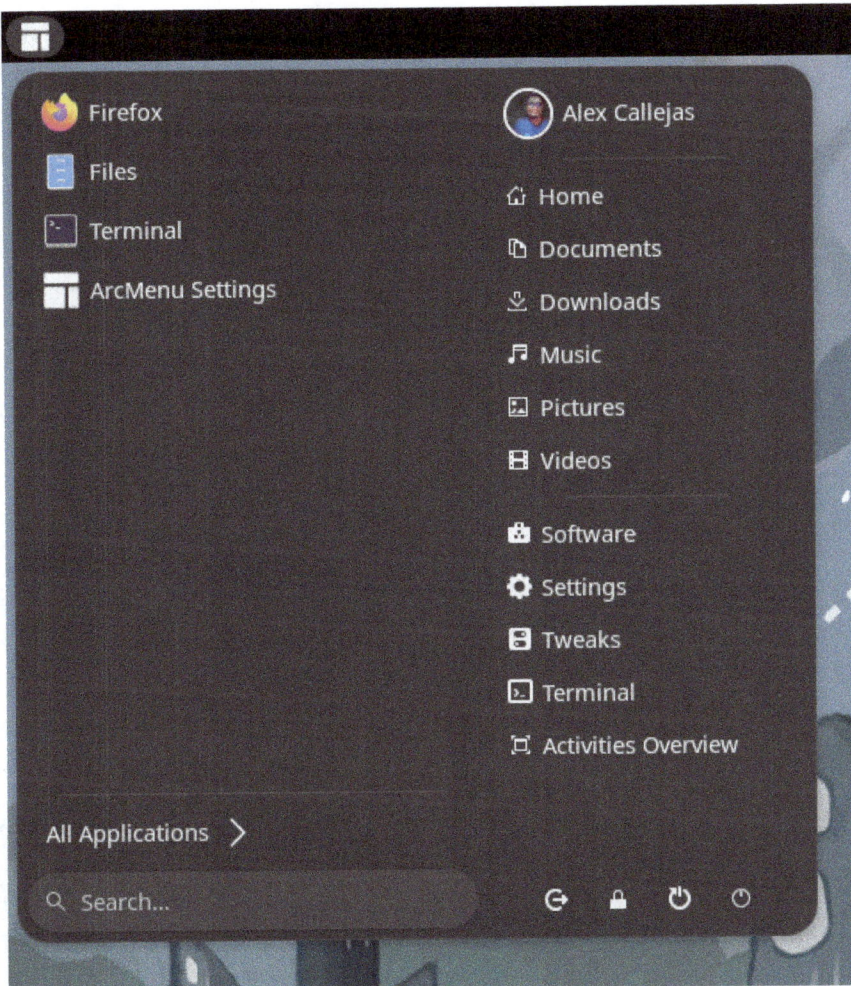

Figure 3.13 – ArcMenu extension

Click on the ArcMenu **Settings** button to change the appearance and organization of the applications, as well as to add or remove shortcuts.

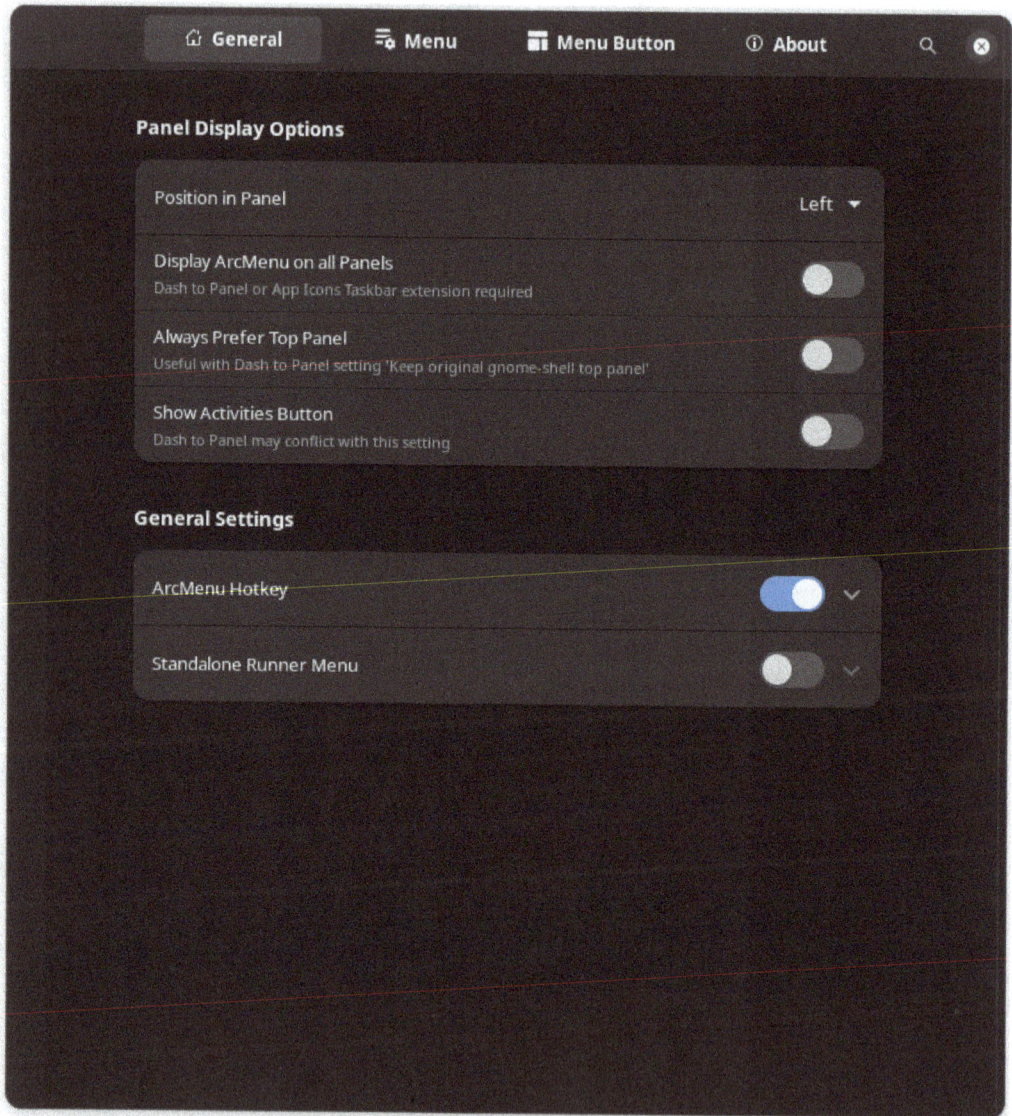

Figure 3.14 – ArcMenu settings

Instead of the *ArcMenu* icon, I prefer the *Fedora* icon to be shown. To do this, click on the **Menu Button** tab and click on the **Browse** button in the **Choose a new icon** section. Then, in the **Distro Icons** tab, choose the **Fedora** icon.

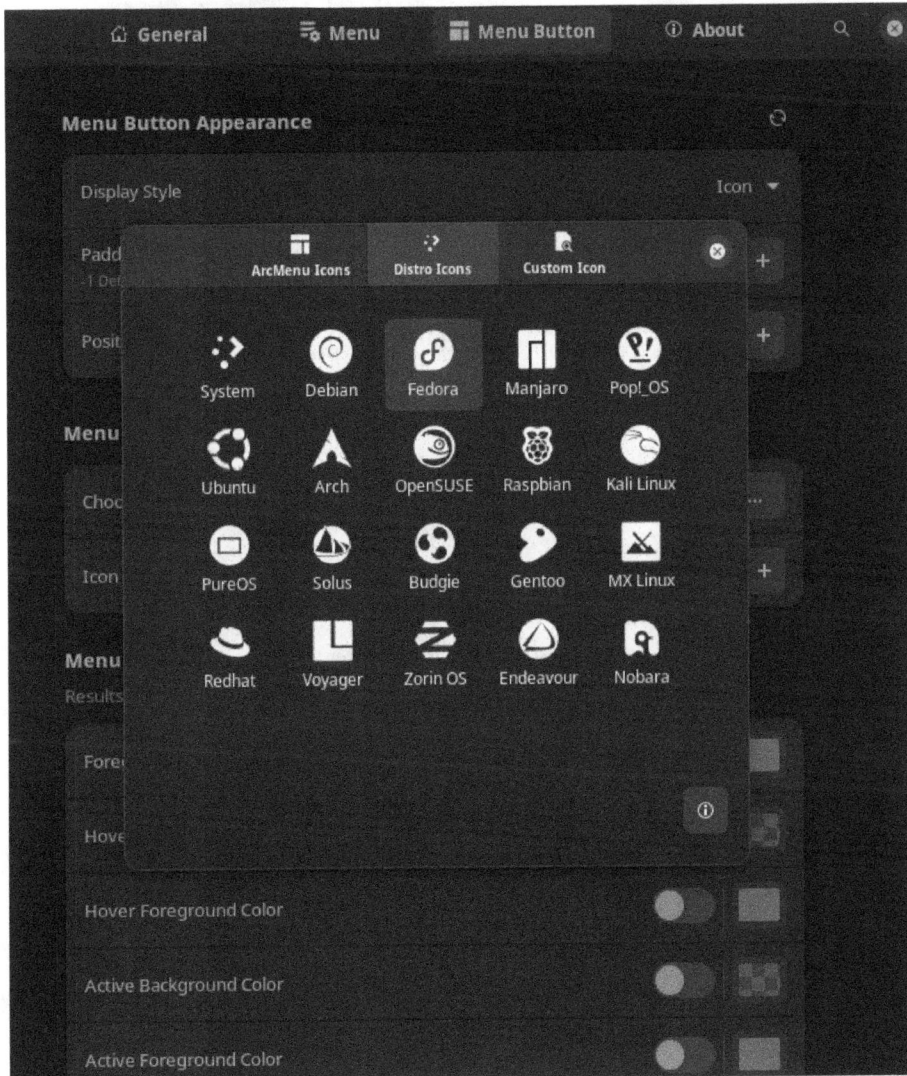

Figure 3.15 – Choosing the Fedora icon

Close the window, and now the Fedora icon shows up as the menu in the top-left corner.

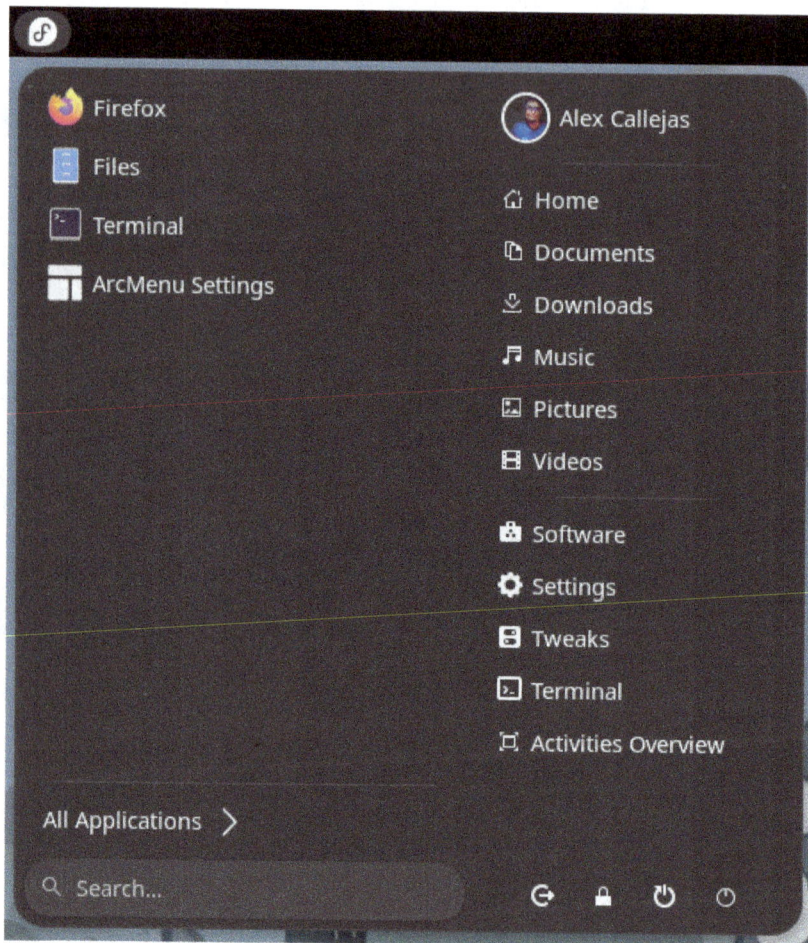

Figure 3.16 – ArcMenu with the Fedora icon

The extension installation procedure is the same in all cases. Let's now look at the extensions that will help us to improve the taskbar.

The taskbar

In the taskbar, the best practices include shortcuts to the most used applications, as well as to the general information and system settings.

On the left side, next to the menu, add the **Frippery Panel Favorites** extension (`https://extensions.gnome.org/extension/4/panel-favorites/`).

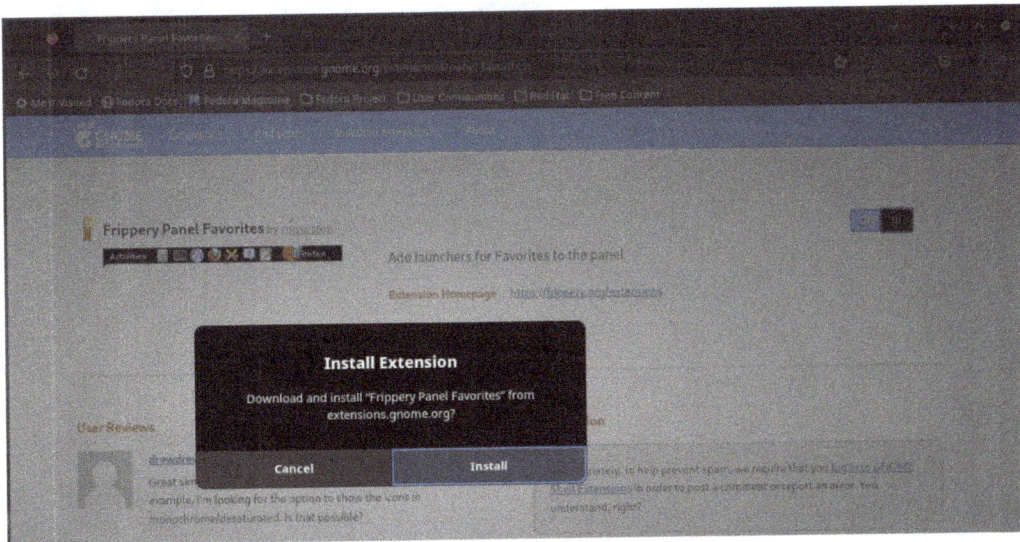

Figure 3.17 – Frippery Panel Favorites

To add or remove favorites, from the menu, click on the **Activities Overview** icon and drag and drop the application icons to the bottom bar.

Figure 3.18 – Favorites applications

To have local weather information, add the **OpenWeather** extension (`https://extensions.gnome.org/extension/750/openweather/`) next to the clock in the center of the taskbar.

Figure 3.19 – OpenWeather extension

To change the location, click on the *settings icon* button in the lower-right corner, and in the **Locations** tab of the **Settings** window, click on the **Add** button to find the location and add it.

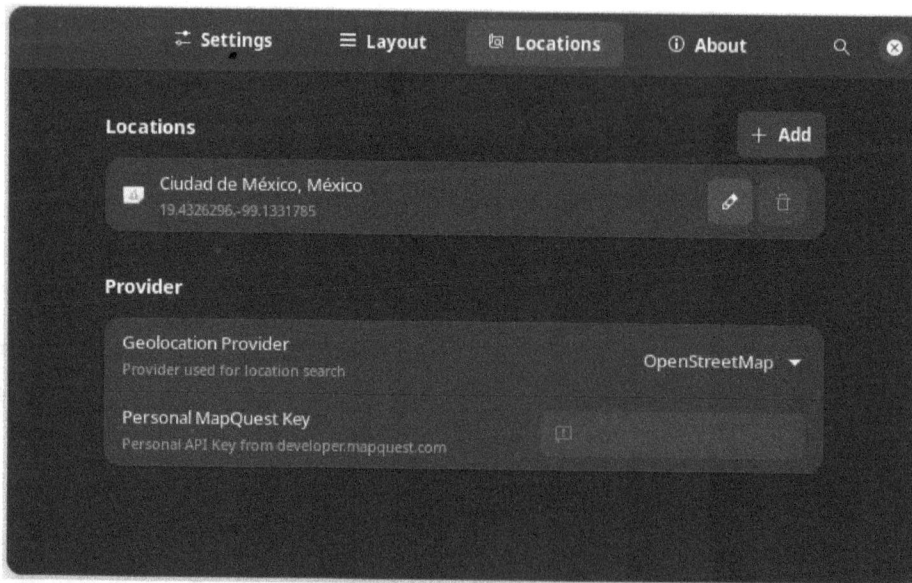

Figure 3.20 – OpenWeather Settings

The extensions that I recommend for the upper-right corner are as follows:

- **Clipboard Indicator** – Saves the text copied for reuse:

  `https://extensions.gnome.org/extension/779/clipboard-indicator/`

- **Extension List** – Provides access to the extension's configuration:

  `https://extensions.gnome.org/extension/3088/extension-list/`

- **Hide Keyboard Layout** – Hides the keyboard layout configuration:

  `https://extensions.gnome.org/extension/2848/hide-keyboard-layout/`

- **Section Todo List** – Adds a simple to-do list:

  `https://extensions.gnome.org/extension/1104/section-todo-list/`

- **Removable Drive Menu** – When inserting a removable disk, it adds a quick access to unmount it:

  `https://extensions.gnome.org/extension/7/removable-drive-menu/`

In the case of a portable computer, the **Battery Time** extension (`https://extensions.gnome.org/extension/5425/battery-time/`) indicates the remaining charge time.

Figure 3.21 – Taskbar – Upper-right corner

Other extensions that help improve the look and feel of the desktop environment are as follows:

- **User Avatar In Quick Settings** – Displays the user's profile picture in the **Settings** part of the upper-right corner:

  `https://extensions.gnome.org/extension/5506/user-avatar-in-quick-settings/`

- **Transparent Shell** – Makes desktop components (top bar, dash, workspace view, etc.) transparent:

  `https://extensions.gnome.org/extension/3518/transparent-shell/`

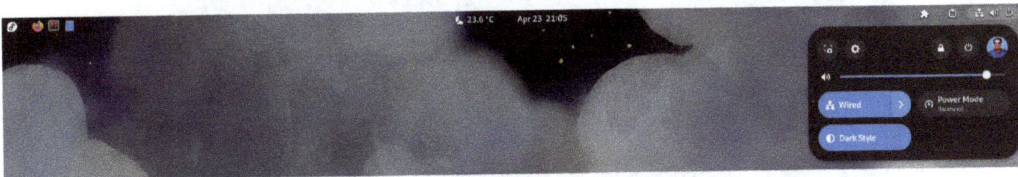

Figure 3.22 – Customized taskbar

Fedora provides an extension that displays the distribution logo on the desktop wallpaper. You can install the `gnome-shell-extension-background-logo` package using the following `dnf` command:

```
[root@workstation ~]# dnf install gnome-shell-extension-background-
logo
```

Click on the **Extensions List** icon in the upper-right corner, then click on the *gear* icon next to the **Background Logo** extension to customize how the Fedora logo is displayed.

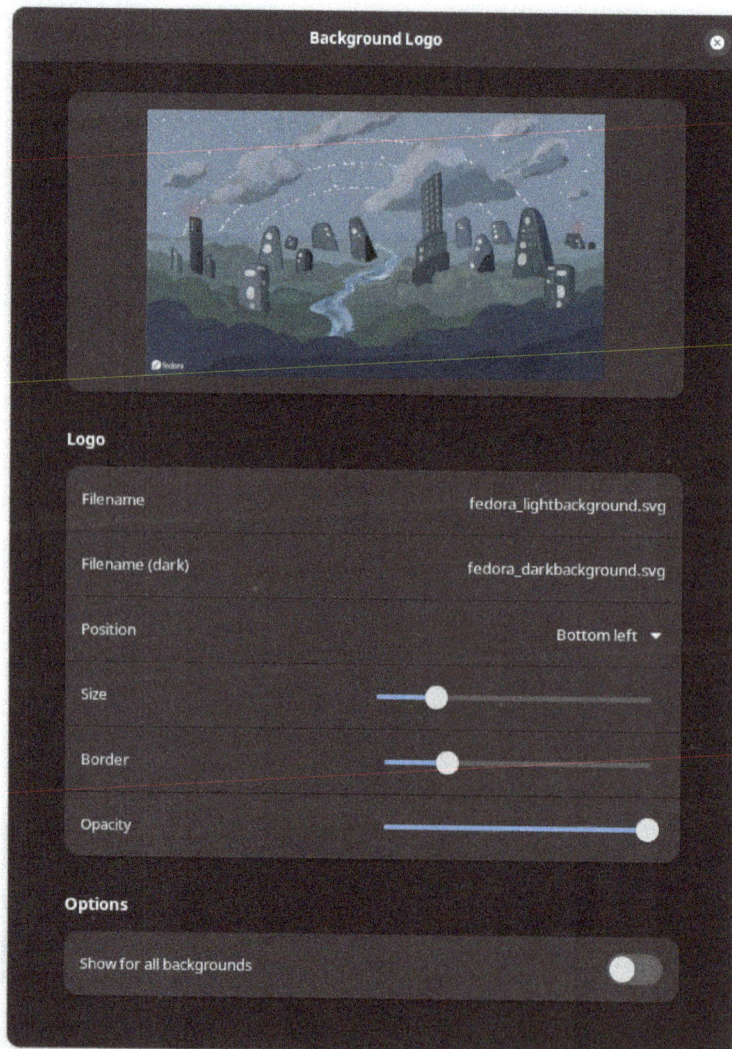

Figure 3.23 – Background Logo settings

Another thing that also improves the look and feel of the desktop environment is the **wallpaper**. One recommendation is to use a neutral background that does not distract our attention. On the `https://pixabay.com/` page, you can find some free-usage minimalist images to use as a wallpaper.

To change the wallpaper, right-click on the desktop background and select **Change background**, then in the **Appearance** section of the **Settings** window, click on the + **Add Picture** button to add the downloaded image and apply the change.

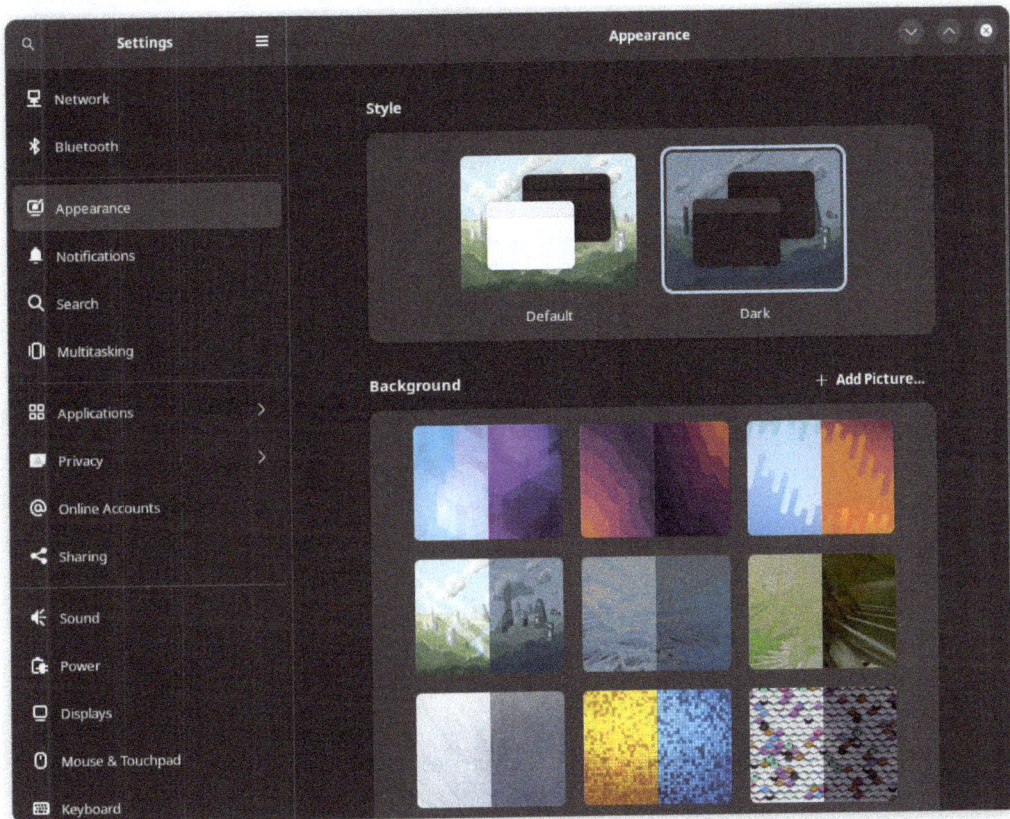

Figure 3.24 – Appearance settings

Now, our custom desktop environment looks and feels better.

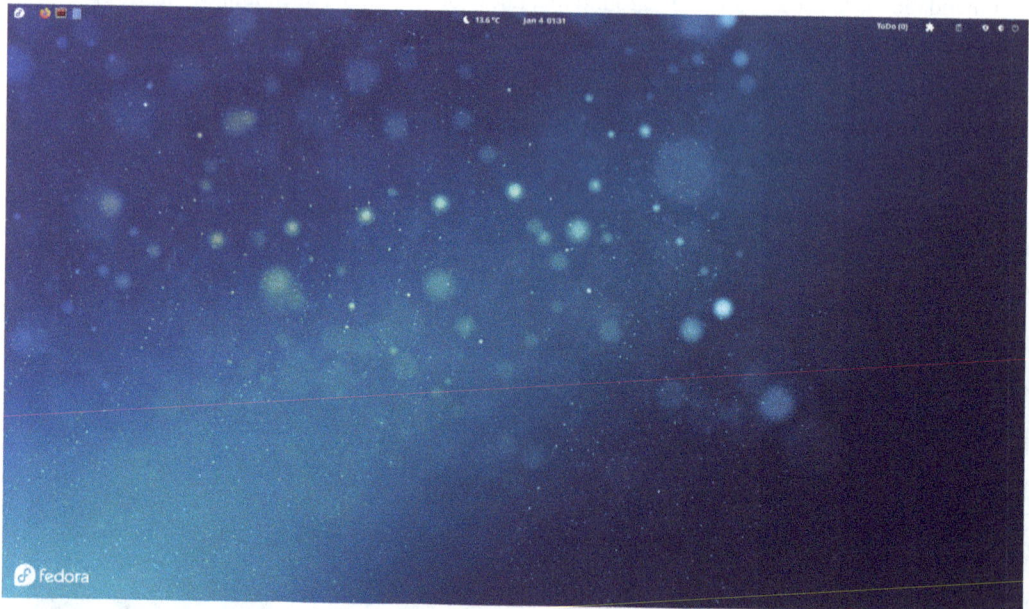

Figure 3.25 – Customized desktop

Our desktop environment looks pretty good, but we could improve it even more with other elements. Let's see how to do that next.

Making tasks easy with widgets

Widgets are small applications designed to ease access or provide information on the desktop.

A to-do list shows a simple list of tasks to do, but if you need more details about the tasks or their development, you can use the GNOME **Task Widget** extension (`https://extensions.gnome.org/extension/3569/task-widget/`).

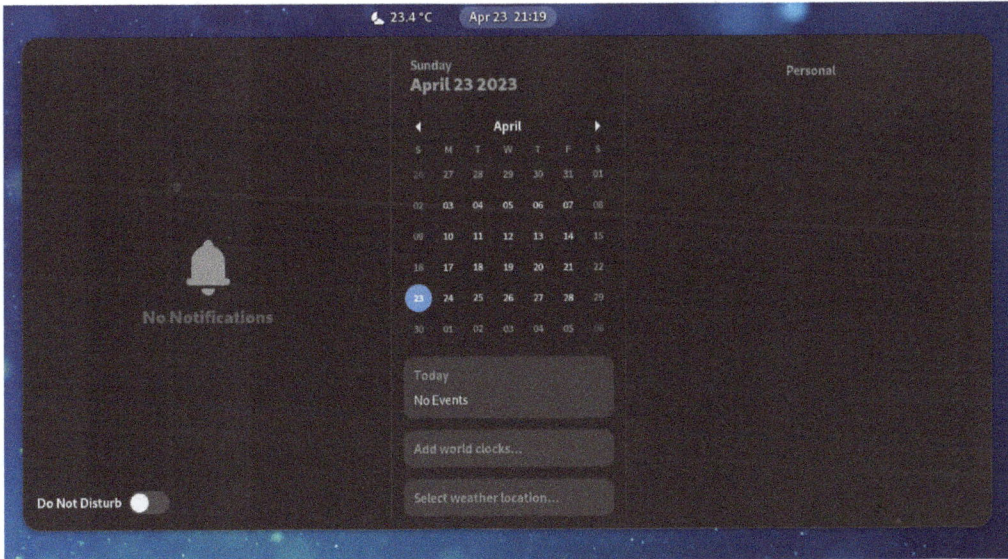

Figure 3.26 – Task widget extension

The **Task Widget** extension displays tasks near the Calendar widget, providing easy access to the task list along with the ability to merge task lists, group them by due date, mark them as completed for historical record, plus integrate with mail application calendars.

In Linux, widgets are generally used to provide computer performance information. There are various extensions that can be used to present information in the taskbar:

- **Resource Monitor** – Displays CPU, memory, storage and network usage:

  `https://extensions.gnome.org/extension/1634/resource-monitor/`

Figure 3.27 – Resource Monitor extension

- **System Monitor** – Shows the use of resources by icons that change color according to their use. By default, it is placed in the center of the taskbar, but its location could be customized:

  `https://extensions.gnome.org/extension/1064/system-monitor/`

Figure 3.28 – System Monitor extension

- **TopHat** – Displays CPU, memory, and network usage in a small graph:

  `https://extensions.gnome.org/extension/5219/tophat/`

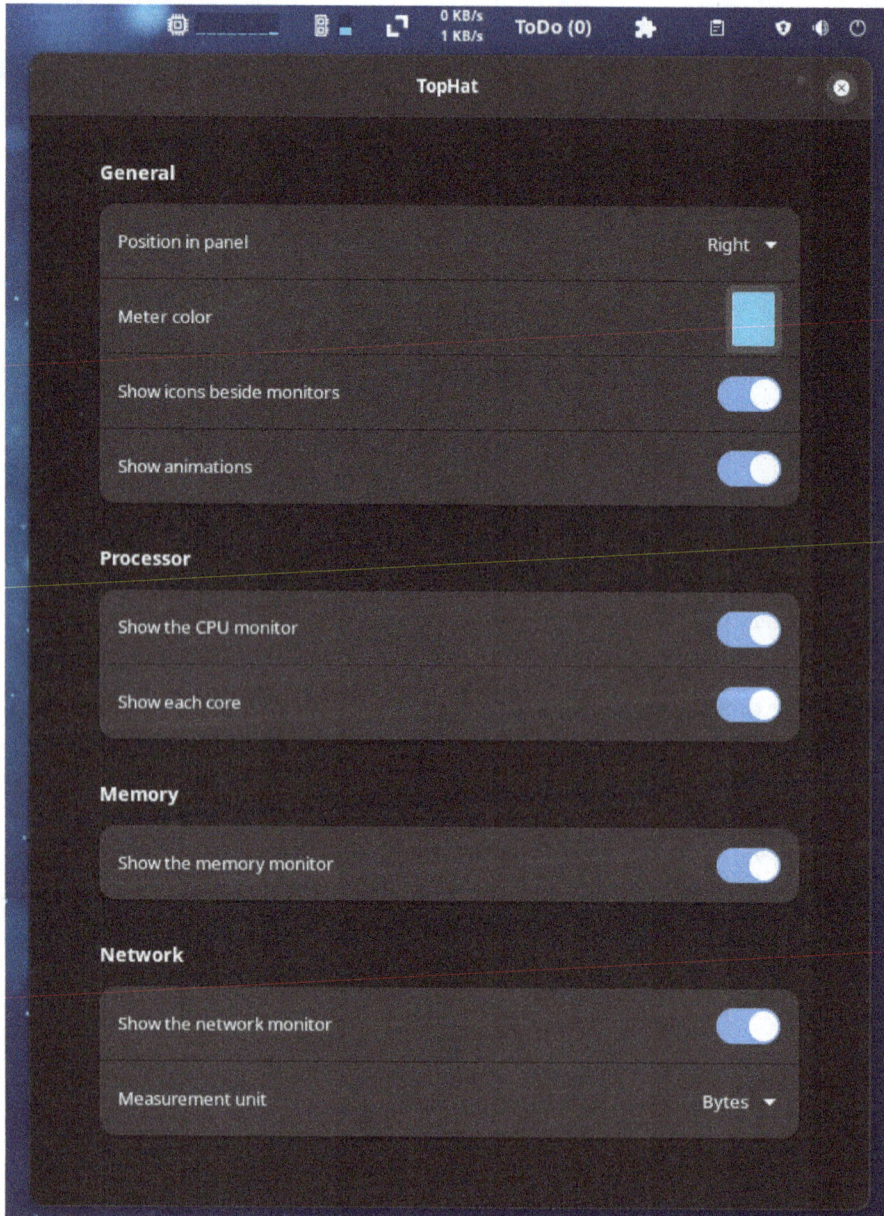

Figure 3.29 – TopHat extension

- **Vitals** – Displays a summary of CPU, memory, and network usage via icons, but clicking on the extension displays all monitored resources:

```
https://extensions.gnome.org/extension/1460/vitals/
```

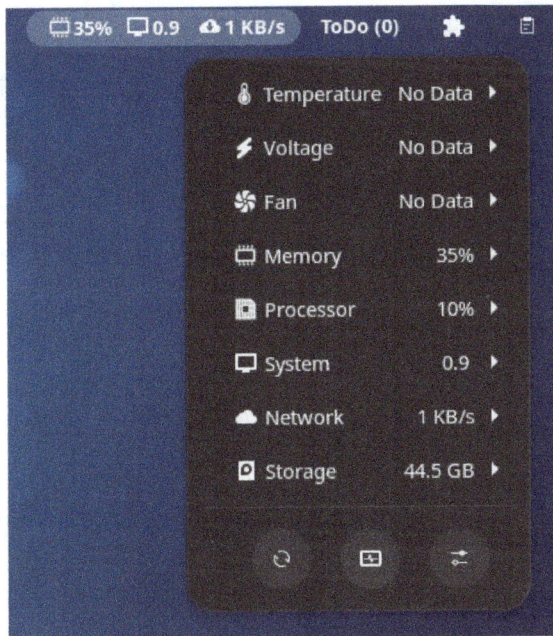

Figure 3.30 – Vitals extension

I do not use these extensions, as they somehow take away space from the taskbar and, in some cases, the taskbar looks like it has collapsed with so much information. In my case, I prefer an option that keeps my taskbar cleaner and displays all the system information I need on the desktop.

Conky

Conky (`https://github.com/brndnmtthws/conky`) is a lightweight system monitor, created for the *X Window System*. It displays any kind of information on the desktop.

You can install Conky using the following `dnf` command:

```
[root@workstation ~]# dnf install conky
```

You can browse the internet to find a lot of templates with different designs that could apply to Conky. I like to use those posted at `https://www.deviantart.com/`.

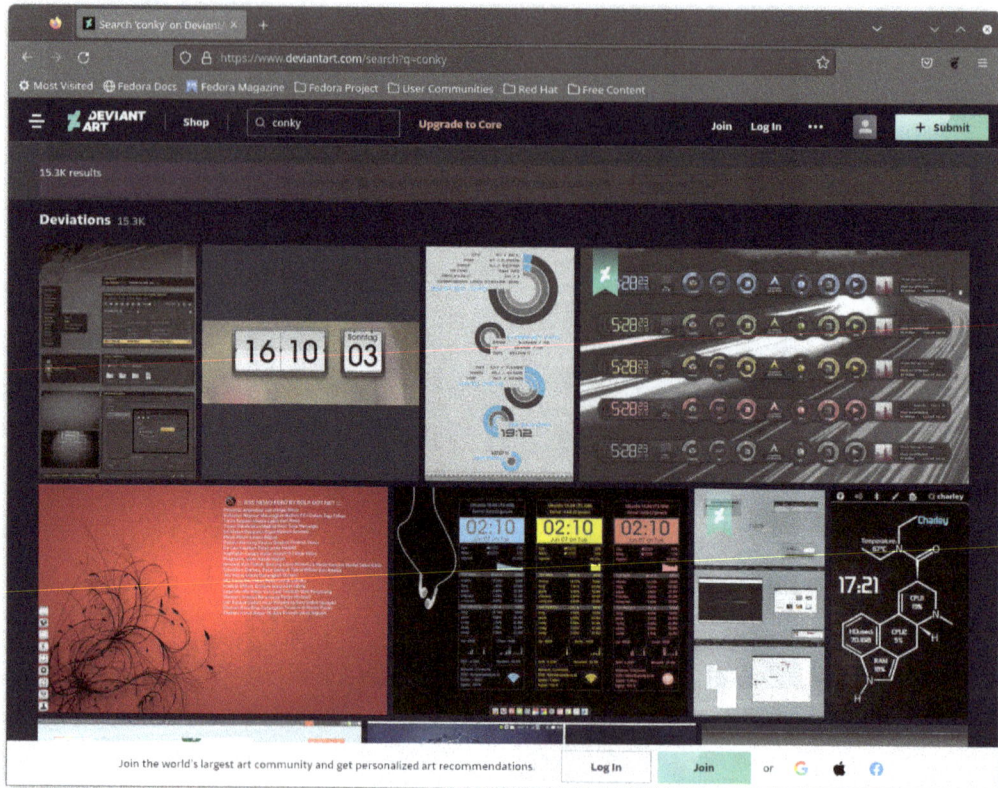

Figure 3.31 – Conky designs at deviantart.com

I found my favorite Conky template, `conky_harmattan`, in a Deviant Art post (`https://github.com/zagortenay333/conky_themes/tree/master/conky_harmattan`). It has many themes included, but we'll use the **Glass theme** in its **God-Mode version**. Clone the `conky_themes` repository in the user's home directory to install it:

```
[acallejas@workstation ~]$ git clone \
```

> **Note**
> We'll talk a bit more about Git in a later chapter.

Change to the `conky_harmattan` directory inside the `conky_themes` directory:

```
[acallejas@workstation ~]$ cd conky_themes/conky_harmattan
```

Copy the `.harmattan-assets` and `.harmattan-themes` directories to the user's home directory, keeping them as hidden directories:

```
[acallejas@workstation conky_harmattan]$ cp -r .harmattan-assets ~/
[acallejas@workstation conky_harmattan]$ cp -r .harmattan-themes ~/
```

> **Note**
> **Hidden directories** are those that have a name beginning with a period (`.`).

We'll create a file in the `.config/autostart` directory in the user's home directory to add `conky` to the system startup. With this, when we start our session, `conky` runs and displays it on the desktop.

Create the `~/.config/autostart/start_conky.desktop` file with the following content:

```
[acallejas@workstation ~]$ vi .config/autostart/start_conky.desktop
[Desktop Entry]
Type=Application
Exec=/bin/sh -c "$HOME/.config/autostart/start_conky.sh"
Hidden=false
NoDisplay=false
Terminal=false
X-GNOME-Autostart-enabled=true
Name=Conky
GenericName=ConkyStartup
Comment=Conky Harmattan Startup
```

Now, create the conky startup script as `~/.config/autostart/start_conky.sh` with the following content:

```
[acallejas@workstation ~]$ cat .config/autostart/start_conky.sh
#!/bin/bash
killall conky
sleep 10
conky -c $HOME/.harmattan-themes/Glass/God-Mode/.conkyrc
```

Add execute permissions to the `start_conky.sh` script:

```
[acallejas@workstation ~]$ chmod +x .config/autostart/start_conky.sh
```

> **Note**
>
> You can find both files in the repository of this book at `https://github.com/PacktPublishing/Fedora-Linux-System-Administration/tree/main/chapter3`.

As indicated in the `conky_harmattan` documentation, register a private API key in **OpenWeatherMap** (`http://openweathermap.org/`) to get the current weather information. On the same page, find the city code by searching for it and copying the code from the URL address of the browser:

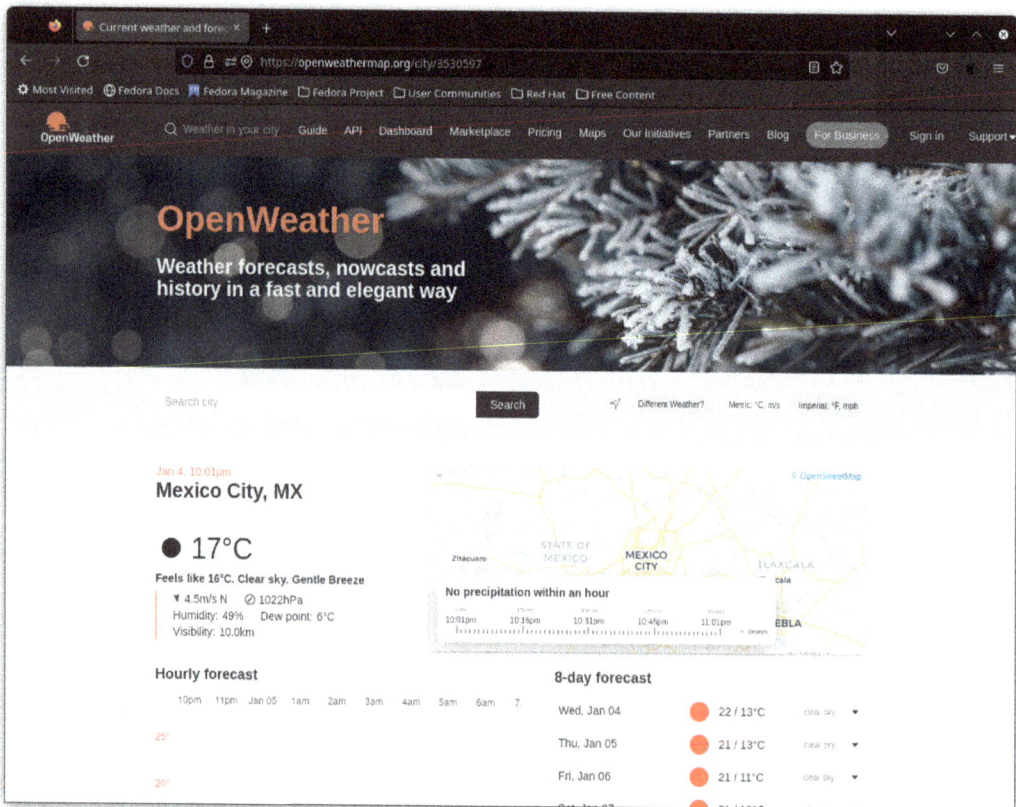

Figure 3.32 – OpenWeatherMap page

Add both pieces of data by editing the ~/.harmattan-themes/Glass/God-Mode/.conkyrc file:

```
[acallejas@workstation ~]$ vi .harmattan-themes/Glass/God-Mode/.
conkyrc
...output omitted...
-----------------------------------
--  API Key
-----------------------------------
template6="d60bb6c3b2b806caf46c43...",

-----------------------------------
--  City ID
-----------------------------------
template7="3530597",
...output omitted...
```

Save the file and test the configuration by running conky from Terminal:

```
[acallejas@workstation ~]$ sh .config/autostart/start_conky.sh
```

Unless it sends an error, conky displays on the desktop:

Figure 3.33 – Conky on the desktop

To customize the `conky` location, edit the `~/.harmattan-themes/Glass/God-Mode/.conkyrc` file in the `Windows Specifications` section by changing the `gap_x` and `gap_y` values, depending on the screen resolution:

```
[acallejas@workstation ~]$ vi .harmattan-themes/Glass/God-Mode/.
conkyrc
...output omitted...
-------------------------------------
--   Window Specifications
-------------------------------------
gap_x=1900,
gap_y=15,
...output omitted...
```

Saving the file displays the change in Conky's position:

Figure 3.34 – Conky monitor

To see the transparent window, uncomment the following lines from the `Windows Specifications` section of the `~/.harmattan-themes/Glass/God-Mode/.conkyrc` file:

```
own_window_argb_visual=true,
own_window_argb_value=0,
```

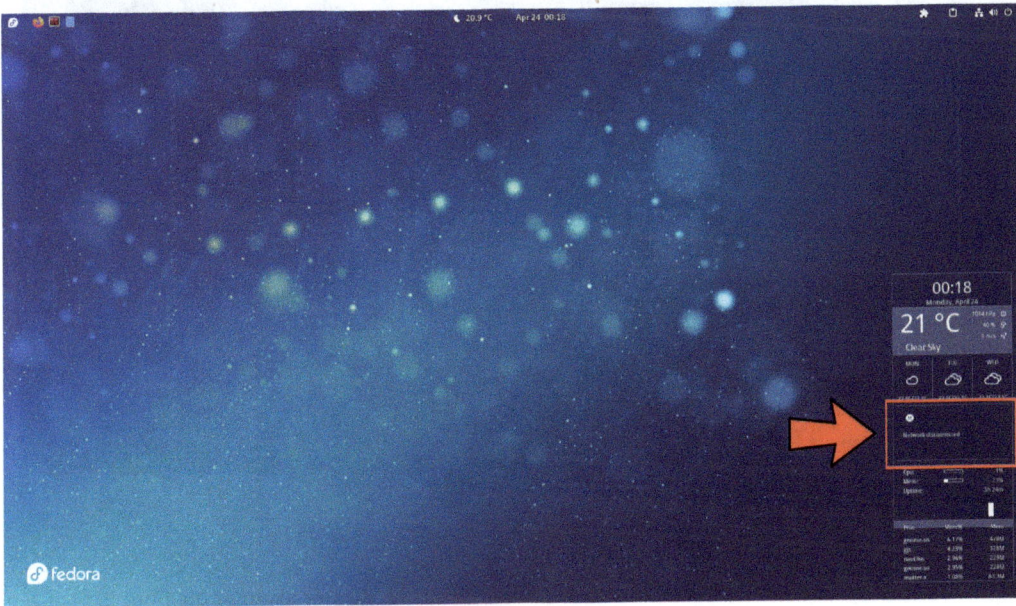

Figure 3.35 – Conky with transparent window

To fix the network graph, check that the device name is correct in the `conky.text` section of the `~/.harmattan-themes/Glass/God-Mode/.conkyrc` file:

```
${if_existing /proc/net/route enp1s0}
${voffset -344}${goto 40}${color5}Up: ${color2}${upspeed
enp1s0}${color5}${goto 150}Down: ${color2}${downspeed enp1s0}
${voffset 10}${goto 40}${upspeedgraph enp1s0 26,80 FFFFFF
FFFFFF}${goto 150}${downspeedgraph enp1s0 26,80 FFFFFF FFFFFF}
${voffset 9}${goto 40}${color5}Sent: ${color2}${totalup
enp1s0}${color5}${goto 150}Received: ${color2}${totaldown enp1s0}
${else}
```

Saving the file displays the graphs in Conky:

Figure 3.36 – Conky graphs

GNOME extensions include many extra ways of customization. A very popular element is **docks**. Let's see some of these options in the following section.

Handy applications with docks

Launchers or **docks** are a convenient way to access favorite and used applications. GNOME does not provide a dock, but you could get one through GNOME extensions.

The most popular are as follows:

- **Dash to Dock** – Provides the classic dock with favorite applications. The dock location could change in the extension settings:

  `https://extensions.gnome.org/extension/307/dash-to-dock/`

Figure 3.37 – Dash to Dock extension

- **Floating Dock** – Provides a dock with a button, which, when pressed, displays favorite applications. The location of the dock could change in the extension settings:

  `https://extensions.gnome.org/extension/2542/floating-dock/`

Figure 3.38 – Floating Dock extension

This customization provides us with a clean desktop for our day-to-day tasks.

These customizations, of course, are not the only ones that exist. A **Linux** system has a *high level* of customization, and even has specialized tools such as `fedy` (`https://github.com/rpmfusion-infra/fedy`), which let us add codecs and third-party or proprietary software from a graphical interface.

> **Important**
>
> **RPM Fusion** is a set of repositories that are not affiliated with or supported by the **Fedora Project**. For more information, refer to *Enabling the RPM Fusion repositories* in the Fedora documentation at `https://docs.fedoraproject.org/en-US/quick-docs/setup_rpmfusion/`.

Before discussing the functionality of the applications involved, the following chapters provide a brief overview of the basic concepts of storage and networking that are needed for later use.

Summary

This chapter offered an overview of desktop environment customization, from resource tuning to tools and tips for a clean and minimalistic desktop.

We divided it into tuning and customization. Keeping that in mind, we customized only the taskbar and its components, as well as added the `conky` system monitor.

Customizing each of the elements of the desktop environment, besides improving the way it looks and feels, allows us to focus on our tasks. It is well known in Linux-based environments, which provide extreme customization of each component, that this task could be endless.

In my experience as a system administrator, not getting distracted by this kind of customization helps me to focus on my daily work.

In the next chapter, we will review the concepts of basic local storage, as well as how to optimize its use.

Further reading

To learn more about the topics that were covered in this chapter, take a look at the following resources:

- *What Is Swappiness on Linux? (and How to Change It)*: `https://www.howtogeek.com/449691/what-is-swapiness-on-linux-and-how-to-change-it/`

- *GNOME 43*: `https://release.gnome.org/43/`

- *GNOME Wiki*: `https://wiki.gnome.org/`

- *GNOME 3 Cheat Sheet*: `https://wiki.gnome.org/Gnome3CheatSheet`

- *GNOME Help*: `https://help.gnome.org/`

- *GNOME Shell Extensions*: `https://extensions.gnome.org/about/`

4

Optimizing Storage Usage

In the previous chapter, during the installation of the OS, we mentioned the importance of the local storage configuration. Local storage resource optimization is vital to the well-being of the system. It is time to review basic storage management concepts that help with optimization, such as the format, filesystem, and sizing, as well as management tools such as logical volumes and Stratis.

In this chapter, we're going to cover the following main topics:

- Understanding file formats and filesystems
- Optimizing storage space size
- Deep diving into Logical Volume Manager
- Discovering Stratis storage

Let's get started!

Technical requirements

To perform some of the configurations included in this chapter, you require free local storage space, if possible, on a local disk independent of the operating system. No matter how large it is, this should do the job. In case of not having extra space, some configurations can be done in local free space on the same disk where the operating system was installed, although it is not recommended.

This will be mentioned when some configuration needs to be performed on a disk independent of the operating system or an alternate disk.

The following table shows the storage arrangement in the test setup:

Device	Size	Used as:
/dev/vda	50 GiB	OS
/dev/vdb	50 GiB	Btrfs, Stratis
/dev/vdc	10 GiB	Stratis
/dev/vdd	20 GiB	Stratis

Understanding file formats and filesystems

A **filesystem** allows the operating system to find the data it stores on its local disk. These basic addressable storage units make a **block** (usually about 4,096 bytes in size). To find the contents of files, among the large number of available storage blocks, it uses inodes. An **inode** contains information about a file in a particular formatted storage block, such as its size, location, access rules (i.e., who can read, write, or execute the file), and much more.

Starting with Fedora Linux 33, the default filesystem format on Workstation Edition is **Btrfs**. Unlike other distributions that still use xfs or even ext4, Btrfs is a **copy-on-write** (**COW**) filesystem for Linux that implements many advanced features.

In a COW filesystem, once modified, a file is not written back to the same block on disk; it's more like a redirect. This is for the preservation of the original data and to ensure writing the new data to unoccupied inodes. This allows for references to the old versions of the file for easy access as in a **snapshot**, keeping a snapshot of the state of the system at a given moment in time.

The downside of this is that this behavior could lead to file fragmentation faster than in other filesystems, although, for regular desktop usage, it is unlikely to make a difference.

To make the modified file appear in the filesystem, all directory entries that contain a reference to it get updated as well, in a recursive way. And because a directory is itself a file pointer with an inode (since it indicates the files inside it), any file modification also creates a new inode for the directory, and this happens through the filesystem to the root directory (/). So, as long as a reference to the old directories remain and is not modified, the entire filesystem could still refer to a previous state, as in a snapshot.

Besides cheap and fast snapshots, Btrfs includes other features such as error detection, fault tolerance, recovery, transparent compression, and integrated volume management, and provides multiple device storage pooling, RAID-like functionality, and checksumming of data and metadata, all with easy-to-use administration.

Let's create a test Btrfs filesystem to show its capabilities.

Creating a Btrfs filesystem

For the development of this example, use an alternative local disk to the OS installed. This introduces you to the capabilities of the Btrfs filesystem from scratch. Follow these steps:

1. Storage administration requires superuser access, so switch to the `root` user using the `sudo` command and create the `/btrfs` directory that will host the filesystem:

```
[user@workstation ~]$ sudo -i
[sudo] password for user: [password]
[user@workstation ~]$ mkdir /btrfs
```

2. Identify the device to use. Ensure that the test storage device is not in use. Formatting implies total destruction of the data.

   Several commands provide information about the use of storage devices. A recommendation is to use more than one command to verify them. These recommendations include the following:

   - `(s)fdisk -l`

   - `parted -l`

   - `cat /proc/partitions`

   - `ls -l /dev/disk/by-path`

   - `lsblk -p`

```
root@workstation:~

[root@workstation ~]# cat /proc/partitions
major minor  #blocks  name

   11        0    1048575 sr0
  252        0   52428800 vda
  252        1       1024 vda1
  252        2    1048576 vda2
  252        3   51377152 vda3
  252       16   52428800 vdb
  251        0    8134656 zram0
[root@workstation ~]# lsblk -p
NAME          MAJ:MIN RM  SIZE RO TYPE MOUNTPOINTS
/dev/sr0         11:0   1 1024M  0 rom
/dev/zram0      251:0   0  7.8G  0 disk [SWAP]
/dev/vda        252:0   0   50G  0 disk
├─/dev/vda1     252:1   0    1M  0 part
├─/dev/vda2     252:2   0    1G  0 part /boot
└─/dev/vda3     252:3   0   49G  0 part /home
                                        /
/dev/vdb        252:16  0   50G  0 disk
[root@workstation ~]#
```

Figure 4.1 – Identifying storage device

In our example, the storage device that is not in use is /dev/vdb, since it shows that it does not contain any partition. Still, it should be managed by **Logical Volume Manager (LVM)**. Run the following command to display the devices managed by LVM:

```
pvs -a
```

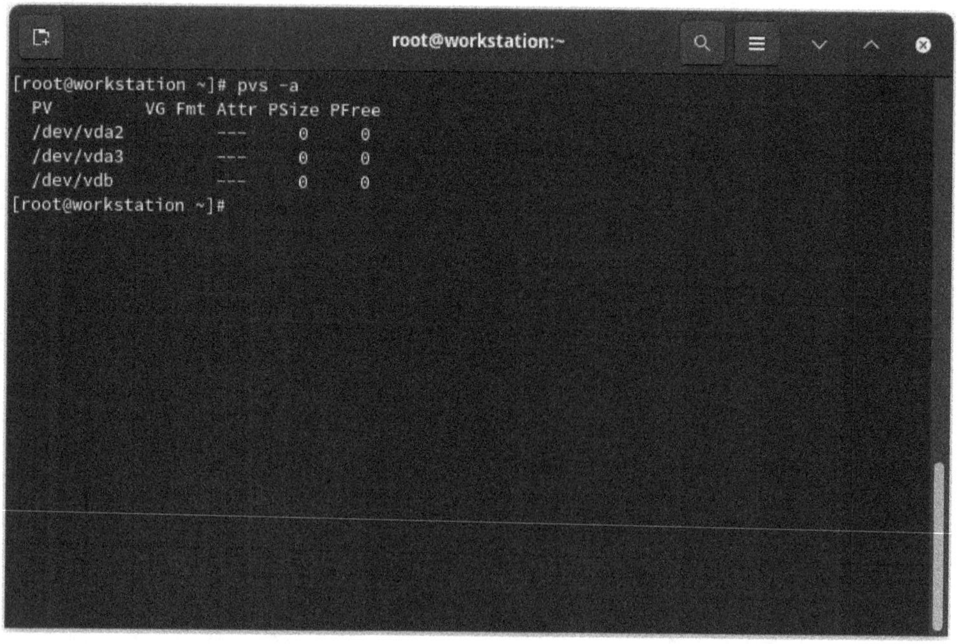

Figure 4.2 – Discarding LVM on the storage device

> **Note**
>
> In case of using a partition, you need to confirm that the partition is not in use by another filesystem and does not have a directory mounted. Use the following basic commands: **fdisk**, **parted**, **mount**, **df**, **lsblk**, and **blkid**.

3. Create a storage pool. With Btrfs, it is not necessary to create physical partitions on the storage device. Create a storage pool and then create subvolumes. These subvolumes can have quotas and snapshots since these resizable partitions can share blocks of data.

    Run the mkfs.btrfs command to format /dev/vdb as Btrfs:

    ```
    mkfs.btrfs -L testbtrfs /dev/vdb
    ```

```
[root@workstation ~]# mkfs.btrfs -L testbtrfs /dev/vdb
btrfs-progs v6.1.2
See http://btrfs.wiki.kernel.org for more information.

Performing full device TRIM /dev/vdb (50.00GiB) ...
NOTE: several default settings have changed in version 5.15, please make sure
      this does not affect your deployments:
      - DUP for metadata (-m dup)
      - enabled no-holes (-O no-holes)
      - enabled free-space-tree (-R free-space-tree)

Label:               testbtrfs
UUID:                def9423d-8684-487f-bd11-4829937752b6
Node size:           16384
Sector size:         4096
Filesystem size:     50.00GiB
Block group profiles:
  Data:              single            8.00MiB
  Metadata:          DUP             256.00MiB
  System:            DUP               8.00MiB
SSD detected:        no
Zoned device:        no
Incompat features:   extref, skinny-metadata, no-holes
Runtime features:    free-space-tree
Checksum:            crc32c
Number of devices:   1
Devices:
   ID        SIZE  PATH
    1     50.00GiB  /dev/vdb

[root@workstation ~]#
```

Figure 4.3 – Creating a Btrfs storage pool

4. Mount the storage device on the directory where subvolumes should be created. Use the mount command:

```
[root@workstation ~]# mount /dev/vdb /btrfs
```

With the Btrfs filesystem mounted, let's analyze the usage of its storage space.

5. To show the structure of a filesystem, run the following:

```
[root@workstation ~]# btrfs filesystem show /btrfs
Label: 'testbtrfs'  uuid: def9423d-8684-487f-bd11-4829937752b6
Total devices 1 FS bytes used 144.00KiB
devid    1 size 50.00GiB used 1.56GiB path /dev/vdb
```

6. To measure the available space on the filesystem, run the following:

```
[root@workstation ~]# btrfs filesystem df /btrfs
Data, single: total=1.00GiB, used=0.00B
System, DUP: total=32.00MiB, used=16.00KiB
Metadata, DUP: total=256.00MiB, used=128.00KiB
GlobalReserve, single: total=3.50MiB, used=0.00B
```

> **Note**
>
> The following section will explain in detail the meaning of the command output.

In Btrfs, a subvolume is similar to a filesystem contained in the host. A Btrfs filesystem contains a single subvolume, but extra subvolumes could exist. The subvolumes appear as directories within the mounted Btrfs filesystem. A subvolume could access it like any other user-accessible directory, or it could mount as a separate filesystem.

Btrfs separates each volume. By default, the Btrfs filesystem contains a subvolume. This is set as the top-level subvolume and is mounted even if not specified. Subvolumes, as they're being created, could nest into each other. But not the top-level subvolume. So each of them has a mountable root and could contain more than one tree of files. This sets a relative location for each subvolume and the mount point of the main subvolume.

A **Btrfs subvolume** is considered more like a namespace.

Some basic layouts exist for subvolumes (including snapshots), and they include the following:

- Flat – Subvolumes are children of the top level
- Nested – Subvolumes are located anywhere in the file hierarchy, below other subvolumes, not the top-level subvolume
- Mixed – The two basic schemes could be mixed, for example, the base structure follows a flat layout, with certain parts of the filesystem placed in nested subvolumes

Let's create a subvolume:

1. Use the `btrfs subvolume create` command to create the `test` subvolume:

```
[root@workstation ~]# btrfs subvolume create /btrfs/test
Create subvolume '/btrfs/test'
```

2. Review the subvolume information with the `btrfs subvolume` command:

```
[root@workstation ~]# btrfs subvolume show /btrfs/test
```

```
[root@workstation ~]# btrfs subvolume show /btrfs/test
test
        Name:                   test
        UUID:                   4bd55120-eb0f-ab46-82fa-e14d185a1f05
        Parent UUID:            -
        Received UUID:          -
        Creation time:          2023-01-19 22:40:51 -0600
        Subvolume ID:           256
        Generation:             8
        Gen at creation:        8
        Parent ID:              5
        Top level ID:           5
        Flags:                  -
        Send transid:           0
        Send time:              2023-01-19 22:40:51 -0600
        Receive transid:        0
        Receive time:           -
        Snapshot(s):
[root@workstation ~]#
```

Figure 4.4 – Subvolume information

3. Create the /test directory and mount the subvolume on it:

    ```
    [root@workstation ~]# mkdir /test
    [root@workstation ~]# mount -o bind /btrfs/test /test
    ```

    In this example, the subvolume doesn't have an allocated space, so it can use all the available space in the pool.

4. Verify the used space of the pool:

    ```
    [root@workstation ~]# btrfs filesystem du /btrfs
         Total     Exclusive  Set shared  Filename
         0.00B        0.00B            -  /btrfs/test
         0.00B        0.00B        0.00B  /btrfs
    ```

    To get more details on space usage, run the following command:

    ```
    btrfs filesystem usage /btrfs
    ```

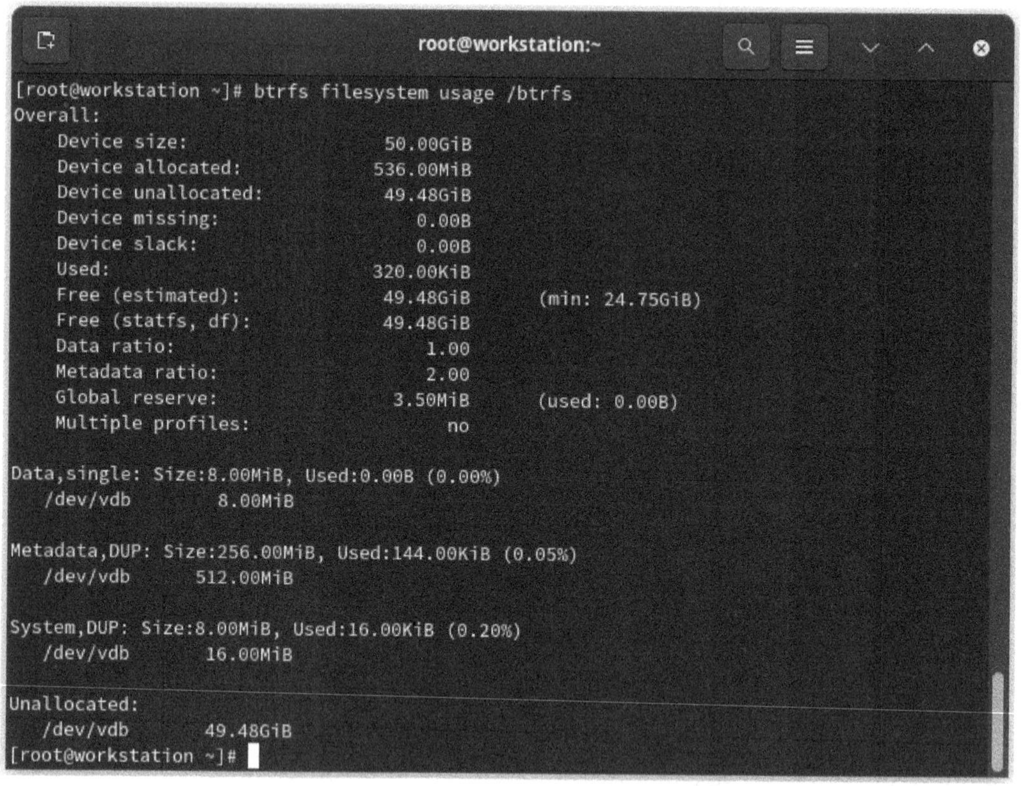

Figure 4.5 – Storage space used by Btrfs pool

Let's create an empty file of 1 GB to observe the change in the allocated usage.

5. Use the dd command to create an empty 1 GB file in the /test directory:

```
[root@workstation ~]# dd if=/dev/zero of=/test/example \
> bs=1M count=1024
```

6. Verify the change of the allocated space in the pool:

```
[root@workstation ~]# btrfs filesystem du /btrfs
[root@workstation ~]# btrfs filesystem usage /btrfs
```

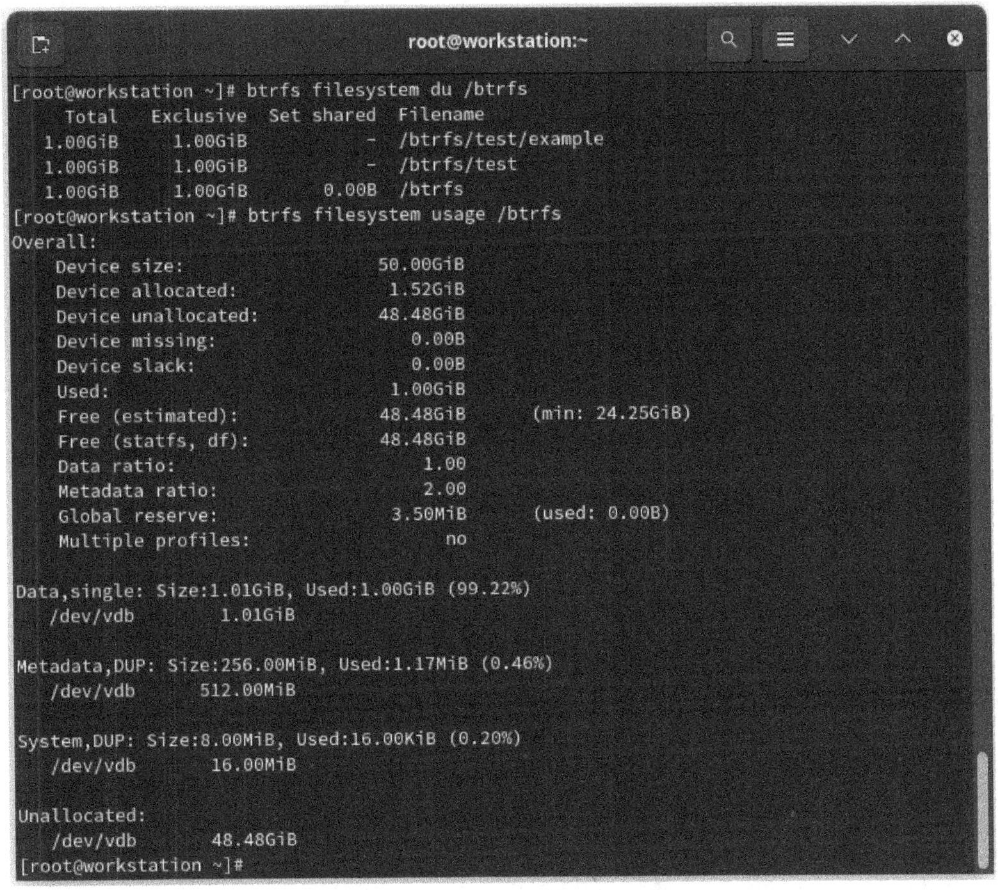

Figure 4.6 – Change in storage space used by the Btrfs pool

This is the end of the example. We started by identifying a free-of-use storage device to format it as Btrfs, created a storage pool on it, created a subvolume, and mounted it in a filesystem and analyzed the storage space usage in detail.

In the next section, we will continue revisiting the basic concepts of storage administration in Fedora Linux.

Optimizing storage space size

In the previous section, we reviewed some of the features of the Btrfs filesystem. Now it is time to learn how to optimize this used storage space in more detail.

Btrfs reserves some raw storage at its lowest level because the volume needs to contain file data or volume metadata. For that, it allocates pieces of raw storage for use by the filesystem. A piece of storage gets referred to as a **chunk**. Its main function is to contain file data or volume metadata to replicate on the same volume or another similar device.

Storage space gets allocated to the chunks, and the space is used by the blocks. A chunk with no blocks used is unallocated; a chunk with one or more blocks used is allocated. All chunks can get allocated even if not all the space is used.

Btrfs uses **delayed allocation** to enable better disk allocation. Btrfs only allocates disk space when the system needs to get rid of dirty pages, so in the end, you get much larger allocations and much larger chunks of sequential data, which makes data reading faster.

Btrfs allocates space on its disks by assigning chunks of 1 GB for data and 256 MB chunks for metadata. This implies that a chunk has a specific profile associated with it: once allocated a chunk for data or metadata, that space is only usable for one or the other. So, Btrfs has different allocation profiles for metadata and data.

This division of metadata and data might get confusing: a filesystem might show 10 GB of data but only 2 GB free. Common operating system commands, such as df or du, do not show the full information about space usage and chunk allocation in Btrfs. For this reason, Btrfs incorporates its own commands that show the used space and allocated chunks.

Using the filesystem created in the previous section, let's take a closer look at storage space usage and chunk allocation. Use the btrfs filesystem df command to display the /btrfs information:

```
[root@workstation ~]# btrfs filesystem df /btrfs
Data, single: total=1.00GiB, used=1.00GiB
System, DUP: total=8.00MiB, used=16.00KiB
Metadata, DUP: total=256.00MiB, used=1.17MiB
GlobalReserve, single: total=3.50MiB, used=16.00KiB
```

Observe the following:

- Data, System, and Metadata are separate block group types:

    - single is the allocation profile, defined at mkfs time.

    - DUP means *duplicate*. It guarantees the existence of two copies on the same disk. This mode protects against data or metadata corruption but not against disk failure.

    - total is the sum of space reserved for all allocation profiles of the given type, that is, all Data/single. Note that *it's not the total size of the filesystem*.

    - used is the sum of the used space of the data, that is, file extents, and metadata blocks.

- GlobalReserve is artificial and internal emergency space:

    - The GlobalReserve space is part of the metadata used. It is used when the filesystem metadata gets exhausted. While it is not allocated, it appears as unused metadata space.

From here, you could add other storage devices to the /btrfs filesystem to make it a single partition that spans all the devices you add. For this, follow these steps:

1. Format the extra devices as Btrfs with the mkfs.btrfs command:

```
mkfs.btrfs /dev/vdc /dev/vdd...
```

2. Add devices to the mounted device:

```
btrfs device add /dev/vdc /dev/vdd...
Performing full device TRIM /dev/vdc (10.00GiB) ...
Performing full device TRIM /dev/vdd (20.00GiB) ...
```

If we rerun the btrfs filesystem df command, the output shows no change:

```
[root@workstation ~]# btrfs filesystem df /btrfs
Data, single: total=1.00GiB, used=1.00GiB
System, DUP: total=8.00MiB, used=16.00KiB
Metadata, DUP: total=256.00MiB, used=1.17MiB
GlobalReserve, single: total=3.50MiB, used=0.00B
```

This is because the disks that are added are neither allocated for data nor metadata. Using the btrfs filesystem show command, the following output shows:

```
[root@workstation ~]# btrfs filesystem show /btrfs
Label: 'testbtrfs'  uuid: 6c8ccaad-f9a0-4957-919e-8d87e02078e3
Total devices 3 FS bytes used 1.00GiB
    devid    1 size 50.00GiB used 1.52GiB path /dev/vdb
    devid    2 size 10.00GiB used 0.00B path /dev/vdc
    devid    3 size 20.00GiB used 0.00B path /dev/vdd
```

The size value is the size of each disk, and the used value is the size of the chunks allocated on that disk. So, the new filesystem size is 80 GB, but no chunks from the new devices are allocated, leaving 79 GB of free space to allocate. Use the usual df command to show this:

```
[root@workstation ~]# df -h /btrfs
Filesystem      Size   Used  Avail  Use%  Mounted on
/dev/vdb        80G    1.1G  79G    2%    /btrfs
```

Btrfs could redistribute space and reclaim any wasted space. If you add a disk, you can run the balance command to make sure everything gets spread across the disks.

It is very useful to balance any Btrfs volume subject to updates and to prevent the allocation of every chunk in the volume. It is usually enough to balance chunks that are 50% or 70% used.

To auto-balance the mounted /btrfs filesystem, run the `btrfs filesystem balance` command:

```
[root@workstation ~]# btrfs filesystem balance /btrfs
Done, had to relocate 3 out of 3 chunks
```

By re-running the `btrfs filesystem df` command, it shows the new distribution of chunks in the filesystem:

```
[root@workstation ~]# btrfs filesystem df /btrfs
Data, single: total=1.00GiB, used=1.00GiB
System, DUP: total=32.00MiB, used=16.00KiB
Metadata, DUP: total=256.00MiB, used=1.16MiB
GlobalReserve, single: total=3.50MiB, used=0.00B
```

When adding a device, it is generally a good idea to run a balance on the filesystem.

Btrfs itself doesn't perform periodic rebalancing on filesystems and might experience problems with disk space management. If left unattended, these error messages could make it impossible to rebalance the partitions or devices on the filesystem.

The issue usually occurs when there is the right pattern of disk I/O and file sizes. This causes inefficient use of disk space and prevents new writes to the disk, generating No space left on device errors.

To prevent this, run a long space allocation check now and then, usually based on the work cycle of our system. The simplest way to explain this period of time could involve a *cash cut* for some businesses. For example: if the business does the cash cut every 30th day of the month, we have a window of time one day before and one day after that date, which leaves us with 28 or 29 *productive* days in which the system cannot change. On both dates, we could check the allocated space to confirm that everything is OK.

Let's see how to perform this space allocation check.

Space allocation check

Btrfs allocates chunks as large as 1/10 of the partition size, up to a maximum of 1 GB. Ideally, at least one chunk must remain unallocated for use during the rebalance operation.

> **Note**
>
> It is not necessary to run a rebalance if Btrfs has not allocated a significant part of the filesystem. A significant part of the filesystem is greater than 80% of the size or the entire filesystem size minus 2 GB.

To determine whether a rebalance would free up space, compare the amount of space allocated to the data with the amount of space used by the data. If the difference between these is greater than the largest chunk size, then a rebalance would probably free up some space.

The `btrfs filesystem usage` command provides the information needed to find both values:

```
[root@workstation ~]# btrfs filesystem usage /btrfs
Overall:
    Device size:                   80.00GiB
    Device allocated:               1.56GiB
    Device unallocated:            78.44GiB
    Device missing:                   0.00B
    Device slack:                     0.00B
    Used:                           1.00GiB
    Free (estimated):              78.44GiB      (min: 39.22GiB)
    Free (statfs, df):             78.43GiB
    Data ratio:                        1.00
    Metadata ratio:                    2.00
    Global reserve:                 3.50MiB      (used: 0.00B)
    Multiple profiles:                   no

Data,single: Size:1.00GiB, Used:1.00GiB (100.00%)
   /dev/vdb          1.00GiB

Metadata,DUP: Size:256.00MiB, Used:1.16MiB (0.45%)
   /dev/vdb        512.00MiB

System,DUP: Size:32.00MiB, Used:16.00KiB (0.05%)
   /dev/vdb         64.00MiB

Unallocated:
   /dev/vdb         48.44GiB
   /dev/vdc         10.00GiB
   /dev/vdd         20.00GiB
[root@workstation ~]#
```

Figure 4.7 – The Btrfs filesystem usage output

Let's create an extra file to better exemplify the check:

```
[root@workstation ~]# dd if=/dev/zero \
> of=/btrfs/test/example2 bs=1M count=49152
49152+0 records in
49152+0 records out
51539607552 bytes (52 GB, 48 GiB) copied, 70.17 s, 734 MB/s
```

Now that we have a filesystem with 49 GB used, let's see how they got allocated:

```
[root@workstation ~]# btrfs filesystem df /btrfs
Data, single: total=50.00GiB, used=48.45GiB
System, DUP: total=32.00MiB, used=16.00KiB
Metadata, DUP: total=256.00MiB, used=54.98MiB
GlobalReserve, single: total=53.69MiB, used=16.00KiB

[root@workstation ~]# btrfs filesystem show /btrfs
Label: 'testbtrfs'  uuid: 6c8ccaad-f9a0-4957-919e-8d87e02078e3
Total devices 3 FS bytes used 48.51GiB
devid    1 size 50.00GiB used 34.56GiB path /dev/vdb
devid    2 size 10.00GiB used 3.00GiB path /dev/vdc
devid    3 size 20.00GiB used 13.00GiB path /dev/vdd
```

Use the `btrfs filesystem usage` command with the `-b` (bytes) parameter to calculate whether rebalancing is necessary:

```
[root@workstation ~]# btrfs filesystem usage -b /btrfs
Overall:
    Device size:                   85899345920
    Device allocated:              54291070976
    Device unallocated:            31608274944
    Device missing:                          0
    Device slack:                            0
    Used:                          52730003456
    Free (estimated):              32682016768      (min: 16877879296)
    Free (statfs, df):             32678871040
    Data ratio:                           1.00
    Metadata ratio:                       2.00
    Global reserve:                   56295424      (used: 0)
    Multiple profiles:                      no

Data,single: Size:53687091200, Used:52613349376 (98.00%)
    /dev/vdb        36507222016
    /dev/vdc         3221225472
    /dev/vdd        13958643712

Metadata,DUP: Size:268435456, Used:58310656 (21.72%)
    /dev/vdb          536870912

System,DUP: Size:33554432, Used:16384 (0.05%)
    /dev/vdb           67108864

Unallocated:
    /dev/vdb        16575889408
    /dev/vdc         7516192768
    /dev/vdd         7516192768
[root@workstation ~]#
```

Figure 4.8 – The Btrfs filesystem usage output

From the output, highlight the size of the device, the allocation on the device, and the size and usage of the data:

```
[root@workstation ~]# btrfs filesystem usage -b /btrfs
Overall:
    Device size:            85899345920
    Device allocated:           54291070976
    Device unallocated:      31608274944
    Device missing:          0
... output omitted...
Data,single: Size:53687091200, Used:52613349376 (98.00%)
... output omitted...
```

With this information, follow these steps to perform the calculation:

1. The device size is 85899345920. Calculate 80%:

    ```
    85899345920 * 0.80 = 68719476736
    ```

2. The device size is 85899345920. Subtract 2 GB (2147483648):

    ```
    85899345920 - 2147483648 = 83751862272
    ```

3. Compare both results. Take the highest amount (83751862272) to compare against the amount allocated on the device:

    ```
    54291070976 < 83751862272
    ```

> **Note**
>
> If the device allocation is smaller than the calculated condition, then this part of the check is negative, and there should be no need to run a rebalance on this filesystem. But a data storage efficiency check must be performed to confirm that a rebalance is not necessary.

4. Estimate the difference between the space allocated and the space used:

    ```
    53687091200 - 52613349376 = 1073741824
    ```

5. Calculate the chunk size:

    ```
    85899345920*0.10 = 8589934592
    ```

6. Compare both results:

    8589934592 > 1073741824

    If the chunk size is greater than the difference, then the check is also negative. Rebalancing is not necessary.

Rebalancing is only necessary if the device allocation is greater than 80% of the device size (or the device size minus 2 GB) and the space allocated and used is greater than the chunk size.

Remember, *both conditions must not meet*. If the first check is negative, it is necessary to run the second check to confirm that rebalancing is not required.

Fedora Linux provides a tool to help us get a detailed report of the Btrfs filesystem's usage. Let's see how to use it.

Using the btrfs-usage-report command

The primary purpose of the `python-btrfs` module is to inspect Btrfs filesystems, acting as a wrapper around low-level kernel calls and Btrfs data structures. This module includes the `btrfs-usage-report` tool to show a report of the Btrfs filesystem usage.

To install the tool, install the `python3-btrfs` package with the `dnf` command:

```
[root@workstation ~]# dnf install python3-btrfs
```

Run the `btrfs-usage-report` command to get the report of the filesystem mounted on `/btrfs`. The report is complete, as shown in *Figure 4.9*.

At the beginning, it shows the following:

- The filesystem ID
- The physical space used
- The profiles

It also shows an estimate of the virtual space available and how much raw disk is allocated per chunk type:

```
[root@workstation ~]# btrfs-usage-report /btrfs
Btrfs usage report for /btrfs
Filesystem ID: 6c8ccaad-f9a0-4957-919e-8d87e02078e3
Mixed groups: False

Total physical space usage:
|
| Total filesystem size: 80.00GiB
| Allocated bytes: 50.56GiB
| Allocatable bytes remaining: 29.44GiB

Target profiles:
|
| type          profile
| ----          -------
| System        DUP
| Metadata      DUP
| Data          single

Estimated virtual space left for use:
|
| type          free
| ----          ----
| Data          28.44GiB
| MetaData      1.20GiB

Virtual space usage by block group type:
|
| type          total         used
| ----          -----         ----
| Data          50.00GiB      49.00GiB
| System        32.00MiB      16.00KiB
| Metadata      256.00MiB     55.61MiB

Allocated raw disk bytes by chunk type.
|
| flags         allocated      used     parity *)
| -----         ---------      ----     ---------
| DATA          50.00GiB       49.00GiB      0.00B
| SYSTEM|DUP    64.00MiB       32.00KiB      0.00B
| METADATA|DUP  512.00MiB      111.22MiB     0.00B
|
| *) Parity is a reserved part of the allocated bytes, limiting the
|    amount that can be used for data or metadata.
```

Figure 4.9 – The Btrfs-usage-report output

The last part of the report adds detailed information about storage space allocation:

```
Allocated bytes per device:
|
| devid        total size    allocated path
| -----        ----------    --------- ----
| 1              50.00GiB      34.56GiB /dev/vdb
| 2              10.00GiB       3.00GiB /dev/vdc
| 3              20.00GiB      13.00GiB /dev/vdd

Allocated bytes per device, split up by chunk type.
|
| Device ID: 1
| | flags              allocated      parity *)
| | -----              ---------      ---------
| | SYSTEM|DUP          64.00MiB         0.00B
| | METADATA|DUP       512.00MiB         0.00B
| | DATA               34.00GiB          0.00B
|
| Device ID: 2
| | flags              allocated      parity *)
| | -----              ---------      ---------
| | DATA                3.00GiB          0.00B
|
| Device ID: 3
| | flags              allocated      parity *)
| | -----              ---------      ---------
| | DATA               13.00GiB          0.00B
|
| *) Parity is a reserved part of the allocated bytes, limiting the
|    amount that can be used for data or metadata.

Unallocatable raw disk space:
|
| Reclaimable (by using balance): 0.00B
| Not reclaimable (because of different disk sizes): 0.00B

Unallocatable bytes per device, given current target profiles:
|
| devid        soft *)       hard **) reclaimable ***)
| -----        -------       -------- ----------------
| 1             0.00B         0.00B            0.00B
| 2             0.00B         0.00B            0.00B
| 3             0.00B         0.00B            0.00B
|
|   *) Because allocations in the filesystem are unbalanced.
|  **) Because of having different sizes of devices attached.
| ***) Amount of 'soft' unallocatable space that can be reclaimed,
|      before hitting the 'hard' limit.
|
```

Figure 4.10 – The Btrfs-usage-report output

Besides checking the allocated space and the efficiency of the data storage check, this tool helps optimize the storage space used on our workstation.

> **Note**
>
> Get the complete output of the `btrfs-usage-report` command from the `/btrfs` filesystem of our GitHub repository at `https://github.com/PacktPublishing/Fedora-Linux-System-Administration/blob/main/chapter4/btrfs-usage-report_btrfs.txt`.

Despite all these advanced features, the use of Brtfs as a filesystem is not the default in distributions other than Fedora Linux or OpenSUSE. Generally, most distributions prefer to use LVM with `ext4` or `xfs` as the filesystem format.

Let's see how different the Brtfs filesystem is from LVM.

Deep diving into Logical Volume Manager

Despite basic differences between Btrfs and LVM, they have a lot in common:

- They focus on protecting against filesystem corruption
- They support single - or multiple-device setup
- They can create quick snapshots
- Several tools exist to help manage them in graphic or command - line form

LVM sits on a layer before the filesystem, so it supports any filesystem. LVM converts *any* device or partition into a physical device (`pv`) that is dynamically manageable. Physical devices get placed in volume groups (`vg`), enabling the creation of logical volumes (`lv`).

This is how an LVM structure gets created sequentially:

1. It creates physical devices with the available devices, using the `pvcreate [device1] [device2] ...` command.
2. It joins the physical devices, creating the volume group, using the `vgcreate [vg_name] [pv1] [pv2] ...` command.
3. It creates the logical volume with the `lvcreate` command.

To remove each layer from the LVM structure, run similar commands in reverse order:

1. To delete the logical volume, use the `lvremove` command.
2. Remove the volume group with the `vgremove` command.
3. Remove the physical devices with the `pvremove` command.

The following figure shows the LVM creation and removal sequence:

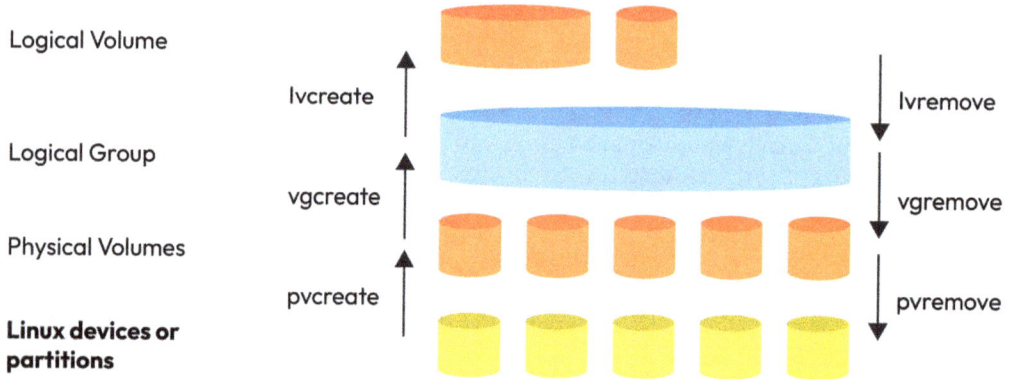

Figure 4.11 – LVM creation and removal sequence and commands

Physical devices could be added or removed to grow or reduce a volume group. In the same way, a logical volume could be extended or reduced but requires data verification before running it. In the case of xfs filesystems on LVM, there is no logical volume reduction.

LVM takes a set of block devices and presents the system with a new block device (lv) with a fixed mapping to physical blocks.

A Btrfs subvolume is different from an LVM logical volume, in the structure and behavior. A Btrfs volume is a mountable filesystem tree, not a block device.

The following figure shows the basic structures:

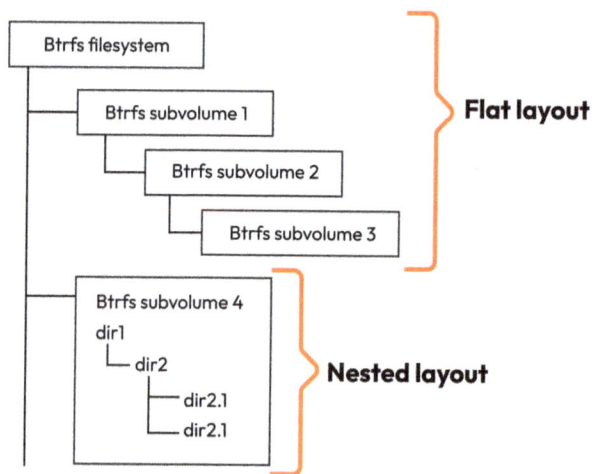

Figure 4.12 – Btrfs subvolumes layouts

The typical Btrfs snapshot structure uses the flat scheme.

Let's compare the snapshots of the Brtfs filesystem and LVM.

Differences between snapshots

LVM supports read-only and read-write snapshots. This eases the creation of consistent backups of active filesystems, with a defined size on the source volume group of the logical volume or an external source. This allows snapshots to belong to a thin provisioned pool when the target LV is a thin LV, which doesn't consume fixed-size chunks of the source volume.

Creating snapshots on LVM is similar to creating a logical volume. Specify the snapshot name and the targeted LV, adding the following parameters to the `lvcreate` command:

```
lvcreate -s -n snapshot_name -L snapshot_size target_lv disk
```

After taking the snapshot, all modifications made on the target LV will be stored in the new snapshot LV, but the old data remains in the source LV.

As needed, use the snapshot LV to roll back some changes in the source LV, mounting it in the affected directory instead of the original LV. Use the usual `mount` and `unmount` commands.

Remove the snapshot as an LV with the `lvremove` command:

```
lvremove /dev/vg_name/snapshot_name
```

> **Note**
> It is possible to deactivate the logical volume before deleting it. Use the `lvchange -an` command. It will *not* show the prompt verifying whether you want to delete an active logical volume.

Snapshots in Btrfs are **COW clones** of a complete subvolume. They look similar to a new subvolume that contains the data of the cloned subvolume, but any changes in one do not affect the other. The space consumed increases as the original subvolume and the snapshot grow apart.

Create a snapshot using the `btrfs subvolume` command stating that it is a snapshot. Observe the following steps to create a snapshot on our `/btrfs` filesystem from the *Creating a Btrfs filesystem* section:

1. List the subvolumes of the filesystem mounted on `/btrfs`:

    ```
    [root@workstation ~]# btrfs subvolume list /btrfs
    ID 256 gen 72 top level 5 path test
    ```

> **Note**
>
> The top-level subvolume with `Btrfs` ID 5 is the root of the volume. All subvolumes mount below it.

2. Create a snapshot of the `test` subvolume:

```
[root@workstation ~]# btrfs subvolume snapshot \
> /btrfs/test /btrfs/test_snapshot
Create a snapshot of '/btrfs/test' in '/btrfs/test_snapshot'
```

3. Listing the subvolumes again displays the snapshot:

```
[root@workstation ~]# btrfs subvolume list /btrfs
ID 256 gen 76 top level 5 path test
ID 257 gen 76 top level 5 path test_snapshot
[root@workstation ~]# ls /btrfs/
test  test_snapshot
```

4. Inspect the directories to verify that they contain the same data:

```
[root@workstation ~]# tree /btrfs/
/btrfs/
├── test
│   └── example
└── test_snapshot
    └── example

3 directories, 2 files
```

With COW, each subvolume could change without changes in one affecting the other.

The differences between Btrfs and LVM are remarkable:

-   A Btrfs subvolume holds the capacity of the filesystem to which it belongs. A logical volume in LVM contains a capacity, which is a space reservation of the volume group it belongs to.

-   A Btrfs snapshot is a full-fledged subvolume, and once created there is no "original" and "snapshot." On LVM, a snapshot depends on the logical volume from the one that it came from.

    For example, it is not possible to resize a logical volume or move its data with the `pvmove` command (from one physical volume to another) while having active snapshots of that logical volume.

> **Note**
>
> For more information about the LVM commands and their Btrfs equivalents, refer to the Fedora wiki article at `https://fedoraproject.org/wiki/User:Chrismurphy/lvm2btrfs`.

Let's now learn about Fedora's latest approach to storage management, Stratis storage.

Discovering Stratis storage

Stratis is a command-line tool designed to simplify storage management. It uses a hybrid approach with both user-space and kernel components, based on existing block device managers, such as `device mapper`, and existing filesystems such as `XFS`.

Here's what you can do with Stratis:

- Create, modify, and destroy storage pools
- Allocate and detach filesystems from storage pools
- Encrypt and decrypt filesystem data

Stratis storage brings together common storage management tools and automates them for ease of use. Here are some things it uses:

- `device-mapper` – A framework for logical to physical mapping of data blocks
- `LUKS` – An on-disk format for encryption that can securely manage multiple passwords
- `XFS` – A scalable, journaling, and performant filesystem
- `Clevis` – A framework for automated decryption

Here are the Stratis components:

- `Blockdev` – Block devices, either a disk or a partition.
- `Pool` – Consists of one or more block devices. A pool has a fixed total size, which represents the sum of all the block devices present in it.
- `Filesystem` – Filesystems don't have a fixed total size, thinly provisioned. The real size of the filesystem grows with the data stored in it. The thin volume and the filesystem increase automatically. Each pool could contain one or more filesystems, formatted with XFS.

The following diagram shows the layout of the components in the Stratis pool:

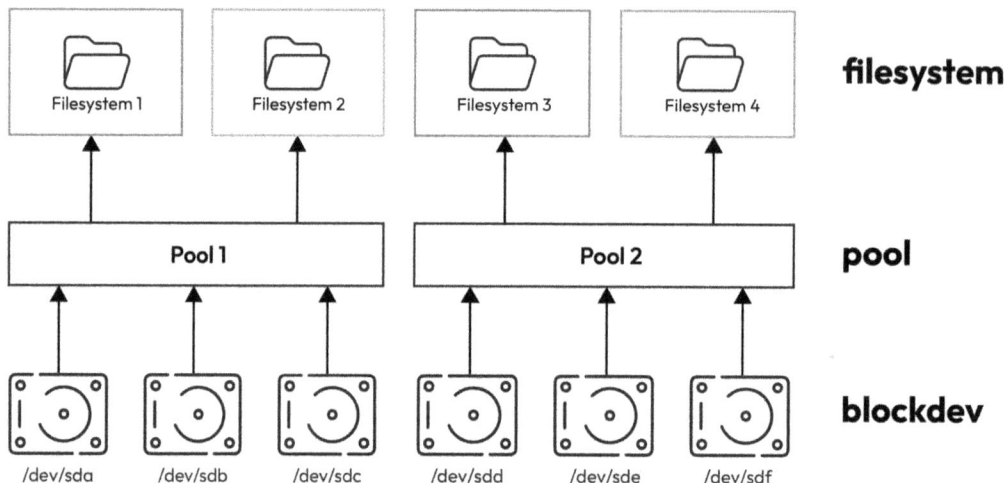

Figure 4.13 – Stratis storage components

Let's create a Stratis test pool to show its capabilities.

Creating a Stratis pool

For this practice example, reuse the disks used in the *Btrfs* section in this chapter.

Follow these steps:

1. Unmount the Btrfs and /test filesystem and remove the /btrfs directory:

    ```
    [root@workstation ~]# umount /btrfs/test
    [root@workstation ~]# umount /btrfs
    [root@workstation ~]# rm -rf /btrfs
    ```

2. Removes the Btrfs filesystem from the storage devices using the wipefs command:

    ```
    [root@workstation ~]# wipefs /dev/vdb --all -f
    [root@workstation ~]# wipefs /dev/vdc --all -f
    [root@workstation ~]# wipefs /dev/vdd --all -f
    ```

    The --all parameter deletes all available signatures.

    The -f parameter forces erasure even if the filesystem is mounted.

3. Install Stratis using the dnf command:

```
[root@workstation ~]# dnf install stratis-cli stratisd
```

4. Use the systemctl command to enable the stratisd service:

```
[root@workstation ~]# systemctl enable --now stratisd
```

5. With the fdisk command, verify the size of the disk:

```
[root@workstation ~]# fdisk -l /dev/vdb /dev/vdc /dev/vdd
Disk /dev/vdb: 50 GiB, 53687091200 bytes, 104857600 sectors
Units: sectors of 1 * 512 = 512 bytes
Sector size (logical/physical): 512 bytes / 512 bytes
I/O size (minimum/optimal): 512 bytes / 512 bytes


Disk /dev/vdc: 10 GiB, 10737418240 bytes, 20971520 sectors
Units: sectors of 1 * 512 = 512 bytes
Sector size (logical/physical): 512 bytes / 512 bytes
I/O size (minimum/optimal): 512 bytes / 512 bytes


Disk /dev/vdd: 20 GiB, 21474836480 bytes, 41943040 sectors
Units: sectors of 1 * 512 = 512 bytes
Sector size (logical/physical): 512 bytes / 512 bytes
I/O size (minimum/optimal): 512 bytes / 512 bytes
[root@workstation ~]#
```

Figure 4.14 – Checking the disk size

6. Use the stratis pool create command to create the pool test on the /dev/vdb device:

```
[root@workstation ~]# stratis pool create test /dev/vdb
```

7. List the Stratis pool using the stratis pool list command:

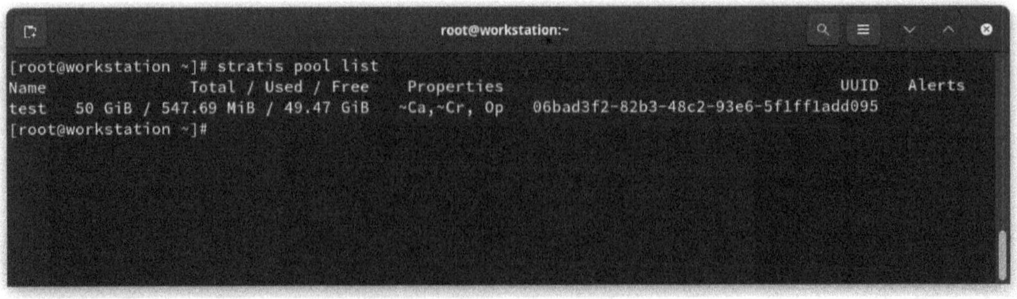

```
[root@workstation ~]# stratis pool list
Name            Total / Used / Free    Properties                                    UUID    Alerts
test   50 GiB / 547.69 MiB / 49.47 GiB   ~Ca,~Cr, Op   06bad3f2-82b3-48c2-93e6-5f1ff1add095
[root@workstation ~]#
```

Figure 4.15 – Stratis pool list

The following table lists the fields of the `stratis pool list` output:

Field	Description
Name	The name of the pool
Total/Used/Free	The physical usage statistics for the pool
Properties	Boolean-valued properties that the pool may have. Each property has a two-letter code in camel case. If the pool does not have the property, add a ~ symbol, which stands for negation, to the property code.
	If the engine has experienced an error in obtaining the property, add a ? symbol, which stands for unknown, to the property code.
	The property codes are as follows:
	• `Ca` - Indicates that the pool has a cache
	• `Cr` - Indicates encrypted pool
	• `Op` - indicates that the pool allows over-provisioning
UUID	Universally Unique IDentifier of the pool
Alerts	Anything unusual or urgent information about the pool that the user needs information on.

Let's now add another device to the pool to see how the available space in the pool increases:

1. Use the `stratis pool add-data` command to add the `/dev/vdc` device to the Stratis pool and list the pool again to observe the change:

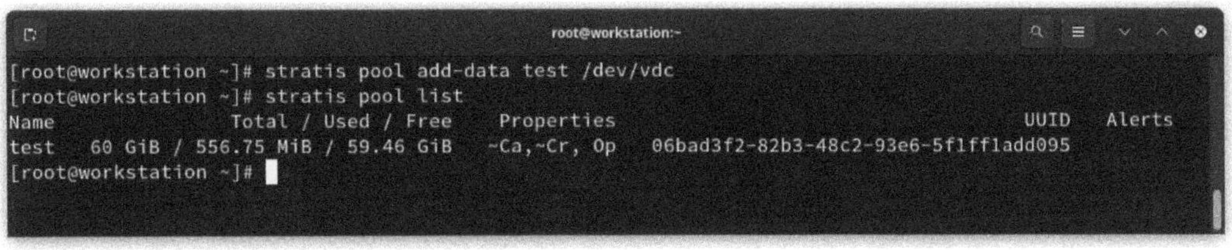

Figure 4.16 – Stratis pool list

Now let's create a filesystem to show the differences from a common filesystem.

2. Create the filesystem data using the `stratis filesystem create` command:

    ```
    [root@workstation ~]# stratis filesystem create test data
    ```

3. List the filesystems in the `test` pool to observe their properties. Use the `stratis filesystem list` command:

Figure 4.17 – Stratis filesystem list

Note that the total size of the filesystem is 1 TiB, even though the sum of the actual available disk space is 60 GiB:

```
[root@workstation ~]# stratis filesystem list test
Pool    Filesystem    Total / Used / Free
test    data          1 TiB / 546 MiB / 1023.47 GiB
...output omitted...
```

As mentioned, the filesystem gets created on a thinly provisioned 1 TiB block device by design. Stratis handles the allocation of blocks from the pool and resizes the XFS filesystem on demand during its lifetime.

Stratis also facilitates the creation of snapshots of filesystems. A Stratis snapshot is a thinly provisioned real-time read/write copy of the source filesystem.

Let's see how to create snapshots.

4. Use the `stratis filesystem snapshot` command to create the snapshot, and then list the filesystems of the pool:

Figure 4.18 – Stratis filesystem list

The filesystems and their snapshots could mount in the traditional way in the operating system. Use the `mount` command and, to keep them mounted permanently, configure an entry in the `/etc/fstab` file.

> **Note**
>
> For more information about Stratis, refer to the Stratis documentation at `https://stratis-storage.github.io/howto/`.

This concludes our review of storage basics. In the following chapters, we will review some other fundamental concepts, such as networking and the use of applications, along with applying system administration of Linux systems.

Summary

This chapter consisted of reviewing the basic concepts of storage management and focused on the Btrfs filesystem, performing practical examples to understand its use and main features, identifying storage devices, formatting storage devices, creating pools, and mounting filesystems.

We clarified some items that assist in optimizing the allocation of storage space and learned the main differences between Btrfs subvolumes and LVM.

As a bonus, we discussed the Fedora Project's new approach to storage management with Stratis, the intention of which is to ease storage management.

In the next chapter, we will cover the fundamental concepts and configurations of network connections and how to optimize them.

Further reading

To learn more about the topics that were covered in the chapter, please visit the following links:

- *Fedora Wiki – Btrfs*: `https://fedoraproject.org/wiki/Btrfs`

- *Btrfs documentation*: `https://btrfs.readthedocs.io/en/latest/`

- *Choose between Btrfs and LVM-ext4*: `https://fedoramagazine.org/choose-between-btrfs-and-lvm-ext4/`

- *Getting started with Stratis – up and running*: `https://fedoramagazine.org/getting-started-with-stratis-up-and-running/`

- *Stratis storage*: `https://stratis-storage.github.io/`

5

Network and Connectivity

Now, it's time to review the basics of network configuration and management on our workstation. This will lead to us knowing about the fundamental points that can be adjusted and fine-tuned in the network configuration. We will get to know in depth about the **NetworkManager** administration tool, as well as the most common tips and examples regarding its use.

We will also walk through the wired and wireless network configuration. In the next section, we will review how to access a **virtual private network** (**VPN**). Finally, we will learn about the tools for monitoring network performance and connectivity.

In this chapter, we're going to cover the following main topics:

- Walking through the basics
- Tuning wireless connectivity
- Improving network connectivity using a VPN
- Network performance monitoring

Let's get to it!

Technical requirements

The configurations mentioned in this chapter require access to the local network, either wired or wireless. It is not necessary to have a dedicated network interface for these tests.

You can find the templates and example files used in this chapter in this book's GitHub repository: https://github.com/PacktPublishing/Fedora-Linux-System-Administration/tree/main/chapter5

Walking through the basics

NetworkManager uses the concept of *connection profiles*, which contain the network configuration. These profiles support a variety of formats for storing properties, such as int32, boolean, uint32, string, array of string, uint64, and many more. As NetworkManager's usage and features grow, ifcfg files may no longer be supported.

NetworkManager uses plugins to read and write this data. NetworkManager added support for new connection types and finally settled on using a more streamlined configuration file format for it, known as the keyfile plugin.

The keyfile plugin supports all connection types and capabilities that NetworkManager has. NetworkManager uses the *INI-key* file format to store connection profile data.

This plugin always remains active and stores any connection that no other active plugin supports. For security, it ignores files that could be read or written by any *non-root* user since private keys and passwords might be stored in plain text inside the file.

Let's take an example of an Ethernet connection profile to understand plugins better:

```
[connection]
id=net_connection
uuid= 9cd8a444-f501-4179-900e-f3754dbbe7c0
type=ethernet
autoconnect=true

[ipv4]
method=auto

[ipv6]
method=auto

[ethernet]
mac-address=48:2a:e3:8f:4b:aa
```

It consists of sections (groups) of key-value pairs that correspond to a configuration name, which is described as a property. Most of the properties in the specification are also written in the same format in the key file. However, some values are unfriendly to use. These are stored in the files listed at /etc/NetworkManager/system-connections/, /usr/lib/NetworkManager/system-connections/ and /run/NetworkManager/system-connections/, in a more readable form.

> **Note**
>
> For more information about the **Description of keyfile settings** plugin, refer to the *GNOME Developer Documentation* at `https://developer-old.gnome.org/NetworkManager/stable/nm-settings-keyfile.html`.

Like any file in Linux, keyfiles can be modified, but NetworkManager must know about these changes so that they can be considered.

Now, let's review the utility that helps us handle NetworkManager and network configuration.

NetworkManager command-line interface (nmcli)

NetworkManager can be managed by the `nmcli` command-line utility (**NetworkManager Command Line Interface**). `nmcli` allows us to create, display, edit, delete, activate, and deactivate network connections. Besides controlling and displaying the status of network devices, it can run as a command from the terminal or be invoked from a script.

As a command running from the terminal, `nmcli` can create, edit, start, and stop network connections or display a network device's status, without the need for the GUI or desktop applet.

For scripts, `nmcli` provides a simple output format that can be adapted to data processing, which integrates network configurations into a process rather than managing network connections manually.

The basic `nmcli` command run format is as follows:

```
nmcli [OPTIONS] OBJECT { COMMAND | help }
```

> **Note**
>
> For a complete list of options, from the terminal, run the `man nmcli` command.

Then, to get the connection overview, run the `nmcli -o conn` command:

Figure 5.1 – Overview of network connections

To get an overview of the `enp1s0` network device, run the `nmcli -o dev show enp1s0` command:

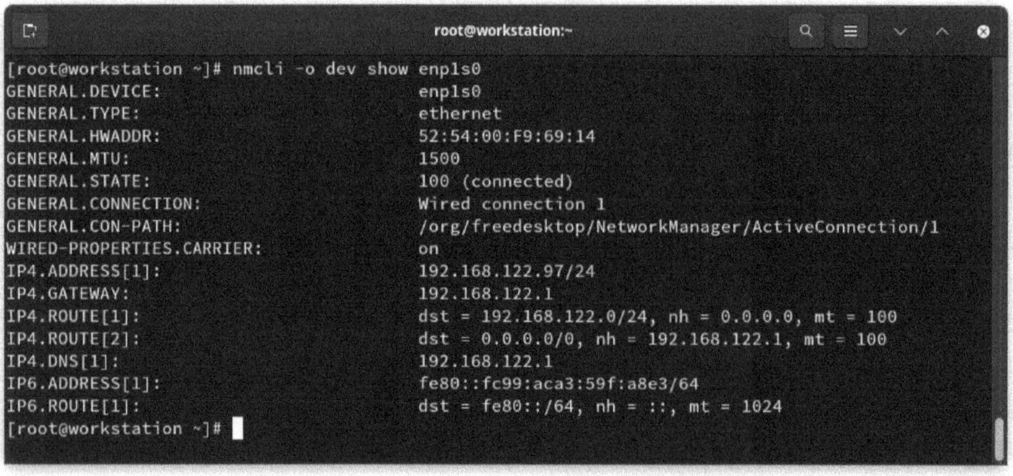
root@workstation:~
[root@workstation ~]# nmcli -o dev show enp1s0
GENERAL.DEVICE: enp1s0
GENERAL.TYPE: ethernet
GENERAL.HWADDR: 52:54:00:F9:69:14
GENERAL.MTU: 1500
GENERAL.STATE: 100 (connected)
GENERAL.CONNECTION: Wired connection 1
GENERAL.CON-PATH: /org/freedesktop/NetworkManager/ActiveConnection/1
WIRED-PROPERTIES.CARRIER: on
IP4.ADDRESS[1]: 192.168.122.97/24
IP4.GATEWAY: 192.168.122.1
IP4.ROUTE[1]: dst = 192.168.122.0/24, nh = 0.0.0.0, mt = 100
IP4.ROUTE[2]: dst = 0.0.0.0/0, nh = 192.168.122.1, mt = 100
IP4.DNS[1]: 192.168.122.1
IP6.ADDRESS[1]: fe80::fc99:aca3:59f:a8e3/64
IP6.ROUTE[1]: dst = fe80::/64, nh = ::, mt = 1024
[root@workstation ~]#

Figure 5.2 – Overview of the network device

You can list the **keyfiles** of network connections by running the `nmcli -f TYPE,FILENAME,NAME conn` command:

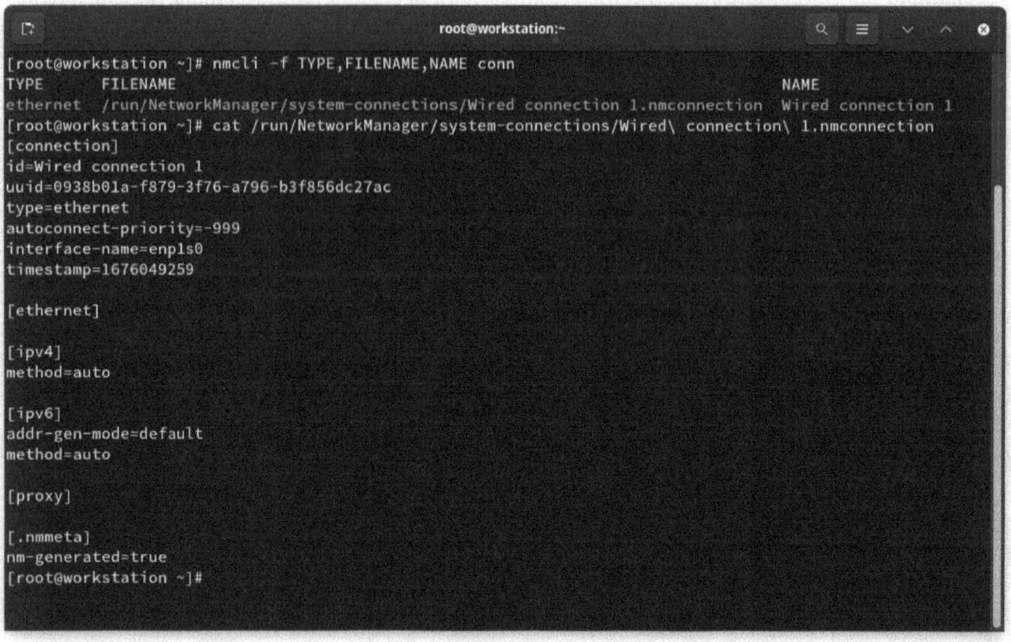
root@workstation:~
[root@workstation ~]# nmcli -f TYPE,FILENAME,NAME conn
TYPE FILENAME NAME
ethernet /run/NetworkManager/system-connections/Wired connection 1.nmconnection Wired connection 1
[root@workstation ~]# cat /run/NetworkManager/system-connections/Wired\ connection\ 1.nmconnection
[connection]
id=Wired connection 1
uuid=0938b01a-f879-3f76-a796-b3f856dc27ac
type=ethernet
autoconnect-priority=-999
interface-name=enp1s0
timestamp=1676049259
[ethernet]
[ipv4]
method=auto
[ipv6]
addr-gen-mode=default
method=auto
[proxy]
[.nmmeta]
nm-generated=true
[root@workstation ~]#

Figure 5.3 – Checking the network connection keyfiles

In this case, observe that the *IP address* of the workstation is set to `auto`, meaning that it uses DHCP as the boot-time protocol:

```
[ipv4]
method=auto
```

To assign a static IP address such as `192.168.122.100` instead of the one assigned by DHCP, follow these steps:

1. Back up the original configuration of the connection:

    ```
    # cat /run/NetworkManager/system-connections/Wired\ connection\
    1.nmconnection >>  wired_connection_1.bkp.txt
    ```

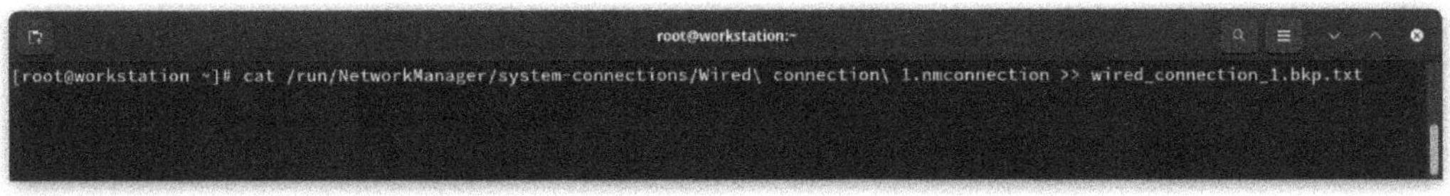

Figure 5.4 – Backing up network connection settings

> **Note**
>
> Running the `cat` command to redirect the output to a file lets us know about and identify the contents of the file.

2. Add the `enp1s0` connection as a new NetworkManager connection profile:

    ```
    # nmcli connection add con-name wired-conn1
    ifname enp1s0 type ethernet
    ```

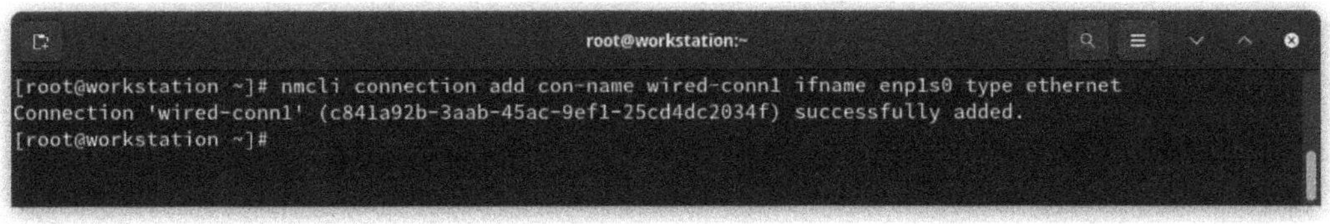

Figure 5.5 – Adding the new NetworkManager connection profile

3. Set the IP address of this profile:

    ```
    # nmcli connection modify wired-conn1
      ipv4.addresses 192.168.122.100/24
    ```

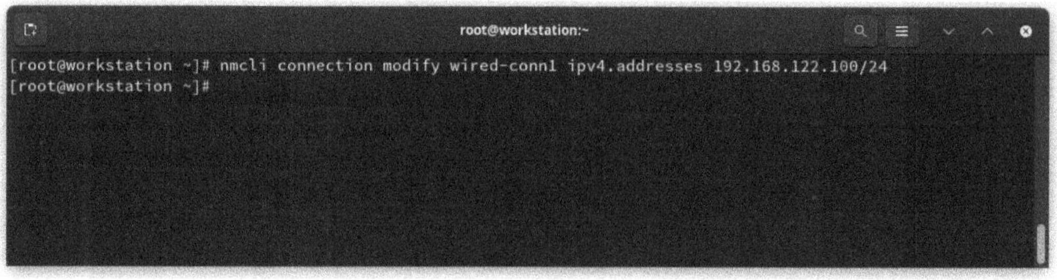

Figure 5.6 – Setting the IP address

4. Set the connection method to `manual`:

    ```
    # nmcli connection modify wired-conn1
      ipv4.method manual
    ```

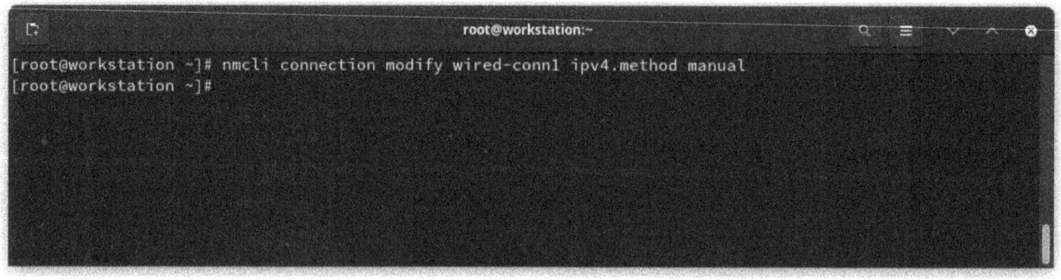

Figure 5.7 – Setting the connection method

5. Set the gateway to `192.168.122.1`:

    ```
    # nmcli connection modify wired-conn1  ipv4.gateway
    192.168.122.1
    ```

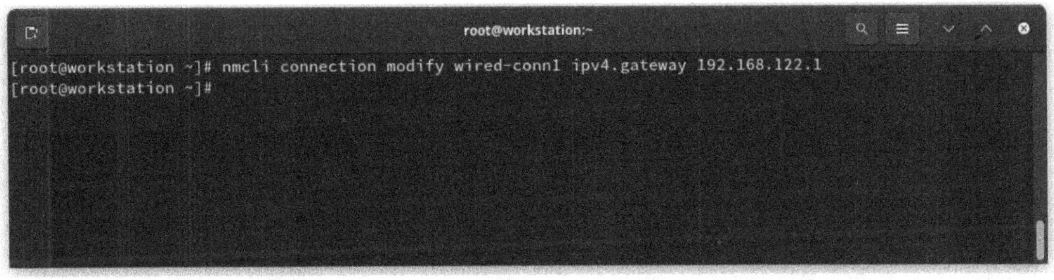

Figure 5.8 – Setting the gateway

6. Set dns to `192.168.122.1`:

```
# nmcli connection modify wired-conn1  ipv4.dns 192.168.122.1
```

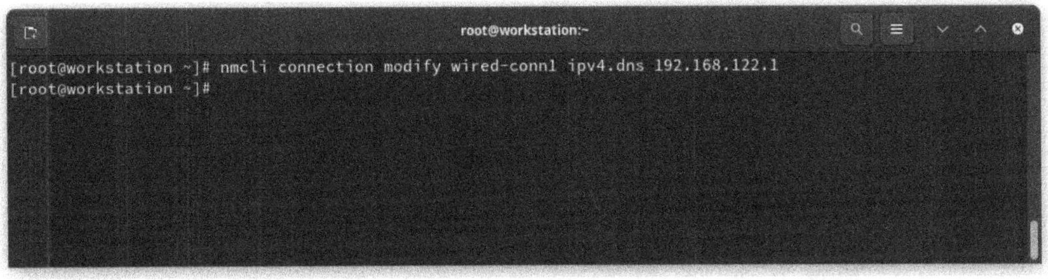

Figure 5.9 – Setting dns

7. Activate the new NetworkManager connection profile:

```
[root@workstation ~]# nmcli connection up wired-conn1
```

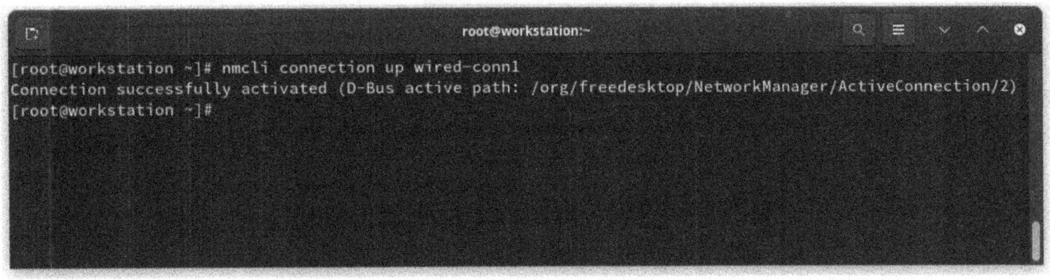

Figure 5.10 – Activating the NetworkManager profile

8. Check the device's status:

```
[root@workstation ~]# nmcli device status
```

```
[root@workstation ~]# nmcli device status
DEVICE   TYPE       STATE       CONNECTION
enp1s0   ethernet   connected   wired-conn1
lo       loopback   unmanaged   --
[root@workstation ~]#
```

Figure 5.11 – Reviewing the device's status

9. Check the network configuration of the workstation. Confirm the changes in the IP address of the enp1s0 device. Then, use the ip command:

```
[root@workstation ~]# ip a
```

```
[root@workstation ~]# ip a
1: lo: <LOOPBACK,UP,LOWER_UP> mtu 65536 qdisc noqueue state UNKNOWN group default qlen 1000
    link/loopback 00:00:00:00:00:00 brd 00:00:00:00:00:00
    inet 127.0.0.1/8 scope host lo
       valid_lft forever preferred_lft forever
    inet6 ::1/128 scope host
       valid_lft forever preferred_lft forever
2: enp1s0: <BROADCAST,MULTICAST,UP,LOWER_UP> mtu 1500 qdisc fq_codel state UP group default qlen 1000
    link/ether 52:54:00:f9:69:14 brd ff:ff:ff:ff:ff:ff
    inet 192.168.122.100/24 brd 192.168.122.255 scope global noprefixroute enp1s0
       valid_lft forever preferred_lft forever
    inet6 fe80::fc6f:fc78:a994:6ebe/64 scope link noprefixroute
       valid_lft forever preferred_lft forever
[root@workstation ~]#
```

Figure 5.12 – Verifying the network configuration

10. Review the workstation connection's keyfiles:

```
# nmcli -f TYPE,FILENAME,NAME conn
```

Figure 5.13 – Checking the keyfiles

Note that the *active configuration* is now highlighted in green.

Let's compare the original backup file with the created one. Use the `diff` command to highlight the differences:

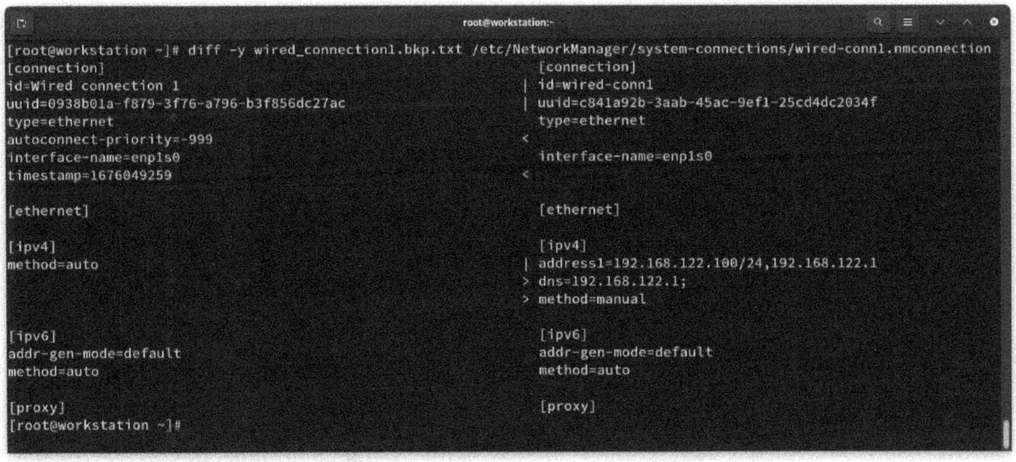

Figure 5.14 – Keyfile differences

The first difference is in the `id` value of the *connection name*. But also, notice that there is a change in the `uuid` value:

```
< id=Wired connection 1
< uuid=0938b01a-f879-3f76-a796-b3f856dc27ac
---
> id=wired-conn1
> uuid=c841a92b-3aab-45ac-9ef1-25cd4dc2034f
```

NetworkManager creates a new *Universally Unique Identifier* (`uuid`) for this connection profile. This allows multiple connections to be applied to the same device, but only one of these can be activated at a time. Extra connections allow you to quickly switch between different networks or configurations.

The connection was *auto-configured* during installation as DHCP. Since this parameter remained unchanged during installation, one of the properties that were assigned by the boot-time protocol was *auto-connection priority*:

```
< autoconnect-priority=-999
```

When the connection is set to `auto-connect`, higher-priority connections are preferred. The default is 0. *A higher number means a higher priority.*

An interesting piece of data that can be found in the original keyfile is `timestamp`, in seconds since the **Unix Epoch**, when the connection was last successfully activated:

```
< timestamp=1687113052
```

The biggest change is in the `ipv4` configuration section:

```
< method=auto
---
> address1=192.168.122.100/24,192.168.122.1
> dns=192.168.122.1;
> method=manual
```

In the original keyfile, the method is set as `auto`. The current keyfile is set to `manual`, plus the configuration of the *IP address*, *gateway*, and *DNS*.

A *wired connection* is the simplest example of network configuration, although several extra properties could be added.

A *wireless connection*, which is used for the kind of work involved in managing Linux servers, is the type of connection we will use the most, given its inherent mobility advantages.

Now, let's see how, besides configuring our *wireless connection*, to optimize it with some fine-tuning settings.

Tuning wireless connectivity

Sometimes, the network's devices are not recognized by the operating system. This is one of the common issues of using wireless networks.

Let's start this section by ensuring that the wireless network device has support from the operating system by identifying which chipset it uses and which drivers work best for its operation.

Identifying the device

In a network device, the main thing is to identify the *Vendor ID* (the 16-bit number of the vendor – that is, the **VID**) and the *Product ID* (the 16-bit number of the product number – that is, the **PID**). Use the following commands for each case, depending on the bus used by the device:

- PCI: `lspci -nn`

- USB: `lsusb`:

```
[root@workstation ~]# lspci -nn
00:00.0 PCI bridge [0604]: Broadcom Inc. and subsidiaries BCM2711 PCIe Bridge [14e4:2711] (rev 10)
01:00.0 USB controller [0c03]: VIA Technologies, Inc. VL805/806 xHCI USB 3.0 Controller [1106:3483] (rev 01)
[root@workstation ~]# lsusb
Bus 002 Device 001: ID 1d6b:0003 Linux Foundation 3.0 root hub
Bus 001 Device 005: ID 0e6a:02c0 Megawin Technology Co., Ltd Defender Gaming Keyboard
Bus 001 Device 006: ID 25a7:fa23 Areson Technology Corp 2.4G Receiver
Bus 001 Device 002: ID 2109:3431 VIA Labs, Inc. Hub
Bus 001 Device 001: ID 1d6b:0002 Linux Foundation 2.0 root hub
[root@workstation ~]#
```

Figure 5.15 – Identifying the network device

As shown in the preceding figure, the output of the `lspci` command provides the required chipset information:

```
00:00.0 PCI bridge [0604]: Broadcom Inc. and subsidiaries BCM2711 PCIe
Bridge [14e4:2711] (rev 10)
```

Now, go to Google and type the chipset information in the form:

```
"14e4 2711" site:cateee.net/lkddb/
```

This search leads to a chipset match in **Linux Kernel Driver DataBase** (`https://cateee.net/lkddb/`), which allows us to identify whether the wireless network device has support and which driver is the correct one to use:

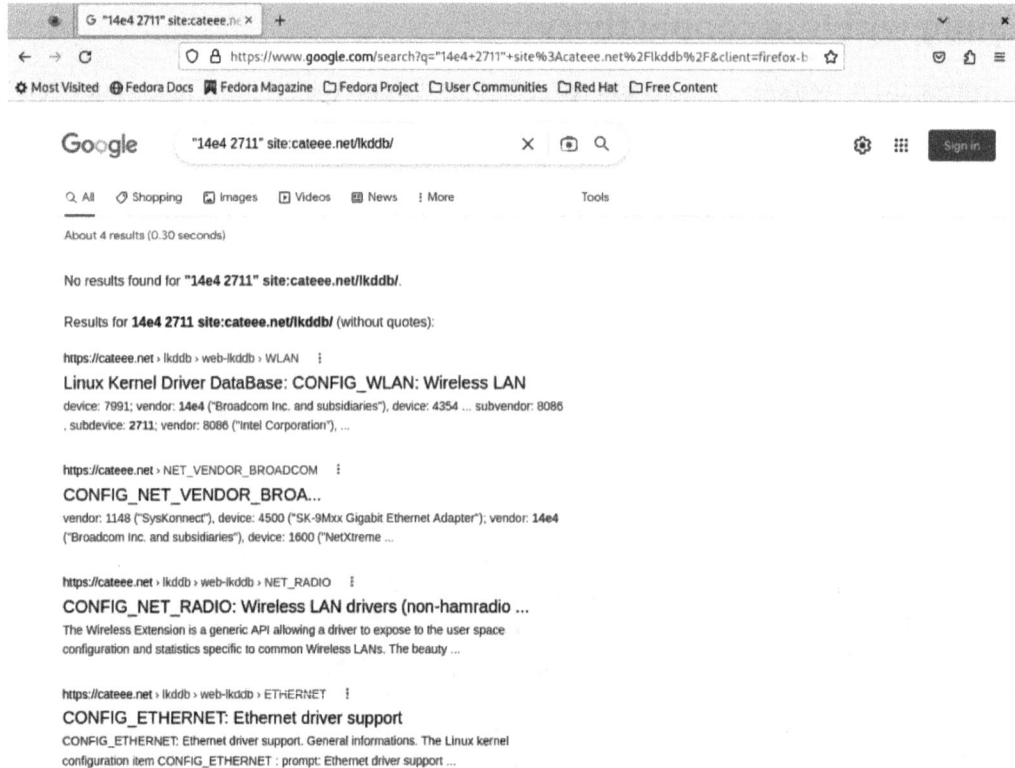

Figure 5.16 – LKDDb search

If you search for chipset information in the form – that is, `"14e4:2711"` – it leads to several useful sites that provide more detailed information. Click on the **Hardware for Linux** page link (`https://linux-hardware.org/`) and find the chipset's details:

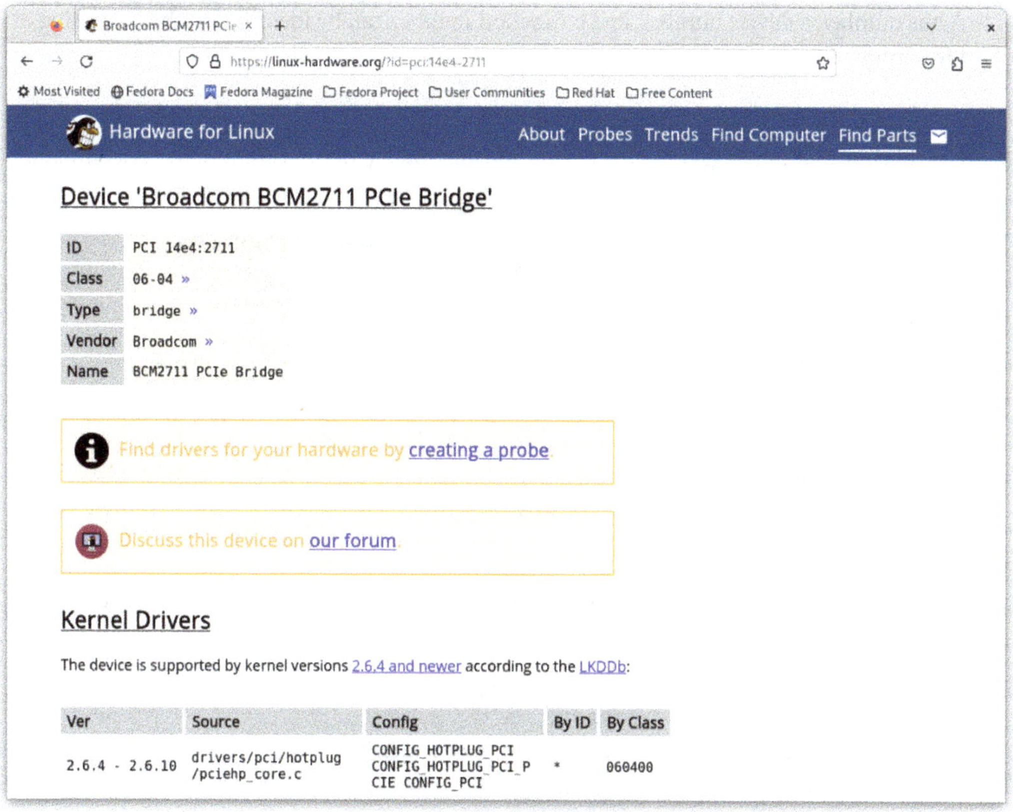

Figure 5.17 – The Hardware for Linux site

With the preceding tools, we can identify the wireless device in our computer. Follow these steps to identify the vendor and its product ID:

1. Run the `lspci` command to identify the card:

    ```
    [root@workstation ~]# lspci | grep -i broadcom
    00:00.0 PCI bridge: Broadcom Inc. and subsidiaries BCM2711 PCIe
    Bridge (rev 10)
    ```

> **Note**
>
> If the card is not integrated into the motherboard of the computer, use the `lsusb` command to identify this device.

A bus number, a device number, and a function number can be identified at the beginning of the output:

```
00:00.0
```

2. Use this information to get detailed device information. To do so, run the `lspci` command:

```
[root@workstation ~]# lspci -vv -s 00:00.0
00:00.0 PCI bridge: Broadcom Inc. and subsidiaries BCM2711 PCIe
Bridge (rev 10) (prog-if 00 [Normal decode])
Device tree node: /sys/firmware/devicetree/base/scb/
pcie@7d500000/pci@0,0
Control: I/O- Mem+ BusMaster+ SpecCycle- MemWINV- VGASnoop-
ParErr- Stepping- SERR- FastB2B- DisINTx-
Status: Cap+ 66MHz- UDF- FastB2B- ParErr- DEVSEL=fast >TAbort-
<TAbort- <MAbort- >SERR- <PERR- INTx-
Latency: 0
Interrupt: pin A routed to IRQ 38
...output omitted...
```

3. List the modules that were loaded in the kernel and search the identified chipset of the wireless card. Use the `lsmod` command:

```
root@workstation ~]# lsmod | grep -i broadcom
broadcom              28672  1
bcm_phy_ptp           24576  1 broadcom
bcm_phy_lib           28672  2 bcm_phy_ptp,broadcom
```

4. Use the `modinfo` command to display the module information:

```
[root@workstation ~]# modinfo broadcom
filename:       /lib/modules/6.1.12-200.fc37.aarch64/kernel/
drivers/net/phy/broadcom.ko.xz
license:        GPL
author:         Maciej W. Rozycki
description:    Broadcom PHY driver
...output omitted...
depends:        bcm-phy-lib,bcm-phy-ptp
intree:         Y
name:           broadcom
vermagic:       6.1.12-200.fc37.aarch64 SMP preempt
    mod_unload aarch64
sig_id:         PKCS#7
signer:         Fedora kernel signing key
sig_key:        4C:FF:C2:28:93:D4:32:A9:E6:E0:32:6A:D9:B0
...output omitted...
```

With these simple steps, we can determine whether the wireless card is using the right, updated driver. This prevents any initial issues when connecting to a network.

Now, let's learn how to identify the available wireless networks and configure our wireless card to get the best connectivity performance.

Finding the best quality network connection

By default, the nmcli command lists the available **Wi-Fi access points** that are no more than *30 seconds old* by enabling a network scan if necessary.

To list the available Wi-Fi access points, run the nmcli dev wifi list command:

```
[root@workstation ~]# nmcli dev wifi list
IN-USE  BSSID              SSID                  MODE   CHAN  RATE         SIGNAL  BARS  SECURITY
        2C:58:4F:7C:4A:1B  innsmouth             Infra  11    405 Mbit/s   100           WPA2
        7C:77:16:47:A5:51  INFINITUM222A_2.4     Infra  1     130 Mbit/s   85            WPA2
        C4:69:F0:F7:45:38  Totalplay-37AA        Infra  1     130 Mbit/s   84            WPA2
        C4:69:F0:F7:45:3B  ClubTotalplay_WiFi_2.4G Infra 1    130 Mbit/s   82            --
        2C:58:4F:7C:4A:1C  ultharcats            Infra  48    540 Mbit/s   82            WPA2
        48:4E:FC:63:EC:8D  IZZI-9844             Infra  6     405 Mbit/s   75            WPA2
        2C:00:AB:67:53:96  IZZI-B761             Infra  11    405 Mbit/s   72            WPA2
        A8:E8:1E:39:2F:18  INFINITUM0BCC         Infra  11    130 Mbit/s   70            WPA2
        F8:F5:32:A2:AB:4F  CasaFiGo              Infra  6     405 Mbit/s   64            WPA2
        C4:69:F0:18:9B:50  Totalplay-36AA        Infra  11    130 Mbit/s   50            WPA2
        9C:C8:FC:44:73:C4  IZZI-9440             Infra  6     405 Mbit/s   47            WPA2
        2C:00:AB:67:53:97  IZZI-B761-5G          Infra  157   540 Mbit/s   39            WPA2
        F8:F5:32:A2:AB:50  CasaFiGo-5G           Infra  157   540 Mbit/s   32            WPA2
        A8:E8:1E:39:2F:1D  INFINITUM0BCC         Infra  149   270 Mbit/s   29            WPA2
        48:4E:FC:63:EC:8E  IZZI-9844-5G          Infra  153   540 Mbit/s   27            WPA2
[root@workstation ~]#
```

Figure 5.18 – Listing the Wi-Fi access points

The nmcli command shows the Wi-Fi access points in different colors. Each one represents different signal strengths.

Soft colors, such as cyan, represent a weak signal (less than 30% intensity). A stronger signal (30-50%) is represented by a magenta color. Orange indicates a better signal (60-80%), whereas green represents an excellent signal (80-100%).

With the --rescan option, the scan could be forced to be disabled, regardless of the age of the access point list.

Use the `nmcli device` command to identify the wireless network device:

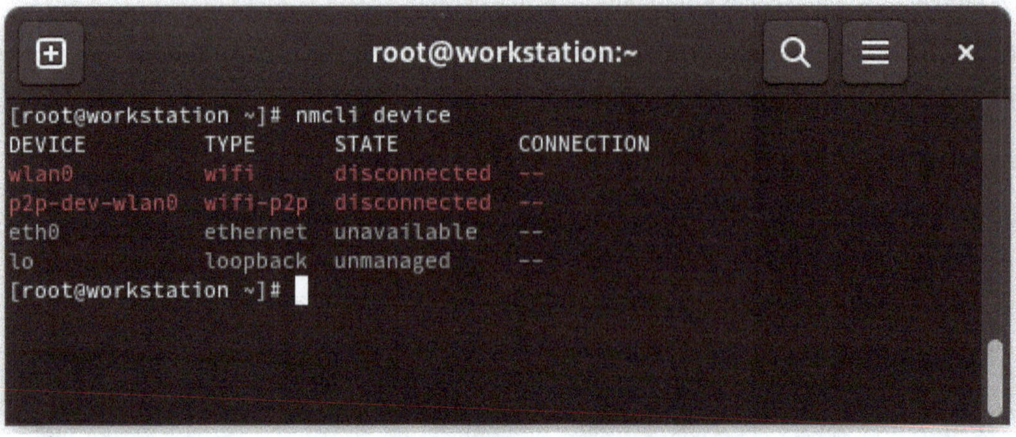

Figure 5.19 – Identifying the wireless network device

From the list of access points, select those that belong to the location of the workstation. Both have good signal quality:

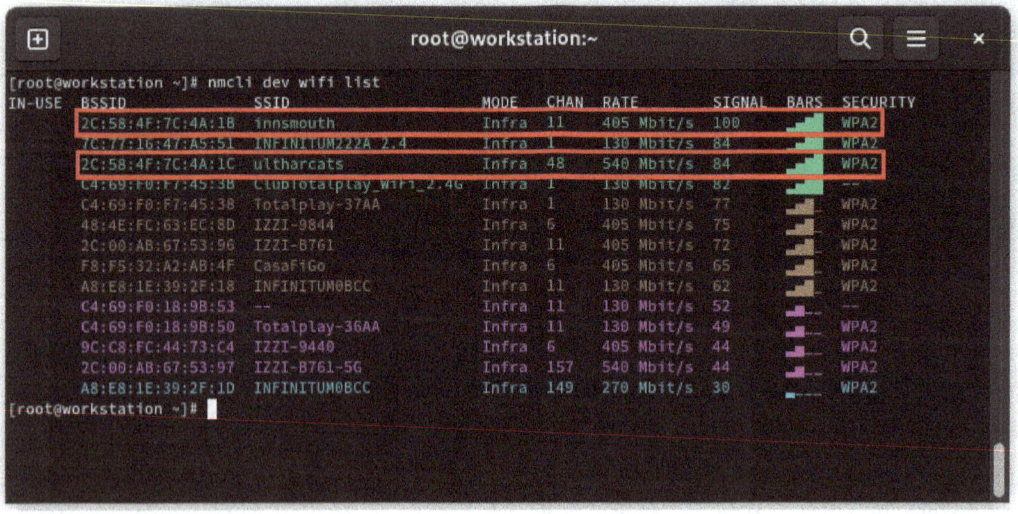

Figure 5.20 – Selecting Wi-Fi access points

Select the access point with the best signal quality and connect to it. Use the `nmcli` command with the following format:

```
# nmcli device wifi connect [SSID] password [SSID-password]
```

> **Note**
>
> This command preserves the **password** in the shell history. To remove it from the history, delete the corresponding line in the `~/.bash_history` file or run the `history -c` command to delete all entries.

Then, use the `nmcli device` command to confirm the device status change:

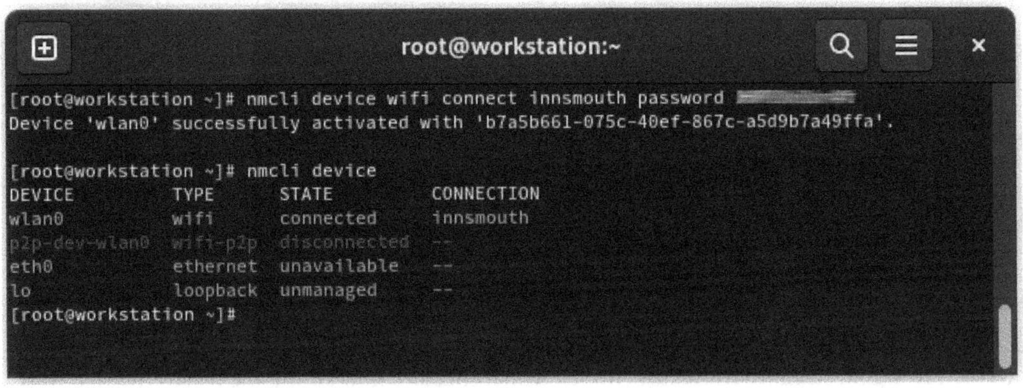
root@workstation:~
[root@workstation ~]# nmcli device wifi connect innsmouth password
Device 'wlan0' successfully activated with 'b7a5b661-075c-40ef-867c-a5d9b7a49ffa'.
[root@workstation ~]# nmcli device
DEVICE TYPE STATE CONNECTION
wlan0 wifi connected innsmouth
p2p-dev-wlan0 wifi-p2p disconnected --
eth0 ethernet unavailable --
lo loopback unmanaged --
[root@workstation ~]#

Figure 5.21 – Connecting to the access point

Repeat the same command and add the show and device options to display the connection details:

```
[root@workstation ~]# nmcli device show wlan0
GENERAL.DEVICE:                         wlan0
GENERAL.TYPE:                           wifi
GENERAL.HWADDR:                         DC:A6:32:AE:8D:8F
GENERAL.MTU:                            1500
GENERAL.STATE:                          100 (connected)
GENERAL.CONNECTION:                     innsmouth
GENERAL.CON-PATH:                       /org/freedesktop/NetworkManager/ActiveConnection/3
IP4.ADDRESS[1]:                         192.168.0.23/24
IP4.GATEWAY:                            192.168.0.1
IP4.ROUTE[1]:                           dst = 192.168.0.0/24, nh = 0.0.0.0, mt = 600
IP4.ROUTE[2]:                           dst = 0.0.0.0/0, nh = 192.168.0.1, mt = 600
IP4.DNS[1]:                             10.2.9.50
IP4.DNS[2]:                             10.2.9.116
IP6.ADDRESS[1]:                         2806:2a0:a16:8274:380f:bb58:98f7:a312/64
IP6.ADDRESS[2]:                         fe80::5de0:9a02:a8eb:b3b8/64
IP6.GATEWAY:                            fe80::2e58:4fff:fe7c:4a1d
IP6.ROUTE[1]:                           dst = fe80::/64, nh = ::, mt = 1024
IP6.ROUTE[2]:                           dst = 2806:2a0:a16:8274::/64, nh = ::, mt = 600
IP6.ROUTE[3]:                           dst = ::/0, nh = fe80::2e58:4fff:fe7c:4a1d, mt = 600
IP6.DNS[1]:                             2806:2a0:23::2
IP6.DNS[2]:                             2806:2a0:2b::2
[root@workstation ~]#
```

Figure 5.22 – Connection details

The **received signal strength indicator** (RSSI), which specifies how strong the received signal is, is measured in *decibels relative to one milliwatt* (**dBm**) or **10-3 W**.

To find the RSSI, it's necessary to interpret the *raw value* given by /proc/net/wireless and then display it in the appropriate unit or greatest value (using 8-bit arithmetic).

Use the iw command to get the device link information:

```
[root@workstation ~]# iw wlan0 link
Connected to 2c:58:4f:7c:4a:1b (on wlan0)
SSID: innsmouth
freq: 2462
RX: 1817351 bytes (8922 packets)
TX: 806585 bytes (3517 packets)
signal: -38 dBm
rx bitrate: 58.5 MBit/s
tx bitrate: 72.2 MBit/s
    bss flags:      short-preamble
dtim period:    1
beacon int:     100
```

The `iw` command grabs the information from the `/proc/net/wireless` file and interprets it. By combining this with the `watch` command, it is possible to directly monitor changes in the file. Here's an example:

```
# watch -n 1 cat /proc/net/wireless
```

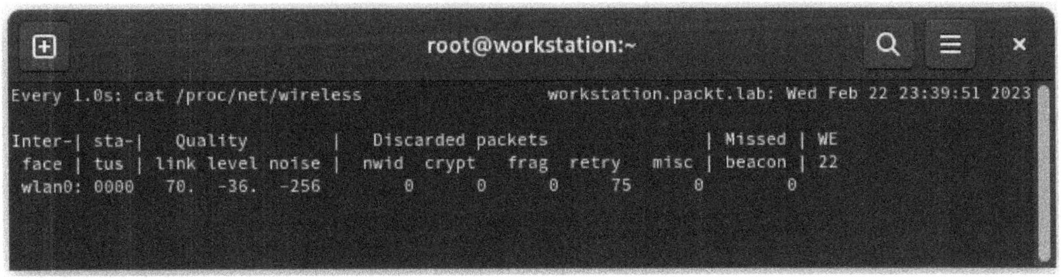

Figure 5.23 – Monitoring the quality of the connection

Monitoring the frequency of changes in quality values and comparing them on different networks could establish the optimal network to use for our system administration tasks. This will help us reduce connectivity interruptions in such tasks.

In the last section of this chapter, we will take a more in-depth look at monitoring connections for better performance and minimizing outages.

The **GNOME** desktop also includes an *applet* to configure the wireless network graphically. `nm-connection-editor` is a *GTK-based* application for adding, deleting, and modifying network connections that NetworkManager stores. Let's see how to do it.

nm-connection-editor

In the top-right corner of the taskbar, there is the control panel for settings, including the network connection. If the workstation is not connected to any network, only the icons for keyboard language, volume, and system power will appear:

Figure 5.24 – The top-right corner of the taskbar

Click on that area to display the control panel:

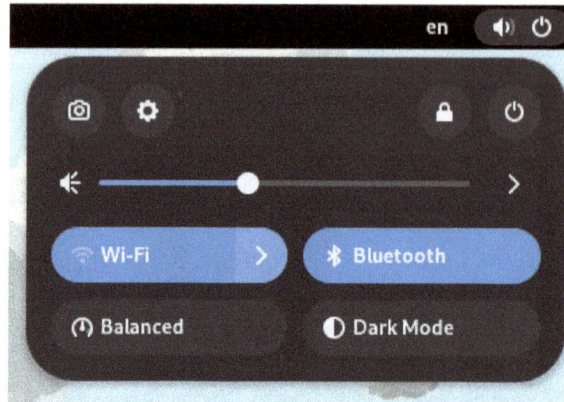

Figure 5.25 – Taskbar control panel

Follow these steps to connect the workstation to the wireless network:

1. Click on the gear icon and select **Wi-Fi** to discover the available wireless networks:

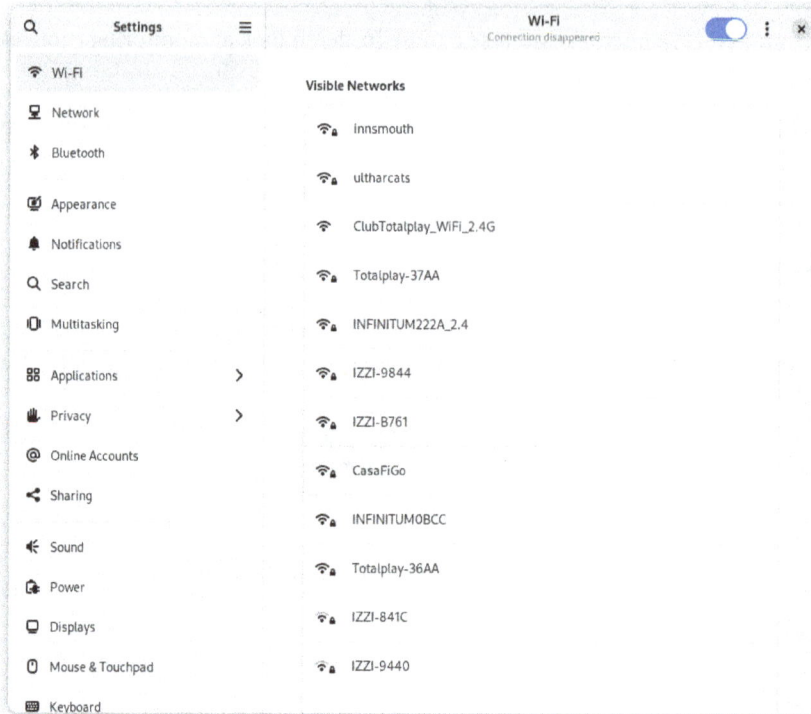

Figure 5.26 – Wi-Fi – Visible Networks

2. Locate the desired wireless network and click on it. If required, you will be prompted to enter the access password:

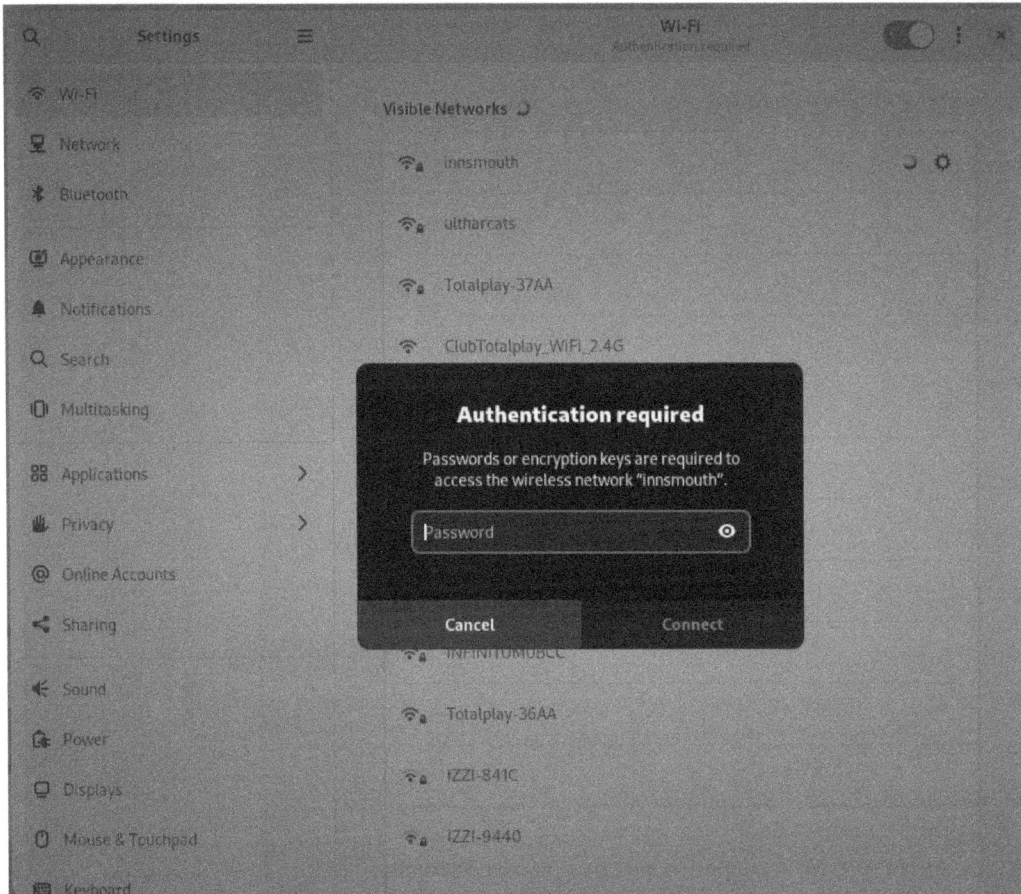

Figure 5.27 – Requesting access to the wireless network

3. If the password you've entered is correct, you will be able to access the wireless network and the connection details will be shown:

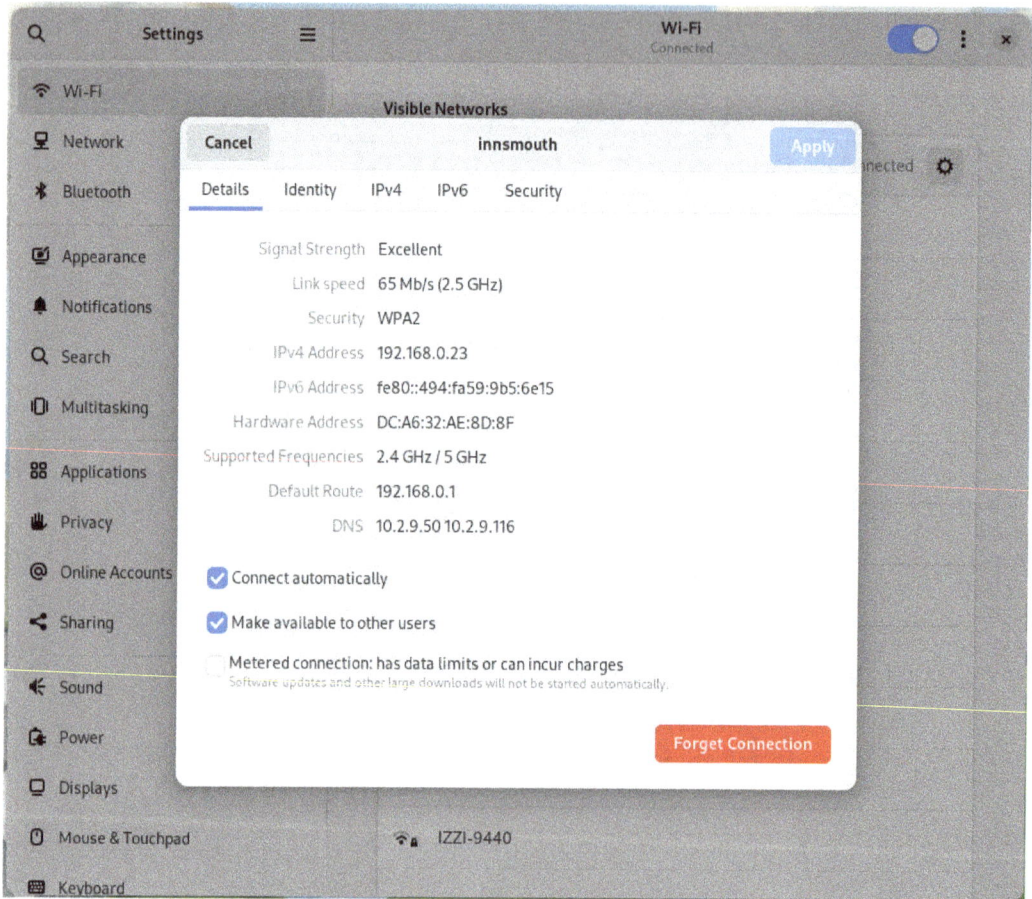

Figure 5.28 – Connection details

4. Now, the wireless connection icon will appear in the top-right corner of the taskbar:

Figure 5.29 – Wireless icon on the taskbar

When we click on it, the control panel will show us an icon that we can use to disable the connection or view the available networks:

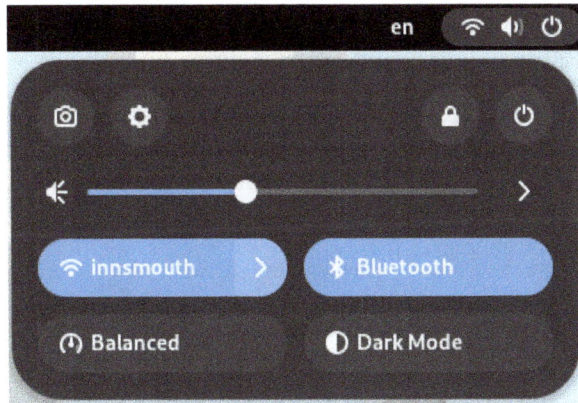

Figure 5.30 – Wireless direct access icon

Now, we can configure the network access to our workstation, either cable or wireless, depending on our needs.

In the examples shown in this chapter, we have focused on setting access and ensuring a healthy connection to the network.

However, we cannot omit the security risks involved in connecting to a network, especially those with public access.

Let's talk about this and how we can mitigate these risks.

What about security?

The use of wireless networks has boosted the mobility of jobs that rely on the use of computers.

Open wireless networks provide many facilities for remote work from anywhere in the world. However, they also include the risk of exposing confidential information about ourselves, our employers, or the clients we work with.

The most basic principle of security is to be aware of what we have open, such as ports, sockets, files, and/or processes. Some processes use the network's open ports to maintain connectivity between the client and server machine. Applying security's basic principle, we must be aware of the ports that have been opened and only allow those that we know must remain that way.

The tool that helps us in these cases is the **network firewall**.

As its name suggests, a network firewall is *a protective barrier that prevents unauthorized network communications*. Its main purpose is to prevent unauthorized access or use of the network services of our system.

Fedora Linux has a *built-in* firewall as part of the networking functions inside the kernel. The firewall management service in Fedora uses `firewalld`.

`firewalld` provides dynamic firewall management with support for network/firewall zones. That support defines the *trust level* of network connections or interfaces. The `firewalld` D-Bus interface uses the `firewall-cmd`, `firewall-config`, and `firewall-applet` firewall configuration tools.

The following diagram shows the firewall management flow with `firewalld`:

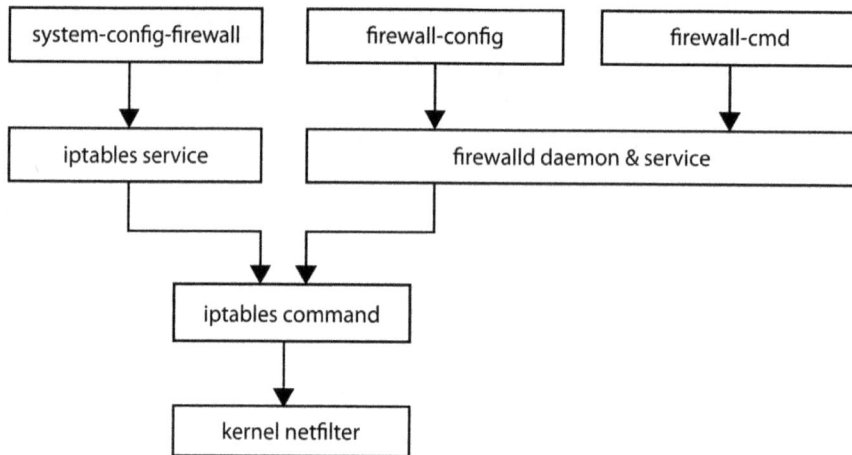

Figure 5.31 – The firewall management flow with firewalld

By default, the `firewalld` service comes installed with Fedora. You can use the **firewall-cmd cli** interface to investigate its status. Run the `firewall-cmd --state` command:

```
[root@workstation ~]# firewall-cmd --state
running
```

To load the configuration into the firewall, use the `firewall-cmd --list-all` command:

```
[root@workstation ~]# firewall-cmd --list-all
FedoraWorkstation (active)
  target: default
  icmp-block-inversion: no
  interfaces: wlan0
  sources:
  services: dhcpv6-client mdns samba-client ssh
  ports: 1025-65535/udp 1025-65535/tcp
  protocols:
  forward: yes
```

```
masquerade: no
forward-ports:
source-ports:
icmp-blocks:
rich rules:
```

The output of the preceding command shows that the configuration allows the `dhcpv6-client`, `mdns`, `samba-client`, and `ssh` services, as well as the `1025-65535/udp` and `1025-65535/tcp` dynamic ports.

In our workstation use case, it is likely that we do not need to have services or ports exposed to the network. So, the best practice is to close them all.

Before closing them, use the `ss` command to investigate the ports that have been opened by the processes to determine whether they refer to the services and ports allowed in the firewall:

```
# ss -tulpn
```

```
[root@workstation ~]# ss -tulpn
Netid State  Recv-Q Send-Q    Local Address:Port      Peer Address:Port Process
udp   UNCONN 0      0               0.0.0.0:50228          0.0.0.0:*     users:(("avahi-daemon",pid=702,fd=14))
udp   UNCONN 0      0               0.0.0.0:5353           0.0.0.0:*     users:(("avahi-daemon",pid=702,fd=12))
udp   UNCONN 0      0               0.0.0.0:5355           0.0.0.0:*     users:(("systemd-resolve",pid=623,fd=10))
udp   UNCONN 0      0             127.0.0.54:53            0.0.0.0:*     users:(("systemd-resolve",pid=623,fd=18))
udp   UNCONN 0      0         127.0.0.53%lo:53            0.0.0.0:*     users:(("systemd-resolve",pid=623,fd=16))
udp   UNCONN 0      0              127.0.0.1:323           0.0.0.0:*     users:(("chronyd",pid=743,fd=5))
udp   UNCONN 0      0                   [::]:5353             [::]:*     users:(("avahi-daemon",pid=702,fd=13))
udp   UNCONN 0      0                   [::]:5355             [::]:*     users:(("systemd-resolve",pid=623,fd=12))
udp   UNCONN 0      0                   [::]:42311            [::]:*     users:(("avahi-daemon",pid=702,fd=15))
udp   UNCONN 0      0                    [::1]:323            [::]:*     users:(("chronyd",pid=743,fd=6))
udp   UNCONN 0      0   [fe80::494:fa59:9b5:6e15]%wlan0:546 [::]:*      users:(("NetworkManager",pid=790,fd=28))
tcp   LISTEN 0      128             0.0.0.0:22             0.0.0.0:*     users:(("sshd",pid=807,fd=3))
tcp   LISTEN 0      4096          127.0.0.54:53            0.0.0.0:*     users:(("systemd-resolve",pid=623,fd=19))
tcp   LISTEN 0      4096            0.0.0.0:5355           0.0.0.0:*     users:(("systemd-resolve",pid=623,fd=11))
tcp   LISTEN 0      128           127.0.0.1:631           0.0.0.0:*     users:(("cupsd",pid=805,fd=7))
tcp   LISTEN 0      128           127.0.0.1:6010          0.0.0.0:*     users:(("sshd",pid=3561,fd=9))
tcp   LISTEN 0      4096      127.0.0.53%lo:53            0.0.0.0:*     users:(("systemd-resolve",pid=623,fd=17))
tcp   LISTEN 0      128                 [::1]:6010            [::]:*     users:(("sshd",pid=3561,fd=8))
tcp   LISTEN 0      128                  [::]:22             [::]:*     users:(("sshd",pid=807,fd=4))
tcp   LISTEN 0      128                 [::1]:631             [::]:*     users:(("cupsd",pid=805,fd=6))
tcp   LISTEN 0      4096                 [::]:5355             [::]:*     users:(("systemd-resolve",pid=623,fd=13))
[root@workstation ~]#
```

Figure 5.32 – Ports and services connections

As a result of this analysis, it is clear that our network is not using the open services allowed in the firewall, so we should close them. Let's look at the main reasons why we should do this:

- The network does not have `ipv6` (`dhcpv6-client`)

- DNS resolution does not use *multicast* on the network. (`mdns`)

- We do not use shared directories by `CIFS` or `samba` (`samba-client`)

- The workstation will be used to connect to other computers via `ssh`, but not in the opposite direction

To permanently remove the services from the configuration, use the `firewall-cmd` command:

```
[root@workstation ~]# firewall-cmd --permanent  --delete-
service={dhcpv6-client,mdns,samba-client}
Error: BUILTIN_SERVICE: 'dhcpv6-client' is built-in service
Error: BUILTIN_SERVICE: 'mdns' is built-in service
Error: BUILTIN_SERVICE: 'samba-client' is built-in service
```

> **Note**
>
> These services come as part of the system and they cannot be removed from the configuration.

The fourth point (from the preceding list) is also optional. We can do this if we need to connect to the workstation and connect to the managed servers from there, either as a *pivot server* or a *jump box*.

With the same command, remove the dynamic ports:

```
[root@workstation ~]# firewall-cmd --permanent  --remove-
port={1025-65535/udp,1025-65535/tcp}
Success
```

> **Note**
>
> The `firewall-cmd --permanent` command only affects the configuration files, not the firewall running in memory.

The service must reload its configuration to consider the changes.

Use the `firewall-cmd --reload` command and verify the configuration change:

```
[root@workstation ~]# firewall-cmd --reload
success
[root@workstation ~]# firewall-cmd --list-all
FedoraWorkstation (active)
  target: default
  icmp-block-inversion: no
  interfaces: wlan0
  sources:
  services: dhcpv6-client mdns samba-client ssh
  ports:
```

```
protocols:
forward: yes
masquerade: no
forward-ports:
source-ports:
icmp-blocks:
rich rules:
```

Thus, by adding services and/or ports, we will have better control of the connections to our workstation.

> **Note**
>
> For more information on the use of `firewalld`, refer to the service manual included in the operating system. Run the `man firewalld` command to access it.

From our side, the workstation has a secure environment that knows and authorizes the services and ports exposed to the network. But, especially in a public network, this communication must have an extra level of security. This could come from using a VPN.

Let's learn how to use a VPN to secure the connection from our workstation to the managed computers.

Improving network connectivity using a VPN

A VPN is a way of connecting to a local network over the internet.

A VPN connection creates a *single virtual private network between two points*. Each bit of data gets encrypted from point to point via **tunneling**. Tunneling refers to the process by which VPN packets reach their destination. VPNs operate at the operating system level, redirecting all their traffic through other servers. All traffic, including its physical location, remains hidden during network browsing. When using a VPN, the VPN router, called the *proxy server*, appears as the origin of the connection, not the real one. So, neither the site offering public access nor anyone else will be able to deduce who you are or what you are doing.

The following diagram shows, with a red line, the tunneling created by the VPN by connecting the workstation to the managed server through the public network:

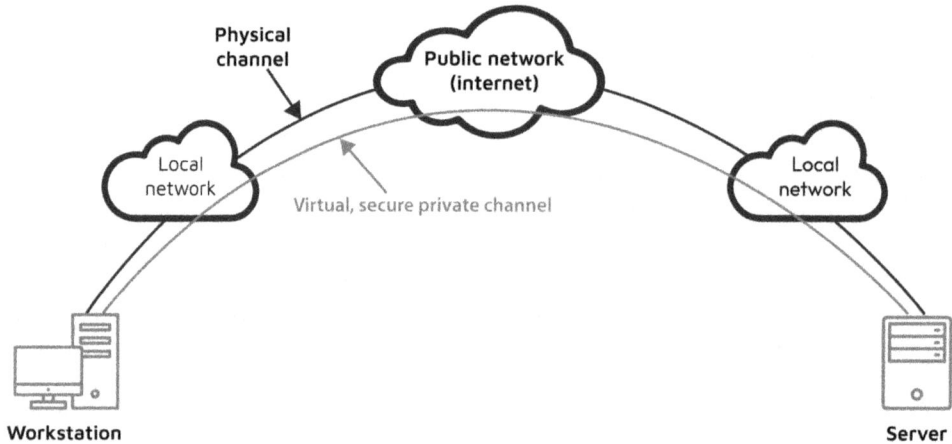

Figure 5.33 – Virtual private network

A VPN could be created with different types of tunneling using a variety of protocols, such as **Secure Shell (SSH)** or **Point-to-Point Protocol (PPP)**. They also support different service providers, such as **Cisco**, **Juniper**, **NetScreen**, and **SonicWall**, and they are multi-compatible.

Now, let's provide an overview of their two most common services: an **IPSec-based VPN** and **OpenVPN**.

IPSec-based VPN

Libreswan is an **IPsec** implementation of userspace for a VPN, which is the preferred method for creating a VPN. A VPN tunnel always uses *authentication* and *encryption*. For cryptographic operations, Libreswan uses the NSS library.

In Fedora, by default, Libreswan is not installed. So, install the NetworkManager-libreswan-gnome package with the dnf command:

```
[root@workstation ~]# dnf install NetworkManager-libreswan-gnome
```

Later, we will describe how to configure the VPN client with this protocol.

OpenVPN

OpenVPN supports client authentication methods based on certificates, smart cards, and/or two-factor authentication. It allows access control policies through firewall rules. OpenVPN *is not* a web application proxy and *does not work* through a web browser. It needs to be set up in the properties of the network connection.

The OpenVPN client integrates into NetworkManager as an *applet*.

Now, let's learn how to connect the workstation as a VPN client.

Configuring a VPN client with the Control Center

Follow these steps to connect the workstation as a VPN client:

1. Go to the top-right corner, click on it, and click on the `gear` icon to open the **Control Center** area:

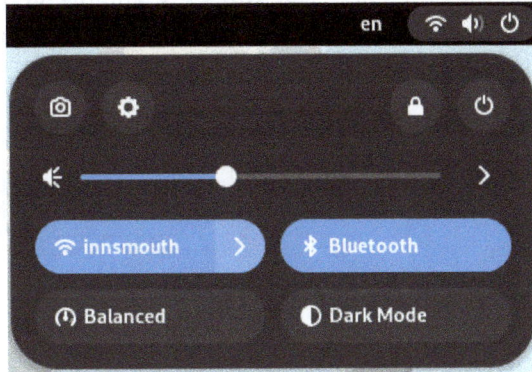

Figure 5.34 – Control Center

2. In **Settings**, in the left column, click **Network**:

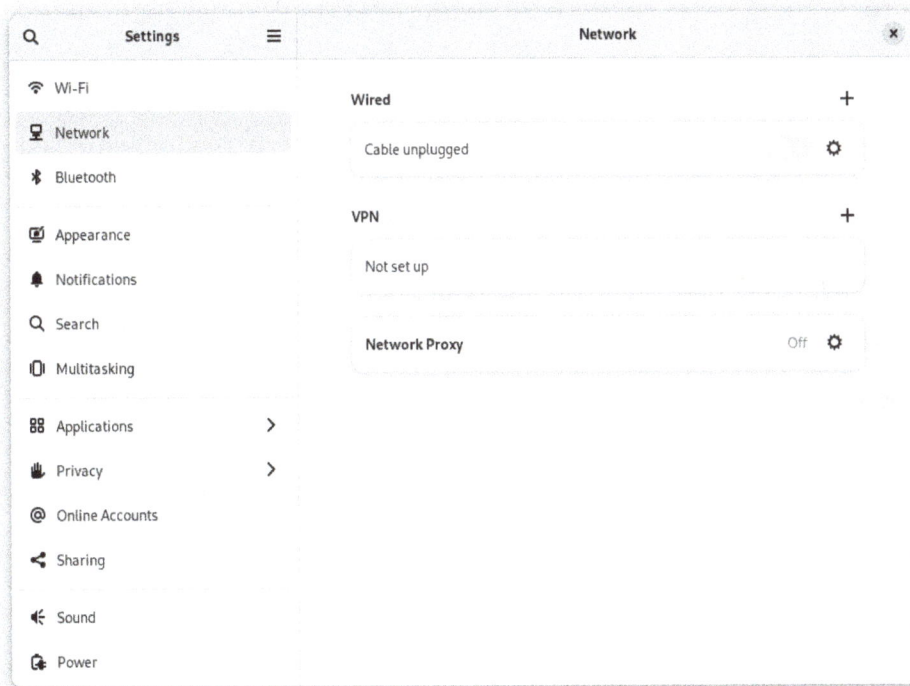

Figure 5.35 – Network settings

3. In the **VPN** section, click on the *plus* (+) symbol to add a new connection.

If the workstation has the `NetworkManager-libreswan-gnome` package installed, the option to add an IPsec-based VPN will appear.

The following figure shows the difference. The **Add VPN** window on the left does have the `NetworkManager-libreswan-gnome` package installed, while the window on the right side does not have the package installed:

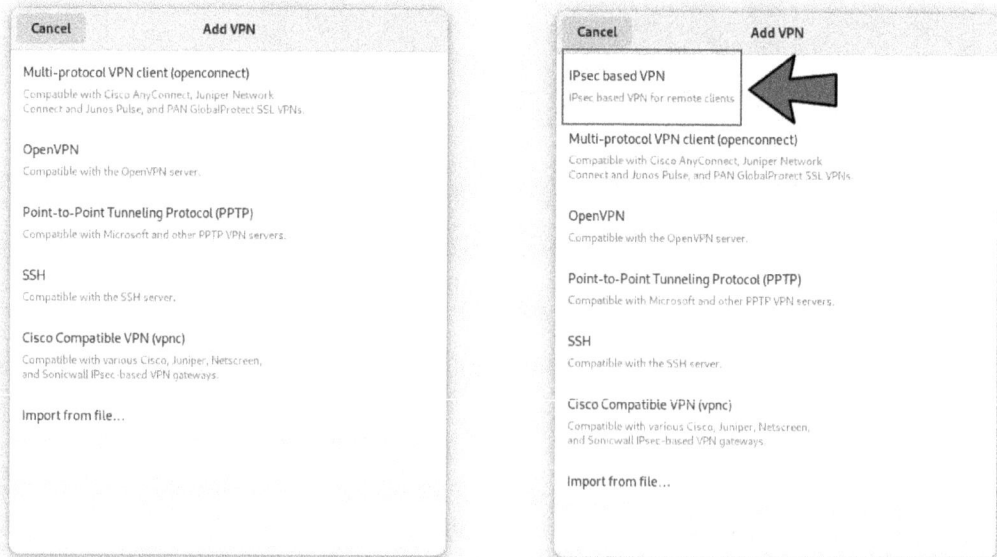

Figure 5.36 – Different VPN connection types available

Let's look at each case.

IPsec-based VPN

The following figure shows the window for adding the **IPsec-based VPN** connection:

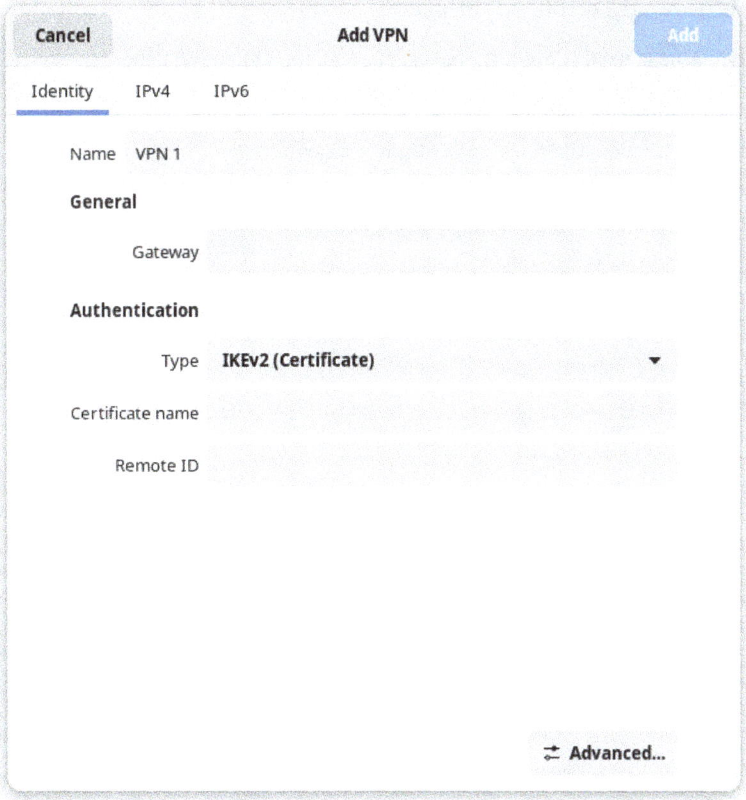

Figure 5.37 – IPsec-based VPN

In the **Identity** tab, add some general configuration properties for the connection:

- **Name**: This will identify the **VPN** connection.

- **General**:

  - **Gateway**: The *name* or IP address of the **VPN** gateway

- **Authentication**:

  - **Type**: IPsec supports two different types of authentication:

    - `IKEv2 (Certificate)`: This authentication uses a *certificate*, so it is the most secure option. This is the **default option** in the connection.

    - `IKEv1 (XAUTH)`: The authentication uses a *username and password* or a *pre-shared key*.

- **Certificate name**: The certificate's filename

- **Remote ID**: This is used if the remote server requires a local identifier for the IKE exchange

By clicking on the **Advanced** button, you can access more specific configuration details. If more details for the connection are needed, they can be set up in this window:

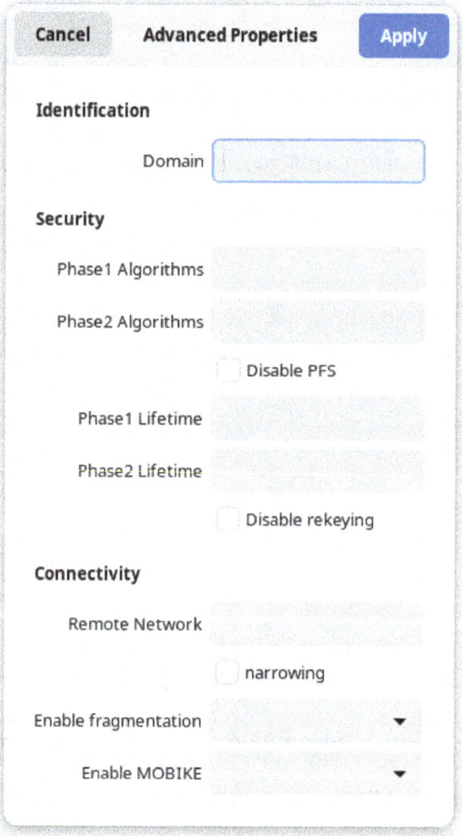

Figure 5.38 – IPsec-based VPN – Advanced Properties

After filling in the required fields, click the **Apply** button. Returning to the previous **Add VPN** screen, click the **Add** button to add the VPN connection.

OpenVPN

Clicking on **OpenVPN** displays a window similar to the IPsec-based screen:

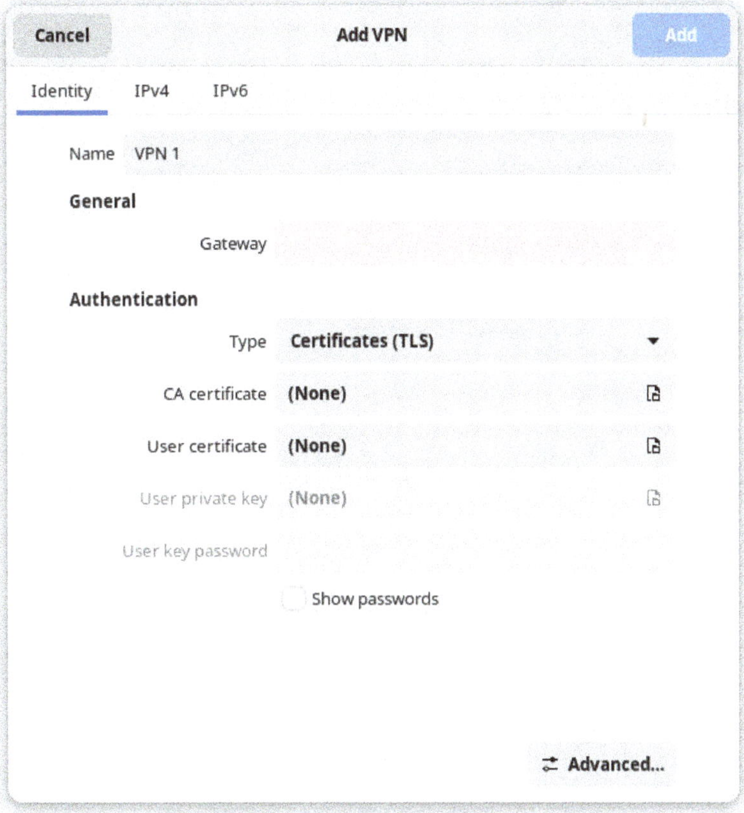

Figure 5.39 – OpenVPN connection

Filling in all the fields, as you did for the previous connection type, allows you to add the OpenVPN connection.

However, adding an OpenVPN connection is typically done by *importing a certificate*. Let's take a look at this process.

In the **Add VPN** connection window, click on the last option, **Import from file…**:

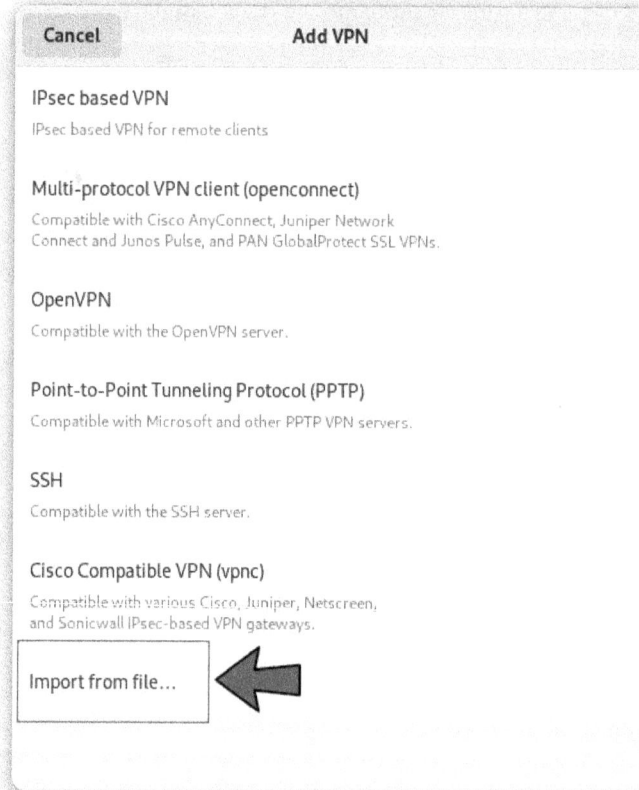

Figure 5.40 – Importing the .ovpn file certificate

Browse to the .ovpn file and click the **Open** button. The configuration window will display the connection information.

For example, in this case, we will import the /home/acallejas/sample.ovpn file.

The following figure shows the **sample vpn** connection information:

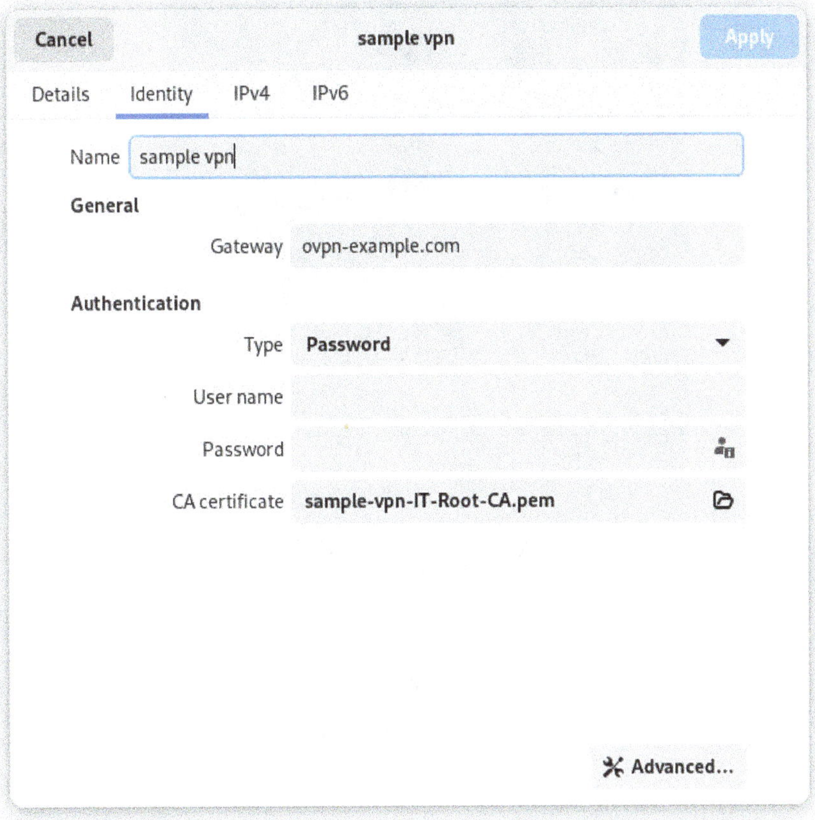

Figure 5.41 – Sample VPN connection

Regarding the connection, note the following:

- The file contains the connection's **Name** and the remote access **Gateway** details.
- Authentication requires **User name** and **Password.**
- **CA certificate** is a .pem file. This file could request a *dynamic passphrase* or **one-time password (OTP)**. This is generated by a physical, virtual, or hybrid device to allow access.

Click on the **Apply** button, if necessary. The OpenVPN connection will be added.

At the end of the VPN connection configuration, go to **Control Center** and select the VPN you want to access:

Figure 5.42 – Choosing a VPN connection

After successfully authenticating, the login icon will appear in the top-right corner:

Figure 5.43 – Workstation connected to the VPN

> **Note**
>
> One of the best practices for secure communications is to have your own VPN. For more information on how to do this, visit the articles published in **Fedora Magazine** at https://fedoramagazine.org/tag/vpn/.

Now that we have improved our network connection, be it wired or wireless, using tuning or a VPN, let's learn about some tools that will help us track the connection's behavior.

Network performance monitoring

There are different and varied network connection monitoring tools, but I prefer those that can be managed via the console. This allows for flexibility and, at the same time, can be used to run test batteries to verify the information that's been received.

The first tool we'll look at is basic but also has enough power to generate a quick analysis of the connection's behavior.

nmon

Nigel's Monitor (nmon) was created for the **IBM AIX** operating system with *release 4.3* in 2006 and was ported to Linux in 2015 under the **GNU General Public License** for use.

nmon is a benchmark tool. It collects operating system statistics, including the following:

- CPU (and CPU thread utilization or CPU frequency)
- GPU stats
- Memory use (physical and virtual, swap and paging)
- Disk (read and write, transfers plus service time and wait times, groups)
- Network (read and write and transfers), and more

This information can be displayed on the screen or saved in a *comma-separated file*. This allows for file backup and analysis to be performed with data extraction tools.

nmon is available in Fedora's repositories. Install nmon using the dnf command:

```
[root@workstation ~]# dnf install nmon
```

Run the tool with the nmon command:

```
[root@workstation ~]# nmon
```

The terminal will display the main nmon window:

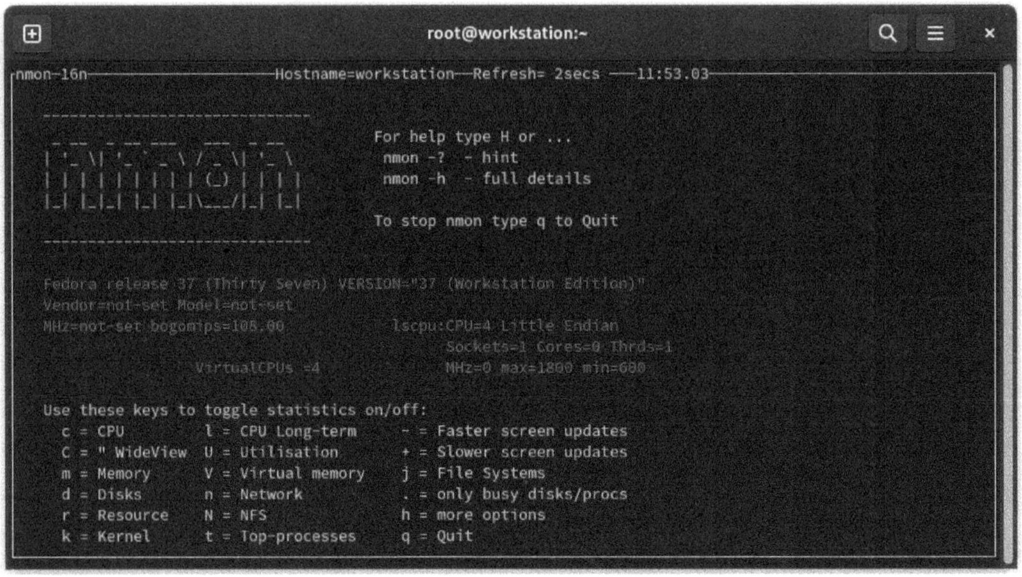

Figure 5.44 – nmon

In the case of network connection analysis, press n to display the connection statistics:

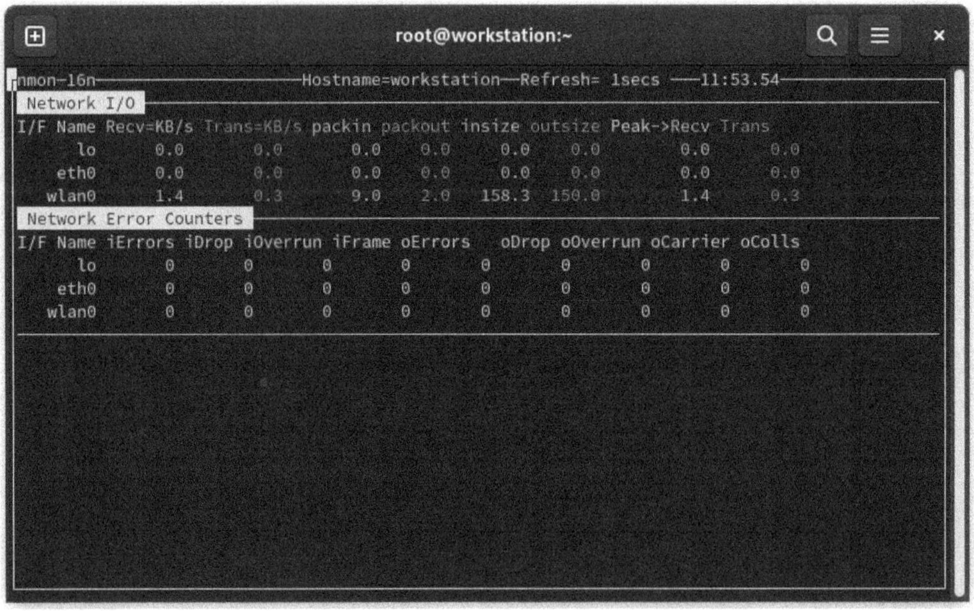

Figure 5.45 – Network stats

> **Note**
>
> nmon can collect a lot of useful information for workstation *performance benchmarking*. To learn more about its uses, refer to the **nmon for Linux** page at `https://nmon.sourceforge.net/`.

Another of my favorite tools is `bashtop`, but it is not included in the Fedora repositories at the time of writing. It must be installed by following the instructions on the project's page on GitHub (`https://github.com/aristocratos/bashtop#installation`).

A **Python** implementation of `bashtop` that's included in the official **Fedora Linux** repositories is bpytop.

Let's learn how to install and use it.

bpytop

bpytop is a *resource monitor* that displays usage and statistics for the processor, memory, disks, network, and processes.

It includes the most common features of resource monitors, such as ease of use and process manipulation at the touch of a key. However, it also has flexible features that allow data and processes to be manipulated simplistically. It can also be used to integrate themes that make it more attractive.

To install bpytop, follow these steps:

1. As the `root` user, use the `dnf` command to install bpytop:

    ```
    [root@workstation ~]# dnf -y install bpytop
    ```

2. On the terminal, run bpytop as **root**:

    ```
    [root@workstation ~]# bpytop
    ```

The main monitor window will appear:

Figure 5.46 – bpytop monitor

> **Note**
>
> To learn more about bpytop monitor usage, refer to the **bpytop GitHub page** at https://github.com/aristocratos/bpytop.

These excellent monitoring tools allow us to track the performance of network connections.

Summary

In this chapter, we reviewed how to connect our workstation to a network, by cable or wirelessly. Besides learning how to fine-tune this connection through best practices, we reviewed how to use VPNs in detail, as well as how to connect our workstation with an IPsec-based VPN and OpenVPN. Finally, we reviewed two monitoring tools that can help us track the performance of the network's connection.

In the next chapter, we will start learning about applications. We will begin by looking at some modern ways of using them, such as using *sandbox containers*.

Further reading

To learn more about the topics that were covered in this chapter, take a look at the following resources:

- *Fedora Linux 36 no longer supports the ifcfg files to configure networking*:

  `https://fedoraproject.org/wiki/Releases/36/ChangeSet#No_ifcfg_by_default`

- *nm-settings-nmcli*:

  `https://developer-old.gnome.org/NetworkManager/stable/nm-settings-nmcli.html`

- *Ask Fedora – Wi-Fi*:

  `https://ask.fedoraproject.org/search?q=wifi%20tags%3Af37%2Cwifi%20order%3Aviews`

- *Fedora Docs: Using firewalld*:

  `https://docs.fedoraproject.org/en-US/quick-docs/firewalld/`

- *Fedora Wiki: OpenVPN*:

  `https://fedoraproject.org/wiki/OpenVPN`

Part 3:
Productivity Tools

In this part, you will learn how to use the most common productivity tools used in a professional business environment, from text editors, office applications, and email clients to web browsers, starting with the different ways to install applications in general on Fedora Linux.

This part contains the following chapters:

- *Chapter 6, Sandbox Applications*

- *Chapter 7, Text Editors*

- *Chapter 8, LibreOffice Suite*

- *Chapter 9, Mail Clients and Browsers*

6

Sandbox Applications

To provide children with a safe place to play, you create a walled area and store their toys inside a small box (or *container*). When this idea moves to the playground, we refer to it as a **sandbox**. The term sandbox in application development comes from this same idea.

In the *sandboxing* approach, each application resides in a sandbox, a controlled and restricted environment for running its code. This environment helps developers isolate and protect system resources.

Developers also use *sandboxed environments* to identify an application's behavior and to detect bugs or other undesirable elements of its behavior.

There are several methods of sandboxing applications for Linux environments. In this book, we focus on some of them, including those considered the *least intrusive* (**AppImage**) and those developed and supported by the **Fedora Project** (**Flatpak**).

In this chapter, we're going to cover the following main topics:

- Inspecting sandbox applications
- Diving deep into AppImage apps
- Examining Flatpak applications

Technical requirements

For sandboxing or development of sandbox applications, you will need to install some packages. Most of them are included in Fedora's official repositories.

In each section, you will see the required packages and how to install each one of them.

If we use any package or code that's not included in the official Fedora repositories, we will include the link to get it and the instructions to install it.

The examples created in this chapter can be found in the book's GitHub repository that you can find at the following URL: `https://github.com/PacktPublishing/Fedora-Linux-System-Administration/tree/main/chapter6`.

Inspecting sandbox applications

Before we begin, we must make a distinction. Application isolation has always been sought as a *security* or *restriction measure*, either in case of intrusions or excessive use of resources.

With this, we can distinguish the development of applications according to the relationship between their use of resources and their interaction with privileged files of the host system.

Then, based on the aforementioned abstraction required to host code in a system, we could typify an application as follows:

- **Native** or **compiled**: It runs on the system with all system restrictions and privileges.
- **Interpret**: Interpreters walk through an application's code line by line and run each instruction into the system. In the past, applications created with interpreted languages were much slower than applications created with compiled languages. But, with the development of *just-in-time compilation*, this difference is reduced.
- **Jailed**: It allows application code to run on the system but from a *restricted location*. This restriction could include system resources or even system files. The structure of the jail could look like the system, but the changes or alterations to the files inside the jail do not affect the behavior of the host system.
- **Sandbox**: This is a more *restrictive* environment than a jail. The sandbox includes *only* the files required to run the application and interact with the system. This feature allows the portability of the application in an efficient way. The distribution of the host system does not affect the runtime of the sandbox application. It only requires that the distribution supports the sandbox type.

The development of a sandbox application could be very simple, from opening an application installed on the system in a controlled environment to porting applications from other distributions, without all the development involved in making it run on each distribution.

Let's see how to create a simple sandbox application. Then, let's learn about the common packaging methods for sandbox applications in Fedora.

SELinux sandbox

SELinux is a set of policies that allow us to add a *security layer* to our system environment. Based on these policies, we could set up a sandbox for applications.

> **Note**
>
> SELinux will be covered in detail in *Chapter 12* of this book.

For example, let's run the **Firefox** browser inside a sandbox isolated from the system environment. To do this, follow the subsequent steps:

1. As a `root` user, install the SELinux sandbox utilities. Install the `policycoreutils-sandbox` package with the `dnf` command:

    ```
    [root@workstation ~]# dnf install policycoreutils-sandbox
    ```

2. Configure SELinux in the `Permissive` mode to allow SELinux sandboxing. Use the `setenforce` and `getenforce` commands to verify the change:

    ```
    [root@workstation ~]# setenforce 0
    [root@workstation ~]# getenforce
    Permissive
    ```

3. As a *non-privileged user*, open a terminal and, inside the SELinux sandbox, run `firefox` in a *1280x1024* window. Use the `sandbox` command:

    ```
    $ sandbox -X -t sandbox_net -t sandbox_web_t -w 1280x1024
    firefox
    ```

    The `sandbox` command runs its own *X server* (`-X`) and enables policy enforcement for network and browser usage (`-t sandbox_net -t sandbox_web_t`). Set up `sandbox` and run `firefox` in a *1280x1024 window* (`-w 1280x1024 firefox`):

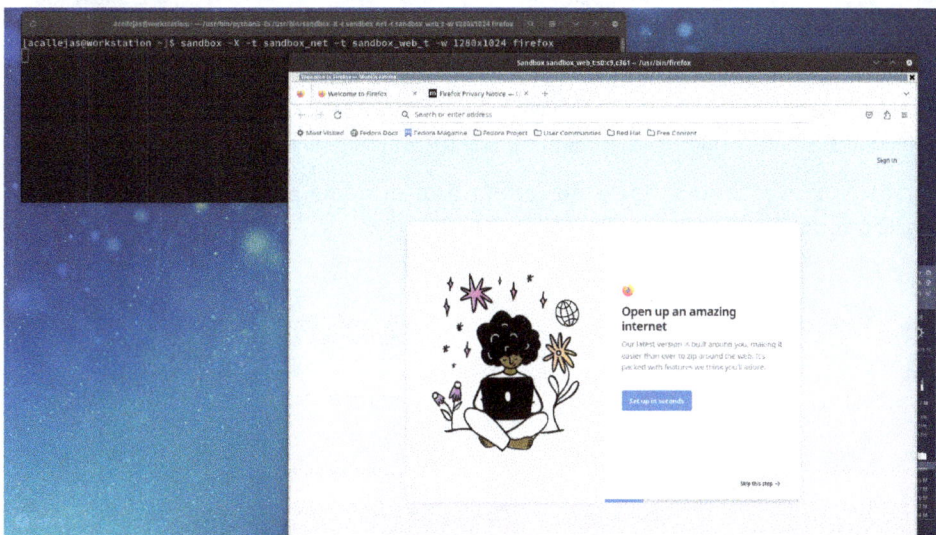

Figure 6.1 – Firefox on SELinux sandbox

Let's find out how to *monitor the performance* of the sandbox.

4. Use the `ps` command to find the sandbox's PID:

```
$ ps auf | grep firefox
acallej+    30511   0.0   0.9 ...output omitted...
```

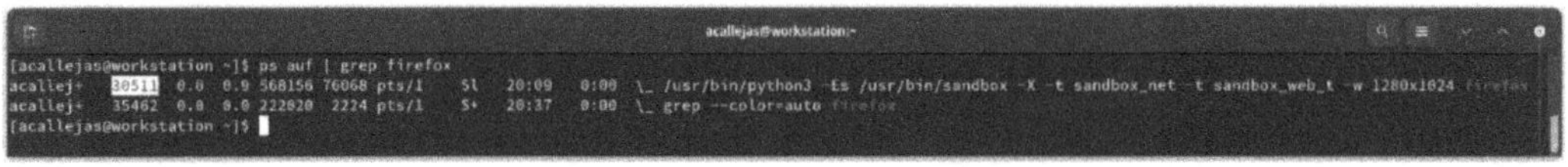

Figure 6.2 – Finding the sandbox pid

5. Use the `top` command to monitor the performance of the found `PID`:

```
$ top -p 30511
```

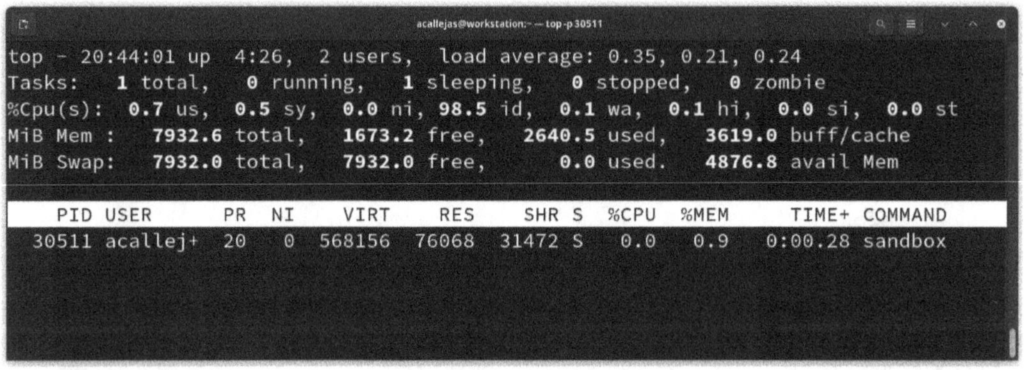

Figure 6.3 – Monitoring sandbox performance

The web browser is isolated, so its behavior does not affect the rest of the system. Let's see how to verify it.

6. On Firefox sandboxing, open the Fedora Project home page (`https://start.fedoraproject.org/`):

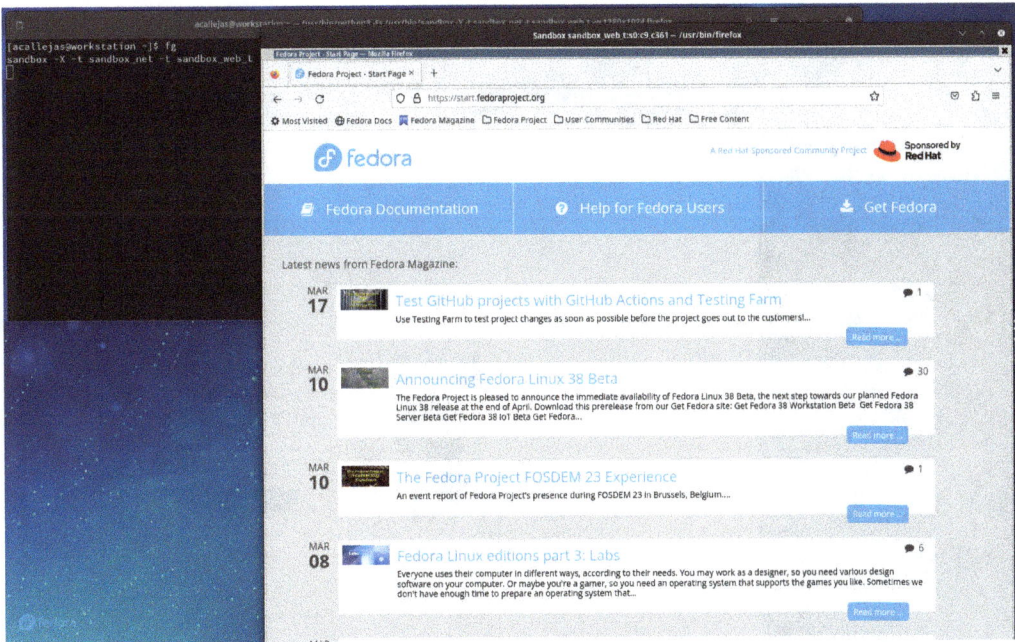

Figure 6.4 – Browsing with Firefox sandboxing

Close Firefox sandboxing by clicking the **X** button in the upper-right corner of the Firefox window.

7. Run Firefox in the sandbox again:

```
$ sandbox -X -t sandbox_net -t sandbox_web_t -w 1280x1024
firefox
```

Use *Ctrl + H* to open the browsing history:

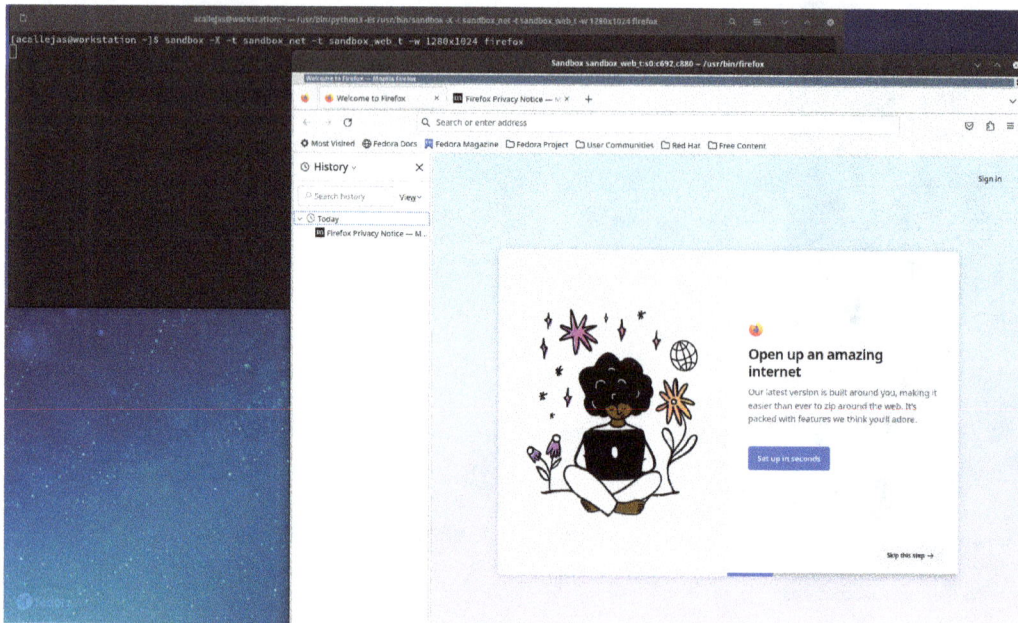

Figure 6.5 – Checking browsing history

8. Close the Firefox sandboxing window again.

Observe that no information about the website visited was saved. This information gets saved in a system file. Firefox runs in isolation and the information is stored inside the sandbox. When the sandbox is closed, the information stored in it is deleted.

The SELinux sandbox has many practical uses, for example, if an *untrusted file* needs to be opened.

With a `pdf` file, as an example, run `evince` in a sandbox to read it. Use the `sandbox` command:

```
$ sandbox -X -i /home/acallejas/findings.pdf evince /home/acallejas/
findings.pdf
```

With the preceding command, an untrusted file is added to the sandbox, indicating the full path to the file (`-i /home/acallejas/findings.pdf`).

> **Note**
>
> For more information on the use of the `sandbox` command, refer to the **manual** by running `man sandbox`.

The SELinux sandbox is one of the most basic ways to isolate an application. Using this idea, it is now taken a step further using different frameworks or forms to package the applications to make them portable to different environments, easing their installation.

Let's look at the most common examples of sandbox applications: **AppImages** and **Flatpaks**.

Diving deep into AppImage apps

Introduced in 2004 as **klik** by *Simon Peter* and renamed in 2011 as **PortableLinuxApp**, it was finally named in 2013 as we know it today: **AppImage**.

AppImage is a universal portable distribution format, also known as *upstream packaging*.

AppImages, as portable applications, do not need installation by the user. They also do not need administrator privileges to run. The user downloads the AppImage and assigns it execution permissions, and the application starts.

For a developer, creating AppImages is quite simple. An AppImage consists of a program package with dependency libraries and all the resources it needs during runtime.

AppImages are unique binaries, following the basic principle of *one application = one file*.

The tools to generate an AppImage from an **AppDir**. They are aware of possible incompatibilities between distributions and try to avoid them.

Once the AppImage is built, it runs on all major desktop distributions.

Let's see how to run an AppImage as a user. Then, let's walk through the development of an AppImage.

Running an AppImage

An AppImage is an image of the application.When you are running it, it mounts on the filesystem in the user space. Just give it *execution permissions* and double-click on it.

AppImages do not have an *application store* from which to download them, but there is a place to find and download hundreds of applications, known as **AppImageHub** (`https://appimage.github.io/apps/`).

For example, to download the developer version of **Firefox Nightly** and test new features without installing it, follow the subsequent steps:

1. Open the Firefox browser and go to `https://appimage.github.io/apps/`. Press the *Ctrl* + *F* key combination and search for the `firefox` string:

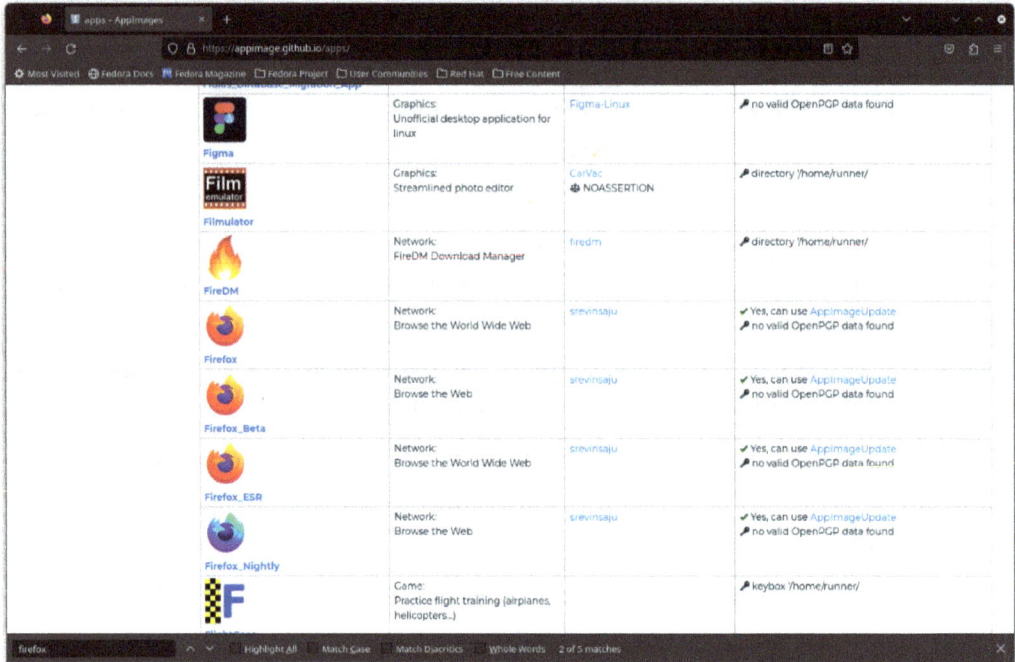

Figure 6.6 – Searching for the Firefox Nightly AppImage

2. Click on the `Firefox_Nightly` link:

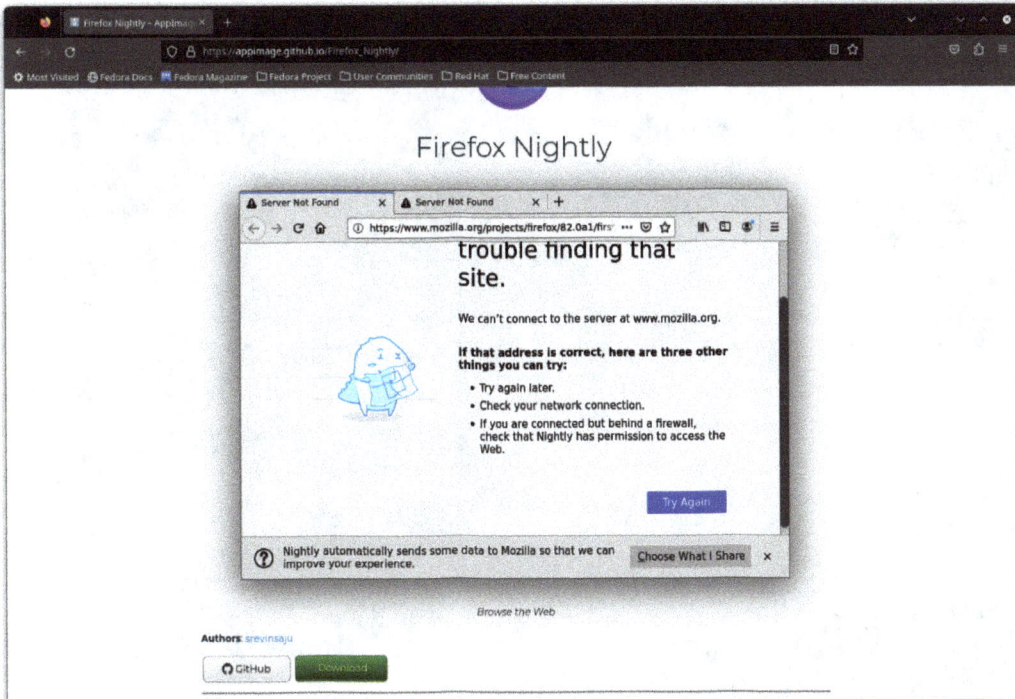

Figure 6.7 – Firefox_Nightly download window

Scroll down and click on the **Download** button.

3. This button takes us to the GitHub repository where the AppImage resides. Click on the *latest version* to download it:

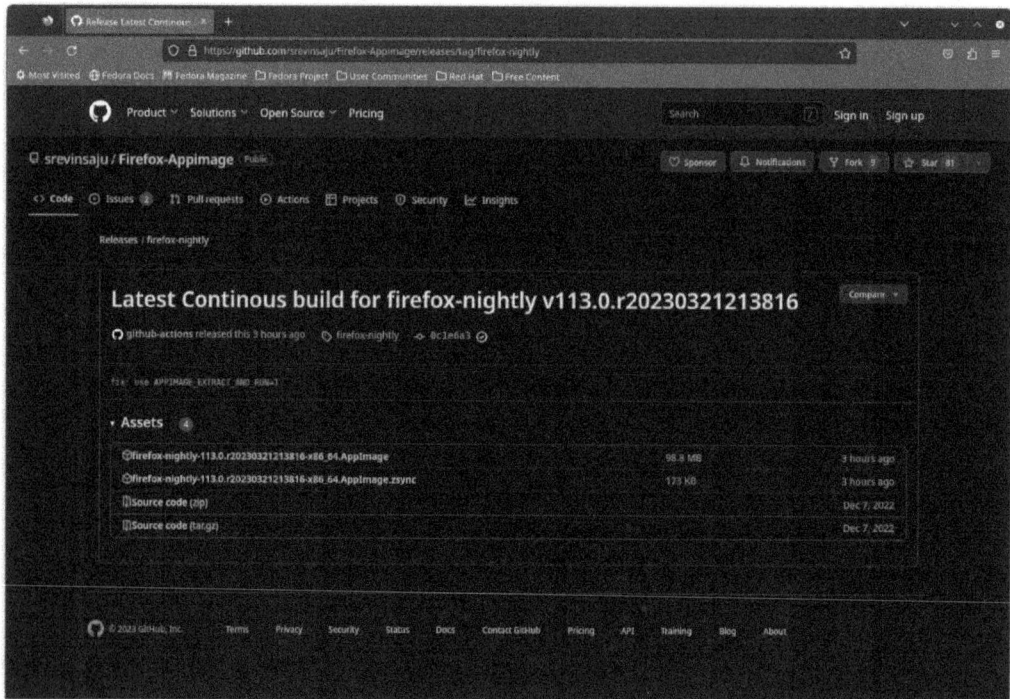

Figure 6.8 – Latest version in AppImage format

Wait for the download to finish.

4. Open a terminal and switch to the Downloads directory. Review the downloaded AppImage by running a long listing. Use the ls command:

Figure 6.9 – Checking the AppImage

5. Grant *execution permissions* to AppImage using the chmod command:

    ```
    $ chmod +x firefox-nightly-113.0.r20230321213816-x86_64.AppImage
    ```

6. Open the file browser and change parent directory to the Downloads directory. Right-click on the AppImage icon and click on **Properties**. Verify that the **Executable as program** switch button is enabled:

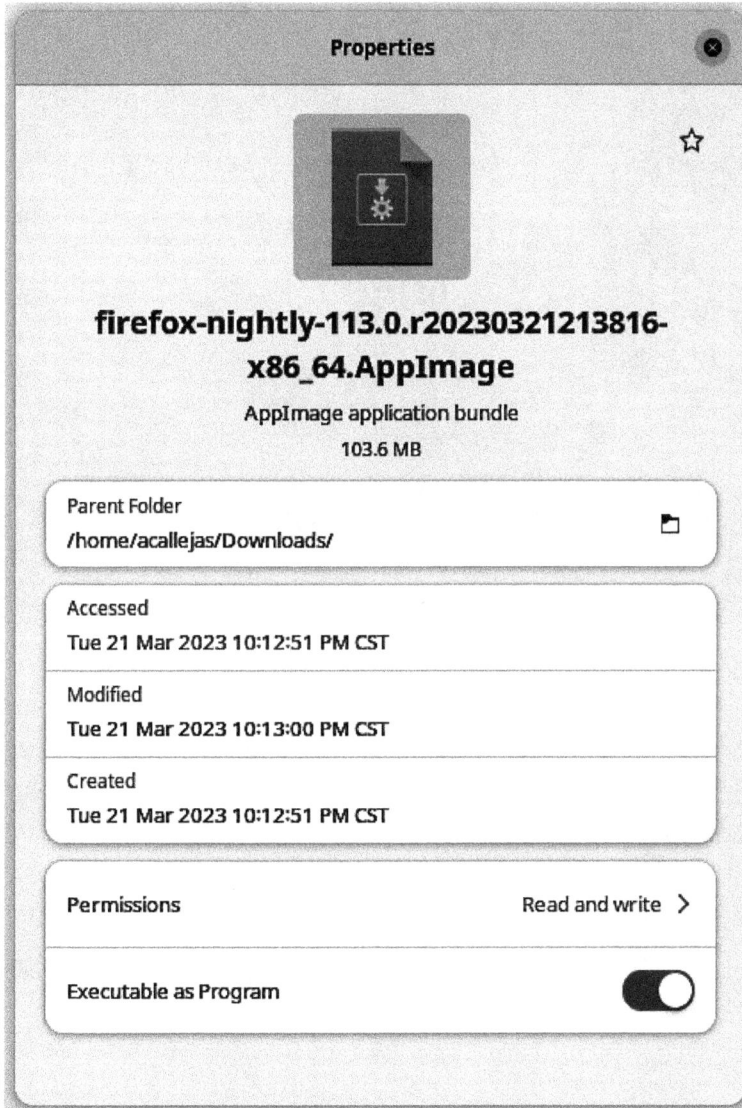

Figure 6.10 – AppImage properties

7. Close the **Properties** window by clicking on **X** in the upper-right corner.

8. Double-click on the AppImage icon. The Firefox Nightly window opens:

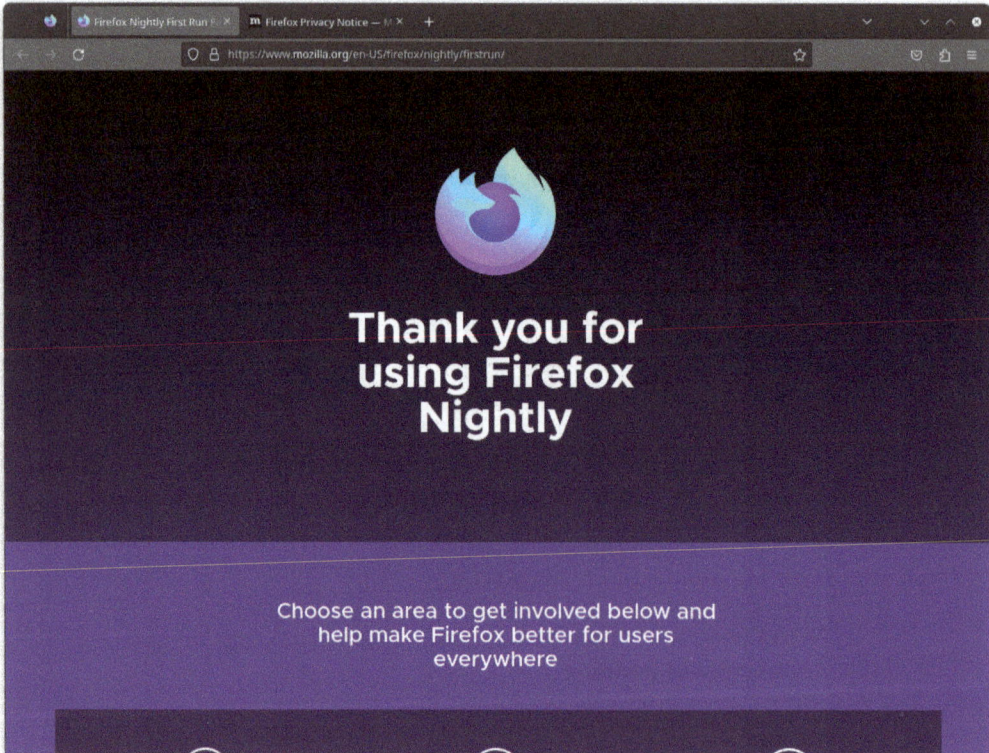

Figure 6.11 – Firefox Nightly on AppImage

With these simple steps, the application runs without being installed. If we prefer, we could create a *launcher* and add it to the shortcuts of the taskbar.

Let's see now how to develop AppImages.

Developing AppImages

Developing AppImages is very simple. The **AppImage** project provides **AppImageKit,** an implementation of the AppImage format focused on the *tiny runtime* of each one.

> **Note**
> AppImageKit is available to download at `https://github.com/AppImage/AppImageKit/releases/continuous`.

The core components of AppImageKit are as follows:

- `runtime`: The runtime provides an executable header for an AppImage. The runtime mounts the filesystem image to a temporary location. Such a filesystem image is called an *AppDir*. It then launches the payload application. Downloading it is not required.

- `Appimagetool`: This creates the AppImages by embedding the runtime and attaching the AppDir inside it. This tool comes as an AppImage.

- `AppRun`: This provides the entry point of the AppImage. The runtime executes this file inside the AppDir. It doesn't need to be a regular file; it could be a symlink to the main binary.

> **Note**
>
> The project adds and deprecates extra tools in the AppImageKit all the time, even those from third parties. So, keep an eye out for updates to the GitHub repository.

To create an AppImage, according to the project documentation, follow these steps:

1. Download `appimagetool` using the `wget` command:

```
$ wget \
> https://github.com/AppImage/AppImageKit/releases/download/
continuous/appimagetool-x86_64.AppImage
```

2. Add execution permissions with the `chmod` command:

```
$ chmod a+x appimagetool-x86_64.AppImage
```

3. To create the AppDir, use a high-level tool such as `linuxdeployqt`. Assuming that the AppDir already has everything needed to run the application, run the `appimagetool` command to generate the AppImage:

```
$ ./appimagetool-x86_64.AppImage some.AppDir
```

With this simple procedure, the new AppImage is created and ready to distribute.

> **Note**
>
> For more information on the use of AppImageKit, refer to the GitHub repository at `https://github.com/AppImage/AppImageKit`.

So, now we know how to create and use AppImages, it's time to look at the proposal drawn up by the Fedora Project itself. Let's take a walk through the **flatpaks**.

Examining Flatpak applications

First is one of Fedora's founding principles, so **Fedora Linux** is always on the *cutting edge.*

Flatpak is a new distribution-independent format for packaging and distributing Linux desktop applications.

The main goals of Flatpak include the following:

- Create a single installation file that could be distributed to users of all distributions
- Run applications that are as isolated as possible from the rest of the system

The biggest benefit to users is the ability to run any application, regardless of the version of Fedora Linux they use.

Its development name was `xdg-app` and it was renamed **Flatpak** in 2016 to reflect the fact that it became ready for wider use.

Flatpak is a system for building, distributing, and running sandboxed desktop applications on Linux.

Flatpak applications are installed through the `flatpak` command or through a GUI such as **GNOME Software** or **KDE Discover**.

Flatpak introduces some basic concepts, such as the following:

- **Runtime**: A platform that provides the basic utilities needed for a Flatpak application to run.
- **BaseApp**: An integrated platform for frameworks such as *Electron*.
- **Flatpak bundle**: A specific export format for a single file. It contains one application. It is also known as *Flatpak runtime.*
- **Sandboxes**: Applications build and run in an isolated environment. Only the content of the sandbox can be accessed by the program. Access to other resources, such as processes other than the sandbox, is not possible.
- **Portals**: The mechanism through which applications interact with the host environment from within a sandbox. It provides interaction with data, files, and services without the need to add permissions to the sandbox.
- **Repositories**: Flatpak applications and runtimes get stored and published via repositories such as Git repositories, which in some cases are named *registries.*

Let's now look at the mechanisms for running Flatpak applications, and then we'll walk a little bit through the development of Flatpak applications.

Using Flatpak applications

Flatpak is installed by default on Fedora desktop variants.

Flatpak applications are *fully integrated* into the operating system's package manager. We can install them using the graphical interface or the command line.

Let's first look at the simplest form of installation using the GUI.

Using the GUI

The origin of installable applications might come as a package built on the OS, not sandboxed or built in a sandbox.

For the end user, there is no difference, but it is possible to find out the installation format of an application from the software manager. It is very simple. For example, let's inspect the format that installed the Firefox browser and its installation options. Follow the subsequent steps:

1. As a *non-root user*, open the **Activities Overview** menu and click on **Software**:

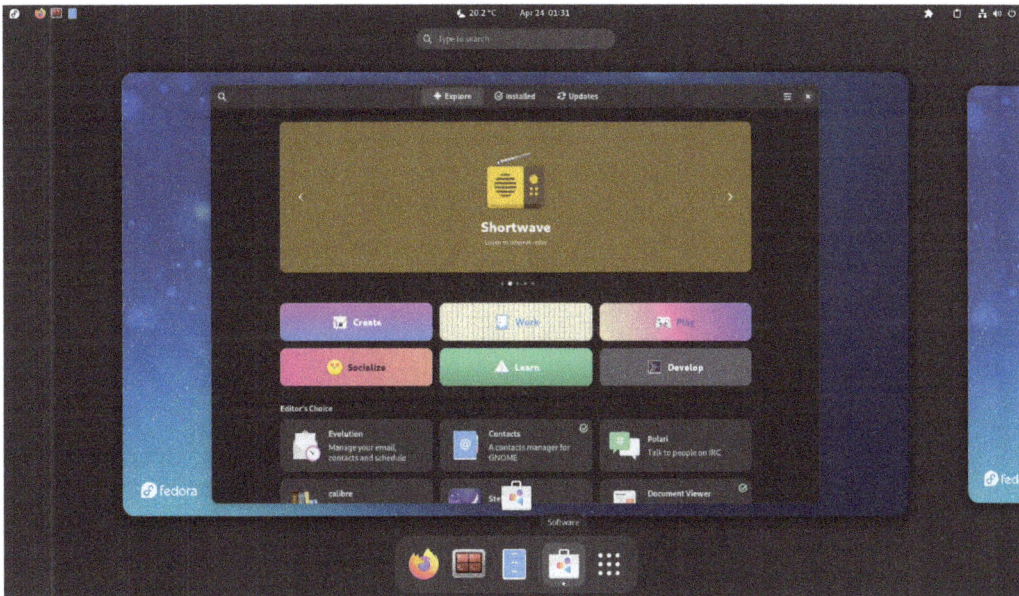

Figure 6.12 – Activities Overview menu

2.   Click on the *search* icon in the upper-left corner. In the search field, type `firefox` and press *Enter*:

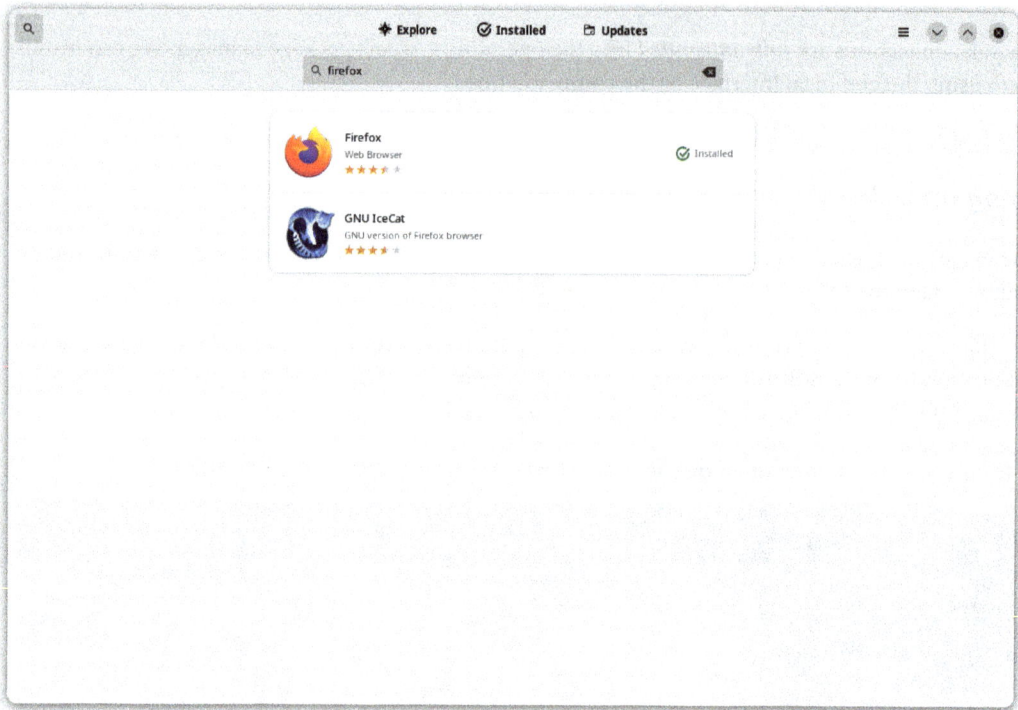

Figure 6.13 – Search for the application

Click on the **Firefox** icon, shown as **Installed**.

3. Below the **Open** button, find the *installation source*. Click on the drop-down list:

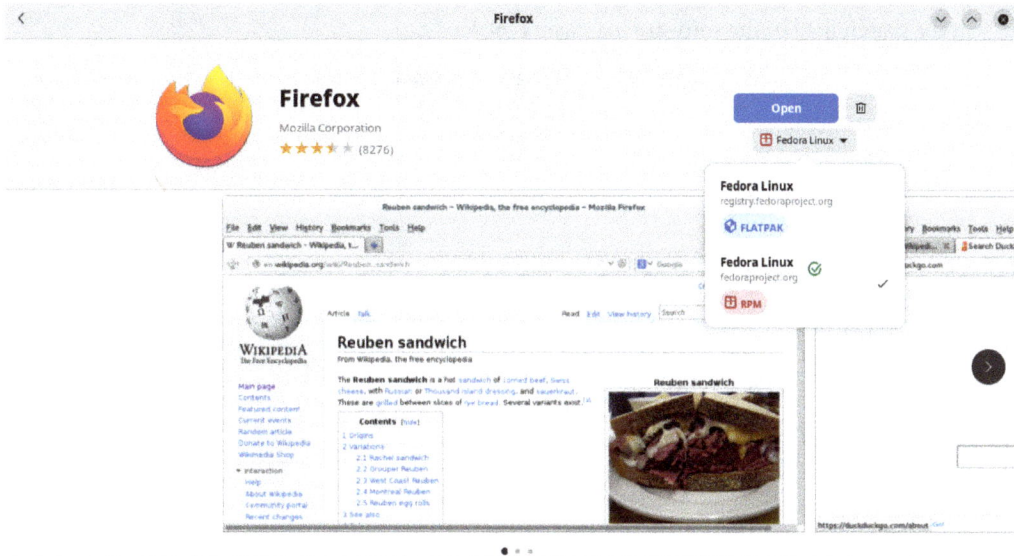

Figure 6.14 – Firefox installation source

Installation options for Firefox include the following:

- **FLATPAK**: From the official Fedora registry (`registry.fedoraproject.org`) as a Flatpak application

- **RPM**: From the official Fedora repositories (`fedoraproject.org`) as RPM

In this case, it shows that Firefox was installed from the official Fedora repositories as a built RPM.

So, to install a Flatpak application with the software manager, just select the installation source.

Let's install a *digital painting editor* as an example. Follow the subsequent steps:

1.   In the search field of the software manager, type `krita`:

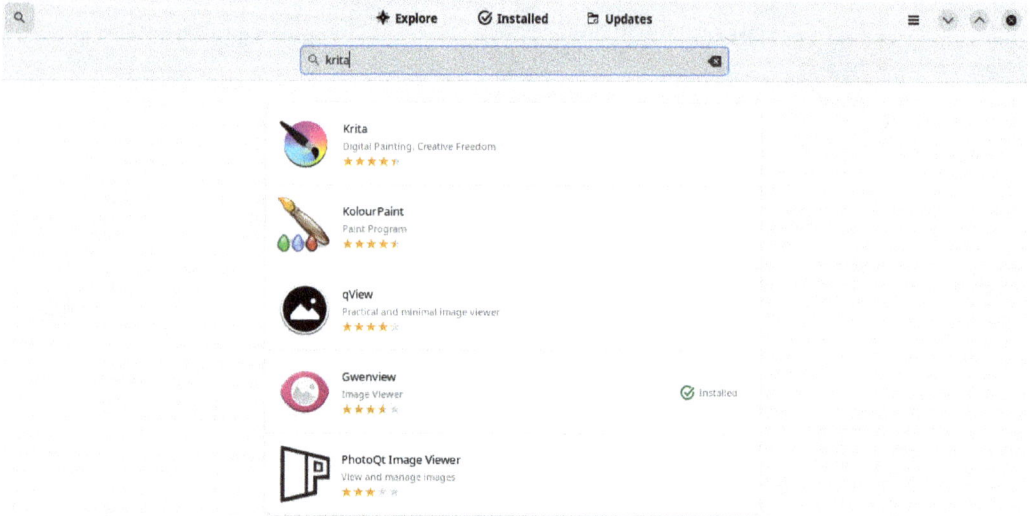

Figure 6.15 – Search for the application

Click on the first result.

2. Verify the installation source as a Flatpak application. Below the **Install** button, click on the drop-down list:

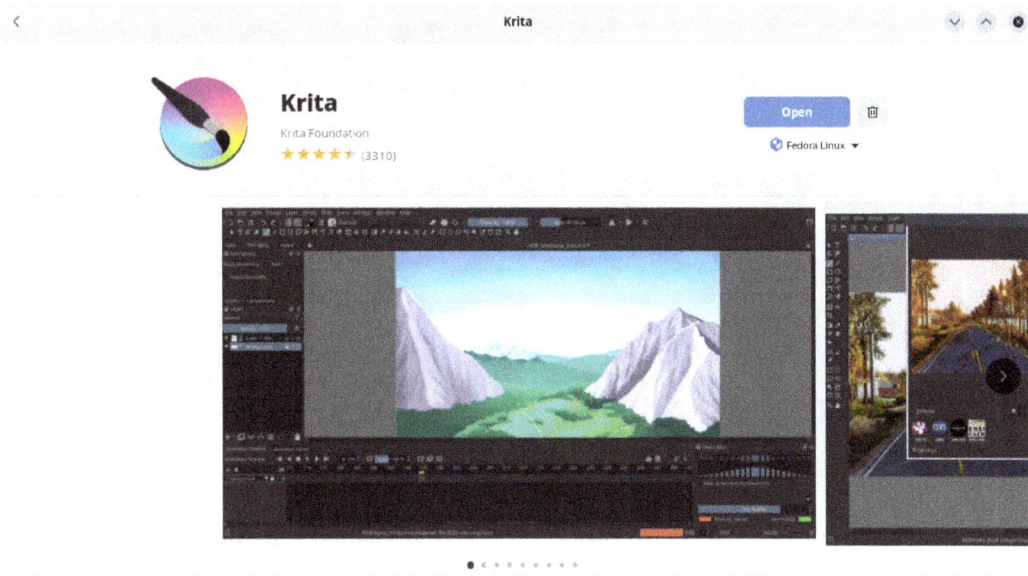

Figure 6.16 – Verifying the installation source

Choose **Flatpak** as the installation source.

3. Click the **Install** button. Wait until the installation is complete.

4.   Click the **Open** button:

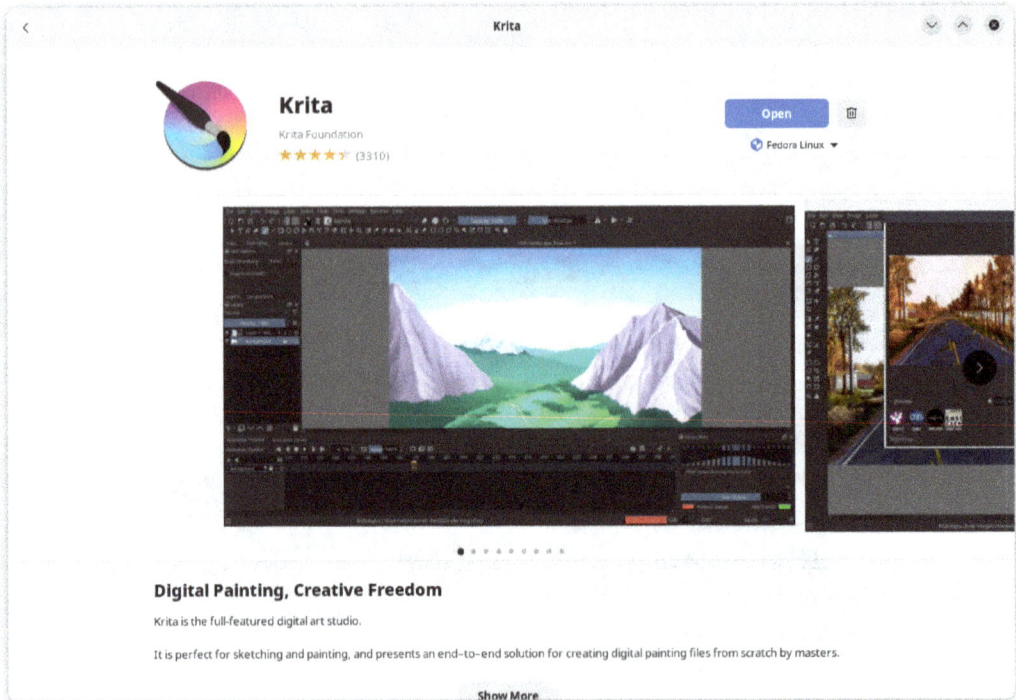

Figure 6.17 – Open the application

The application opens and is ready for use:

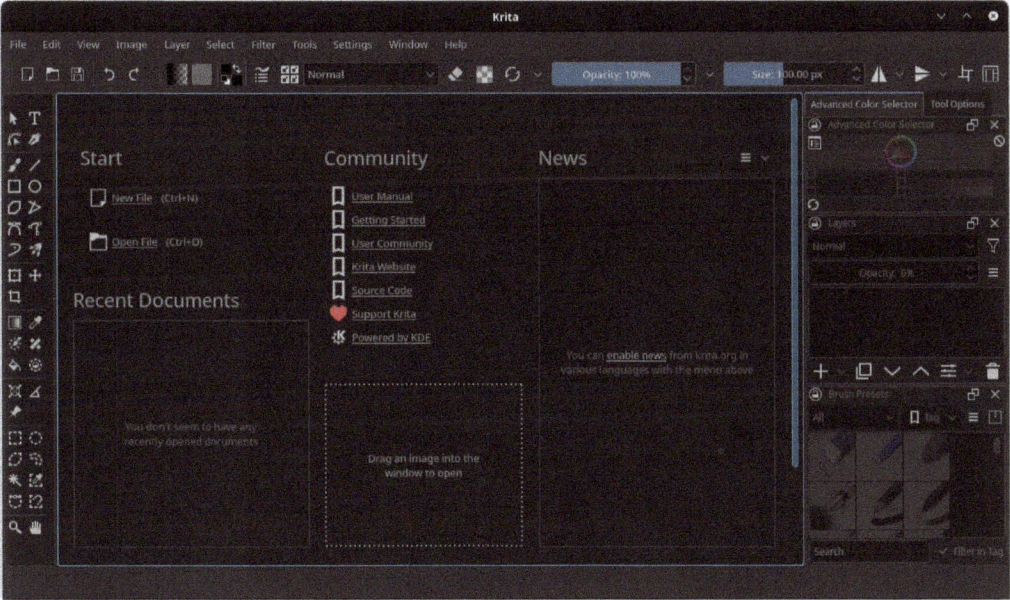

Figure 6.18 – Krita as a Flatpak application

As mentioned earlier, the end user experiences no difference with applications built on `rpm`. Through the command line, it is possible to inspect the resources used and the isolation of the application from the system along with other options such as adding other repositories of Flatpak applications.

Let's now see how to use the command line to manage Flatpak applications.

Using the CLI

As mentioned in *Chapter 1*, the use of the command line expands the system administration capabilities. Let's analyze the performance of the Flatpak application installed in the previous section. Follow the subsequent steps:

1. As a `root` user, open a terminal and use the `ps` command to search for the `xdg-dbus-proxy` and `krita` processes:

```
[root@workstation ~]# ps axf | egrep "krita|xdg-dbus-proxy"
  13340 ?        S      0:00  |      \_ bwrap --args 42 krita
  13359 ?        S      0:00  |          \_ bwrap --args 42 krita
  13360 ?        Sl     0:04  |              \_ krita
  13353 ?        S      0:00  \_ bwrap --args 42 xdg-dbus-proxy --args=44
  13354 ?        Sl     0:00       \_ xdg-dbus-proxy --args=44
```

xdg-dbus-proxy is a filtering proxy for *D-Bus* connections. It is the portal through which the krita application interacts with the system.

2. Using the method of the first section of this chapter, track the performance of both processes. Use the top command:

```
[root@workstation ~]# top -p 13353,13360
```

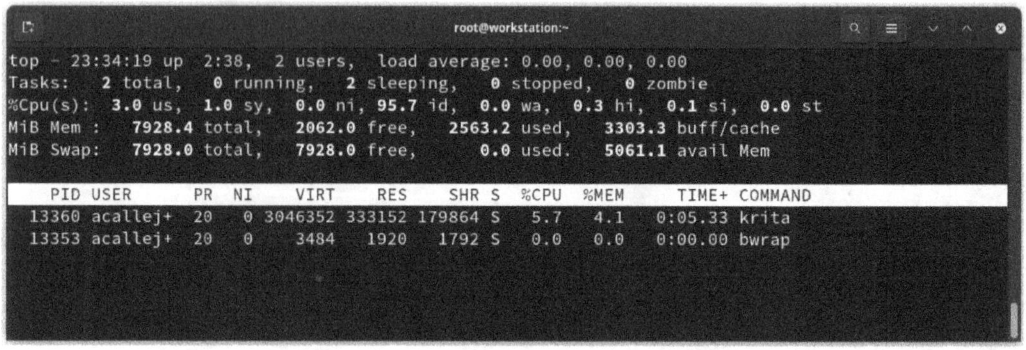

Figure 6.19 – Flatpak application performance

As mentioned at the beginning of this section, flatpak comes installed by default in Fedora Linux. It is available as a command to build, install, and run applications and runtimes. It could operate at the local or wide level, as a root or *non-root* user.

Let's start to explore the capabilities of the flatpak command line.

3. Use the flatpak command to list the Flatpak applications installed:

```
[root@workstation ~]# flatpak list --app
```

Figure 6.20 – Listing Flatpak applications

4. To inspect the changes to Flatpak applications on the system, use the `flatpak` command with the `history` option:

```
[root@workstation ~]# flatpak history
```

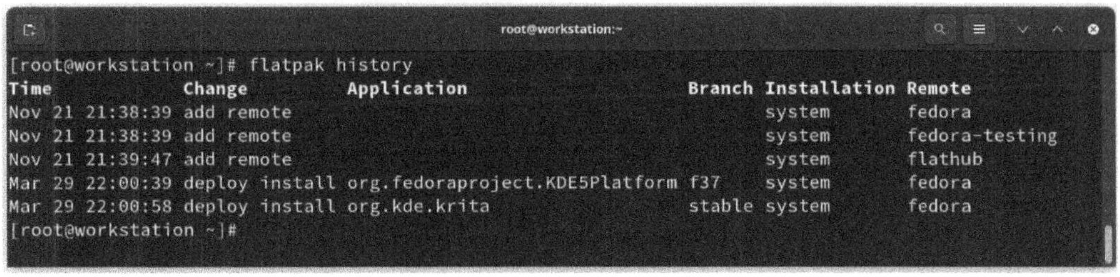

Figure 6.21 – Flatpak history

These changes include installation, update, or removal, covering applications and runtimes.

5. To show the application details, use the `flatpak` command with the `info` option and the `Application ID` of the application:

```
[root@workstation ~]# flatpak info org.kde.krita
```

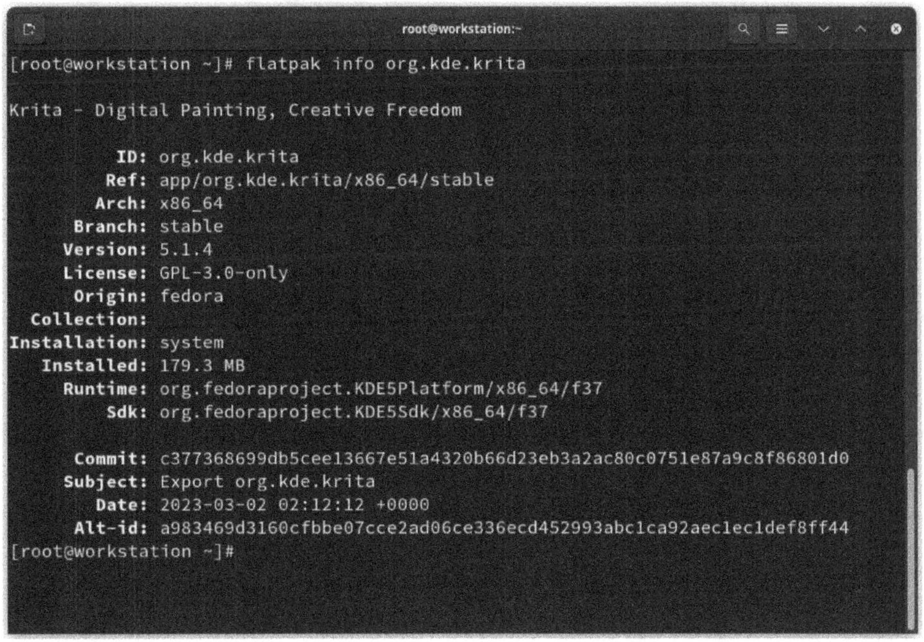

Figure 6.22 – Flatpak application info

6. To display the running applications, use the `flatpak` command with the `ps` option:

```
[root@workstation ~]# flatpak ps
```

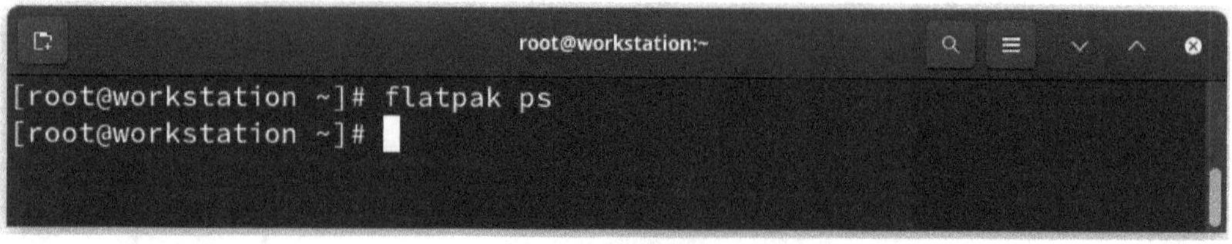
root@workstation:~
[root@workstation ~]# flatpak ps
[root@workstation ~]#

Figure 6.23 – Running Flatpak applications

Observe that the `root` user is not running any Flatpak applications.

Switch to the *non-root* user and run the same command:

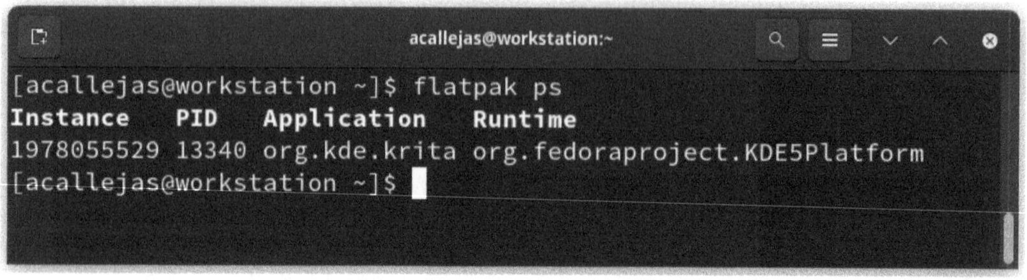
acallejas@workstation:~
[acallejas@workstation ~]$ flatpak ps
Instance PID Application Runtime
1978055529 13340 org.kde.krita org.fedoraproject.KDE5Platform
[acallejas@workstation ~]$

Figure 6.24 – Running Flatpak applications

Let's now see how we can add Flatpak applications from the command line. But before that, it is important to identify the installation source.

As mentioned before, Flatpak applications in Fedora Linux are set by default and point to the official registry of the distribution.

Through the command line, it's possible to add other repositories as installation sources and install more Flatpak applications because they are not in the Fedora registry, the version is different, or just to have more installation sources.

Let's verify the general repository of Flatpak applications as an installation source. Follow the subsequent steps:

1. As a root user, open a terminal and use the flatpak command to list the repositories:

```
[root@workstation ~]# flatpak remotes
```

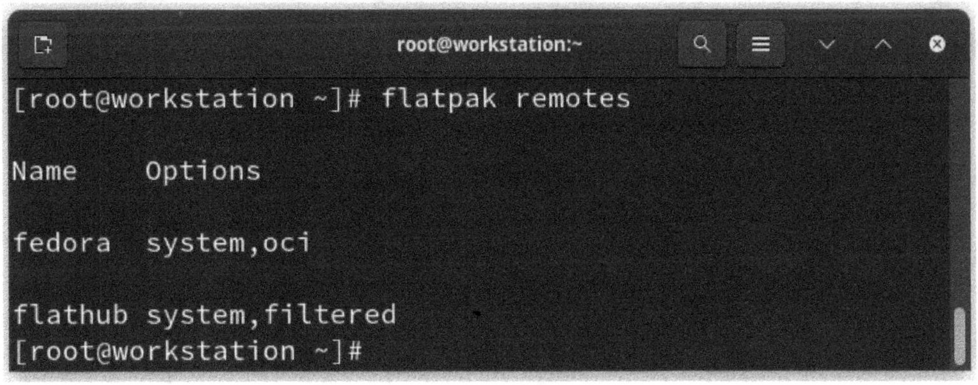

Figure 6.25 – Flatpak repositories

2. Add more columns to show the details of the repositories.
   Use the - -columns=name,title,url,homepage parameter:

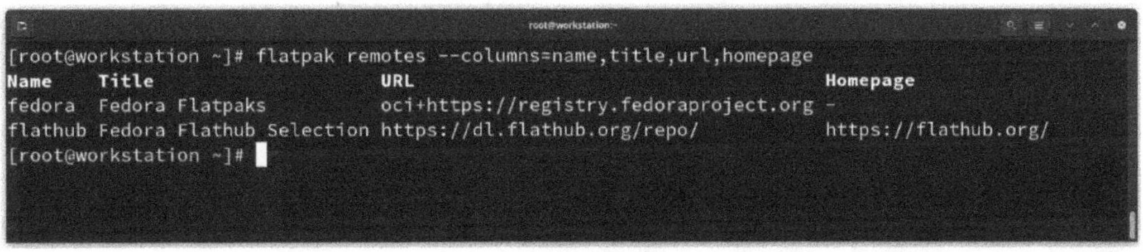

Figure 6.26 – Flatpak application repositories

3. To list the applications available in a repository, use the flatpak command with the remote-ls option and the Name repository. To avoid *runtimes* and only list the applications, add the -app parameter:

```
[root@workstation ~]# flatpak remote-ls flathub --app
```

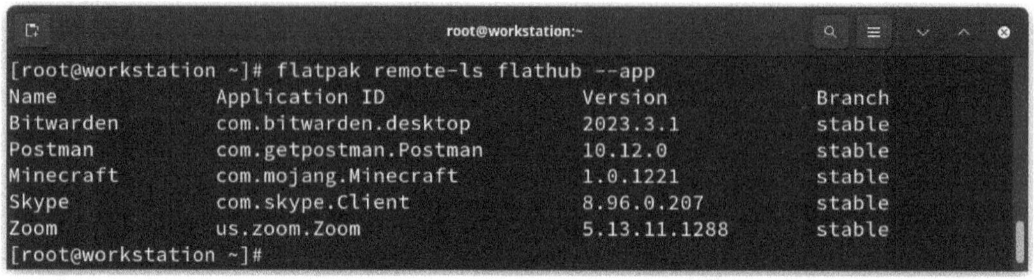

Figure 6.27 – Applications available on Flathub

In *step 1*, *Figure 6.25* shows that the `flathub` repository appears as *filtered*.

> **Note**
>
> This is true for versions before Fedora Linux 38, where the Flathub filter was removed.

This is because the Fedora Linux configuration points to `Fedora Flatpaks`. `Fedora Flatpaks` is the remote Flatpak repository of the Fedora Project.

The difference is that Flathub makes applications and tools *as accessible as possible*, no matter what distribution they're used in.

On the other hand, `Fedora Flatpaks` pushes RPMs from the Fedora Project and makes them accessible through Fedora Linux as Flatpak applications.

To have access to all the Flathub applications, let's add the repository again without restrictions.

4. Add the `flathub` repository using the `flatpak` command with the `remote-add` option. Add the `--if-not-exists` parameter to prevent *registry overwriting* (the repository URL is `https://flathub.org/repo/flathub.flatpakrepo`):

    ```
    # flatpak remote-add --if-not-exists flathub \
    > .org/repo/flathub.flatpakrepo
    ```

Figure 6.28 – Adding the Flathub repository

5. List the repositories again using the `flatpak remotes` command:

```
[root@workstation ~]# flatpak remotes
```

Figure 6.29 – Flatpak repositories

Note that Flathub is no longer *filtered*. Let's now see what Flatpak applications offer us.

6. List the applications available in the `flathub` repository. Use the `flatpak remote-ls flathub -app` command:

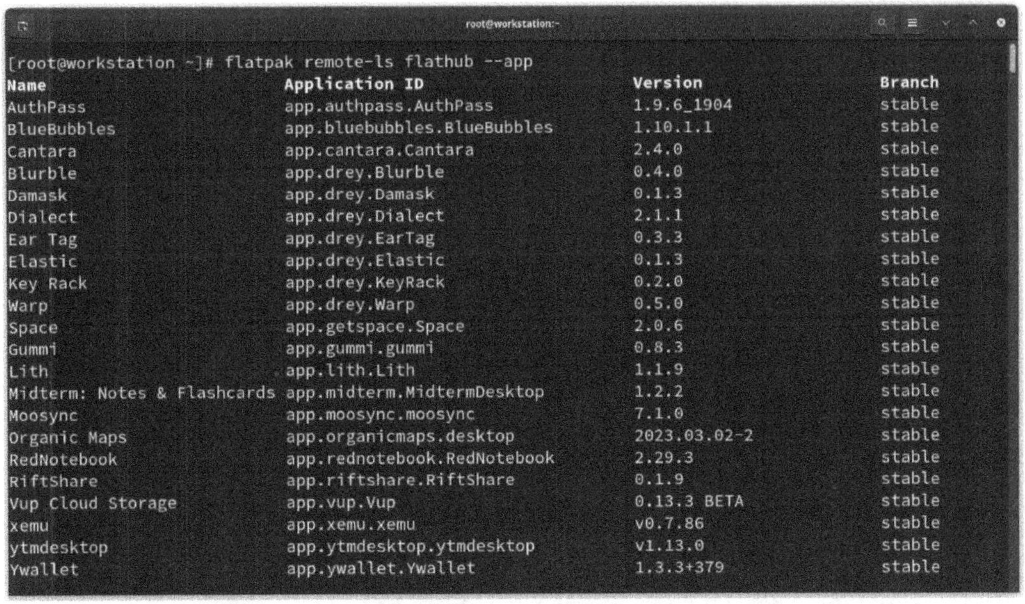

Figure 6.30 – Flathub applications

If we get the number of applications, we find that it has increased:

```
# flatpak remote-ls flathub --app | wc -l
```

- **2164**

Let's install an application.

7. Switch to a *non-root* user and search for the Telegram Desktop app. Use the flatpak remote-ls flathub -app command and filter the Telegram Desktop string:

```
$ flatpak remote-ls flathub --app | grep "Telegram Desktop"
```

[acallejas@workstation ~]$ flatpak remote-ls flathub --app | grep "Telegram Desktop"
Telegram Desktop   org.telegram.desktop   4.7.1   stable
[acallejas@workstation ~]$

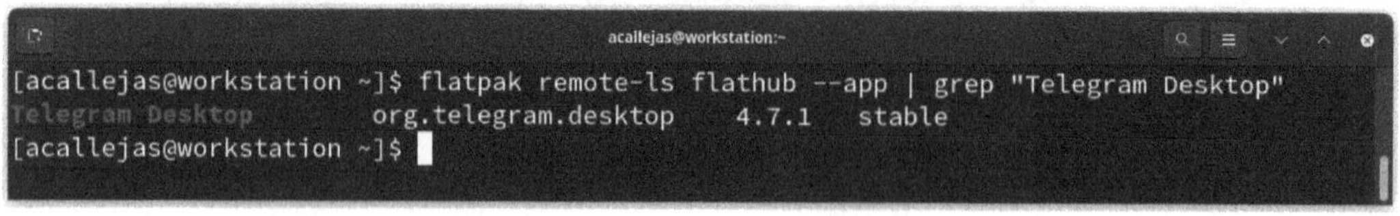

Figure 6.31 – Searching for the Telegram Desktop Flatpak application

Before installing it, let's get the details of the Flatpak application.

8. Use the flatpak remote-info command with the flathub repository option and the Application ID from Telegram Desktop:

```
$ flatpak remote-info flathub org.telegram.desktop
```

```
[acallejas@workstation ~]$ flatpak remote-info flathub org.telegram.desktop
        ID: org.telegram.desktop
       Ref: app/org.telegram.desktop/x86_64/stable
      Arch: x86_64
    Branch: stable
Collection: org.flathub.Stable
  Download: 78.4 MB
 Installed: 199.3 MB
   Runtime: org.freedesktop.Platform/x86_64/22.08
       Sdk: org.freedesktop.Sdk/x86_64/22.08

    Commit: c779ebef5304ca28baa5792249a28a5260971b0681efd79fc471b11fd1a4d770
    Parent: 1d03f448b3f4e66b87ea21968f1479675a6d3bbc374f9a0ec72d3330c44bb7e4
   Subject: Update to commit with abstract socket support (0fef1c56)
      Date: 2023-04-03 18:49:06 +0000
[acallejas@workstation ~]$
```

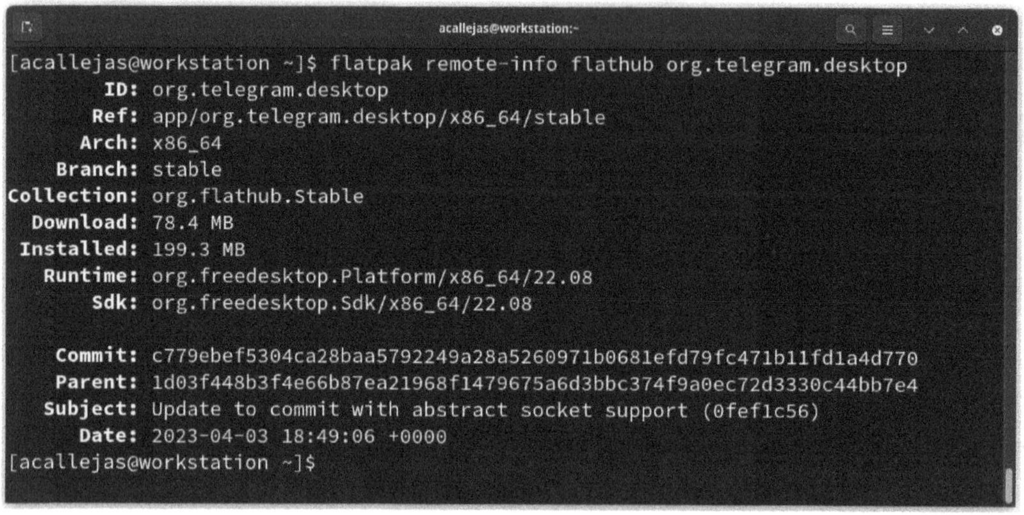

Figure 6.32 – Telegram Desktop info

9. To install the application, use the `flatpak install` command with the `flathub` repository option and the `Telegram Desktop Application ID`:

```
$ flatpak install flathub org.telegram.desktop
```

Here's the output:

```
Looking for matches…
Required runtime for org.telegram.desktop/x86_64/stable
(runtime/org.freedesktop.Platform/x86_64/22.08) found in remote
flathub
Do you want to install it? [Y/n]: Y
```

Since it requires a *runtime* to be installed first, the command asks us whether we want to install it. Type Y to install.

Wait for the installation to finish:

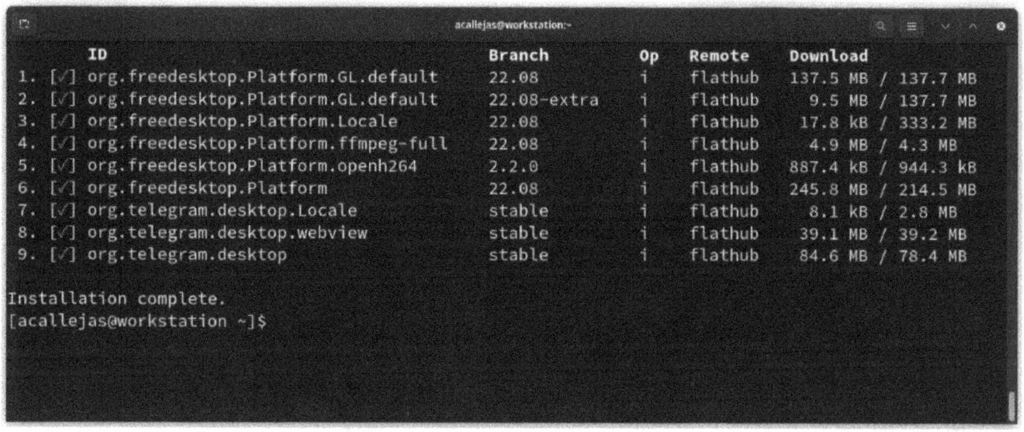

Figure 6.33 – Telegram Desktop installation

10. Once installed, use the `flatpak  run` command with the `Application  ID` to run the application:

```
$ flatpak run org.telegram.desktop
```

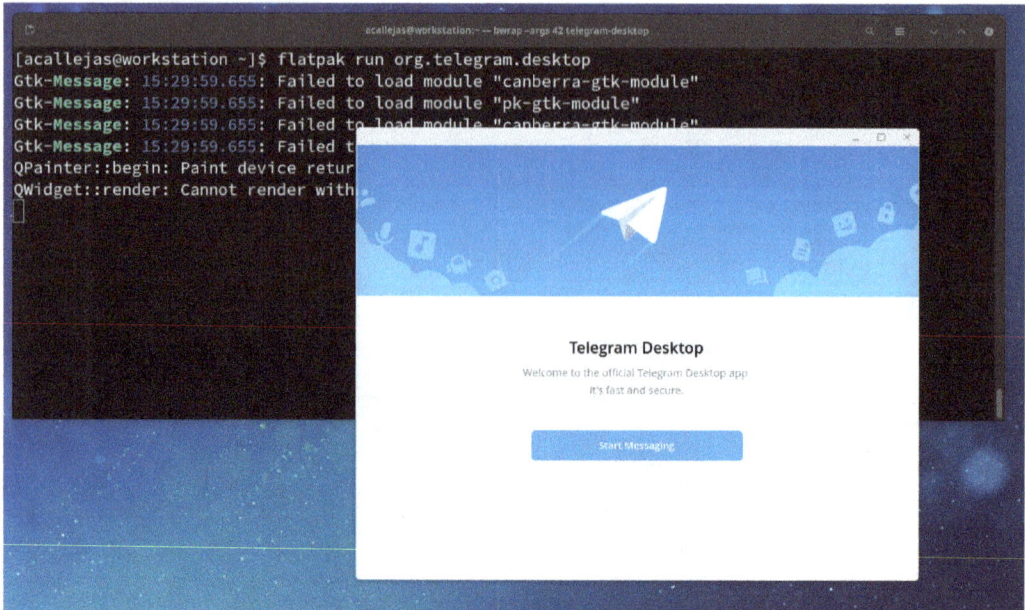

Figure 6.34 – Telegram Desktop Flatpak application

11. After installation, it is possible to find it in the **Activities** menu and/or add it to **Favorites** to display the icon in the top bar:

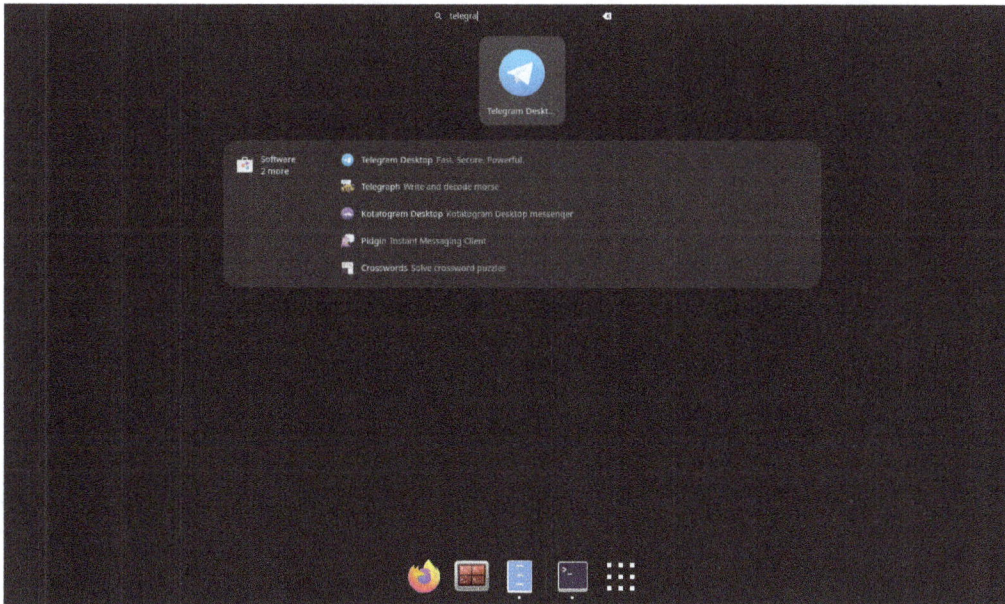

Figure 6.35 – Searching for Telegram Desktop in the Activities menu

Both procedures, graphical and CLI, provide an intuitive way to use Flatpak applications, regardless of the distribution or version installed.

> **Note**
>
> For more information on the use of Flatpak applications, refer to the *Using Flatpak* section of Flatpak's documentation at `https://docs.flatpak.org/en/latest/using-flatpak.html`.

Now, let's walk through the process of creating Flatpak applications.

Building Flatpak applications

Building Flatpak applications is relatively simple. As a prerequisite, you must install, as a `root` user, the `flatpak-builder` package, either as an RPM or Flatpak application:

- RP

  ```
  # dnf list flatpak-builder
  ```

- Flatpak application

  ```
  # flatpak install flathub org.flatpak.Builder
  ```

As an example, let's create a Flatpak application based on a simple `bash` script. To create our Flatpak application, follow the subsequent steps:

1. Identify the runtime using the `flatpak remote-ls` command with the `-a` (*all*) parameter. To search both runtimes and applications in the `flathub` repository, filter the `freedesktop platform` string to find the latest version. As an optional filter, add a parameter to avoid `translations`:

    ```
    # flatpak remote-ls flathub -a | grep -i \
    > "freedesktop platform" | grep -v translations
    ```

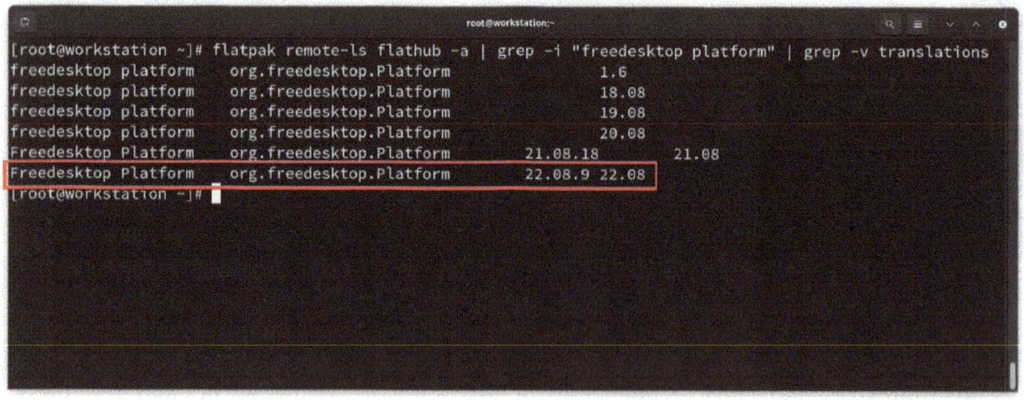

    Figure 6.36 – Identifying the runtime

    From the preceding figure, we can see that the last version is `22.08`. Next, we'll search for the same version of the SDK.

2. Use the `flatpak remote-ls` command with the `-a` (*all*) parameter in the `flathub` repository. Filter the `freedesktop SDK` string and the `22.08` version:

    ```
    # flatpak remote-ls flathub -a | grep -i \
    > "freedesktop SDK" | grep 22.08
    ```

    Figure 6.37 – Searching the SDK

3. Use the `flatpak install` command to install both:

```
# flatpak install flathub \
org.freedesktop.Platform//22.08 \
org.freedesktop.Sdk//22.08
```

- Looking for matches...

```
Skipping: org.telegram.desktop/x86_64/22.08 is already installed
```

Since we installed the runtime in a previous step, the `flatpak` command skips its installation. Type Y to install the SDK:

```
Do you want to install it? [Y/n]: Y
```

Wait for the installation to finish:

```
[root@workstation ~]# flatpak install flathub org.freedesktop.Platform//22.08 org.freedesktop.Sdk//22.08
Looking for matches...
Skipping: org.freedesktop.Platform/x86_64/22.08 is already installed

        ID                          Branch      Op      Remote      Download
1. [✓] org.freedesktop.Sdk.Locale   22.08       i       flathub     18.0 kB / 339.0 MB
2. [✓] org.freedesktop.Sdk          22.08       i       flathub     395.9 MB / 513.0 MB

Installation complete.
[root@workstation ~]#
```

Figure 6.38 – SDK installation

4. Create a `bash` script. For example, as a *non-root* user, copy the following and save it as `script.sh`:

```
#!/bin/sh
echo "Hello world, I'm a flatpak application"
```

5. Add the *manifest*. Each Flatpak application includes a file with basic build information known as the *manifest*. Create a file with the following and save it as `org.flatpak.script.yml` in the same directory as the `bash` script:

```
app-id: org.flatpak.script
runtime: org.freedesktop.Platform
runtime-version: '22.08'
sdk: org.freedesktop.Sdk
command: script.sh
modules:
  - name: script
    buildsystem: simple
```

```
build-commands:
  - install -D script.sh /app/bin/script.sh
sources:
  - type: file
    path: script.sh
```

6. Build the Flatpak application using the `flatpak-builder` command with the target directory and the *manifest*:

```
$ flatpak-builder build-dir org.flatpak.script.yml
```

```
[acallejas@workstation Devel]$ flatpak-builder build-dir org.flatpak.script.yml
Downloading sources
Initializing build dir
Committing stage init to cache
Starting build of org.flatpak.script
===================================================================
Building module script in /home/acallejas/Devel/.flatpak-builder/build/script-1
===================================================================
Running: install -D script.sh /app/bin/script.sh
Committing stage build-script to cache
Cleaning up
Committing stage cleanup to cache
Finishing app
Please review the exported files and the metadata
Committing stage finish to cache
Pruning cache
[acallejas@workstation Devel]$ ls
build-dir  org.flatpak.script.yml  script.sh
[acallejas@workstation Devel]$
```

Figure 6.39 – Building the Flatpak application

7. Install the Flatpak application using the `flatpak-builder` command. Add the `--user` option to install dependencies on the user's local installation. With the `--force-clean` option, delete the previously created directory. This removes the contents of the directory and creates new build content:

```
$ flatpak-builder --user --install --force-clean \
> build-dir org.flatpak.script.yml
```

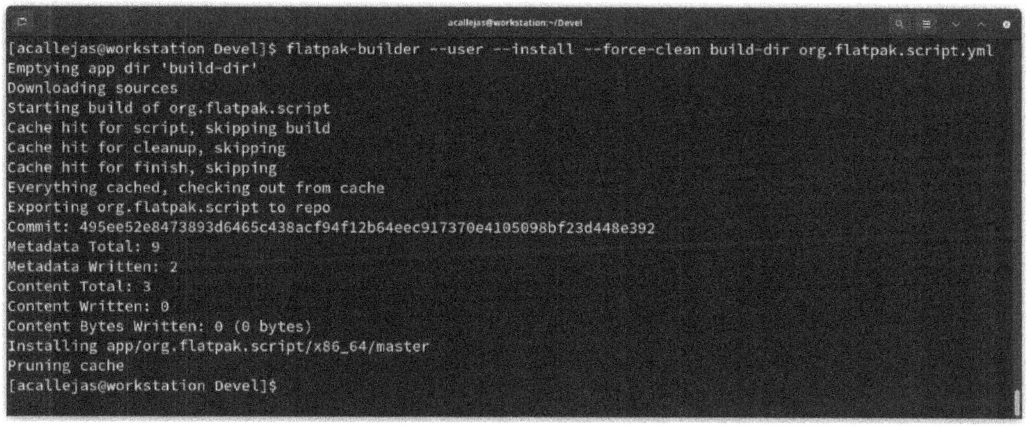

Figure 6.40 – Installing the Flatpak application

8. Run the Flatpak application using the `flatpak run` command:

```
$ flatpak run org.flatpak.script
```

Figure 6.41 – Running the Flatpak application

This way, we have a Flatpak application based on a simple script with all the necessary sandbox and isolation features.

In a more complex case, the *manifest* should include all the necessary dependencies and files, declared as *modules*.

> **Note**
>
> For more information on the build of Flatpak applications, refer to the *Building* section of Flatpak's documentation at https://docs.flatpak.org/en/latest/building.html.

This concludes our tour of sandbox applications. In the following chapters, we will discuss the installation options for different applications. Some should be installed via RPM and some others should be available as AppImages or Flatpak applications.

Summary

In this chapter, we learned how sandbox applications work, from a very illustrative example using SELinux and Firefox, to portable application formats widely used today.

We explored AppImage apps, from how to run them to using the AppImageKit to generate AppImages.

Finally, we took a deep look at Flatpak applications, a format that supports the Fedora Project and even maintains its own version of Fedora Flatpaks based on RPMs.

We also learned how to use the command line to extend the administration and use of sandboxed applications.

In the next chapter, we will take a walk through the most popular terminal-based text editors, plus look at some usage tricks and customizations.

Further reading

To learn more about the topics covered in this chapter, you can visit the following links:

- *Flatpak*: `https://flatpak.org/`
- *Getting Started with Flatpak*: `https://fedoramagazine.org/getting-started-flatpak/`
- *An introduction to Fedora Flatpaks*: `https://fedoramagazine.org/an-introduction-to-fedora-flatpaks/`
- *Comparison of Fedora Flatpaks and Flathub remotes*: `https://fedoramagazine.org/comparison-of-fedora-flatpaks-and-flathub-remotes/`
- *Flatpak Usage*: `https://developer.fedoraproject.org/deployment/flatpak/flatpak-usage.html`
- *Flathub*: `https://flathub.org/home`

7
Text Editors

In *Chapter 1*, we recommended that you always use the command line to edit files. Since practice is the only way to develop our console skills, we should take every opportunity to do so. File editing is the most basic and most common skill used during the configuration of a system.

Some text editors even allow us to execute commands on the operating system. This gives us an advantage of being able to practice them. We can also extend their capabilities by installing plugins or customizing their configuration. These modifications allow us to format files, verify syntax, and execute tasks.

Besides their use, we will discuss basic configuration tips and customizations of the most popular text editors.

In this chapter, we're going to cover the following main topics:

- Text editors and the command line
- Emacs overview
- Nano basics
- The mighty Vim

Let's get started!

Technical requirements

To perform the configurations, customizations, and examples mentioned in this chapter, the installed **Fedora Workstation** image in *Chapter 2* includes the vim and nano packages in their *basic form*. emacs and some other packages may need to be installed. Most of them are included in Fedora's official repositories.

In each section, you will see the required packages and how to install each of them.

When using a package or code not included in the official Fedora repositories, we will provide a link to get it and instructions to install it.

The examples created in this chapter are available for download in the book's GitHub repository: `https://github.com/PacktPublishing/Fedora-Linux-System-Administration/tree/main/chapter7`.

Text editors and the command line

The **UNIX** operating system has some unique of ideas and concepts that shape its design. UNIX was the first operating system to abstract all I/O operations under a unified concept. The fathers of UNIX called this concept a **file**. Each *file* exposes itself through the same **Application Programming Interface (API)**. This abstraction provides many advantages, such as preventing duplicate code and increasing reusability.

To read/write to a disk, keyboard, document, or network device, it is possible to use the same basic set of commands (such as the `cat`, `more`, `grep`, `sed`, and `echo` commands).

This principle is encapsulated in the phrase: *everything is a file*.

This fundamental concept has two sides:

- In UNIX, everything is a *stream of bytes*.

  With reference to a file, called a *file descriptor*, the I/O access uses the same set of operations and the same API (whatever the device type and the underlying hardware is). As a byte stream, it allows the following:

  - `read`

  - `write`

  - `search`

  - `close`

- In UNIX, the filesystem serves as a universal *namespace*.

  Files are not only a stream of bytes with a consistent API, but they can also reference each other in a uniform way. UNIX filesystem *paths* provide a consistent, global scheme for labeling resources, regardless of their nature. This global namespace is often viewed as a *hierarchy of files and directories*. This is a convenient abstraction; a file path could refer to *almost anything*: a filesystem, a device, a network share, or a communication channel.

This means that in UNIX, and so in Linux, anything is accessible as a *file* in the filesystem space. The point of all this is to make it possible to use common tools for different things.

The tool used to change the content of the text files is the text editor. The files contain *plain text* or *source code* either for a program or for text formatters, which reads the typed input and produces a printable output.

The main advantage of text editors on UNIX/Linux systems is the ability to use them without a graphical environment, in the terminal. This advantage allows their use on *remote machines*. Since there's no need to transfer the entire graphical environment, working with text editors improves the speed of the network. As a system administrator, you need to know how to edit files from the terminal like an expert.

`nano` or `vim` come as a base package with any Linux distribution. In some cases, either package is available out of the box, and some distributions also include `emacs`.

These packages achieve the same thing (edit text files) but they do it in very different ways:

- `nano`: Easiest to use, but with the fewest features.
- `vim`: Steepest learning curve, but powerful once it's mastered.
- `emacs`: Midway between `nano` and `vim` in difficulty of use. Powerful and customizable. Does not always come as a base package.

Let's take a deep dive into each of them. We'll start with the one that has the most historical weight, **GNU Emacs**, created by Richard Stallman. In Fedora Workstation, it needs to be installed to use it. Let's start by getting an overview of it.

Emacs overview

Early text editors were very rudimentary, so much so that they could not open an entire text document. To solve that, a text editor turned out to be more of a command that could generate words and dump them into a file, find and replace words in a file, delete lines in a file, and so on.

Editing large documents in this way could become quite boring. So, people started to develop **macros** to perform common related tasks.

In 1983, Richard Stallman released a package of his macros under the name **Editing Macros**, or **Emacs** for short. When Dr. Stallman started the GNU project, GNU Emacs became his most successful application.

GNU Emacs is a text editor designed for POSIX operating systems. It is often considered complex since it was developed long before modern computer conventions and terminology existed.

However, GNU Emacs offers efficient commands for common but complex actions, plus plugins and configuration *hacks* developed around it over 40 years. Once you learn the basic use of GNU Emacs, it is a powerful, efficient, and hackable editor for life.

The most common version of emacs is GNU Emacs.

To install it on our Fedora Workstation, using the software application from main menu, choose between **RPM** or **FLATPAK** for its installation source, as we covered in *Chapter 6*:

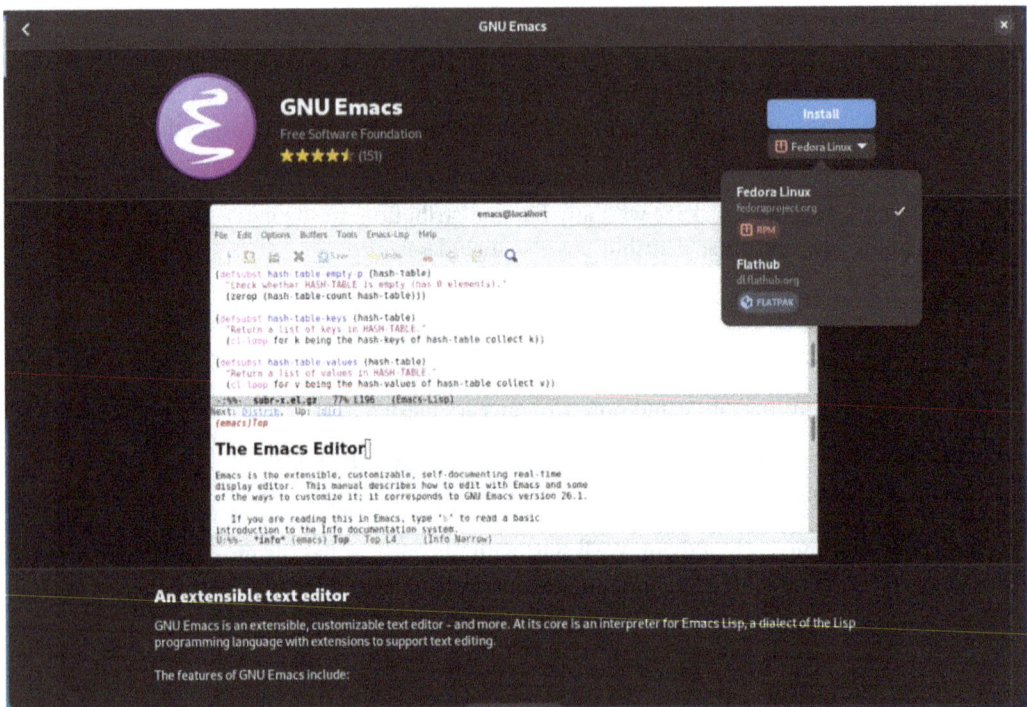

Figure 7.1 – Installing emacs

Using the console allows you to list the available plugins too. Switch to the `root` user and run the following:

```
# dnf list emacs*
```

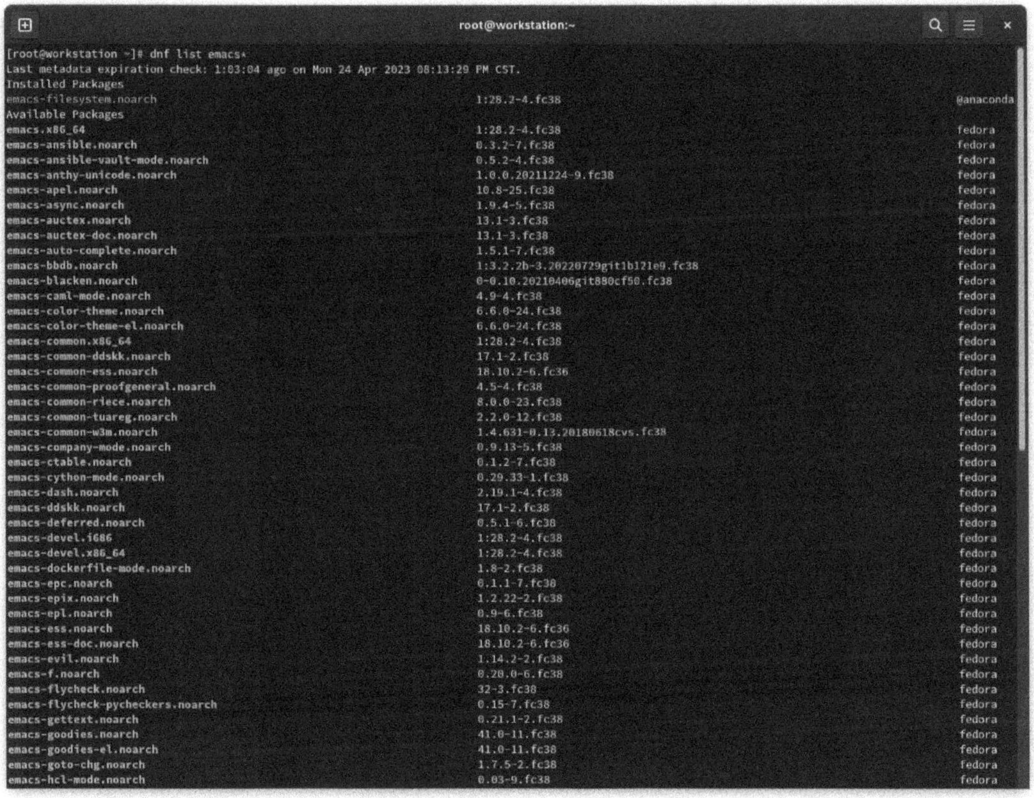

Figure 7.2 – emacs and plugins

Listing and counting the plugins, there are under 100 of them:

```
# dnf list emacs-* | wc -l
85
```

Install GNU Emacs by your preferred method and let's start with the basics.

The basics

At the beginning, the usability of the program seems complicated. But it's only a little different because it was created in another era. Follow these instructions to start getting used to the user interface.

Open **GNU Emacs** from the menu by typing `Emacs` in the search box:

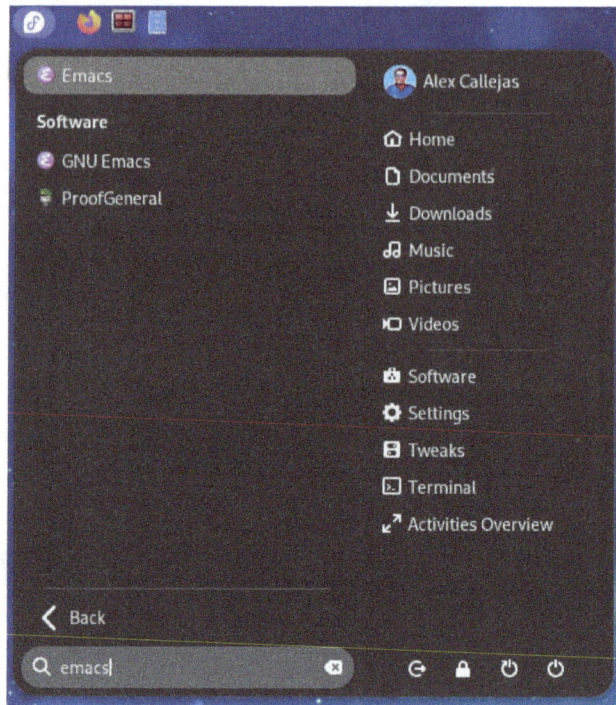

Figure 7.3 – Open emacs from menu

It can also be opened using the `emacs` command as a *non-root* user from the terminal:

```
$ emacs
```

In both cases, the **GNU Emacs** window opens:

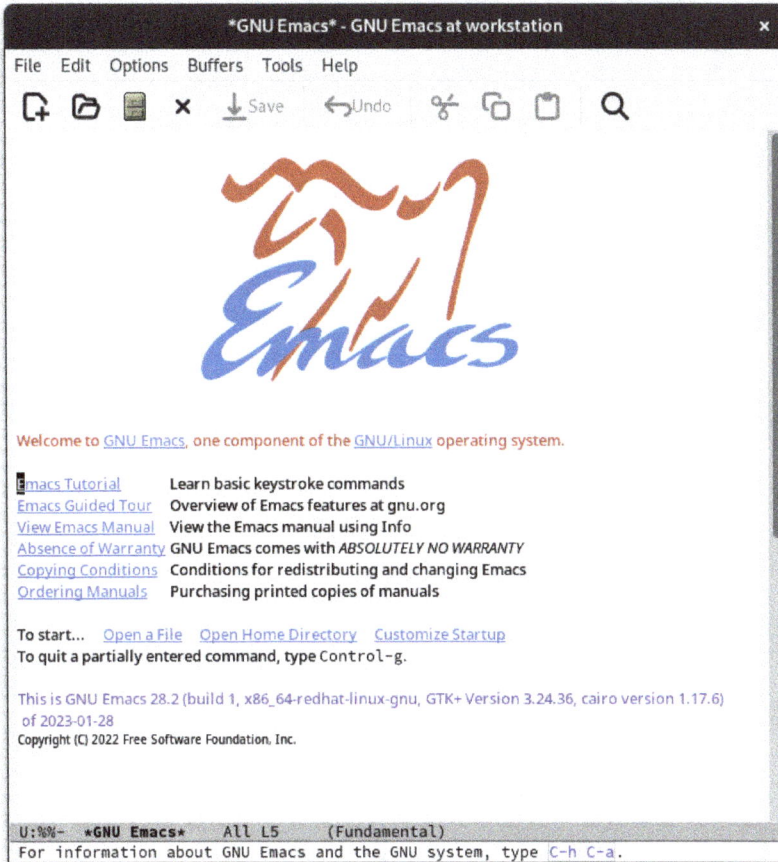

Figure 7.4 – GNU Emacs

On the welcome screen, the first link, **Emacs Tutorial**, takes you to the help tutorial of the application:

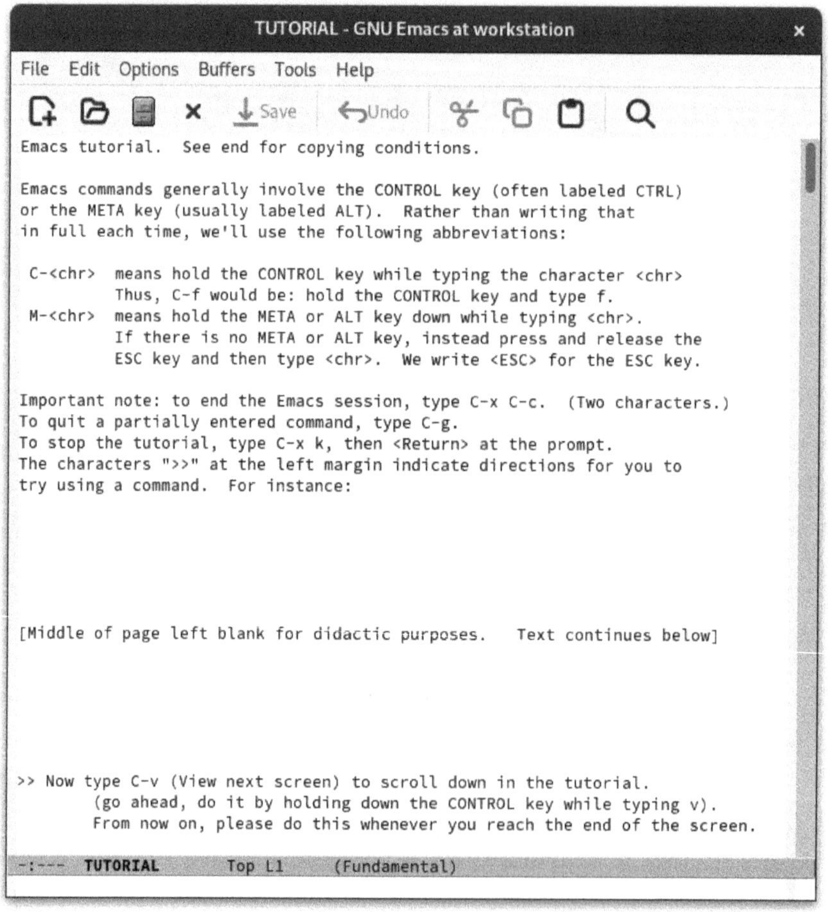
TUTORIAL - GNU Emacs at workstation
File Edit Options Buffers Tools Help
Save
Undo
Emacs tutorial. See end for copying conditions.
Emacs commands generally involve the CONTROL key (often labeled CTRL)
or the META key (usually labeled ALT). Rather than writing that
in full each time, we'll use the following abbreviations:
C-<chr> means hold the CONTROL key while typing the character <chr>
Thus, C-f would be: hold the CONTROL key and type f.
M-<chr> means hold the META or ALT key down while typing <chr>.
If there is no META or ALT key, instead press and release the
ESC key and then type <chr>. We write <ESC> for the ESC key.
Important note: to end the Emacs session, type C-x C-c. (Two characters.)
To quit a partially entered command, type C-g.
To stop the tutorial, type C-x k, then <Return> at the prompt.
The characters ">>" at the left margin indicate directions for you to
try using a command. For instance:
[Middle of page left blank for didactic purposes. Text continues below]
>> Now type C-v (View next screen) to scroll down in the tutorial.
(go ahead, do it by holding down the CONTROL key while typing v).
From now on, please do this whenever you reach the end of the screen.
-:--- TUTORIAL Top L1 (Fundamental)

Figure 7.5 – Emacs tutorial

You can return to it as many times as you need with its key combination.

Most of the key combinations use the *Ctrl* key, along with the required combination. For example, to open the tutorial, the combination is *C-h* + *C-t*, which means pressing the *Ctrl* key plus the *h* key, followed by the *Ctrl* key plus the *t* key; that is, you could hold down the *Ctrl* key and press the *h* key followed by the *t* key.

In some cases, the *Alt* key is also used for key combinations. But the notation is different, noted by an *M*. For example, to use the *Alt-x* combination, the notation is *M-x*.

This is because the *Alt* key was known as *Meta* in the past. Remember, when GNU Emacs was developed, some of the current terms were not in use back then.

> **Note**
>
> The letter *M* refers to the *Meta* key, which on x86 PCs is the *Alt* key. There are also ports of emacs on other platforms, such as macOS where *Meta* refers to the ⌘ *Cmd* key.

Using the graphical interface helps when getting started with GNU Emacs. The menus include the key combinations used for each task:

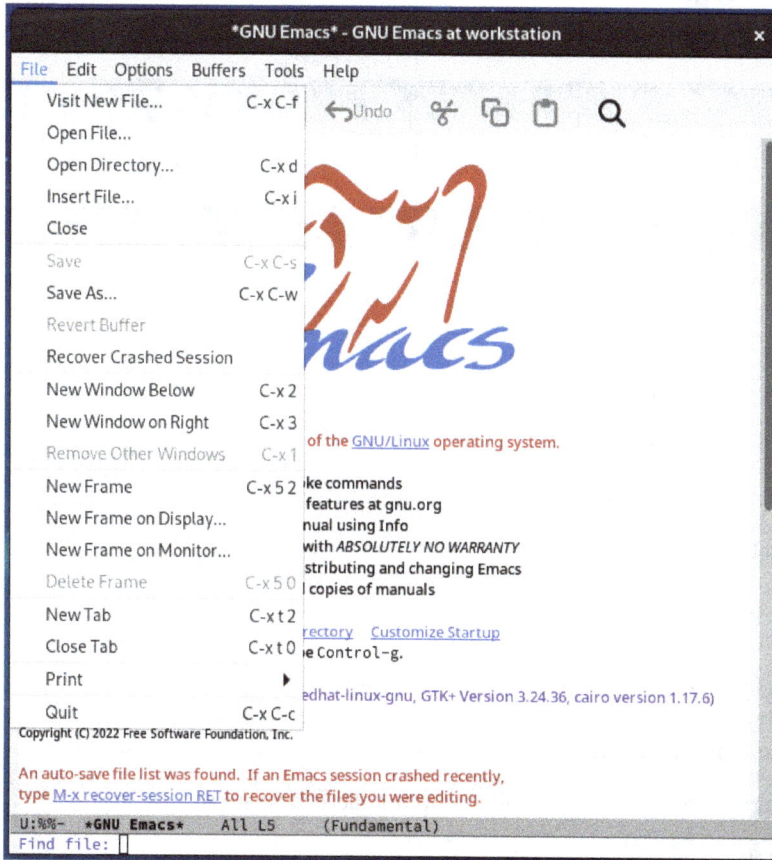

Figure 7.6 – GNU Emacs menus

The following table shows the most common tasks with their corresponding key combination:

Open a file	`C-x C-f`
Save file	`C-x C-s`
Save as	`C-x C-w`
Close file	`C-x C-k`
Quit	`C-x C-c`
Cut	`C-w`
Copy	`M-w`
Display all key bindings	`C-h b`
Tutorial	`C-h C-t`

Table 7.1 – GNU Emacs common key combinations

GNU Emacs is very flexible and runs without a graphical interface, in the terminal. This is where it becomes an essential tool in system administration.

Let's now take a look at an overview of the advanced usage of GNU Emacs.

Mastering GNU Emacs

At first glance, GNU Emacs looks like a very complex way to edit files because it uses different keyboard combinations than those used by other text editors. But for the day-to-day tasks of the system administrator, running from the terminal, GNU Emacs is a powerful solution.

Let's give an overview of this using a small example. Follow these steps:

1. Open **GNU Emacs** in the terminal by running the emacs command with the `--no-window-system` parameter:

```
$ emacs --no-window-system
```

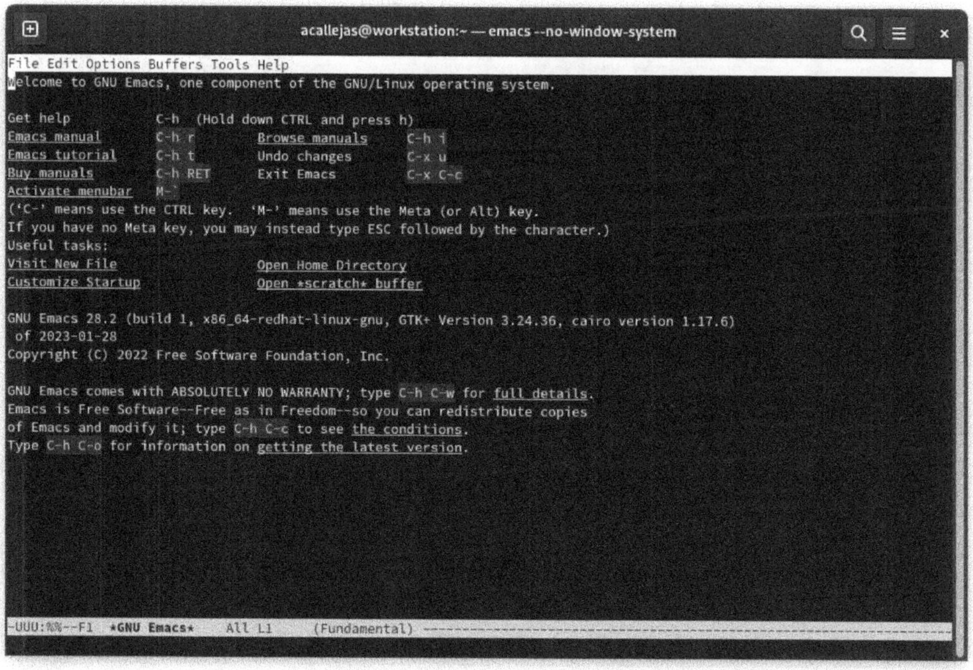

Figure 7.7 – GNU Emacs on the terminal

2. From the start screen, browse to the test file to be modified.

3. Press the *Ctrl* key plus the *x* key (*C-x*) to enter command mode, followed by the *Ctrl* and *f* keys (*C-f*) to find the file to edit. Press the *Tab* key to display the contents of the directory:

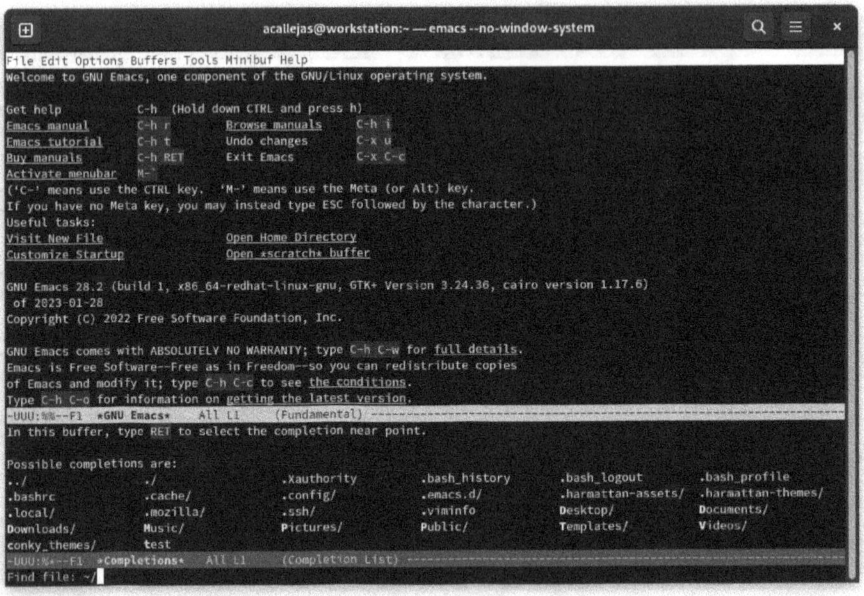

Figure 7.8 – Find the file to edit

4. The file to edit is the `test` file. Type `test` in `Find file` at the bottom to open the file.

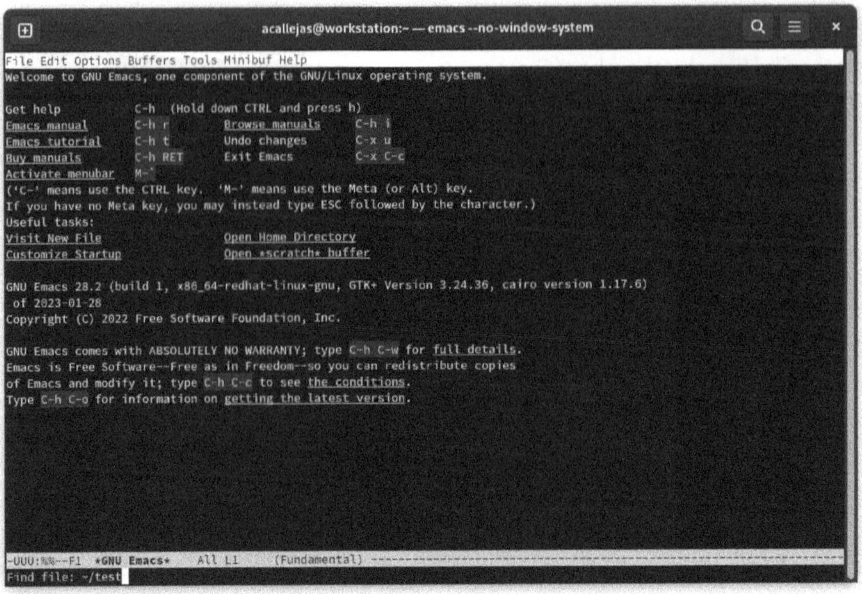

Figure 7.9 – Opening the test file

> **Note**
>
> The file mentioned previously is available in the book's GitHub repository at `https://github.com/PacktPublishing/Fedora-Linux-System-Administration/tree/main/chapter7`.

This `test` file is a combination of the `/etc/group` and `/etc/passwd` files.

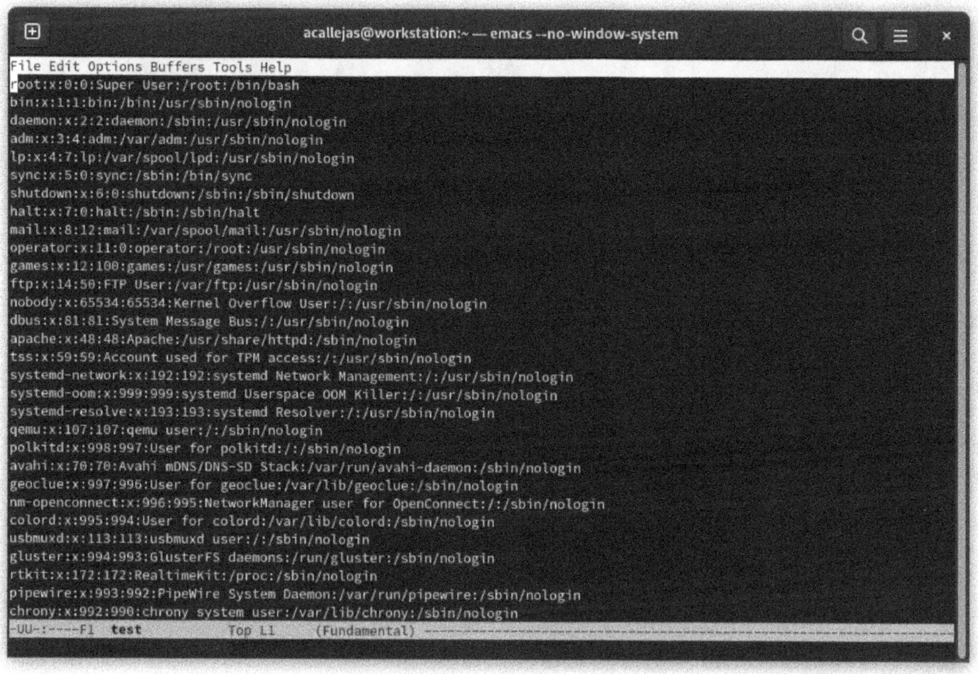

Figure 7.10 – test file

5. Suppose that you need to see the contents of both files within the `test` file. On the line where one of them ends, split the screen and move between the contents of each of them.

To split the screen, press *Ctrl* plus the *x* and *2* keys (*C-x-2*):

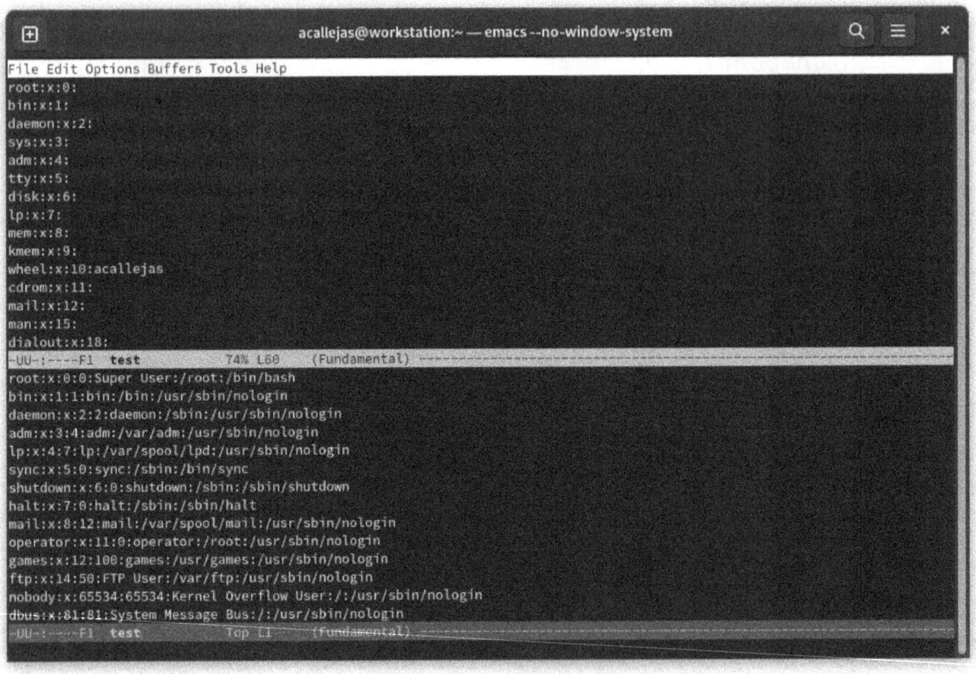

Figure 7.11 – Split screen

6.   In Emacs, a **buffer** contains a process or a file. A **window** is the view of a buffer. The **frame** is the desktop window.

The following figure shows these concepts:

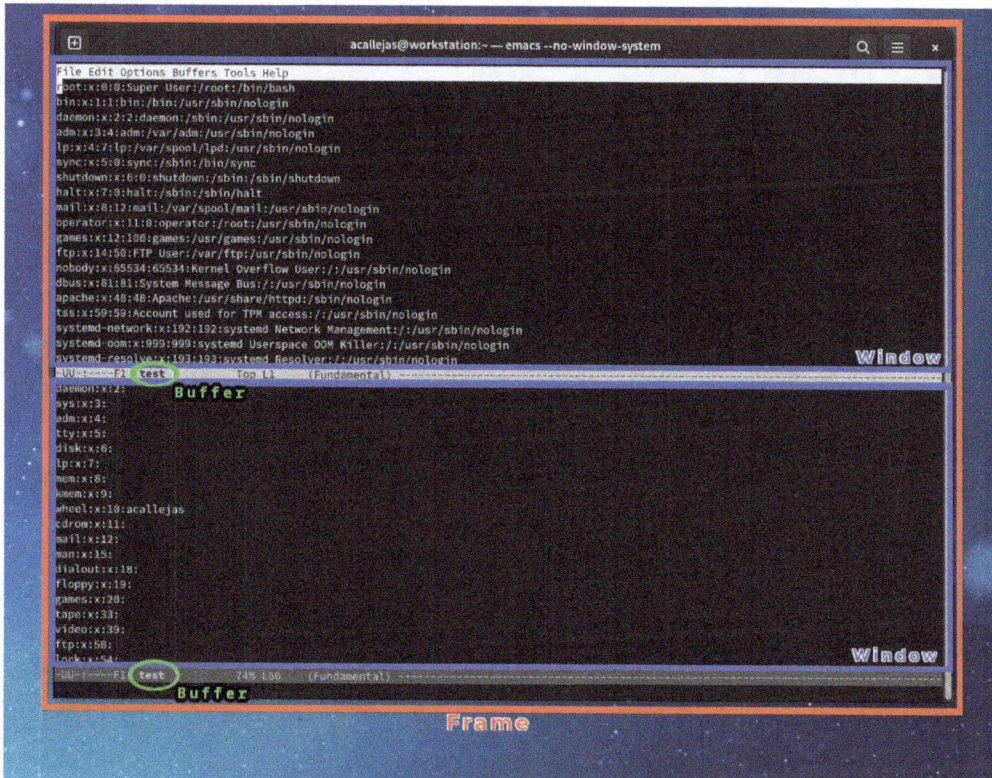

Figure 7.12 – Buffers, windows, and frame

This means that we split the frame into two windows. Each buffer edits the same `test` file.

If needed, each buffer could open different files, split the frame into more horizontal and vertical windows, or open other frames.

7. To change the buffer, press the *Ctrl* key with the *x* key plus the *o* key (*C-x-o*).

8. This adds a line of plus signs (+) to separate the contents of the files. Save the file by pressing the *Ctrl* key with the *x* key (*C-x*) plus the *Ctrl* key with the *s* key (*C-s*).

Figure 7.13 – Saving changes

9. Quit the saved file by pressing the *Ctrl* key with the *x* key (*C-x*) plus the *Ctrl* key with the *c* key (*C-c*).

The following table shows advanced tasks with their corresponding key combinations:

Text Selection	
Start selection	C-<space> or C-@
Deselect	C-g
Undo	
Undo	C-/ or C-x-u
Panic!	
Cancel a command or operation in progress ,	C-g
Copy & Paste	
Yank	C-y
Cut line after cursor	C-k
Cut word after cursor	M-d

Navigation	
Previous line	C-p
Next line	C-n
Back a character	C-b
Back a word	M-b
Forward a character	C-f
Forward a word	M-f
Go to start of line	C-a
Go to end of line	C-e
Frames, windows, and buffers	
Vertical split	C-x-3
Horizontal split	C-x-2
No splits	C-x-1
Remove window	C-x-0
Visit other window	C-x-o
Open a new frame	C-x-5-2

Table 7.2 – GNU Emacs advanced key combinations

Now let's see how to add enhancements to the text editor.

Powering GNU Emacs

GNU Emacs has some essential features. Not all implemented, but conceptualized:

- *It has lots of plugins.* Not all text editors have plugins, and not all need them. Sometimes the only feature needed is simplicity. For a text editor used for hours a day, plugins add valuable enhancements and improvements.

- *It is a customizable environment that could become a complete desktop environment,* for example, keeping track of projects, tasks, and events, organizing emails and chats, and managing remote servers.

- *Provides powerful and flexible key combinations and keymaps configurable for specific modes.*

- *Every aspect of the environment is customizable.* It allows modifying the user interface of all applications: the help system, the file and workspace tabs, and the fonts and colors of the user interface elements.

Install these enhancements through GNU Emacs. Follow these steps:

1. List the available packages, inside GNU Emacs, by pressing the *Meta* (*Alt*) key and the *x* key. Enter the package command mode, distinguished at the bottom of the window by the *M-x* combination:

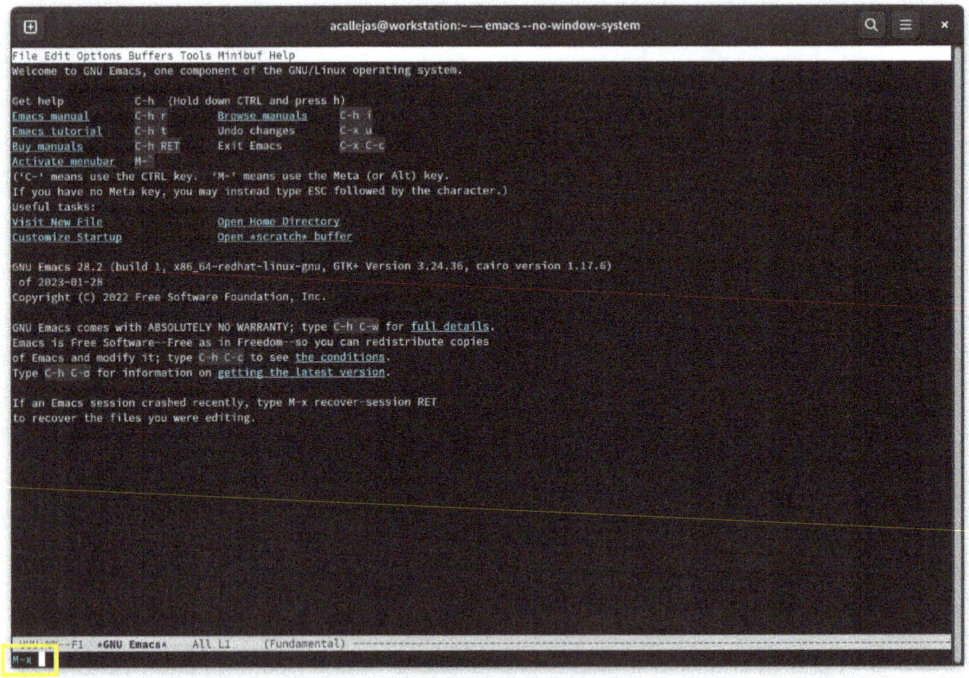

Figure 7.14 – Package command mode

2. Type `list-packages` and hit *Enter*:

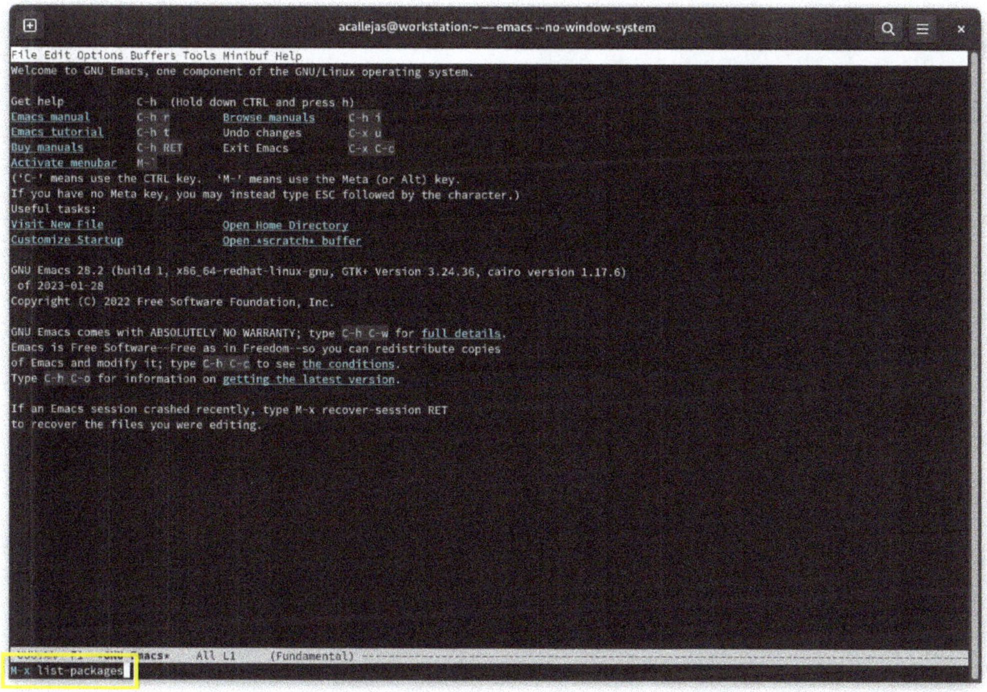

Figure 7.15 – List packages

The window shows the packages available for installation:

Figure 7.16 – List of available packages

3. To find a package, for example, yaml-mode, to help us with YAML syntax. In the list, press the *Ctrl* key and the *s* key (*C-s*). Type yaml-mode at the bottom to find the selected package:

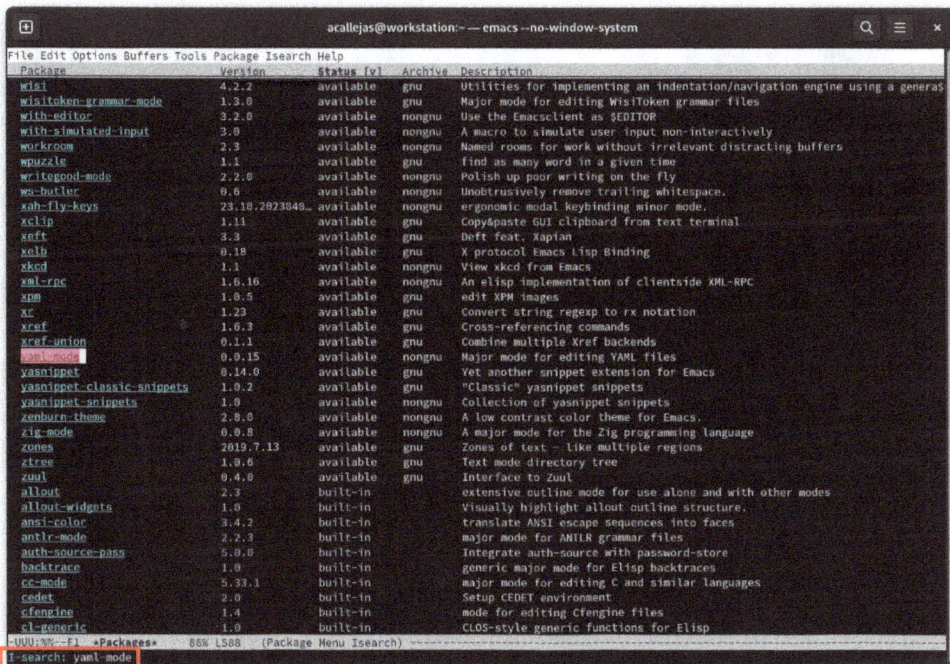

Figure 7.17 – Searching for the package to install

> **Note**
>
> This requires the `emacs-yaml-mode.noarch` package installed to work.

4. To view the package description, press the *Meta* (*Alt*) key plus the *x* key (*M-x*) and type `describe-package`.

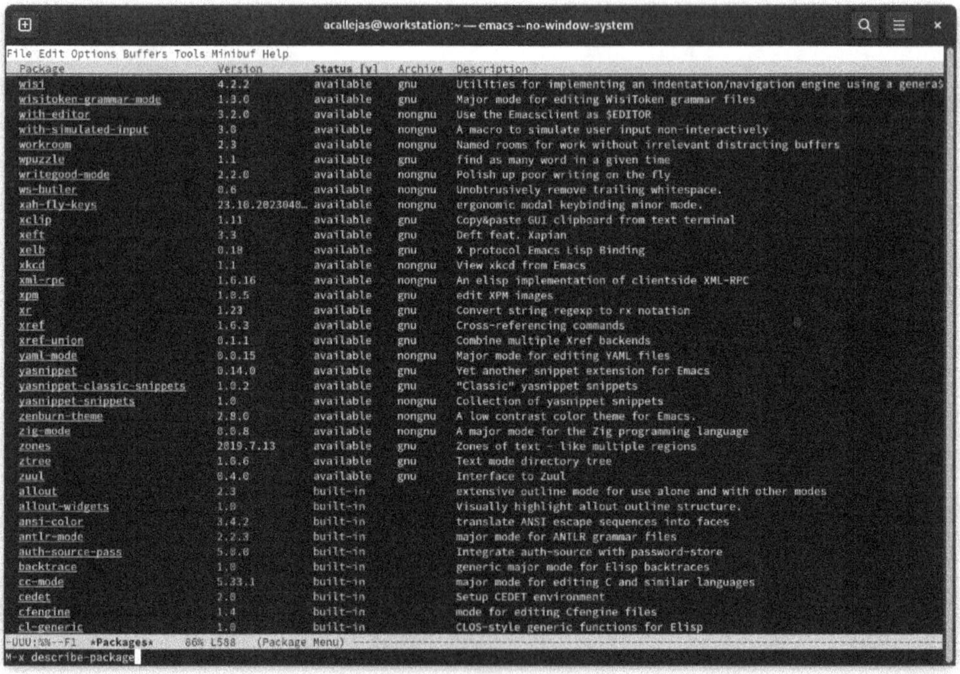

Figure 7.18 – Describing package

5.   This splits the window horizontally. To switch to the *description window*, press the *Ctrl* key and the *x* key, followed by the *o* key (*C-x-o*):

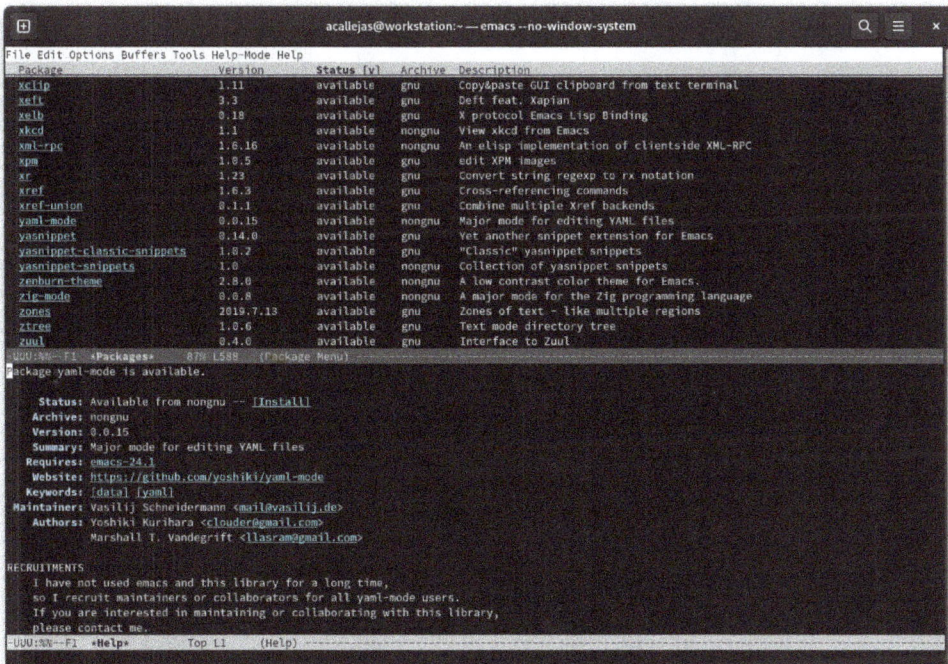

Figure 7.19 – Description window

6. Close the window by pressing the *Ctrl* key and the *x* key, followed by the *0* key (*C-x-0*).

7. Mark the `yaml-mode` package for installation by pressing the *Meta* (*Alt*) key and the *x* key (*M-x*) and type `package-menu-mark-install`.

Figure 7.20 – Marking the package to install

This adds an I to the left side of the package:

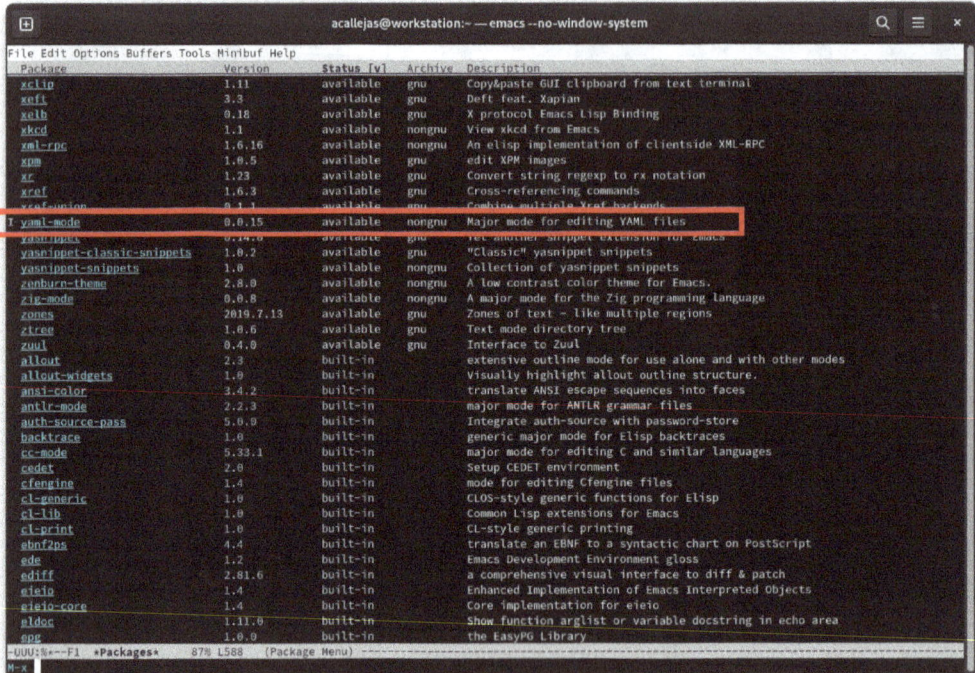

Figure 7.21 – Package marked for installation

8. To install the package, press the *Meta* (*Alt*) key and the *x* key, and type `package-install-selected-packages`.

Figure 7.22 – Installing marked packages

9. Exit Emacs using *C-x* + *C-c* .

The installation is very fast. Open a YAML file to see the *help* menu with the syntax of the package:

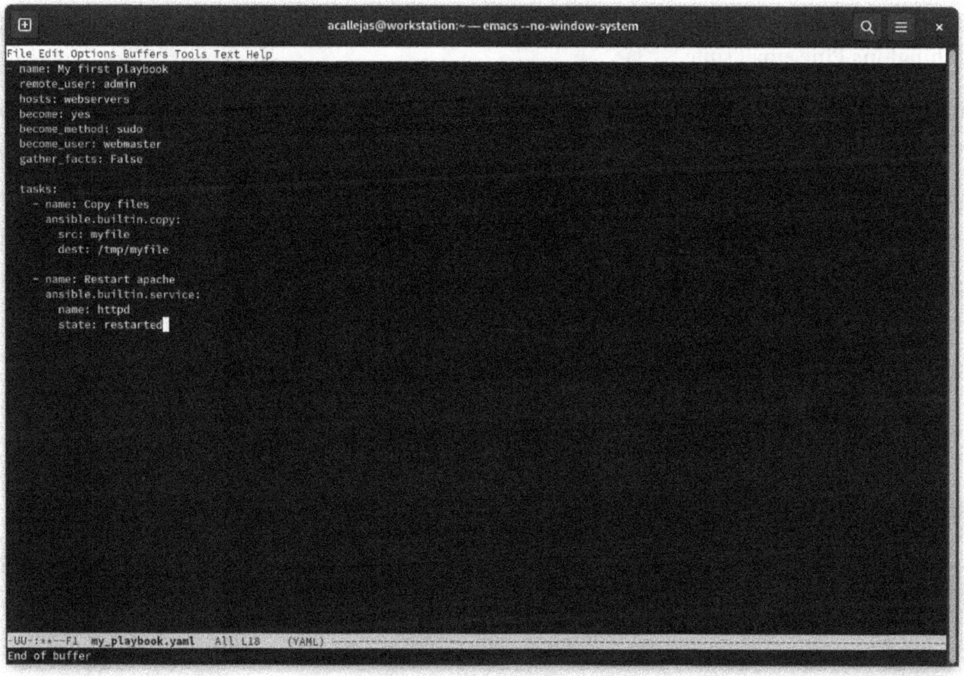

Figure 7.23 – YAML file

As shown in the previous figure, a lot of packages and plugins could be installed to help us with a particular feature.

> **Note**
>
> On the internet, you will find many examples of packages and plugins. As a personal recommendation, check out this Reddit thread, with the must-have packages according to the community: `https://www.reddit.com/r/emacs/comments/w4gxoa/what_are_some_musthave_packages_for_emacs/`.

GNU Emacs, especially for a novice user, seems very complex to use. This led to the popularization of simpler text editors. One of the most popular ones, which became the default text editor in Fedora Linux, is **Nano**.

Let's now review the basic principles of its use.

Nano basics

GNU nano was designed as a free replacement for the Pico text editor, which was part of the University of Washington's Pine email suite.

At the end of 1999, **Chris Allegretta** left **Slackware** for **Debian**. He missed having a package that included **Pine** and **Pico**. So, he decided to make a Pico clone, at that time called **Tip Isn't Pico (TIP)**.

In January 2000, TIP was renamed **nano** due to a conflict with another program called **tip**, included with many older Unix systems.

In February 2001, nano received an official GNU declaration from Richard Stallman. nano also reached its first production release on March 22, 2001.

To create a new file, as a *non-root* user, run the nano command from the terminal:

```
$ nano
```

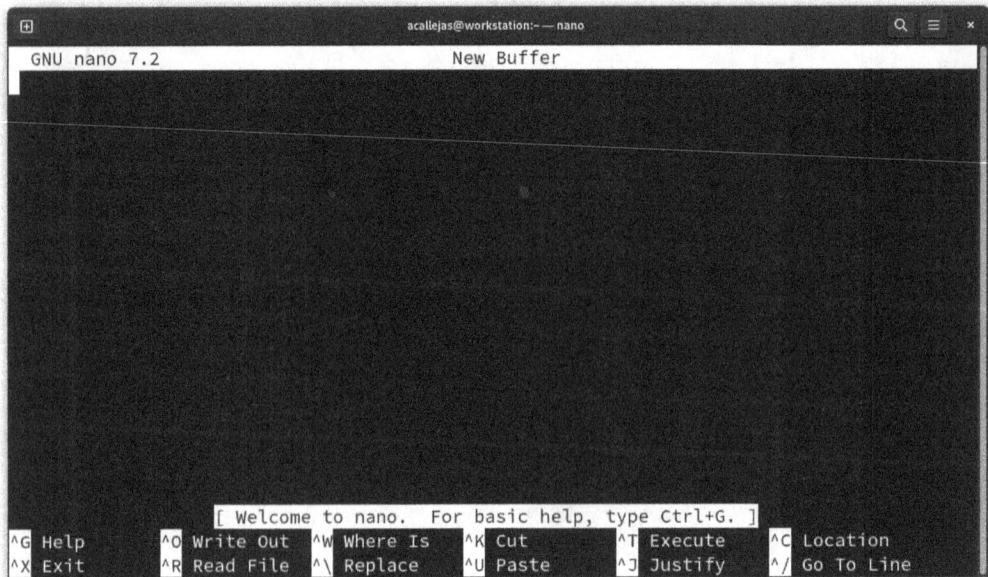

Figure 7.24 – Nano text editor

At the bottom taskbar of the window, there are help commands for the editor:

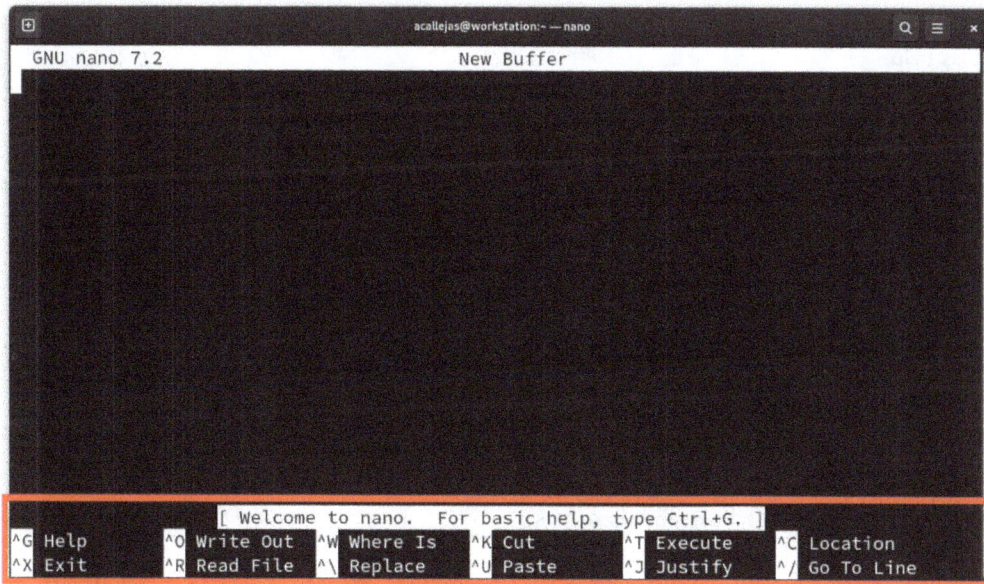

Figure 7.25 – Help commands for nano

Unlike emacs, nano denotes the *Ctrl* key with the circumflex accent symbol (^), so the help menu is displayed by pressing the *Ctrl* key with the *G* key. To exit, press the *Ctrl* and *X* keys.

> **Note**
>
> For more information about why the circumflex accent symbol (^) is used for *Ctrl*, please refer to https://retrocomputing.stackexchange.com/questions/10925/why-do-we-use-caret-as-the-symbol-for-ctrl-control.

Besides the *Ctrl* key, nano also uses the *Alt* key and some symbols as part of its commands for specific tasks.

The following table shows the most common tasks with their corresponding key combination:

File Management	
Display help	^G
Exit	^X
Write the current file	^O
Insert another file into the current one	^R
Editing	
Insert a new line at the cursor position	^M
Delete the character under the cursor	^D
Delete the character to the left of the cursor	^H
Insert a tab at the cursor position	^I
Justify the current paragraph	^J
Justify the entire file	Alt+J
Count the number of words, lines, and characters	Alt+D
Search and Replace	
Search for a string or a regular expression	^W
Replace a string or a regular expression	^\
Repeat the last search	Alt+W

Table 7.3 – GNU nano common key combinations

GNU nano stands out for its *simplicity*, in terms of its interface and use.

Another text editor, not as simple as `nano`, nor as complex as `emacs`, is the vim editor.

Let's step through the Vim editor and its customization possibilities.

The mighty vim

Vim (an acronym for **Vi IMproved**) is an *enhanced* version of the **Vi** text editor, present in all UNIX systems. Bram Moolenaar introduced the first version in 1991.

Vim is a powerful editor that offers many out-of-the-box features. The use of plugins adds new features, making it easier to adapt Vim to specific workflows. Many plugins focus on general functionality, such as locating files, providing information, and dealing with different file syntaxes or Git versioning.

Vim comes included in the Fedora Linux base installation, although not as the default text editor. To change it to the default text editor, add it to the shell configuration file. In Bash, this file is `~/.bashrc` or `~/.bash_profile`.

Add the following global variables to set the vim editor as the default editor:

```
export VISUAL=vim
export EDITOR="$VISUAL"
```

Both global variables cover the general use of the EDITOR variable.

A VISUAL editor is a full-screen editor such as vim or emacs.

An EDITOR editor works without using the terminal's functionality (such as the old ed or ex mode of vi).

For example, when invoking an editor through Bash, Bash tries the VISUAL editor first. If VISUAL fails (because the terminal doesn't support a full-screen editor), it tries EDITOR.

With both variables set to vim, grant their use as the default text editor.

Unlike emacs or nano, vim does not use key combinations. The vim editor works in two modes: *Command* and *Insert*. Now let's review its basic usage.

The basics

The vim modes are essential in its use. To switch between modes, use the *Esc* key. The following figure shows the editing flow for a file with vim:

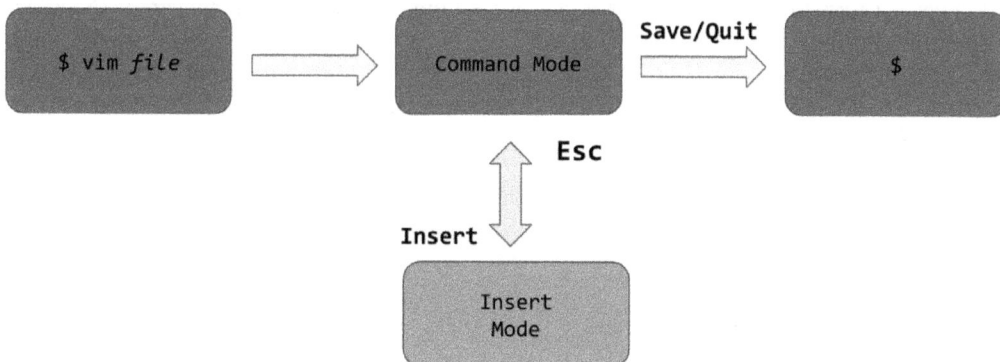

Figure 7.26 – Vim workflow

To create or open a file with vim, run the vim command in the terminal. This opens vim to its splash screen, in command mode:

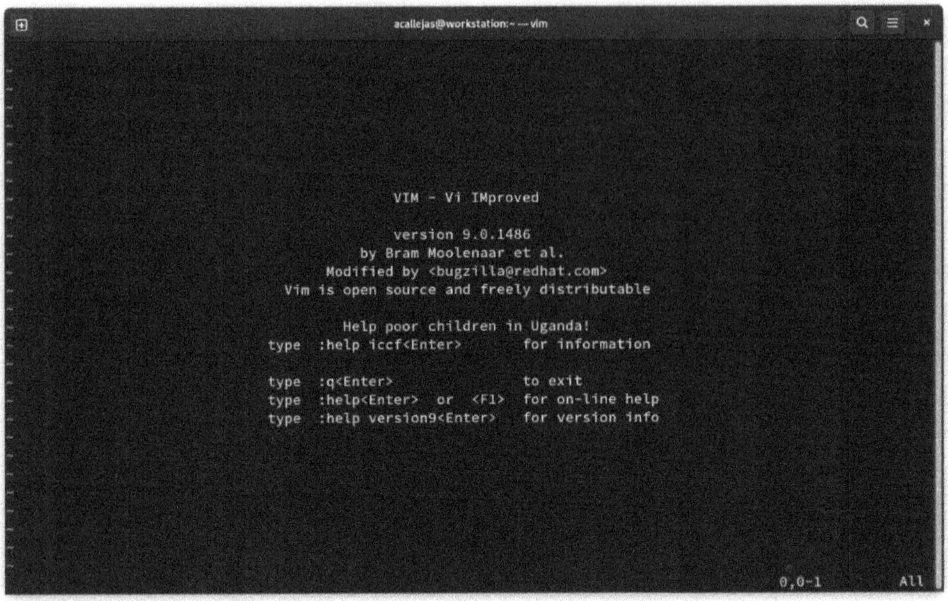

Figure 7.27 – Vim splash screen

To start typing, and to switch to insert mode, press the *Esc* key and then the *I* key. The screen changes. In the upper-left corner the cursor appears, and in the bottom taskbar, the mode appears as **INSERT**:

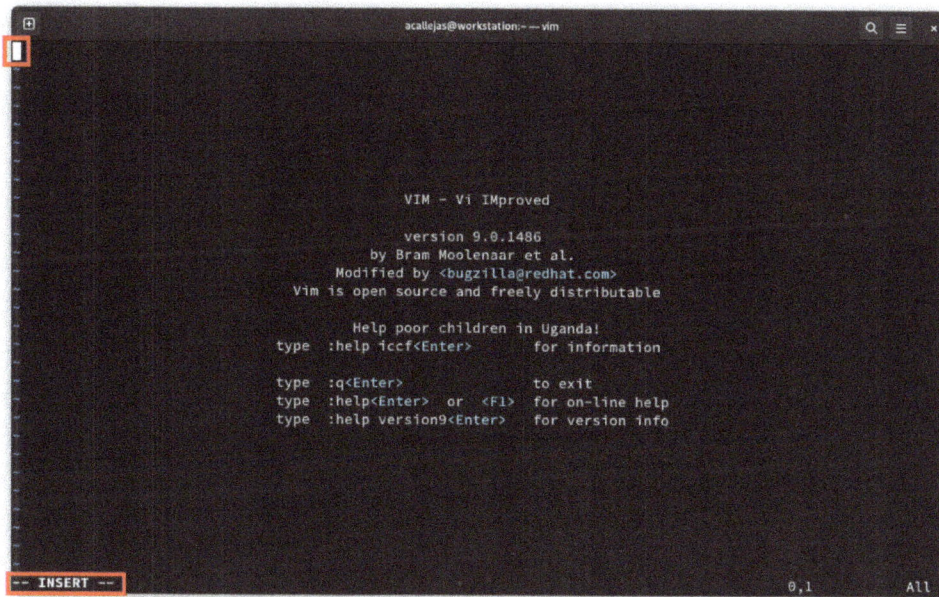

Figure 7.28 – Insert mode

After typing, to return to command mode, press the *Esc* key. This clears the mode in the bottom bar.

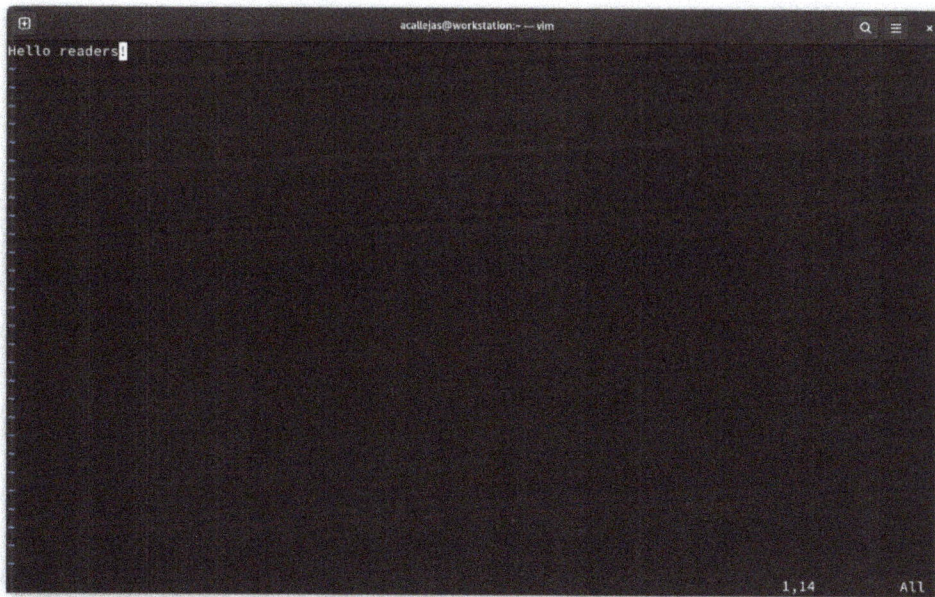

Figure 7.29 – Command mode

The normal mode contains a command-line mode. Here, a variety of tasks, such as saving or quitting the file, can be run.

To enter command-line mode, press the colon key (`:`) and type the command for the desired task. The following table shows the commands for the most common tasks:

Save/Quit	
Write buffer	`:w`
Quit	`:q`
Write and quit	`:wq`
Abandon buffer	`:q!`
Other	
Find down	`:/[string]`
Set numbers	`:se nu`
No numbers	`:se nonu`

Table 7.5 – Commands for common tasks

In normal mode, also, file editing tasks can be run. No need to press the colon key (`:`). Just run the command for the editing task needed. The following table shows the most common editing commands:

Insert	
After cursor	`a`
At the end of line	`A`
Before cursor	`i`
At beginning of line	`I`
Open line below	`o`
Open line above	`O`
Yank word	`yw`
Yank line	`yy`
Put (paste)	`p`
Change	
Word	`cw`
Line	`cc`
Rest of line	`C`
Under cursor	`s`
Replace character	`r`

Delete	
Word	dw
Line	dd
Rest of line	D
Under cursor	x
Before cursor	X
Transpose	xp

Table 7.6 – Commands for editing tasks

> **Note**
> Vim includes a *tutor* to learn how to use it. To start the tutor, run the `vimtutor` command.

The flexibility and power of Vim make it an essential tool in system administration.

Let's now get an overview of the advanced use of Vim.

Mastering vim

For many people, `vim` seems as complex as `emacs`. But in practice, with reference to *Figure 7.26*, the editing flow is simpler. The only thing to get used to is switching between modes.

As proof of this, let's use the same example used earlier with `emacs` to edit the `test` file, composed of the contents of the `/etc/passwd` and `/etc/group` files. Follow these steps:

1. In the terminal, as a *non-root user*, run the `vim` command. To browse for the file, type a colon (`:`) and the letter `e` with a space. Type the letter `t` to browse for the `test` file and then press the *Tab* key. Vim shows in the bottom bar the files whose names begin with `t`:

Figure 7.30 – Browse for the test file

2. To split the screen, as in emacs, type a colon (:) and then the split command:

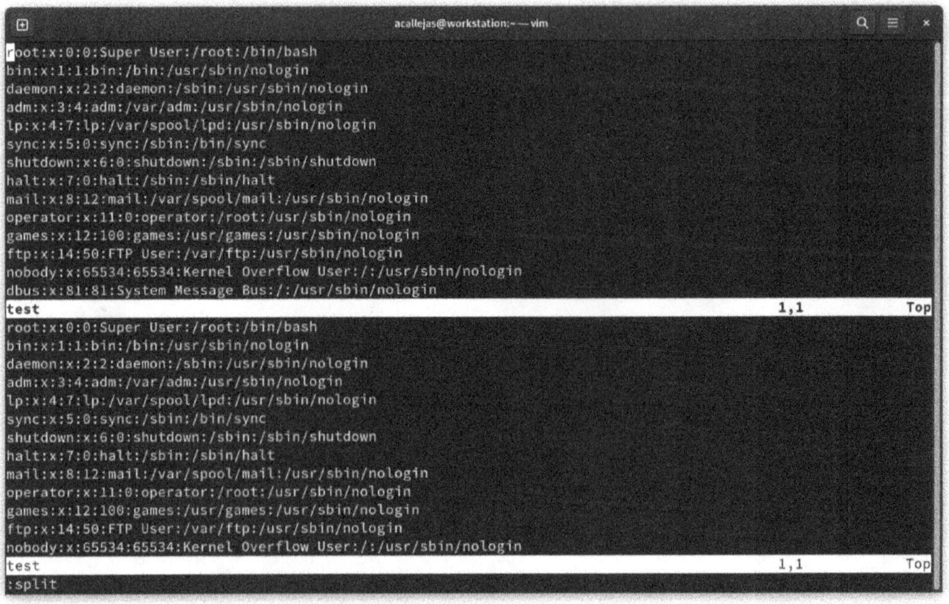

Figure 7.31 – Split screen

3. To switch screens, press the *Ctrl* key plus the *w* key twice (*Ctrl+ww*). Scroll down until you find the plus sign (+) characters added in the emacs example:

```
root:x:0:0:Super User:/root:/bin/bash
bin:x:1:1:bin:/bin:/usr/sbin/nologin
daemon:x:2:2:daemon:/sbin:/usr/sbin/nologin
adm:x:3:4:adm:/var/adm:/usr/sbin/nologin
lp:x:4:7:lp:/var/spool/lpd:/usr/sbin/nologin
sync:x:5:0:sync:/sbin:/bin/sync
shutdown:x:6:0:shutdown:/sbin:/sbin/shutdown
halt:x:7:0:halt:/sbin:/sbin/halt
mail:x:8:12:mail:/var/spool/mail:/usr/sbin/nologin
operator:x:11:0:operator:/root:/usr/sbin/nologin
games:x:12:100:games:/usr/games:/usr/sbin/nologin
ftp:x:14:50:FTP User:/var/ftp:/usr/sbin/nologin
nobody:x:65534:65534:Kernel Overflow User:/:/usr/sbin/nologin
dbus:x:81:81:System Message Bus:/:/usr/sbin/nologin
test                                                    5,1          Top
++++++++++++++++++++++++++++++++++++++++++++++++++++++++++++++++++++++++++++++++++
++++
root:x:0:
bin:x:1:
daemon:x:2:
sys:x:3:
adm:x:4:
tty:x:5:
disk:x:6:
lp:x:7:
mem:x:8:
kmem:x:9:
wheel:x:10:acallejas
test                                                    53,1         43%
```

Figure 7.32 – Search for plus characters

4. Let's replace these plus signs (+) with asterisks (*). Type a colon (:) and type the percent sign (%) plus the s letter. This indicates to vim that this is a substitution. Next, type a slash (/) to state the string to be replaced and again another slash (/) to type the characters that will replace the original string. Type another slash (/) and then the letter g to tell vim that the substitution must take place *globally*:

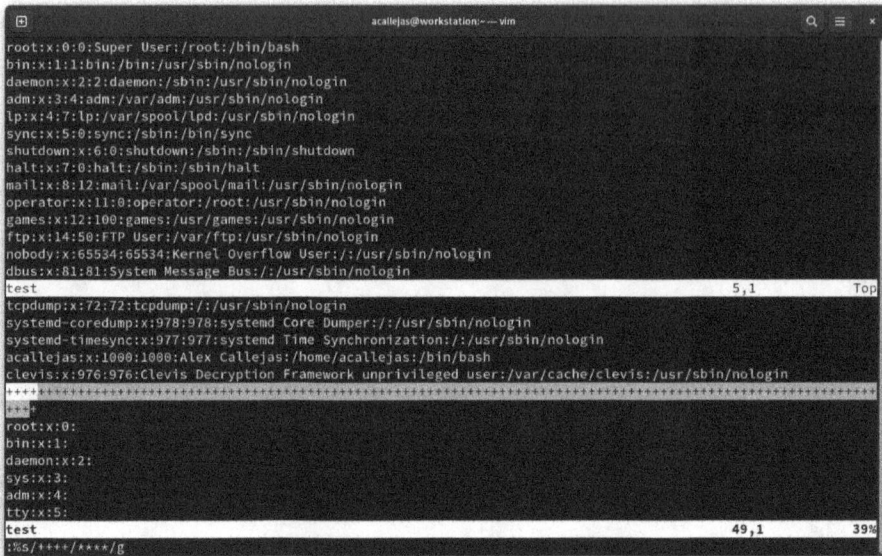

Figure 7.33 – Replacing characters

5. Press the *Enter* key and `vim` performs the substitution. The bottom bar displays a message of the completed task:

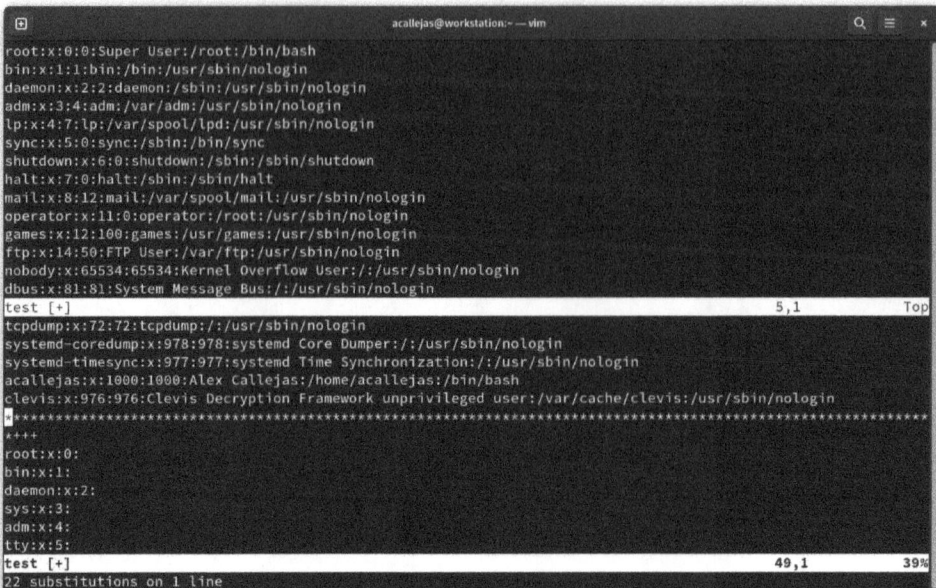

Figure 7.34 – Modifying the test file

6. To save and quit the file, type a colon (:) followed by the letters w and q, and then press the *Enter* key.

> **Note**
>
> On the internet, you can find more commands and advanced uses of vim. A very useful resource is the post *50 Useful Vim Commands*: https://vimtricks.com/p/50-useful-vim-commands/.

Pimp my vim

Like emacs, Vim expands its capabilities with the installation of plugins and packages, in addition to customizing the interface to provide information or help edit the file. Beyond the look and feel, it adds features that increase the usability of the editor.

Unlike emacs, Vim uses a variety of initialization files where settings and customizations are included. Some of the most relevant files are as follows:

- /usr/share/vim/vim90/doc/*.txt

  The Vim documentation files. Use :help doc-file-list to get the complete list.

- /usr/share/vim/vim90/doc/tags

  The tags file used to find information in the documentation files

- /usr/share/vim/vim90/syntax/syntax.vim

  System-wide syntax initializations

- /usr/share/vim/vim90/syntax/*.vim

  Syntax files for various languages

- /usr/share/vim/vimrc

  System-wide Vim initializations

- ~/.vimrc

  Personal Vim initializations

- /usr/share/vim/vim90/optwin.vim

  Script used for the :options command. A nice way to view and set options.

The file that contains the Vim initializations is `vimrc`. The `vimrc` file is a collection of the following:

- Configurations
- Custom commands
- Custom functions
- Mappings
- Plugins

Let's take a look at some examples of each of them.

Configurations

In normal mode, it is possible to configure Vim to add some features. For example, to add numbers to lines to identify them, type a colon (:) followed by `set nu`:

```
⊕                                    acailejas@workstation:~ — vim test                          Q  ≡   ×
 1 root:x:0:0:Super User:/root:/bin/bash
 2 bin:x:1:1:bin:/bin:/usr/sbin/nologin
 3 daemon:x:2:2:daemon:/sbin:/usr/sbin/nologin
 4 adm:x:3:4:adm:/var/adm:/usr/sbin/nologin
 5 lp:x:4:7:lp:/var/spool/lpd:/usr/sbin/nologin
 6 sync:x:5:0:sync:/sbin:/bin/sync
 7 shutdown:x:6:0:shutdown:/sbin:/sbin/shutdown
 8 halt:x:7:0:halt:/sbin:/sbin/halt
 9 mail:x:8:12:mail:/var/spool/mail:/usr/sbin/nologin
10 operator:x:11:0:operator:/root:/usr/sbin/nologin
11 games:x:12:100:games:/usr/games:/usr/sbin/nologin
12 ftp:x:14:50:FTP User:/var/ftp:/usr/sbin/nologin
13 nobody:x:65534:65534:Kernel Overflow User:/:/usr/sbin/nologin
14 dbus:x:81:81:System Message Bus:/:/usr/sbin/nologin
15 apache:x:48:48:Apache:/usr/share/httpd:/sbin/nologin
16 tss:x:59:59:Account used for TPM access:/:/usr/sbin/nologin
17 systemd-network:x:192:192:systemd Network Management:/:/usr/sbin/nologin
18 systemd-oom:x:999:999:systemd Userspace OOM Killer:/:/usr/sbin/nologin
19 systemd-resolve:x:193:193:systemd Resolver:/:/usr/sbin/nologin
20 qemu:x:107:107:qemu user:/:/sbin/nologin
21 polkitd:x:998:997:User for polkitd:/:/sbin/nologin
22 avahi:x:70:70:Avahi mDNS/DNS-SD Stack:/var/run/avahi-daemon:/sbin/nologin
23 geoclue:x:997:996:User for geoclue:/var/lib/geoclue:/sbin/nologin
24 nm-openconnect:x:996:995:NetworkManager user for OpenConnect:/:/sbin/nologin
25 colord:x:995:994:User for colord:/var/lib/colord:/sbin/nologin
26 usbmuxd:x:113:113:usbmuxd user:/:/sbin/nologin
27 gluster:x:994:993:GlusterFS daemons:/run/gluster:/sbin/nologin
:set nu                                                          5,1            Top
```

Figure 7.35 – Numbered lines

This setting only remains enabled as long as the editor is open. Closing the editor disables it.

Keep this setting enabled by adding it to the `.vimrc` file.

These settings could help with syntax while editing the file. For example, when editing YAML files, you could configure the `.vimrc` file in a basic way as follows:

```
set ts=2  ← [1]
set et    ← [2]
set ai    ← [3]
```

- [1] A tab is two spaces
- [2] Expand tabs
- [3] Auto-indenting

Custom commands

In Vim, we can create custom commands to perform tasks. For example, we could create a command that tells us today's date in various formats:

- In the `.vimrc` file, add the following line:

  ```
  :command! TellDate echo call("strftime", [<args>])
  ```

- In Vim command mode, run the `TellDate` command as follows:

  ```
  :TellDate "%F"
  ```

```
2023-05-07                                              0,0-1          All
```

Figure 7.36 – Custom date

- To get the current time, run the `TellDate` command as follows:

  ```
  :TellDate "%H:%M"
  ```

```
20:38                                                   0,0-1          All
```

Figure 7.37 – Current time

Custom functions

As seen previously, Vim allows us to run a built-in or custom command from command mode. But it is not limited to one; it could run a set of commands or series of instructions within the same command mode. Or they get written to a file and generated in a running Vim instance (`:source path/to/file`). Some of these files come up as part of the configuration from the `.vimrc` file.

These scripts use **Vimscript** (also called **VimL**). This **Vim** ex-command subset provides many features that could be expected from a scripting language, such as values, variables, functions, and loops.

It is very common for a script to mix features of a scripting language and raw ex-commands.

The `.vimrc` file includes some files describing functions that extend the capabilities of the text editor. These functions get called using the native Vimscript `let` function, which assigns a value to a variable.

The function structure uses the following syntax:

```
{functionName}() function.
  {some_tasks}
endfunction
```

The following table shows the most common functions of Vimscript:

Buffer			Marks	
Current line number	`line('.')`	Position of a mark	`getpos("'a")`	
	`col('.')`		`setpos("'a",...)`	
	`col('$')`	Position of selection start	`getpos("'<")`	
Current line as string	`getline('.')`	Cursor		
Get line 1	`getline(1)`	Moves cursor	`cursor(line,col)`	
Get lines 1-5	`getline(1, 5)`		`cursor(line,col, off,curswant)`	
Next blank line, returns line number	`search('^$')`	Returns [bufnum, line, col, off, curswant]	`getcurpos()`	
Search but don't move cursor	`search('^$','n')`	Date/time	`strftime('%c')`	
			`strftime('%c', getftime('file.c'))`	

Table 7.7 – Vimscript common functions

Mappings

Vim allows us to customize key mappings. It is useful to change the definition of the keys typed on the keyboard. The most common use is to define a sequence of commands for a function key. For example, if want to map the x key to the dd command to delete lines, in normal mode, in the .vimrc file, add the following line:

```
nmap x dd
```

Mapping applies in four modes: *normal*, *visual*, *selection*, and *operator-pending*.

For help with mapping, commands, and modes, run the following in command mode:

```
:help map.txt
```

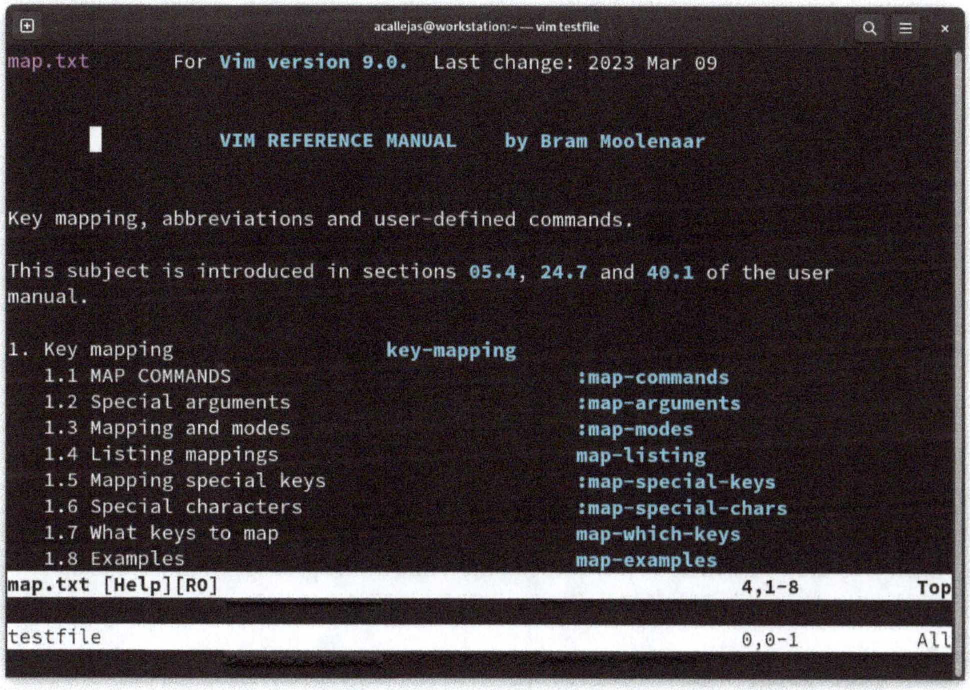

Figure 7.38 – Mapping help

Plugins

Vim plugins are installed via packages. A Vim package is a *directory* or *repository* that contains one or more plugins that depend on each other. Among its main features are the following:

- Downloaded as a compressed file and unzipped in its own directory, which avoids it mixing with others and makes it easy to update and remove

- Contain plugins loaded at startup and others that are only loaded when needed with `:packadd`

The directory recommended to install Vim packages inside is the user's `.vim` directory.

To exemplify the process, let's install the most used plugin: **Vim Airline**.

Vim Airline is a plugin that replaces the standard Vim status line with a useful status bar, and provides useful information about the working file, including the following:

- Filename

- Save status

- File type

- Encoding

- Position

- Word count

Vim mode

To install Vim Airline, follow these steps:

1. In the home directory of the *non-root user*, as the *non-root user*, create the `.vim` directory:

   ```
   [acallejas@workstation ~]$ mkdir -p .vim
   ```

2. Change to the `.vim` directory. Download the Vim Airline package from its repository on GitHub (`https://github.com/vim-airline/vim-airline`):

   ```
   $ cd .vim
   $ wget https://github.com/vim-airline/vim-airline/archive/refs/
   tags/v0.11.tar.gz
   ```

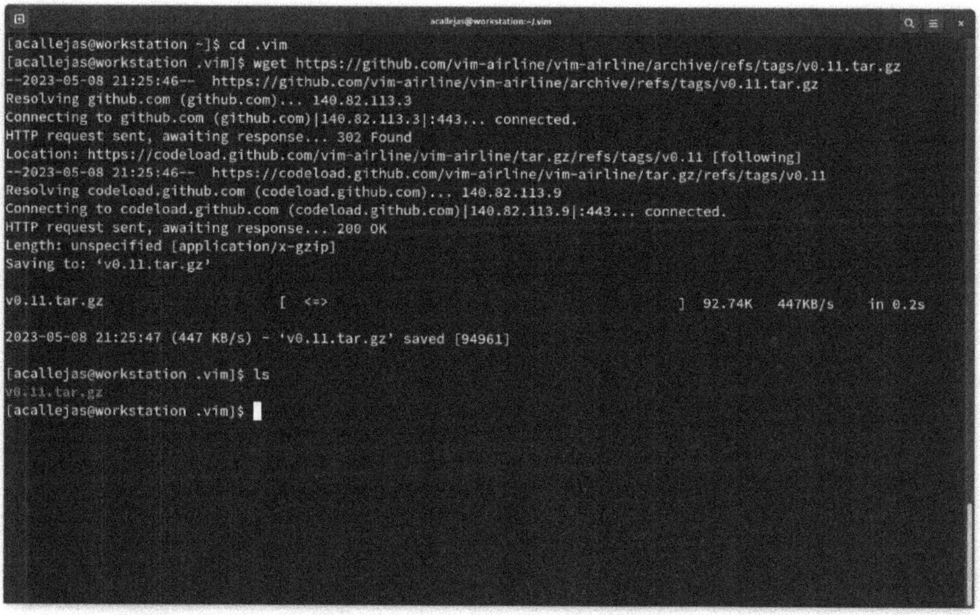

Figure 7.39 – Download Vim Airline

3. Decompress the Vim Airline package:

```
$ tar xzf v0.11.tar.gz
```

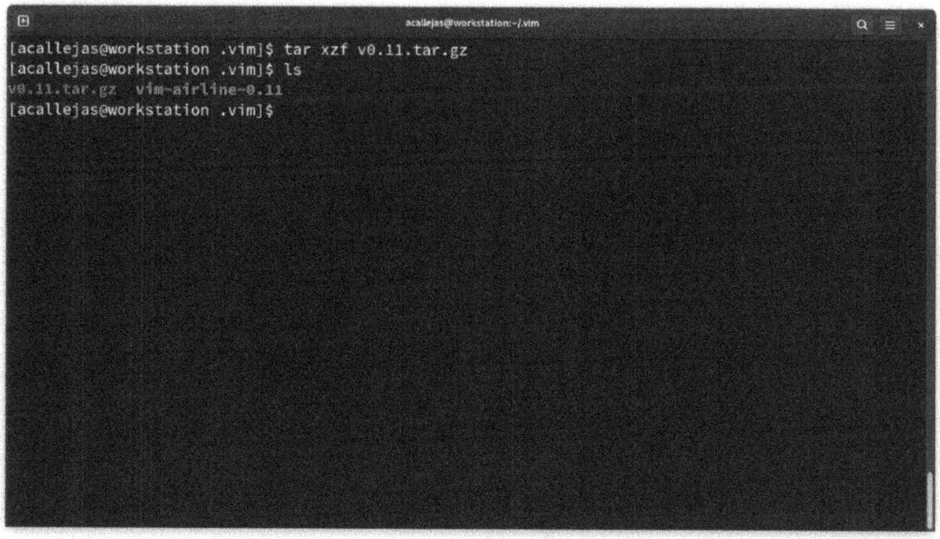

Figure 7.40 – Decompressing the package

4. Move the Vim Airline version directory as `vim-airline`

```
$ mv vim-airline-0.11 vim-airline
```

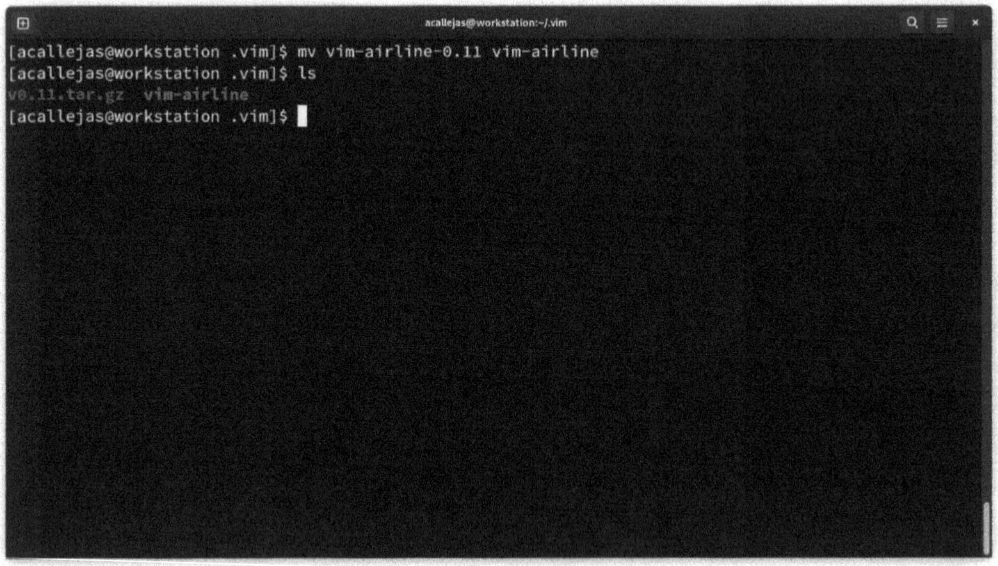
acallejas@workstation:~/.vim
[acallejas@workstation .vim]$ mv vim-airline-0.11 vim-airline
[acallejas@workstation .vim]$ ls
v0.11.tar.gz vim-airline
[acallejas@workstation .vim]$

Figure 7.41 – Renaming a directory

5. Create the `pack/dist/start` path. Move the `vim-airline` directory into the `pack/dist/start` path:

```
$ mkdir -p pack/dist/start
$ mv vim-airline pack/dist/start/
```

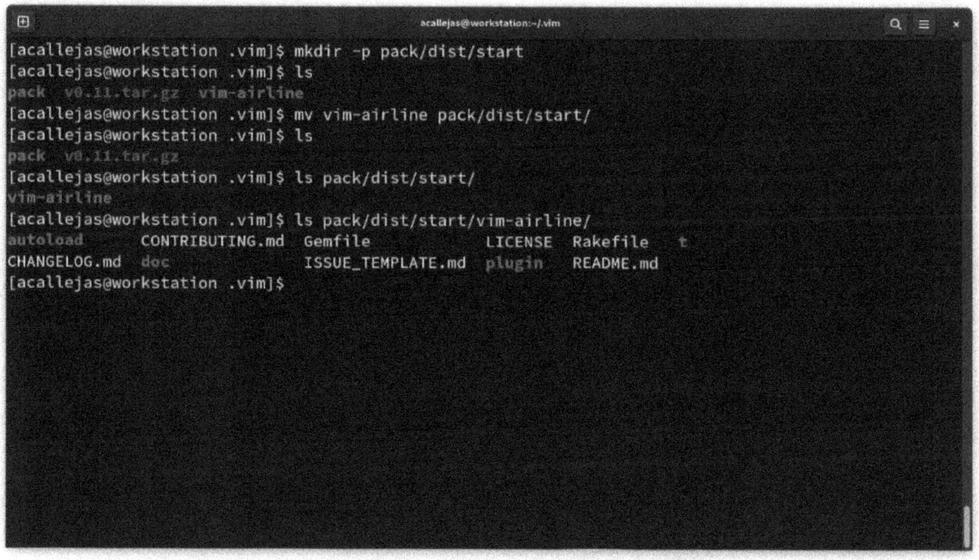

Figure 7.42 – Relocating the vim-airline directory

Vim Airline is a Vimscript version of Powerline (https://github.com/powerline/powerline) written in Python.

Powerline includes a font with pretty symbols. To get these symbols with Vim Airline, install the patched font.

6. As the root user, or with sudo if a non-root user has the privileges, install the powerline-fonts package using the dnf command:

```
$ sudo dnf install powerline-fonts
```

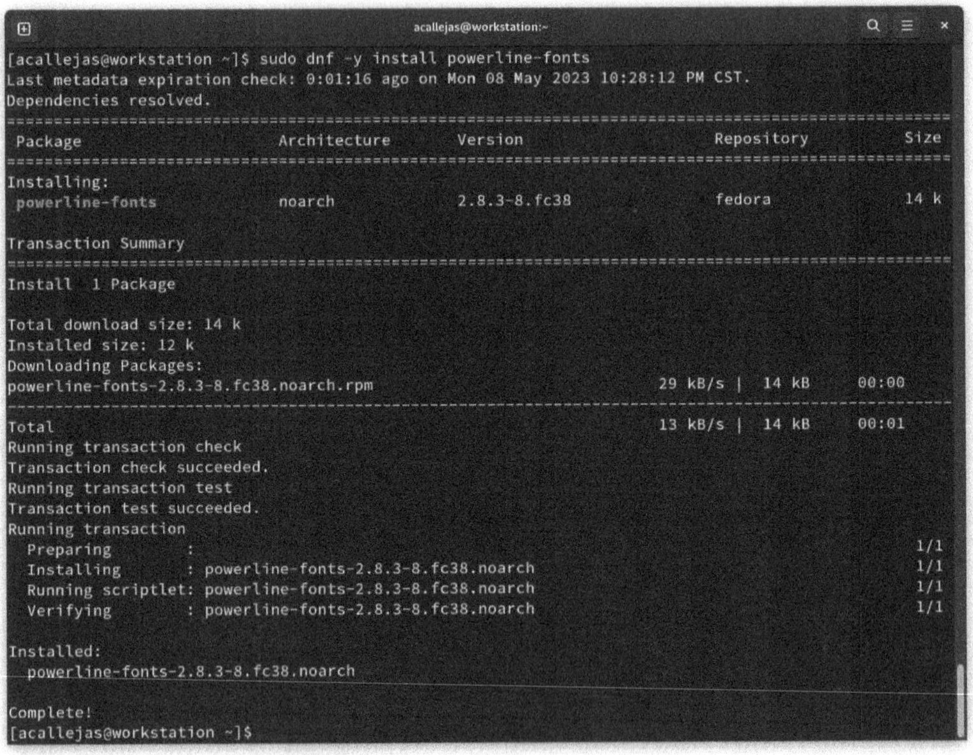

Figure 7.43 – Installing the Powerline font

7. Switch to the home directory and edit the `.vimrc` file to enable the font use. Add the line
    `let g:airline_powerline_fonts = 1`:

    ```
    $ cd
    $ vim .vimrc
    ```

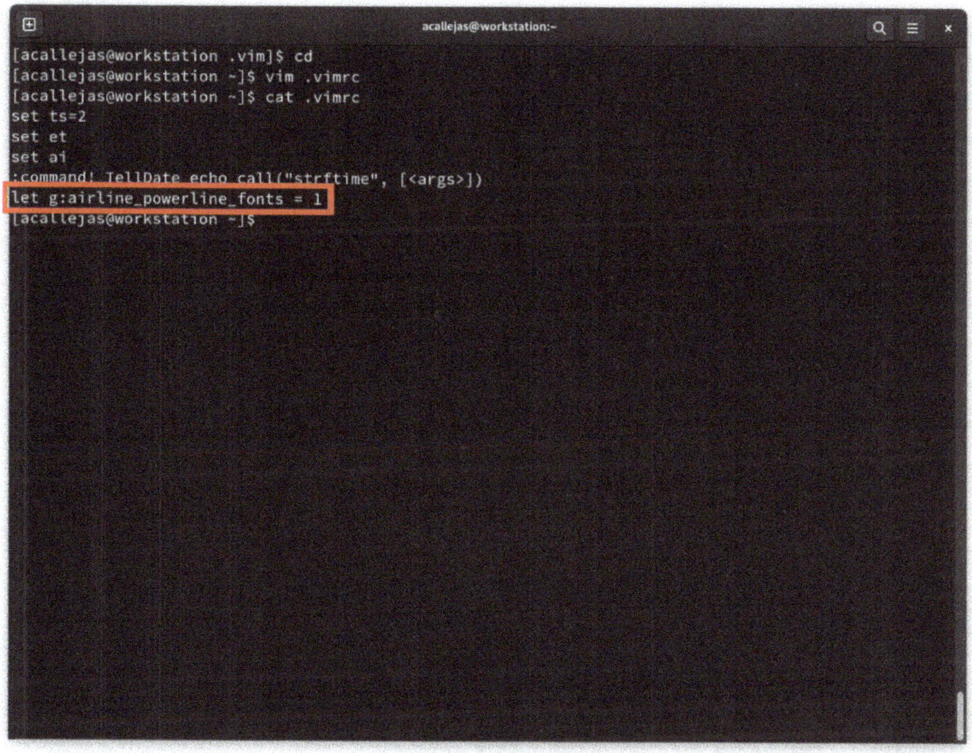

Figure 7.44 – Enabling font usage

8. Edit the `test` file and check the new status bar:

    ```
    $ vim test
    ```

Figure 7.45 – vim-airline status bar

9.   When changing modes, the bar also changes its color to differentiate between the modes:

- This is what it looks like in Insert mode:

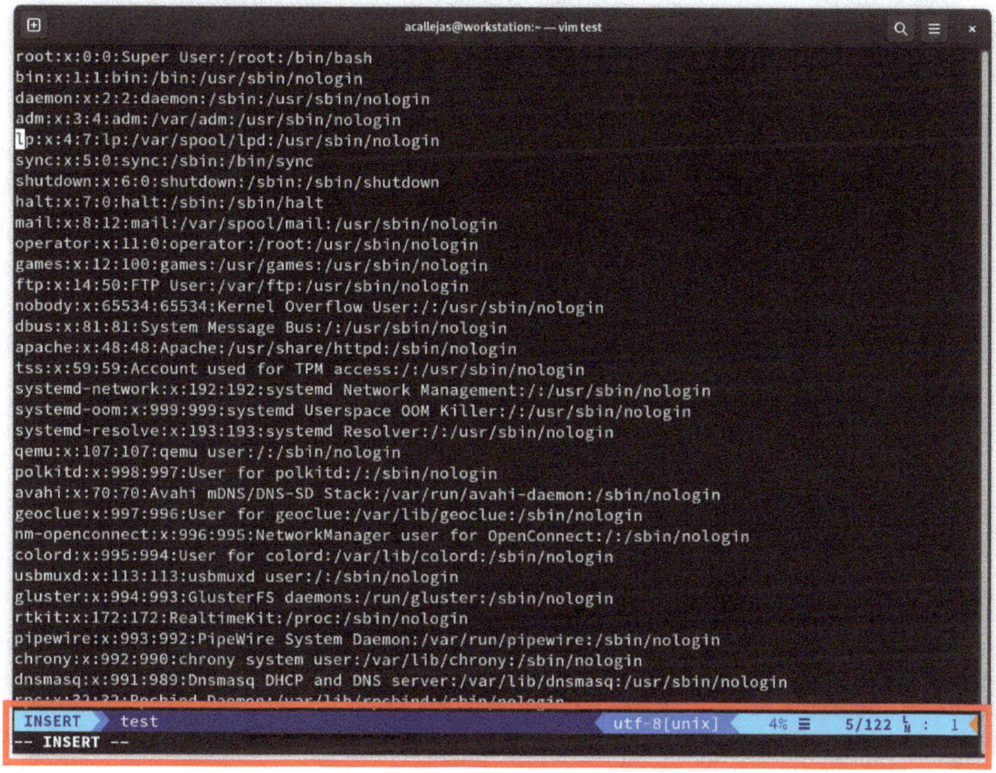

Figure 7.46 – Insert mode

- The following is what it looks like in Command mode:

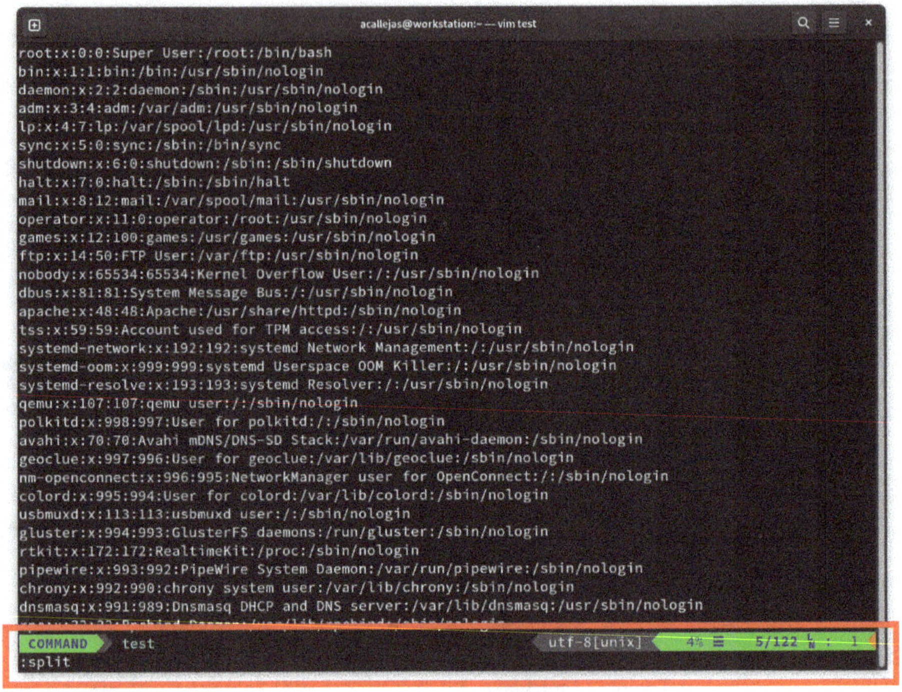

Figure 7.47 – Command mode

> **Note**
>
> Changing or customizing the color scheme is available. For further reference, visit the `vim-airlines-themes` repository on GitHub: `https://github.com/vim-airline/vim-airline-themes`.

This way, the plugin installation and configuration work in our editor.

There are many plugins, some very specialized, that complement Vim, with a similar installation.

> **Note**
>
> On the internet, you'll find many examples of packages and plugins. As a personal recommendation, visit these posts with specialized recommendations to improve Vim:
>
> - *5 useful Vim tplugins for developers*: `https://opensource.com/article/19/1/vim-plugins-developers`
> - *Top five Vim plugins for sysadmins*: `https://www.redhat.com/sysadmin/five-vim-plugins`

This concludes our walk-through of the text editors. In the following chapters, we'll make use of them, adding plugins or packages for specialized tasks to help us with the system administration of our Linux systems.

Summary

In this chapter, we learned in depth about text editors, beginning with the fundamental understanding that in Unix/Linux, *everything is a file*. Thus, the use of the terminal as a tool to edit files eases the tasks of system configuration.

We took our first steps in **Emacs**. While it is known to be a very complex editor for novices, we offered a basic guide to get started with it.

We also reviewed the use of **Nano**, the default text editor in several distributions, including Fedora Linux.

We also deep-dived into the use of **Vim**, a well-known and recommended file editing tool for file management.

The decision is up to you, dear reader, to choose an editor of your preference.

In the next chapter, we will review the **LibreOffice** suite and its different programs for creating and editing commonly used file formats.

Further reading

To learn more about the topics covered in this chapter, you can visit the following links:

- The Linux Documentation Project: Text editors

    `https://tldp.org/LDP/intro-linux/html/sect_06_01.html`

- *9 Best Text Editors for the Linux Command Line*

    `https://itsfoss.com/command-line-text-editors-linux/`

- *Linux skills: 9 tutorials to get more from your text editor*

    `https://www.redhat.com/sysadmin/text-editor-roundup-2022`

- *A beginner's guide to text editing with Emacs*

    `https://www.redhat.com/sysadmin/beginners-guide-emacs`

- *How to get started with the Vi editor*

    `https://www.redhat.com/sysadmin/get-started-vi-editor`

8

LibreOffice Suite

GNU/Linux supports the standardization, optimization, and improvement of organizations that operate with an *office suite*. The office suite is one of the most common tools in any industry, with the goal of making work more practical and dynamic. An office suite is a set of programs that allows you to create, modify, organize, store, send, receive, scan, and print files. The basic programs of an office suite include word processors, spreadsheets, and image and/or presentation editors for projects.

LibreOffice is an open source office suite by excellence. It was originally called OpenOffice, but when Apache acquired it, some users created a fork, which became LibreOffice.

All distributions and users adopted LibreOffice, accelerating its development. LibreOffice is present in the most popular GNU/Linux distributions, besides Flatpak packages, making its installation very simple.

In this chapter, we will cover the following main topics:

- Exploring Office tools on Fedora Linux
- Getting used to Writer and Calc
- Creating slides and image management

Let's get started!

Technical requirements

LibreOffice comes installed by default in the Workstation version of Fedora Linux, which we installed in *Chapter 2*. The development of the topics in this chapter only requires you to confirm that you have followed the steps of the aforementioned chapter. If not, ensure that you install LibreOffice on your Fedora Linux Workstation.

The examples created in this chapter are available for download in the book's GitHub repository, which you can find at the following URL: `https://github.com/PacktPublishing/Fedora-Linux-System-Administration/tree/main/chapter8`.

Exploring office tools on Fedora Linux

The **Fedora Project** has not developed its own office suite, but it provides a default set of office applications designed to have broad appeal and deliver useful functionality. The official repositories include the LibreOffice components.

Besides LibreOffice, Fedora Linux offers you the possibility to install other office suites, including add-ons such as templates or fonts.

Before diving into the components of LibreOffice, let's take a brief look at these packages.

WPS Office

WPS Office is a *cross-platform* (Windows, Linux, Android, and iOS) productivity suite available for computers and mobile devices. It is considered a high-performance but *proprietary* solution, compatible and comparable to Microsoft Office. Its **Writer**, **Presentation**, and **Spreadsheet** components are robust solutions, like Microsoft's **PowerPoint**, **Excel**, and **Word**.

The WPS Office suite is produced by WPS Office Software, a subsidiary of the Kingsoft Corporation, which is a leading internet services and software company in China. It is fully compatible with Microsoft Office formats and has a spell checker available in more than 10 different languages.

On Fedora Linux, it is available through a Flatpak package provided by Flathub.

> **Note**
>
> The Flatpak package comes with a warning, saying that this Flatpak package is not verified, affiliated, or supported by the Kingsoft Office Corporation.

ONLYOFFICE

ONLYOFFICE Desktop Editors is an open source office suite available for Linux, Windows, and macOS, freely distributed under the terms of **AGPLv3**. It consists of three editors for text documents, spreadsheets, and presentations that are natively compatible with Microsoft Office formats.

ONLYOFFICE Desktop Editors offers you the possibility to connect to cloud platforms, such as ONLYOFFICE, Nextcloud, ownCloud, Seafile, Liferay, and kDrive, and collaborate on team documents, including co-editing in real time, reviewing, commenting, and interacting using chat.

> **Note**
>
> The **Affero General Public License** is a *copyleft license* derived from the **GNU General Public License**. It is designed to ensure community cooperation on software running on a network, and it adds an obligation to distribute the software if it provides services over a network.
>
> The **Free Software Foundation** recommends the use of **GNU AGPLv3** for any software that runs over a network. You can find more information at `https://www.gnu.org/licenses/agpl-3.0.html`.

On Fedora Linux, ONLYOFFICE Desktop Editors is available through a Flatpak package provided by Flathub.

Calligra

Calligra is an office suite created by KDE. You don't need to have the Plasma desktop environment installed to use it, as it works fine on other desktop environments, such as Fedora Workstation using GNOME.

Calligra adopts the OASIS OpenDocument format as its native file format. The **OpenDocument Format (ODF)** is an XML-based open document file format for office applications. It is used for documents containing text, spreadsheets, diagrams, and graphical elements.

> **Note**
>
> For more information on the **OASIS Open Document Format for Office Applications**, refer to `https://www.oasis-open.org/committees/tc_home.php?wg_abbrev=office`.

The main components of Calligra are as follows:

- **Calligra Words**: A word processor, organized around a main window, for editing and writing text, and a panel on the right that provides access to the most common tools.

- **Calligra Stage**: A presentation editor that highlights its templates, which, although there are few, are a good basis for a customized presentation.

- **Calligra Sheets**: Used for spreadsheet editing. As in the previous cases, it offers templates for specific cases.

- **Calligra Plan**: A tool that helps you to organize and hierarchize tasks.

- **Karbon**: A vector graphics editor that supports documents with multiple pages and imports PDF files.

On Fedora Linux, each component is available individually as an RPM package or a Flatpak package, provided by Fedora Flatpaks.

Fonts

Fedora Linux installs by default more than 70 fonts. However, in its repositories, it has more than 1,000 fonts available. To install more fonts from the official repositories, follow these steps:

1. As a *non-root user*, open the menu in the upper-left corner and click on **Software**:

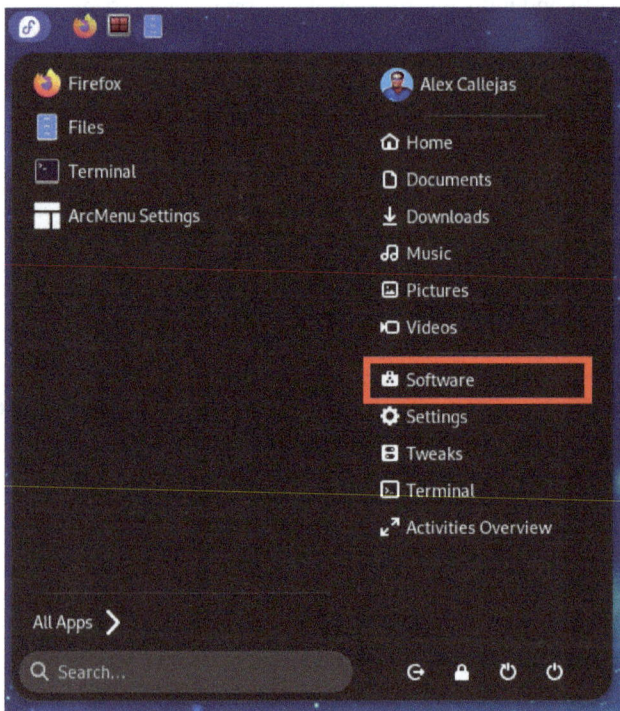

Figure 8.1 – Opening the menu

2. Click on the search icon in the upper-left corner. In the search field, type fonts, and then press *Enter*.

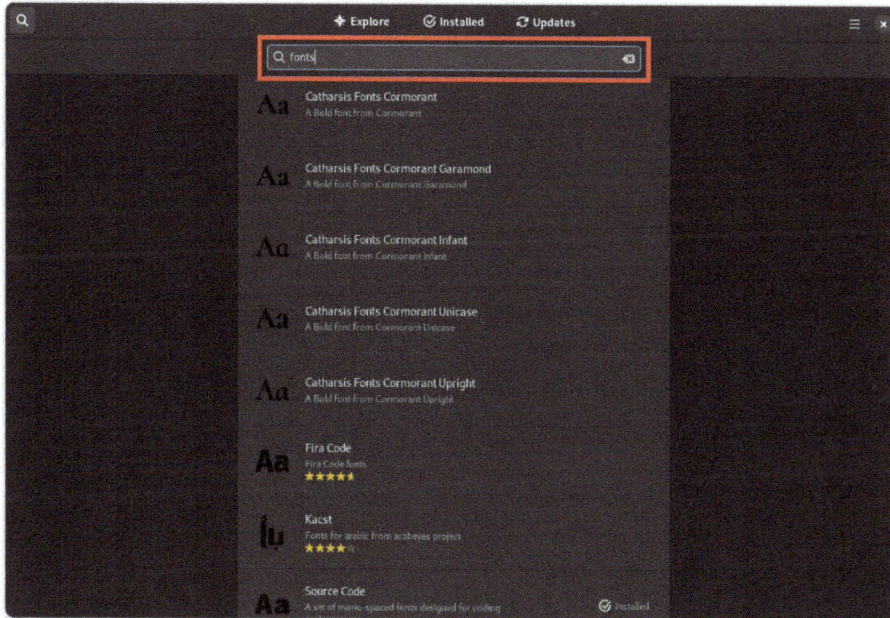

Figure 8.2 – Searching the fonts

3.   Select the desired font and install it – for example, search for the font `julietaula Montserrat Alternates`, and then click on the font icon. Click on the **Install** button:

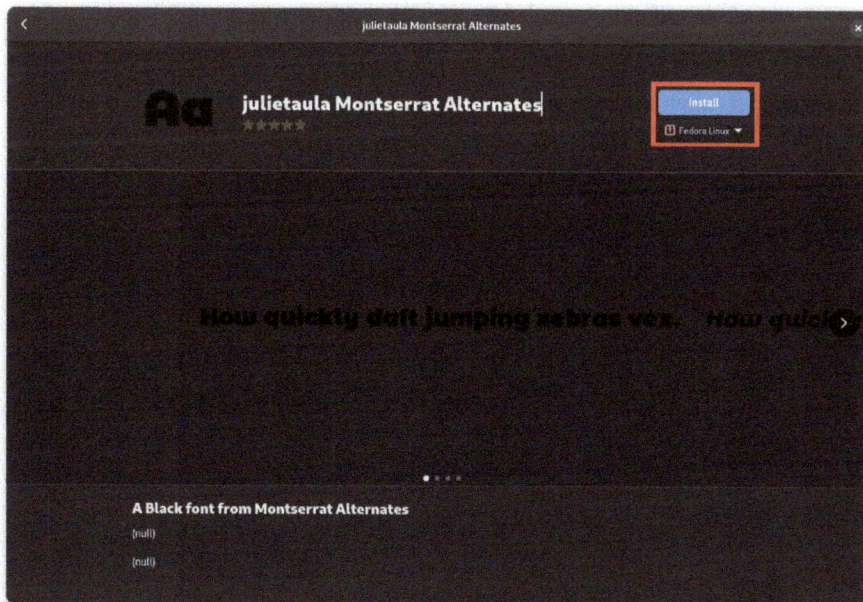

Figure 8.3 – Installing the font

Wait for the installation to complete.

At the end of the installation, the font is available for use in the office suite.

> **Note**
>
> For more information on the **Montserrat Font Project**, refer to its repository on GitHub at `https://github.com/JulietaUla/Montserrat`.

Now that we know the alternative options to LibreOffice and how to install more fonts, let's take a look at the default office suite of Fedora Linux.

LibreOffice

LibreOffice is the successor project to `OpenOffice.org`, commonly known as **OpenOffice**.

`OpenOffice.org` started in the year 2000, after Sun Microsystems released the StarOffice 5.2 code as a free download for personal use.

In 2010, Oracle Corporation acquired Sun Microsystems. This concerned members of the `OpenOffice.org` community because of the *well-known behavior* of Oracle towards open source software (as in the **Java lawsuit against Google**: `https://en.wikipedia.org/wiki/Google_LLC_v._Oracle_America,_Inc`).

In the same year, members of the `OpenOffice.org` community announced the Document Foundation, a *non-profit* foundation intended to provide continuity in the development of the office suite. The foundation's main project is LibreOffice, a fork of `OpenOffice.org`.

LibreOffice adds extra features and improves compatibility with Microsoft Office, with regular releases and security updates.

The main components of LibreOffice are as follows:

- **Writer**: A word processor
- **Calc**: A spreadsheet editor
- **Impress**: A slide show editor

Fedora Linux includes in its repositories extra components for the LibreOffice suite:

- **Base**: A database manager
- **Draw**: A drawing tool

Any installed LibreOffice component programs can be accessed from the **Activities Overview** menu. Type `Libre` in the search bar, as shown in the following figure:

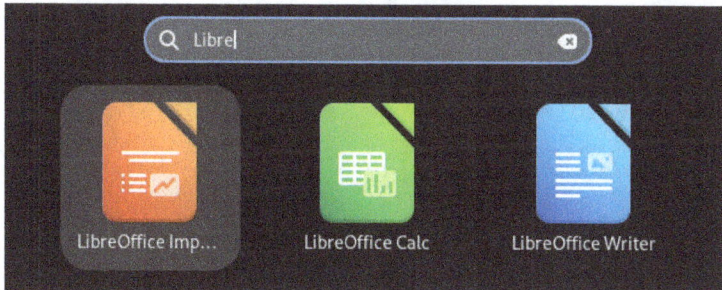

Figure 8.4 – Searching for LibreOffice components

The LibreOffice components are also grouped as an **Office** category in the menu. To access them, follow these steps:

1. As a *non-root user*, open the menu in the upper-left corner, and click on the **All Apps** icon:

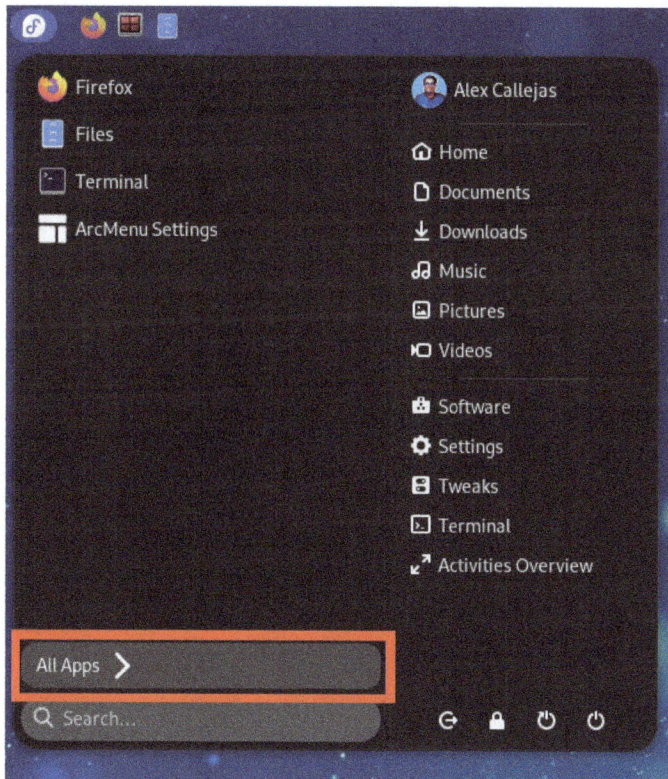

Figure 8.5 – All Apps on the menu

2.   Within the categories offered by the menu, click on the **Office** category:

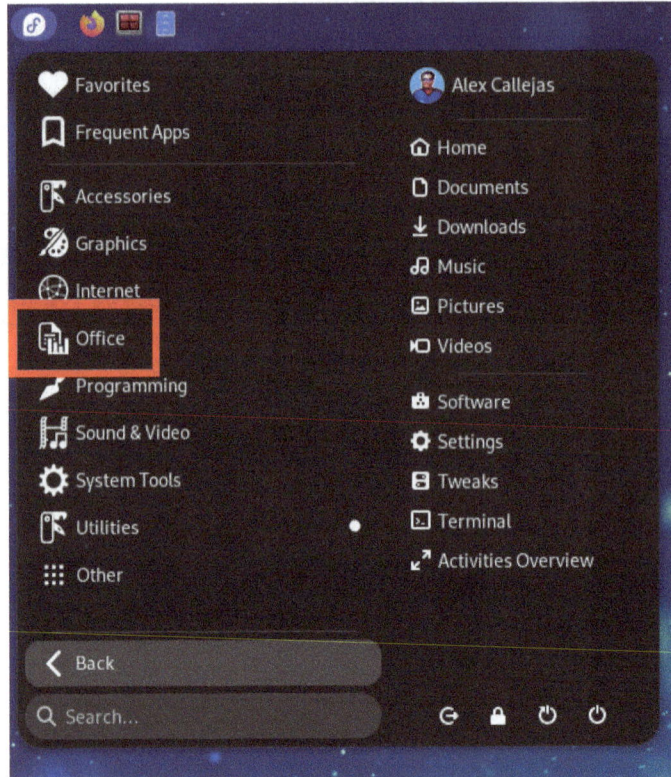

Figure 8.6 – The Office category

3. Within the **Office** category, find the installed LibreOffice components:

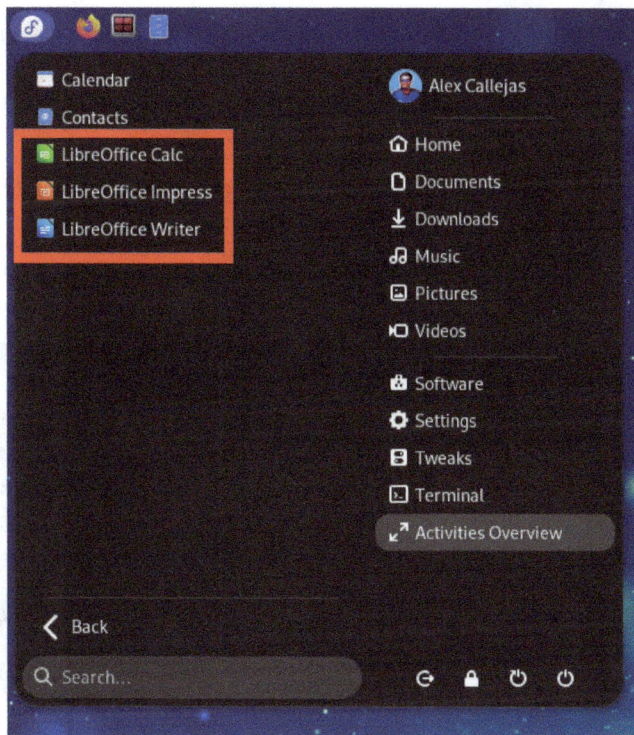

Figure 8.7 – The installed LibreOffice components

4. To access the desired component, click on its icon.

Either access method allows you to open LibreOffice components and use them to create and edit documents.

Let's take a closer look at each of the LibreOffice components.

Getting used to Writer and Calc

Text editors and spreadsheets are the most used tools in an office suite. With them, documentation related to managed systems comes to life, which we'll talk about in a later chapter when covering **Linux** system administration.

Let's take a look at each of these LibreOffice components.

Writer

LibreOffice Writer is the word processor of the suite. **Writer** is a word processor, like **Microsoft Word** and **Corel's Word Perfect**, with similar functions and file format compatibility. The default file format of Writer is **OpenDocument (ODT)**, but it is capable of opening and editing Microsoft Word files such as *DOC, DOCX, RTF,* and *XHTML*.

LibreOffice Writer is like Microsoft Word (as shown in the following figure), since it has many options that can be found in Microsoft's products.

Upon opening Writer to create or edit a text file, you will be shown the active page, along with various editing resources.

Figure 8.8 – LibreOffice Writer

Editing resources include the following:

- A *menu* with different tabs:

  - **File**, with commands that open or close existing documents or create a new document, besides closing an application.

  - **Edit**, with commands to edit the active document.

  - **View** includes commands to display the interface view and toolbars.

  - **Insert**, with commands for inserting elements into the active document. These elements include *images, objects* from other applications, *hyperlinks, comments, symbols, footnotes,* and *sections*.

- **Format**, with commands to format the content of the active document.

- **Styles**, with commands to apply, create, edit, load, and manage styles in text documents. Styles come in several categories, such as *paragraph*, *character*, *frame*, *page*, and *list*.

- **Table**, with commands to insert, edit, and delete tables and their elements in text documents.

- **Form** contains commands to activate the form design mode, and it allows you to enable or disable control wizards or control forms in the document.

- **Tools** contains several tools, including a spell checker, redaction options, a mail merge wizard, and an extensions manager, besides other tools to configure or customize the program's menus and preferences.

- **Window** includes commands to display and manipulate document windows.

- **Help** provides access to the LibreOffice *help* resource.

- Various *toolbars*:

  - The **Standard** toolbar is available in every **LibreOffice suite** application. Its functions include the following:

    - **New** (document)
    - **Open File**
    - **Save** and **Save As**
    - **Email Document**
    - **Edit Mode**
    - **Export as PDF**
    - **Print File Directly** and **Print Preview**
    - **Spelling**
    - **Cut**, **Copy**, **Paste**, and **Clone Formatting**
    - **Undo** and **Redo**
    - **Hyperlink**

  - **Formatting** contains a variety of functions for text formatting.

- The **Properties** *sidebar*:

  - The sidebar sits to the right or left of the active document display area. It provides *contextual properties*, *style management*, *document navigation*, and *media gallery functions*.

The preceding functions and accessible commands load by default when Writer opens, but more functions and commands can added by enabling other toolbars. Enable these toolbars through the **View** menu under the **Toolbars** option:

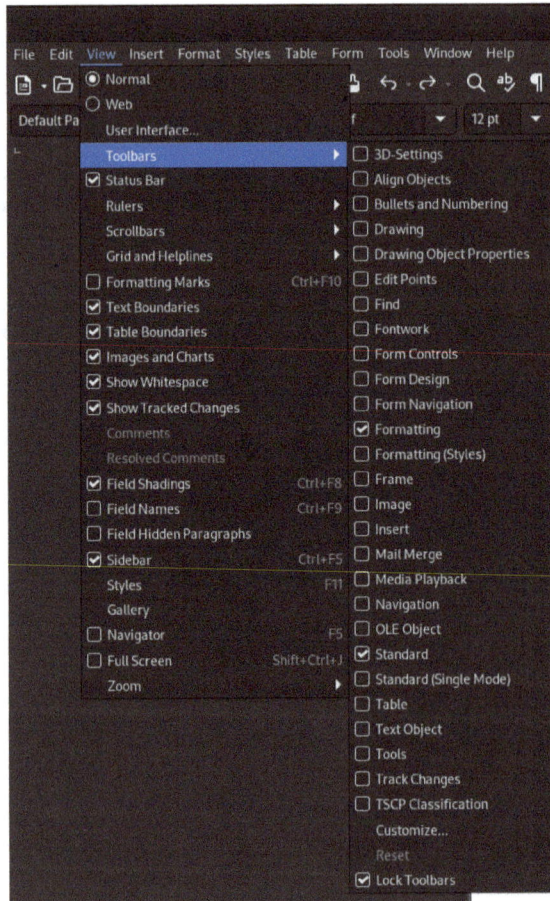

Figure 8.9 – The available toolbars in Writer

> **Note**
> For more information about the toolbar options available in LibreOffice Writer, refer to **LibreOffice Writer Help** at `https://help.libreoffice.org/latest/en-US/`.

Writer helps us document our processes in Linux system administration. It can improve the documentation with a variety of applicable styles. It can also create its own styles and/or change or customize existing ones.

Let's see an example of how to use styles in LibreOffice Writer.

Applying styles in LibreOffice Writer

While creating documentation, we format text and paragraphs to get a certain look and feel. However, this could turn into a tedious and time-consuming task, which can be solved by applying styles.

LibreOffice Writer links the formatting attributes of paragraphs, characters, and other similar elements by applying styles. This not only creates uniform and professional-looking documents but also saves you time, by calculating the table of contents in a document.

Let's use some small text as an example, named `Lorem Ipsum Doc.txt`, which you can find in the GitHub repository of the book, in the `chapter 8` directory (`https://github.com/PacktPublishing/Fedora-Linux-System-Administration/blob/main/chapter8/Lorem%20Ipsum%20Doc.txt`).

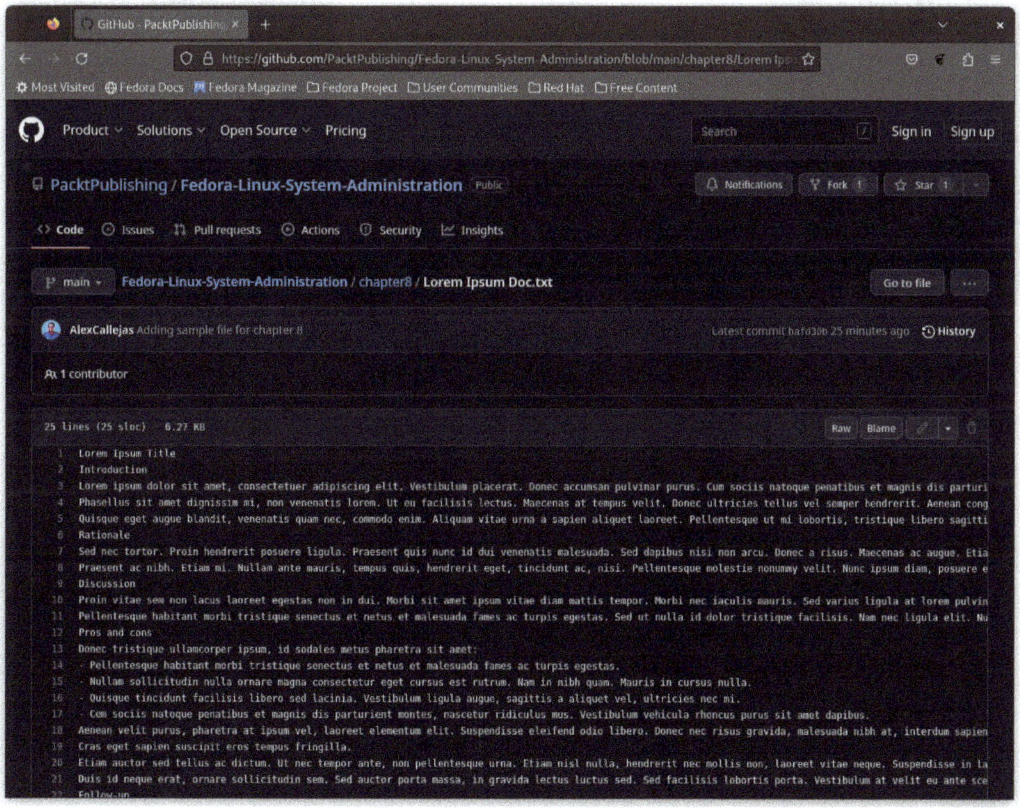

Figure 8.10 – Sample text in the GitHub repository

Follow these steps to apply a style to the text:

1. Open LibreOffice Writer. Copy the text into a new file. Save it to a known location, such as $HOME/Documents:

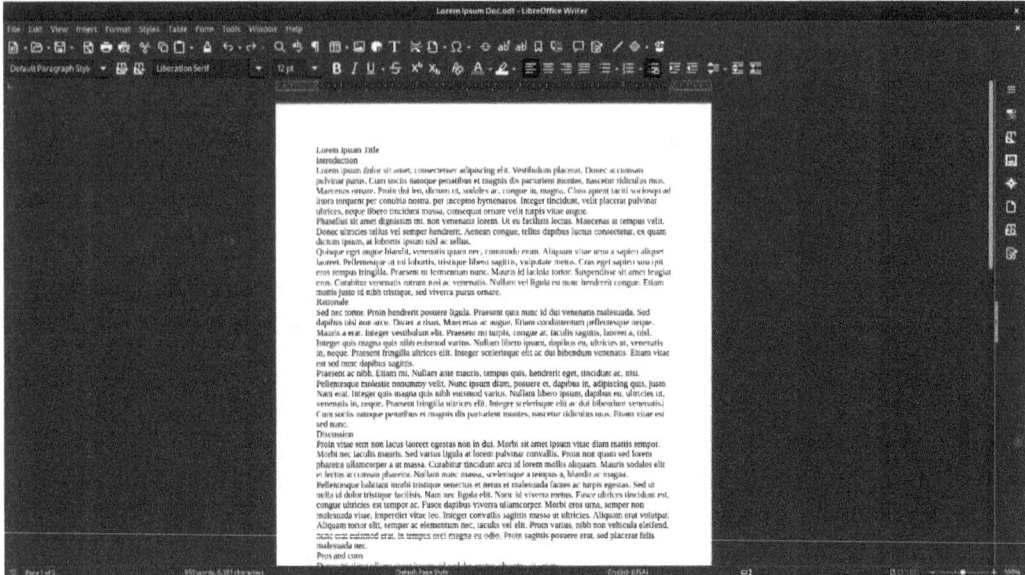

Figure 8.11 – Lorem Ipsum doc

> **Note**
>
> To avoid highlighting spelling errors in this exercise, disable automatic spell-checking. From the **Tools** menu, disable the **Automatic Spell Checking** checkbox or press the *Shift + F7* keys.

2. Increase the visibility of the text on the screen. From the **View** menu, click on **Zoom** and then **Page Width**. Note that some parts of the text, such as lines or words, appear separate from the paragraph. This indicates that there are sections that divide the paragraphs:

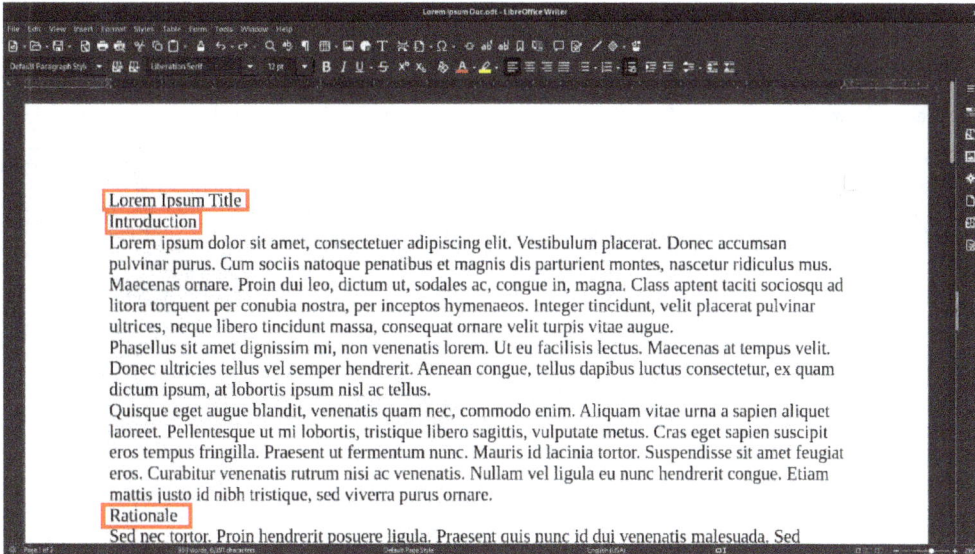

Figure 8.12 – Paragraph section separators

In LibreOffice Writer, section titles are called *headings*. Headings come in hierarchical order – first-level headings are called *Heading 1*, second-level headings are called *Heading 2*, third-level headings are called *Heading 3*, and so on. Let's tell Writer which titles and headings we have in the example text.

3.   Press the *F11* key to display the **Styles** sidebar:

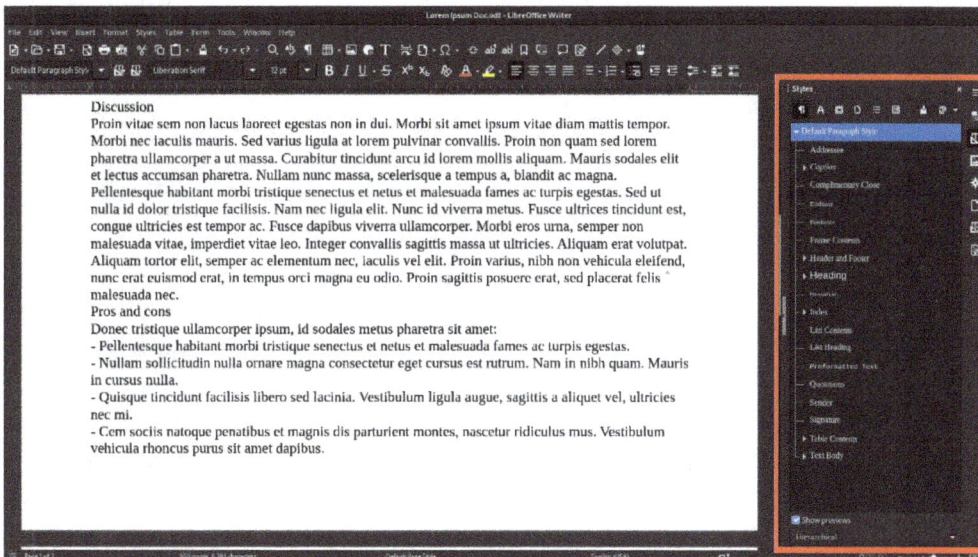

Figure 8.13 – The Styles sidebar

Because we paste *plain text* into our document, it's important to tell Writer that the text is the *body* of the document.

4. Select all the text using the *Ctrl + A* key. Double-click on **Text Body** in the **Style** sidebar:

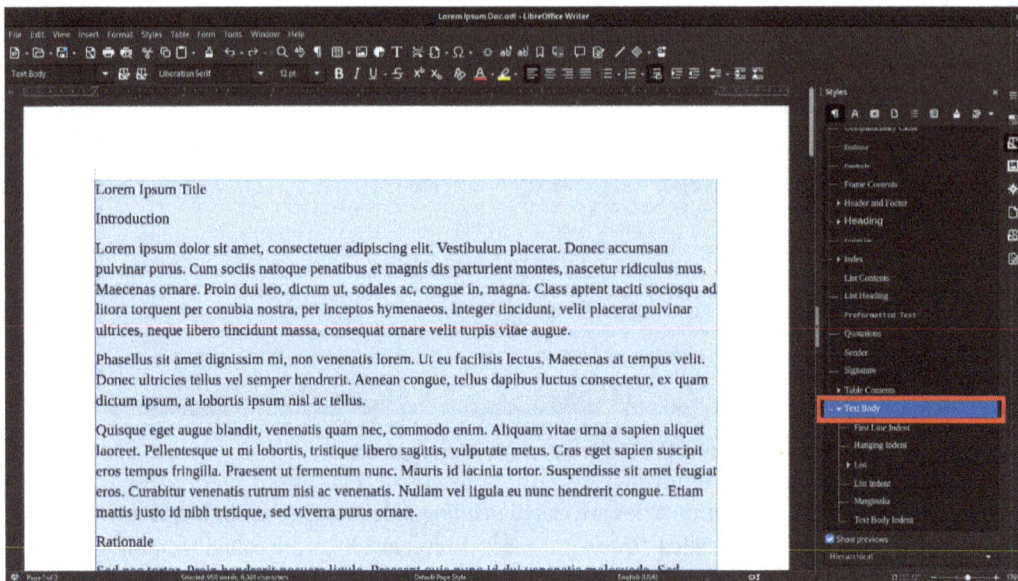

Figure 8.14 – Applying the Text Body style

Note that the paragraphs separate automatically, since the style has a spacing of **0.10"** between paragraphs. If you want to change this default spacing, right-click on the **Text Body** style and select **Modify**. Then, in the **Indents & Spacing** tab, modify the **Below paragraph** value, and then click the **OK** button.

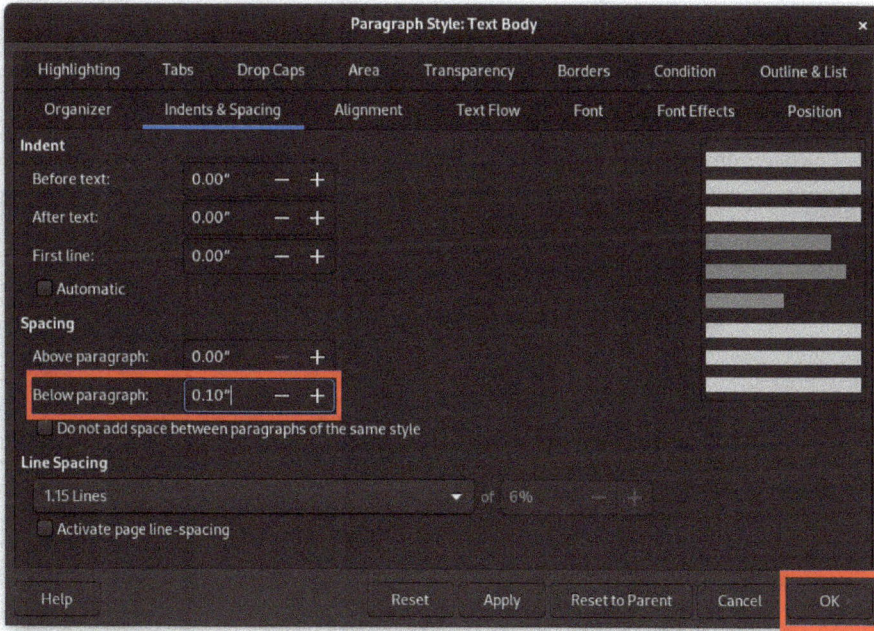

Figure 8.15 – Modifying the Below paragraph value

5. Turn the first line into the title of the document. Position the cursor on the first line, and click on the **Headings** section of the **Style** sidebar. Double-click on **Title**.

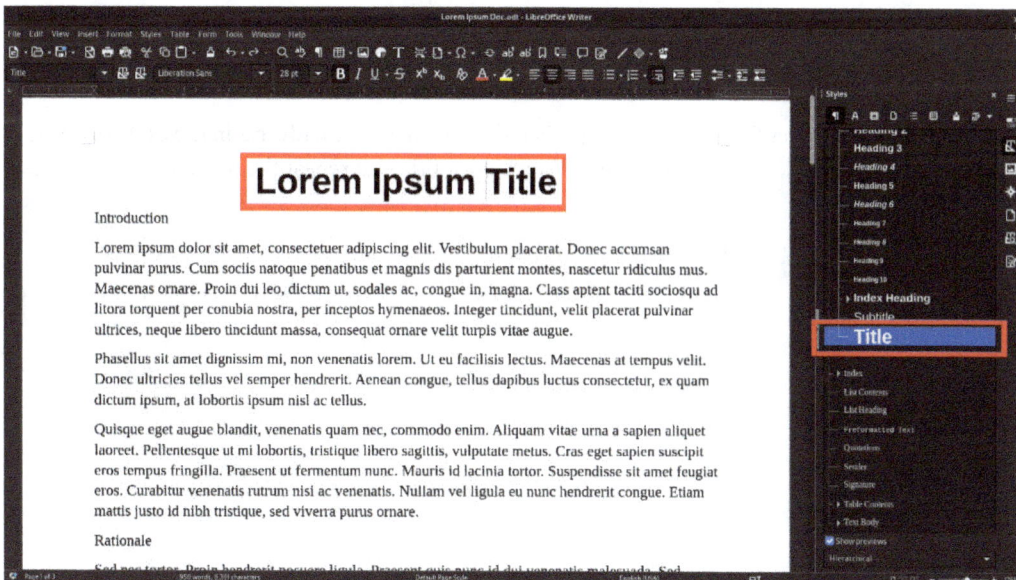

Figure 8.16 – Formatting title

Now, format the titles of the sections and subsections of the text.

The words **Introduction**, **Rationale**, and **Discussion** are *section headings*. The lines **Pros and cons** and **Follow up** are subtitles within the **Discussion** section.

6. Place the cursor on the **Introduction** line, and double-click on **Heading 1** in the **Style** sidebar.

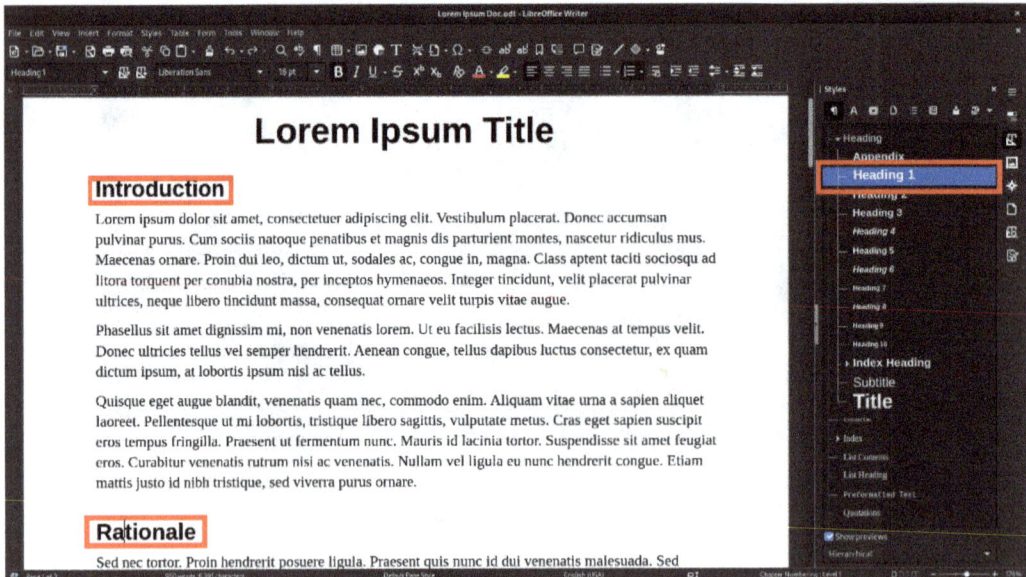

Figure 8.17 – Applying the Heading 1 style

Using the *Ctrl + 1* keys, apply the same style by placing the cursor over the words **Rationale** and **Discussion**.

7. Place the cursor over **Pros and cons**, and then double-click on **Heading 2** in the **Styles** sidebar. Then, add a sentence that follows the **Follow Up** subtitle and repeat the procedure, or use the *Ctrl + 2* keys.

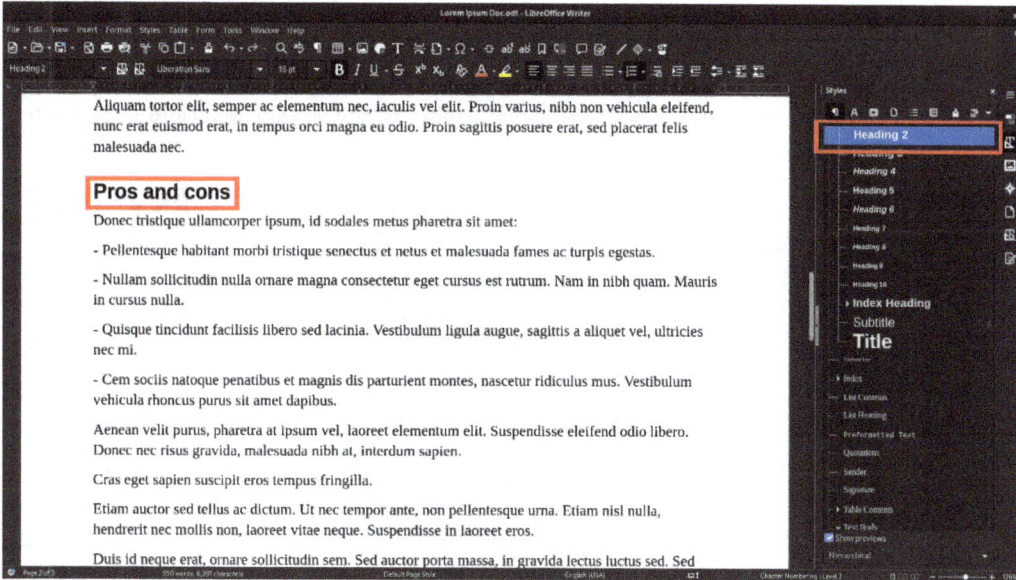

Figure 8.18 – Applying the Heading 2 style

8. In the **Pros and cons** subsection, some lines start with a *dash* (-), which means that those lines make a list. Select these lines, and double-click on the **List 1** style in the **Style** sidebar. This style adds an indentation to the lines, and if you add more lines, they become part of the list.

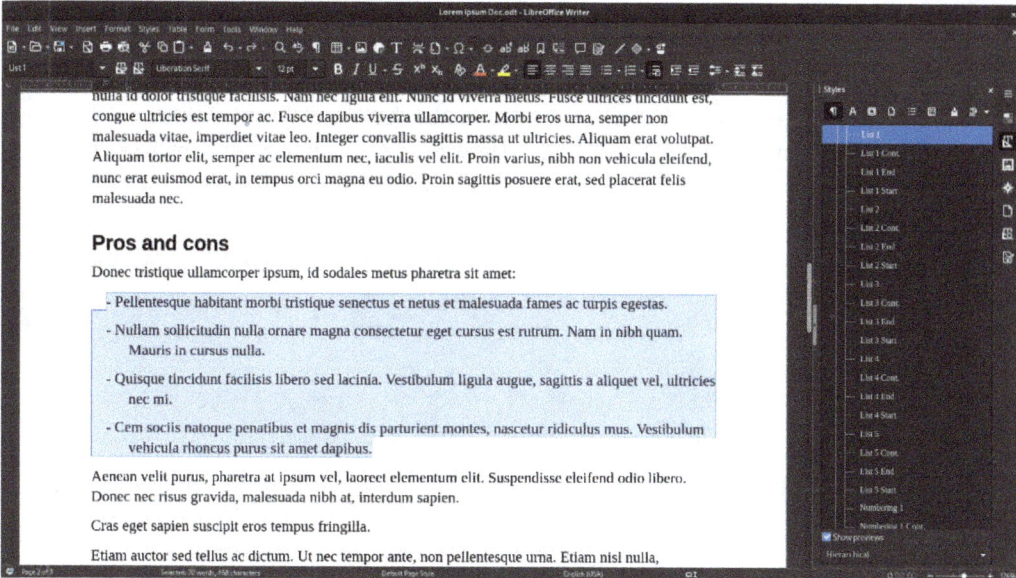

Figure 8.19 – Creating a list

Finally, let's add a *table of contents* to our formatted document.

9. Place the cursor at the end of the title, and press *Enter*. Click on the **Insert** menu, and select **Table of Contents and Index**. Click on **Table of Contents, Index or Bibliography**. The **Table of Contents, Index or Bibliography** window will appear:

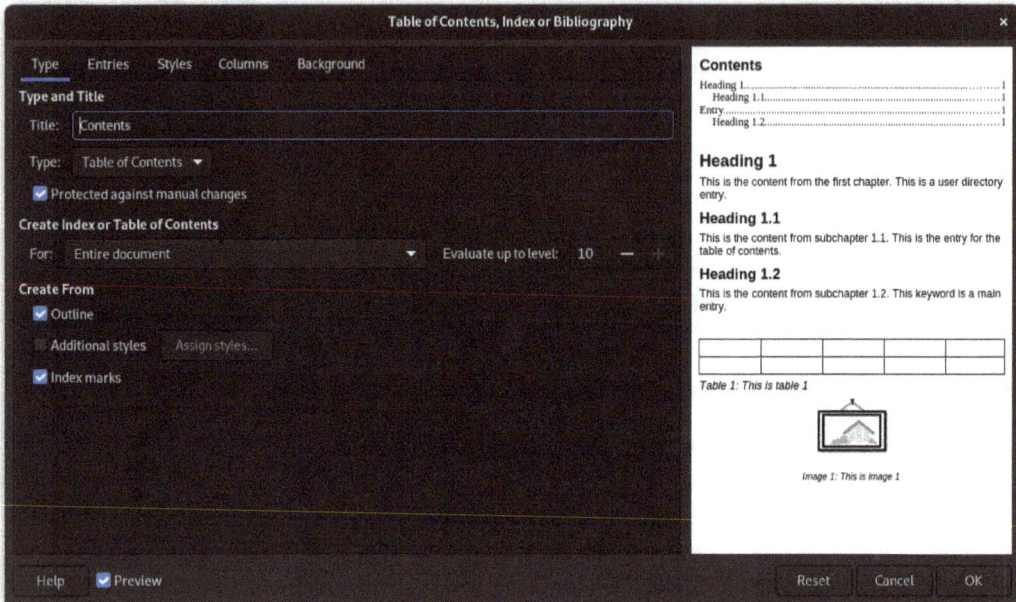

Figure 8.20 – The Table of Contents, Index or Bibliography window

10. Edit the title if desired. In the tabs of the window, make changes to the appearance of the table. Click on the **OK** button to insert the table of contents on the document, completing the example.

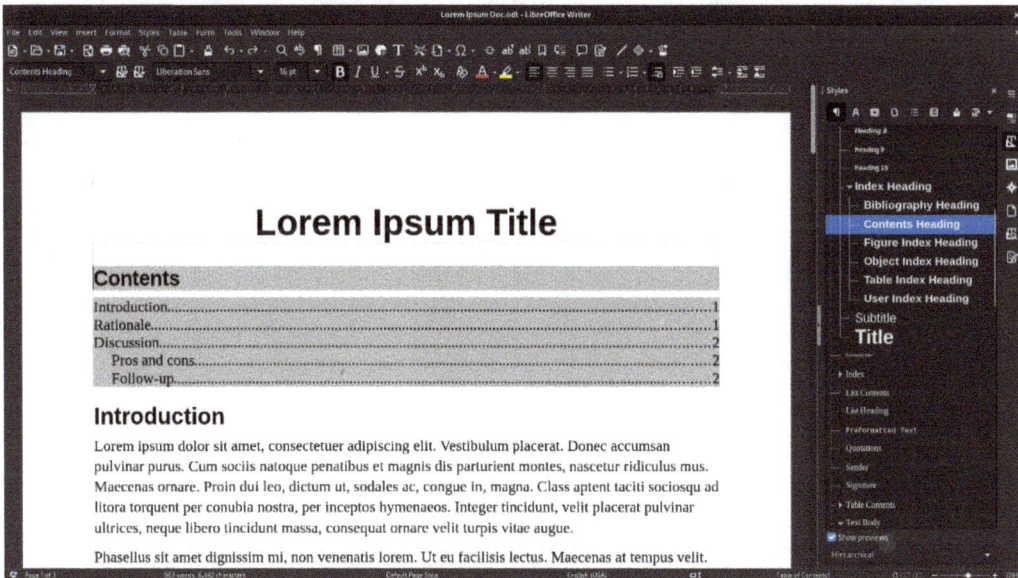

Figure 8.21 – Adding a table of contents

With these simple style changes, you can produce more professional and uniform documentation. The selected styles can be applied automatically, and you can update the table of contents by right-clicking on the table and selecting the **Update Index** option.

> **Note**
>
> For more information about applying styles in LibreOffice Writer, refer to the third-party resources on the **Document Foundation Wiki** under **Writer | Libre Office Styles Tutorial** at https://wiki.documentfoundation.org/Documentation/Third_Party_Resources.

The *properties sidebar*, some *toolbars*, and the process to *apply styles* remain the same in other **LibreOffice** components.

Now, let's get an overview of the other components and the differences in their available editing toolbars.

Calc

LibreOffice Calc is the spreadsheet component of the suite and is used to calculate, analyze, and manage data. It supports importing and modifying Microsoft Excel spreadsheets. The LibreOffice Calc interface resembles the Microsoft equivalent:

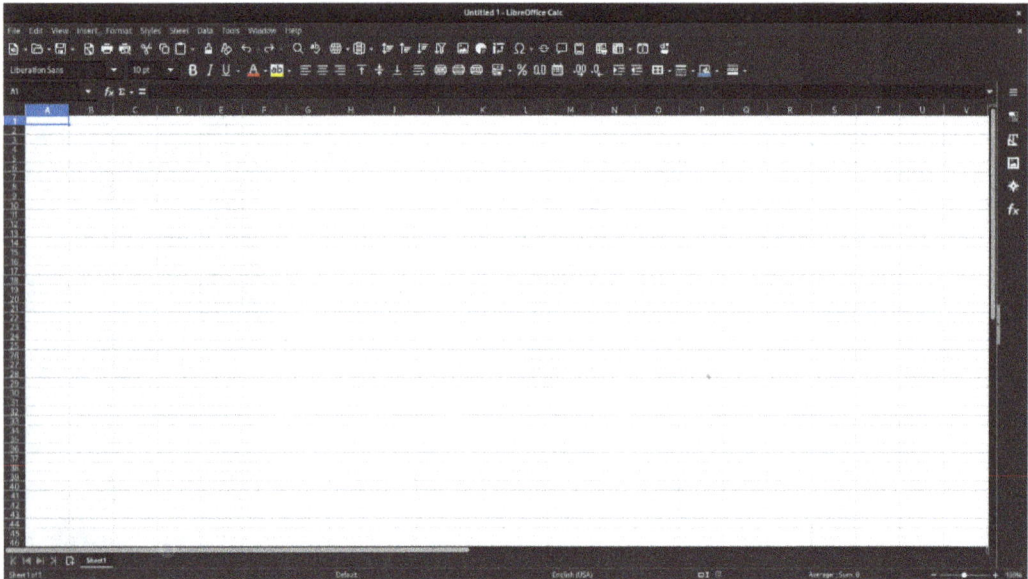

Figure 8.22 – LibreOffice Calc

Its main features include the following:

- **Calculations**: LibreOffice Calc provides functions, including statistical and banking functions, to create formulas and perform complex calculations on data. It also includes a **Function Wizard** that helps you create formulas.

- **What-if calculations**: Visualize immediate results of changes made to a calculation factor composed of several factors, as well as managing large tables using different predefined scenarios.

- **Database functions**: Use spreadsheets to organize, store, and filter data. LibreOffice Calc supports exports from databases, using drag and drop, or using a spreadsheet as a data source or as an inserted object in LibreOffice Writer.

- **Organize data**: Reorder a spreadsheet to show or hide certain ranges of data, format ranges according to special conditions, or work out quick subtotals and total calculations.

- **Dynamic charts**: LibreOffice Calc shows spreadsheet data in dynamic charts that update when data changes.

- **Opening and saving Microsoft Excel files**: Convert Microsoft Excel files and save them in a variety of other formats. The default format for LibreOffice Calc is the **ODF spreadsheet** (.ods).

The LibreOffice Calc interface looks similar to the LibreOffice Writer interface. Its main difference from the LibreOffice Writer interface is that LibreOffice Calc provides an extra **Data** menu. The **Standard** and **Formatting** toolbars include a couple of options for *cell formatting*. Calc also includes a **Formula bar**, from which *formulas for calculations* can be added:

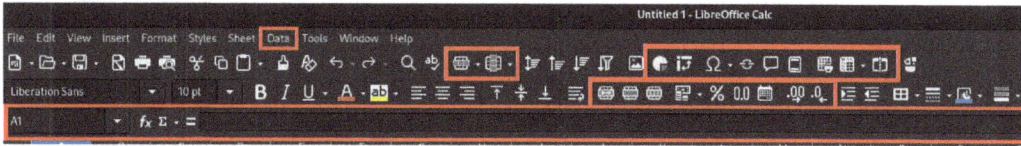

Figure 8.23 – The LibreOffice Calc interface

Let's take a look at the details of each of the differences in the **Calc** interface:

- The **Data** menu, with commands to edit the data on the current sheet – that is, define ranges, sort and filter data, calculate results, outline data, and create pivot tables:

  - **Inserting a chart**: Creates a chart in the current spreadsheet.

  - **Inserting or editing a pivot table**: Enables you to combine, compare, and analyze large amounts of data. Data can either be organized, reordered, or summarized, according to different viewpoints.

  - **Defining a print area**: Defines the range of cells in a spreadsheet to print.

  - **Freezing rows and columns**: Splits the sheet in the upper-left corner of the active cell or column. This area becomes no longer scrollable.

- The **Formatting** toolbar includes functions for Calc such as the following:

  - **Merging and centering or unmerging cells, depending on the current toggle state**: Use these options to select adjacent cells and then merge them into a single centered cell. Conversely, a large cell can be split into individual cells.

  - **Formatting as currency**: The cell receives the default currency formatting set in **Tools | Options | Language settings | Languages**.

  - **Formatting as percentage**: Applies percentage formatting to the selected cells.

  - **Formatting as number**: Applies default numeric formatting to the selected cells.

  - **Formatting as date**: Applies the default date format to selected cells based on the LibreOffice locale settings.

  - **Adding or removing decimal places**: Adds or removes a decimal place to the numbers in the selected cells.

- Use the **Formula** bar to enter formulas. Buttons are used to access the commands:

  - The **Name Box** shows a reference to the active cell, the range of selected cells, or the name of the active area.

  - The **Function Wizard** opens the wizard to help create functions.

- The **Select Function** inserts a function from a range of cells into the active cell. The function includes *Sum*, *Average*, *Minimum*, *Maximum*, and *Count*.

- **Function** adds a formula to the active cell.

> **Note**
>
> For more information about the commands and options available in **LibreOffice Calc**, refer to **LibreOffice Help** at `https://help.libreoffice.org/latest/en-US/`.

All these spreadsheet editing tools help us to document processes in the administration of Linux systems, when creating and/or editing inventories or databases of administration elements, such as servers, routers, users, and passwords.

Now, let's take a look at the component that manages slide shows and images in the LibreOffice suite.

Creating slides and image management

Following the documentation of processes, assisted by Writer, and the inventory of administrable elements, supported by Calc, it is time to present a summary of the status, advancement, or performance of our projects. The LibreOffice component to help us create professional presentations is **LibreOffice Impress**.

LibreOffice Impress enables us to create professional slide shows, which can include graphics, drawing objects, text, multimedia, and a lot of other elements, as well as importing and changing Microsoft PowerPoint presentations.

For onscreen slide shows, LibreOffice Impress includes features such as animation, slide transitions, and multimedia playback.

As in the case of Writer and Calc, the Impress interface is similar to its Microsoft product peer, Microsoft PowerPoint.

One of the few differences occurs upon opening LibreOffice Impress. Impress displays the **Select a Template** window:

Figure 8.24 – Opening LibreOffice Impress

LibreOffice includes a set of built-in templates to create documents, presentations, spreadsheets, or drawings. Using the templates available in the template manager, you can create your own templates or search online for extra templates.

Templates save editing time by opening new documents with the content and formatting already complete. The **Template Manager** provides access to and the organization of templates in LibreOffice.

Previews of available templates appear in the *main window* of the Template Manager, based on the search and filtering options. Double-click on any template icon to open a new document with the template content and formatting.

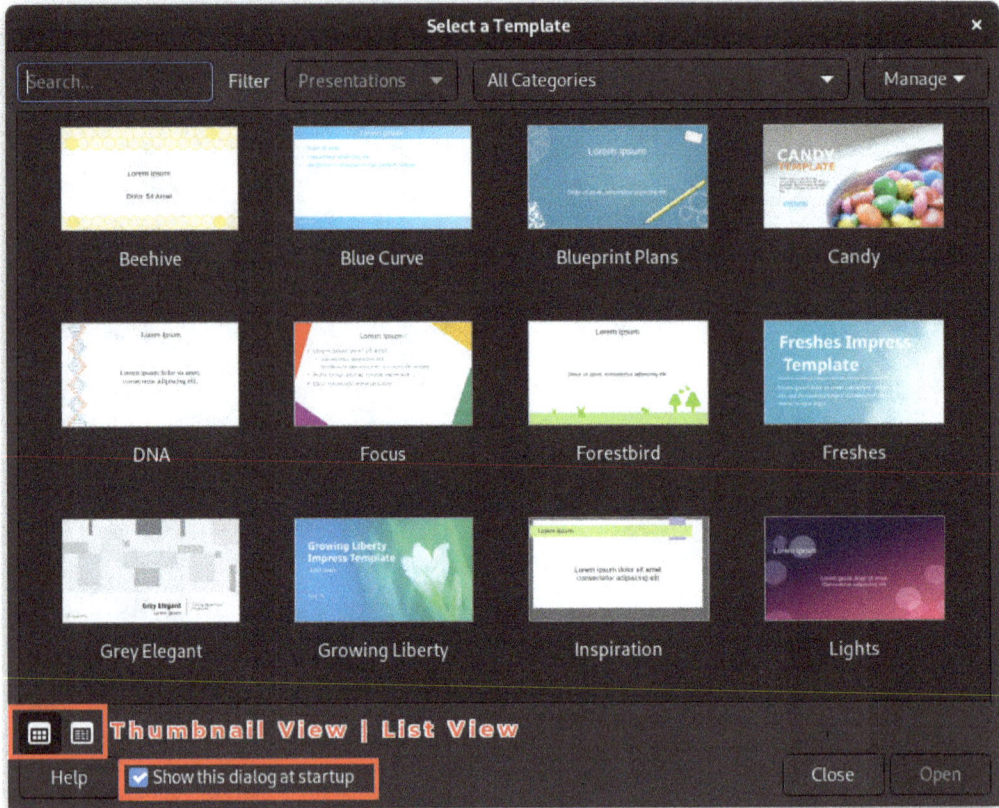

Figure 8.25 – The Template Manager

Select **Thumbnail View** or **List View** at the bottom-left to change the way the templates appear.

You can disable the display of the Template Manager window by clicking on the **Show this dialog at startup** checkbox.

The main differences between the **Writer** and **Calc** interface are that LibreOffice Impress provides a couple of extra menus – **Slide** and **Slide Show**. On Impress, the **Formatting** toolbar does not load at startup and instead displays the **Drawing** toolbar. It also includes the **Standard** toolbar, access to commands to present slides, and the **Presentation** toolbar:

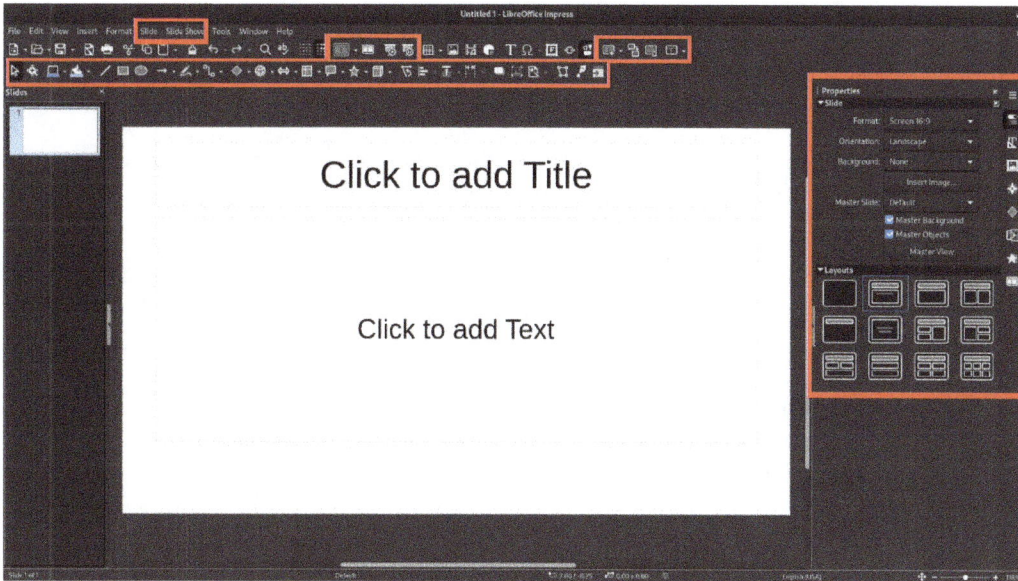

Figure 8.26 – The LibreOffice Impress interface

The **Properties** sidebar is also different, as it focuses on slides.

Let's take a look at the details of each of the differences in the Impress interface:

- The **Slide** menu provides navigation and slide management commands – you can *create*, *edit*, *duplicate*, and *delete* slides, as well as *insert slides from another presentation*.

- The **Slide Show** menu contains commands and options to play a presentation. This includes *starting* the slide show, *defining settings*, adding a *timer*, and defining *object interaction*, *animations*, and *transitions*.

- The **Standard** toolbar includes functions for Impress, such as the following:

  - **Display Views**, in **Edit Modes** or **Master Modes**.

  - **Master Slide** switches to **Master Slide View**, where we can add desired elements that appear on all slides using the same master slide.

  - **Start from First Slide** and **Start from Current Slide** state the origin point to display the slide show.

  - Use the **Slide** bar buttons to manage slides – **New Slide**, **Duplicate Slide**, **Delete Slide**, and **Slide Layout**.

- The **Drawing** bar contains common editing tools. The **Drawing** bar is also available in a text document or a spreadsheet. The set of visible icons could differ depending on the type of active document. Editing tools include the following:

  - The **Select** tool (a *white arrow*) allows you to select an object on the active slide
  - **Zoom & Pan**
  - **Line Color**
  - **Fill Color**
  - **Insert Line**
  - **Inserting different shapes**: Basic, Rectangle, Ellipse, Lines and Arrows, Symbol, Block Arrows, Connectors, Curves and Polygons, Flowchart, Callouts, Stars and Banners, and 3D Objects
  - **Object management**: Rotate, align, arrange, and distribute
  - **Image management**: Add shadow, crop, filter, points, and glue points functions (the point where a connection line could be set)
  - **Toggle Extrusion**

> **Note**
>
> For more information about the commands and options available in LibreOffice Impress, refer to **LibreOffice Help** at `https://help.libreoffice.org/latest/en-US/`.

The LibreOffice components help us to improve the documentation of our managed systems. In the following chapters, we will use them to establish a standardized system baseline.

Summary

In this chapter, we provided an overview of Linux office suites. Some of them are integrated into the official Fedora Linux repositories, and we added some fonts that could help us to improve the look and feel of the documentation made with an office suite.

We walked through the main components of LibreOffice, included by default in the Workstation version of Fedora Linux. **Writer**, the *text editor*, helps us to create process documentation, and we learned how to apply styles to documents, improving the appearance and organization of our documentation.

With **Calc**, the *spreadsheet editor*, we can create inventories and databases of our managed devices. We reviewed the main differences between the available tools to edit spreadsheets and the text editor.

Finally, we learned how to make *slide shows* of our documentation, using **Impress**. We also discussed the differences between its editing tools and those of the other components of LibreOffice.

In the following chapter, we will review mail clients and browsers, closing the journey of the productivity tools offered by Fedora Linux. These tools will help us to organize the documentation of administration processes using Linux systems.

Further reading

To learn more about the topics covered in this chapter, you can visit the following links:

- *Office Suites for Fedora*: `https://flylib.com/books/en/1.303.1.85/1/`
- *Fedora Magazine – Apps for daily needs part 2: office suites*: `https://fedoramagazine.org/apps-for-daily-needs-part-2-office-suites/`
- Fedora Docs – *Adding New Fonts in Fedora*: `https://docs.fedoraproject.org/en-US/quick-docs/fonts/`
- *LibreOffice Timeline*: `https://www.libreoffice.org/about-us/libreoffice-timeline/`
- *LibreOffice Help*: `https://help.libreoffice.org/latest/en-US/`
- LibreOffice – *Documentation/Third Party Resources*: `https://wiki.documentfoundation.org/Documentation/Third_Party_Resources`

9
Mail Clients and Browsers

The internet began as ARPAnet, a packet-switched network sponsored by the US government, in September 1969. *Linus Torvalds* wouldn't be born until December of that same year. In 1991, when Linux emerged, only academics, researchers, and the military were on the internet. For most people, *being online* meant connecting with a **v.32 modem**, at the astonishing speed of **9600 BPS (baud per second)** to a **Bulletin Board System (BBS)**, or an online service. The internet as we knew it could be accessed through ASCII-based applications such as `Pine` and `Elm` for email, using command line programs such as `ftp` and `Archie` to search and share files. The most advanced tool available was `Gopher`, a Yahoo-like guide to internet resources. Then, *Tim Berners-Lee* invented the World Wide Web, and everything changed.

Today, internet access has improved a lot with higher speeds. This has led to the emergence of different tools for reading emails and surfing the web.

In this chapter, we will discuss the most common tools available in Fedora Linux, covering the following main topics:

- Mailing with Evolution
- Mailing with Thunderbird
- Trusty old Firefox
- Expanding browsing with Google Chrome

Technical requirements

For the development of the topics in this chapter, it is necessary to install the packages indicated in each section. The Firefox browser is the only package installed by default in the Workstation version of Fedora Linux.

In each section, you will find instructions for the different types of installation of each package as required.

Mailing with Evolution

In 2000, Linux distributions didn't have an email client that provided the functionality and interoperability needed for corporate users. Then, *Ximian* decided to develop **Evolution**. Evolution version 1.0 was released in December 2001. It offered Ximian a *proprietary plug-in* that allows users to connect with Microsoft Exchange Server. Evolution was open source software from the beginning, but Ximian's connector was sold as proprietary software. Thus, Ximian could generate revenue. When Novell acquired Ximian in August 2003, Novell decided to integrate the Exchange plugin as open source, starting in May 2004 on **Evolution 2.0**.

Novell was acquired by **the Attachmate Group** in 2011. As a result, Novell's developers moved to **SUSE**. In 2012, SUSE decided to withdraw funding for Evolution development.

Red Hat continued with Evolution development. This resulted in the active development of Evolution and the need for an email client with good support for Microsoft Exchange.

Evolution works as the default personal information manager in most Linux distributions that use GNOME by default, especially Debian and Fedora Linux.

In December 2018, the Fedora Project decided to drop Evolution from the default installation of the Workstation version, starting on Fedora Linux 30. However, Evolution is still available in the official repositories, allowing you to install and use it as a personal information manager.

Now, let's see how to install and configure Evolution on our workstation. Follow the following steps:

1. To install Evolution, Fedora Linux offers several options. From the **Software** application, select **Evolution** for installation, from your preferred source:

    *   **RPM**
    *   **Fedora Flatpak**

- **Flathub**

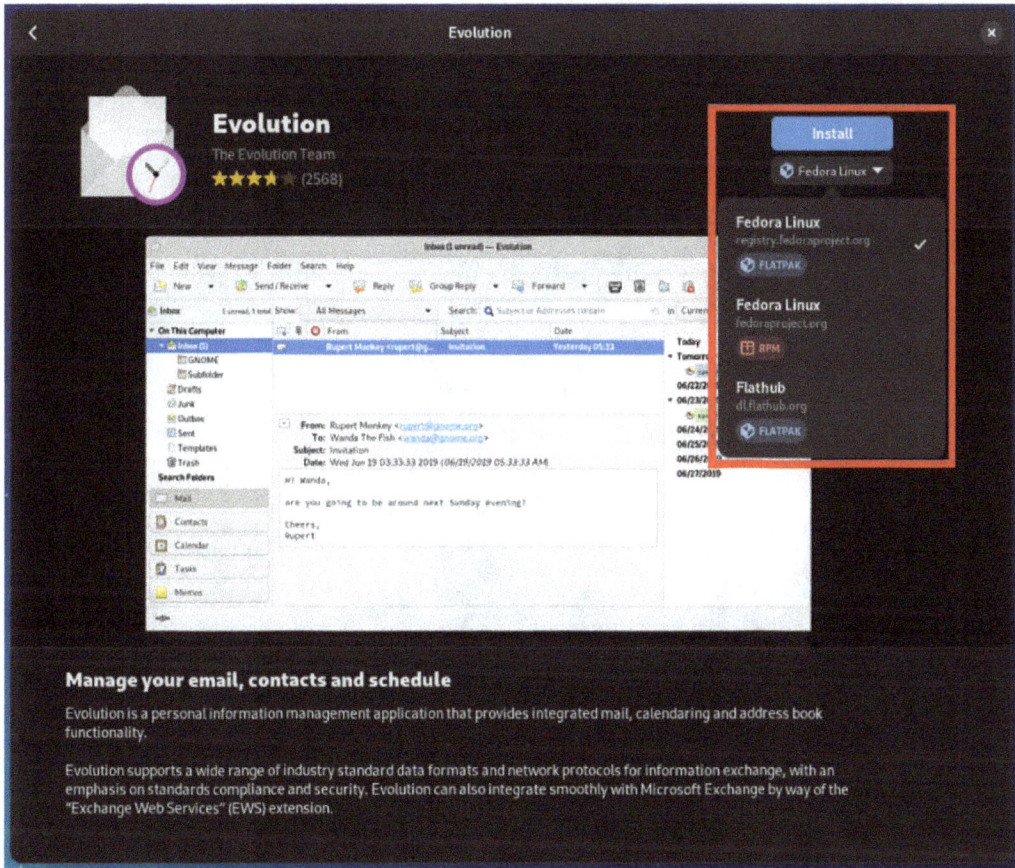

Figure 9.1 – Installing Evolution from a software application

2. Using the terminal, with the `dnf` command, you can see the available packages and plugins. Switch to the `root` user and run the following:

```
# dnf list *evolution*
```

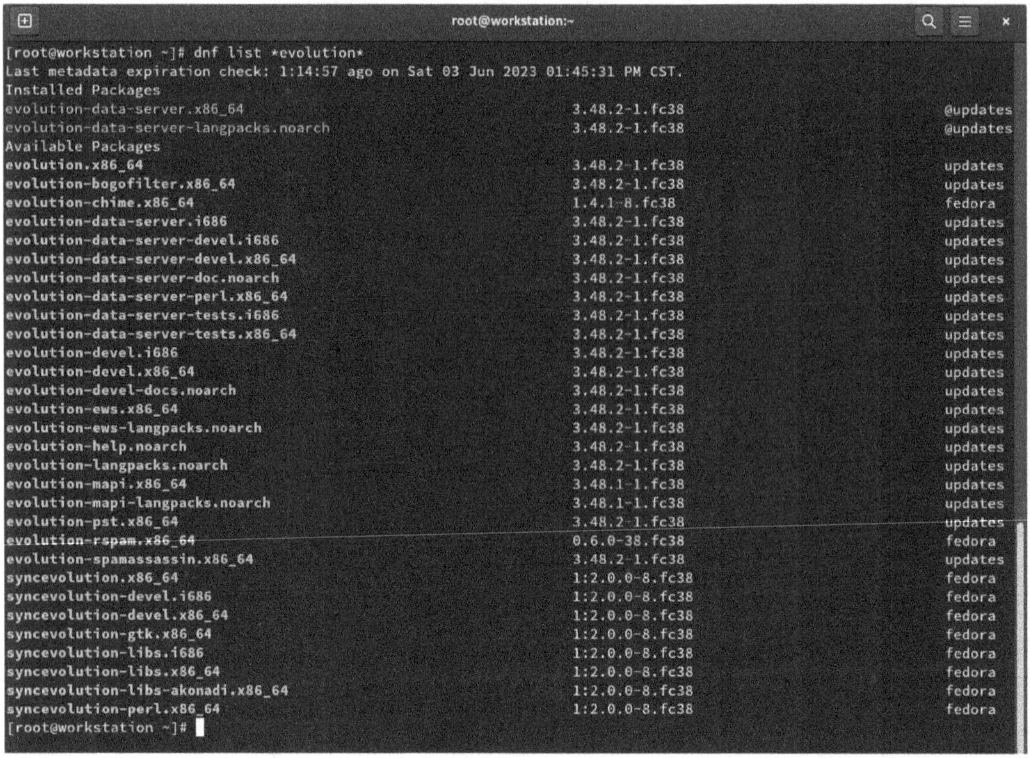

Figure 9.2 – Evolution and plugins

Install **Evolution** by your preferred method, and then we'll start with the mail client configuration.

3. To open **Evolution**, launch it from the menu. As a *non-root user*, open the menu in the upper-
    left corner and type `Evolution` in the search box:

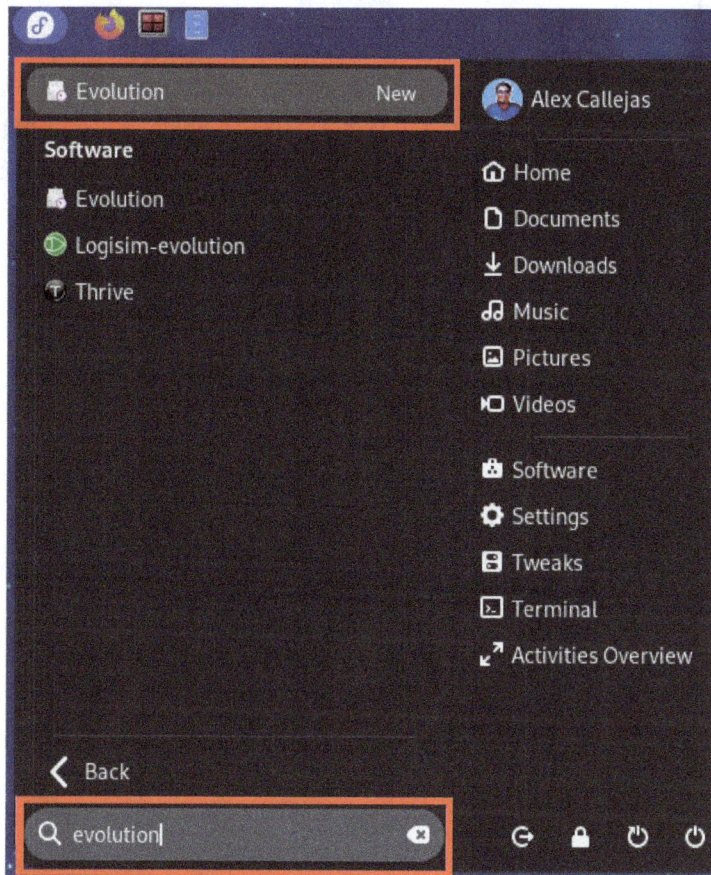

Figure 9.3 – Evolution from the menu

Evolution can also be accessed from the **Activities Overview** menu. Type `evolution` in the search bar:

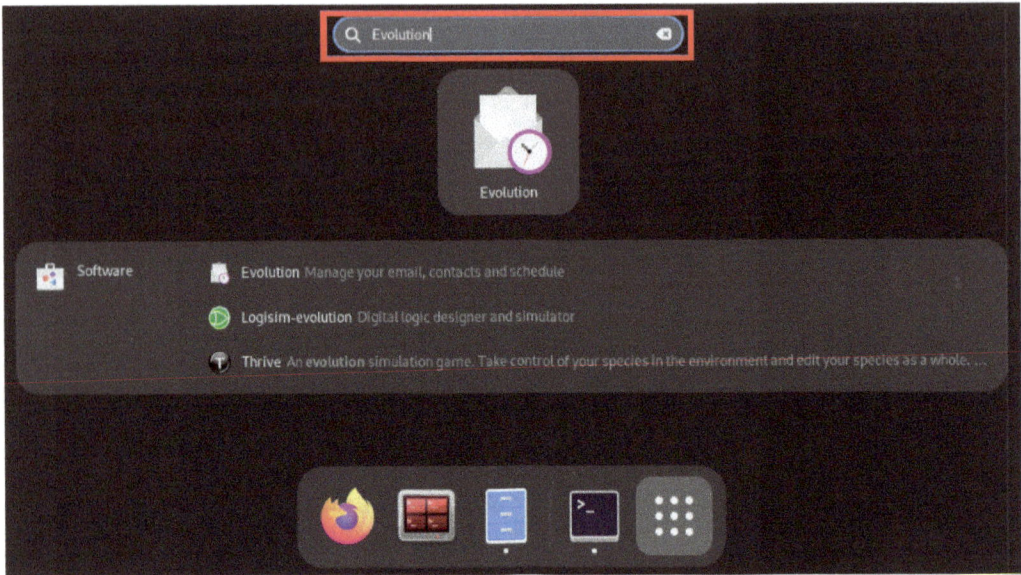

Figure 9.4 – Evolution from the Activities Overview menu

4.   When **Evolution** opens for the first time, set it as the default email client if you like:

Figure 9.5 – Configuring Evolution as the default email client

5. In the **Welcome** screen, it'll ask you to set up an email account. Click the **Next** button to start the configuration:

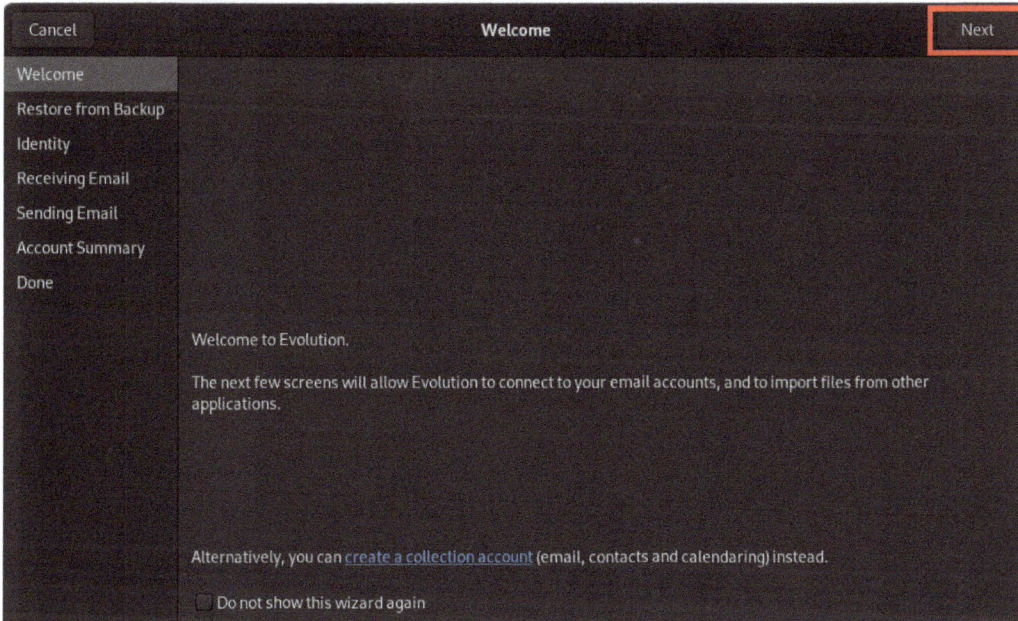

Figure 9.6 – The Evolution configuration wizard

6. The first option offered is to restore a backup of the Evolution configuration to set up the email account.

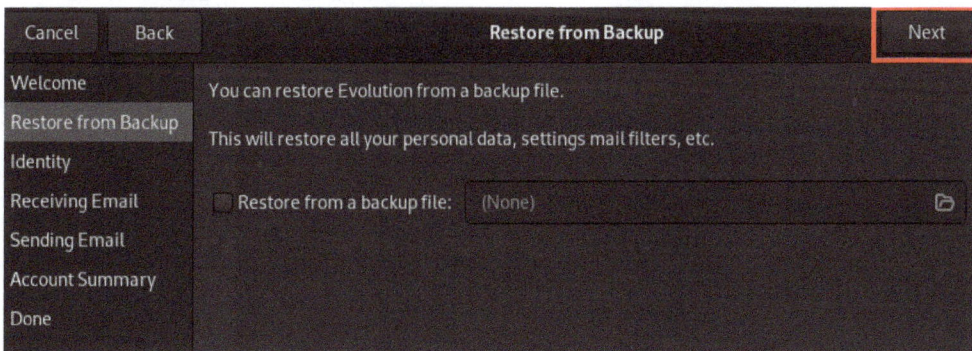

Figure 9.7 – The Restore from backup window

If you have a backup, check the **Restore from a backup file** box, and click on the **Browse** icon to select the file and restore the backup.

If don't have an Evolution backup, click on the **Next** button to continue with the configuration.

7. In the following window, fill in the requested data – **Full Name** and **Email Address**:

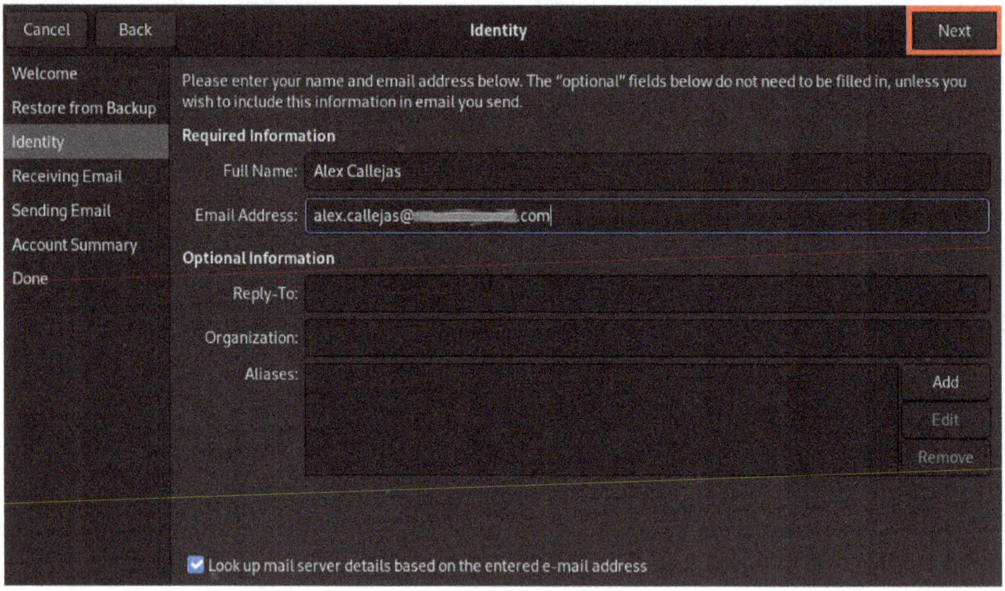

Figure 9.8 – The Identity window

More information can be added, such as the *name of the organization* or the *aliases* managed by the account.

When finished, click the **Next** button to continue with the configuration.

8. If Evolution activates, it will search for the mail service information for the account entered. If this is not found, it will provide configuration options for receiving mail:

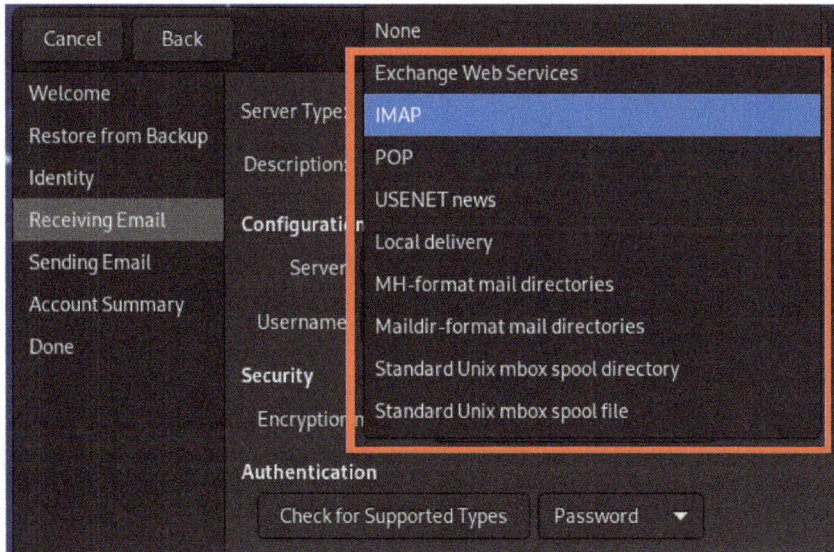

Figure 9.9 – Receiving mail options

The options are as follows:

- **Exchange Web Services**: Connects to **Microsoft Exchange** servers to synchronize email, calendar, and contact information.

- **IMAP**: Maintains email on the server, so email can be accessed from multiple systems through the IMAP protocol. **IMAP** stands for **Internet Message Access Protocol**.

- **POP**: Downloads email to the hard disk for permanent storage as an option, freeing up space on the email server. **POP** stands for **Post-Office Protocol**.

- **USENET news**: It connects to a news server and downloads a list of available news summaries.

- **Local delivery**: Move the email from the spool and store it in the home directory.

- **MH-format mail directories**: Downloads emails using mh (**Message Handling System**) or an *mh-style* program. mh consists of several different programs designed to work from the command line. Instead of storing many messages in a single file, each message has its own separate file in a special directory.

- **Maildir-format mail directories**: Downloads emails using a *Maildir-style* program. The Maildir email format is a common way of storing email messages. Each message is stored in a separate file with a unique name, and each mail folder is a filesystem directory.

- **Standard Unix mbox spool directory**: Downloads emails in the format used by Unix hosts to store mail messages. The mbox files usually live in the *system mail spool*, under various names in users' mail directories and under the name mbox in users' home directories.

- **Standard Unix mbox spool file**: This is the same case as the previous option, but the *mail spool* is created in a single file.

> **Note**
>
> Confirm general mail access data, such as **server type** and **security,** with the staff of the corresponding area to avoid connectivity problems.

9. After selecting the option to receive mail, enter the access data, as shown in the following figure:

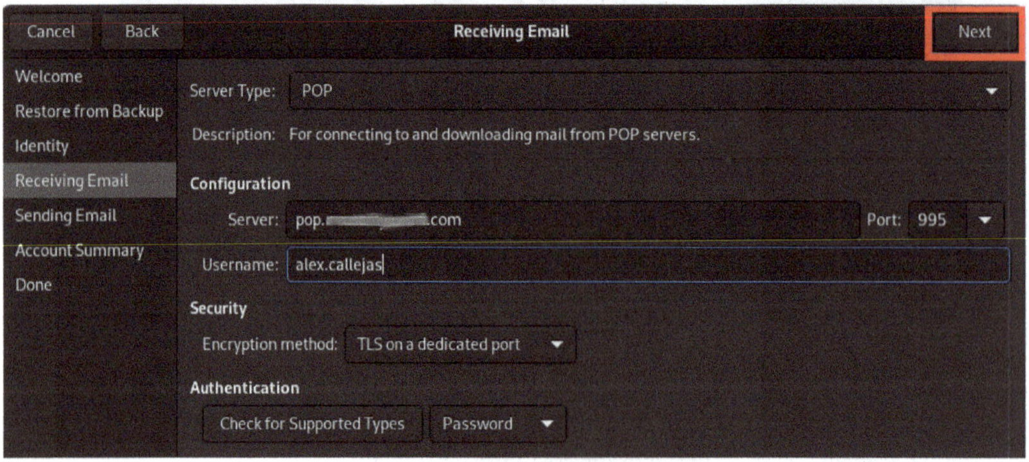

Figure 9.10 – The Receiving Email window

Click the **Next** button to continue with the configuration.

10. In the following window, configure the mail reception options, such as the time interval to check new mails, or whether a copy of the mail should be left on the server, as well as enabling or disabling functions:

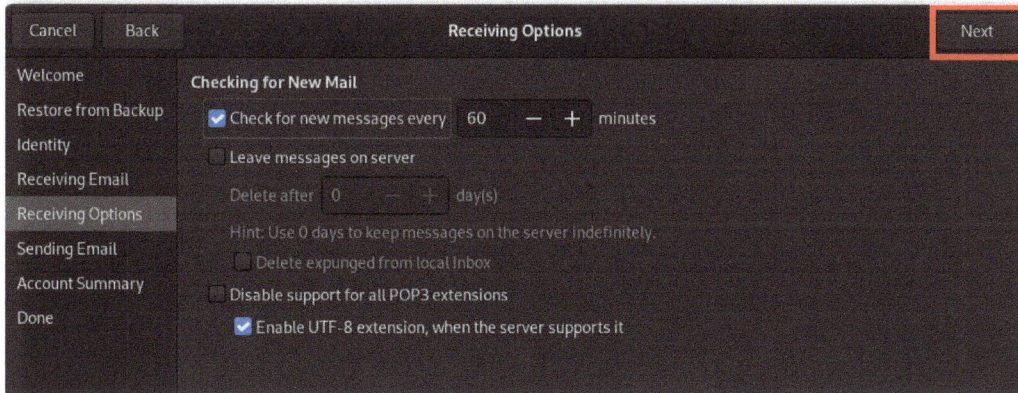

Figure 9.11 – The Receiving Options window

Click the **Next** button to continue with the configuration.

11. In the following window, configure the **Sending Email** options:

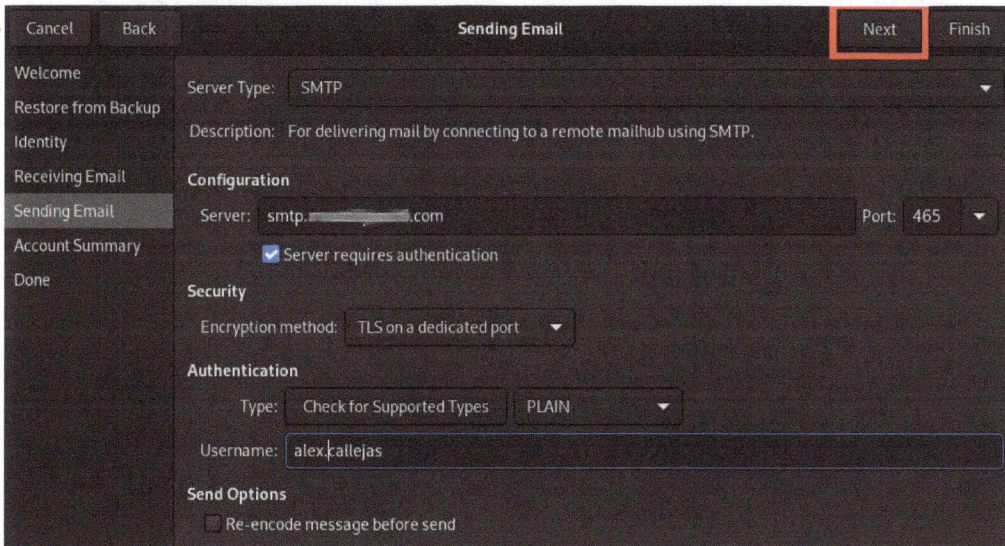

Figure 9.12 – The Sending Email window

By default, the wizard fills the **Sending Email** fields with the login information provided for the mail reception. If this information is correct and enough for sending emails, click the **Finish** button to end the configuration.

If you want to review all the information provided, click the **Next** button.

12. The following window shows a summary of the data configured for the account:

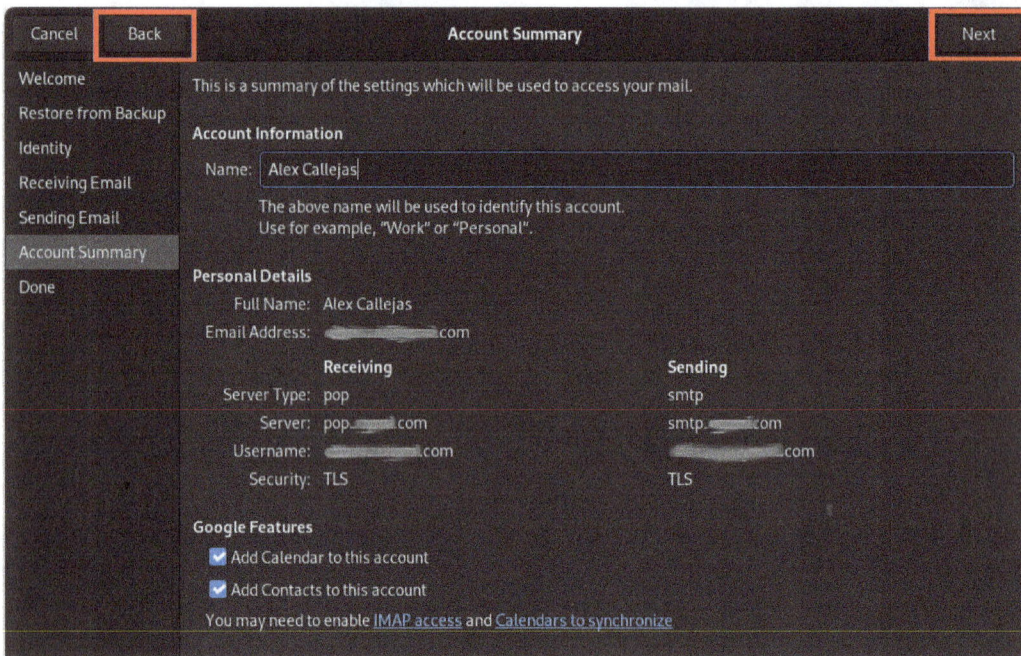

Figure 9.13 – The Account Summary window

If any information needs to be changed, click on the **Back** button to return to the window where it is required to change the data.

If the information is correct, click the **Next** button.

13. The following window confirms the end of the mail account configuration:

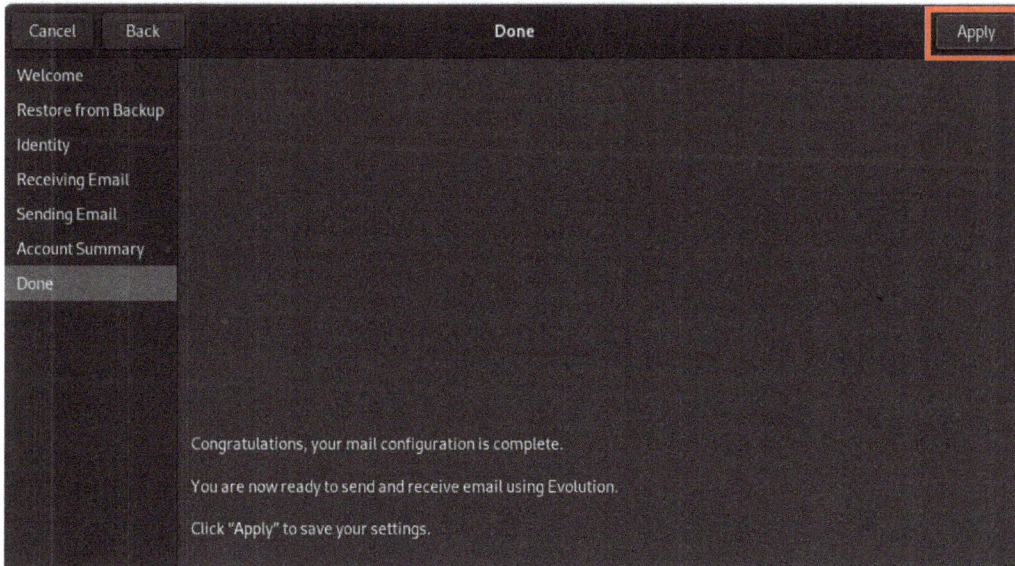

Figure 9.14 – The completed mail configuration window

14. Click the **Apply** button to save the settings.

With the account now set up, email is ready to be checked and sent.

In the main window of Evolution, in the upper-left corner, there are buttons to send/receive mail and create a new mail.

To send or receive mail, click on the **Send/Receive** button:

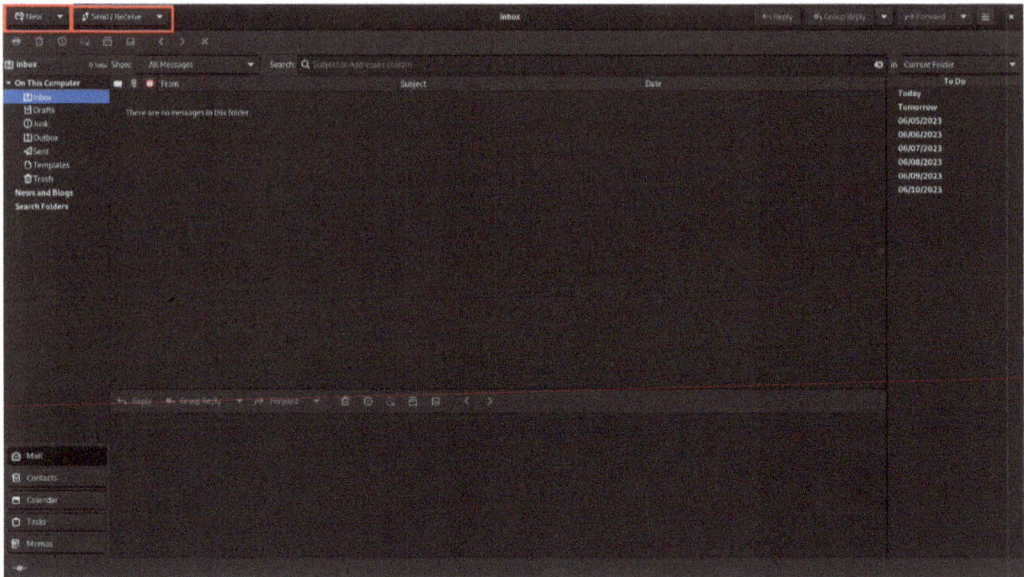

Figure 9.15 – The Evolution main window

To create an email, click the **New** button:

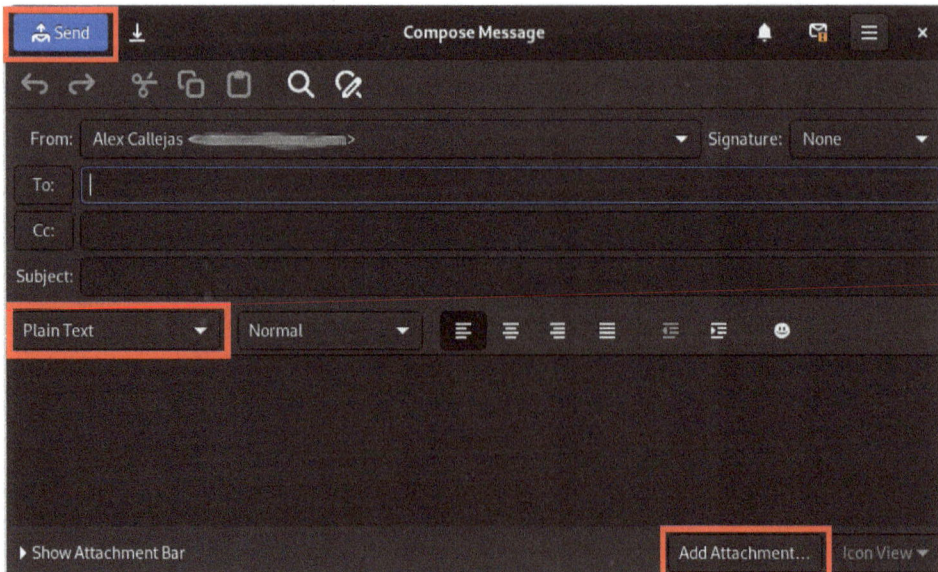

Figure 9.16 – The Compose Message window

In the *new message composition* window, fill in the recipient and subject of the email. Additionally, choose the format of the email (*plain text*, *rich text*, or *HTML*), as well as add attachments with the button in the lower-right corner.

When the email message is ready for delivery, click on the **Send** button.

Evolution is currently the default client in several Linux distributions. Some alternative mail clients exist, but they do not have all the options that Evolution has.

One of the clients with more options, which is an alternative to Evolution, is Mozilla Thunderbird.

Let's now take a walk through this mail client and see its main differences with Evolution.

Mailing with Thunderbird

Mozilla Thunderbird is a cross-platform, free, and open source email, news, RSS, and chat client, developed by the Mozilla Foundation. It uses the XUL interface language. **XML User Interface Language (XUL)** is an XML-based user interface language developed by Mozilla. XUL works as an XML dialect, providing graphical user interfaces such as web pages. XUL is not a public standard.

On December 7, 2004, *version 1.0* was released and received over 500,000 downloads in its first 3 days of release, and 1 million in 10 days.

On July 6, 2012, Mozilla announced that the company was dropping the Thunderbird development priority because the ongoing effort to expand Thunderbird's feature set was unsuccessful. On December 1, 2015, Mozilla's CEO announced that the development of Thunderbird should be separated from Firefox.

Recently, Thunderbird announced on its official blog that one of the same Mozilla subsidiaries (**MZLA Technologies Corporation**) will continue with the project, with new updates, a new design, and a mobile application.

Thunderbird is installed by default on the desktop systems of several Linux distributions. It is not installed by default in Fedora Linux, but it is available in the official repositories.

Let's see how to install and configure Thunderbird on our Fedora Linux Workstation. Follow the following steps:

1. To install Mozilla Thunderbird, Fedora Linux offers several options, but it is only available as a Flatpak package. From the software application, to install Mozilla Thunderbird, select your preferred option:

    *   **Fedora Linux** (Flatpak)
    *   **Flathub**

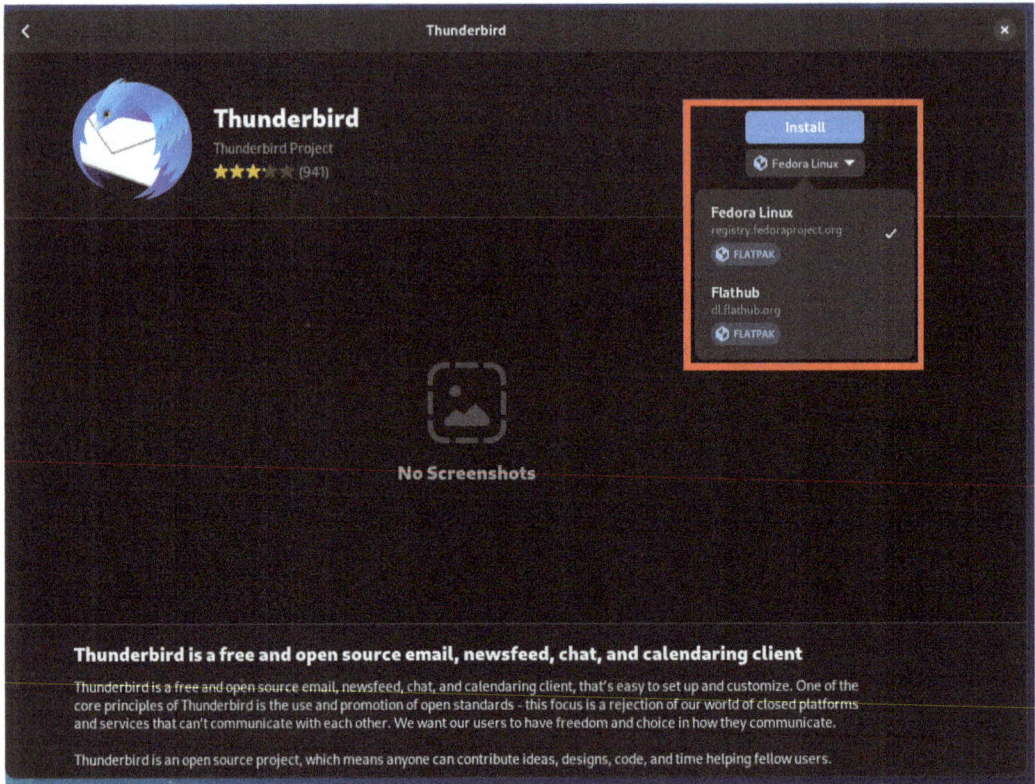

Figure 9.17 – Installing Thunderbird from a software application

2. Using the terminal, with the `dnf` command, you can see the available packages and plugins. Switch to the `root` user and run the following:

```
# dnf list *thunderbird*
```

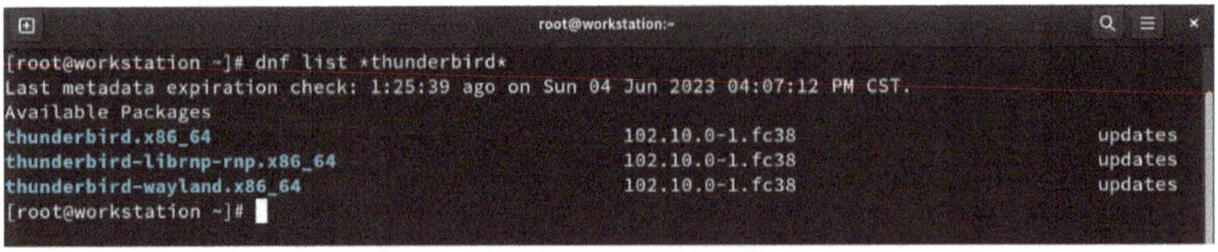

Figure 9.18 – Thunderbird and plugins

Install Mozilla Thunderbird by your preferred method, and then we'll start with the mail client configuration.

3. To open Mozilla Thunderbird, launch it from the menu. As a *non-root user*, open the menu in the upper-left corner and type `Thunderbird` in the search box:

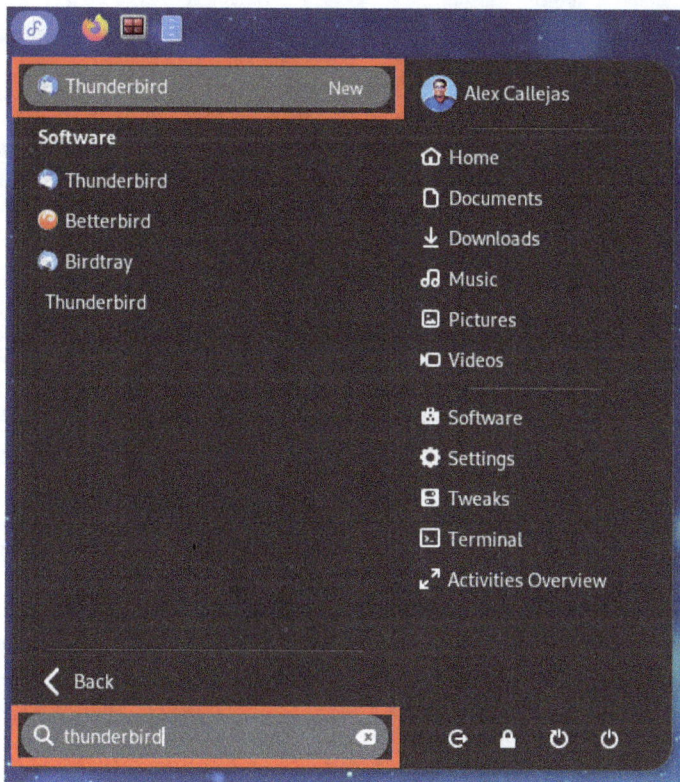

Figure 9.19 – Launching Thunderbird from the menu

Mozilla Thunderbird can also be accessed from the **Activities Overview** menu. Type `thunderbird` in the search bar:

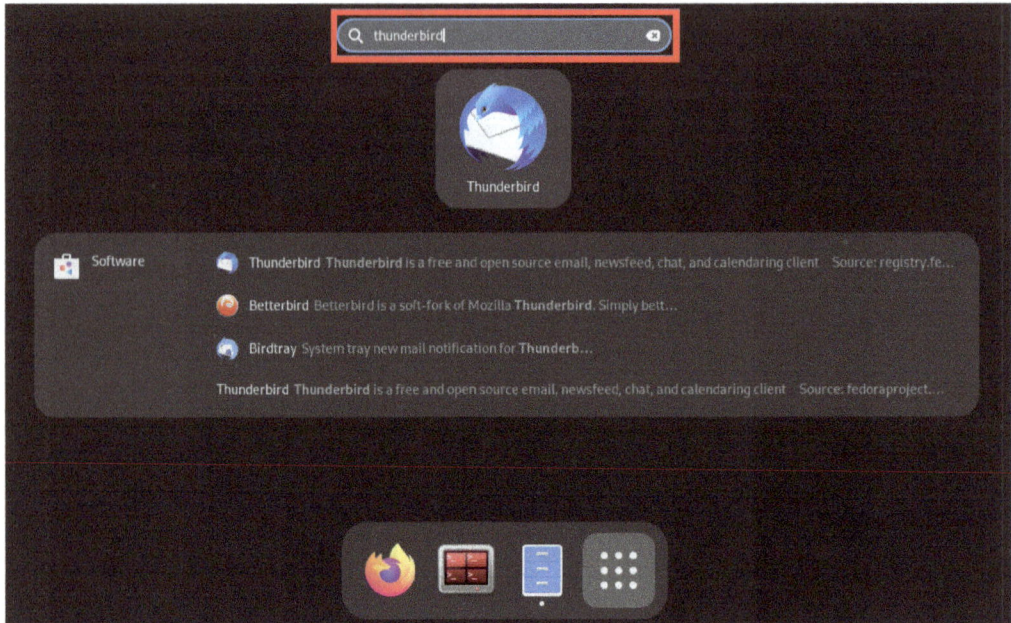

Figure 9.20 – Thunderbird from the Activities Overview menu

4.   When Mozilla Thunderbird opens for the first time, it will ask you to set up an email account:

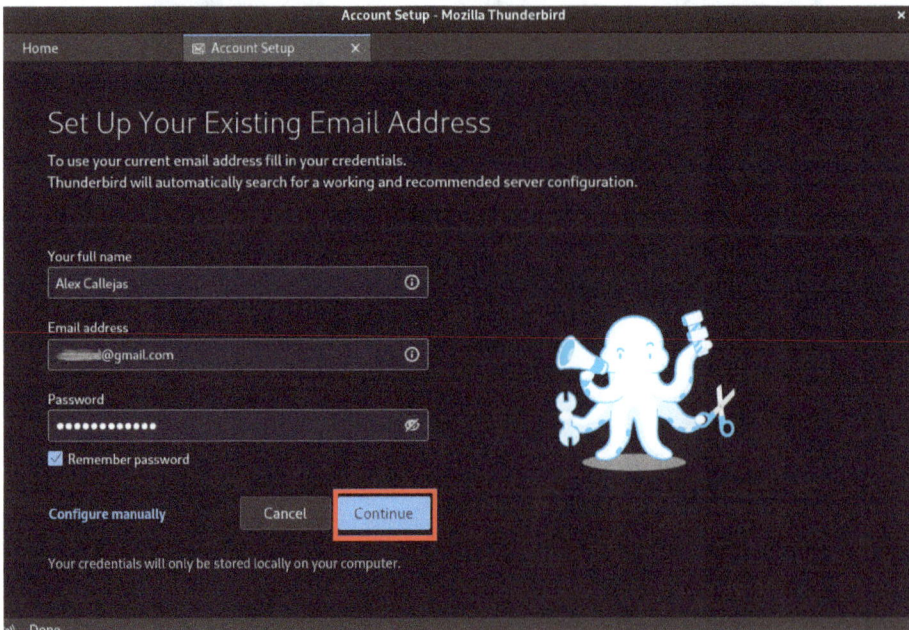

Figure 9.21 – The Account Setup window

Fill in the requested data, and click on the **Continue** button.

> **Note**
>
> In my case, I entered a Google email account. If your workstation is connected to the internet, Mozilla Thunderbird will try to get the information from the servers of the mail service. It will only get the information if it is accessible.

The following window shows the data of the available configurations downloaded. Select the configuration of your preference, and click on the **Done** button:

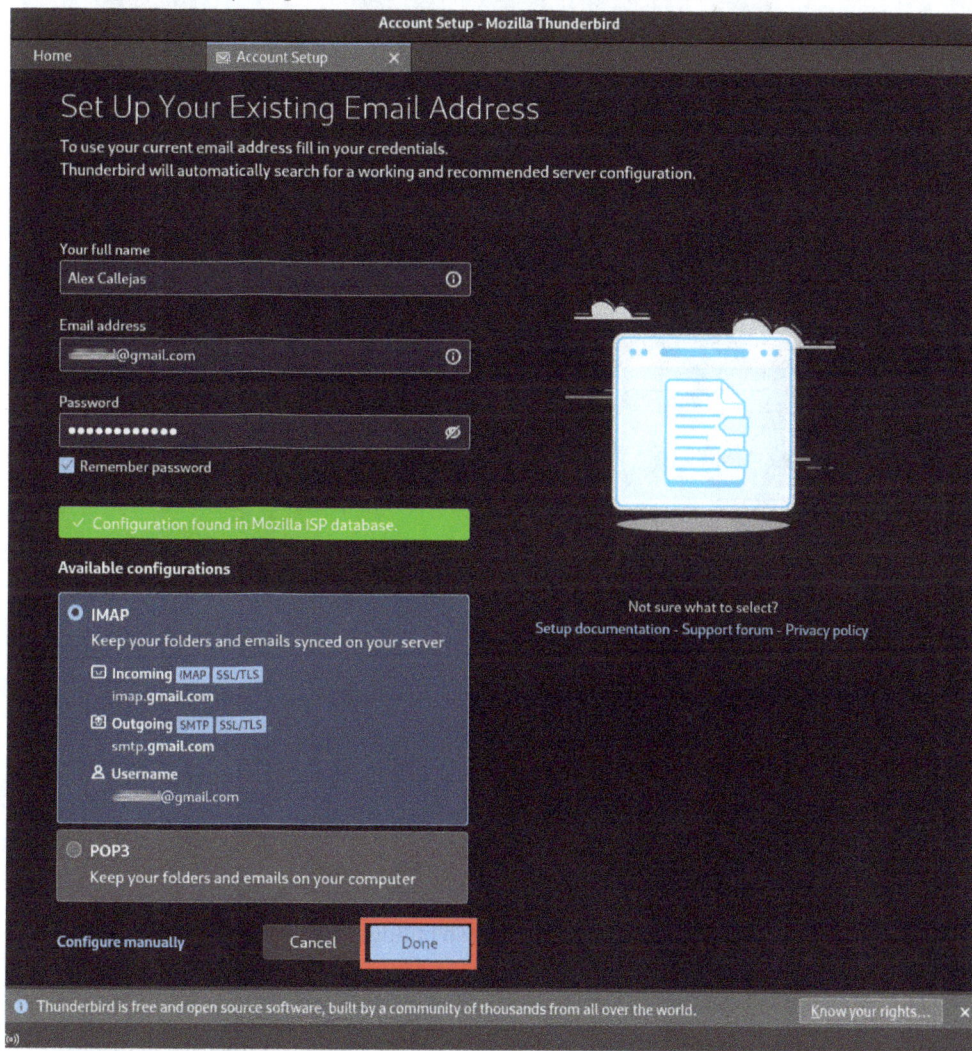

Figure 9.22 – The available configurations downloaded

Mozilla Thunderbird will offer to connect the services found in the account, such as the address books or calendars:

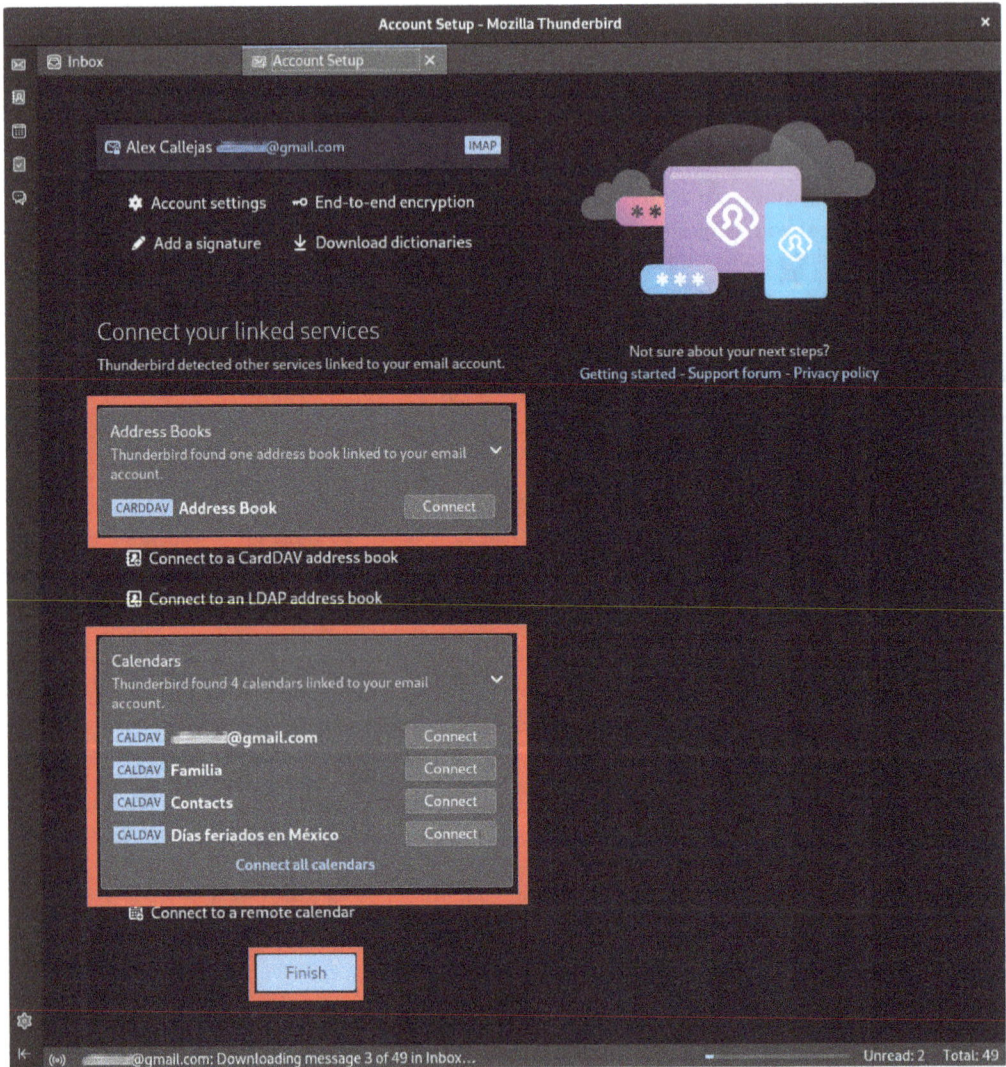

Figure 9.23 – Automatic setup completed

To complete the configuration, click on the **Finish** button.

> **Note**
>
> If Mozilla Thunderbird can't find service configuration information, you will need to manually configure the mail account.

This ends the *automatic configuration* of the mail account. To specify the mail account settings manually, follow the following steps:

1. In the **Account Setup** window, click the **Configure manually** link:

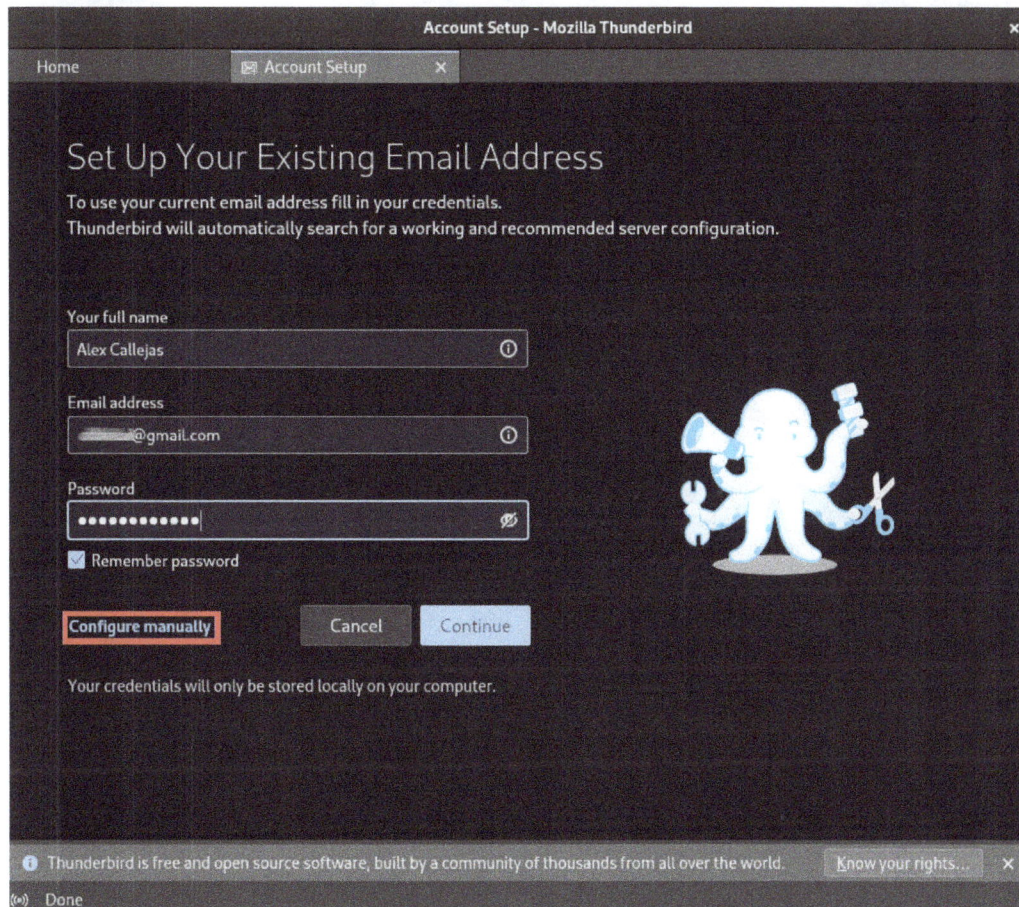

Figure 9.24 – The Account Setup window

> **Note**
>
> Confirm the general mail access data, such as server type, service ports, and security, with the staff of the corresponding area to avoid connectivity issues.

Mozilla Thunderbird supports connection to a mail server, by IMAP or POP3 protocols or local mail, as described in the previous section.

2.   Select the protocol to be used and the access data of the *incoming* and *outgoing* mail servers:

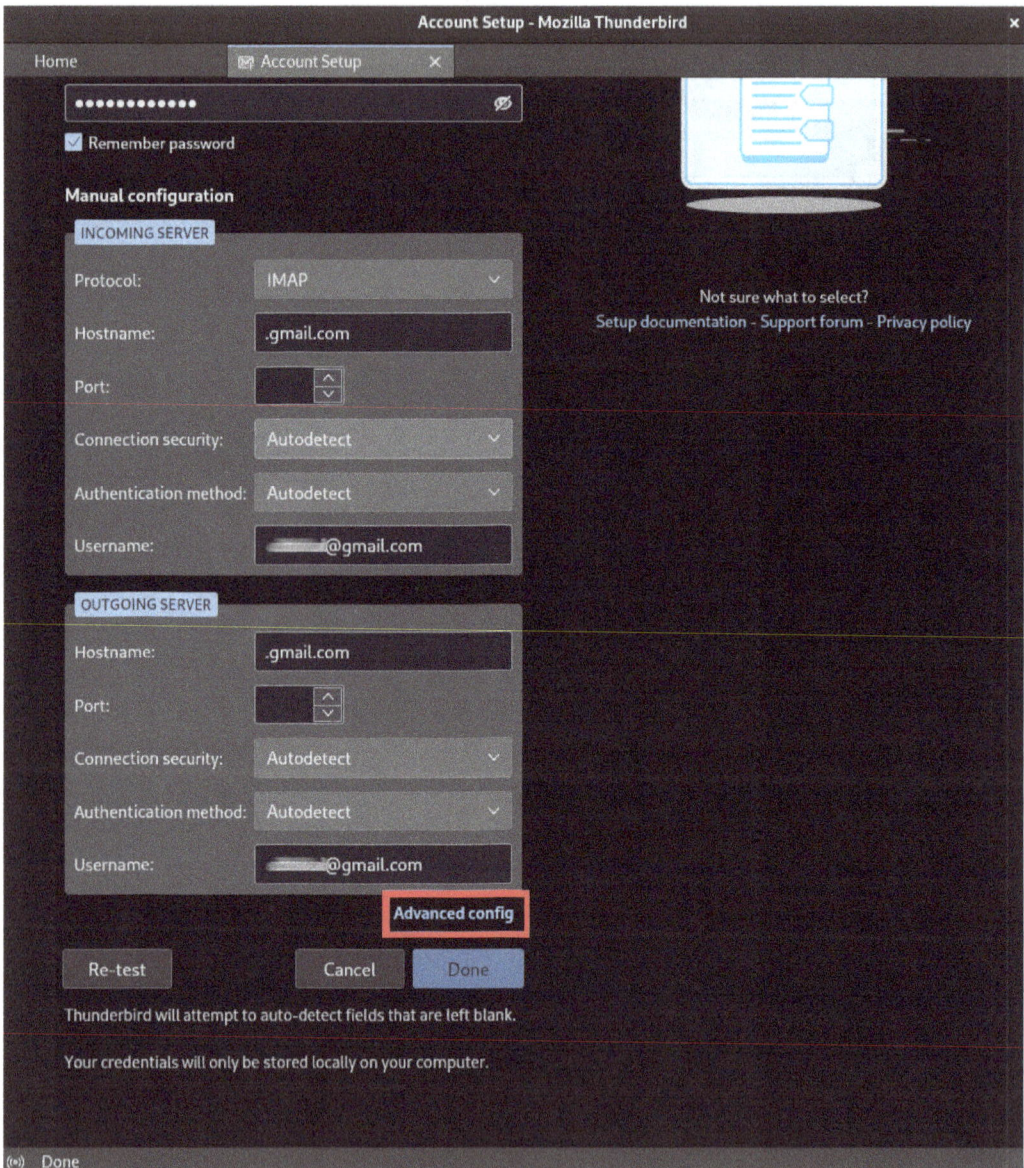

Figure 9.25 – The manual Account Setup window

3. If further configuration options are required, click on the **Advanced config** link.

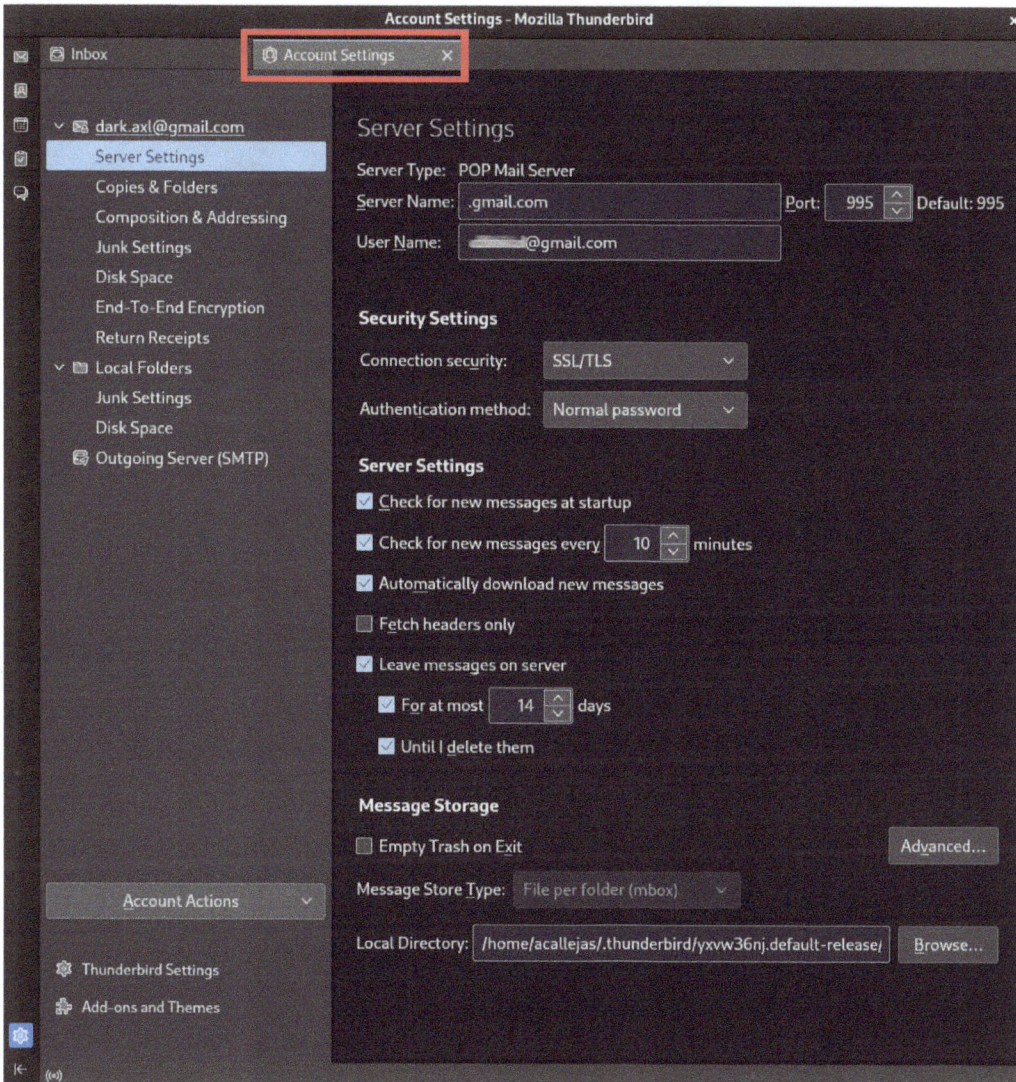

Figure 9.26 – The advanced Account Settings window

This window contains granular settings for the account connection details.

Once the configuration is complete, click on the **x** symbol in the **Account Settings** tab to close it.

4.   After completing the account setup, Mozilla Thunderbird's main window appears:

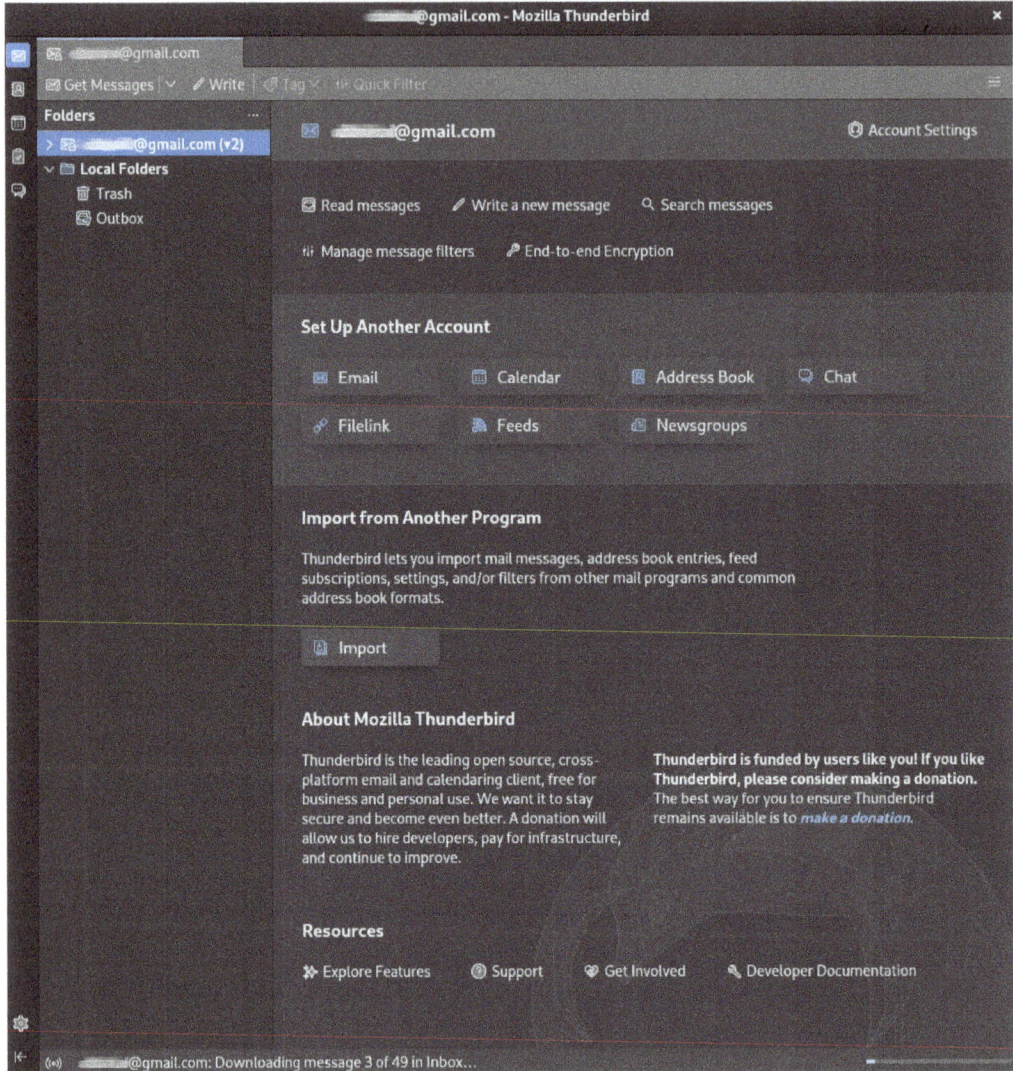

Figure 9.27 – The Mozilla Thunderbird main window

5. From the main window, it is possible to configure more accounts for mail, calendars, address books, chat, file links, feeds, or newsgroups. It also imports these accounts from other email clients and provides access to support resources. To retrieve mail messages, click on the **Get Messages** button:

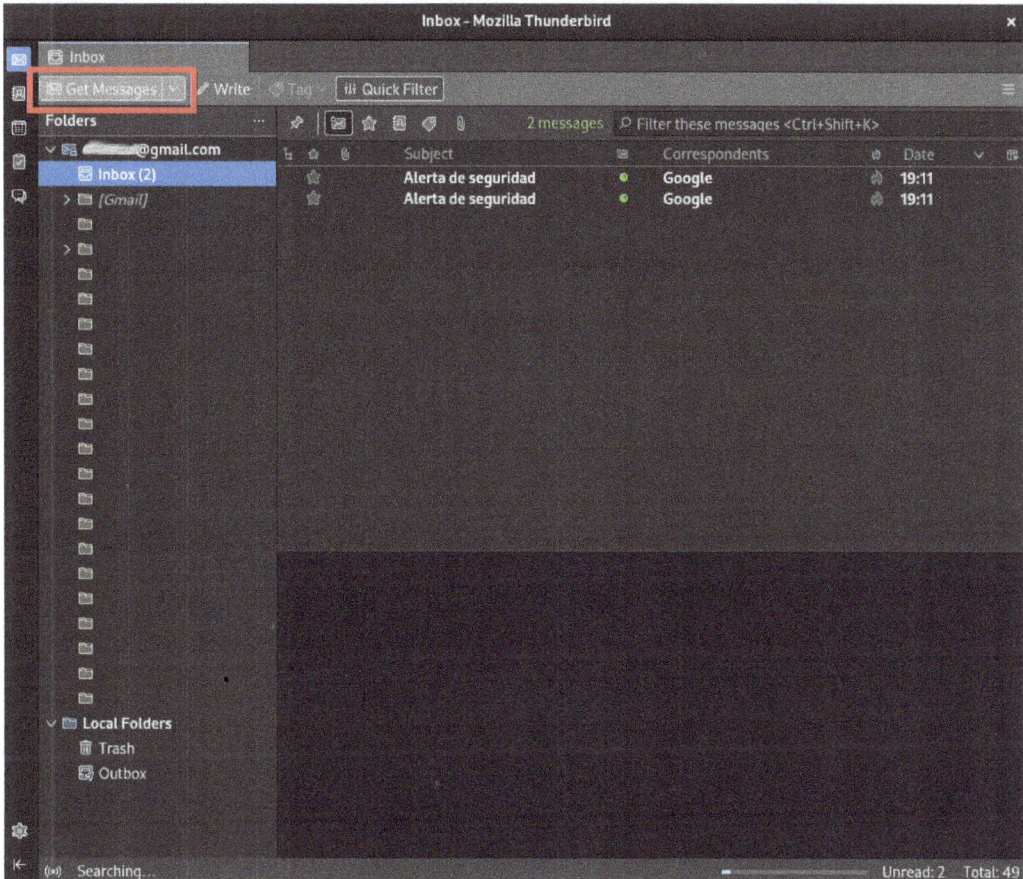

Figure 9.28 – Retrieving mail messages

Now, let's see how to send an email:

1. To create a new email message, click the **Write** button on the Mozilla Thunderbird toolbar:

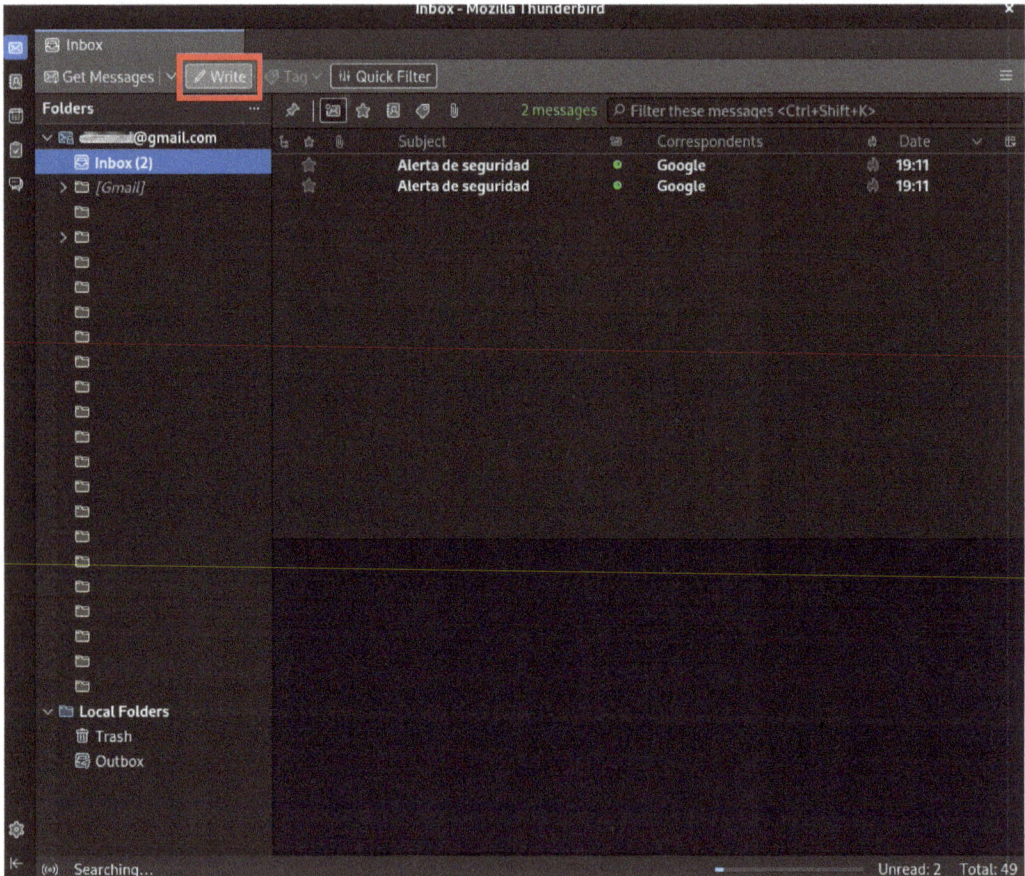

Figure 9.29 – The Mozilla Thunderbird main window

2. In the **Write** message window, fill in the recipient and subject of the email. If you need to send attachments, click on the **Attach** button on the toolbar:

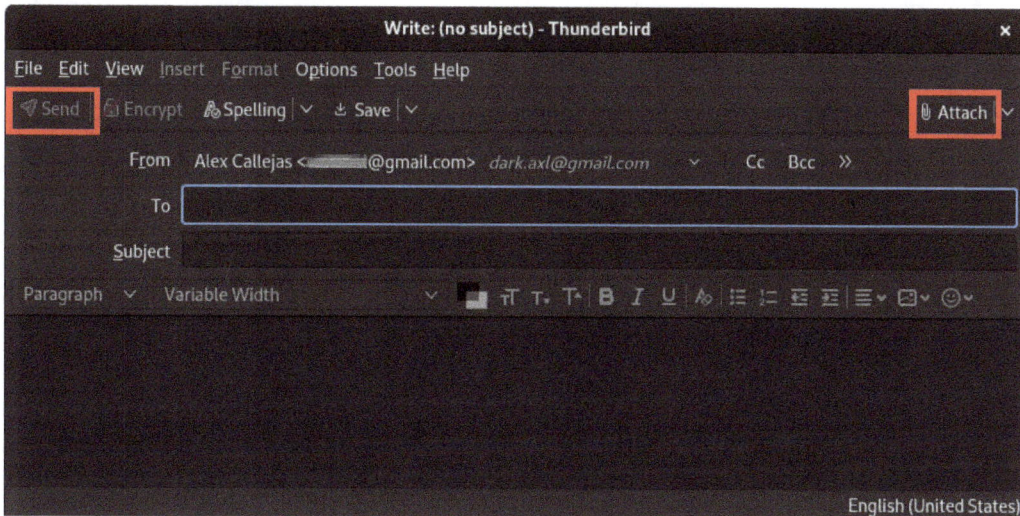

Figure 9.30 – The Write message window

3. When the email message is ready for delivery, the **Send** button gets enabled. Click the **Send** button to dispatch the email message.

According to `opensource.com`, these two mail clients, **Evolution** and **Mozilla Thunderbird**, represent the most used desktop mail clients in enterprise environments.

However, the most common method to get access to email on Linux is through a web browser.

Let's now take a look at the two most used web browsers in Fedora Linux.

Trusty old Firefox

In January 1998, the **Netscape Communications Corporation** (**NSCP**) announced plans to release the source code for its **Netscape Communicator software** on the internet. The company released the source code for the first developer version of **Netscape Communicator 5.0** in the first quarter of 1998. This aggressive move allowed Netscape to harness the creative power of thousands of internet programmers by incorporating enhancements for future versions of Netscape software.

This announcement led to the creation of the **Mozilla Project**.

Phoenix 0.1 was released in *September 2002*. That was the first version of a browser that was later called **Firebird** and then **Firefox**. **Firefox 1.0** was launched in 2004 and became a huge success.

In November 2003, Red Hat announced **Fedora Core 1**, the first software release of the Fedora Project. GNOME was Fedora Linux's default desktop. Mozilla Suite was the web browser of choice at the time. Mozilla had not yet started the Firefox browser project, so this suite included an *email client* and a *Usenet newsreader*.

Fedora Core 3 was released one year later, in 2004. This was the first version to include the Mozilla Firefox web browser.

In 2019, Fedora Linux 31 Workstation came with a Firefox backend, moved from X11 to Wayland by default, and had a new *display server*. This was another step in the ongoing effort to move to Wayland. This affected only GNOME.

Firefox comes installed as the default RPM on Fedora Linux Workstation, alongside Firefox installed as a Flatpak application and another package that lets you run Firefox in Wayland.

Let's see the difference between each of these installation options:

1. From the software application, search for Firefox, and click on the *installed* option:

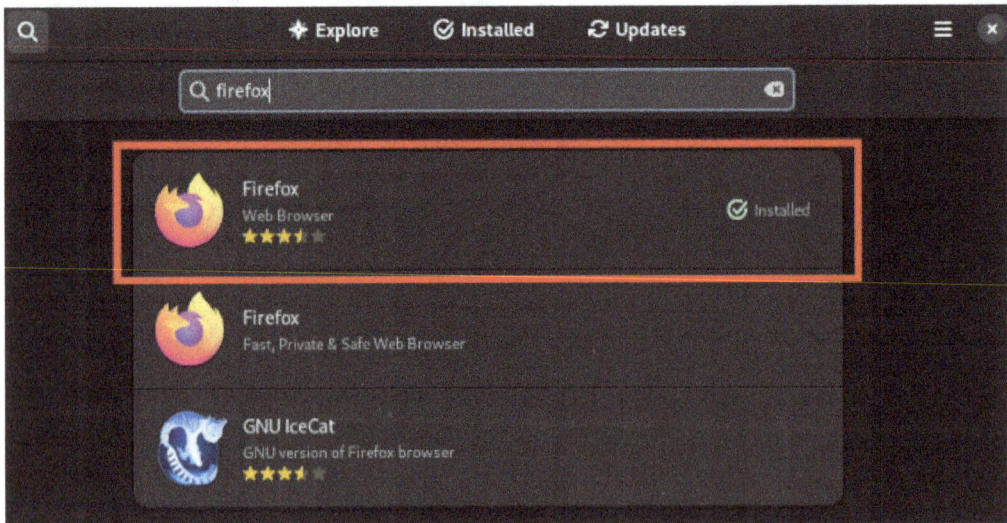

Figure 9.31 – Firefox on a software application

2. After clicking on the installation sources, find RPM and the Fedora Flatpak application:

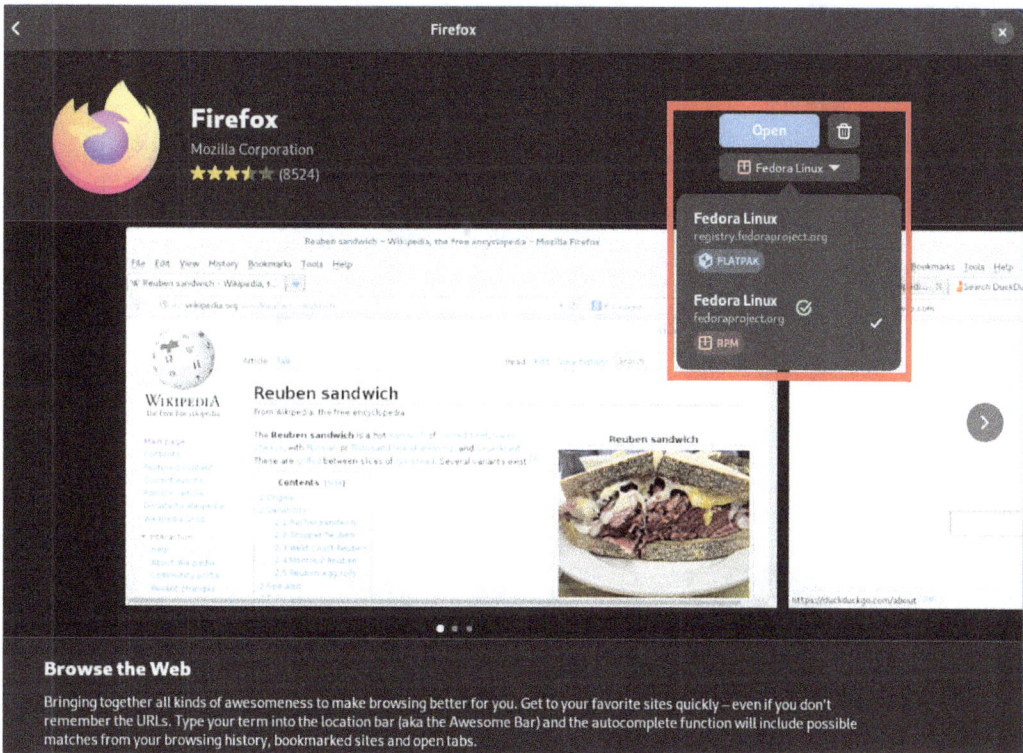

Figure 9.32 – The Firefox installation source

3. Also in the terminal, use the `dnf` command to list the available Firefox packages:

```
# dnf list *firefox*
```

```
root@workstation:~
[root@workstation ~]# dnf list *firefox*
Last metadata expiration check: 2:16:32 ago on Sat 10 Jun 2023 04:36:58 PM CST.
Installed Packages
firefox.x86_64                              114.0-1.fc38             @updates
firefox-langpacks.x86_64                    114.0-1.fc38             @updates
Available Packages
firefox-pkcs11-loader.x86_64                3.13.6-9.fc38            fedora
firefox-wayland.x86_64                      114.0-1.fc38             updates
firefox-x11.x86_64                          114.0-1.fc38             updates
[root@workstation ~]#
```

Figure 9.33 – The Firefox packages on the terminal

4. To open the **Firefox** browser, by default, a launcher will appear in the favorites of the **Activities Overview** window:

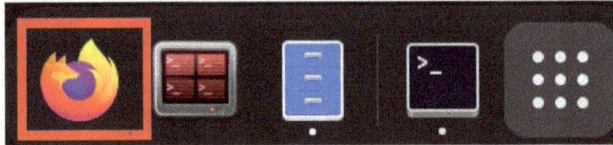

Figure 9.34 – The Firefox launcher on Activities Overview

From the menu, you can also find the **Firefox** launcher within the favorites:

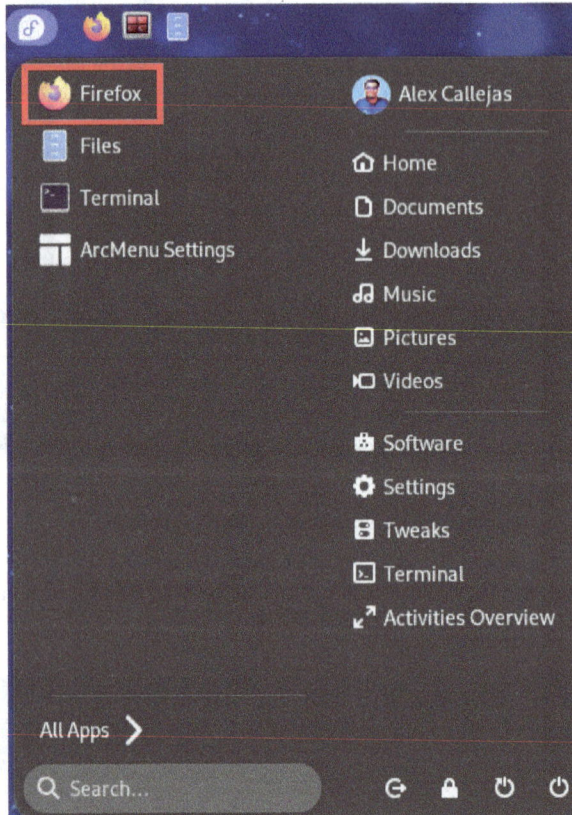

Figure 9.35 – The Firefox launcher on the menu

In *Chapter 3*, I mentioned that installing the **Gnome Frippery Panel Favorites extension** (`https://extensions.gnome.org/extension/4/panel-favorites/`) adds the favorites to the taskbar, so the **Firefox** launcher appears on the desktop:

Figure 9.36 – The Firefox launcher on the desktop

5. Opening Firefox shows the **Fedora Project** page as the *home page*:

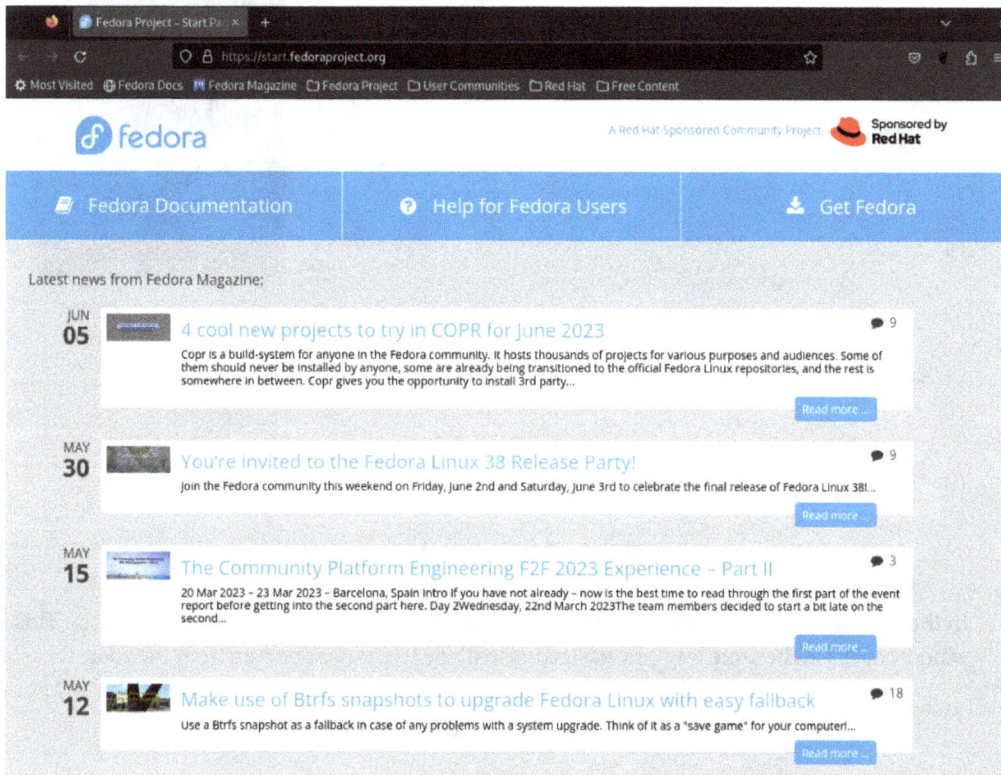

Figure 9.37 – The Firefox browser

6. You can choose to change the home page, which can be done from the Firefox settings. To do this, click on the icon with three horizontal lines, as shown here:

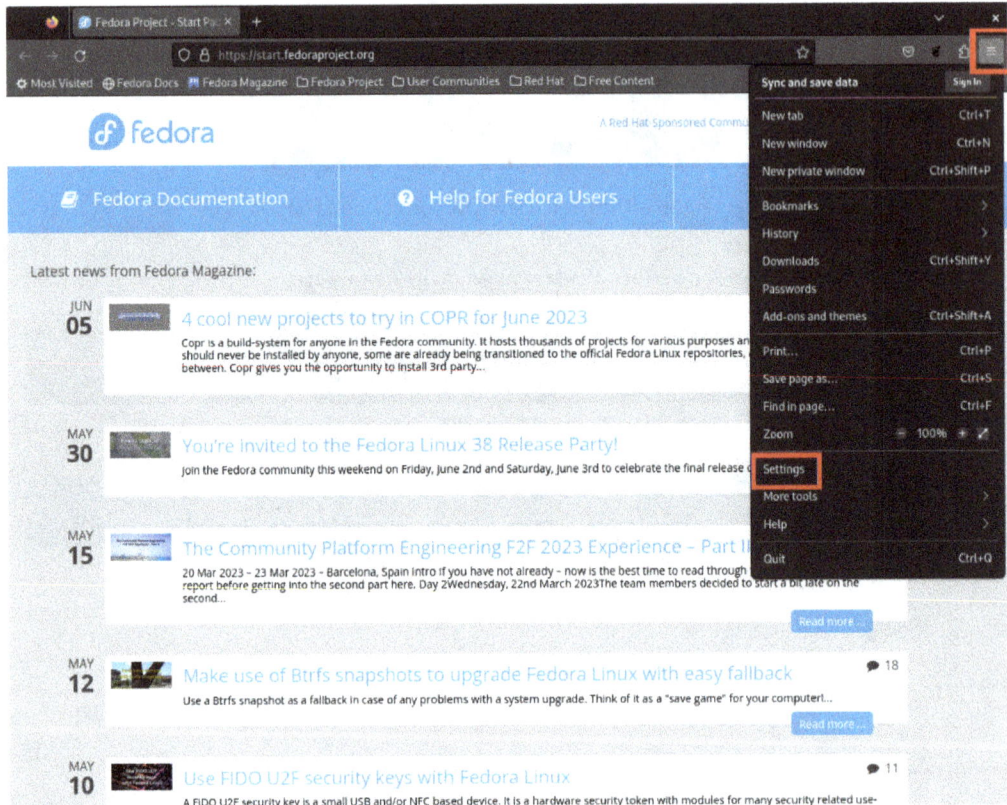

Figure 9.38 – The Firefox settings

7. In the drop-down menu, select **Settings** to open the window with the Firefox preferences. This window opens in the same way – by navigating to about:preferences from the address bar:

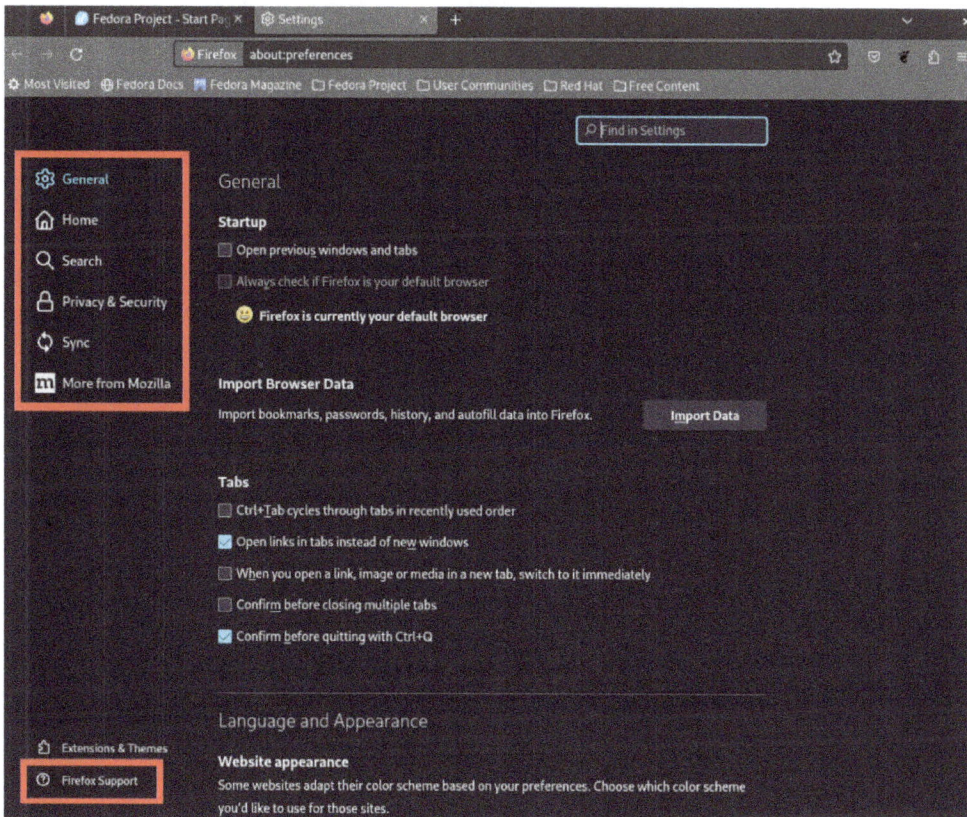

Figure 9.39 – Firefox preferences

8. Firefox settings appear in sections, and each one has several sections:

   •   **General**: General configuration options such as the following:

      ◦   **Language and appearance**: Changes the appearance of the website, with automatic, light or dark color schemes, colors, fonts, zoom, as well as the language. It also changes the display of Firefox menus, messages, and notifications.

      ◦   **Files and applications**: Changes the handling of files, such as downloads, including where to save them and which applications to open them with.

      ◦   **Firefox updates**: Verifies the browser version.

      ◦   **Performance**: Changes or verifies the recommended performance settings.

      ◦   **Browsing**: Changes or adds options to the browsing behavior, such as a scroll display or media file handling. It also controls extensions and features.

      ◦   **Network settings**: Configures how Firefox connects to the internet.

- **Home**: Controls the launch options when opening Firefox:

  - **New windows and tabs**: Configuration of the home page, new windows, and tabs

  - **Firefox Home Content**: Configuration of the home screen content

- **Search**: Configuration of the search options, including the following:

  - **Search bar**: A tool to perform a search

  - **Default search engine**: The preferred search engine (the default is Google)

  - **Search suggestions**: The behavior of the suggestions in searches

  - **Search shortcuts**: Alternative search engines

- **Privacy & Security**: Privacy and security settings, which include the following:

  - **Enhanced tracking protection**: A tool to block malicious trackers and scripts. It allows different levels of security.

  - **Cookies and site data**: The management of cookies and saved site data.

  - **Logins and passwords**: The management of site access data and passwords.

  - **History**: Browsing history management.

  - **Address bar**: The customization of the address bar view.

  - **Permissions**: The customization of access to resources, such as location, devices, or notifications.

  - **Firefox data collection and use**: The management of data collected by Firefox.

  - **Security**: The customization of the general security of navigation.

- **Sync**: The configuration of sync options – bookmarks, history, tabs, passwords, and add-ons. Create a sync account if required.

- **More from Mozilla**: Allows you to try other Mozilla products:

  - **Firefox Mobile**: A browser for mobile phones

  - **Firefox Relay**: Email masking to protect online identity

- **Extensions & themes**: Firefox customization options. This window can also be opened by navigating to `about:addons` from the address bar:

  - **Extensions**: The extensions include programs that expand Firefox's functions, such as *pop-up blockers*, *online translation*, and *cookie handling*

- **Themes**: Changes the color scheme or add a custom background to the browser

- **Plugins**: Plugins add features to the browser, such as playing some video or image formats

- **Firefox Support**: Opens the **Mozilla Support** window (`https://support.mozilla.org`). This can also be accessed in the **Firefox Options, Preferences and Settings** section.

9. In the drop-down menu shown in *Figure 9.38*, find some shortcuts to various sections of the Firefox settings or preferences. For example, to view the version of Firefox, click on the drop-down menu, click on the **Help** option, and then click on **About**:

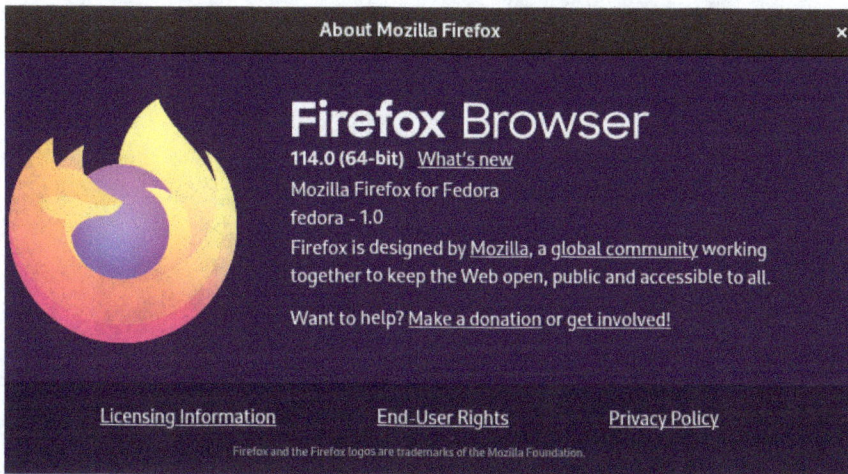

Figure 9.40 – About Mozilla Firefox

One of the best feel and look-related options that Firefox has is customizing the browser theme.

Let's see how to add a theme to our browser.

Customizing Firefox

A theme changes the appearance of Firefox, such as the color scheme and the background image of the toolbars. Not all Firefox themes are *light* (background), and in some cases, they are *not compatible*. Before installing a theme, verify the compatibility and size of it.

Now, let's see how to install a Firefox theme on our workstation. Follow the following steps:

1. Open the Firefox **Settings** window and click on the **Extensions & Themes** section:

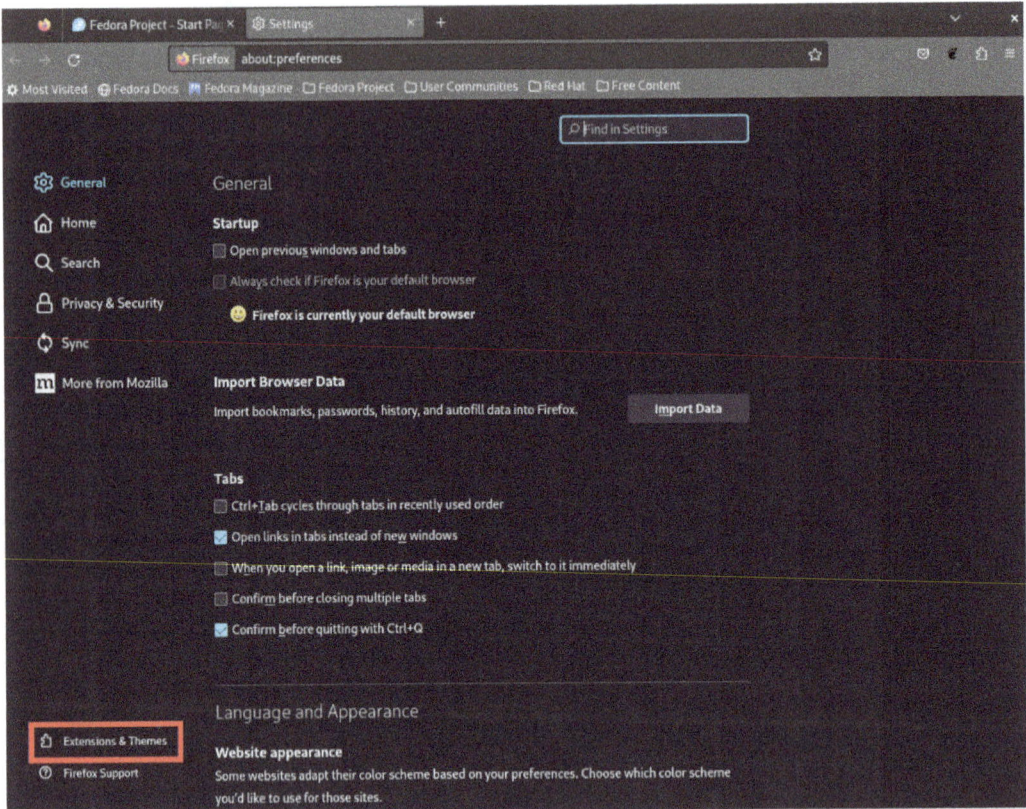

Figure 9.41 – Firefox Extensions & Themes

2.   The Firefox **Add-ons Manager** window displays a sub-menu with **Recommendations**, **Extensions**, **Themes**, and **Plugins** customization options.

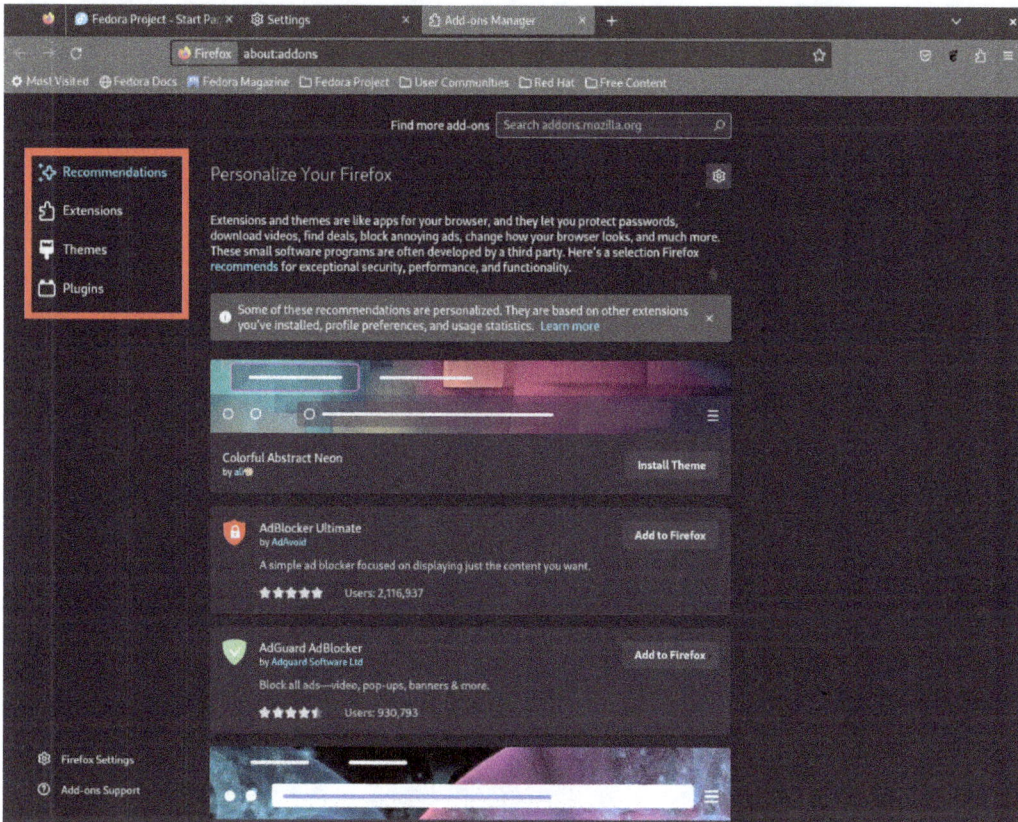

Figure 9.42 – Firefox add-ons

Click on **Themes**.

3.   In the **Themes** window, browse through the theme recommendations offered by Firefox:

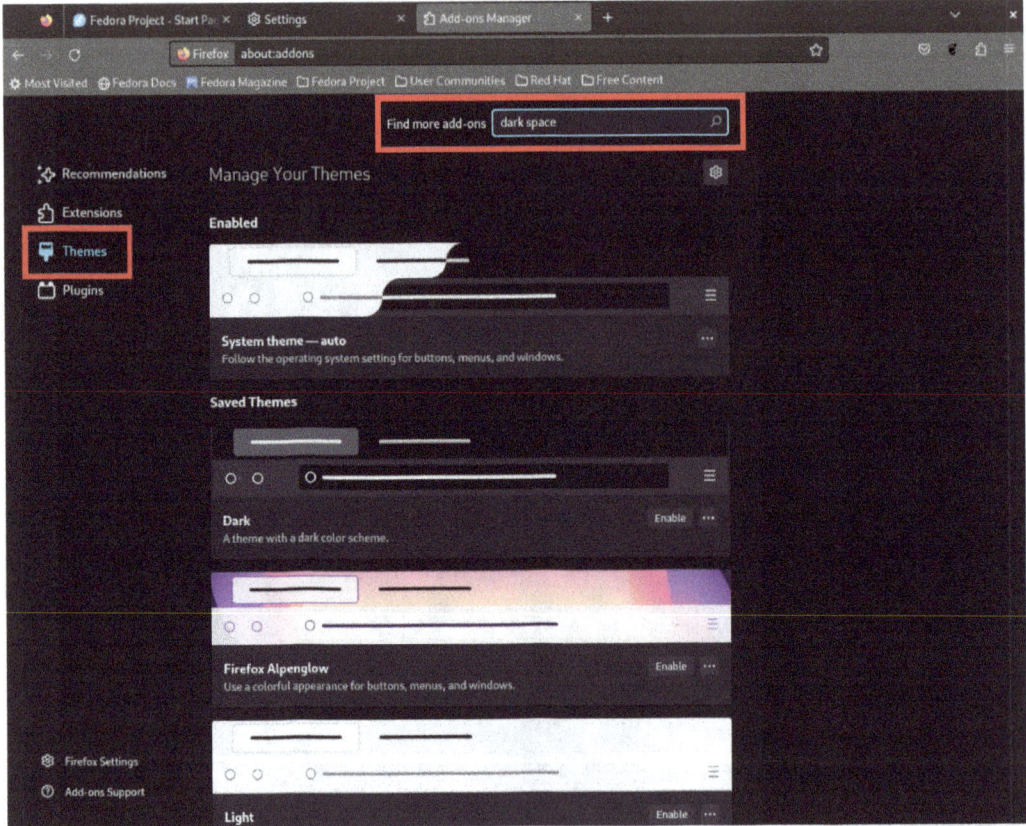

Figure 9.43 – Firefox themes

It is also possible to search for themes. In the search bar called **Find more add-ons**, type `dark space`.

4.   Firefox displays a window with the results for the theme search:

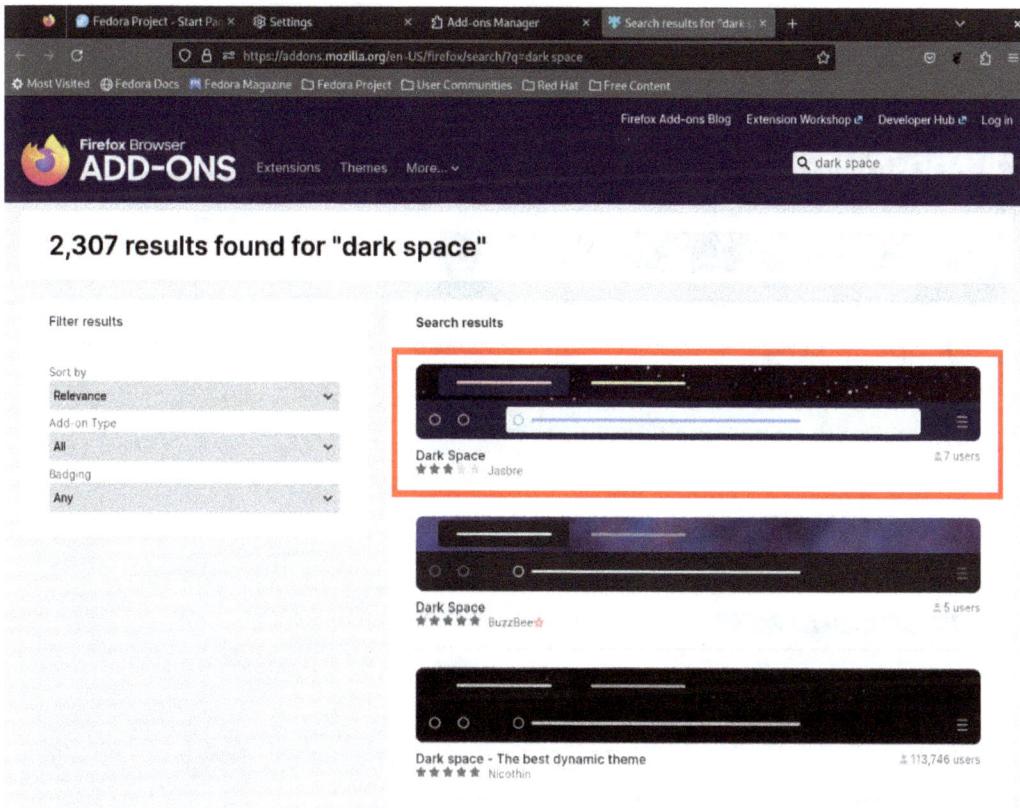

Figure 9.44 – Searching for a theme

Click on the first theme.

5. To add the theme, install and enable it, and then click on the **Install Theme** button:

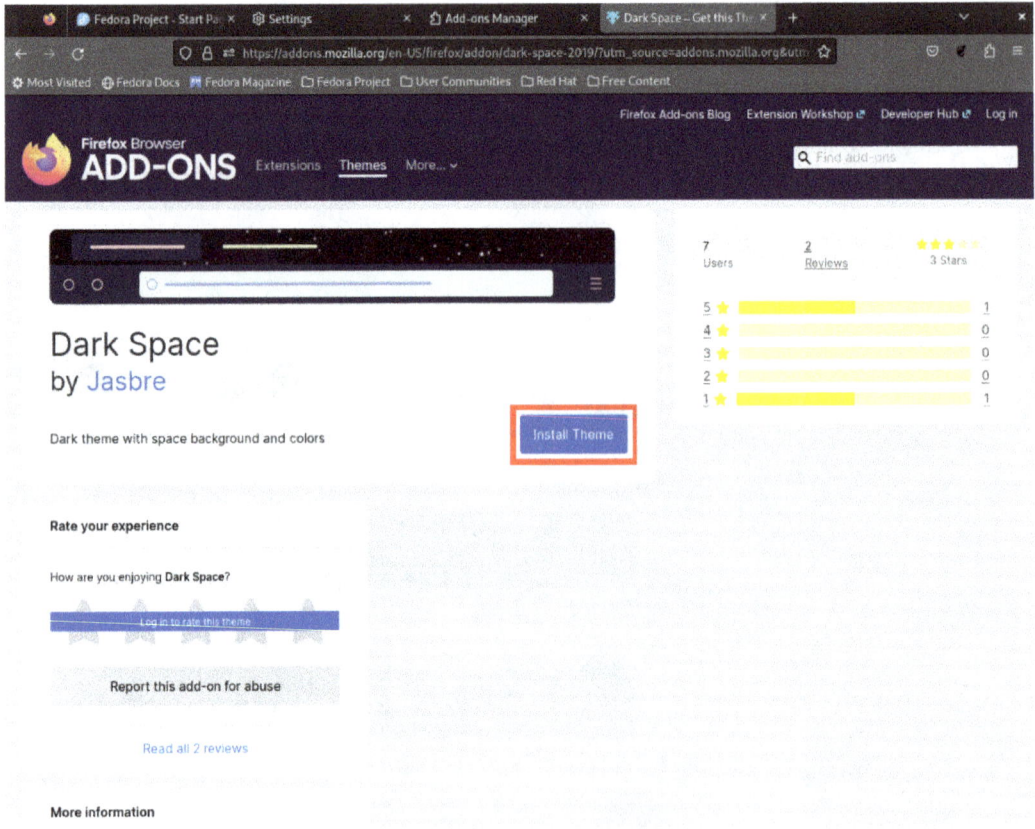

Figure 9.45 – Installing a theme

6. A notification window will appear to confirm the add-on installation:

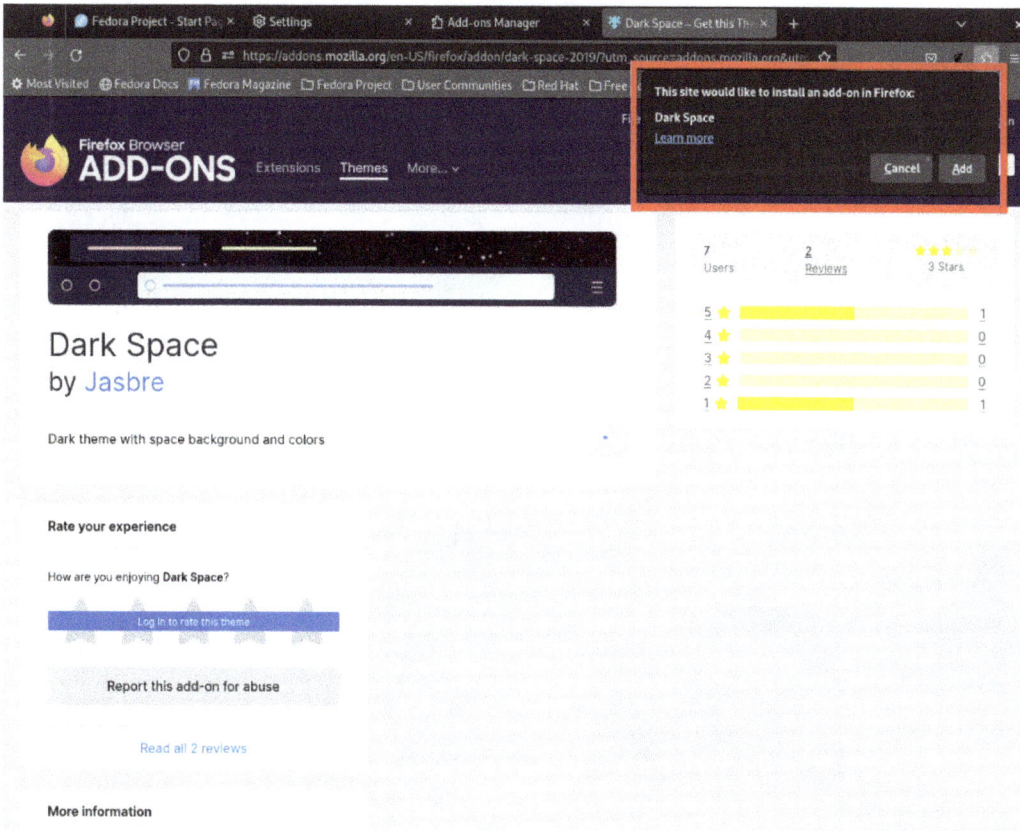

Figure 9.46 – Installing an add-on

Click the **Add** button.

7.   The appearance of Firefox will change in the *tab bar* and *toolbar*:

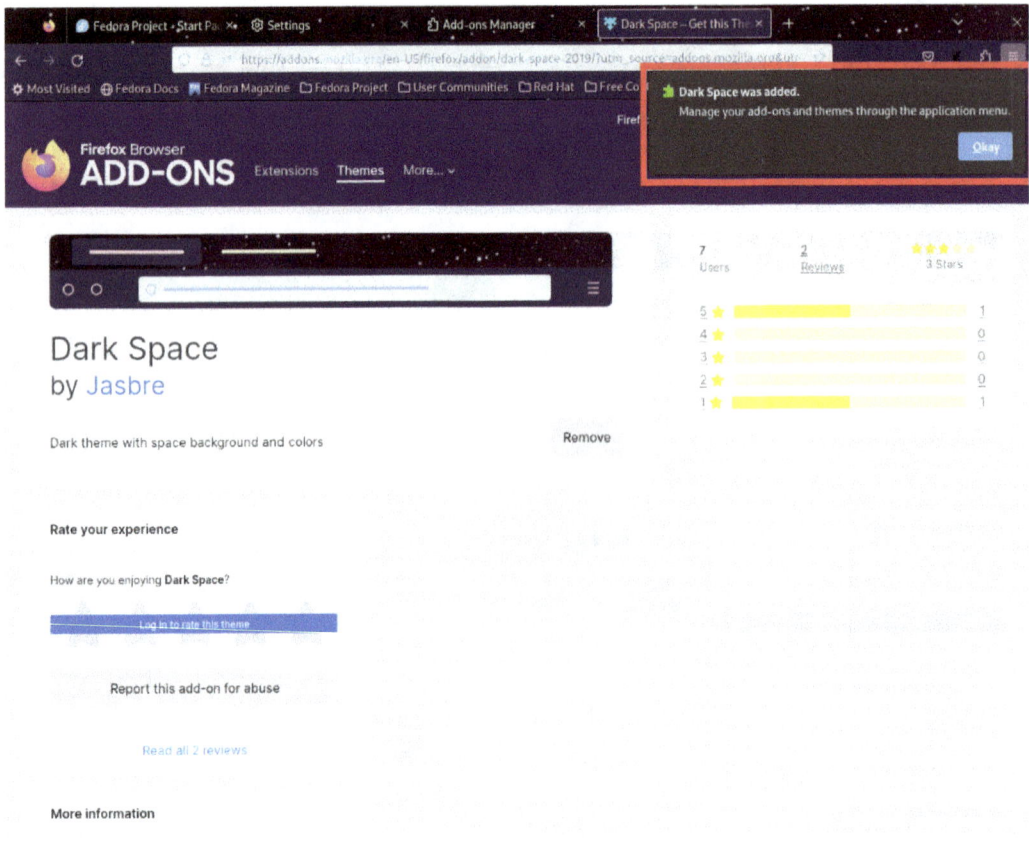

Figure 9.47 – Adding a theme

A notification window will inform you about the theme application. Click the **Okay** button to accept the change.

Once you have finished customizing Firefox, it is ready to open our email via the web.

Following the example in the previous section, open the Google Mail URL (`https://mail.google.com`):

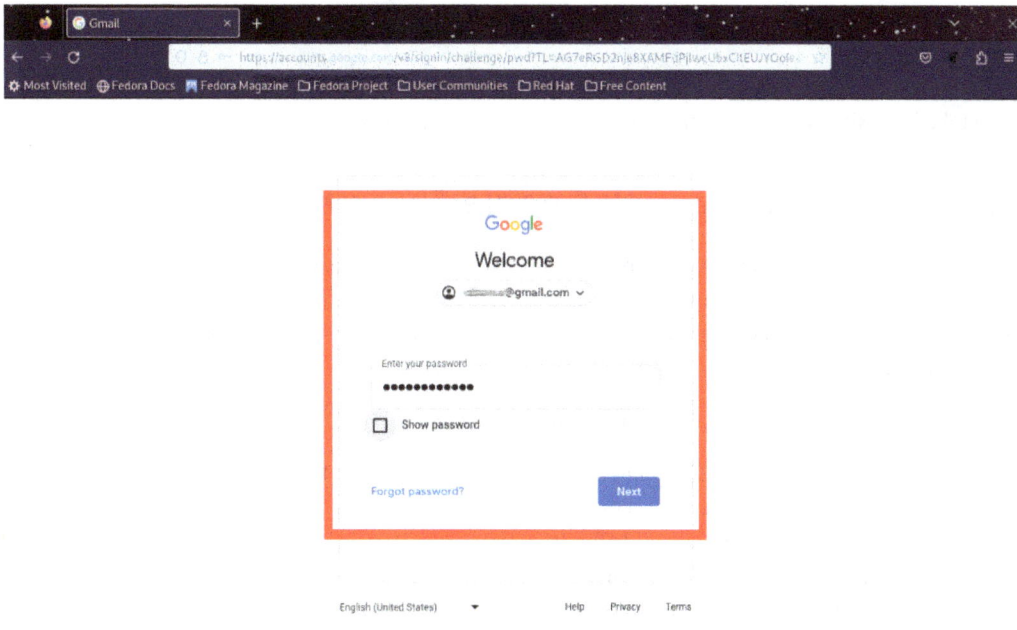

Figure 9.48 – Accessing mail via the web

Enter your email address and password. Click the **Next** button. Firefox will open the email folder so that you can check and send mail:

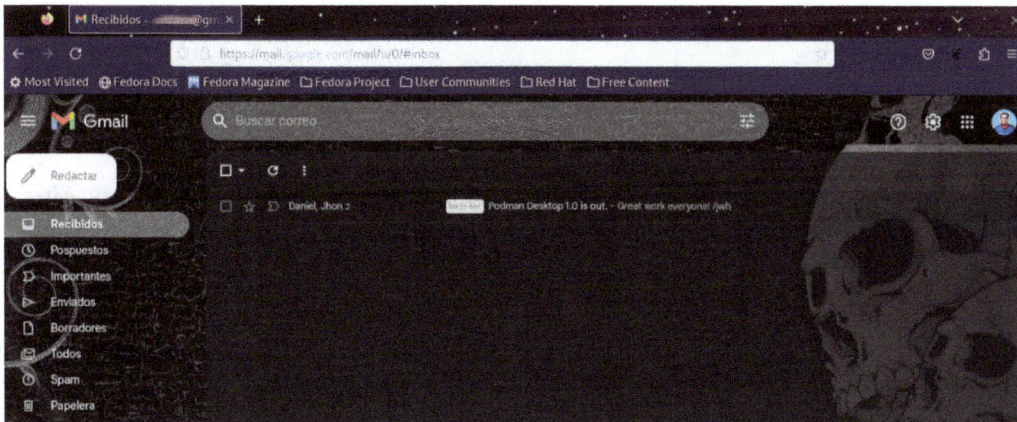

Figure 9.49 – Accessing email via the web

Firefox is one of the best and most stable browser options available on Linux.

Another of the best and most popular options is to use Google's browser – **Google Chrome**. Let's see how to take browsing one step further, using Google's Chrome browser.

Expanding browsing with Google Chrome

Google Chrome is a *proprietary* web browser developed by Google, although derived from *open source projects*. Chrome builds on the Chromium open source browser project. Chrome draws from different code libraries from Google and others from third parties, such as Netscape. Chrome releases are sourced from Chromium.

Regardless of this, Google Chrome is available free of charge.

Google Chrome was launched in 2008, and along with its release, the Chromium source code became available. This allowed the code set to serve as the basis for the development of other browsers. The initial version of the code included builds for Windows, macOS, and Linux at a very early stage of development, lacking full functionality. **Chromium 1.0** was released in December 2008 and removed Chrome from beta status for Windows only.

In May 2009, the first *alpha version* of Chromium for Linux was released. That July, Chromium incorporated native themes for Linux, using the GTK+ toolkit, which allowed it to integrate with the GNOME desktop environment.

Chromium 5.0 was released in January 2010. **Google Chrome 5.0** followed in May 2010 and provided a stable (*non-beta*) version for all platforms.

Chrome includes extra features, such as support for *proprietary media files* (such as **H.264** or **AAC**) and playback of *rights-protected media* (Netflix, etc.). Chrome also includes support for other Google services, such as browser synchronization and location services not supported by Chromium.

Google Chrome is available on Fedora Linux Workstation through a third-party repository. After enabling this repository, Chrome can be installed via the software application or the command line.

Let's verify the options to install Chrome on our workstation:

1. Open the software application, and in the search option, type `Google Chrome`:

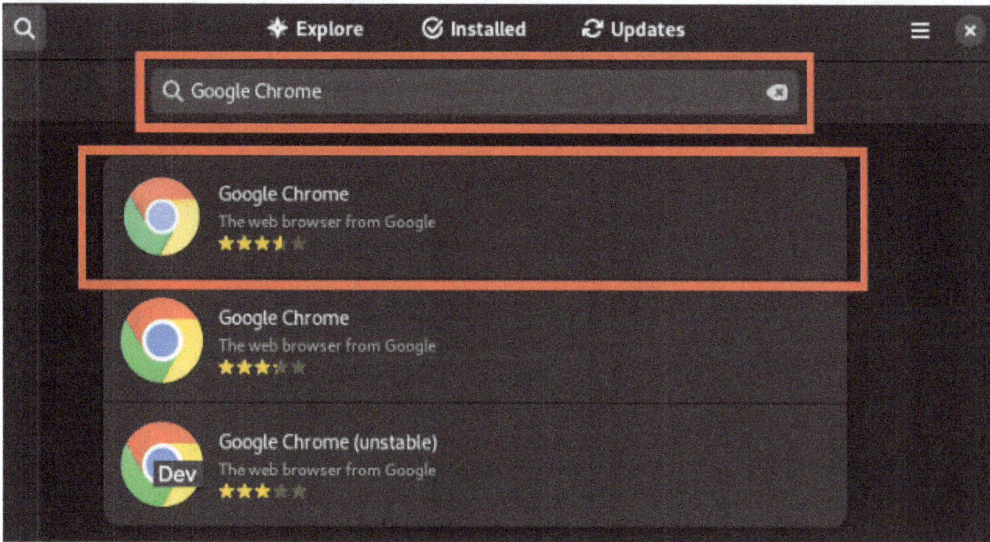

Figure 9.50 – Searching for Chrome on the software app

2.   Click on the first result and verify the installation source:

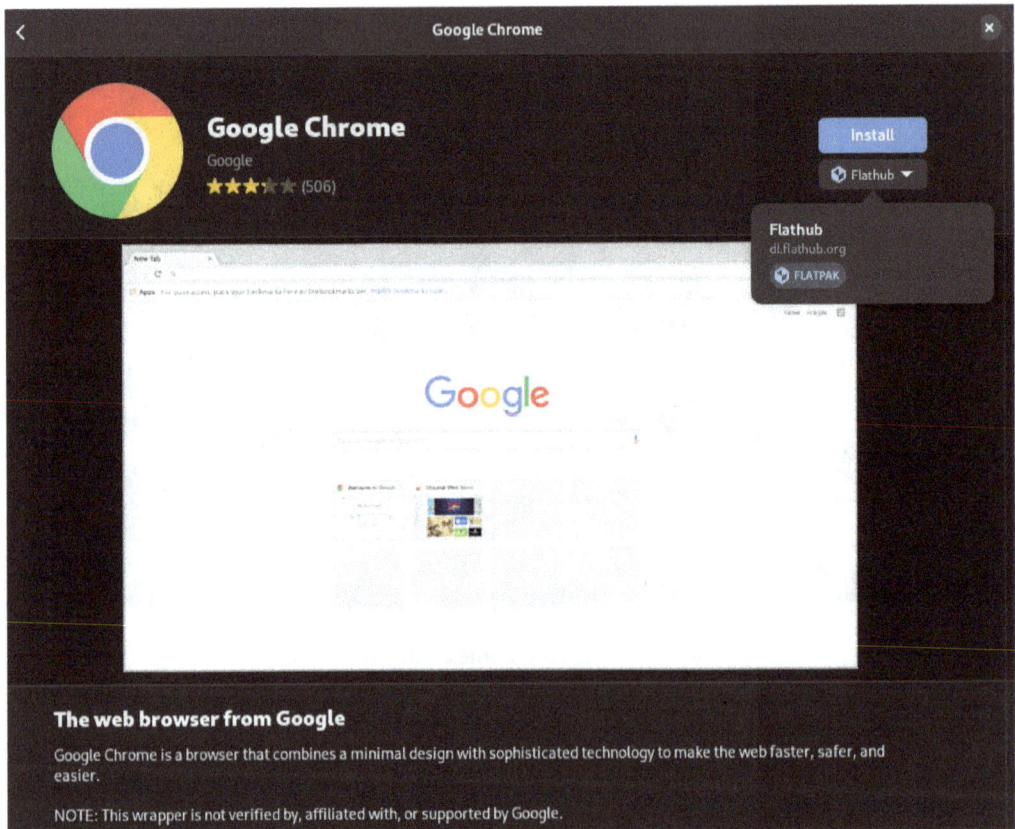

Figure 9.51 – The Google Chrome source installation options

3. To enable the Google third-party repository, return to the main window of the software application. Click the collapsed menu icon with three horizontal lines, next to the close (**x**) button:

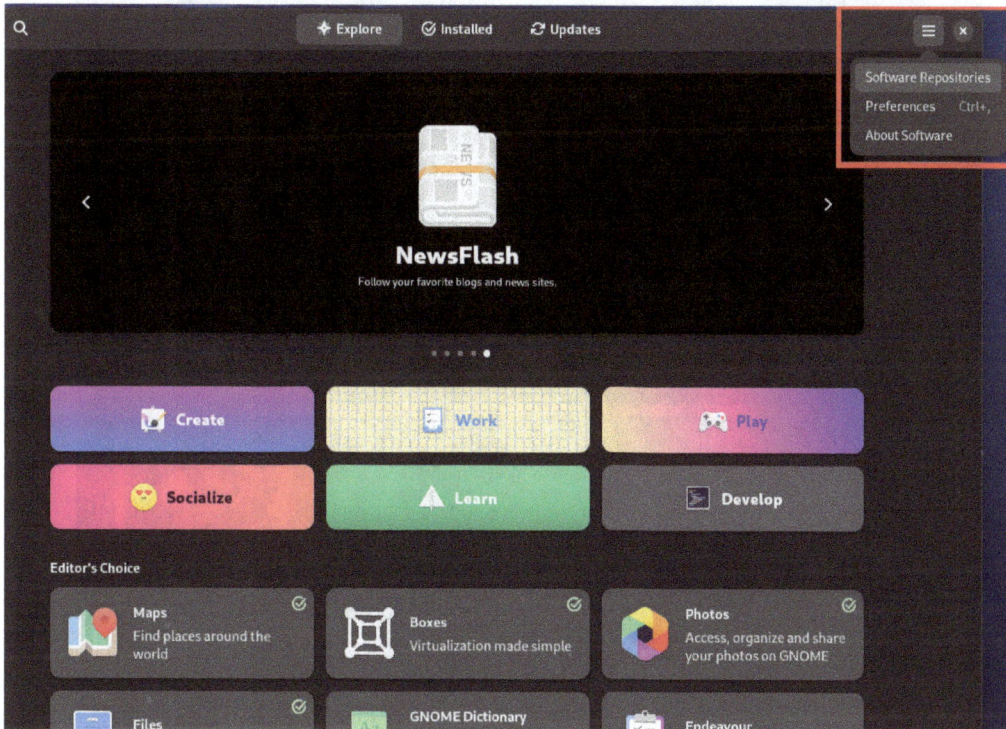

Figure 9.52 – Software repositories on the software app

4. Click on **Software Repositories**.

5.   Scroll down until you find the `google-chrome` repository, and toggle the button to enable it:

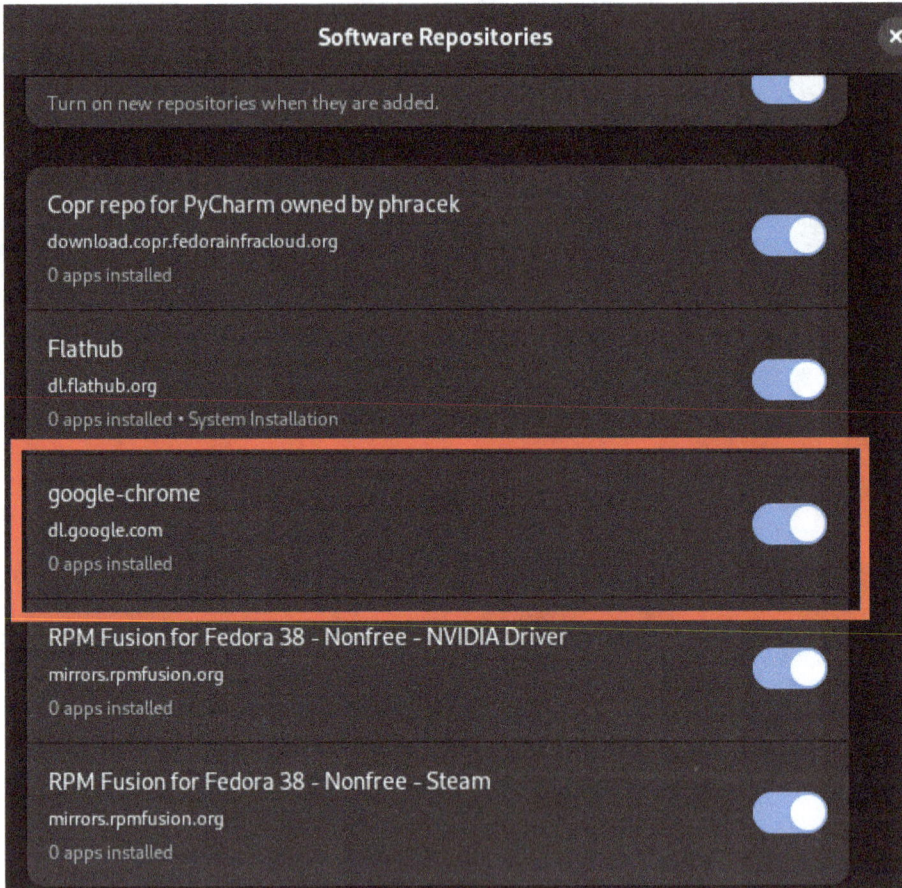

Figure 9.53 – The Software Repositories window

6.   Run the search again, and verify that the installation source is RPM:

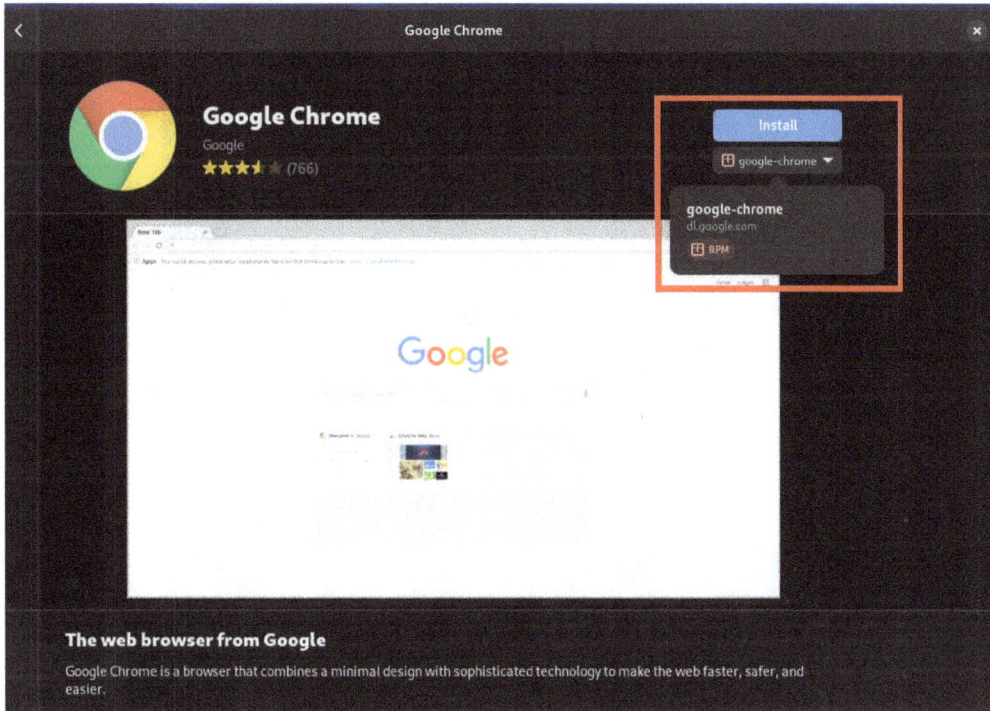

Figure 9.54 – The Google Chrome source installation options

7.   Open the terminal, and as the root user, use the dnf command to list the google-chrome browser packages:

```
# dnf list *google-chrome*
```

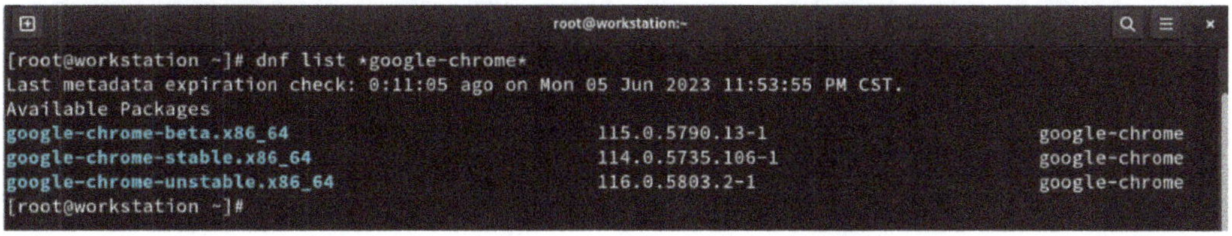

Figure 9.55 – The Google Chrome packages

Install Google Chrome by your preferred method, and then we'll start the browser configuration.

8. To open Google Chrome, launch it from the menu. As a *non-root* user, open the menu in the upper-left corner, and type `Google Chrome` in the search box:

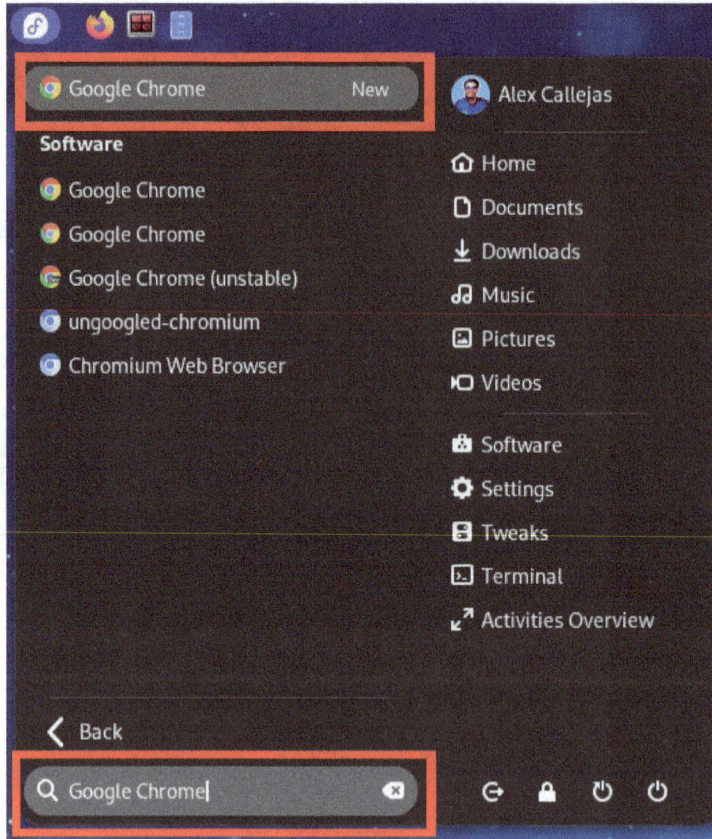

Figure 9.56 – Google Chrome launched from the menu

Google Chrome can also be accessed from the **Activities Overview** menu. Type `Google Chrome` in the search bar:

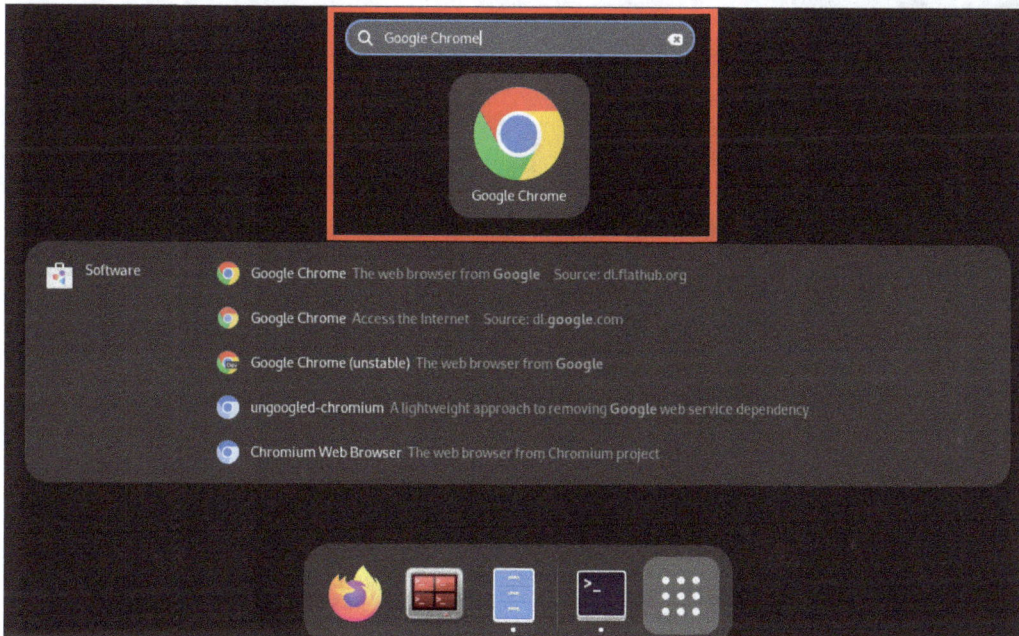

Figure 9.57 - Google Chrome from the Activities Overview menu

9. If needed, add **Chrome** to the **Favorites** tab. Drag and drop the **Chrome** icon from the **Activities Overview** menu to the **Favorites** dash.

A notification window will confirm that Google Chrome is now pinned to the **Favorites** dash:

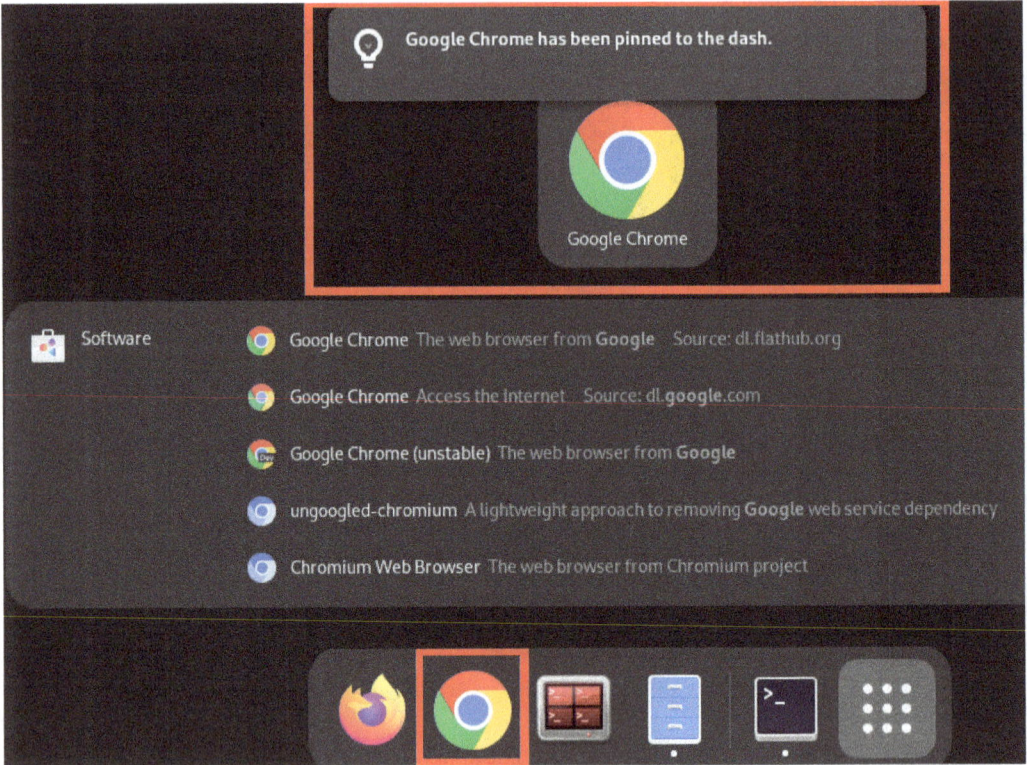

Figure 9.58 – Google Chrome pinned to Favorites

The icon can also be placed in the **Favorites** dash in your preferred location. From now on, it will appear as a **Favorites** item:

Figure 9.59 – The Favorites dashboard

Thus, the Google Chrome icon also appears in the taskbar, which was enabled by the previously installed extension:

Figure 9.60 – Google Chrome on the taskbar

10. When Chrome opens for the first time, you can set it as the default browser:

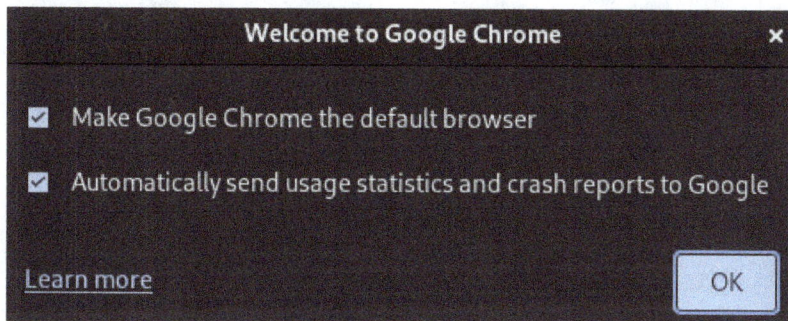

Figure 9.61 – Configure Google Chrome as the default browser

11. Enable the checkboxes and click the **OK** button if you agree with the settings. Otherwise, close the window.

To configure Google Chrome, let's take advantage of the fact that the email account currently being used is from Google Mail.

12. When the Chrome window opens, click on the **Already a Chrome user? Sign in** link to use the email account and *synchronize* the Chrome settings.

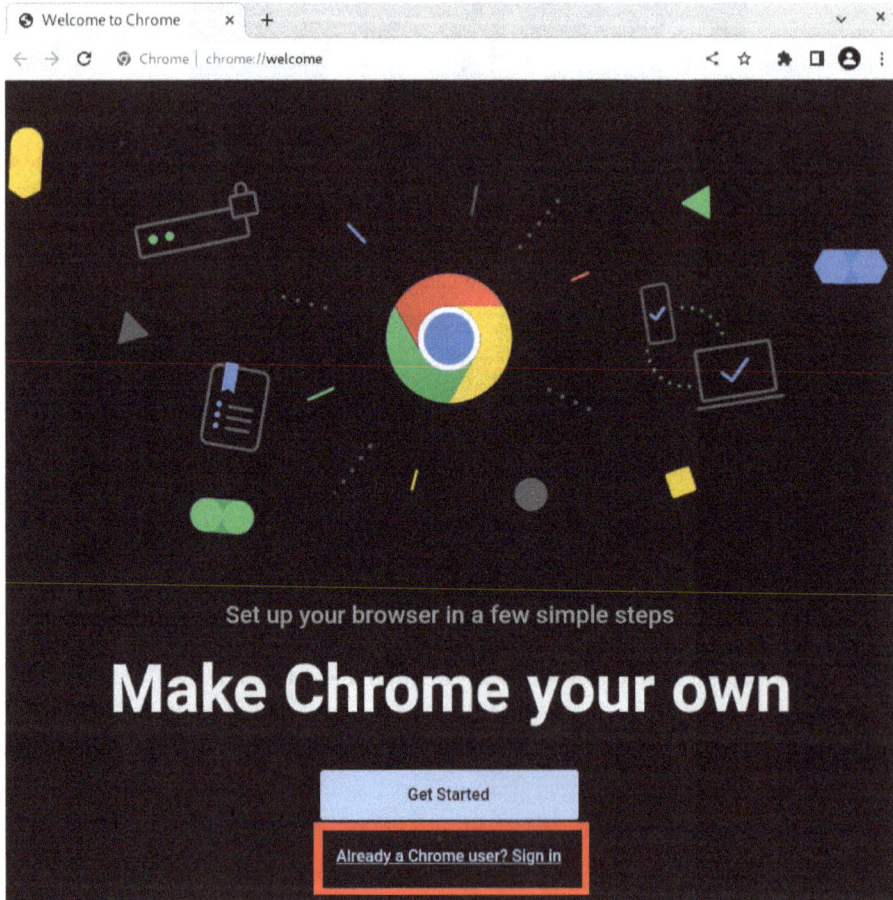

Figure 9.62 – The Google Chrome welcome screen

13. Enter the email address in the following dialog box, and click on the **Following** button:

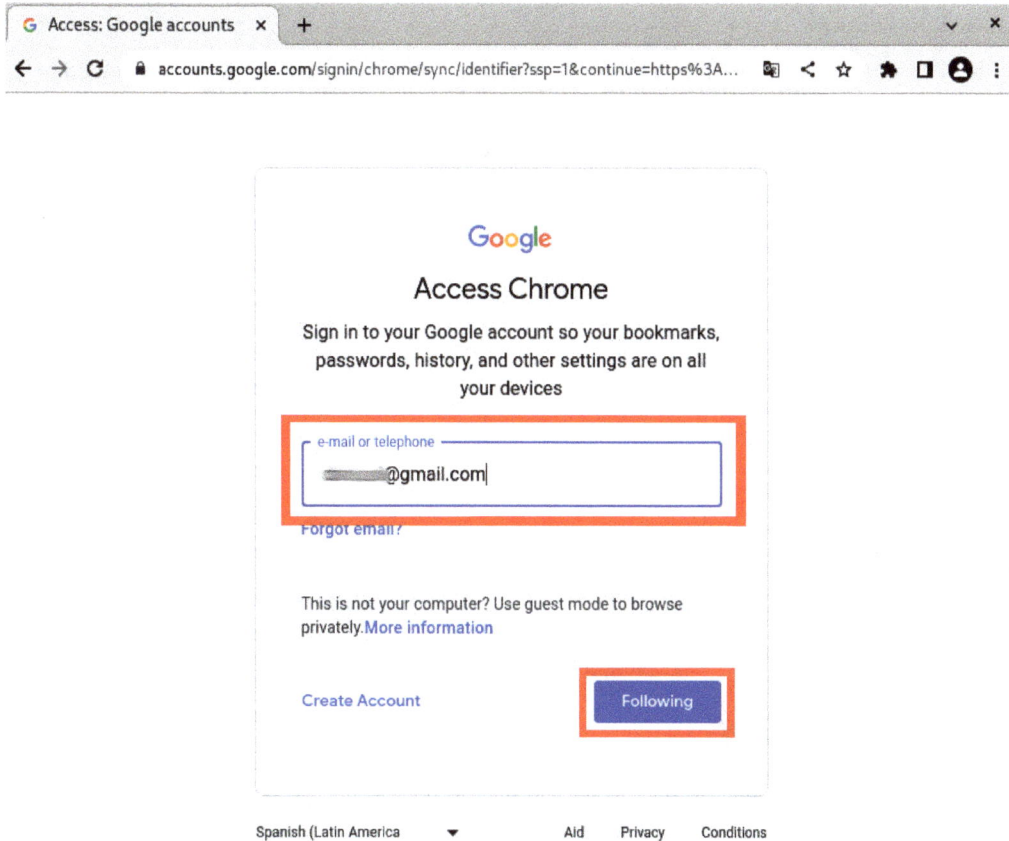

Figure 9.63 – The Google Chrome access screen

14. On the following screen, enter your password, and click on the **Following** button:

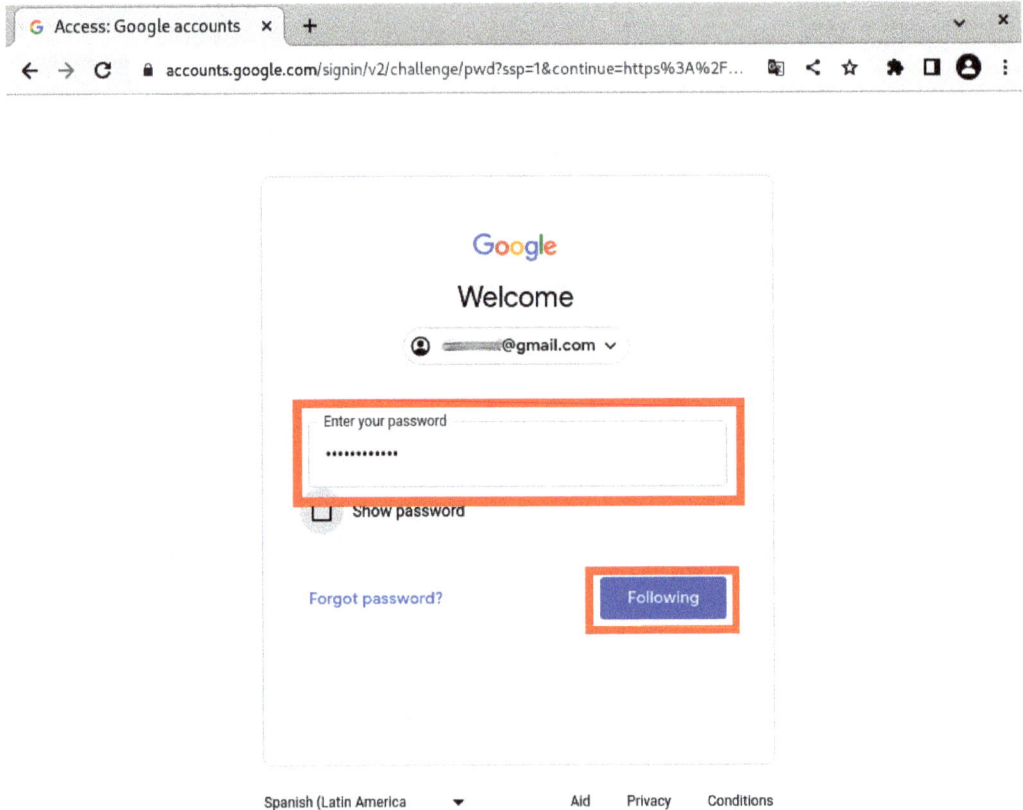

Figure 9.64 – The Google Chrome access screen

15. If you customized Chrome on another device and enabled sync, Chrome will configure automatically.

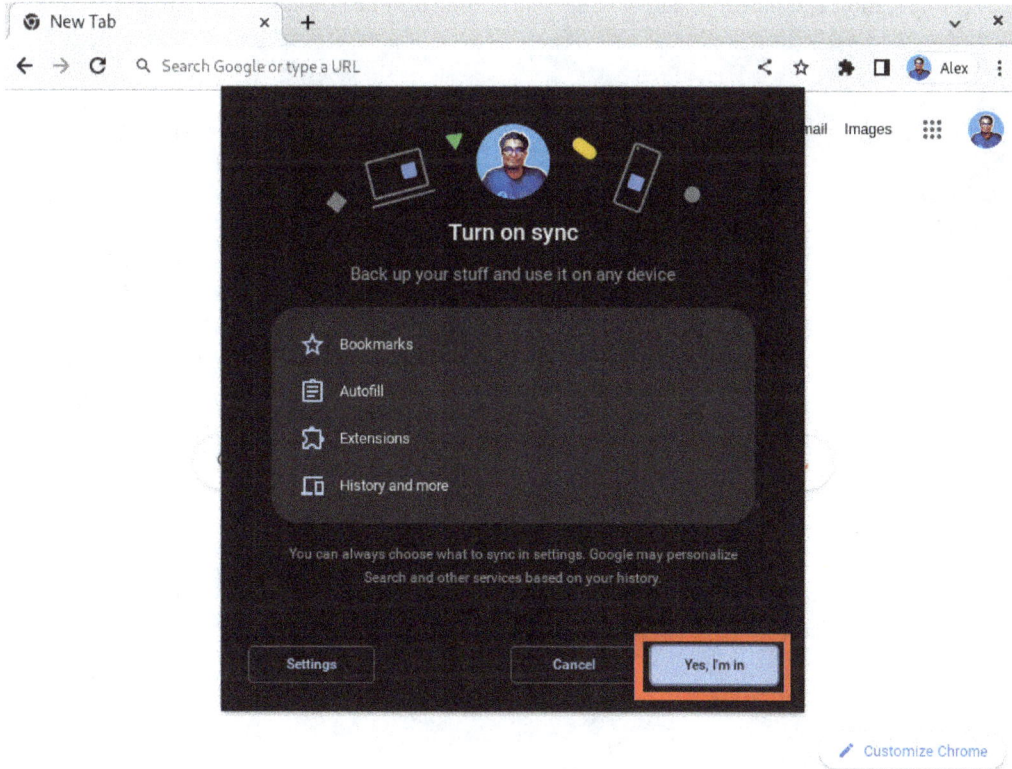

Figure 9.65 – The Google Chrome sync screen

16. Click the **Yes, I'm in** button to start the synchronized customization.

The automatic *application of your theme, installation of extensions and plugins*, as well as the configuration and downloading of your *history* and *bookmarks* will start running:

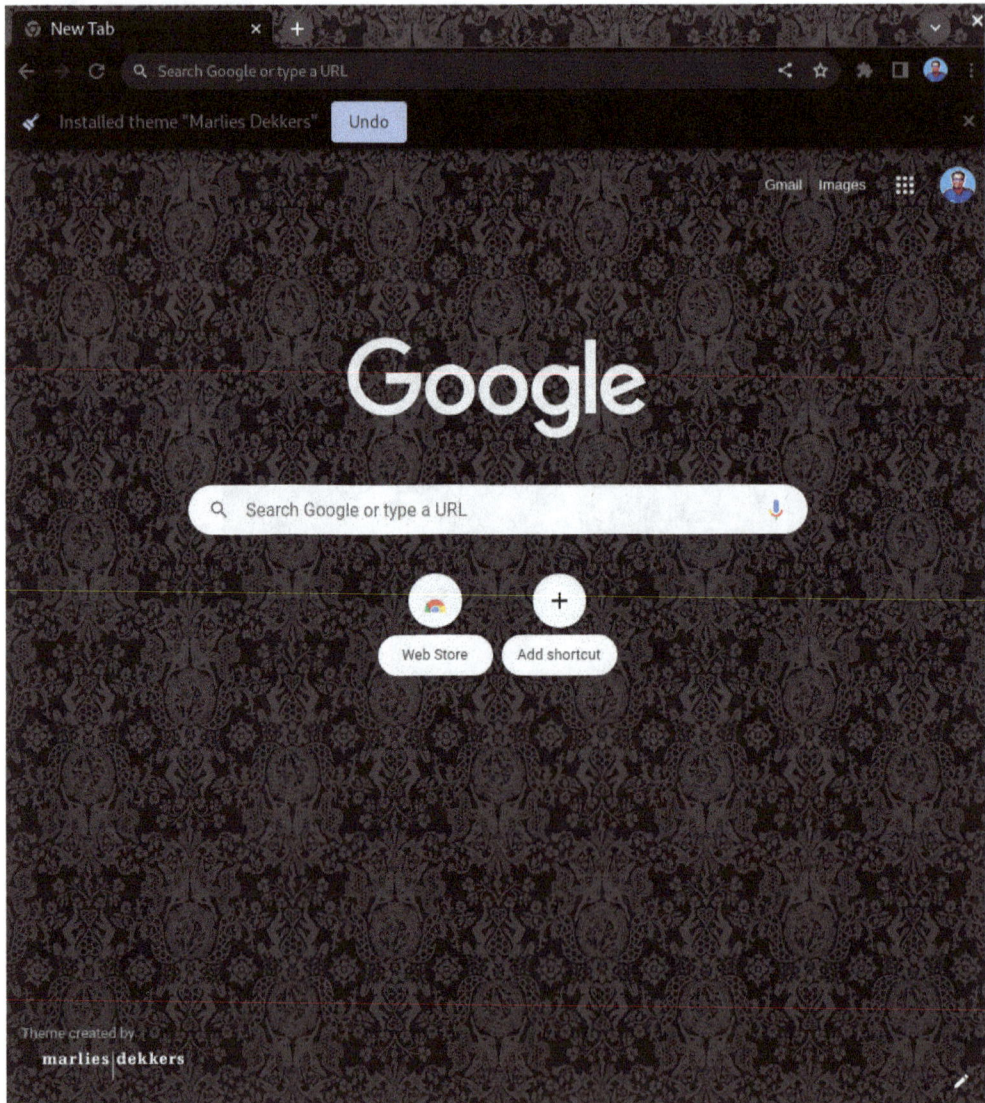

Figure 9.66 – Running the Google Chrome sync

17. After finishing the sync, Google Chrome will display the completed customization:

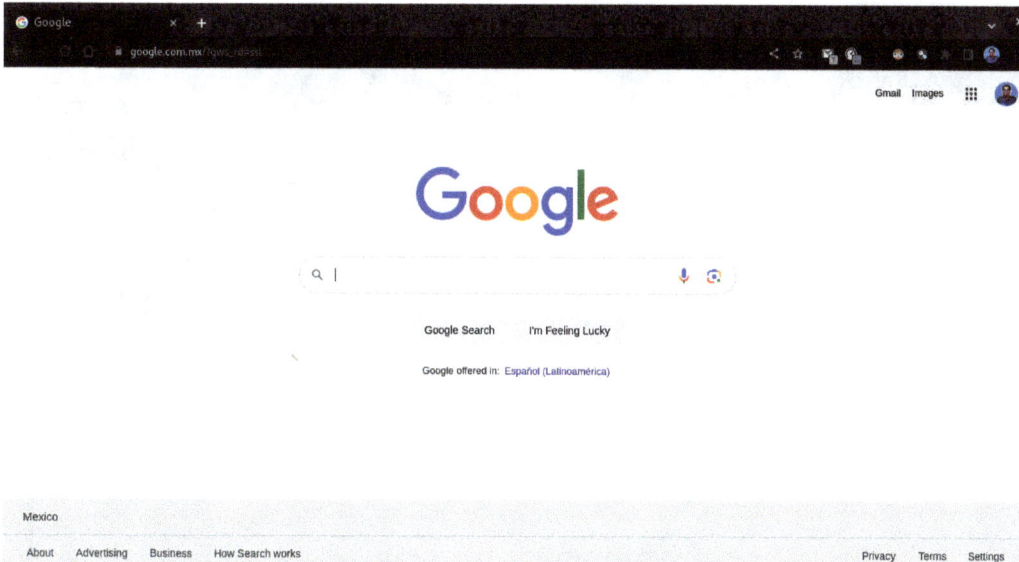

Figure 9.67 – Google Chrome customized

Like Firefox, Google Chrome offers the configuration and synchronization between devices. Chrome takes advantage of the use of Google services for configuration sync. The configuration and customization of Chrome is pretty similar to Firefox.

To access the Chrome settings, click on the button with the *three dots* icon (aka a vertical ellipsis) below the **x** button:

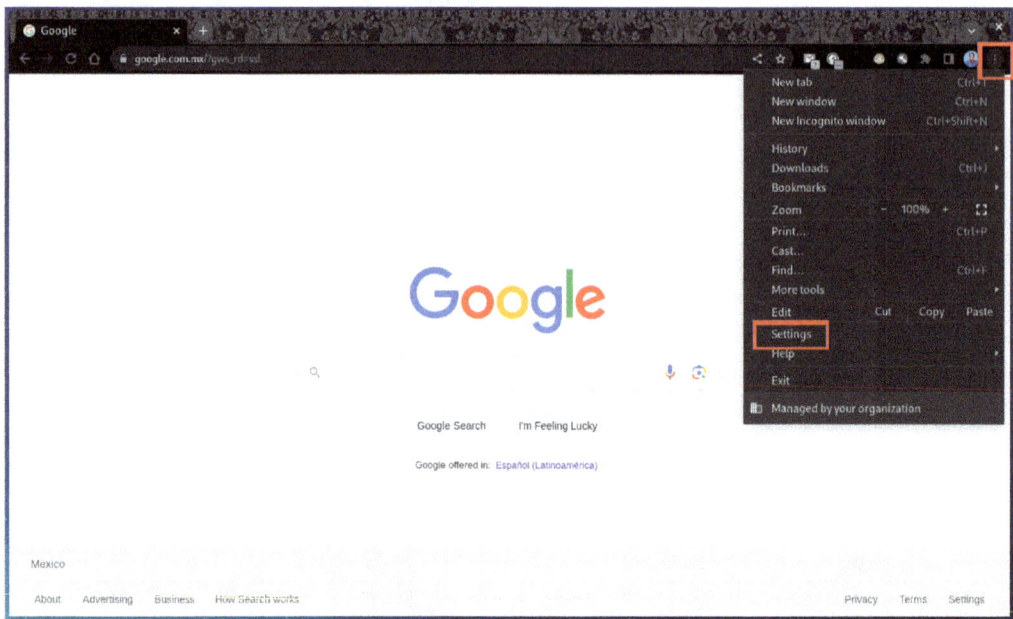

Figure 9.68 – Chrome settings

The Chrome settings appear in sections, and each one has several sections, among them the following:

- **You and Google**: Configures access account and syncs with **Google** services. From here, you can customize the profile, as well as import bookmarks and settings.

- **Autofill and passwords**: Manages the password manager, payment methods, and stored addresses and data.

- **Privacy and security**: Includes a security check option to detect security breaches, malicious extensions, and so on. It also manages privacy and security options.

- **Performance**: Adds a memory saver option, a type of *power saving mode*, for inactive open tabs.

- **Appearance**: Configures the appearance of the browser, such as the theme, the home page, as well as how to display the bookmarks bar or the side panel.

- **Search engine**: Configures the browser's search engine (which might differ from **Google**) and its behavior.

- **Default browser**: Detects the system default browser.

- **On startup**: Configures browser behavior at startup.

- **Languages**: Configures the preferred languages to display website content, as well as offering to spell-check when you type on websites.

- **Downloads**: Manages file downloads.

- **Accessibility**: Configures the browser accessibility options.

- **System**: Configures the browser behavior options in the operating system.

- **Reset settings**: Resets the browser settings to factory defaults.

- **Extensions**: Manages browser extensions and add-ons.

- **About Chrome**: Displays the browser version.

The following figure shows the sections of the Chrome settings:

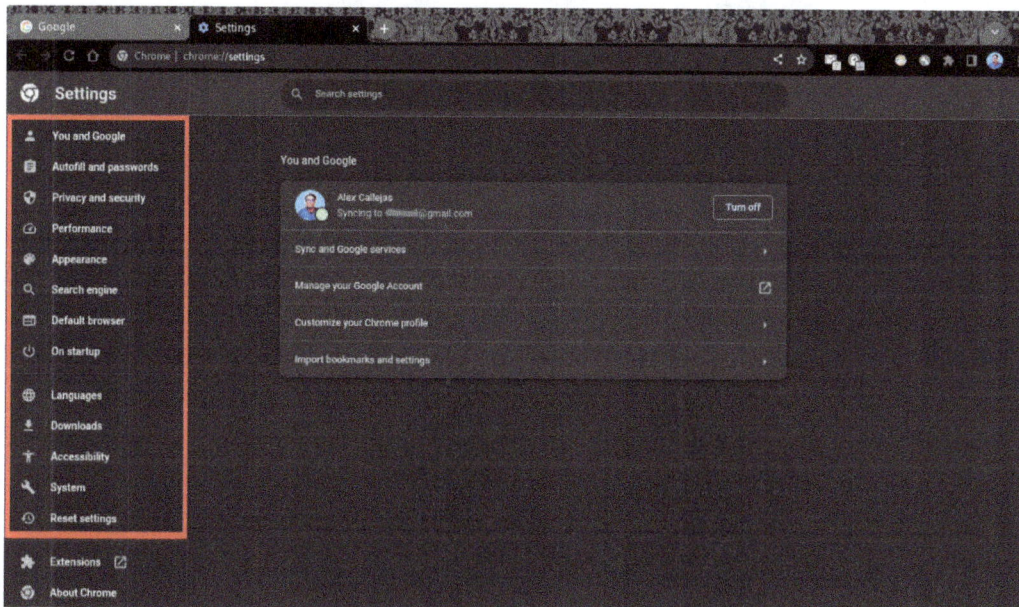

Figure 9.69 – The Chrome settings sections

Like in Firefox, you can access the **Settings** section of Chrome directly. For example, to view the browser version, type `chrome://settings/help` in the address bar:

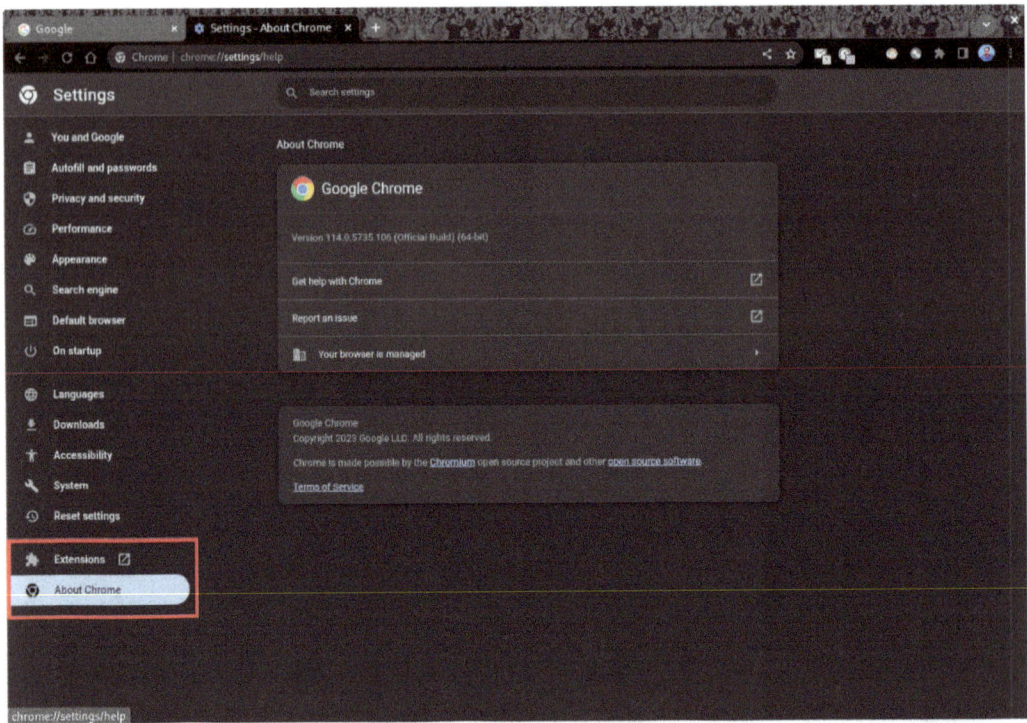

Figure 9.70 – The Chrome version

In this particular case, Chrome was customized with the **Google Mail Checker** extension (`https://chrome.google.com/webstore/detail/google-mail-checker/mihcahmgecmbnbcchbopgniflfhgnkff`), which adds a button to directly access Google Mail:

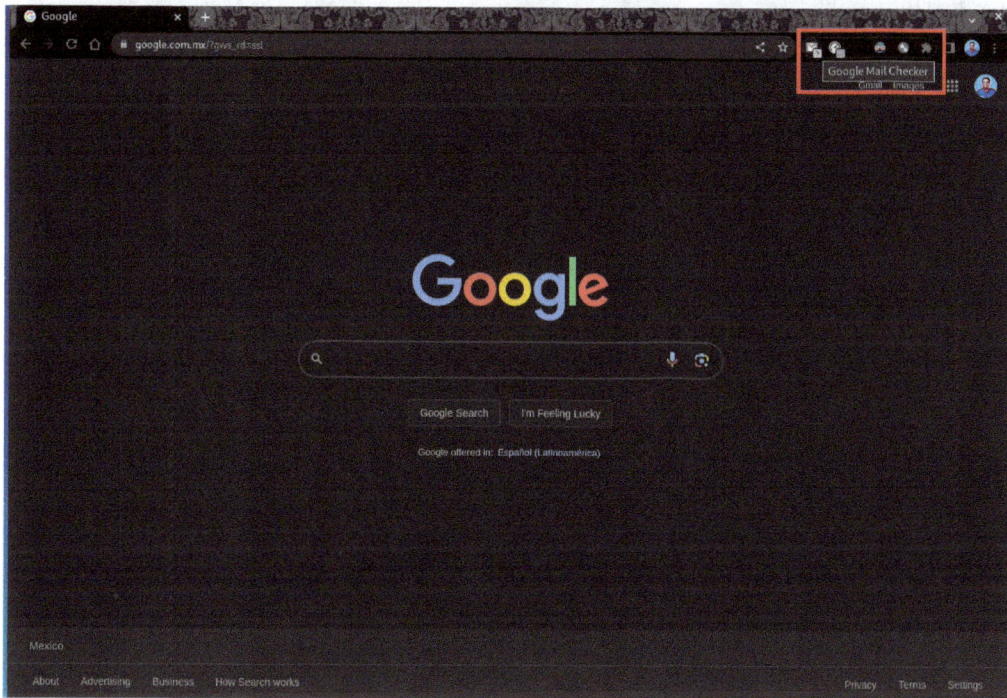

Figure 9.71 – The Google Mail Checker extension

To manage and add extensions in Chrome, click on the **Extensions** section of the Chrome settings, or type `chrome://extensions/` in the address bar:

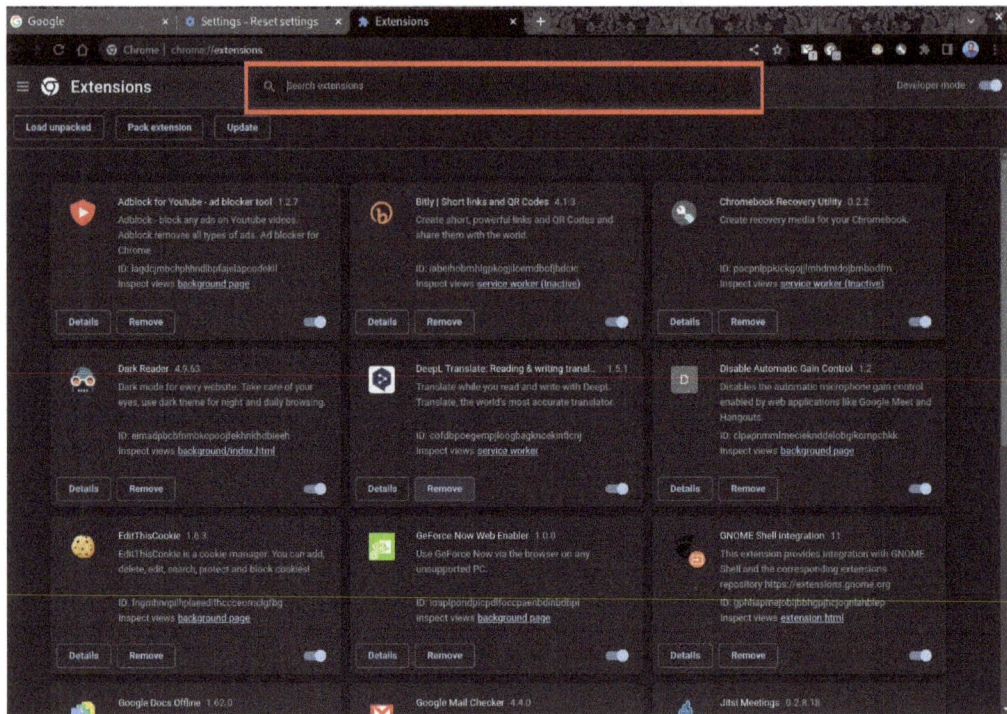

Figure 9.72 – Chrome extensions

From the search bar, you can find and install extensions with one click.

These applications are those most used for email and internet browsing in Fedora Linux Workstation.

With these applications, we have covered all the basic tools, establishing a baseline for the standardization of the managed systems' documentation.

In the following chapters, we will discuss the processes and best practices to generate the baseline, as well as a standardized system administration.

Summary

In this chapter, we learned how to install, configure, and use the most common Linux options for email and web browsing.

Evolution, supported by Red Hat and GNOME, is one of the most common mail clients in enterprise environments (according to opensource.com). This is because it allows you to connect to the Microsoft Exchange mail service.

The Mozilla Project provides us with two options for both services. The **Thunderbird** email client is an excellent alternative for email management, whereas **Firefox**, the most used web browser, is included in all Linux distributions.

Google Chrome proves a dynamic choice as a web browser. Based on open source projects, it offers the best of both worlds, with the integration of proprietary plugins. The use of a mail account in the services offered by Google provides mobility between devices, as well as flexibility when accessing them.

In the following chapter, we will look at the fundamentals of the concepts and processes for the administration of Linux systems, taking advantage of having a workstation with a compatible operating system.

Further reading

To learn more about the topics covered in this chapter, you can visit the following links:

- *Fedora Magazine – Email clients in Fedora*:

  https://fedoramagazine.org/email-clients-fedora/

- *Fedora docs – Mail Servers*:

  https://docs.fedoraproject.org/en-US/fedora/latest/system-administrators-guide/servers/Mail_Servers/

- *GNOME Wiki – Evolution*:

  https://wiki.gnome.org/Apps/Evolution

- *Thunderbird*:

  https://www.thunderbird.net/en-US/

- *Fedora Wiki – Firefox*:

  https://fedoraproject.org/wiki/Firefox

- *Fedora docs – Installing Chromium or Google Chrome browsers*:

  https://docs.fedoraproject.org/en-US/quick-docs/installing-chromium-or-google-chrome-browsers/

Part 4:
System Administration Tools

In this part, you will learn the best practices to perform system administrator tasks, starting from the basic principles. You will also receive tips on how to tune a system, use hardened security, and use virtualization and containers.

This part contains the following chapters:

- *Chapter 10, System Administration*
- *Chapter 11, Performance Tuning Best Practices*
- *Chapter 12, SELinux*
- *Chapter 13, Virtualization and Containers*

10

System Administration

Unlike many professions, there is no single path to becoming a system administrator. Many **SysAdmins** have a degree in a wide range of fields: **computer science**, **systems engineering**, **Information Technology**, **software engineering**, **mechanical engineering**, **meteorology**, and so on.

Plus, given the hands-on nature of system administration, and the availability of open source server software, many SysAdmins enter this field on a self-taught basis. Generally, it requires some prior experience with the system expected to be managed. In some cases, SysAdmin candidates must hold a certificate before they can be considered for the position.

This profession becomes more difficult if you don't have the habit of undertaking *best practices*.

But where do you learn them? Where are they written down?

In this chapter, we intend to clear up those doubts and help you on your way to becoming a **Linux system administrator**.

We're going to cover the following main topics:

- The three laws of the SysAdmin
- A little bit of Git and programming
- Don't forget to back up
- Automating with Ansible
- Never-ending study

Technical requirements

To complete the topics in this chapter, you will need to install the packages indicated in each section. In each section, you will find instructions for the different types of packages you will need to install.

The examples for this chapter can be downloaded from this book's **GitHub** repository: `https://github.com/PacktPublishing/Fedora-Linux-System-Administration/tree/main/chapter10`.

The three laws of the SysAdmin

"Because, if you stop to think of it, the three laws of robotics are the essential guiding principles of a good many of the world's ethical systems. [...] To put it simply, if Byerley follows all the laws of robotics, he may be a robot, or may simply be a very good man."

Dr. Susan Calvin in Evidence from Isaac Asimov

For more than 20 years, I was a SysAdmin for different companies. In those years, some young people asked me what the best practices were and if could they apply them to consider themselves a good SysAdmin. Over the years, I have read different articles about these *best practices*: **Ethics Code for SysAdmins**, **The 10 Commandments of the SysAdmin**, and even **Fundamental Laws of Computing**.

This job of becoming a platform SysAdmin is an arduous task that becomes complicated if we don't get into the habit of applying best practices. But where do you learn them? Where are they written down?

One of the best philosophies, in my experience, is to follow the **KISS principle** and, based on it, simplify the recommendations into fundamental principles that help us develop our skills.

Let's provide an overview of this principle.

The KISS principle

The KISS principle (an acronym for *Keep It Simple, Stupid!*) is a design principle that was outlined by the US Navy in 1960. It states that most systems work better if they're kept simple than if they become complicated. Thus, simplicity should be a key aim in design, and unnecessary complexity should be avoided.

A text attributed to *Leonardo Da Vinci* gives us a broad outline of the principle:

"Simplicity is the ultimate sophistication.

When once you have tasted flight, you will forever walk the Earth with your eyes turned skyward, for there you have been, and there you will always long to return.

Learning never exhausts the mind."

– Leonardo da Vinci

In most cases, simple solutions are more effective. Over the years, I have seen young SysAdmins fall into applying complex solutions that lead to more issues.

> **Note**
>
> For more information on how to apply the KISS principle in code creation, refer to *The Kiss Principle* at `https://people.apache.org/~fhanik/kiss.html`.

Based on this, let me share with you the fundamental principles that guide me in my work as a SysAdmin.

Let's see how these fundamental principles originated, and then delve deeper into them.

Knowing the basic tasks

This is from Wikipedia (`https://en.wikipedia.org/wiki/System_administrator`):

"A System Administrator is the person who handles implementing, configuring, maintaining, monitoring, documenting, and ensuring the proper functioning of a computer system, or some aspect of it."

Their purpose is to guarantee the *uptime, performance, resource usage*, and *security* of the servers that they manage.

They have different roles, such as *server administrator, database administrator, network administrator, email server administrator, web server administrator, security administrator, backup administrator,* and so on.

Depending on the role, the tasks change, but they converge on fundamental points.

Let's start with the most basic point, which is to *always use the command-line interface*. As mentioned in *Chapter 1*, the Terminal is the primary tool for operating system administration. Its use extends the capabilities of system administration and operation.

From my own experience, *any productive system will fail one day*, no matter how many precautions we have provided or maintenance we've undertaken. The best solution is to prepare for that day with a valid backup.

If we do not know what is critical in our system, then we should investigate what is critical and, thus, plan to have a backup. How do we know that a backup will serve us in case of disaster? Here are some questions you should ask when planning:

- What software (or script) is used for backing up?
- How much space do we have for backups (internal and external, on disk, or on tape)?
- How often should we rotate the backups?
- Regardless of the total backup (full backup), do we need incremental backups?

Once we have a clear idea of how we make the backup, we must take the necessary time to verify it. Although we have a good plan for creating backups, this does not mean that they won't be corrupted.

Backing up, and how often we do it, is *the most basic and generic task* in all types of system administration.

The majority of backup solutions allow us to handle this task via the command line. Thanks to this facility, the task could become *automated*, like many others. Automating tasks streamlines SysAdmins' work.

The statement *Lazy SysAdmin is the best SysAdmin* is well known. This means that if you are proactive enough to automate all processes, you will have a lot of *free time* and be considered lazy. The best SysAdmin never seems to be very busy and prefers relaxing and letting the system do the work for them. *Work smarter, not harder.*

But the free time we can get from *automating processes* should be used productively – maybe by studying some new language or emerging technologies we haven't mastered (Perl, Python, Kubernetes, and so on) or optimizing some script to turn it into an *orchestration*.

The following figure shows the evolution of these principles:

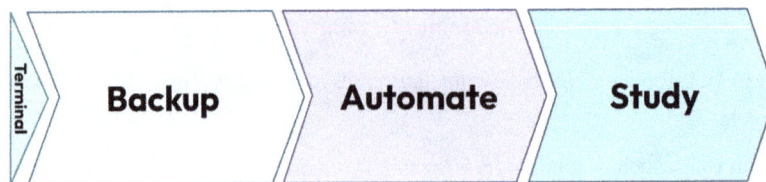

Figure 10.1 – Fundamental principles

Following these basic principles helped me improve many systems administration skills. Although they do not cover all aspects of systems administration per se, they create good habits that could develop many skills needed for this job.

These principles constitute my *fundamental laws of effective management* – that is, my three laws of the SysAdmin:

- **Back up**: A SysAdmin must back up the entire system and always verify the backup
- **Automate**: A SysAdmin should automate as much as possible, except if it conflicts with the first law
- **Study**: A SysAdmin must have free time to study, so long this free time does not conflict with the first or second law

Before we dive deep into each of the laws of system administration, let's take a quick look at a couple of indispensable tools for implementing them.

First, we'll look at programming and version management.

A little bit of Git and programming

Typical system administration tasks involve command-line tools. Tasks of greater complexity often need to chain several commands and share the results with each other. Linux commands can be combined to solve repetitive and difficult tasks using the Bash shell environment and basic programming functions.

As a command interpreter and a programming language in its own right, the Bash shell environment allows you to run routines and use expressions, besides running other programming languages.

These routines simplify the lists of commands, which can be included in a file called a *Bash script*.

Next, we'll learn how to create Bash scripts.

Bash scripting

Bash scripting consists of programming using commands as the program's instructions. This strategy automates repetitive tasks, reducing them to a single line through expressions such as logic gates, conditions, loops, and so on. Thus, it facilitates the consolidation of several long commands into a *single piece of code to run*.

It provides a structured, formatted, and modular sequence of activities, as well as commands with dynamic values through the use of command-line arguments.

In its simplest form, a Bash script consists of a runnable file containing a list of commands, and with programming logic to control decision-making in the task. Skill in shell scripting is essential for administering systems in any operating environment.

There is a lot of literature and many references on how to write a Bash script in the best way. However, by following the principle of simplicity mentioned at the beginning of this chapter, it could summarized as follows:

```
#!/bin/bash  ← [1]
#
# IDENTIFICATION  ← [2]
#

# VARIABLES  ← [3]

# COMMANDS  ← [4]
```

Let's take a closer look:

- [1] she-bang or sh-bang: The first line of a script starts with the #! notation. This is a *two-byte magic number* that indicates an interpretative script. The syntax that follows is the name of the command interpreter needed to run the lines of this script.

> **Note**
>
> To understand how magic numbers indicate file types in Linux, refer to the `file(1)` and `magic(5)` man pages.

- [2] IDENTIFICATION: The identification section of the script is essential and indispensable. This is the documentation of the script and includes the description of the routines run, as well as the version and even the author's details and license of use.

- [3] VARIABLES: This section declares the variables that run the script during its operation. The variables store information in the system's memory. The script uses local variables. These variables store information for short periods. Local variables exist and are valid only for the shell or session in which the script runs.

- [4] COMMANDS: This section lists the routines and commands to run. It also includes functions used to specify *run* commands in specific situations.

Let's see an example of a Bash script. Create a script that covers the following routines:

1. Name the file `mytasks.sh`.

2. Create a *working directory* named `class`.

3. Concatenate the following files as a `data` file in the working directory:

   - `/etc/passwd`

   - `/etc/group`

   - `/etc/shadow`

4. Create the following users:

   - `John`

   - `Peter`

   - `Mark`

5. Copy the `data` file to the users' home.

6. Generate an *activity log*.

The routines are simple: creating a *working directory* gives the administrator a single point of consolidation of working files. This makes backing up much easier. And, from system files, we create a data file, which must exist in each of the users' home directories – the same users that, if they do not exist in the system, must create them. All routines and activities performed by the Bash script should be recorded in the log for documentation purposes.

The Bash script involves creating users, so the user running the script must have the *appropriate privileges* to do so. One of the best options is to use the `sudo` command. Then, you can grant the *non-root user* the privilege to create users and assign the permissions needed to the files involved in the activities.

To make this example a little simpler, we'll use the `root` user. To switch to the `root` user, use the `sudo` command:

```
$ sudo -i
```

To create the Bash script, follow these steps:

1. Create and change to the `class` working directory:

    ```
    # mkdir class
    # cd class
    ```

2. Use your preferred text editor to create the `mytasks.sh` script file. In this example, we will use the `vim` editor:

    ```
    # vim mytasks.sh
    ```

3. As a `she-bang`, add the `#!/bin/bash` line:

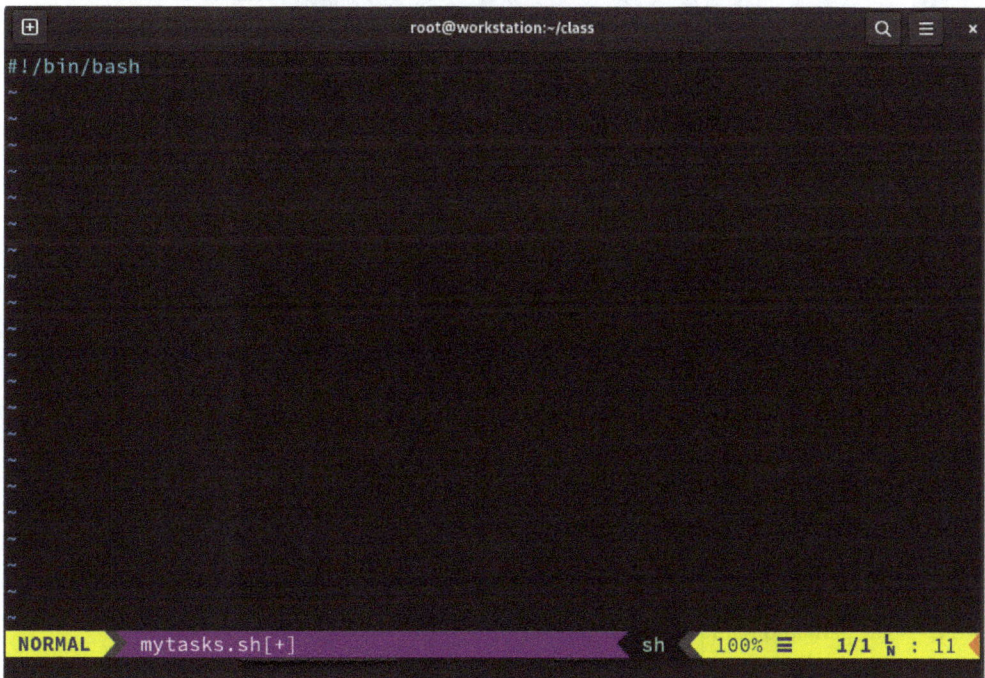

Figure 10.2 – Creating the mytasks.sh script

4. Fill in the IDENTIFICATION section with descriptive information about the script routine, including the version and the author of the script:

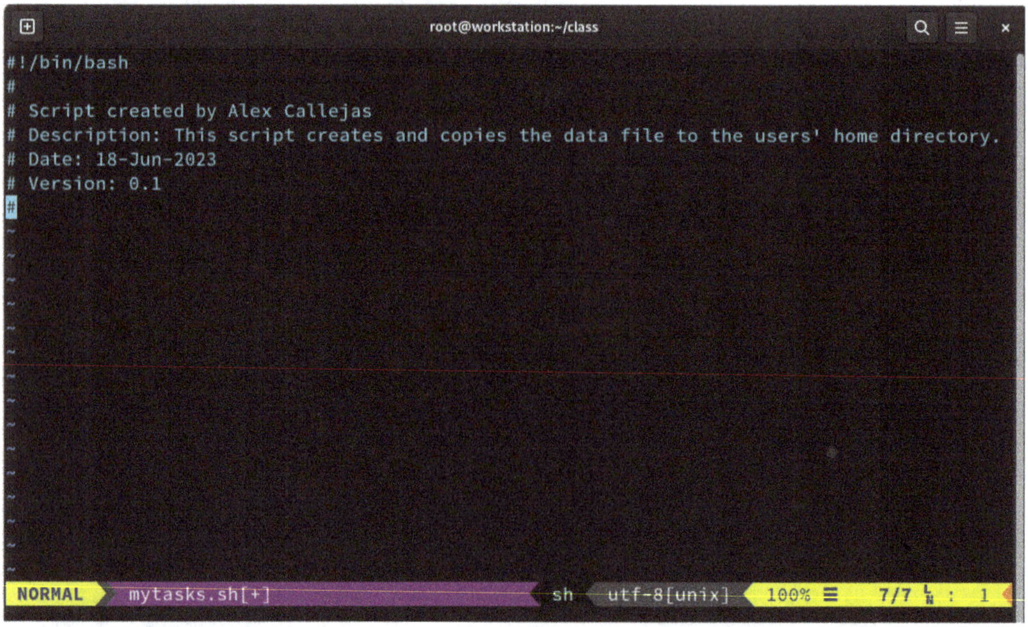

Figure 10.3 – Script identification section

5. In the VARIABLES section, we need to declare the static information, which won't change:

I.   The path and name of the class working directory:

WDIR=/root/class

II. The path and name of the log file:

LOG=**$WDIR**/mytasks.log

Please note how the working directory variable serves as the file path origin point.

III. The selected timestamp for the log record of the runs:

TIMESTAMP=$(**date** +'%Y-%m-%d %H:%M')

This output of the date command gets formatted as 2023-06-18 20:50.

IV. The path and name of DATA_FILE:

DATA_FILE=**$WDIR**/data

6. In the command section, test the use of variables and how tasks are logged and run by creating the data file:

    I.   Start recording a header with symbols to separate the activities in `log`:

        ```
        echo "+++++++++++++++++++++++++++++++++++++++" >> $LOG
        ```

        To record the activities in `log`, run an `echo` command with the activity and direct the output to the `log` file.

    II. Record the start of the script so that you can count the time it takes to perform the routine:

        ```
        echo "$TIMESTAMP [INFO] Start running mytasks.sh" >> $LOG
        ```

        Using `log` levels (`info`, `error`, `warn`, and so on) allows you to distinguish the outputs of the activities.

> **Note**
>
> To learn more about kernel log levels, refer to the `syslog(2)` man page.

    III. Record the first activity – that is, creating the data file:

        ```
        echo "$TIMESTAMP [INFO] Create data file" >> $LOG
        cat /etc/passwd >> $DATA_FILE
        cat /etc/group >> $DATA_FILE
        cat /etc/shadow >> $DATA_FILE
        ```

        This same first activity can be seen in the following screenshot:

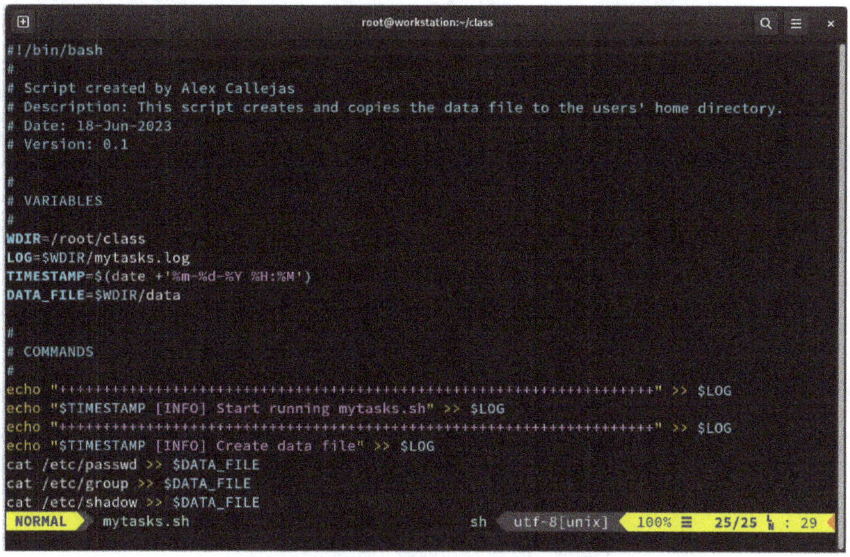

Figure 10.4 – The first version of mytasks.sh

Now, let's test this first version of the Bash script:

1. Set *run rights* to the `mytasks.sh` script:

    ```
    # chmod +x mytasks.sh
    ```

    ```
    [root@workstation class]# ls -l mytasks.sh
    -rw-r--r--. 1 root root 667 Jun 18 20:30 mytasks.sh
    [root@workstation class]# chmod +x mytasks.sh
    [root@workstation class]# ls -l mytasks.sh
    -rwxr-xr-x. 1 root root 667 Jun 18 20:30 mytasks.sh
    [root@workstation class]#
    ```

    Figure 10.5 – Setting run rights to mytasks.sh

2. Run the `mytasks.sh` script:

    ```
    # ./mytasks.sh
    ```

3. Verify the creation of the `data` file:

    ```
    [root@workstation class]# ./mytasks.sh
    [root@workstation class]# ls
    data  mytasks.log  mytasks.sh
    [root@workstation class]# cat data
    root:x:0:0:Super User:/root:/bin/bash
    bin:x:1:1:bin:/bin:/usr/sbin/nologin
    daemon:x:2:2:daemon:/sbin:/usr/sbin/nologin
    adm:x:3:4:adm:/var/adm:/usr/sbin/nologin
    lp:x:4:7:lp:/var/spool/lpd:/usr/sbin/nologin
    sync:x:5:0:sync:/sbin:/bin/sync
    shutdown:x:6:0:shutdown:/sbin:/sbin/shutdown
    halt:x:7:0:halt:/sbin:/sbin/halt
    mail:x:8:12:mail:/var/spool/mail:/usr/sbin/nologin
    operator:x:11:0:operator:/root:/usr/sbin/nologin
    games:x:12:100:games:/usr/games:/usr/sbin/nologin
    ftp:x:14:50:FTP User:/var/ftp:/usr/sbin/nologin
    nobody:x:65534:65534:Kernel Overflow User:/:/usr/sbin/nologin
    dbus:x:81:81:System Message Bus:/:/usr/sbin/nologin
    apache:x:48:48:Apache:/usr/share/httpd:/sbin/nologin
    tss:x:59:59:Account used for TPM access:/:/usr/sbin/nologin
    systemd-network:x:192:192:systemd Network Management:/:/usr/sbin/nologin
    systemd-oom:x:999:999:systemd Userspace OOM Killer:/:/usr/sbin/nologin
    systemd-resolve:x:193:193:systemd Resolver:/:/usr/sbin/nologin
    qemu:x:107:107:qemu user:/:/sbin/nologin
    polkitd:x:998:997:User for polkitd:/:/sbin/nologin
    avahi:x:70:70:Avahi mDNS/DNS-SD Stack:/var/run/avahi-daemon:/sbin/nologin
    geoclue:x:997:996:User for geoclue:/var/lib/geoclue:/sbin/nologin
    nm-openconnect:x:996:995:NetworkManager user for OpenConnect:/:/sbin/nologin
    ```

    Figure 10.6 – Verifying the data file

4. Verify that activities are recorded in the `log` file:

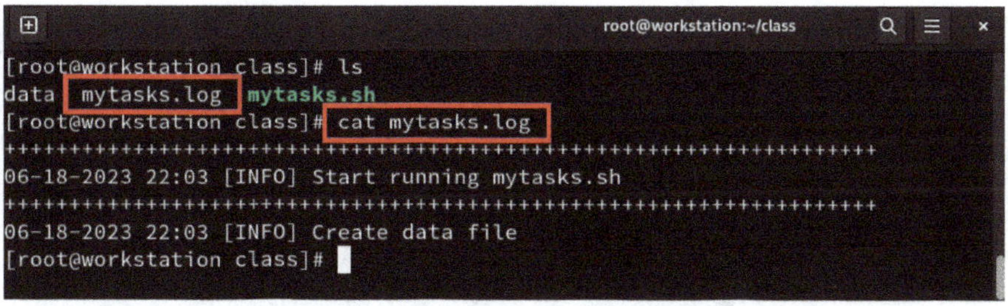

Figure 10.7 – Verifying the log file

As we can see, the `data` file was created and the activities were recorded in the `log` file.

The next step is to create the users. However, note that every time the Bash script runs, the `data` file must be created. Before continuing, now is a good time to add a validation:

- If the `data` file exists, continue with the following instruction.

- If the `data` file is not present, then you can create it.

5. For validation, use an `if-else` statement. A basic effective `if-else` statement indicates that if a particular test is `true`, then it performs a given set of commands. If it is `false`, then perform a different set of commands.

In the COMMANDS section, add the following `if-else` statement:

```
echo "$TIMESTAMP [INFO] Verify the data file" >> $LOG
if [ -f $DATA_FILE ];
then
    echo "$TIMESTAMP [OK] The data file exists" >> $LOG
else
    echo "$TIMESTAMP [INFO] Create data file" >> $LOG
    cat /etc/passwd >> $DATA_FILE
    cat /etc/group >> $DATA_FILE
    cat /etc/shadow >> $DATA_FILE
fi
```

Note that the commands that create the `data` file can be turned into a basic `for` loop:

```
for i in passwd group shadow
do
    cat /etc/$i >> $DATA_FILE
done
```

A `for` loop in Bash is a statement that allows code to run repeatedly.

The COMMANDS section looks as follows:

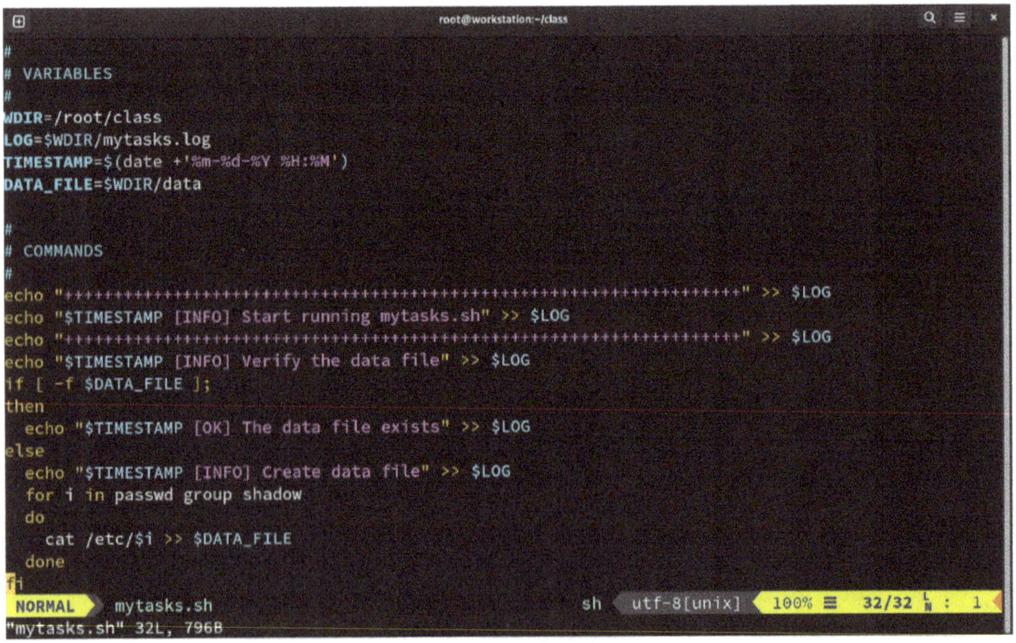

Figure 10.8 – The COMMANDS section of mytasks.sh

Save the changes and test them.

6. Verify the run in the log file record:

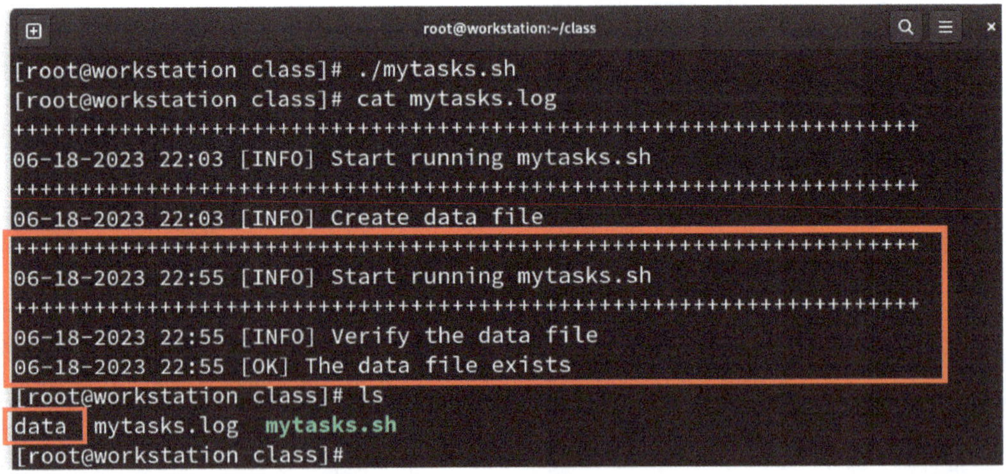

Figure 10.9 – Verifying the run on the log file

7. Delete the data file and rerun the mytasks.sh script to confirm the creation of the data file:

```
# rm -rf data
```

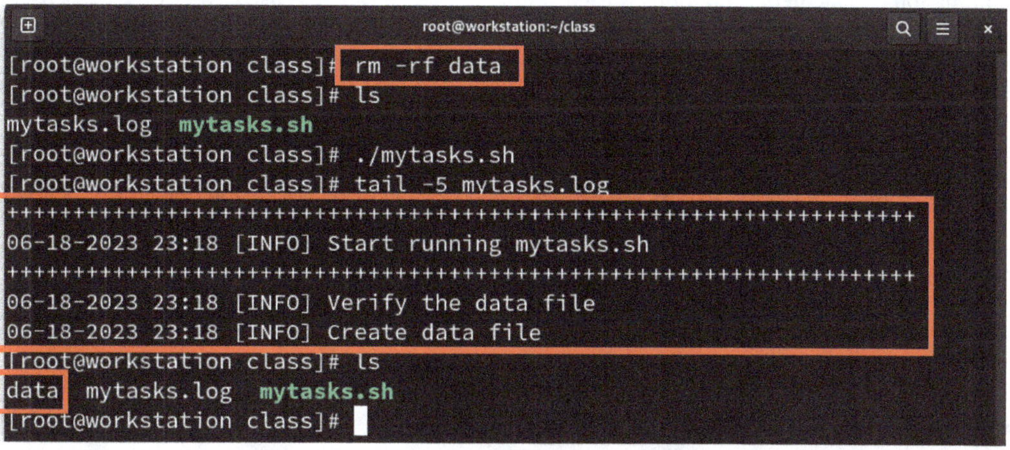

Figure 10.10 – Validating the creation of the data file

Since this change worked, the version of the Bash script could change:

```
# Version: 0.2 → Add data file validation
```

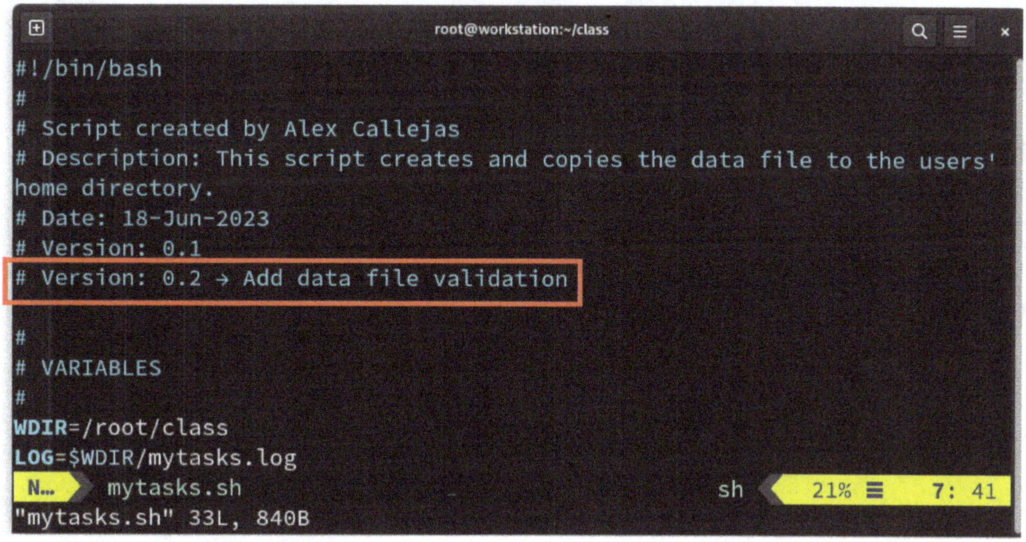

Figure 10.11 – Modifying the version of mytasks.sh

Let's continue by adding the routine activities.

The routine includes creating users and copying the data file to their home directories. Here, a combination of statements and loops is used so that the script can be reused every time extra users are added to it:

1. Begin by recording the activity in the log file:

    ```
    echo "$TIMESTAMP [INFO] Verify users" >> $LOG
    ```

2. Use a for loop to confirm the users and the data file in their home directories. Instead of adding the usernames to the script, instruct the loop to take the reading of a users file as input. So, add the users file to the VARIABLES section:

    ```
    USER_FILE=$WDIR/users
    ```

3. Create the users file with the requested usernames:

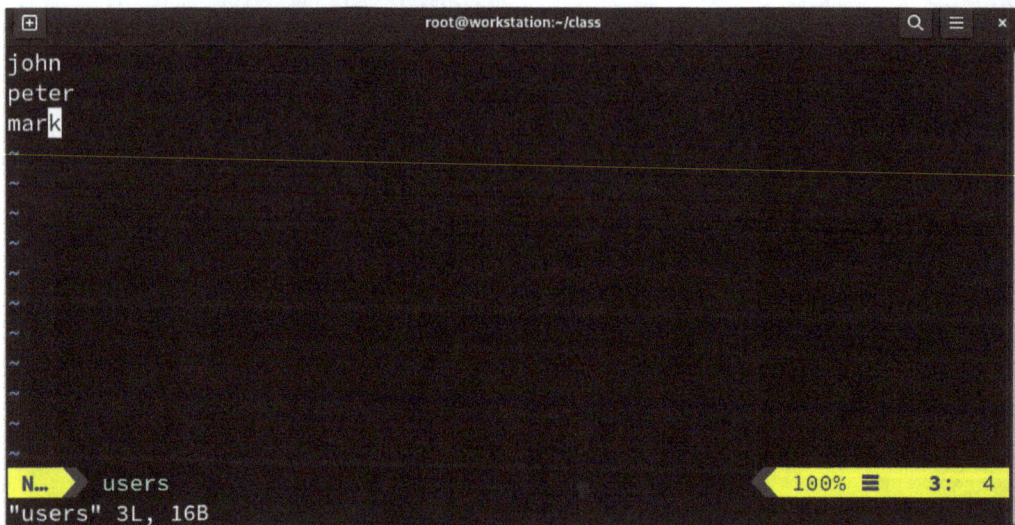

Figure 10.12 – The users file

4. In the for loop, for each line representing a user, first, confirm the user's existence in the /etc/passwd file. If the user exists, then confirm the data file in the user's home directory. If both statements are positive, only then both statements are recorded in the log file.

    If either statement is negative, then create the user and copy the data file to the user's home directory. Alternatively, you can copy the data file to its home directory, in case the user exists but the data file doesn't. This statement takes the form of a *nested if statement*:

```
echo "$TIMESTAMP [INFO] Verify users" >> $LOG
for i in $(cat $USER_FILE)
do
  grep $i /etc/passwd
  if [ $? == 0  ];
  then
    echo "$TIMESTAMP [WARN] The user $i exists" >> $LOG
    if [ -f /home/$i/data ];
    then
      echo "$TIMESTAMP [OK] The data file exists on $i's home directory" >> $LOG
    else
      echo "$TIMESTAMP [INFO] Copy data file on $i's home directory" >> $LOG
      cp $DATA_FILE /home/$i/
    fi
  else
    echo "$TIMESTAMP [INFO] Create the user $i" >> $LOG
    useradd $i
    echo "$TIMESTAMP [INFO] Copy data file on $i's home directory" >> $LOG
    cp $DATA_FILE /home/$i/
  fi
done
```
NORMAL   mytasks.sh   sh   utf-8[unix]   100% ≡   55/55 L : 4   ☰ [38]tra…

Figure 10.13 – A nested if statement

5. Run the `mytasks.sh` script and confirm that the users were created and that the `data` file was copied to their home directories:

```
[root@workstation class]# ./mytasks.sh
[root@workstation class]# tail mytasks.log
++++++++++++++++++++++++++++++++++++++++++++++++++++++++++++
06-19-2023 00:56 [INFO] Verify the data file
06-19-2023 00:56 [OK] The data file exists
06-19-2023 00:56 [INFO] Verify users
06-19-2023 00:56 [INFO] Create the user john
06-19-2023 00:56 [INFO] Copy data file on john's home directory
06-19-2023 00:56 [INFO] Create the user peter
06-19-2023 00:56 [INFO] Copy data file on peter's home directory
06-19-2023 00:56 [INFO] Create the user mark
06-19-2023 00:56 [INFO] Copy data file on mark's home directory
[root@workstation class]#
```

Figure 10.14 – Testing user creation and data file copying

6. Rerun the test for user creation and data file copy to confirm the condition:

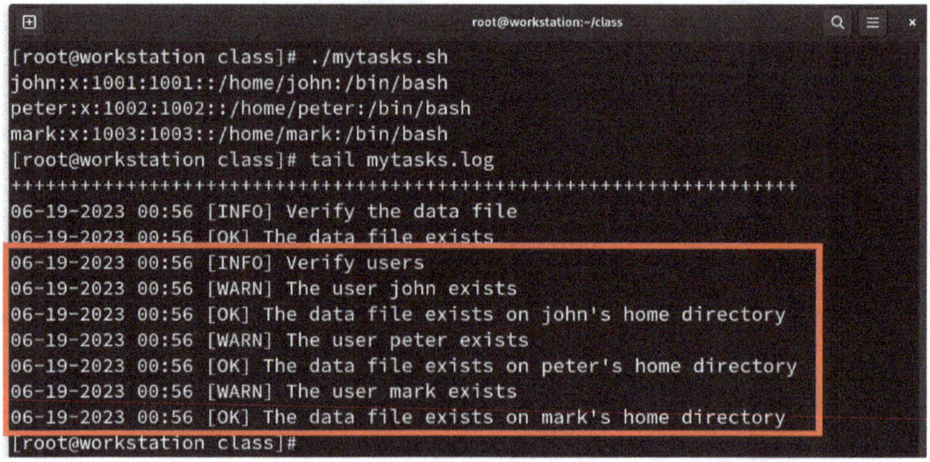

Figure 10.15 – Creation and copy condition confirmed

7. Add the `lucas` user to the `user` file and run the `mytasks.sh` script to confirm the creation of the user and that the `data` file was copied:

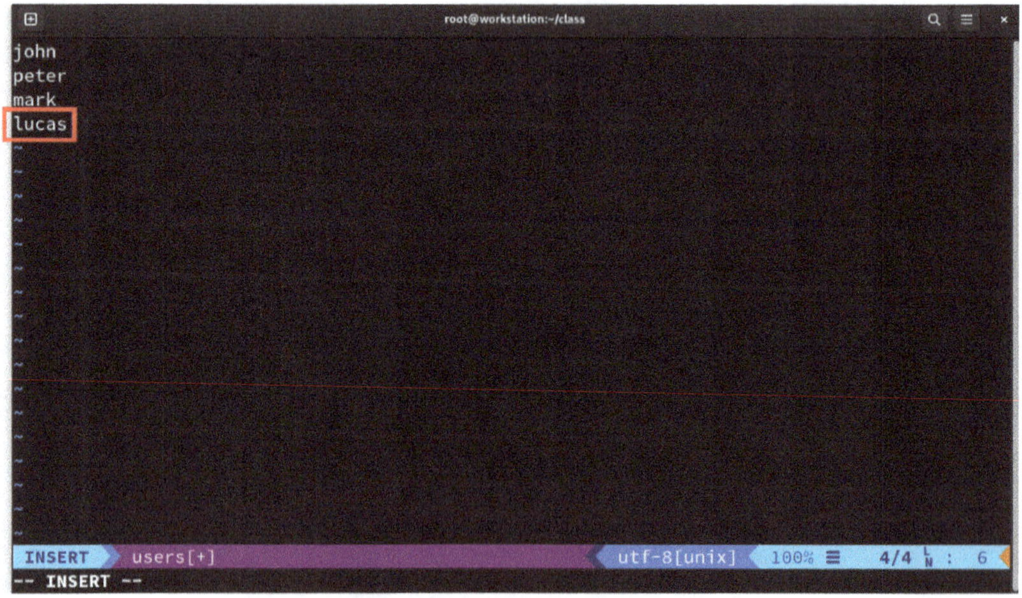

Figure 10.16 – Adding the lucas user

8. Run the script and review the `log` file:

```
[root@workstation class]# ./mytasks.sh
john:x:1001:1001::/home/john:/bin/bash
peter:x:1002:1002::/home/peter:/bin/bash
mark:x:1003:1003::/home/mark:/bin/bash
[root@workstation class]# tail mytasks.log
06-19-2023 01:02 [OK] The data file exists
06-19-2023 01:02 [INFO] Verify users
06-19-2023 01:02 [WARN] The user john exists
06-19-2023 01:02 [OK] The data file exists on john's home directory
06-19-2023 01:02 [WARN] The user peter exists
06-19-2023 01:02 [OK] The data file exists on peter's home directory
06-19-2023 01:02 [WARN] The user mark exists
06-19-2023 01:02 [OK] The data file exists on mark's home directory
06-19-2023 01:02 [INFO] Create the user lucas
06-19-2023 01:02 [INFO] Copy data file on lucas's home directory
[root@workstation class]#
```

Figure 10.17 – Reviewing user creation and copying the data file

9. The nested `if` statement works and results in the version of the script being changed. Since this is a working version that meets the needs of the routine, this makes it the first version of the script:

    ```
    # Version: 1.0 → Add user creation and customization
    ```

> **Note**
>
> You can find the `mytasks.sh` script in this book's GitHub repository at `https://github.com/PacktPublishing/Fedora-Linux-System-Administration/tree/main/chapter10/`.

This small script exemplifies how to simplify routine day-to-day tasks. If you have any doubts about whether a routine could be a Bash script, remember one of the most well-known statements among SysAdmins:

"*If you typed it twice, you should have scripted it once.*"

The problems come when you're modifying the scripts and managing their versions.

A tool that could help us when we need to manage different versions of scripts or configuration files is Git.

Let's learn a little bit about this tool.

Git

Git is a form of control version software designed by *Linus Torvalds* and released in 2007. It maintains versions of applications, prioritizes *efficiency*, *reliability*, and *compatibility*, and provides a record of changes to the files. It also coordinates the work that several people do on shared files in a code repository.

Git has supported the growth of open source software in recent years, making collaboration between programmers around the world easier.

Version control allows you to record changes that have been made to a file or set of files over time so that specific versions can be retrieved later.

Git is a *distributed version control system*. Besides the central repository, the clients replicate the entire repository, including its complete history. Thus, if a server fails, any of the repository clients could get copied back to the server to restore it. Each clone is a complete backup of all data.

GitLab and **GitHub** provide the most important *Git-based* web services. Each of them allows us to share repositories of our projects, both *private and public*.

To access GitHub, use your preferred browser and navigate to `https://github.com/login`. Log in or create your account by following the instructions on the page:

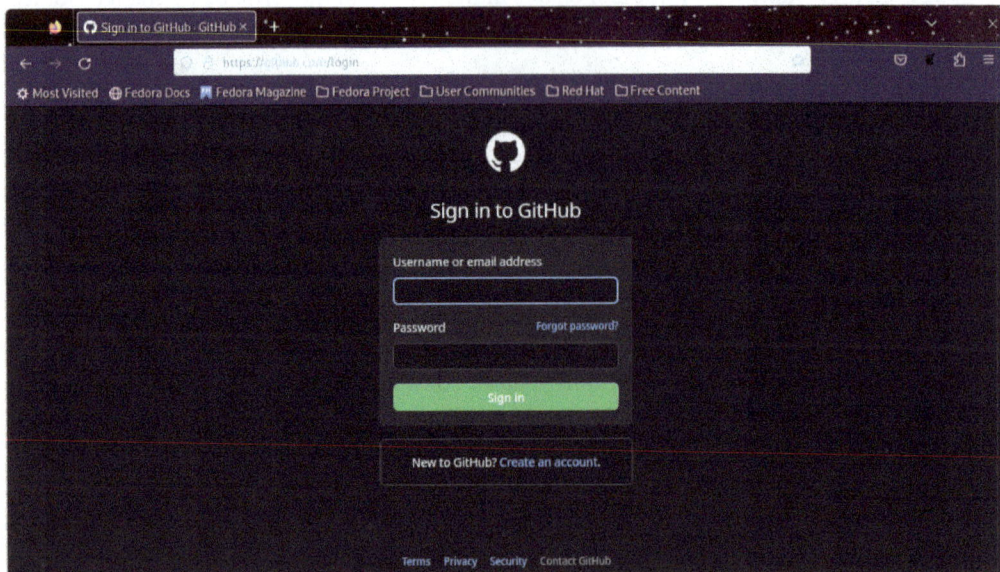

Figure 10.18 – GitHub login page

To access GitLab, use your preferred browser and navigate to `https://gitlab.com/users/login`. Log in or register to create your account by following the instructions on the page. Also, consider signing in using other web services such as **Google**, **GitHub**, **Twitter**, **Bitbucket**, or **Salesforce** for authentication. Each service will ask you if you want GitLab to access your account:

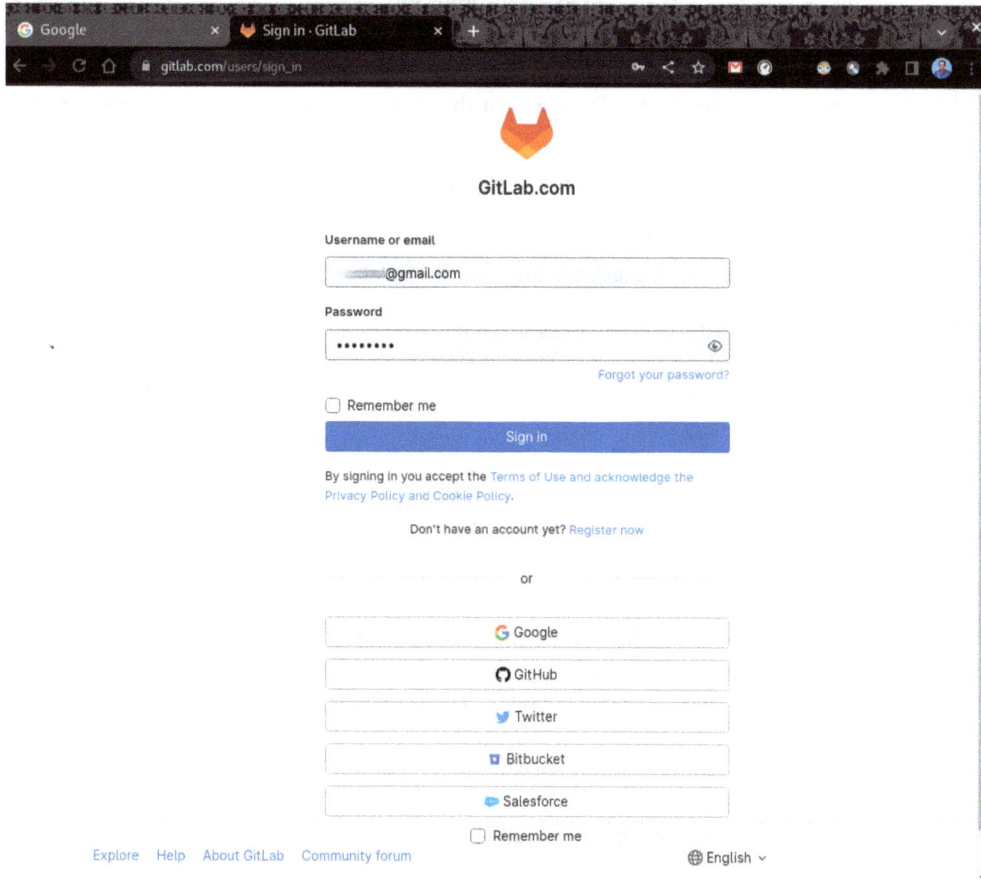

Figure 10.19 – GitLab – The Sign in page

Now, let's learn how to work with Git. We use a local repository, but it could live on a dedicated server or a web service platform.

> **Note**
>
> The examples that follow illustrate how to use Git, so the public repository on the web could use either of the two free services. *Choose wisely*.

Let's start with the basics.

The basics

Git handles files as a set of snapshots of a mini filesystem. Most operations in Git only need local files and resources to work. Everything in Git gets verified before storage. Therefore, it is identified by a *checksum* (as an identification number). Git generally adds information.

Git has three main states that files come in: *modified*, *staged*, and *committed*:

- **Modified** means that the file has changed but the changes have not been committed to the database yet

- **Staged** means that a modified file, in its current version, gets marked to go to the next commit instance

- **Committed** means that the changes are stored in the local database

The following figure illustrates the state changes of a file within Git:

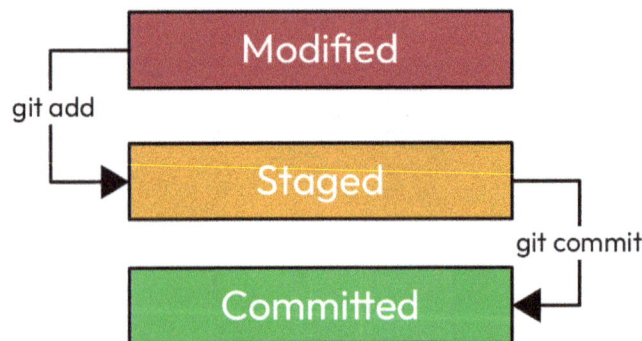

Figure 10.20 – File state change flow in Git

In *Chapter 2*, we installed Git on our workstation. Let's set up our session and create a sample repository. Follow these steps:

1. As a *non-root user*, set up a username and associate it with an email address. This data gets saved with the changes that are made. Use the `git config` command:

   ```
   $ git config --global user.name "username"
   $ git config --global user.email user@your-mail.com
   ```

2. Create a directory and switch to it:

   ```
   $ mkdir git-basics ; cd git-basics
   ```

3. Initialize the directory as a `git` repository:

    ```
    $ git init .
    Initialized empty Git repository in /home/username/git-basics/.
    git/
    ```

    The `git-basics` directory is now a `git` repo, so it might contain one of the states mentioned previously:

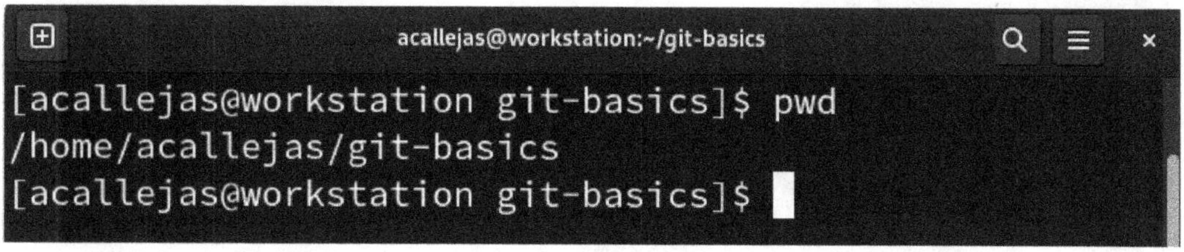

    Figure 10.21 – The git-basics directory

    To be able to see the state of the repository, add a custom configuration in the user's profile.

4. Add the following lines to the `.bashrc` file of the user:

    ```
    #
    # Lines added for git-prompt
    #
    git_prompt_sh='/usr/share/git-core/contrib/completion/
    git-prompt.sh'
    if [ -f ${git_prompt_sh} ]; then
      source ${git_prompt_sh}
      export GIT_PS1_SHOWDIRTYSTATE=true
      export GIT_PS1_SHOWUNTRACKEDFILES=true
      export PS1='[\u@\h \W$(declare -F __git_ps1 &>/dev/null && __
    git_ps1 " (%s)")]\$ '
    fi
    ```

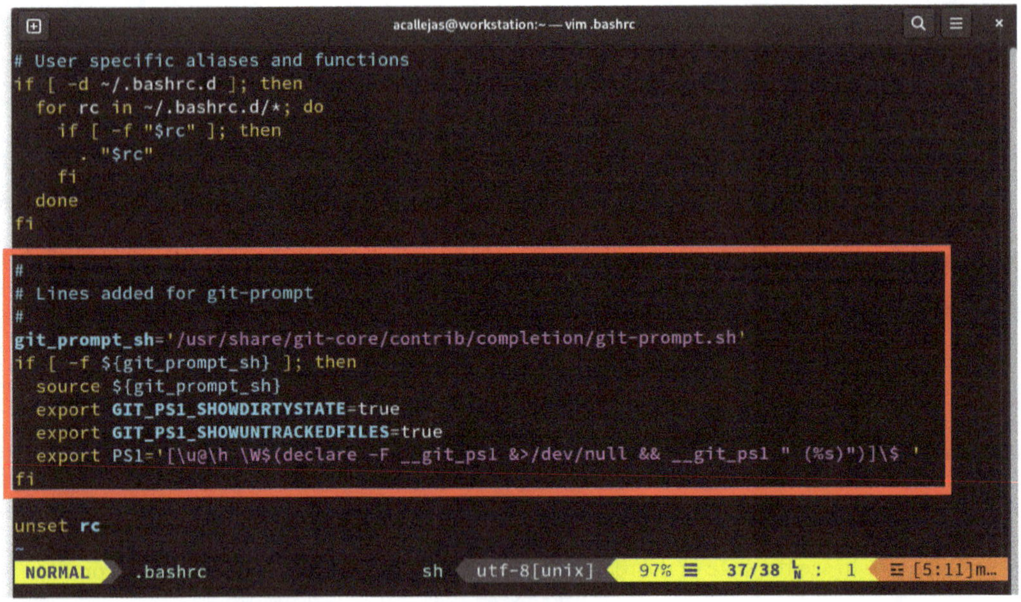

Figure 10.22 – Adding git-prompt to the .bashrc file

5.   After saving this change to the `.bashrc` file, return to the `git-basics` directory:

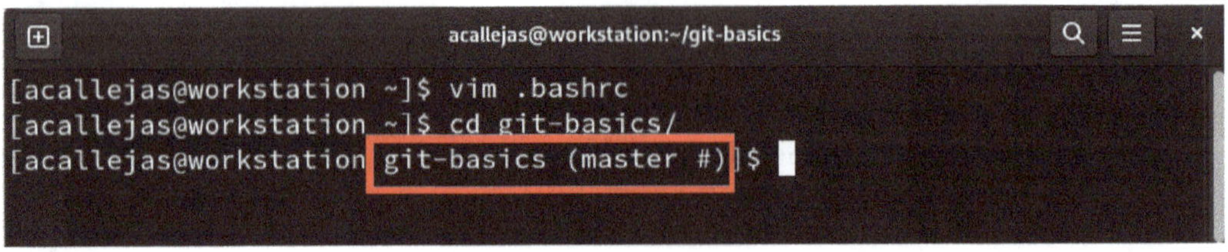

Figure 10.23 – git-basics

Note that the prompt now shows the initial branch of the repo, which is named `master`.

`master` is the initial name of the branch by default. Before we start adding files, let's rename the branch.

6.   Use the `git branch` command to change the branch's name from `master` to `main`:

```
$ git branch -m master main
```

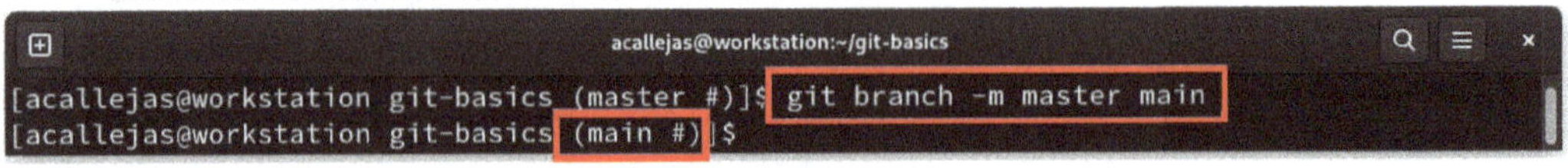

Figure 10.24 – Renaming the initial branch

Now, it's time to add files to the repository.

7. Create a Python script called my-script.py with the following content:

```
name = input("What's your name? ")
print(name + " Welcome!")
```

Upon running this script, you will asked for your name and you'll see a welcome message.

8. After saving the file, review the status of the repository by running the git status command:

```
$ git status
```

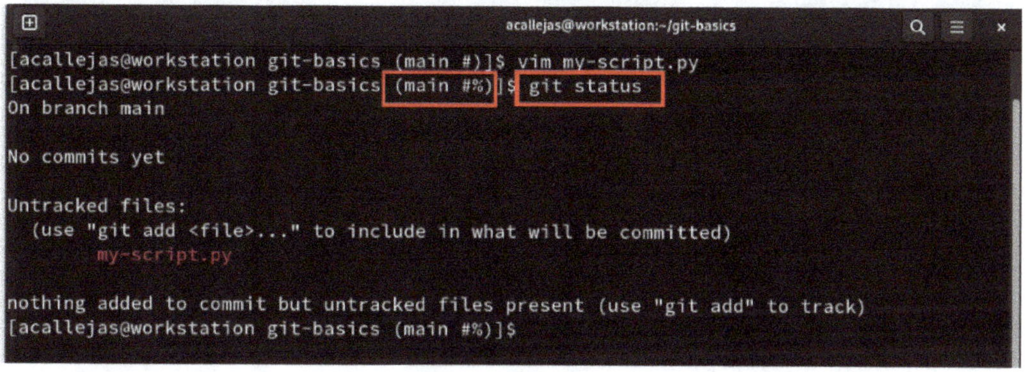

Figure 10.25 – Reviewing the status of the repository

The output of the command shows that the repository has changed. Note that some files are not *tracked* until their status changes.

At the *prompt*, you should now see the % symbol, which indicates that a file has been added to the repository.

Let's look at some other symbols that were added to the prompt concerning the repository's status:

* Unstaged (*)
* Staged (+)

Note

To learn more about git-prompt, refer to the documentation of the git-prompt.sh script at /usr/share/git-core/contrib/completion/git-prompt.sh.

Now, let's change the repository's status.

9. Use the `git add` command to add the file to the repository:

```
$ git add my-script.py
```

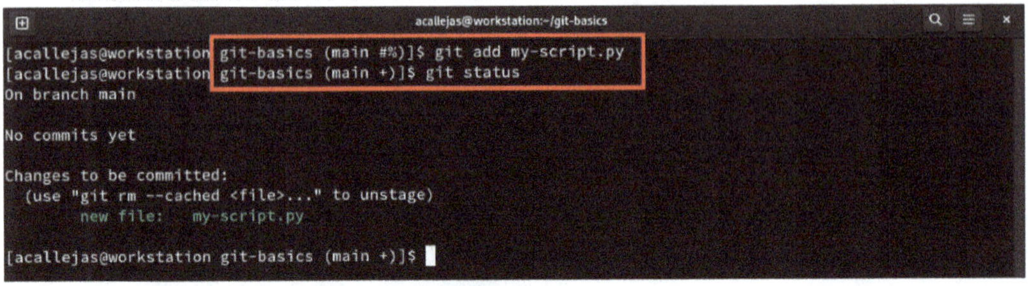

Figure 10.26 – Changing the repository's status

Now, the repository's status appears as `staged`, and the prompt displays the respective symbol (+).

Before we store the changes in the database, we need to test the file and review that no other changes need to be made.

10. Run the `my-script.py` script and verify that it works fine:

```
$ python my-script.py
```

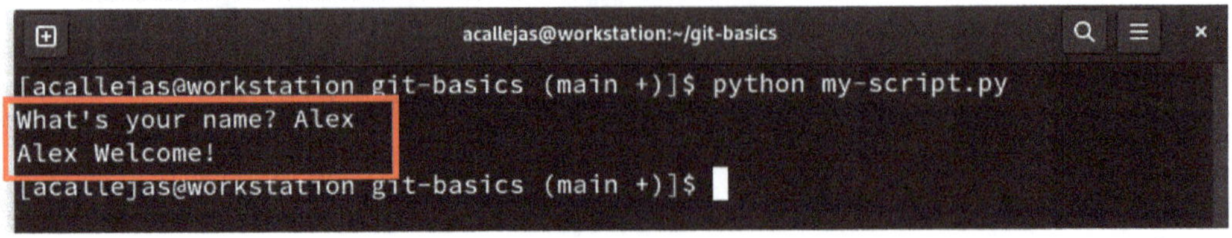

Figure 10.27 – Testing the my-script.py script

Since the script ran successfully, let's commit to adding the file to the repository.

11. Use the `git commit` command to change the status of the branch to `committed` so that you can apply the change that was made to the repository. This command supports adding a comment. This comment helps notify you about the modifications that are made in the repository by providing a brief description of the changes:

```
$ git commit -m "Adding my-script.py script"
```

Review the history of changes that were made to the repository by running the `git log` command:

```
$ git log
```

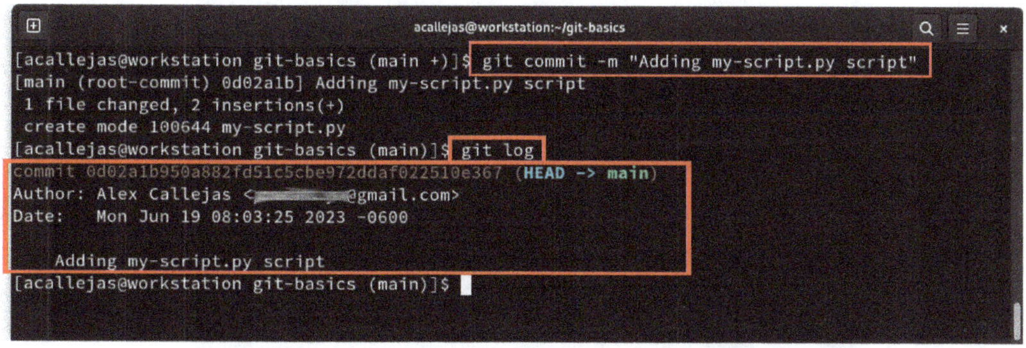

Figure 10.28 – Committing and reviewing the repository's history

> **Note**
>
> If you have doubts about how to add a good commit message, please visit the online resource *Conventional Commits* at https://www.conventionalcommits.org/.

With these simple steps, our script repository has *version control* and is managed by Git.

Having a repository that contains the scripts that are used for daily tasks, aside from acting as a backup, can be turned into a collaborative resource for our area. If we wish to publish it on a web platform, we need to *remove sensitive data* from it so that we can turn it into a valuable resource for the community.

Now, let's learn how to publish both script directories in a public repository on the internet.

> **Note**
>
> For this example, I'm using a repository on GitHub, but it could be created the same way on any *Git-based web platform* of your choice.

To create the repository on any web platform, follow these steps:

1. Log into the web platform:

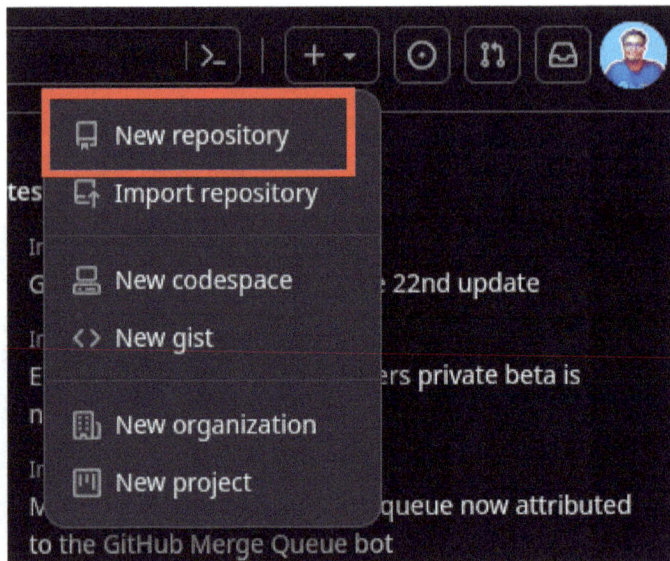

Figure 10.29 – Web platform dashboard

Click on the plus (+) button and click on **New repository**.

2. The **Create a new repository** screen will appear:

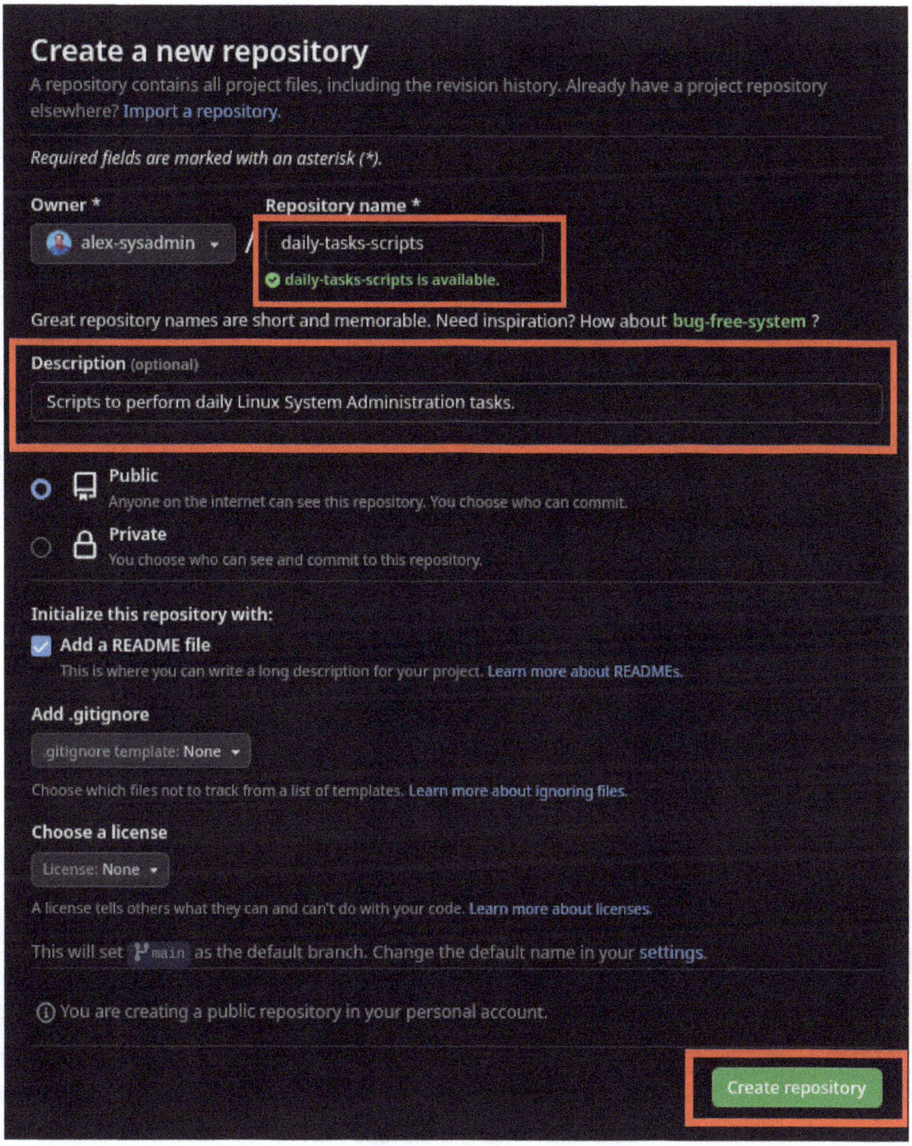

Figure 10.30 – The Create a new repository screen

Enter the repository's name and a brief description of its use. Leave the repository set to **Public** and choose to **Add a README file**. This file provides a welcome message or a detailed description of the repository's usage.

Once you're finished, click **Create repository**.

3.   The repository will be created. Click the **Code** button and copy the **HTTPS** address of the repository:

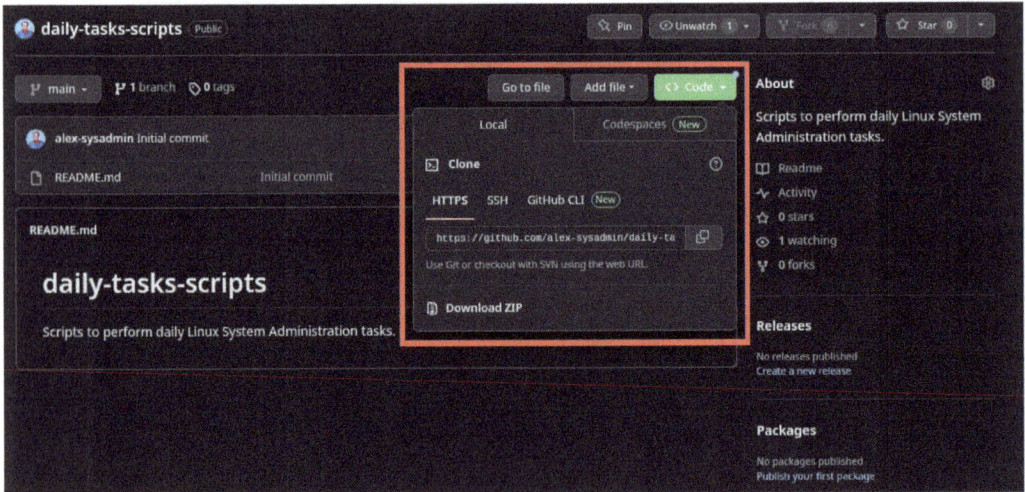

Figure 10.31 – Public repository

Let's copy the remote repository as local.

4.   Create a working directory and switch to it. Use the `git clone` command to download a copy of the repository:

```
$ git clone https://github.com/alex-sysadmin/daily-tasks-
scripts.git
```

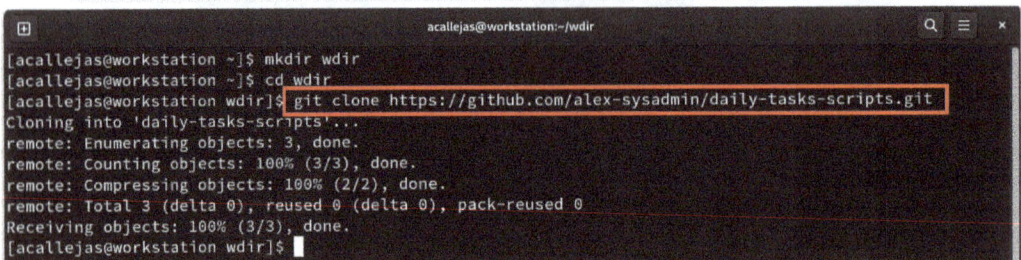

Figure 10.32 – Cloning the repository

5. Switch to the repository, verify the *main branch*, and review the files contained within:

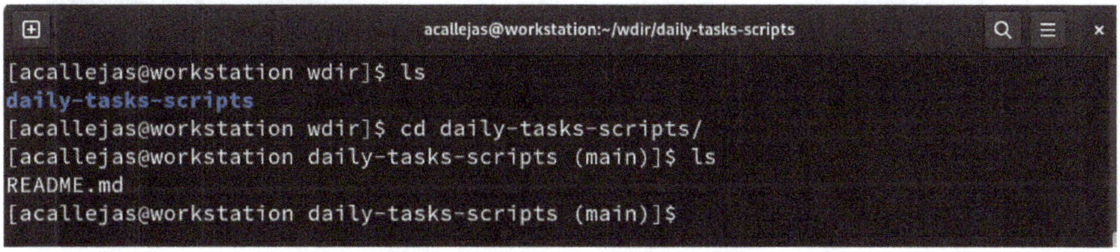

Figure 10.33 – Verifying the repository

6. Copy the directory of the Bash script example and the preceding example script into this directory:

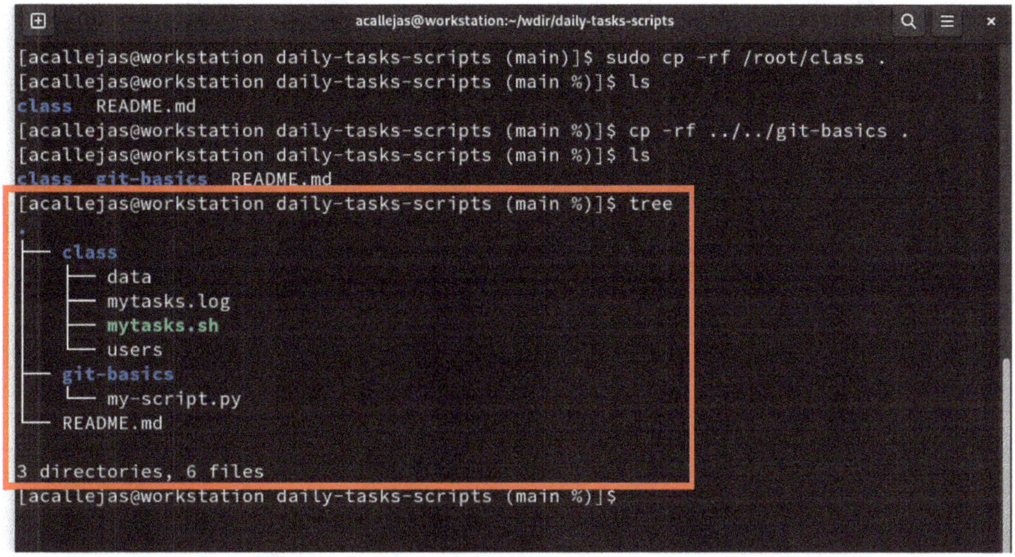

Figure 10.34 – The daily-tasks-scripts repository

Before adding the files with Git, note that the `class` directory, from the Bash script, has some ownership issues. Also, take note of the `log` file, which is not needed in the repository but is created when the script is run. The `users` file contains *sensitive information* about the users that have been created. Both files must remain, but their contents must be restarted (this is referred to as *blanking*). Fix these issues:

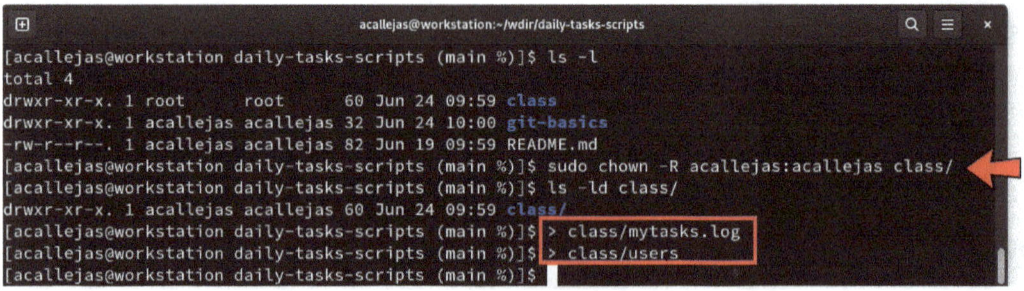

Figure 10.35 – Fixing issues

The preceding example directory, `git-basics`, is also a repository. Remove the hidden `.git` directory inside it so that Git doesn't take it as a *submodule* of the main repository. A backup of our scripts is all we need:

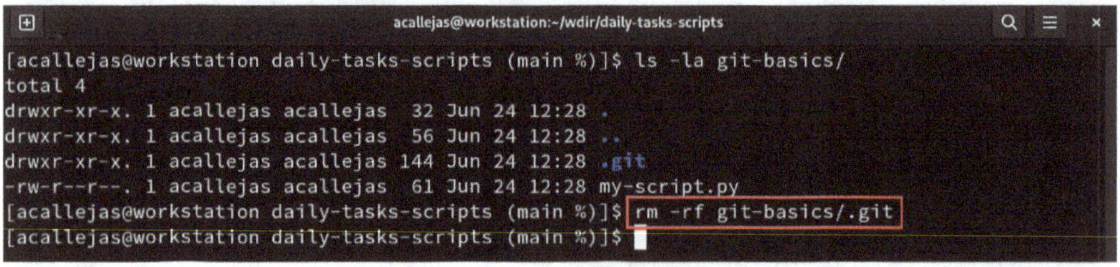

Figure 10.36 – Removing the .git directory

With the files ready, let's add them to the repository.

7. Use the `git add` command to add all the files to the repository:

    ```
    $ git add .
    ```

8. Commit the changes to the repository by adding the corresponding comment. Then, run the `git commit` command:

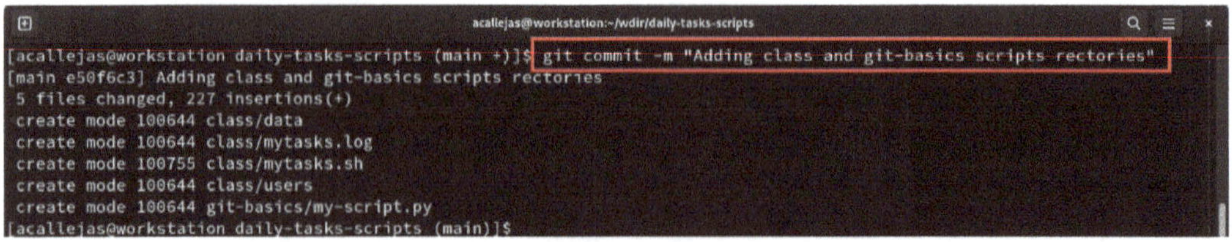

Figure 10.37 – Committing changes to the repository

9. Let's synchronize the *local changes* with the *remote repository*. Set the *original repository* as the *upstream repository* to reference it. Use the `git push` command to set up the upstream repository:

```
$ git push --set-upstream origin main
```

```
[acallejas@workstation daily-tasks-scripts (main)]$ git push --set-upstream origin main
Username for 'https://github.com': alex-sysadmin
Password for 'https://alex-sysadmin@github.com':
Enumerating objects: 9, done.
Counting objects: 100% (9/9), done.
Delta compression using up to 8 threads
Compressing objects: 100% (6/6), done.
Writing objects: 100% (8/8), 2.86 KiB | 584.00 KiB/s, done.
Total 8 (delta 0), reused 0 (delta 0), pack-reused 0
To https://github.com/alex-sysadmin/daily-tasks-scripts.git
   db1e329..e50f6c3  main -> main
branch 'main' set up to track 'origin/main'.
[acallejas@workstation daily-tasks-scripts (main)]$
```

Figure 10.38 – Pushing changes to the repository

> **Note**
>
> The authentication for the repository depends on the web platform in use. In the case of GitHub, it requests a *token*. To generate one, go to **Settings | Developer settings | Personal access token | Generate new token** and copy it to a safe place.

10. The modified files will appear on the web platform:

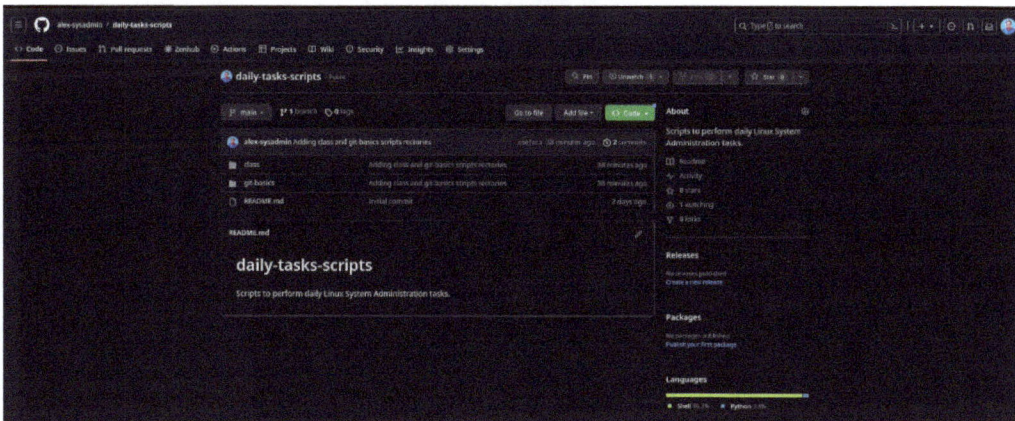

Figure 10.39 – The repository on GitHub

With that, we have a collaborative repository of the scripts that will be used in our day-to-day tasks.

At the same time, the repository serves as a backup of our scripts.

Let's take a walk through the alternatives that could help us make a backup.

Don't forget to back up

Back up: A SysAdmin must back up the entire system, and always verify the backup.

Backing up is the most basic task.

Good practice begins with good habits. One of the habits that I have made over the years is to back up a file before editing it, either in the file path or by creating a backup directory:

```
[acallejas@workstation ~]$ mkdir Bkp
[acallejas@workstation ~]$ cd Bkp
[acallejas@workstation Bkp]$ sudo cp /etc/passwd etc.passwd.bkp
[acallejas@workstation Bkp]$ vim /etc/passwd
[acallejas@workstation Bkp]$ ls -l
total 4
-rw-r--r--. 1 root root 2966 Jun 19 15:02 etc.passwd.bkp
[acallejas@workstation Bkp]$
```

Figure 10.40 – Backing up before modifying

On the surface, it doesn't seem like a big task. However, if you incorporate this step into your tasks, then you have a simple backup of the files that you work with.

Besides copying files to change, another good habit is to create a package that contains archives or compressed files.

Let's see how this works.

Archiving and compression

First of all, note the difference between an **archive** file and a **compressed** file:

- An **archive** file consists of *files and directories* stored in a single file. The archive file remains uncompressed – it uses the same disk space as all the individual files and directories are combined.

- A **compressed** file also consists of files and directories stored in a single file. However, they are stored in such a way that they use less disk space than all the individual files and directories combined.

An archive file itself is not compressed, but a compressed file could contain an archive file.

Linux provides several utilities for compressing and decompressing files. The following table shows the most used utilities:

Utility	Syntax	Examples
gzip	gzip <file>	$ gzip test
	gunzip <file>	$ gunzip test.gz
bzip2	bzip2 <file>	$ bzip2 test
	bunzip2 <file>	$ bunzip2 test.bz2
xz	xz <file>	$ xz test
	xz -d <file>	$ xz -d test.xz
zip	zip .zip-file <file>	$ zip test.zip test
	unzip <.zip-file>	$ unzip test.zip

Table 10.1 – Compress and decompress utilities

Let's look at the difference between the utilities in the compression algorithms that are used by each:

- The gzip utility compresses the size of files using **Lempel-Ziv (LZ77)** encoding. Each file gets replaced by one with the .gz extension.

- bzip2 compresses files using the *Burrows-Wheeler* block-sorting text compression algorithm and *Huffman encoding*. Each file gets replaced with another file with the .bz2 extension.

- xz uses the **Lempel-Ziv-Markov chain algorithm** (LZMA) for compression/decompression.

- The .zip format uses a *32-bit CRC algorithm*. It includes two copies of the metadata for each entry to provide greater protection against data loss.

> **Note**
> To learn more about compression utilities, refer to the gzip, bzip2, xz, and zip man pages.

In practical use cases, compression utilities share the same goal: *to reduce the space usage* of the file in question. Beyond the algorithm, what needs to be considered is the size of space usage that the file reduces. This is due to portability reasons. The following illustrative example shows the differences practically. However, note that more compression or decompression requires more resources (CPU and memory).

Another best practice habit is to *compress* backups so that any space that's used doesn't become an issue. This can also be enhanced if we compress file archives.

In Linux, we can use the `tar` tool to create, manage, and extract archive files. With this command, many files that are stored in a single archive file become portable. A `tar` archive is a structured sequence of metadata and file data with an index.

Archives might be compressed when they're created using one of the supported compression algorithms. Besides creating archive files, the `tar` command provides further options, such as listing the contents of an archive without extracting it or extracting files from compressed and uncompressed archives.

The `tar` command's options provide us with *three different styles*:

- In the *traditional style*, the first argument is a group of option letters, and the arguments that follow supply arguments to those options that need them.

- In the *UNIX or short option style*, each option letter comes preceded by a single hyphen (`-`). If an option has an argument, the argument follows it, either as a separate word on the command line or immediately after the option.

- In *GNU or long option style*, each option begins with two hyphens (`--`) and has a meaningful name, consisting of lowercase letters and hyphens. The long option could be abbreviated to its initial letters. Long option arguments are supplied as separate words on the command line, immediately following the option, or separated from the option by an equals (`=`) sign with no intervening whitespace. Optional arguments should always use the latter method.

The `tar` command requires an action with at least one option. The most common actions and options are shown in the following table:

Description	Traditional Style	Short Style	Long Style
Creates an archive file	c	-c	--create
Lists the content of an archive file	t	-t	--list
Extracts an archive file	x	-x	--extract
Shows the currently archived or extracted files	v	-v	--verbose
Use this option with the name of the file to create or open	f	-f	--file
Keeps the original permissions of the files by extracting them	p	-p	--preserve-permissions
Uses the file suffix to determine the algorithm to use for compression	a	-a	--auto-compress
Uses the `gzip` compression algorithm	z	-z	--gzip
Uses the `bzip2` compression algorithm	j	-j	--bzip2
Uses the `xz` compression algorithm	J	-J	--xz
Uses an LZ-variant algorithm	Z	-Z	--compress

Description	Traditional Style	Short Style	Long Style
Enables extended attribute support and stores file-extended attributes	NA	NA	`--xattrs`
Enables SELinux context support and stores SELinux contexts	NA	NA	`--selinux`

Table 10.2 – Common tar command actions and options

Let's analyze an example of how to create an archive of compressed files with two different compression algorithms so that we can compare the space that's used.

As a non-root user, in our backup directory, use the `tar` command to create an archive file of the day-to-day script repository.

Follow these steps:

1. First, use the `gzip` compression algorithm option. Run the following `tar` command:

    ```
    $ tar czvf daily-tasks-scripts.bkp.tar.gz ../wdir/daily-tasks-
    scripts
    ```

```
[acallejas@workstation -]$ cd Bkp/
[acallejas@workstation Bkp]$
[acallejas@workstation Bkp]$ tar czvf daily-tasks-scripts.bkp.tar.gz ../wdir/daily-tasks-scripts
tar: Removing leading '../' from member names
../wdir/daily-tasks-scripts/
../wdir/daily-tasks-scripts/.git/
../wdir/daily-tasks-scripts/.git/branches/
../wdir/daily-tasks-scripts/.git/hooks/
../wdir/daily-tasks-scripts/.git/hooks/applypatch-msg.sample
../wdir/daily-tasks-scripts/.git/hooks/commit-msg.sample
../wdir/daily-tasks-scripts/.git/hooks/post-update.sample
../wdir/daily-tasks-scripts/.git/hooks/pre-applypatch.sample
../wdir/daily-tasks-scripts/.git/hooks/pre-commit.sample
../wdir/daily-tasks-scripts/.git/hooks/pre-merge-commit.sample
../wdir/daily-tasks-scripts/.git/hooks/pre-push.sample
../wdir/daily-tasks-scripts/.git/hooks/pre-receive.sample
../wdir/daily-tasks-scripts/.git/hooks/push-to-checkout.sample
../wdir/daily-tasks-scripts/.git/hooks/sendemail-validate.sample
../wdir/daily-tasks-scripts/.git/hooks/update.sample
../wdir/daily-tasks-scripts/.git/hooks/fsmonitor-watchman.sample
../wdir/daily-tasks-scripts/.git/hooks/pre-rebase.sample
../wdir/daily-tasks-scripts/.git/hooks/prepare-commit-msg.sample
../wdir/daily-tasks-scripts/.git/info/
../wdir/daily-tasks-scripts/.git/info/exclude
../wdir/daily-tasks-scripts/.git/description
../wdir/daily-tasks-scripts/.git/refs/
../wdir/daily-tasks-scripts/.git/refs/heads/
../wdir/daily-tasks-scripts/.git/refs/heads/main
../wdir/daily-tasks-scripts/.git/refs/tags/
```

Figure 10.41 – Creating an archive with the tar command

2. Now use the `bzip2` compression algorithm and create the file archive from the same directory by running the following `tar` command:

```
$ tar cjvf daily-tasks-scripts.bkp.tar.bz2 ../wdir/daily-tasks-
  scripts
```

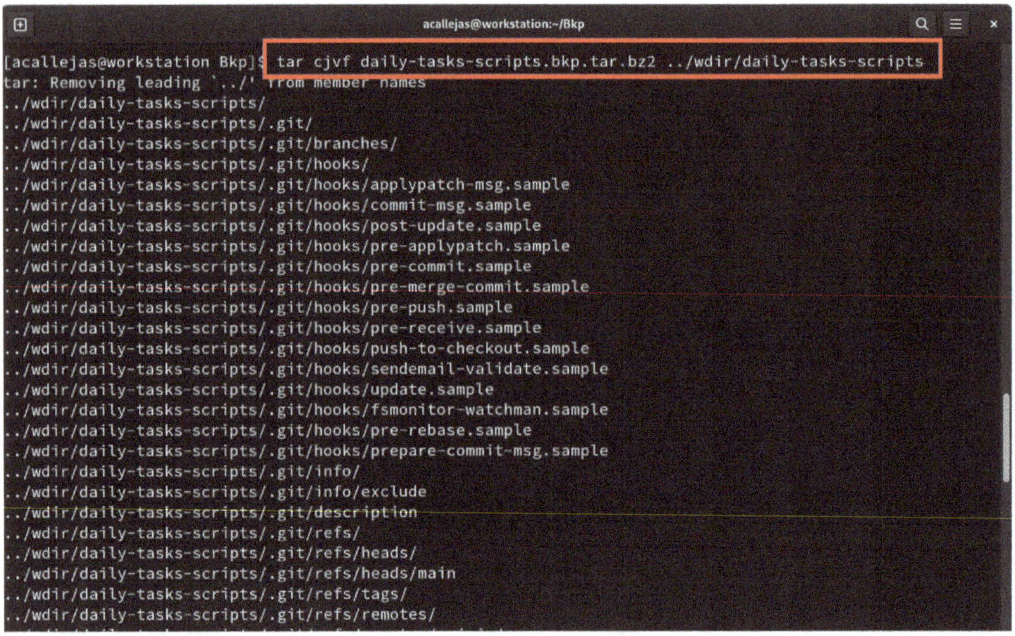

Figure 10.42 – Using the bzip2 compression algorithm with the tar command

3. Check the size of both file archives to compare the compression rate:

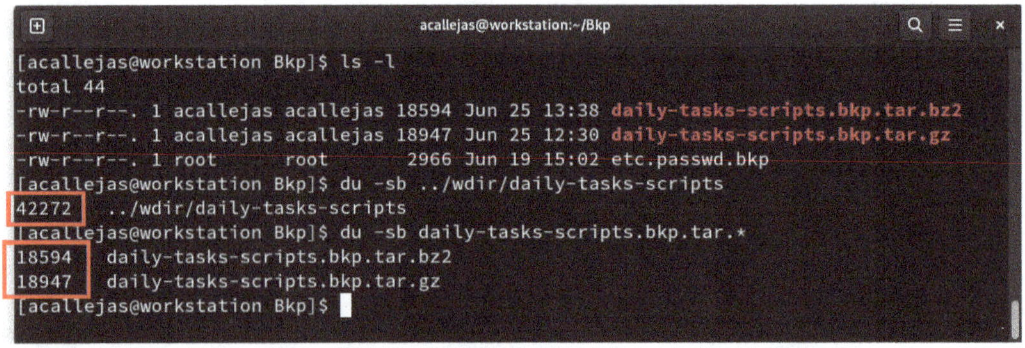

Figure 10.43 – Comparing file sizes

As we can see, the repository's directory size is 42272 bytes:

```
$ du -sb ../wdir/daily-tasks-scripts
42272 ../wdir/daily-tasks-scripts
```

The size of the archive file, when compressed with the gzip algorithm, is 18947 bytes:

```
$ du -sb daily-tasks-scripts.bkp.tar.gz
18947 daily-tasks-scripts.bkp.tar.gz
```

The size of the archive file, when compressed with the bzip2 algorithm, is 18594 bytes:

```
$ du -sb daily-tasks-scripts.bkp.tar.bz2
18594 daily-tasks-scripts.bkp.tar.bz2
```

Let's take a closer look at what this means:

- The gzip compression algorithm reduced the size of the repository by 44.82%
- The bzip2 compression algorithm reduced the size of the repository by 43.98%

The difference is minimal, and these are the most used formats for backups. It is up to you to decide which one to use – just remember: *don't forget to back up!*

> **Note**
>
> To learn more about archiving files, refer to the tar man page.

As mentioned in the previous section, the Git repository also helps us back up the information contained in it. It also provides us with a snapshot of the data at the time it was taken.

So, let's learn how to manage versions with Git.

Version management with Git

To learn how Git handles versioning, we'll use the example from the previous section. As a *non-root user*, switch to the daily-tasks-scripts repository directory and follow these steps:

1. As a good habit, ensure that the local repository keeps updated and in sync with the remote repository before starting. Use the git fetch and git pull commands to do so:

```
$ git fetch --all
$ git pull --all
```

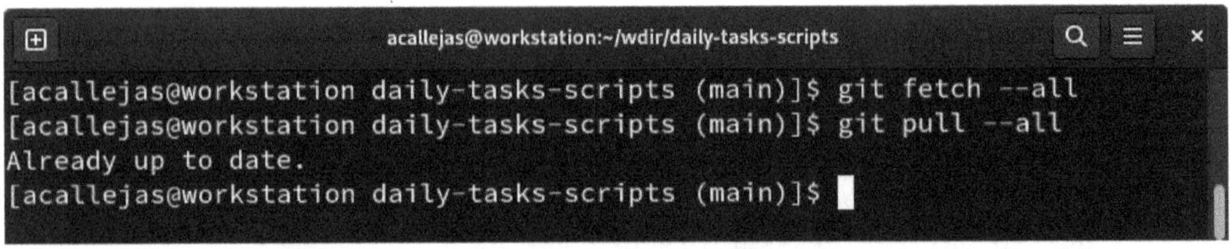

Figure 10.44 – Keeping the repository updated and in sync

The git fetch command extracts all the data from a remote project that doesn't already exist locally. The git fetch command only downloads the data to the local repository – it doesn't merge it or change anything you're currently working on. The changes have to be merged manually.

The git pull command incorporates changes from a remote repository into the current branch of the local repository.

As another good practice, Git gives you the option to branch the repository. Branching means deviating from the main line of development and continuing to work without altering that main line.

To change the repository without altering its original content, let's create a branch.

2. Create the enhancement branch of the daily-tasks-scripts repository. Use the git branch command and the appropriate branch name:

    ```
    $ git branch acallejas/repo-enhancement
    ```

> **Note**
> Include the author of the changes in the *branch name* as good practice.

The git branch command only creates the branch. To switch to it, use the git switch command and the branch's name.

Both commands can be combined to create the branch and switch to it. To do this, use the git switch command with the -c option:

```
$ git switch -c acallejas/repo-enhancement
```

When creating the repository, we added a README.md file that serves to document the use of the repository. Let's update this file so that we can document our repository.

3. Update the README.md file so that it documents the repository:

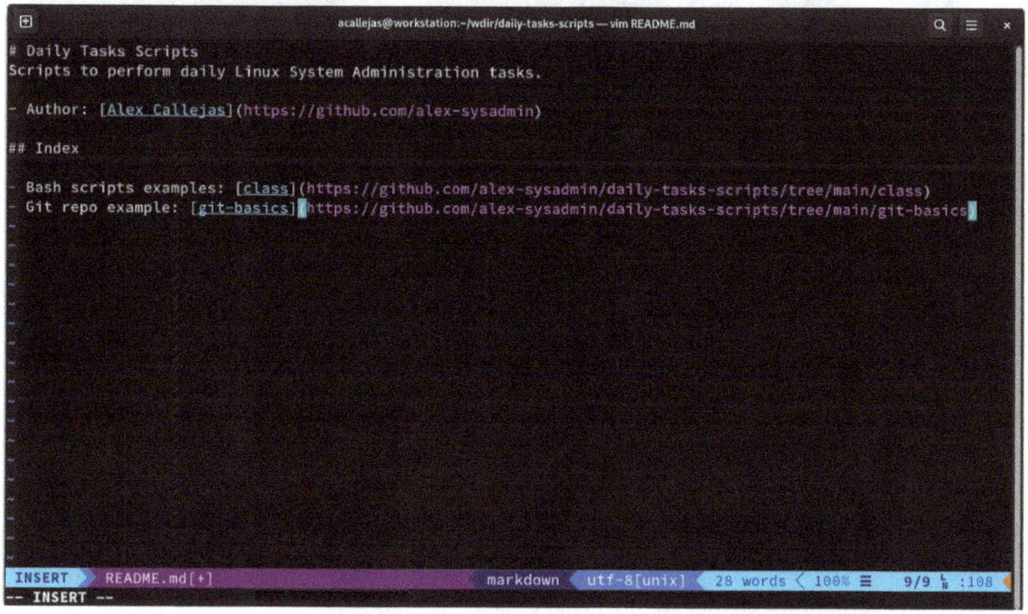

Figure 10.45 – Updating the README.md file

Note that the README.md file format uses the Markdown language. Markdown is a *markup language* that appears to human readers when it's in its source code form.

> **Note**
> To learn more about the basic syntax of the Markdown language, refer to the *Markdown guide* at https://www.markdownguide.org/basic-syntax.

Save the changes and compare the differences between this branch and the main branch.

4. Use the git diff command to display the differences between the branches:

```
$ git diff
```

```
acallejas@workstation:~/wdir/daily-tasks-scripts                    Q  ≡  ×

[acallejas@workstation daily-tasks-scripts (main)]$ git checkout -b acallejas/repo-enhancement
Switched to a new branch 'acallejas/repo-enhancement'
[acallejas@workstation daily-tasks-scripts (acallejas/repo-enhancement)]$ ls
class  git-basics  README.md
[acallejas@workstation daily-tasks-scripts (acallejas/repo-enhancement)]$ vim README.md
[acallejas@workstation daily-tasks-scripts (acallejas/repo-enhancement *)]$ git diff
diff --git a/README.md b/README.md
index 59da754..519cf34 100644
--- a/README.md
+++ b/README.md
@@ -1,2 +1,9 @@
-# daily-tasks-scripts
+# Daily Tasks Scripts
 Scripts to perform daily Linux System Administration tasks.
+
+- Author: [Alex Callejas](https://github.com/alex-sysadmin)
+
+## Index
+
+- Bash scripts examples: [class](https://github.com/alex-sysadmin/daily-tasks-scripts/tree/main/class)
+- Git repo example: [git-basics](https://github.com/alex-sysadmin/daily-tasks-scripts/tree/main/git-basics)
[acallejas@workstation daily-tasks-scripts (acallejas/repo-enhancement *)]$
```

Figure 10.46 – Displaying the differences between the branches

The lines that begin with plus (+) signs state the differences in the README.md file between the versions of the branches.

5. Add and commit the changes to the file to update the branch:

    ```
    $ git add README.md
    $ git commit -m "Updating README.md file"
    ```

6. Update the remote repository with the local enhancement branch. Use the git push command and the branch's name to do so:

    ```
    $ git push -u origin acallejas/repo-enhancement
    ```

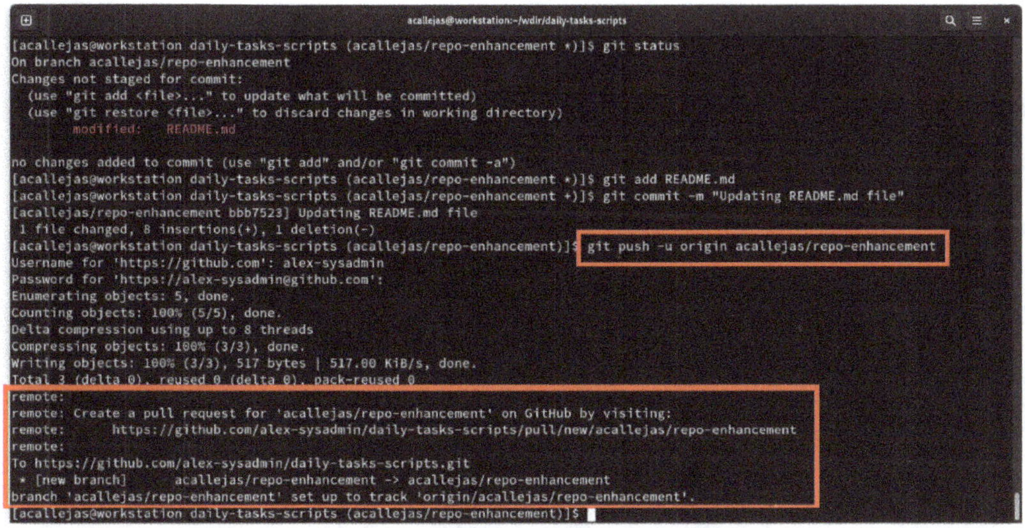

Figure 10.47 – Updating the remote repository

7. For the local repository, use the `git branch` command to show the branches of the local repository. The `-r` option lists the remote branches while `-a` lists all branches:

```
$ git branch
$ git branch -r
$ git branch -a
```

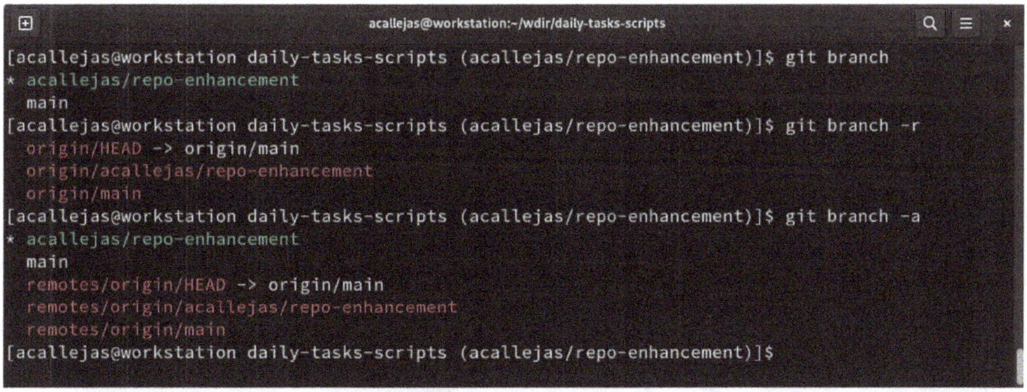

Figure 10.48 – Listing the branches

8. The web platform also displays the branches. Navigate to the repository and click on the **Branches** link:

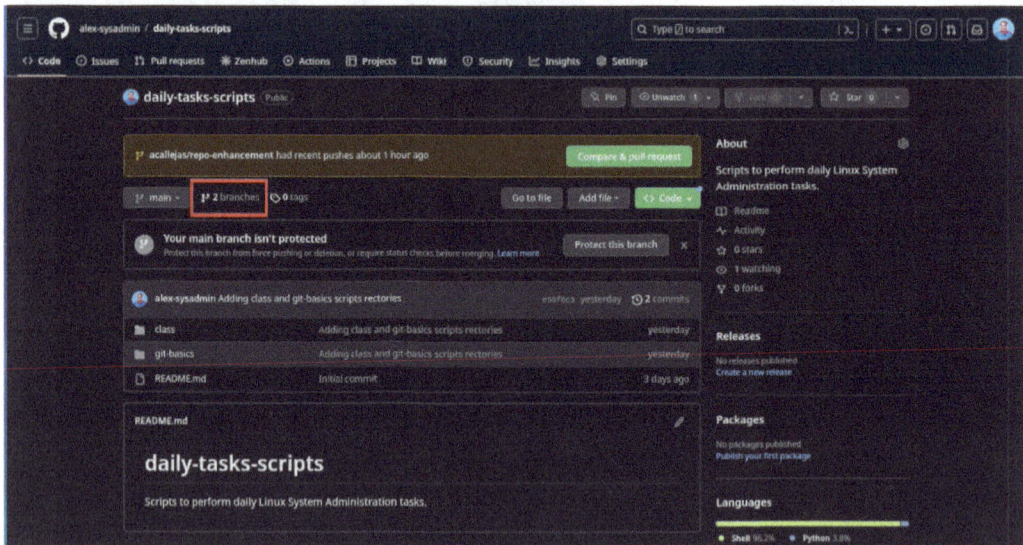

Figure 10.49 – Branches

The changes haven't been applied to the *main branch* yet. To do this, we need to *merge* the branch with the enhancements. This should be done through a pull request.

Let's integrate the enhancements into the *main branch*.

9. In the **Branches** window, click on the **New pull request** button:

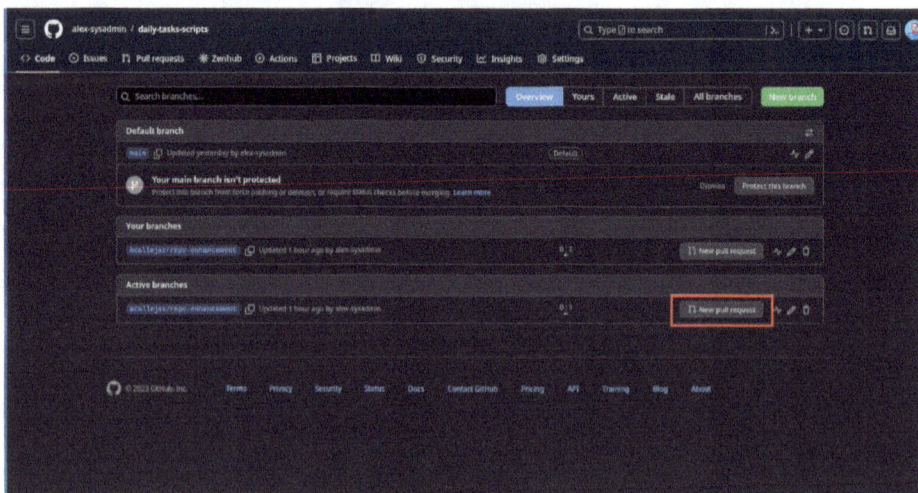

Figure 10.50 – The Branches window

10. In the **Open a pull request** window, fill in the title and description fields of the change:

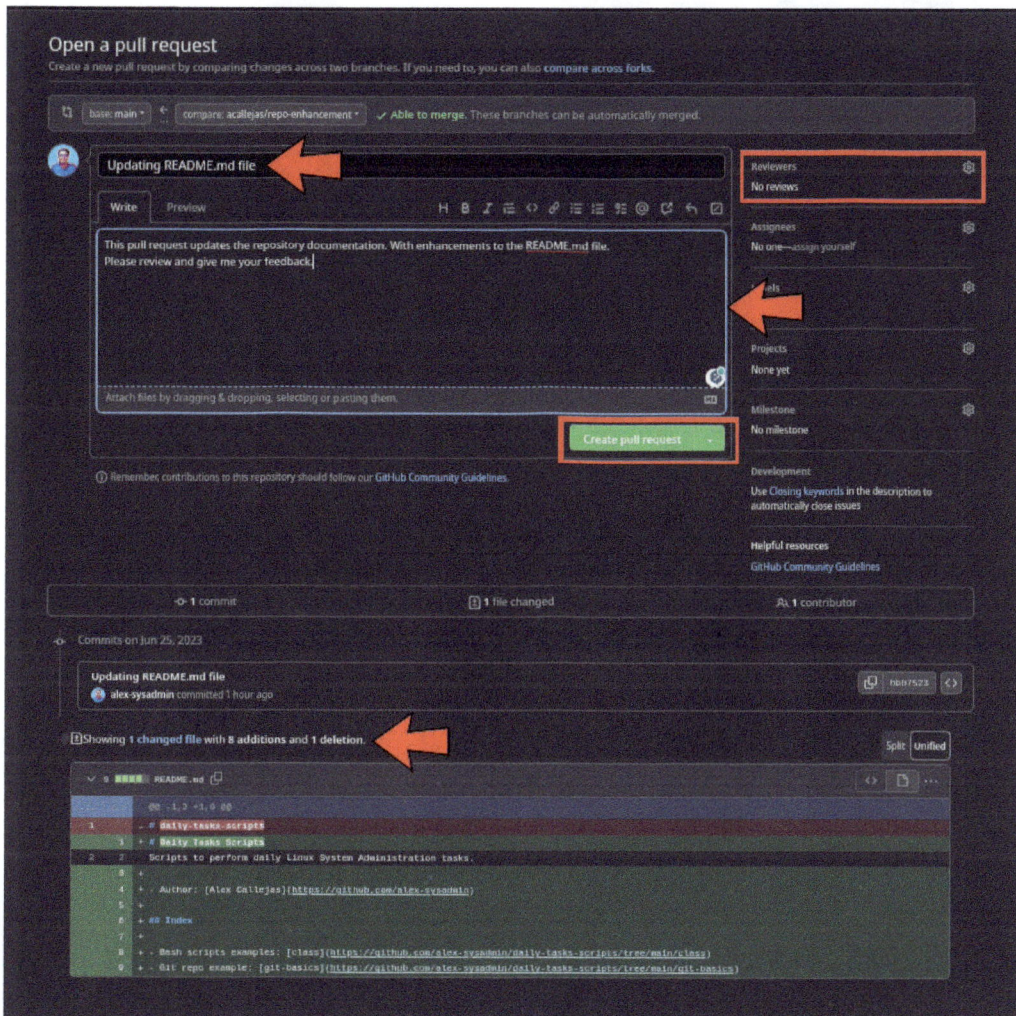

Figure 10.51 – The Open a pull request window

11. In this window, at the bottom, find and verify the details of the change.

12. In the right column, in the **Reviewers** section, select members of the team to *review the changes before merging them*, as good practice.

13. Once the request is ready, click on the **Create pull request** button.

14. The **Pull requests** window will appear, providing an overview of the change:

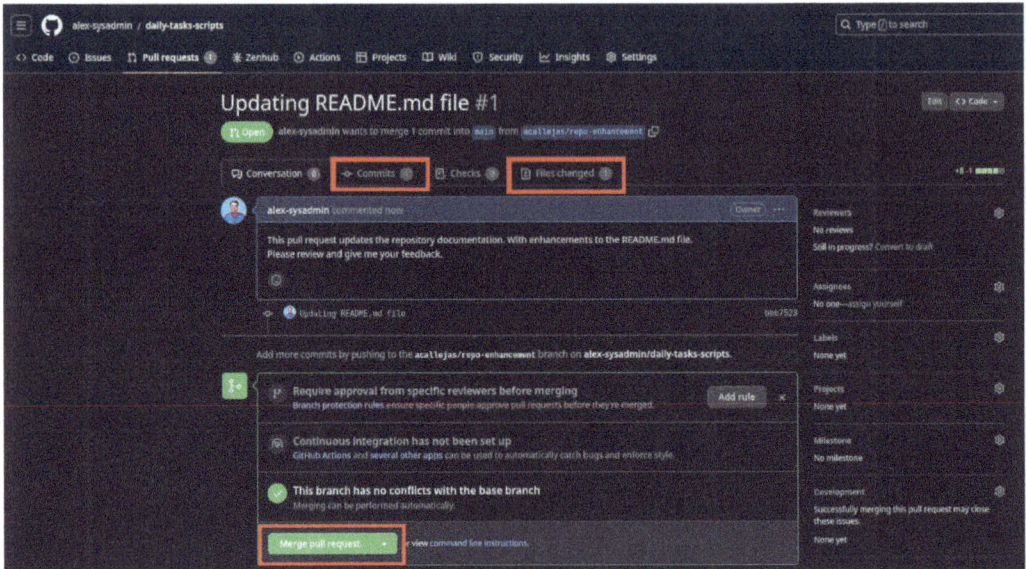

Figure 10.52 – The Pull requests screen

The **Commits** tab lists the changes committed, while the **Files changed** tab displays the difference between versions of the changed files.

15. If you agree with the merger of the branches, click on the **Merge pull request** button.

16. On confirming the merge, the repository on the web platform will display the changes that have been made:

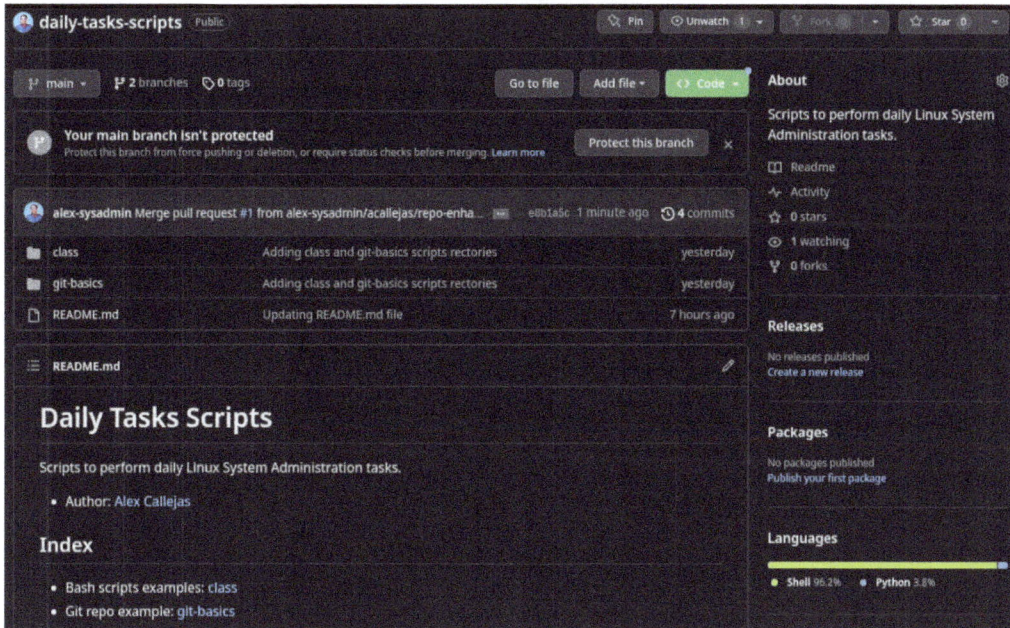

Figure 10.53 – Remote repository updated

Let's update the local repository.

17. In the local repository, switch to the main branch and update it:

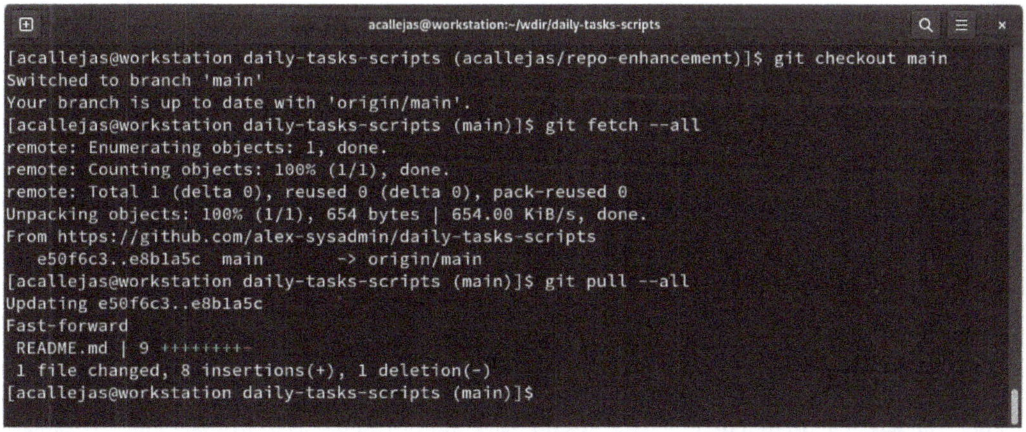

Figure 10.54 – Local repository updated

By using the branches of the repository, a backup of our script directory of day-to-day tasks becomes available.

By archiving files to Git repositories, a backup could exist. Of course, there are software solutions that ease this task, even IT areas in charge of it. But the best practice is, regardless of these solutions, as the first law of the SysAdmin says: *always back up*. These activities, like many others, can be run in an automated fashion using scripts and/or scheduled tasks.

Now, let's look at a tool that might make it easier to automate tasks in Linux.

Automating with Ansible

Automate: A SysAdmin should automate as much as possible, except if it conflicts with the first law.

Previously, we discussed one of the most well-known statements among SysAdmins:

"If you typed it twice, you should have scripted it once."

If a task gets scripted, it could be scheduled and, with this, automated. This means that the task must run without the SysAdmin's intervention.

However, not all scheduled tasks might be automated. The easiest way to determine this is by applying the *principles of automation*:

- The rule of **algorithmic thinking**

    Everything is a system. Algorithmic thinking is a way of getting to a solution through a clear definition of the steps needed – *nothing happens by magic*.

- The rule of **bottlenecks**

    Bad decisions propagate. Every system, regardless of how well it works, has at least one constraint (*a bottleneck*) that limits performance.

- The rule of **autonomy**

    Humans always play a role. This challenges the idea that automation means completely eliminating the human element. Using the rule of algorithmic thinking, humans are another layer of abstraction in the system.

Taking these principles into account and applying them allows us to define an ideal automation solution.

The **Ansible project** is an open source community sponsored by Red Hat, the developer of the automation tool. Ansible is available in the official Fedora Linux repositories.

Ansible is an automation tool that focuses on simplicity and ease of use as its primary goals. Ansible enables us to configure systems, manage packages, and, in an advanced way, orchestrate tasks that support the continuous delivery cycle.

Ansible works in two separate layers:

- *Control plane* (in the cloud): Generate instances and manage their resources
- *On instance*: Syart and stop services, push configuration files, install packages, and more

Through OpenSSH, an agentless service, Ansible manages systems and performs the tasks described previously.

Let's start with the basics of Ansible.

The basics

The Ansible use cases approach deals with automating processes. Let's look at some of the most common options:

- Provisioning
- Configuration management
- Application deployment
- Continuous delivery
- Security and compliance
- Orchestration

Ansible divides process automation into a variety of work unit levels:

- **Tasks**: A task is the smallest unit of work. It could consist of an action such as *install a database, install a web server*, or *copy this configuration file to the server*.
- **Plays**: A play consists of several tasks. For example, the play *Prepare a database for a web service* could consist of the following tasks:

    A. Install the database package.

    B. Set the password for the database administrator.

    C. Create the database.

    D. Define the access to the database.

- **Playbook**: A playbook consists of several plays. For example, the playbook *Install a website with a database backend* could consist of the following tasks:

    A. Configure the database server.

    B. Configure the web server.

The task automation process within Ansible requires two types of nodes to be defined: *control* and *managed*. The control node is the machine from where Ansible is running and the managed nodes are the machines where the tasks take place:

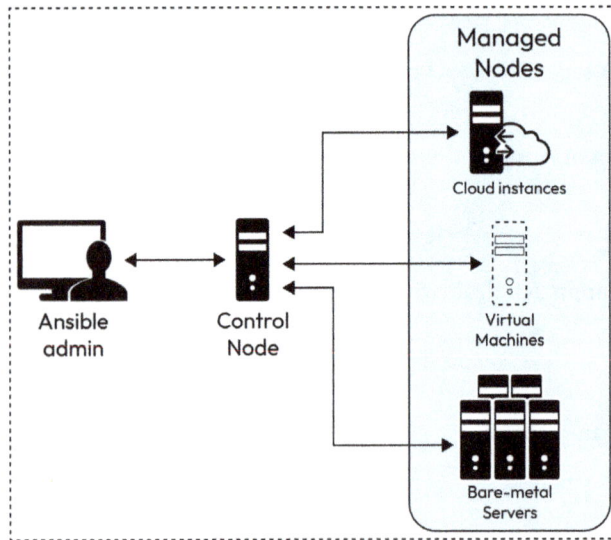

Figure 10.55 – Ansible nodes

Let's learn how to prepare our workstation as the Ansible control node.

First steps

So, let's start with installing and configuring Ansible. Follow these steps:

1. Ansible is available in the official Fedora Linux repositories. Install the `ansible` package using the `dnf` command:

    ```
    $ sudo dnf install ansible
    ```

    The default configuration file of Ansible resides in the `/etc/ansible/ansible.cfg` file, but as a best practice, create a custom file to get better control of automated tasks.

2. Inside the working directory, create a directory named `ansible` and switch to it:

    ```
    $ mkdir ansible; cd ansible
    ```

3. Inside the `ansible` directory, create a configuration file called `ansible.cfg`. Only add the `defaults` section and set up the name of the `inventory` file, something like this:

    ```
    [defaults]
    inventory = inventory
    ```

Ansible does not install an agent on the managed nodes. Instead, it bases its communication with them through **SSH keys**. So, let's create a key that we'll use to manage the nodes.

4. Create an `ssh` key pair and specify `rsa` with `2048` bits. Use the `ssh-keygen` command to do so:

    ```
    $ ssh-keygen -t rsa -b 2048
    ```

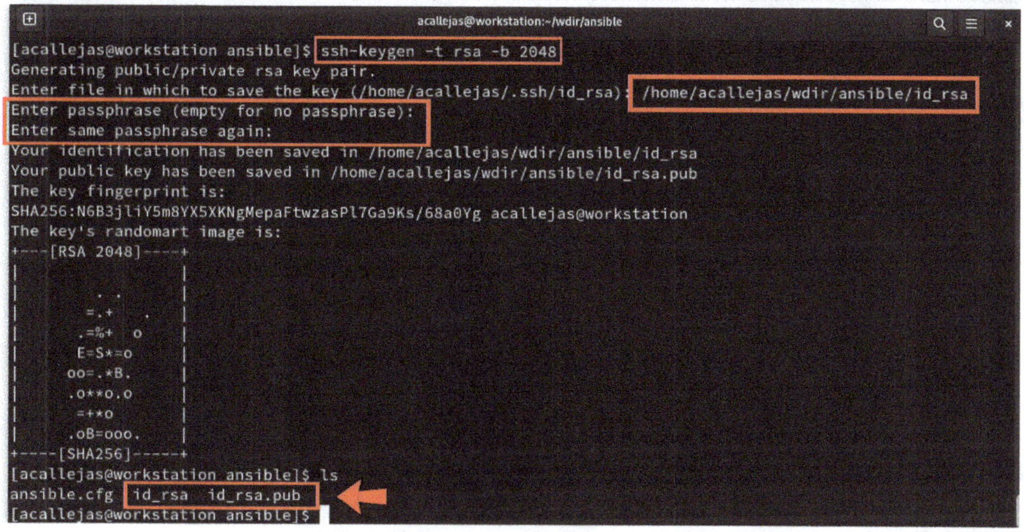

Figure 10.56 – Generating the ssh key pair

The `ssh-keygen` command will ask you to confirm the path where the key should be generated. Note that the path must not be the *default path* but inside the working directory in the `ansible` directory.

After this, the command prompts you to enter a passphrase instead of the user's login password. As the connection must run *unattended*, leave this field empty and hit *Enter* twice to confirm the creation of the key pair.

Note

To learn more about creating SSH keys, refer to the `ssh-keygen` man page.

This command generates the SSH key pair, which consists of a *public key* and a *private key*.

Let's test the communication with the key without using the user's access password.

5. To test communication with the SSH key, copy the key to the same workstation. Use the `ssh-copy-id` command to do so:

    ```
    $ ssh-copy-id -i id_rsa.pub localhost
    ```

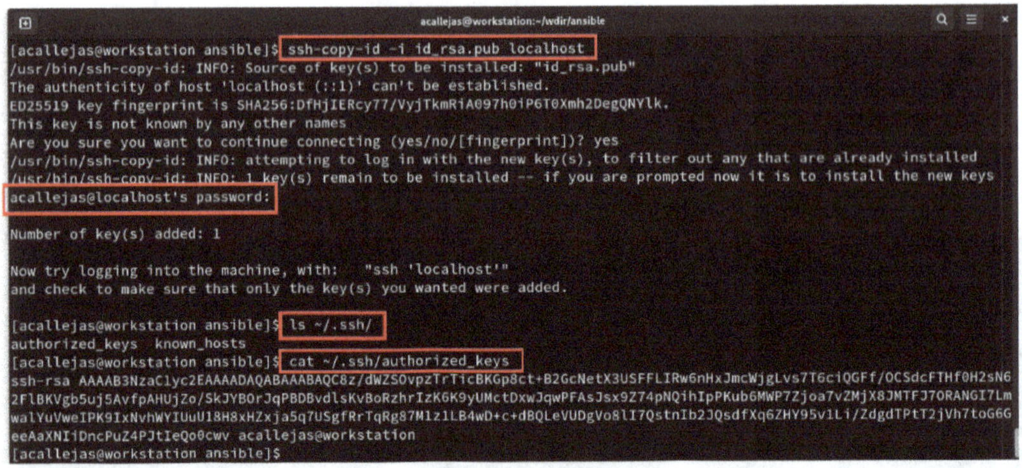

Figure 10.57 – Copying the ssh public key

The `ssh-copy-id` command copies the public key to the machine where the trust relationship gets established. In our case, this is the workstation itself.

To copy the key, the command asks for the user's one-time login password.

Once access is granted, the command copies the content of the public key to the `authorized_keys` file in the hidden `.ssh` directory inside the user's home directory.

6. To test the connection, use the `ssh` command to offer the private key:

```
$ ssh -i id_rsa localhost
```

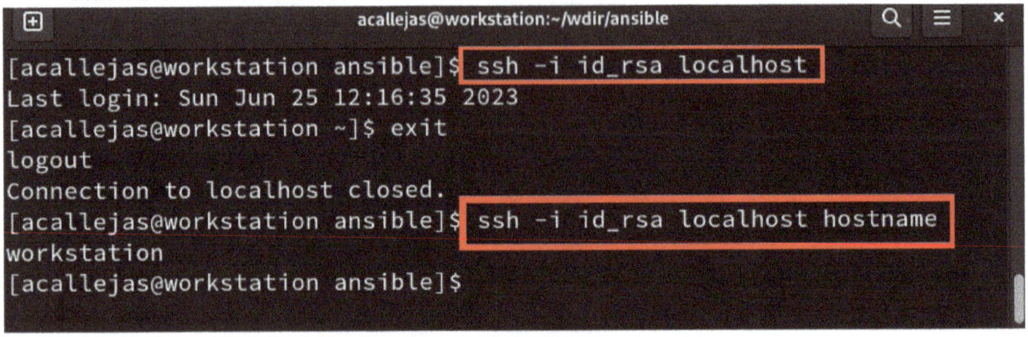

Figure 10.58 – Testing the trust relationship

The connection that uses the private key must allow access and run remote commands without requesting the user's password.

Now, let's configure and automate simple tasks with Ansible.

7. Create the `inventory` file, adding `workstation` as a managed node, indicating the private key as a variable for the host. In the `inventory` file, add the following lines:

```
[workstation]
localhost
[workstation:vars]
ansible_ssh_private_key_file=/home/acallejas/wdir/ansible/id_rsa
```

Let's test the communication to the managed nodes using ad hoc commands. Ad hoc commands allow us to run basic tasks from the command line.

8. Use the `ansible` command, along with the `ping` module, to verify the connection to all managed nodes:

```
$ ansible all -m ping
```

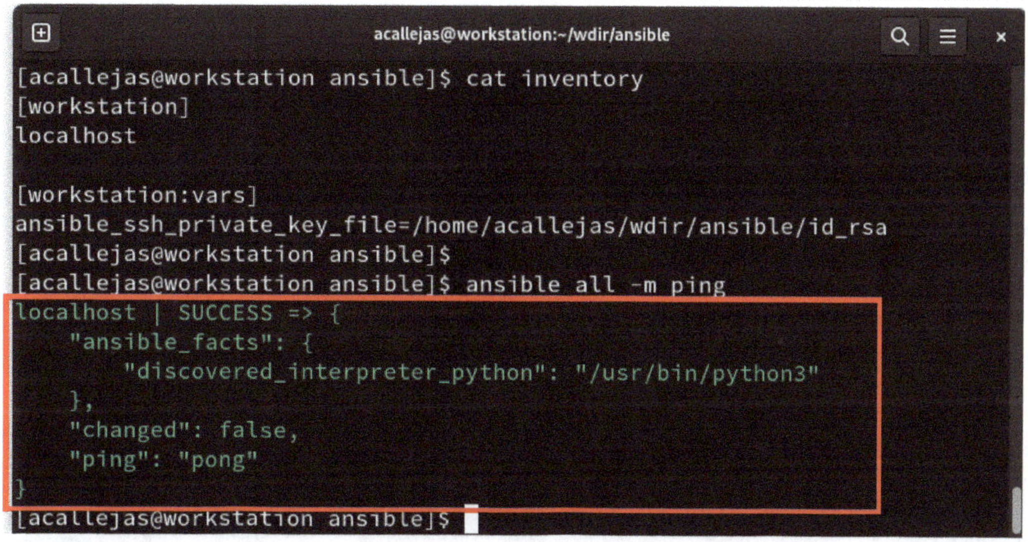

Figure 10.59 – Testing communication with all managed nodes

This ad hoc command allows us to run any operating system command by passing it as an argument using the `-a` or `--args` option:

```
$ ansible workstation -a "hostname"
```

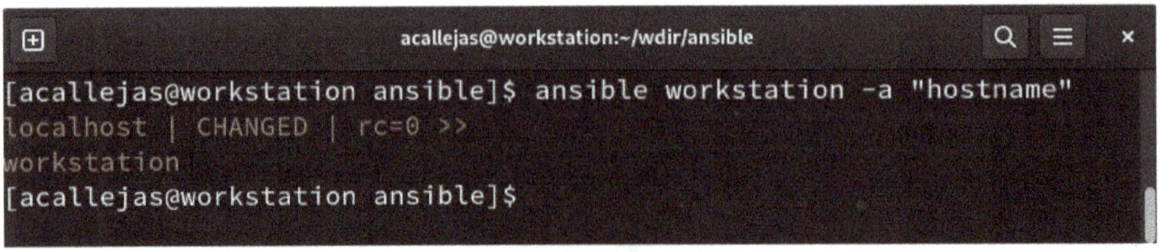

Figure 10.60 – Using ad hoc commands

> **Note**
>
> For more information, refer to the *Introduction to ad hoc commands* section of the Ansible documentation at `https://docs.ansible.com/ansible/latest/command_guide/intro_adhoc.html`.

As mentioned previously, the *tasks* and the set of them (*plays*) get grouped into a file. This file allows us to run them *sequentially or selectively*. These files are called *playbooks*.

Playbooks come written in YAML format. This format, due to its simplicity, is based on a tree structure, which makes it more human-readable than a JSON or XML file. This means that it maintains its ideal of being the simplest implementation tool.

Let's analyze a *playbook* through a simple example. The following *playbook* runs the *tasks* to verify that a web server has the `httpd` package installed and running:

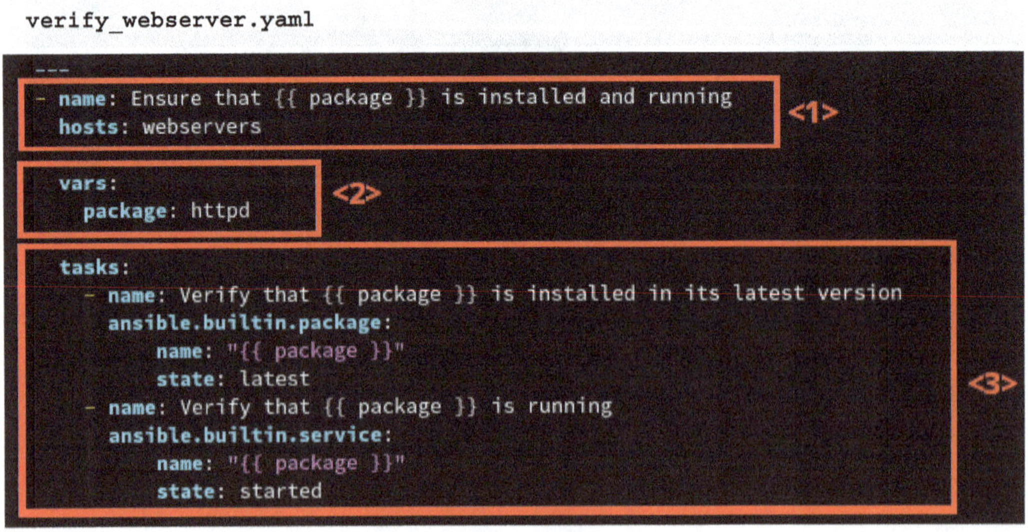

`verify_webserver.yaml`

Figure 10.61 – Ansible playbook

Let's take a closer look:

- **<1> Identification block**: This assigns a *name* to the play and the *hosts* in the inventory where the play applies.

- **<2> Variables block**: This declares the *variables* used in the play.

- **<3> Tasks block**: This declares the *tasks* to run in the play.

In the preceding example, the *play* consists of two *tasks*:

- Verify that the httpd package has been installed as the latest version

- Verify that the httpd service has been enabled and started

For each of these tasks, the play uses two modules: ansible.builtin.package and ansible. builtin.service.

The modules consist of small units of code that perform tasks using instructions from the operating system. In the preceding example, the ansible.builtin.package module uses the dnf command to determine the *installation status* of the package.

The ansible.builtin.service module uses the systemctl command to determine the *status of the service*.

Since the syntax of the playbooks uses the YAML file format, they are prone to indentation failures. Ansible provides a tool to check the syntax of playbooks – that is, the ansible-playbook command with the --syntax-check option:

```
$ ansible-playbook --syntax-check verify_webserver.yaml
```

```
$ ansible-playbook --syntax-check verify_webserver.yaml
ERROR! Syntax Error while loading YAML.
  mapping values are not allowed in this context

The error appears to be in '/home/acallejas/wdir/ansible/verify_webserver.yaml': line 6, column 8, but may
be elsewhere in the file depending on the exact syntax problem.

The offending line appears to be:

  vars:
      ^ here
```

Figure 10.62 – Verifying the syntax of the playbook

The output of this command explains the syntax error. The error message shows where you can find the runtime error.

> **Note**
>
> Although the error message displays the error's location, it could be a result of an error that wasn't caused by the displayed location. As a best practice, confirm the correct indentation on the lines before the error message.

After editing the playbook and fixing the error, run the syntax check again:

```
$ ansible-playbook --syntax-check verify_webserver.yaml
```

```
$ ansible-playbook --syntax-check verify_webserver.yaml
playbook: check_service.yml
```

Figure 10.63 – Running the syntax check on the playbook once more

This output indicates that our playbook has the correct syntax and is ready to run.

Another test tool provided by Ansible consists of running it in *dry-run mode*. Use the `ansible-playbook` command with the `--check` option to run in dry-run mode:

```
$ ansible-playbook --check verify_webserver.yaml
```

```
$ ansible-playbook --check check_service.yml

PLAY [Ensure that httpd is installed and running] ************************************

TASK [Gathering Facts] **************************************************************
ok: [192.168.0.101]

TASK [Verify that httpd is installed in its latest version] *************************
changed: [192.168.0.101]

TASK [Verify that httpd is running] ************************************************
changed: [192.168.0.101]

PLAY RECAP *************************************************************************
192.168.0.101 : ok=3 changed=0 unreachable=0 failed=0 skipped=0 rescued=0 ignored=0
```

Figure 10.64 – Running the playbook in dry-run mode

Dry-run mode doesn't send any error message, so it is considered positive. Note that no change occurred; the playbook only tested if the tasks could be run on the managed node.

Now that there are no errors in the tests, run the playbook:

```
$ ansible-playbook verify_webserver.yaml
```

```
$ ansible-playbook check_service.yml

PLAY [Ensure that httpd is installed and running] **********************************

TASK [Gathering Facts] ************************************************************
ok: [192.168.0.101]

TASK [Verify that httpd is installed in its latest version] ***********************
changed: [192.168.0.101]

TASK [Verify that httpd is running] **********************************************
changed: [192.168.0.101]

PLAY RECAP **********************************************************************
192.168.0.101 : ok=3 changed=2 unreachable=0 failed=0 skipped=0 rescued=0 ignored=0
```

Figure 10.65 – Running the playbook

The `failed=0` output indicates that the tasks were finished successfully.

As predicted, in dry-run mode, the playbook does not generate errors.

Confirm this by logging into the host and verifying that the tasks are running:

```
[root@webserver1 ~]# rpm -qa | grep httpd
fedora-logos-httpd-36.0.0-3.fc38.noarch
httpd-filesystem-2.4.57-1.fc38.noarch
httpd-tools-2.4.57-1.fc38.x86_64
httpd-core-2.4.57-1.fc38.x86_64
httpd-2.4.57-1.fc38.x86_64
[root@webserver1 ~]# ps auxf | grep httpd
root      2059  0.0  1.1  35008 11624 ?        Ss   06:58   0:00 /usr/sbin/httpd -DFOREGROUND
apache    2060  0.0  0.7  47816  7176 ?        S    06:58   0:00  \_ /usr/sbin/httpd -DFOREGROUND
apache    2061  0.0  0.8 1236584 8860 ?        Sl   06:58   0:00  \_ /usr/sbin/httpd -DFOREGROUND
apache    2062  0.0  0.8 1105448 8864 ?        Sl   06:58   0:00  \_ /usr/sbin/httpd -DFOREGROUND
apache    2063  0.0  0.8 1105448 8864 ?        Sl   06:58   0:00  \_ /usr/sbin/httpd -DFOREGROUND
```

Figure 10.66 – Verifying tasks

> **Note**
>
> To learn more about Ansible, refer to the Ansible documentation at `https://docs.ansible.com/index.html`.

Automating with Ansible simplifies day-to-day tasks.

Automate as much as possible, so long as that automation impacts backups.

Automating enables us to get free time. Free time must be used to develop or learn new skills. *A SysAdmin never stops learning.*

Finally, let's take a look at a few resources where we can learn about and develop new skills.

Never-ending study

Study: A SysAdmin must have free time to study, so long this free time does not conflict with the first or second law.

Infrastructure profiles have been evolving the most in recent years. It is not that it is going to disappear as a job role, but it is reinventing itself and new skills are emerging. Thus, professionals must gain new knowledge.

The best advice is to always go back to the basics – that is, to programming and coding. Knowing all sides of the system is what assures the *SysAdmin* that they can continue to play a fundamental role. Each new technology can mean better work in less time with greater control of the system.

When new technology comes along, it takes time to study and implement it while keeping the system active, all while increasing productive leisure time.

A SysAdmin needs commitment to continuous learning while keeping up to date with the latest technology trends and best practices.

In these same years, the boom of online education took place. Among the many resources available, there are several to take advantage of.

Let's review those that could develop our skills as a SysAdmin:

- A great place to develop `vim` editor skills is VimTricks. **VimTricks** (`https://vimtricks.com/`) collects the necessary tricks, how-tos, guides, videos, links, and plugins and posts them on their social networks and as an e-newsletter. The site offers an extensive archive of published material, as well as a book and the possibility to register to receive the e-newsletter regularly:

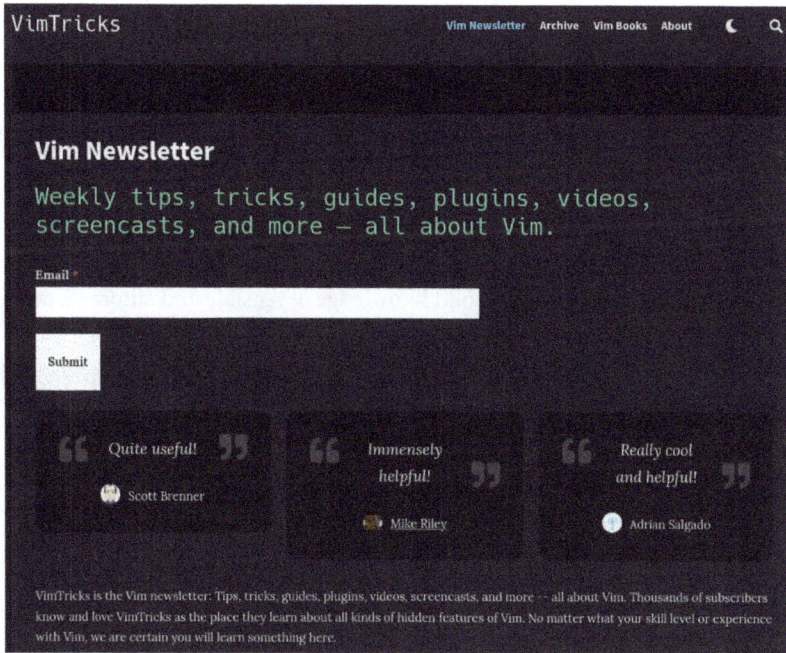

Figure 10.67 – The VimTricks web page

- Another recommendation is a page that brings together the tools and training needed to develop with the new **Red Hat** technologies – that is, `https://developers.redhat.com/`:

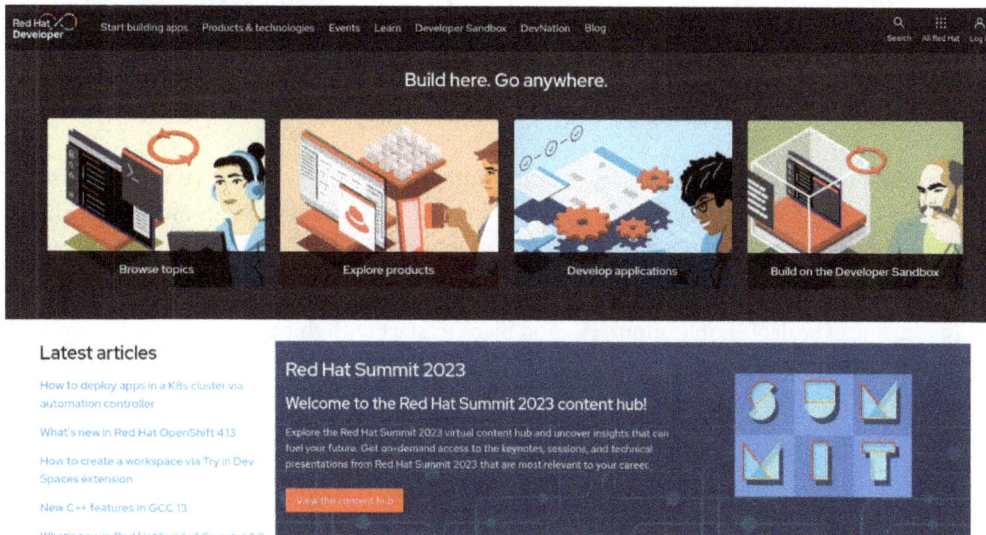

Figure 10.68 – The Red Hat Developer web page

Red Hat Developer is a community that provides tools, training, and technical talks designed to help developers improve their skills and keep up-to-date on the technologies that are shaping the future.

Subscribers have access to weekly DevNation technical talks, technology deep dives, and open source tutorials.

The subscription is free – just sign up and you'll also get access to other official Red Hat learning and reference sites.

- As a form of support to help you get solid knowledge of Ansible and automate tasks with this tool, you can go to `https://www.ansiblepilot.com/`:

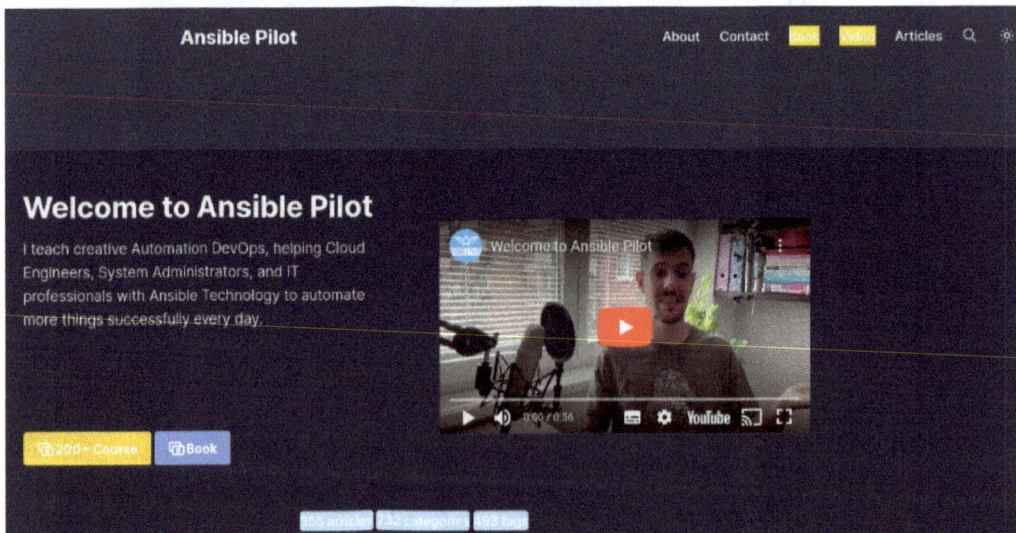

Figure 10.69 – The Ansible Pilot learning page

Luca Berton, Ansible automation expert and author of several books on automation, offers many examples, pieces of code, and videos of automating tasks of all kinds on his site. This is a great place to learn and practice task automation.

- **Kubernetes** is the *new paradigm of technology*. It is an open source container orchestrator that manages scalable applications. A good place to start with this technology is `https://kubebyexample.com/`:

Figure 10.70 – The Kube by Example web page

With Kube by Example, you can learn about Linux principles, the basics of Kubernetes, developing applications deployed on the platform, and applicable security best practices. It includes lots of downloadable code, practical examples, and videos so that learning can flow naturally.

- At **Packt Publishing** we don't lag behind. You can access free learning content at `https://www.packtpub.com/free-learning`:

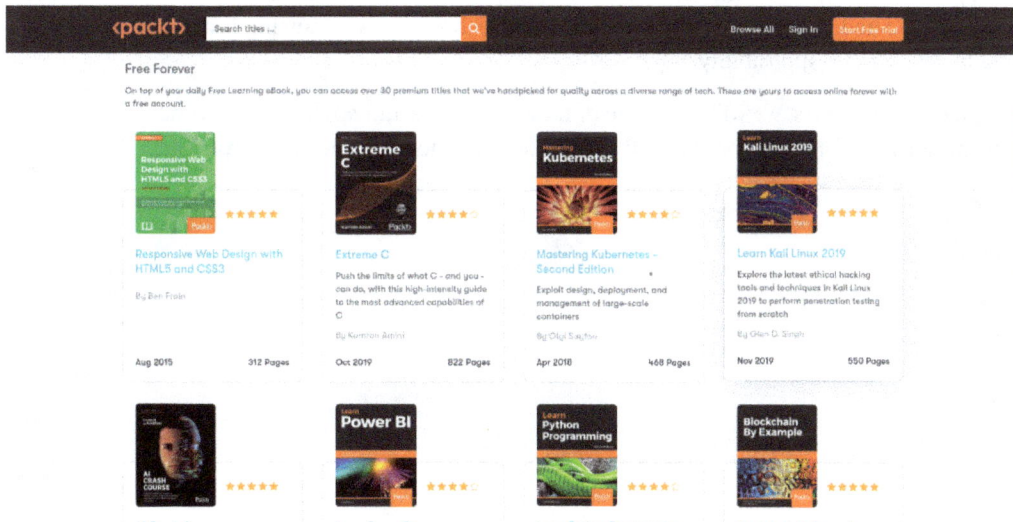

Figure 10.71 – Packt free learning

By registering, you will have unlimited access to thousands of learning materials such as e-books and video courses – free content forever! Don't miss the opportunity and sign up for your free trial.

Remember, a SysAdmin is always reinventing themselves.

It's not magic. It's talent and sweat.

There is a lot of reference material that could guide you in your development as a *SysAdmin*. However, if you want to look at it from a simple point of view, these three principles should help you create good habits that generate good practices.

I hope you find them useful.

In the next chapter, we will discuss the use and practical application of operating system tuning.

Summary

In this chapter, we reviewed the path to becoming a SysAdsmin and proposed three basic rules for the acquisition of good habits.

First, we looked at *backing up* any information with which we have contact with the system. This backup will ensure that changes that are made can be returned safely in case they're needed. It also provides a snapshot of the system at a certain point in time. Next, we looked at various task *automation* techniques to streamline our daily routine. This principle lightens your workload and allows SysAdmins to get free time that might be occupied with expanding their knowledge. The last point we considered was to *never stop learning*. Since technology is advancing faster and faster, this should be taken as a responsibility.

In the following chapters, we will make use of these principles and apply them to various particular aspects of *systems administration*. We will start by learning how to tune operating systems.

11
Performance Tuning Best Practices

Performance tuning system resources is one of the main (or even the most important) tasks of any system administrator. Performance tuning is the process of tweaking a system's configuration to improve the use of computing resources, data throughput, or user experience. It requires a thorough understanding of the hardware and software components of a system, as well as the many interactions between them.

Performance tuning is often confused with troubleshooting, but there are significant differences between them. In a troubleshooting process, the main goal is finding and solving a problem to make the system work. In performance tuning, the goal is to get the system running with the best possible performance while taking advantage of the resources and environment it operates in.

In this chapter, we are going to cover the following main topics on how to get the best performance regarding the key aspects of the system:

- Understanding kernel tuning
- Main tuning – CPU and memory
- Don't ignore storage tuning
- Boosting performance with network tuning

Technical requirements

To complete the topics in this chapter, you will need to install the packages indicated in each section. There, you will find instructions for each package that needs to be installed.

The examples that were created for this chapter can be downloaded from this book's GitHub repository: `https://github.com/PacktPublishing/Fedora-Linux-System-Administration/tree/main/chapter11`.

Understanding kernel tuning

The Linux kernel exposes *user-space tunable information and configurations* through the /proc directory. The /proc filesystem acts as an interface to the **kernel** data structures and runtime information. It provides a way to access detailed information about processes, system configuration, hardware, and more, exposing this data through a hierarchy of virtual files.

The files in the /proc directory contain system information such as memory (meminfo), CPU (cpuinfo), and available filesystems.

The /proc/sys subdirectory contains configurable parameters to adjust kernel behavior and activity. Most files in /proc/sys can be modified by the root user. Modifying files in /proc/sys causes immediate changes to the running system.

> **Note**
> Changing the files in /proc/sys could improve the performance of the running system, but it could also degrade it. Be careful when applying any changes to these files. Remember to back up before making any changes to them.

Within /proc/sys, the files get organized into a subdirectory tree by tunable kernel type:

- /proc/sys/dev: Contains tunables for **system devices**
- /proc/sys/fs: Contains tunable variables related to the **filesystem**
- /proc/sys/kernel: Includes tweaks that change the **internal kernel operation**
- /proc/sys/net: Contains tunables that change the **network configuration**
- /proc/sys/vm: This contains parameters that change the management of the **virtual memory of the kernel**

> **Note**
> Remember, not all files in /proc/sys are writable. Some of them only get altered by the operating system itself.

Let's see how we can change these kernel tunables.

Tuning kernel parameters

The following figure illustrates how the kernel parameters can be changed in different ways:

Linux Performance Tuning Tools

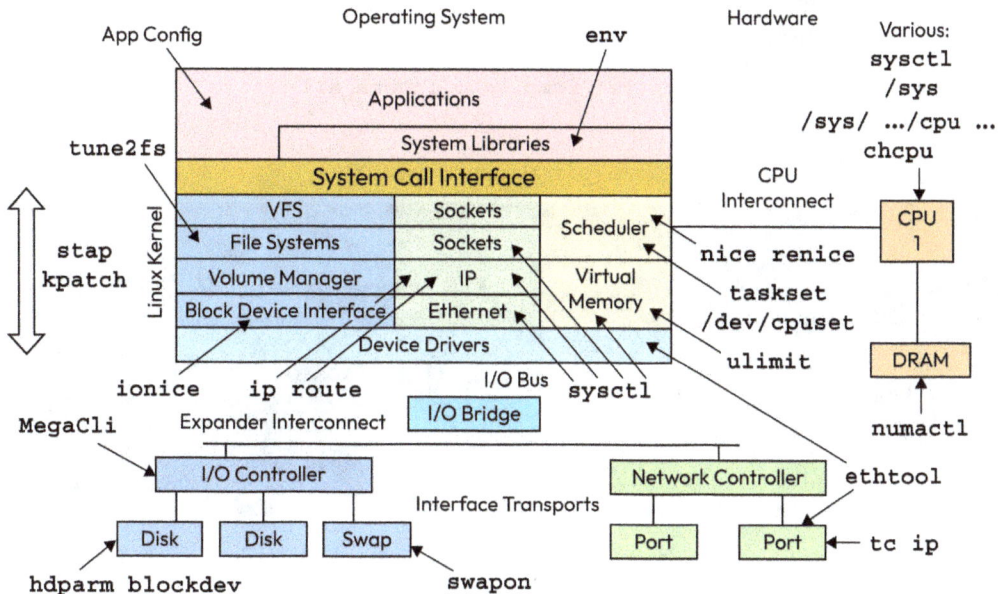

Figure 11.1 – Linux Performance Tuning Tools, by Brendan Gregg (CC BY-SA 4.0)

As system administrators, the best practice is to make changes through the command line, as follows:

- Using a text editor to change /proc/sys files

- Using the echo command to set simple values in the tunables

- Using the sysctl command to set a parameter by name

- Create files with the desired parameters in the /etc/sysctl.d directory

> **Note**
>
> Changing the configurable values in the kernel tunables directly does not make them *persistent* at reboot. To do this, you must use the sysctl command or create a file with the change in the /etc/sysctl.d directory.

Let's see an example of each of the different ways we can do this. Follow these steps:

1. Review the content of the tunable `icmp_echo_ignore_all` inside the `/proc/sys/net/ipv4` directory:

    ```
    # cat /proc/sys/net/ipv4/icmp_echo_ignore_all
    0
    ```

    This value (0) indicates that `icmp` (`ping`) support exists:

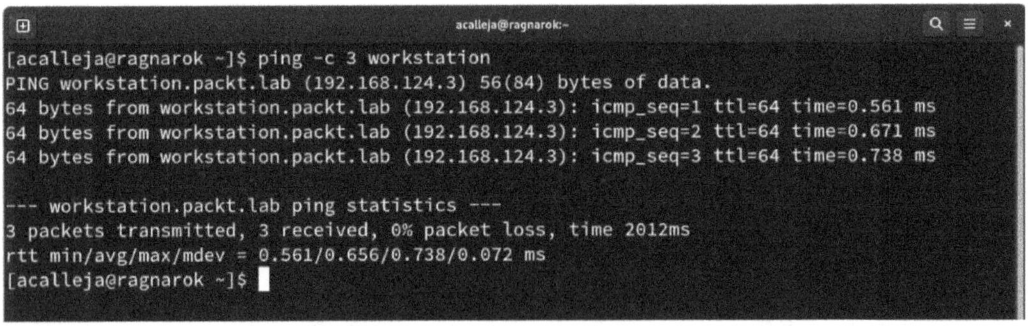

Figure 11.2 – The workstation supports ping

    Let's change it.

2. Use the `echo` command to change the value of the tunable from *false* (0) to *true* (1):

    ```
    # echo "1" > /proc/sys/net/ipv4/icmp_echo_ignore_all
    ```

    Confirm the change of the tunable:

    ```
    # cat /proc/sys/net/ipv4/icmp_echo_ignore_all
    1
    ```

    As you will see, the operating system no longer allows *pinging*:

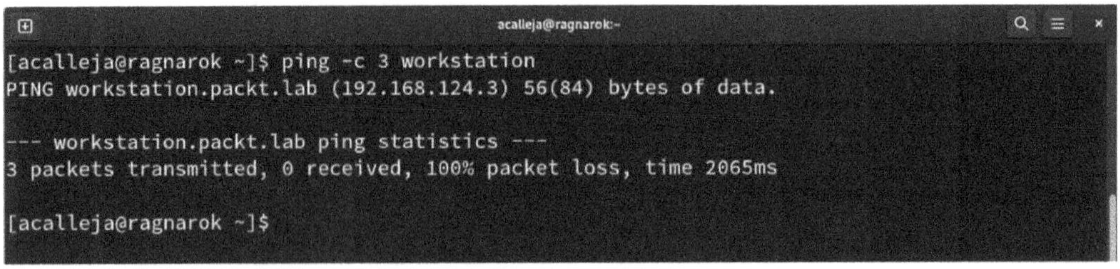

Figure 11.3 – Ping not allowed by the operating system

This change can also be made using the `sysctl` command.

Let's do it.

3. The path of the tunable to change can be represented by replacing the slashes under `/proc/sys` with dots. In our example, the tunable is as follows:

    net.ipv4.icmp_echo_ignore_all

    Use the `sysctl` command with the `-w` option to enable `ping`:

    ```
    # sysctl -w net.ipv4.icmp_echo_ignore_all="0"
    net.ipv4.icmp_echo_ignore_all = 0
    ```

    Confirm that `ping` support is already enabled:

```
[acalleja@ragnarok ~]$ ping -c 3 workstation
PING workstation.packt.lab (192.168.124.3) 56(84) bytes of data.
64 bytes from workstation.packt.lab (192.168.124.3): icmp_seq=1 ttl=64 time=0.482 ms
64 bytes from workstation.packt.lab (192.168.124.3): icmp_seq=2 ttl=64 time=0.689 ms
64 bytes from workstation.packt.lab (192.168.124.3): icmp_seq=3 ttl=64 time=0.340 ms

--- workstation.packt.lab ping statistics ---
3 packets transmitted, 3 received, 0% packet loss, time 2073ms
rtt min/avg/max/mdev = 0.340/0.503/0.689/0.143 ms
[acalleja@ragnarok ~]$
```

Figure 11.4 – Ping allowed

However, this change is not persistent on reboot.

Let's see how to do this.

4. On boot, the kernel loads the tunable settings from the configuration files found in these directories:

    - `/etc/sysctl.d/`
    - `/run/sysctl.d/`
    - `/usr/lib/sysctl.d/`

    Create a configuration file with the `.conf` extension, with the tunable set to `true`:

    ```
    # echo "net.ipv4.icmp_echo_ignore_all=1" > /etc/sysctl.d/ping.conf
    ```

    Use the `sysctl` command with the `-p` option to apply the setting:

    ```
    # sysctl -p /etc/sysctl.d/ping.conf
    net.ipv4.icmp_echo_ignore_all = 1
    ```

Confirm the `ping` behavior change:

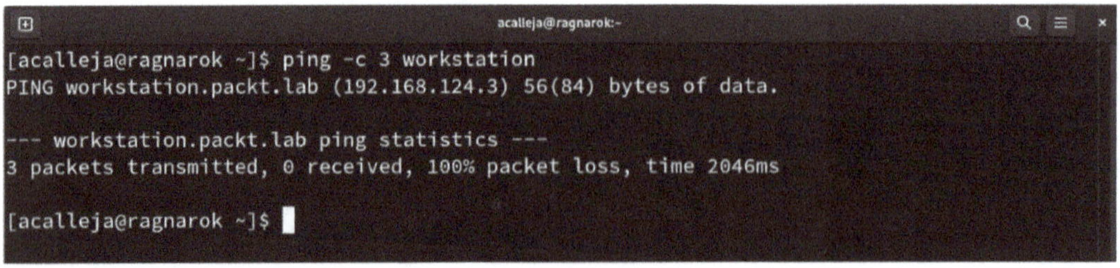

Figure 11.5 – Ping not allowed

These are the different ways to change the kernel tunables. To get the list of kernel tunables, use the `-a` option of the `sysctl` command:

```
# sysctl -a
```

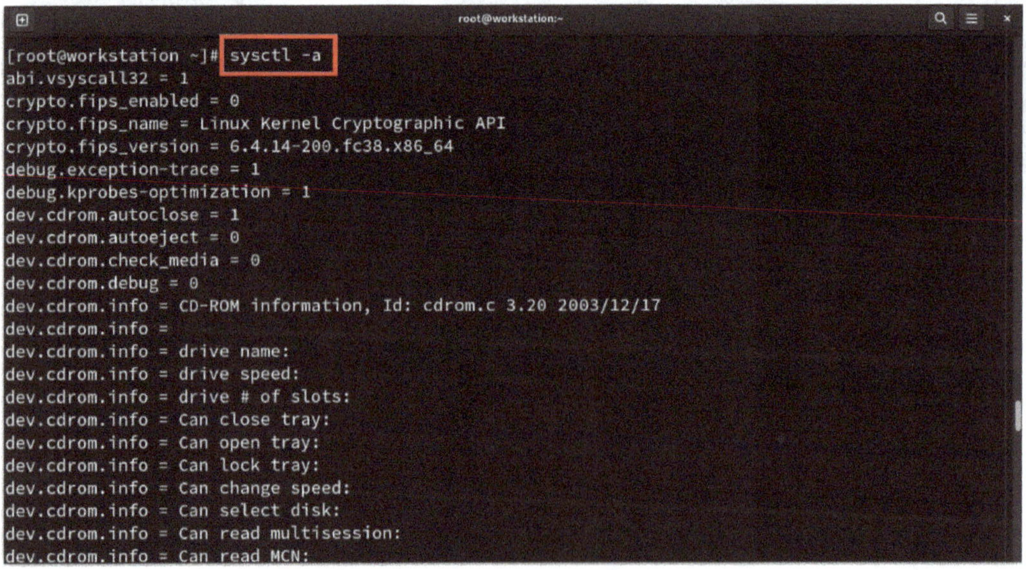

Figure 11.6 – Kernel tunables list

Changes that are made to the kernel tunables modify the behavior of the operating system. Now, let's take a look at the changes in some specific aspects of the main components of the operating system.

Main tuning – CPU and memory

In the previous section, *Figure 11.1* illustrated the different tools that help us collect performance information on the use of system resources.

The tools display system information such as free disk space, CPU temperature, and other essential components, as well as network information such as the system's IP address and current upload and download rates.

Monitoring the resources of the running system represents one of the many main tasks of a system administrator. The goal of system monitoring is to determine whether the current performance meets the specified technical requirements.

Monitoring the performance of resources helps us know about the areas that need improving.

Before changing the CPU and memory usage configuration, let's take a brief look at the basic monitoring tools included in Fedora Linux.

Overview of monitoring tools

Monitoring tools provide per-process statistics and are based on process structures or system-wide statistics from the kernel. Monitoring tools usually become available to *unprivileged users*, but for a more granular level of detail, system administrator privileges are required.

The ps and top commands are the most common commands that provide process statistics, including CPU and memory.

As the root user, running the ps command with the aux option lists the processes with extended details by user:

```
# ps aux
```

Figure 11.7 – Output of the ps aux command

The following table describes the output of the `ps  aux` command column by column:

Column	Description
USER	The user running the process.
PID	Process ID of this process.
%CPU	CPU time used (in percent) by this process.
%MEM	Physical memory used (in percentage) by this process.
VSZ	Virtual memory used (in bytes) by this process.
RSS	Resident Set Size, *non-swappable* physical memory used (in KiB*) by this process.
TTY	Terminal from which the process started. The *question mark* (?) indicates that the process wasn't started from a terminal.
STAT	Process state.
START	Starting time and date of the process.
TIME	Total CPU time used by this process.
COMMAND	The command, with all its arguments, that started the process.

Table 11.1 – The ps aux command's output description column by column

*More details will be provided in the following section.

> **Note**
>
> For more information about the *process stat codes*, refer to the `ps` manual pages. Use the `man ps` command.

Unlike the `ps` command, where the output is static, the `top` command provides a real-time report of process activity. It also provides an interface for filtering and manipulating the monitoring data:

```
# top
```

```
⊞                                          root@workstation:~                                    Q  ≡  ×
top - 15:21:55 up 6 min,  1 user,  load average: 0.00, 0.00, 0.00
Tasks: 155 total,   1 running, 154 sleeping,   0 stopped,   0 zombie
%Cpu(s):  0.0 us,  0.1 sy,  0.0 ni, 99.8 id,  0.0 wa,  0.1 hi,  0.1 si,  0.0 st
MiB Mem :   7927.3 total,   7451.4 free,    232.3 used,    243.6 buff/cache
MiB Swap:   7927.0 total,   7927.0 free,      0.0 used.   7457.1 avail Mem

    PID USER      PR  NI    VIRT    RES    SHR S  %CPU  %MEM     TIME+ COMMAND
     70 root      20   0       0      0      0 I   0.3   0.0   0:00.78 kworker/0:2-events
      1 root      20   0  220540  27088  10644 S   0.0   0.3   0:00.80 systemd
      2 root      20   0       0      0      0 S   0.0   0.0   0:00.00 kthreadd
      3 root       0 -20       0      0      0 I   0.0   0.0   0:00.00 rcu_gp
      4 root       0 -20       0      0      0 I   0.0   0.0   0:00.00 rcu_par_gp
      5 root       0 -20       0      0      0 I   0.0   0.0   0:00.00 slub_flushwq
      6 root       0 -20       0      0      0 I   0.0   0.0   0:00.00 netns
      8 root       0 -20       0      0      0 I   0.0   0.0   0:00.00 kworker/0:0H-ttm
     11 root       0 -20       0      0      0 I   0.0   0.0   0:00.00 mm_percpu_wq
     12 root      20   0       0      0      0 I   0.0   0.0   0:00.31 kworker/u8:1-events_unbound
     13 root      20   0       0      0      0 I   0.0   0.0   0:00.00 rcu_tasks_kthread
     14 root      20   0       0      0      0 I   0.0   0.0   0:00.00 rcu_tasks_rude_kthread
     15 root      20   0       0      0      0 I   0.0   0.0   0:00.00 rcu_tasks_trace_kthread
     16 root      20   0       0      0      0 S   0.0   0.0   0:00.00 ksoftirqd/0
     17 root      20   0       0      0      0 I   0.0   0.0   0:00.04 rcu_preempt
     18 root      rt   0       0      0      0 S   0.0   0.0   0:00.00 migration/0
     19 root     -51   0       0      0      0 S   0.0   0.0   0:00.00 idle_inject/0
```

Figure 11.8 – Output of the top command

The command output header provides general information on the current behavior of the system:

- The first line includes the current time, how long the system runs for, the number of users connected, and the average load in the last 1, 5, and 15 minutes

- The second line shows the number of tasks and their statuses: running, sleeping, stopped, or zombies

- The third line shows different CPU usage values (at runtime):

  - us: Time that CPU spends running processes for users in *user space*

  - sy: Time spent running *system kernel space* processes

  - ni: Time spent running processes with a manually set nice value

  - id: CPU idle time

  - wa: Time that CPU spends waiting for I/O tasks to complete

  - hi: Time spent servicing *hardware interrupts*

  - si: Time spent servicing *software interrupts*

  - st: Time lost due to running virtual machines (*steal time*)

- The fourth line shows the total amount (in KiB) of physical memory, and how much is free, used, and buffered or cached

- The fifth line shows the total amount (in KiB) of swap memory, and how much is free, used, and available

The following table describes the output of the `top` command column by column:

Column	Description
PID	Process ID
USER	User owner of the process
PR	Process priority
NI	Nice value of the process
VIRT	Virtual memory used by the process
RES	Resident memory used by the process
SHR	Shared memory used by the process
S	Status of the process
%CPU	Share of CPU time used (in percentage) by the process since the last update
%MEM	Share of physical memory used (in percentage)
TIME+	Total CPU time used by the task in hundredths of a second
COMMAND	The command, with all its arguments, that started the process

Table 11.2 – The top command's output description column by column

> **Note**
>
> For more information about the process status codes, refer to the `top` manual pages. Use the `man top` command to do so.

Regarding memory, the `free` command lists the free and used *physical* and *swap* memory. By using the `-b`, `-k`, `-m`, and `-g` options, the output will be displayed in bytes, KB, MB, and GB, respectively:

```
# free
```

Figure 11.9 – Outputs after running the different options of the free command

The GNOME desktop provides a graphical tool for resource monitoring. From the main menu, under **Activities Overview**, type `system monitor`:

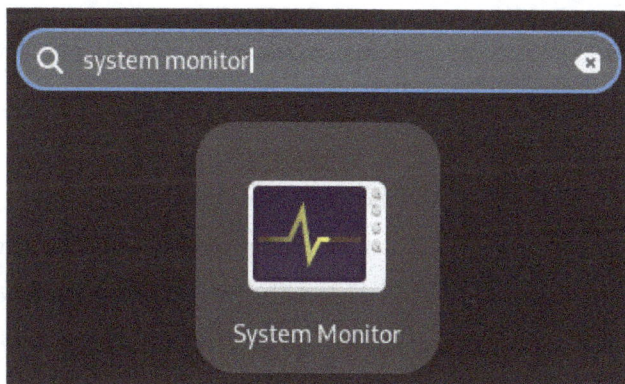

Figure 11.10 – GNOME System Monitor from Activities Overview

You can also open the utility from the Terminal by running the `gnome-system-monitor` command:

```
$ gnome-system-monitor
```

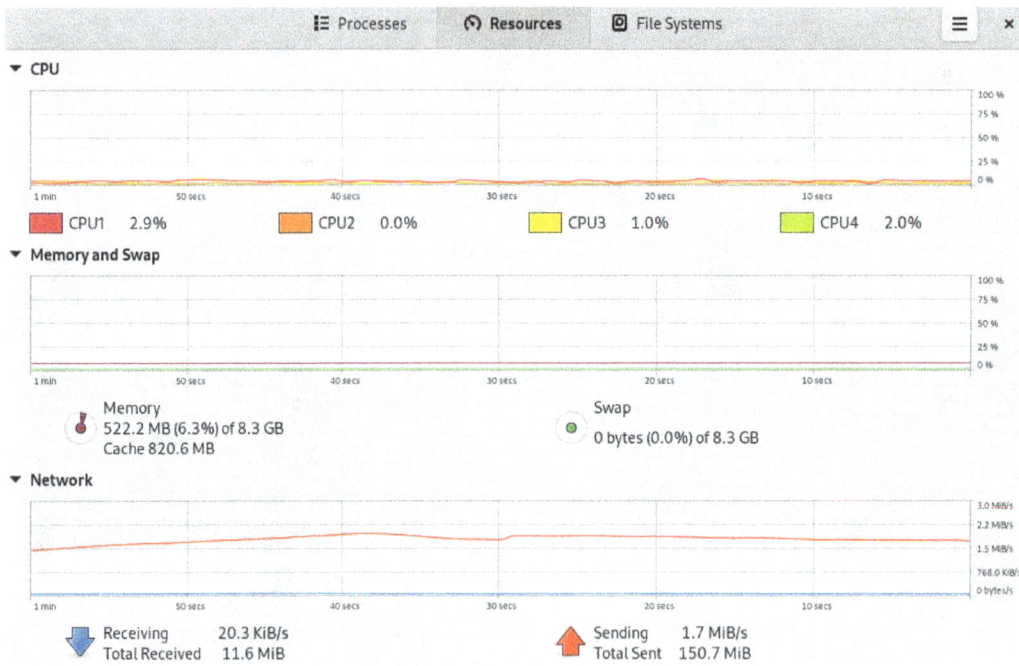

Figure 11.11 – GNOME System Monitor

Fedora Linux, through its official repositories, provides a package that integrates several monitoring tools. The `sysstat` package takes the *raw data* from the kernel counters and allows you to display and store the metrics in a historical *process running* database.

The following utilities are included in this package:

- `mpstat`: Reports individual or combined CPU-related statistics
- `iostat`: Reports CPU and I/O statistics for devices, partitions, and the network filesystem
- `pidstat`: Reports statistics for processes, including disk `I/O`, `CPU`, and `memory` usage
- `cifsiostat`: Reports statistics about shared filesystems, printers, or network serial ports
- `sar`: Collects, reports, and stores system activity

To install the package, from the Terminal, run the following command:

```
# dnf install sysstat
```

All these tools are useful for measuring and storing system resource usage information. And with this, we can determine which aspect of the resources has points for improvement.

Let's start with CPU usage.

Improving CPU usage

To find points of improvement in CPU usage, first, observe the behavior of the CPU. Let's learn how to check CPU usage with the different monitoring tools. Follow these steps:

1. Use the ps command to list the processes with the highest CPU usage:

    ```
    # ps ax --format pid,%cpu,cmd --sort -%cpu
    ```

```
[root@workstation ~]# ps ax --format pid,%cpu,cmd --sort -%cpu
  PID %CPU CMD
 1547  0.2 sshd: root@pts/0
  665  0.1 /usr/lib/systemd/systemd-oomd
 1543  0.1 [kworker/3:0-events]
    1  0.0 /usr/lib/systemd/systemd --switched-root --system --deserialize=31
    2  0.0 [kthreadd]
    3  0.0 [rcu_gp]
    4  0.0 [rcu_par_gp]
    5  0.0 [slub_flushwq]
    6  0.0 [netns]
   11  0.0 [mm_percpu_wq]
   13  0.0 [rcu_tasks_kthread]
   14  0.0 [rcu_tasks_rude_kthread]
   15  0.0 [rcu_tasks_trace_kthread]
   16  0.0 [ksoftirqd/0]
   17  0.0 [rcu_preempt]
   18  0.0 [migration/0]
   19  0.0 [idle_inject/0]
   20  0.0 [cpuhp/0]
   21  0.0 [cpuhp/1]
```

Figure 11.12 – Output of the ps command listing the processes with the highest CPU usage

This mode of the ps ax command formats the output by process identifier (pid), percentage of CPU usage, and the command that started the process, sorting by the percentage of CPU usage.

The output shows that the process with the highest CPU usage is SSH, which should be considered normal for administrative tasks.

In our system, a web server is running. Let's analyze its CPU usage.

2. Use the ps command to identify the httpd process and its CPU usage:

    ```
    # ps auxf | grep "[h]ttpd"
    # ps ax --format pid,%cpu,cmd --sort -%cpu | grep "[h]ttpd"
    ```

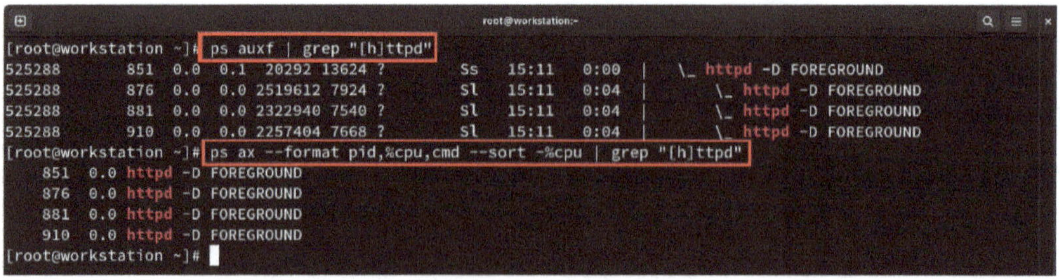

Figure 11.13 – Identifying the httpd process and its CPU usage

> **Note**
>
> Enclosing the first character of the process in square brackets limits the search, ignoring the `grep` command itself at the output.

Note that the CPU usage displayed is not significant, so further research needs to focus on finding the real value of CPU usage.

3. Use the process identifier (`pid`) to find the resource usage with the `top` command:

    ```
    # top -p 851,876,881,910
    ```

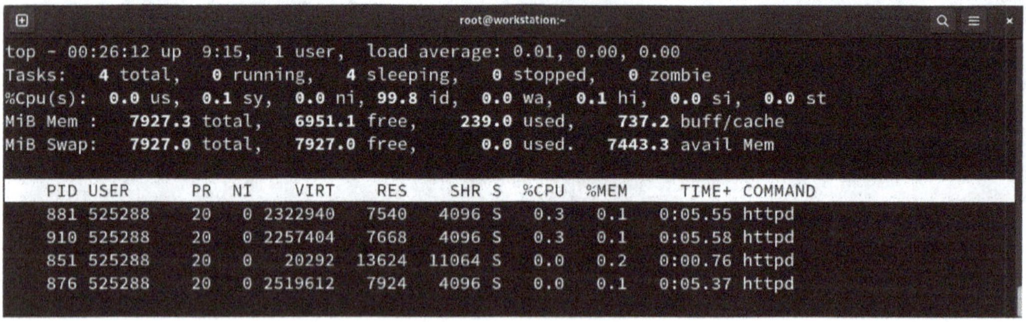

Figure 11.14 – Monitoring resource usage with the top command

Now, let's use the utility included in the `sysstat` package to get more information about the process's performance.

4. Use the `pidstat` command with the process identifier (`pid`) to get the CPU usage of the process at the *1-second interval*:

    ```
    # pidstat -p 851,876,881,910 1 1
    ```

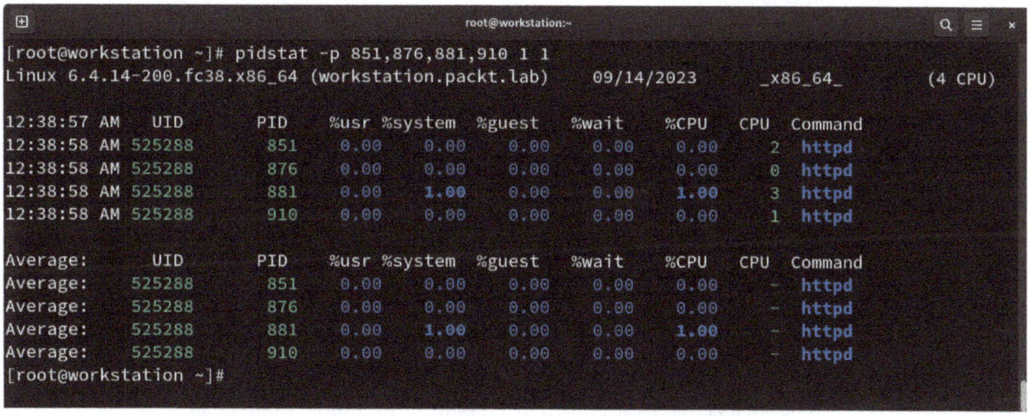

Figure 11.15 – Process CPU usage percentage

A single CPU can only run *one process at a time*. To make the Linux system run multiple processes simultaneously, through multitasking, processes interleave their running on the CPU.

The kernel uses the *process scheduler* to determine which process to run at any given time. The process scheduler must balance several options, based on certain criteria, such as determining which process gets the next turn of execution, getting a fair share of CPU time but allowing high-priority processes a larger share and preempting lower-priority processes, or being predictable and scalable under different workload conditions.

The scheduler controls the order of running based on the scheduling priority policy assigned to each thread or process. These scheduling policies are divided into two groups: **non-real-time policies** and **real-time policies**.

> **Note**
>
> **Real-time computing (RTC)** guarantees the response of a system from the event to the response itself, within specified time constraints. A *real-time system* describes a system that controls an environment. It receives data, processes it, and returns the results fast enough to affect the environment at that time.

The priority of the process using real-time policies is a value between 1 (*lowest*) and 99 (*highest*) and is known as a **static priority**. Processes using non-real-time policies that do not use static priorities are set to 0.

The priority of the process could *increase* and *decrease* during the lifetime of the process; this is known as the **dynamic priority**. The value for determining which non-real-time process takes precedence over other non-real-time processes comes under the name of **nice value**. A user could change the priority of a process by using the nice or renice commands.

Since the static priority of non-real-time processes is set to 0, the nice value determines the *relative scheduling* of non-real-time processes. The nice value ranges from -20 (*highest*) to 19 (*lowest*).

Fedora Linux provides six scheduling policies divided into two groups: real-time and non-real-time scheduling classes. The following table lists the policies available in each scheduling class:

Class	Policies	Definition
Real-time scheduler	SCHED_FIFO	Uses the *first-in, first-out* scheduling algorithm without timeslices.
	SCHED_RR	Uses the *round-robin* scheduling algorithm with timeslices.
Completely Fair Scheduler (CFS)	SCHED_NORMAL (*also known as* SCHED_OTHER)	Defines the *round-robin* style time-sharing schedule.
	SCHED_BATCH	Benefits *batch-oriented* workloads.
	SCHED_IDLE	Benefits running low-priority applications.
Deadline scheduler	SCHED_DEADLINE	The scheduler guarantees real-time task scheduling, even under high load conditions. It does so by using three parameters – period, deadline, and runtime – to define a task in nanoseconds.

Table 11.3 – Scheduling policies

Let's continue using the previous example of the web server to analyze the priority of its process. Follow these steps:

1. Use the ps command to list the priority of processes:

```
# ps axo pid,pri,rtprio,ni,cls,comm | grep -e "PID" -e "[h]ttpd"
```

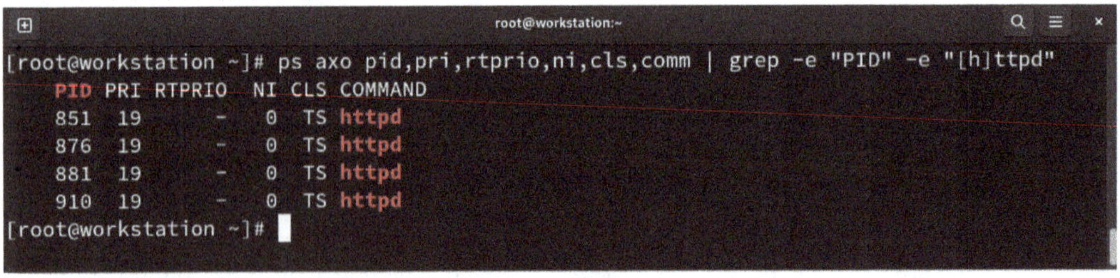

Figure 11.16 – Reviewing process priority

Here, the `pri` column shows **static priority** (19), the `rtprio` column shows real time priority (-), the `ni` column shows **nice value** (0), and the `cls` column shows the **scheduling policy**. Here, TS represents **time-sharing**.

The preceding output indicates that the process has low priority in its run. Let's change this.

2. Use the `chrt` command to display the scheduling policy and priority of the web server processes:

```
# chrt -p [PID]
```

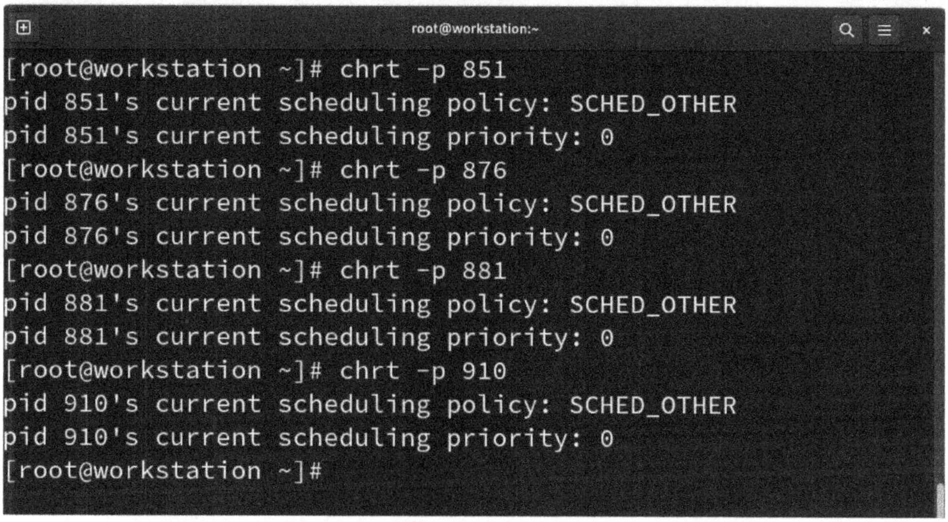

```
[root@workstation ~]# chrt -p 851
pid 851's current scheduling policy: SCHED_OTHER
pid 851's current scheduling priority: 0
[root@workstation ~]# chrt -p 876
pid 876's current scheduling policy: SCHED_OTHER
pid 876's current scheduling priority: 0
[root@workstation ~]# chrt -p 881
pid 881's current scheduling policy: SCHED_OTHER
pid 881's current scheduling priority: 0
[root@workstation ~]# chrt -p 910
pid 910's current scheduling policy: SCHED_OTHER
pid 910's current scheduling priority: 0
[root@workstation ~]#
```

Figure 11.17 – Scheduling the policy and priority of web server processes

The scheduled priority of all processes is 0 and their scheduling policy is SCHED_NORMAL (or SCHED_OTHER). Let's improve the process run.

3. Stop the web server service and restart it by changing the scheduled policy to SCHED_FIFO and the scheduled priority to 38. Use the `chrt` command and the process binary:

```
# systemctl stop httpd
# chrt -f 38 /usr/sbin/httpd
```

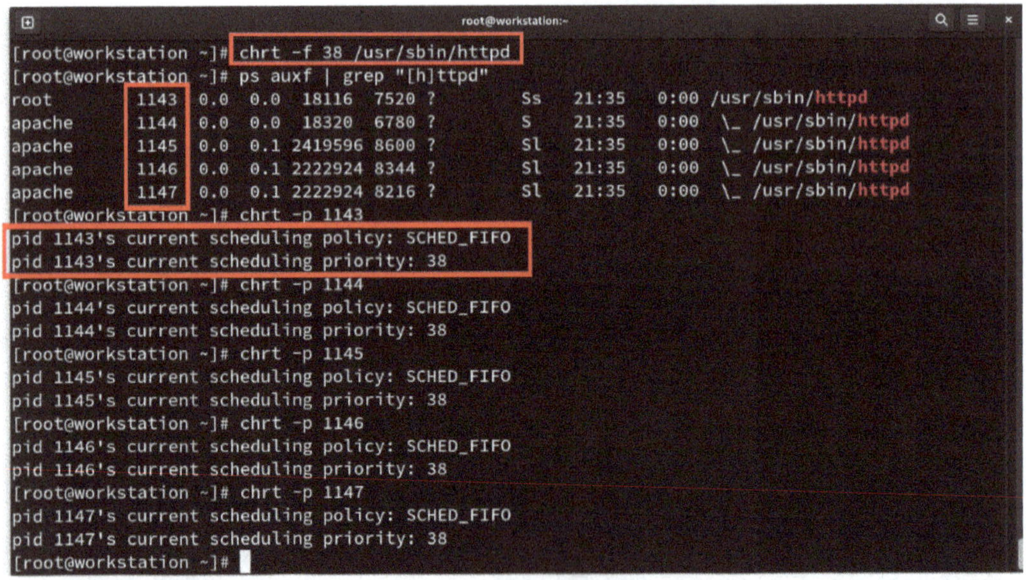

Figure 11.18 – Changing the scheduling policy and priority

Review the scheduling policy and priority of the web server processes.

> **Note**
>
> For more information about the `chrt` command's options, refer to the manual pages by running the `man chrt` command.

This change is temporary. When the process restarts, the scheduled policy and scheduled priority should apply again.

To set a scheduled policy and priority to improve the performance of the process each time it starts, it must be added to the service's `unit` file.

Let's do it.

4. Create a scheduled configuration file for the `httpd` service with the following content:

    ```
    # vim /etc/systemd/system/httpd.service.d/10-scheduler.conf
    [Service]
    CPUSchedulingPolicy=rr
    CPUSchedulingPriority=10
    ```

```
[root@workstation ~]# mkdir -p /etc/systemd/system/httpd.service.d
[root@workstation ~]# vi /etc/systemd/system/httpd.service.d/10-scheduler.conf
[root@workstation ~]# cat /etc/systemd/system/httpd.service.d/10-scheduler.conf
[Service]
CPUSchedulingPolicy=rr
CPUSchedulingPriority=10
[root@workstation ~]# systemctl daemon-reload
[root@workstation ~]#
```

Figure 11.19 – Creating the service configuration file

Unit configuration policies are set to change the priority of a service during the boot process. The directives in the [Service] section change the scheduling policy and priority:

- CPUSchedulingPriority (**Nice**): Sets the default nice level for the service. The *nice* level is set as a number between -20 (*highest priority*) and 19 (*lowest priority*).

- CPUSchedulingPolicy: Sets the CPU scheduling policy for the service. The policy is set with the other, batch, idle, fifo, and rr values.

> **Note**
>
> At the time of writing, the CPUSchedulingPolicy variable does not support the SCHED_DEADLINE policy setting.

Reload the configuration of the services that were loaded in by systemd before restarting the web server service. Use the systemctl command:

```
# systemctl daemon-reload
```

Restart the service to apply the policy and priority changes.

5. Use the systemctl command to restart the web server service:

```
# systemctl restart httpd
```

```
[root@workstation ~]# systemctl restart httpd
[root@workstation ~]# ps auxf | grep "[h]ttpd"
root       2698  0.3  0.1  18116 11244 ?          Ss   00:22   0:00 /usr/sbin/httpd -DFOREGROUND
apache     2699  0.0  0.0  18320  6648 ?          S    00:22   0:00  \_ /usr/sbin/httpd -DFOREGROUND
apache     2700  0.0  0.1 2419596 8724 ?          Sl   00:22   0:00  \_ /usr/sbin/httpd -DFOREGROUND
apache     2701  0.0  0.1 2222924 8340 ?          Sl   00:22   0:00  \_ /usr/sbin/httpd -DFOREGROUND
apache     2702  0.0  0.1 2222924 8468 ?          Sl   00:22   0:00  \_ /usr/sbin/httpd -DFOREGROUND
[root@workstation ~]# chrt -p 2698
pid 2698's current scheduling policy: SCHED_FIFO
pid 2698's current scheduling priority: 10
[root@workstation ~]# chrt -p 2699
pid 2699's current scheduling policy: SCHED_FIFO
pid 2699's current scheduling priority: 10
[root@workstation ~]# chrt -p 2700
pid 2700's current scheduling policy: SCHED_FIFO
pid 2700's current scheduling priority: 10
[root@workstation ~]# chrt -p 2701
pid 2701's current scheduling policy: SCHED_FIFO
pid 2701's current scheduling priority: 10
[root@workstation ~]# chrt -p 2702
pid 2702's current scheduling policy: SCHED_FIFO
pid 2702's current scheduling priority: 10
[root@workstation ~]#
```

Figure 11.20 – Restarting the web server service

Review the scheduling policy and priority of the web server processes.

The change of priority and scheduled policy should apply when the service starts. This change improves the performance of the service.

What we've covered here applies to the case of processing. Now, let's learn how to improve memory usage.

Improving memory usage

The ps and top utilities differentiate between two statistics: VIRT (or VSZ), the total amount of virtual memory a process has requested, and RES (or RSS), the total amount of virtual memory a process is currently mapping into physical memory. RSS is the most critical value.

Using the preceding example, observe the virtual memory value mapped to the web server process with the ps command:

```
# ps -o pid,vsz,rss,comm -C httpd
```

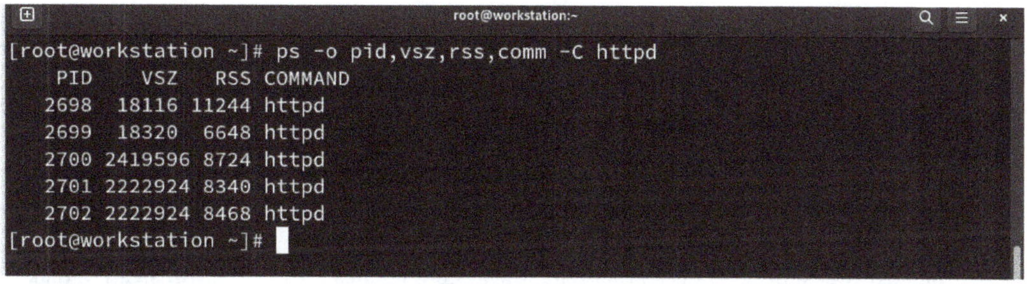

```
root@workstation:~
[root@workstation ~]# ps -o pid,vsz,rss,comm -C httpd
    PID     VSZ   RSS COMMAND
   2698   18116 11244 httpd
   2699   18320  6648 httpd
   2700 2419596  8724 httpd
   2701 2222924  8340 httpd
   2702 2222924  8468 httpd
[root@workstation ~]#
```

Figure 11.21 – Reviewing the virtual memory mapped to the web server

When a process requests memory, virtual memory addresses get reserved, but the kernel doesn't allocate them to physical page frames. The kernel only allocates physical page frames when the process starts using `memory`.

In the same way that the priority and scheduled policy are changed for processing, the memory that an application consumes could change.

Follow this step to adjust the `MemoryLimit` parameter of the `sshd` process:

1. Using the `sysctl` command, adjust the `MemoryLimit` parameter:

   ```
   # systemctl set-property sshd.service MemoryLimit=1G
   ```

> **Note**
>
> A memory size can be specified in kilobytes, megabytes, gigabytes, or terabytes using the `K`, `M`, `G`, or `T` suffix, respectively.

This command changes the service startup configuration file.

Use the `sysctl` command to display the service unit file. Filter the `Memory` parameter:

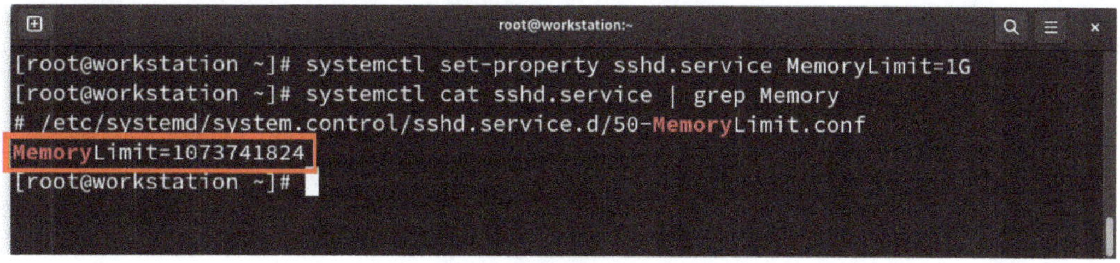

```
root@workstation:~
[root@workstation ~]# systemctl set-property sshd.service MemoryLimit=1G
[root@workstation ~]# systemctl cat sshd.service | grep Memory
# /etc/systemd/system.control/sshd.service.d/50-MemoryLimit.conf
MemoryLimit=1073741824
[root@workstation ~]#
```

Figure 11.22 – Reviewing the MemoryLimit parameter

In *Figure 11.22*, we find that the kernel assigned the service 10 MB of memory and, by setting the MemoryLimit parameter, ensures that it only uses up to 1 GB.

Keeping control of the resources assigned to the services allows them to improve their performance and that of the operating system as well.

Managing unallocated memory is the task that requires the most intense monitoring in Linux. The kernel uses most of the unallocated memory as a cache to store data that gets read from or written to disk. The next time a process needs that data, the system fetches it from RAM instead of disk. The caching mechanism improves performance in general since storage is usually much slower than physical memory.

Besides cache pages, the system uses anonymous pages. Anonymous pages have no data associated with them on disk. These anonymous pages represent the pages that processes allocate and use to store their work data.

We have different tools and utilities that help us monitor both.

Let's have a brief overview of these tools and utilities.

Inspect the memory usage with the free and vmstat commands:

```
# free -m
```

```
[root@workstation ~]# free -m
               total        used        free      shared  buff/cache   available
Mem:            7927         228        6229           9        1468        7447
Swap:           7926           0        7926
[root@workstation ~]#
```

Figure 11.23 – Output of the free command

In this system, there's 8 GiB of RAM. The cache pages (the buff/cache column) consume 1 GiB.

Let's compare this with the output of the vmstat command:

```
# vmstat --unit M 1
```

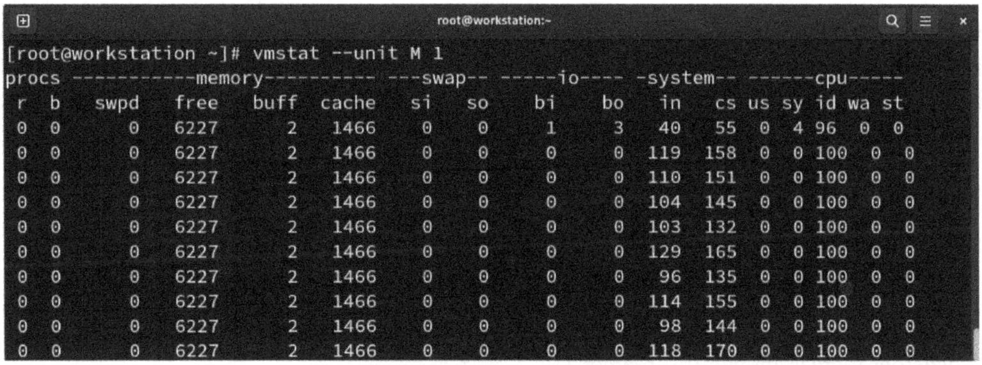

Figure 11.24 – Output of the vmstat command

From the output of the `vmstat` command, note that the size of the page cache is the sum of the `buff` and `cache` columns. Buffers are part of the page cache. Buffers store blocks of data read *directly* from a block device, not from the filesystem.

Anonymous pages get moved to the swap area when the system is under memory pressure. The kernel chooses between retrieving anonymous pages or pages from the page cache. The availability of swap increases the amount of effective memory.

From the output of the `vmstat` command (*Figure 11.24*), in the `swap` section, we can see the values of the anonymous pages:

- `si`: Pages *swapped in* per second
- `so`: Pages *swapped out* per second

The *swap area* was a subject of discussion for many years. At the beginning of the computer era, several myths about how to calculate the swap area were created among system administrators from those days. They were not only taken as good practices but as a must-have during the creation of the swap area. This was because, in those days, physical storage was expensive.

Nowadays, with new technologies, storage has become cheaper and more affordable. So, the creation of the swap area is considered under the use case criteria.

Red Hat proposes the following table as a basis for use cases for sizing when creating the swap area:

RAM	Swap Space
2 GiB or less	*Two times* the RAM
Between 2 GiB and 8 GiB	Equal to RAM
Between 8 GiB and 64 GiB	At least 4 GiB
More than 64 GiB	At least 4 GiB

Table 11.4 – Basic guidance on swap area sizing

Keep in mind that when a process requests memory, the kernel only reserves virtual memory and doesn't consume any RAM. Since the kernel only allocates physical page frames when the process starts, this allows applications to allocate more memory than what's available in the system. This feature function is called memory overcommitment.

The memory overcommit policy of the system can be tuned using the `sysctl` variable, `vm.overcommit_memory`. You can set it to one of the following values:

- 0: The kernel uses a *heuristic overcommit algorithm*. This is the configured system default.

- 1: The kernel *always* overcommits memory. It always grants memory allocations, regardless of whether there is enough free memory.

- 2: The kernel strictly controls memory overcommitment. It only commits an amount of memory equal to the *amount of swap space plus a percentage* (the default is 50%) of physical memory. This percentage gets defined with the `vm.overcommit_ratio` variable.

Use the `sysctl` command to verify both variables:

```
# sysctl vm.overcommit_memory
# sysctl vm.overcommit_ratio
```

```
[root@workstation ~]# sysctl vm.overcommit_memory
vm.overcommit_memory = 0
[root@workstation ~]# sysctl vm.overcommit_ratio
vm.overcommit_ratio = 50
[root@workstation ~]#
```

Figure 11.25 – Reviewing the memory overcommit variables

Monitoring these basic aspects of memory helps improve the performance of the system and the services it provides.

Let's see how to do the same with storage.

Don't ignore storage tuning

Unlike other system resources, storage may optimize its performance as soon it gets sized. It can also be tuned when its usage gets analyzed.

For this, it is necessary to consider that the correct sizing depends on differentiating the measures used in the storage allocation process.

A very common mistake is to size with the wrong storage measurements, causing storage space to go unused or wasted.

The key point to consider is how disk manufacturers overcome the challenge of creating a device that lives in two worlds. A disk is a raw physical device with no virtual or data structures before creating a filesystem. A raw disk becomes a block disk structure when it gets formatted as a filesystem. Filesystems are binary structures.

This means that we must create a physical device, created under the physical rules of the real world, and turn it into a data structure in the digital world.

The **International System of Units (SI)** is the most widely used measurement system in the world. The **International Electrotechnical Commission (IEC)** constructed an alternative standard using the SI decimal prefixes that involves taking the first two letters of the analogous decimal prefix (for example, *ki-* for *kilo-*) and adding the letters - *bi* - for *binary*.

The point of error occurs when the values get confused. Note the difference in the following comparison table:

SI decimal prefixes			
Prefix	**Nomenclature**	**base**	**Bytes**
kilo-	k	10^3	1,000
mega-	M	10^6	1,000,000
giga-	G	10^9	1,000,000,000
tera-	T	10^{12}	1,000,000,000,000
IEC binary prefixes			
kibi-	Ki	2^{10}	1,024
mebi-	Mi	2^{20}	1,048,576
gibi-	Gi	2^{30}	1,073,741,824
tebi-	Ti	2^{40}	1,099,511,627,776

Table 11.5 – Prefixes comparison

So, how many bytes are on a 1 TB disk?

1 TB is 1 x 1,012 bytes = 1,000,000,000,000.

As mentioned previously, to create a filesystem on disk, binary structures use a block size (by default) of 4,096 (4 KiB). Using this nomenclature, a terabyte means 1,012 bytes.

Thus, some operating system tools could report in TB, but actually, they measure in binary tebibytes (TiB).

A tool that reports disk size in TB, but measures TB as tebibytes, would report that a 1 TB disk is only 0.91 TB in size (equal to 0.91 TiB), a difference of almost 10%.

Thus, it is very important to clearly state which units get used to analyze the sizing in a system report – otherwise, significant errors could occur in the analysis.

Now, let's learn how to analyze storage space usage.

Improving storage space usage

A big issue in analyzing storage space usage involves identifying it correctly. A stable identifier that maps to a filesystem is its **UUID**. This is a hexadecimal number that acts as a **Universal Unique Identifier**.

The UUID is part of the filesystem and remains the same so long as the filesystem is not regenerated again.

The utility for listing block devices is the lsblk command.

The lsblk command with the -fp option displays the full path to the device, as well as the UUIDs and mount points, plus the filesystem type of the physical disk partition:

```
# lsblk -fp
```

```
[root@workstation ~]# lsblk -fp
NAME          FSTYPE FSVER LABEL   UUID                                   FSAVAIL FSUSE% MOUNTPOINTS
/dev/sda
├─/dev/sda1
├─/dev/sda2 ext4   1.0   boot    c2457f56-74ee-4fb3-9748-b79bb5f6c1bc    793.1M    11% /boot
├─/dev/sda3 vfat   FAT16         6C81-19BE                                 88.2M    12% /boot/efi
├─/dev/sda4
└─/dev/sda5 btrfs        fedora  a280b604-6023-4ba5-bb9e-80d612f84b0d      2.4G    27% /home
                                                                                        /
/dev/zram0                                                                                  [SWAP]
[root@workstation ~]#
```

Figure 11.26 – Output of the lsblk command

> **Note**
>
> If the filesystem is not mounted, the mount point appears blank.

The most used tool for obtaining information about total filesystem usage is the df command. With the -h option, the output is displayed in a human-readable format:

```
$ df -h
```

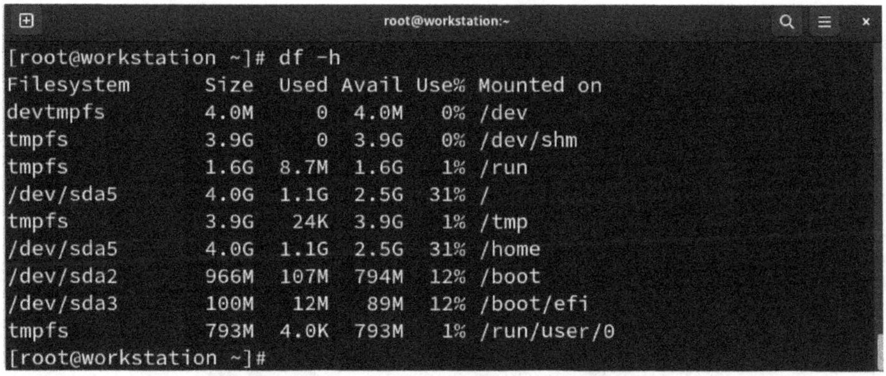

Figure 11.27 – Output of the df -h command

By installing the `sysstat` package, as mentioned previously, we receive tools for monitoring system performance. In the case of storage, the `iostat` command displays I/O statistics per disk, as well as workload, usage, and saturation metrics.

Running the `iostat` command without arguments returns the CPU usage and disk I/O metrics:

```
# iostat
```

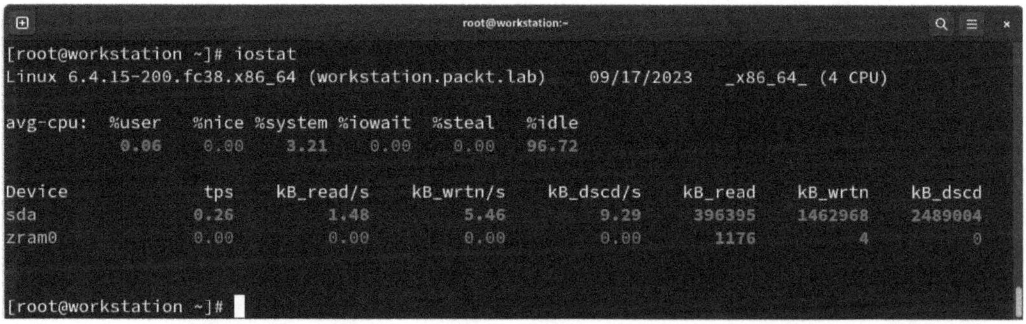

Figure 11.28 – Output of the iostat command

By combining the different options of the `iostat` command, we can generate very useful statistics for usage analysis. Here's an example:

```
# iostat -dyz  1 3
```

```
[root@workstation ~]# iostat -dyz  1 3
Linux 6.4.15-200.fc38.x86_64 (workstation.packt.lab)     09/17/2023     _x86_64_       (4 CPU)


Device           tps    kB_read/s    kB_wrtn/s    kB_dscd/s    kB_read    kB_wrtn    kB_dscd
sda         11573.00         0.00         0.00         0.00          0          0          0


Device           tps    kB_read/s    kB_wrtn/s    kB_dscd/s    kB_read    kB_wrtn    kB_dscd
sda         12544.00         0.00         0.00         0.00          0          0          0


Device           tps    kB_read/s    kB_wrtn/s    kB_dscd/s    kB_read    kB_wrtn    kB_dscd
sda         12808.00         0.00         0.00         0.00          0          0          0


[root@workstation ~]#
```

Figure 11.29 – Output of the iostat -dyz command

Let's look at the options that were used:

- -d displays the disk I/O usage report
- -y skips the first report with statistics since when the system started
- -z skips inactive devices
- The interval is a second
- The count is an output of three reports every interval

> **Note**
>
> For more information about the iostat command options, refer to the manual pages. You can find them by running the man iostat command.

As mentioned in the previous section, having swap space increases the effective amount of memory. Let's learn how to create a swap space in the system with effective sizing.

We'll use the /dev/sdc disk we used in *Chapter 4* to create the filesystem with Stratis. Please follow the instructions in the aforementioned chapter to remove the pool and wipe the filesystem from the disk.

Then, follow these steps:

1. Use the wipefs command:

   ```
   # wipefs /dev/sdc
   ```

> **Note**
>
> This command destroys the filesystem information of the device. Please be very careful and verify that the device you wish to wipe is the correct one.

Now, let's create the partition for the swap area.

2. Inspect the `/dev/sdc` disk to confirm that no partitions have been created. Use the `parted` command:

```
# parted /dev/sdc print
```

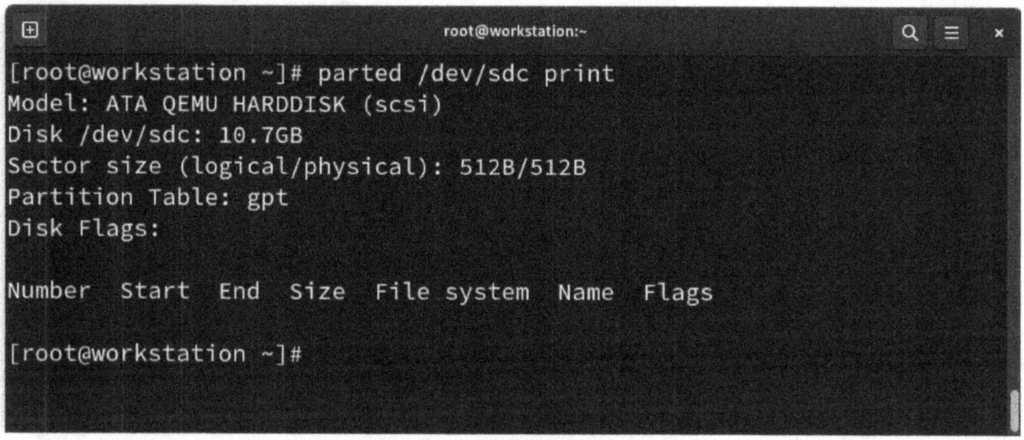
root@workstation:~
[root@workstation ~]# parted /dev/sdc print
Model: ATA QEMU HARDDISK (scsi)
Disk /dev/sdc: 10.7GB
Sector size (logical/physical): 512B/512B
Partition Table: gpt
Disk Flags:
Number Start End Size File system Name Flags
[root@workstation ~]#

Figure 11.30 – Listing the /dev/sdc disk partitions

Create a 512 MB partition.

3. Use the `parted` command:

```
# parted /dev/sdc
```

```
⊞                                    root@workstation:~                          Q  ≡  ×
[root@workstation ~]# parted /dev/sdc
GNU Parted 3.5
Using /dev/sdc
Welcome to GNU Parted! Type 'help' to view a list of commands.
(parted) print
Model: ATA QEMU HARDDISK (scsi)
Disk /dev/sdc: 10.7GB
Sector size (logical/physical): 512B/512B
Partition Table: gpt
Disk Flags:

Number  Start  End  Size  File system  Name  Flags

(parted) mkpart
Partition name?  []? swap1
File system type?  [ext2]? linux-swap
Start? 1049kb
End? 513MB
(parted) print
Model: ATA QEMU HARDDISK (scsi)
Disk /dev/sdc: 10.7GB
Sector size (logical/physical): 512B/512B
Partition Table: gpt
Disk Flags:

Number  Start    End     Size   File system    Name   Flags
 1      1049kB   513MB   512MB  linux-swap(v1)  swap1  swap

(parted) quit
Information: You may need to update /etc/fstab.

[root@workstation ~]#
```

Figure 11.31 – Creating a swap partition

Using the `parted` command without a subcommand opens an interactive `parted` session. Inside the interactive session, do the following:

I.   Run the `mkpart` subcommand to create the partition.

II.   Set `swap1` as the partition's name.

III.   Set the filesystem type to `linux-swap`.

IV.   The partition should start at 2,049 KB and end at 513 MB so that the size is 512 MB.

Note

It is important to start a partition in the first block of the underlying storage. Starting at sector `2048` is the default value for modern Linux and is stored on all storage types. This is known as the initial offset or partition alignment.

Verify that the partition was created by running the `print` subcommand.

Type `quit` to exit the interactive `parted` session.

> **Note**
>
> The `parted` command can display output on a *binary basis* as well.

Run the `# parted /dev/sdc unit MiB print` command:

```
[root@workstation ~]# parted /dev/sdc unit MiB print
Model: ATA QEMU HARDDISK (scsi)
Disk /dev/sdc: 10240MiB
Sector size (logical/physical): 512B/512B
Partition Table: gpt
Disk Flags:

Number  Start     End      Size     File system  Name    Flags
 1      1.00MiB   489MiB   488MiB                 swap1   swap

[root@workstation ~]#
```

Figure 11.32 – Output of the parted command displayed on a binary basis

Ask the system to detect the new partition and create the associated device file in the /dev directory.

4. Run the `udevadm settle` command to observe the `udev` event queue and update it:

    ```
    # udevadm settle
    ```

    Now, format the partition.

5. Use the `mkswap` command:

    ```
    # mkswap /dev/sdc1
    ```

```
[root@workstation ~]# mkswap /dev/sdc1
Setting up swapspace version 1, size = 488 MiB (511700992 bytes)
no label, UUID=1b753f6f-7aa4-4f25-b603-1ddc1ffdd124
[root@workstation ~]#
```

Figure 11.33 – Formatting the partition

Review the swap area of the system.

6. Use the `free` command:

    ```
    # free -m
    ```

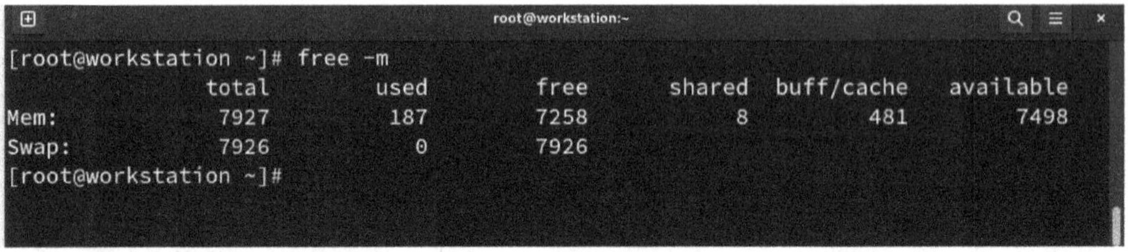

Figure 11.34 – Reviewing swap memory

Activate the swap partition in the system.

7. Use the `swapon` command:

    ```
    # swapon /dev/sdc1
    ```

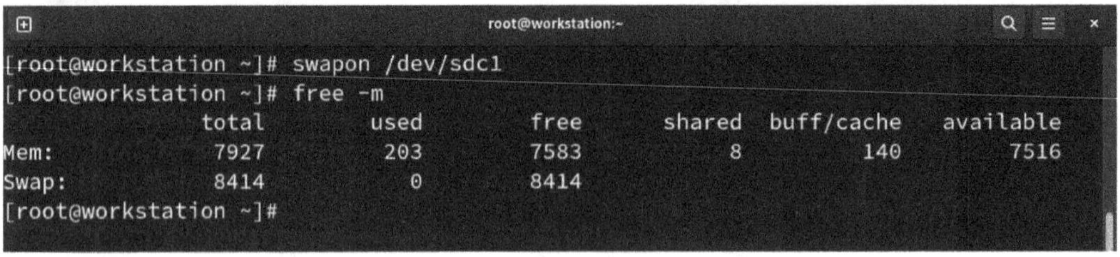

Figure 11.35 – Activating the swap partition

Now, verify the swap area of the system.

The new swap area partition is active and available to the system. To make it persistently active, we need to create an entry in the /etc/fstab file.

8. Identify the UUID of the swap partition and create an entry in the /etc/fstab file. Use the lsblk command to do so:

    ```
    # lsblk -fp
    ```

Figure 11.36 – Identifying the UUID of the swap partition

Add the following line to the /etc/fstab file:

```
UUID=6f53144d-fe12-4fc3-bb69-6469012592dc  swap  swap  defaults
0 0
```

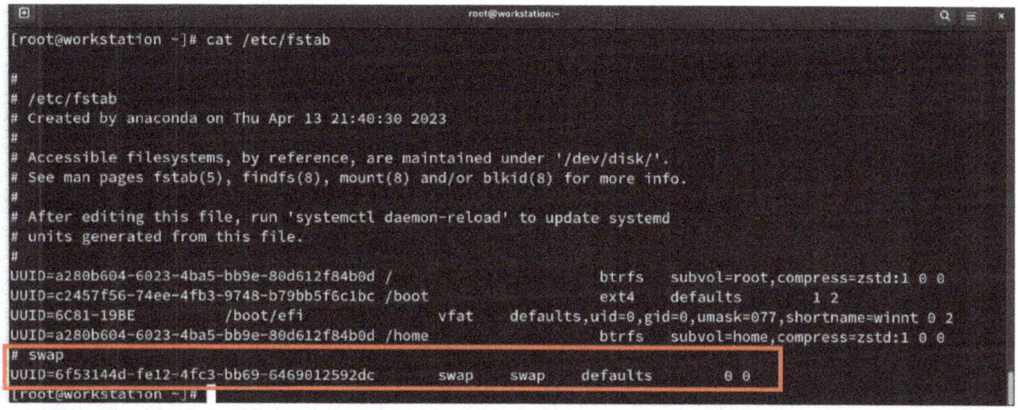

Figure 11.37 – Adding the swap partition to the /etc/fstab file

In this way, the swap partition remains persistently available to the system. With this, the system's performance improves since physical memory becomes available. At this stage, the storage space is optimized for the swap space.

Finally, let's learn how to improve the performance of the network connection to the system.

Boosting performance with network tuning

The network represents one of the most complex and key elements involved in tuning the system. Being an externally self-organizing element, some network elements could affect performance. To identify and adjust them, it is necessary to know the flow that a packet follows both when transmitted and received by a system, as well as the tuning options available for them.

The transmission and reception flow of the packet is roughly as follows:

- **Transmission:**

    I.   Data gets written to a socket (an object such as a file) and sent to the transmit buffer.

    II.   The kernel encapsulates the data in a **protocol data unit** (**PDU**).

    III. The PDUs go to the device's transmit queue.

    IV.   The network device driver copies the PDU from the transmit queue header to the NIC.

    V.   The NIC sends the data and triggers an interrupt when transmitted.

- **Reception:**

    I.   The NIC receives a frame and uses DMA to copy the frame to the receive buffer.

    II.   The NIC triggers a hard interrupt.

    III. The kernel handles the hard interrupt and schedules a soft interrupt to handle the packet.

    IV.   The soft interrupt handles and moves the packet to the IP layer.

    V.   If the packet is intended for local delivery, the PDU is de-encapsulated and placed in a socket receive buffer:

    VI.   If a process is waiting in this socket, it processes the data in the receive buffer

The tunables for the case of improving network flow consist of buffer limits. The kernel adjusts the size of these buffers based on the current network use but within the limits specified by the kernel tunables. The default values of these variables get calculated at boot time based on the amount of available memory.

The kernel tunables, which could change when running the `sysctl` command, are as follows:

- `net.ipv4.tcp_mem`: This specifies the TCP system memory limits. It considers three fields: `min`, `max`, and `pressure` (when the amount of memory used in TCP/UDP exceeds this number, pages get moderated until they drop and return to the `min` value). These values represent the number of pages, not bytes.

- `Net.ipv4.udp_mem`: This specifies the UDP system memory limits. It considers three fields: `min`, `max`, and `pressure`. These values represent the number of pages, not bytes.

- `net.core.rmem_max`: The maximum network core socket receive/send (`read/write`) buffers. Values are in bytes.

- `net.core.wmem_max`: The maximum network core socket receive/send (`read/write`) buffers. Values are in bytes.

- `net.ipv4.tcp_rmem`: The maximum TCP socket receive/send (`read/write`) buffers. It considers three fields: `min`, `default`, and `max`. Values are in bytes.

- `net.ipv4.tcp_wmem`: The maximum TCP socket receive/send (`read/write`) buffers. It considers three fields: `min`, `default`, and `max`. Values are in bytes.

> **Note**
>
> The change of these values should take place after a behavioral analysis.

In general, tunable values should be changed after the system's behavior has been analyzed.

For this purpose, several tools and utilities exist, which we have used throughout this chapter.

Now, let's look at a tool that complements the use of `sysstat` and provides a graphical display of the collected metrics.

Analyzing metrics

Besides installing the `sysstat` package to monitor tools, it can also be run as a service:

```
# systemctl enable --now sysstat
```

```
[root@workstation ~]# systemctl status sysstat
● sysstat.service - Resets System Activity Logs
     Loaded: loaded (/usr/lib/systemd/system/sysstat.service; enabled; preset: enabled)
    Drop-In: /usr/lib/systemd/system/service.d
             └─10-timeout-abort.conf
     Active: active (exited) since Mon 2023-09-18 14:59:25 UTC; 8h ago
    Process: 674 ExecStart=/usr/lib64/sa/sa1 --boot (code=exited, status=0/SUCCESS)
   Main PID: 674 (code=exited, status=0/SUCCESS)
        CPU: 2ms

Sep 18 14:59:25 workstation.packt.lab systemd[1]: Starting sysstat.service - Resets System Activity Logs...
Sep 18 14:59:25 workstation.packt.lab systemd[1]: Finished sysstat.service - Resets System Activity Logs.
[root@workstation ~]#
```

Figure 11.38 – Reviewing the status of the sysstat service

The `sysstat` service collects, reports, or saves information about system activity. It stores operating system counters in the `/var/log/sa/sadd` file. From the data that's been collected, a lot of information about the system can be received:

- CPU usage

- Memory paging and usage

- Network I/O and transfer statistics

- Process creation activity

- The activity of all block devices

- Interrupts per second

We can get the collected data with the `sar` command:

- Use the `sar` command with the `-u` option to get the CPU usage report:

    ```
    # sar -u 1 3
    ```

```
[root@workstation ~]# sar -u 1 3
Linux 6.4.15-200.fc38.x86_64 (workstation.packt.lab)     09/18/2023     _x86_64_     (4 CPU)

11:47:58 PM     CPU     %user     %nice     %system     %iowait     %steal     %idle
11:47:59 PM     all      0.00      0.00       0.25        0.00        0.00      99.75
11:48:00 PM     all      0.25      0.00       0.00        0.00        0.00      99.75
11:48:01 PM     all      0.00      0.00       0.25        0.00        0.00      99.75
Average:        all      0.08      0.00       0.17        0.00        0.00      99.75
[root@workstation ~]#
```

Figure 11.39 – Output of the sar –u command

This command is also used to read the history files where the daily data is recorded.

- Use the `sar` command to read one of the log files from `/var/log/sa`:

    ```
    # sar -q -f /var/log/sa17
    ```

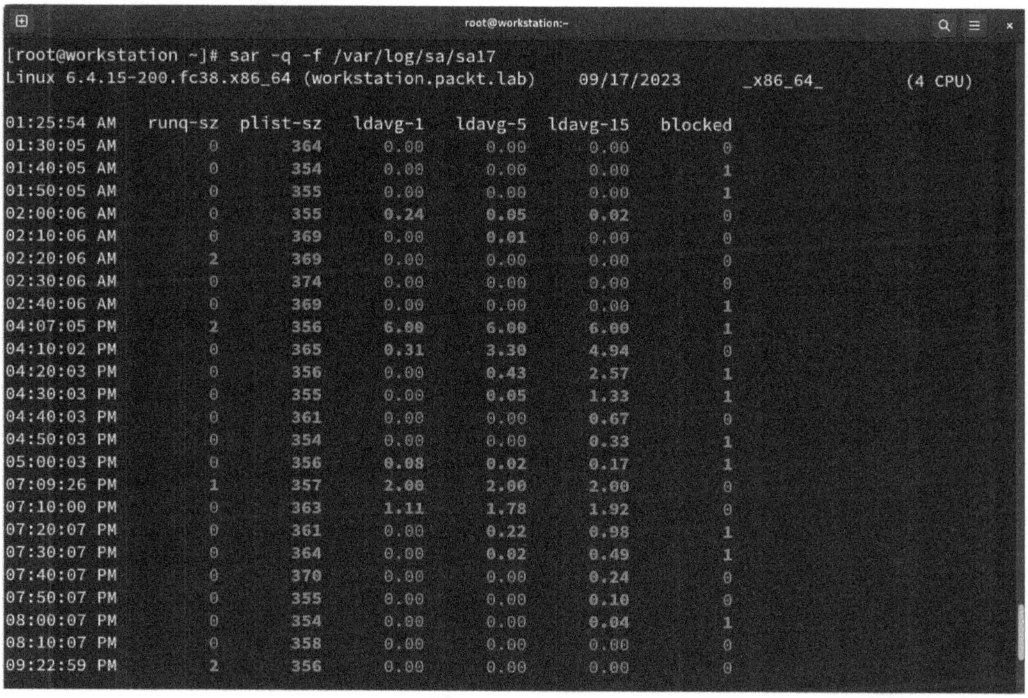

Figure 11.40 – The log file's content

> **Note**
>
> For more information about `sar` command options, refer to the manual pages by running the `man sar` command.

From these files, it is possible to generate graphs and export them as images or even a PDF report. The most commonly used tool for this is `ksar`.

To get `ksar`, download it from their website at `https://sourceforge.net/projects/ksar/`:

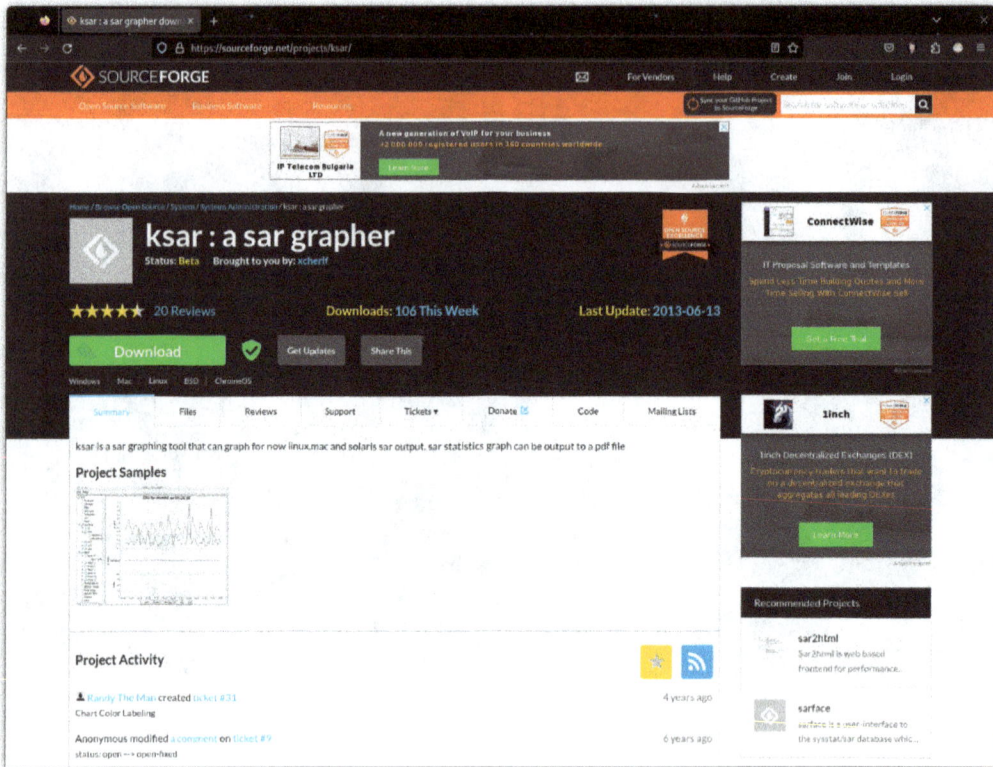

Figure 11.41 – The ksar website

> **Note**
>
> A more updated version of the `ksar` tool can be downloaded from its GitHub repository: `https://github.com/vlsi/ksar/releases`.

The `ksar` tool comes as a `jar` file, so it requires the `java-17-openjdk` package to be installed:

```
# dnf install java-17-openjdk
```

The best practice is to make a copy of the `log` files to analyze, either by period or by a known event. A copy of the file can be used to generate the performance graphs. Follow these steps:

1. Use the `sar` command to redirect the contents of the log files to a text file:

    ```
    # LC_ALL=C sar -A > /tmp/sar.data.txt
    ```

2. Use the `java` command to open the `ksar` tool:

```
$ java -jar kSar.jar
```

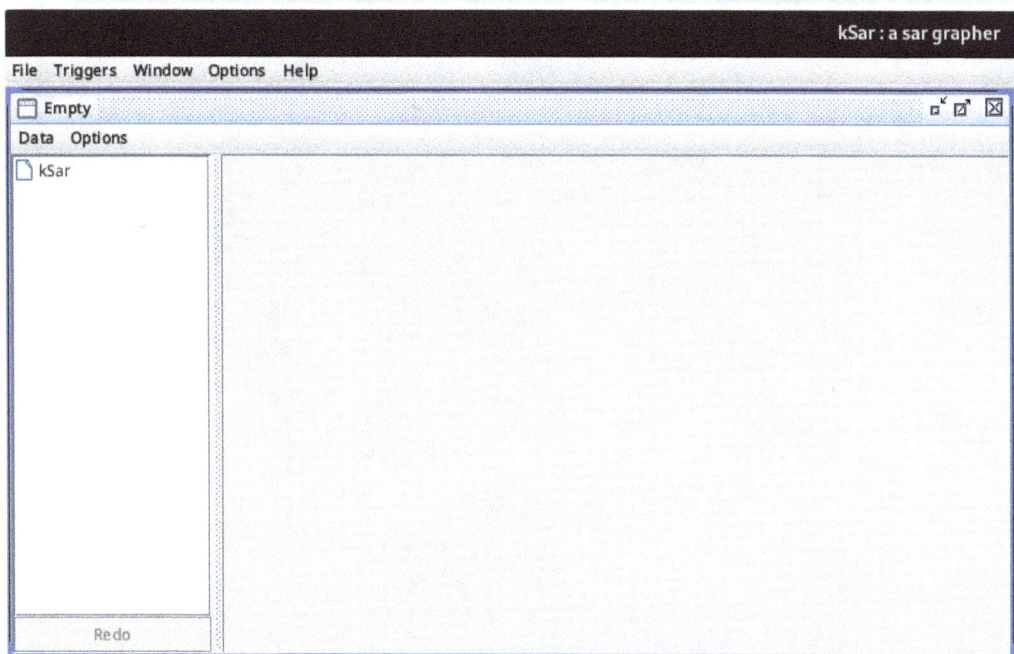

Figure 11.42 – The ksar tool's main window

Load the `data` file created from the `log` files to generate the system performance graphs.

3.   From the **Data** menu, click on **Load from a text file...**:

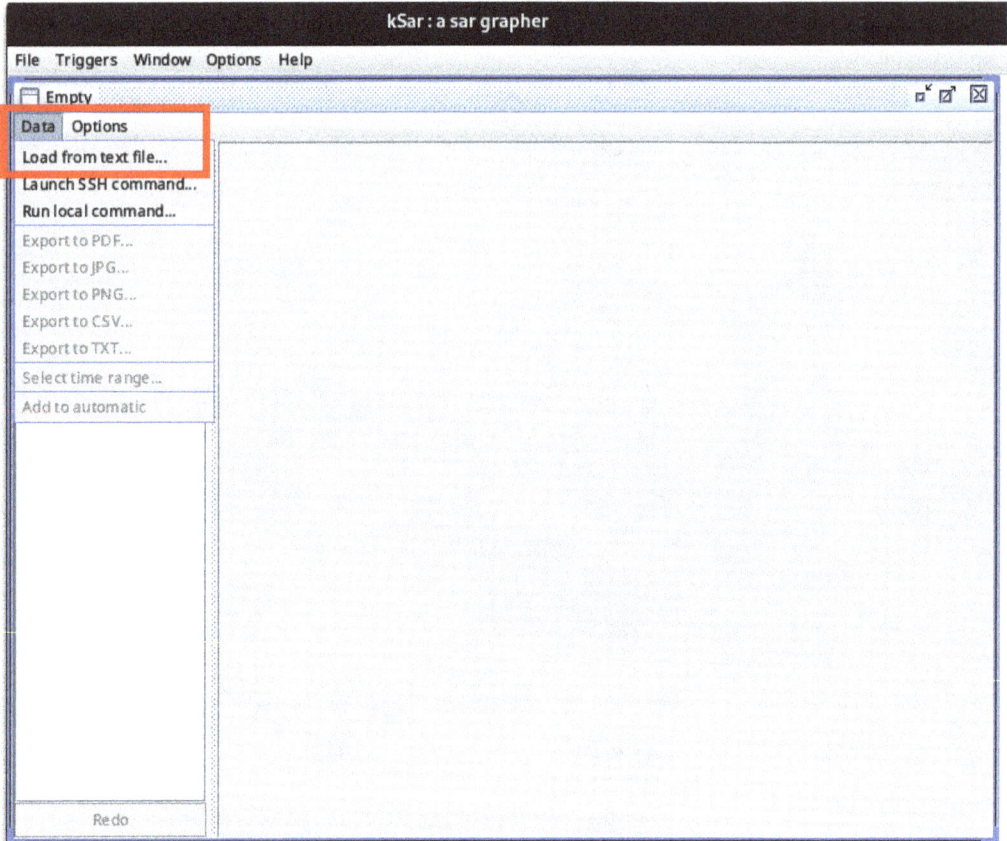

Figure 11.43 – The Load from a text file... option

The file selection window will open.

4.   Navigate to the directory where the generated file resides:

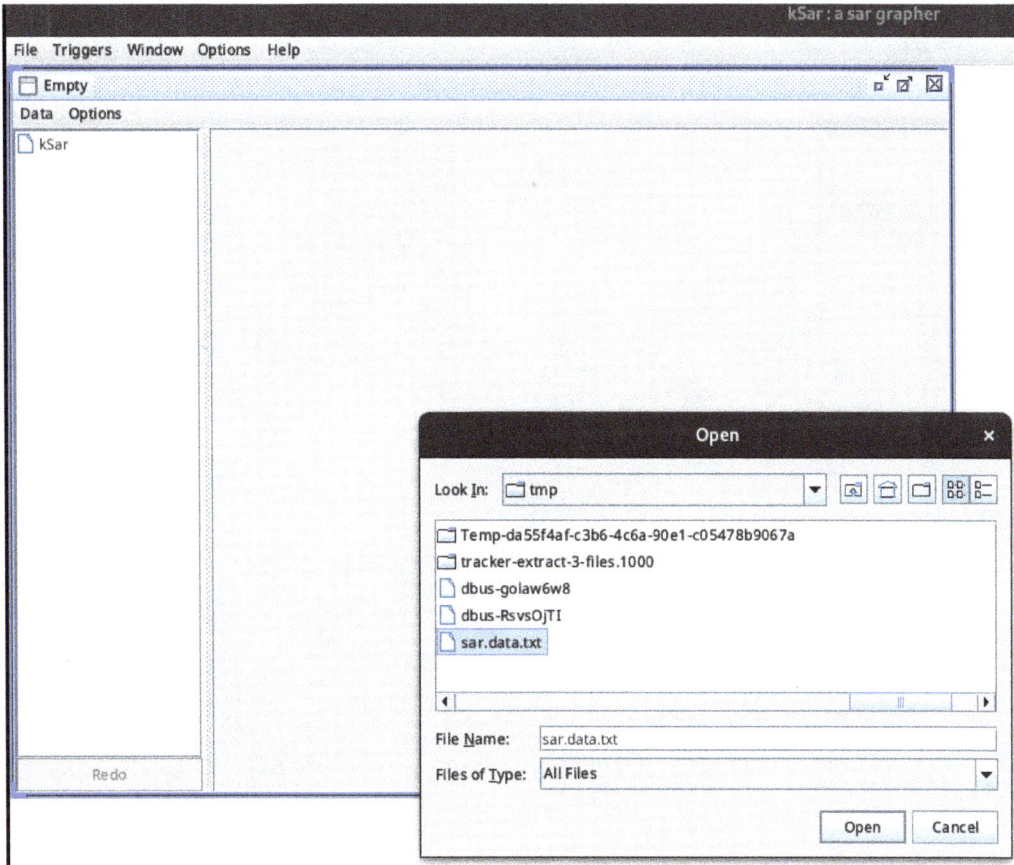

Figure 11.44 – Selecting the sar file

Select the sar file and click **Open**.

The file will take some time to load, depending on its size and the amount of data to analyze.

5. After loading finishes, the window will display the data column for filtering by resource:

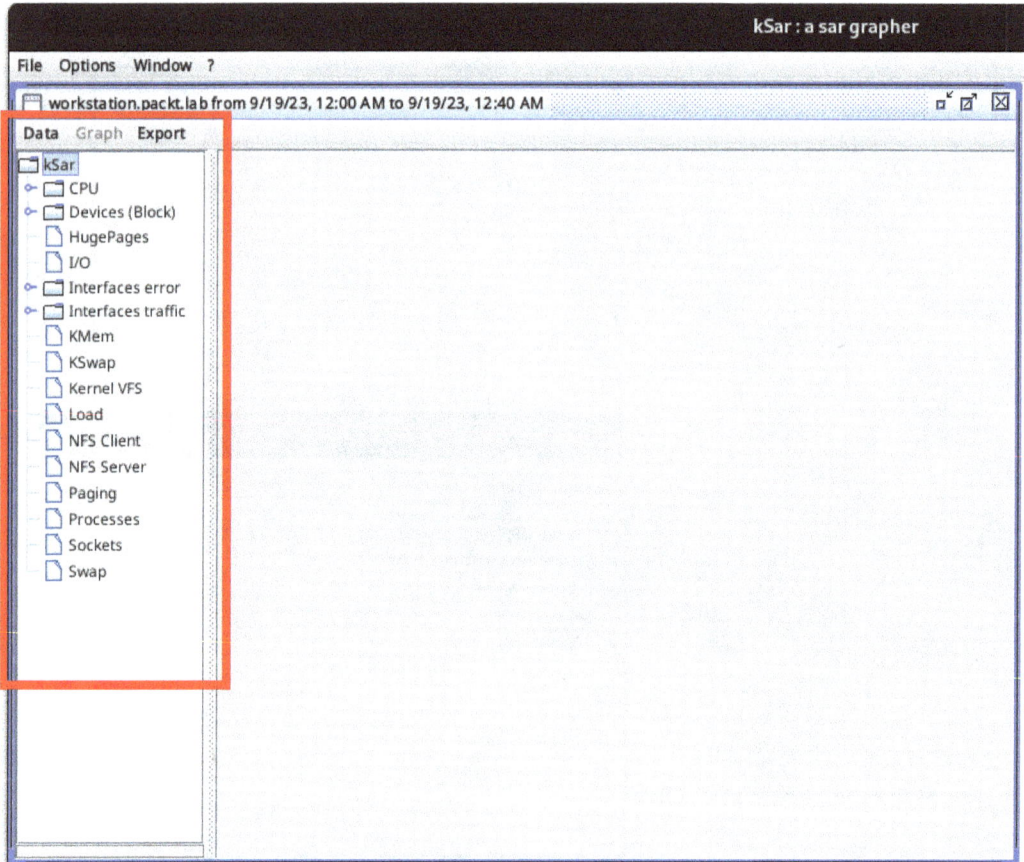

Figure 11.45 – Data analyzed window

Navigate to **NIC** to review the network behavior.

6.   Click **Interfaces traffic** and then **eth0**:

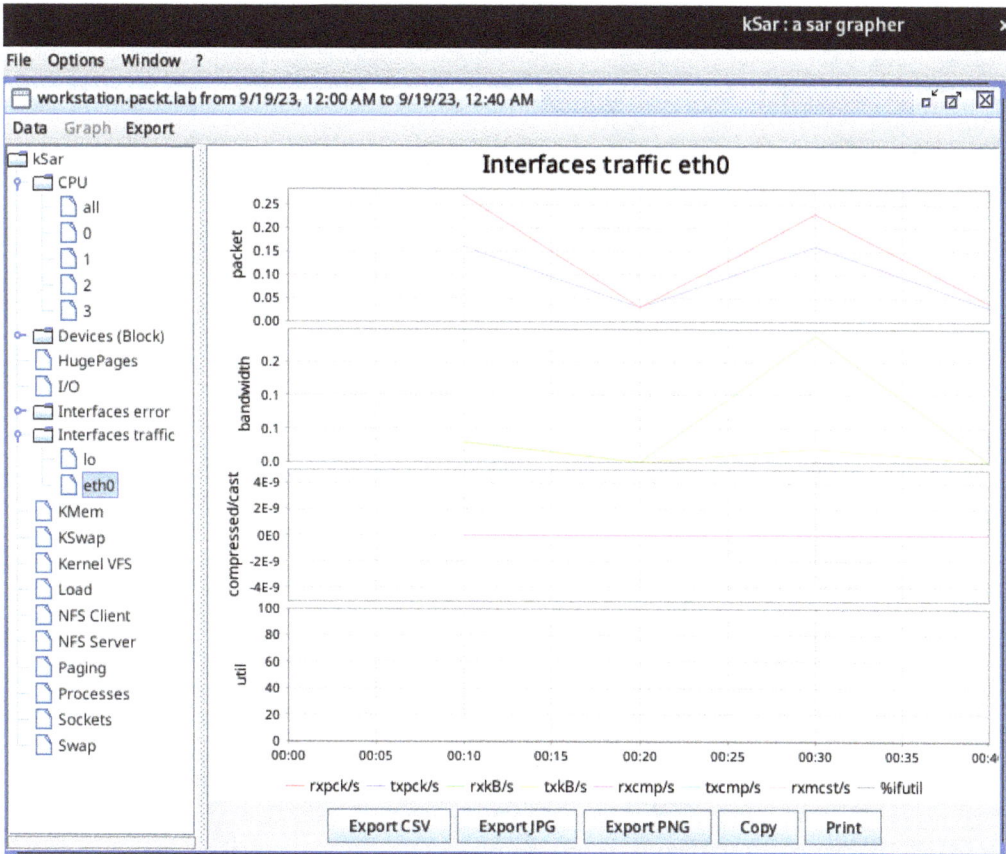

Figure 11.46 – NIC performance graph

> **Note**
>
> On your system, the device may be different. Please confirm the device information that we will analyze.

This way, the behavior could be better visualized.

Let's export these graphs.

7. Click on the **Export** menu and then **Export to PDF…**:

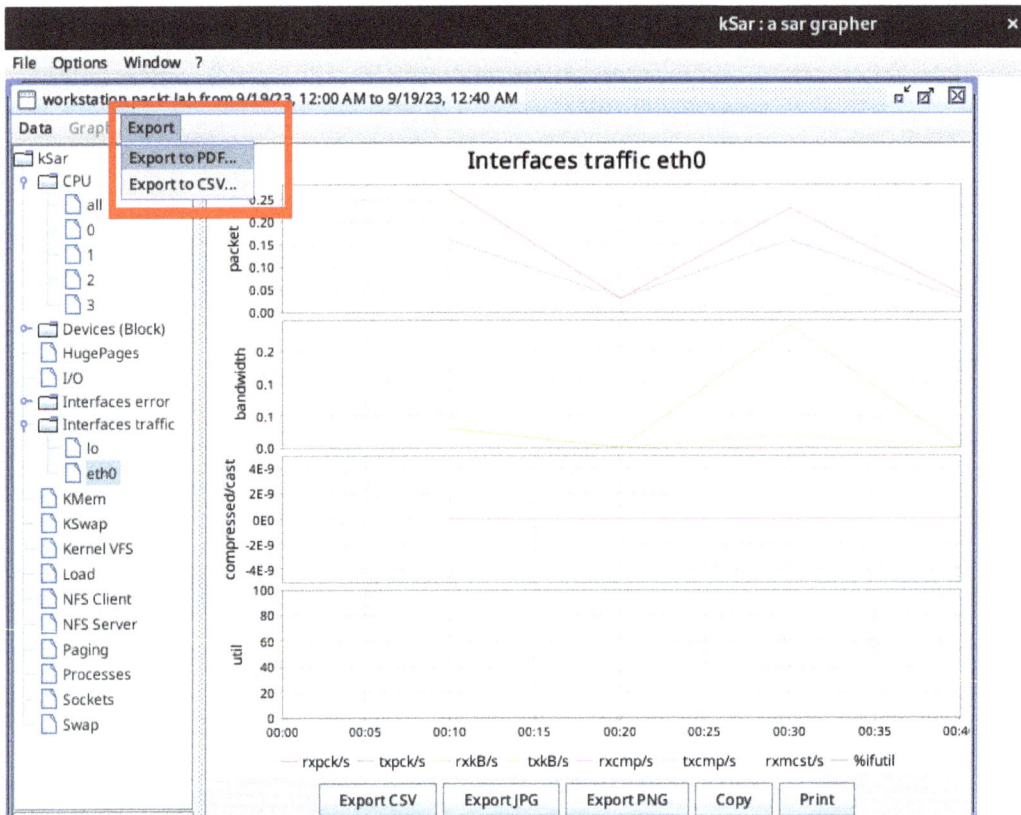

Figure 11.47 – The Export menu

The window for selecting the data to export will open.

8.   Select the data to export and click the **OK** button:

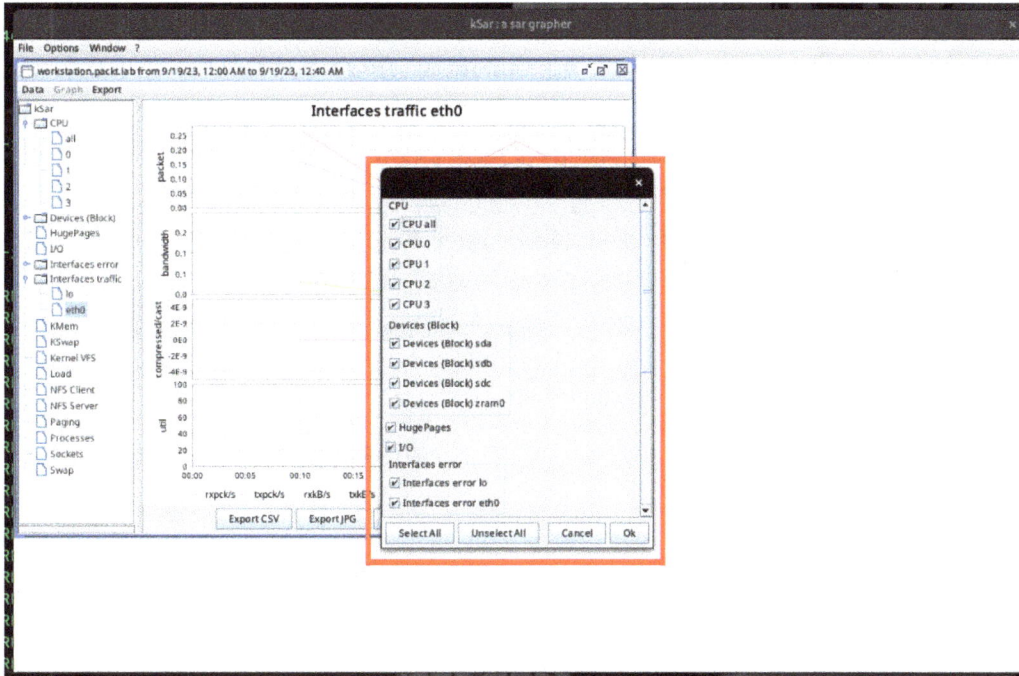

Figure 11.48 – Selecting data to export

Name the file, as is best practice, with the system's name, and save it in the directory of your choice.

> **Note**
>
> You can get the export report from our GitHub repository at `https://github.com/`
> `PacktPublishing/Fedora-Linux-System-Administration/blob/main/`
> `chapter11/workstation.packt.lab.pdf`.

This concludes the best practices for improving system performance. In the next chapter, we will talk about the security provided by Fedora Linux.

Summary

In this chapter, we provided an overview of best practices in system tuning. Beyond configurations, we looked at the tools that are available in Fedora Linux to analyze system behavior.

System tuning, in most cases, is performed after a failure incident. It is at this point that it gets confused with troubleshooting. System tuning is about more than resolving a failure – it is about collecting metrics and performing analysis using the right tools.

First, we learned how to change the kernel tunables using the `sysctl` command to understand their origin and the scope of these changes in their original configuration.

Then, we learned how to use the system tools and utilities, including the `ps`, `top`, and `free` commands. We also covered the suite of utilities provided by installing the `sysstat` package, including the `mpstat`, `iostat`, `pidstat`, and `sar` commands.

After that, we briefly reviewed the *units of measurement*, which cause failures when sizing resources, particularly in storage.

Finally, we touched on network tuning and discussed the limitations of the operating system. While doing so, we learned how to use `ksar`, a tool that helps us graph the metrics collected by `sysstat` when it's running as a service.

In the next chapter, we will take a walk through the hardened security layer offered by Fedora Linux: SELinux. In most cases, this is not activated due to ignorance of how it works. We will clarify how it operates so that we can implement it in our systems.

12
Untangling Security with SELinux

Security, *Hardening*, *Compliance*, and *Policy*: these are the four horsemen of the SysAdmin apocalypse. One of the big battles is maintaining the security of the systems. Besides the daily tasks, the security of the systems is part of the job, even those systems where the third-party provider asks us to deactivate the *enhanced security*. In most of these cases, an analysis is enough to find the right troubleshooting method or a workaround.

Security-Enhanced Linux (**SELinux**) is a code that runs in the user space, leveraging kernel code (**Linux Security Modules**) to provide **mandatory access control** (**MAC**) over system resources. The access to system objects and features takes place on a per-domain basis following the principle of *least privilege*.

In this chapter, we are going to learn how to take advantage of the benefits of SELinux to secure managed systems, covering the following main topics:

- Learning about mandatory access control
- Labeling and type enforcement
- How to troubleshoot SELinux issues

Technical requirements

For the development of the topics in this chapter, it is necessary to install the packages indicated in each section. In each section, you will find the instructions for the different types of installation of each package as required.

Learning about mandatory access control

Linux file permissions control which users or groups of users access specific files. But a user with read or write access to a specific file could use that file in any way desired, even if that use is not what the file should be used for.

Linux *standard file permissions* succeed when files get used by a single owner and a single designated group of people.

File permissions fail to prevent some forms of unwanted access. They were not designed to control how a file gets used, but only who to allow to read, write, or run a file.

Linux standard file permissions are ownership-based, also known as **discretionary access control** (DAC).

The MAC rules are *policy* based, not by ownership.

There are two types of MAC:

- **Multi-level security systems**: The original and simplest form of MAC consists of a vertical structure of protection and security levels. Information only flows within this area. A level of protection is also assigned to users, who can thus only access the same or lower levels.

- **Multi-lateral security systems**: These systems are more complex and assign access based on segments. Those segments form associations, which in turn consist of protection levels and code words. This results in a horizontal security system that also includes vertical levels of protection.

SELinux is an example of a MAC application on Linux.

SELinux offers a special security architecture based on the principles of MAC. SELinux *minimizes access* to operating system processes and files through strict access control methods and corresponding security measures. The module aims to ensure data confidentiality and integrity. Furthermore, with SELinux, the operating system and user programs remain delimited.

SELinux also relies on two other implementations: **type enforcement** (TE) and **role-based access control** (RBAC). With RBAC, access rights map according to a defined role model. The defined user roles abstract the work processes of an organization. On a MAC model, TE is the notion that access gets governed through clearance based on a *subject-access-object set of rules*.

SELinux defines security measures and sets extra attributes that state under what conditions and in what situations a rights holder could access certain operating system processes or files. If these conditions or relationships (i.e., attributes) are not met, access is denied.

SELinux consists of sets of policies that declare exactly what *actions and accesses* are allowed for each object used by an application. It is also known as a *targeted policy* since the policy covers the activities of a single application. Policies declare predefined labels that apply to individual programs, files, and network ports.

SELinux enforces a set of access rules that prevent a security flaw in one application from affecting other applications or the system itself. SELinux provides an extra layer of security, but it also adds a level of complexity that might seem confusing to those unfamiliar with it.

To better understand how it works, let's walk through the basic concepts that SELinux works with.

Labeling and type enforcement

SELinux is a *labeling system*, which tells us that each file, directory, or object in the system has a corresponding label. Each file, process, directory, and port has a *special security label* called an SELinux context. A **context** is a tag name used by the SELinux policy to determine whether a process can access a file, directory, or port. Policies control the interaction between these elements. By default, the policy does not allow any interaction unless an explicit rule grants access. If no permission rule exists, access is not allowed. The Linux kernel enforces these rules.

SELinux contexts have different labels in their format, separated by colons: *user*, *role*, *type*, and *sensitivity level*. They are formed as follows:

`user:role:type:level` (optional)

> **Note**
> The *sensitivity level* is the part that is optional.

The targeted policy bases its rules on the third context component: the *type* context. Type context names usually end with _t.

Let's look at the following example:

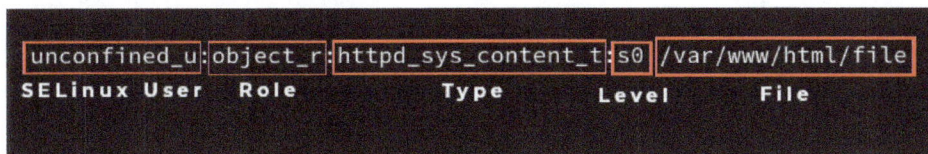

Figure 12.1 – SELinux label example

In the preceding example, the `/var/www/html/file` file has the following context components: `unconfined_u` is the SELinux user, the role is `object_r`, the type is `httpd_sys_content_t`, and the sensitivity level is `s0`. So, the context on which the access of this file depends is `httpd_sys_content_t`.

Let's use a demo example with this file to learn how the SELinux policy works.

How SELinux works

Before analyzing the operation of SELinux, let's determine how SELinux is running on the system.

SELinux runs in three modes:

- **Enforcing**: SELinux enforces access control rules. This is the Fedora Linux default enabled mode.

- **Permissive**: SELinux is active but instead of enforcing access control rules, it *logs warnings* of rules violated. This mode gets used for testing and troubleshooting.

- **Disabled**: SELinux is completely *disabled*; no SELinux violations are denied or even logged. *This is not recommended under any circumstances.*

To find out how SELinux is running, use the `sestatus` command:

```
$ sestatus
SELinux status:                 enabled
SELinuxfs mount:                /sys/fs/selinux
SELinux root directory:         /etc/selinux
Loaded policy name:             targeted
Current mode:                   enforcing
Mode from config file:          enforcing
Policy MLS status:              enabled
Policy deny_unknown status:     allowed
Memory protection checking:     actual (secure)
Max kernel policy version:      33
```

The SELinux running mode gets configured in the `/etc/selinux/config` file:

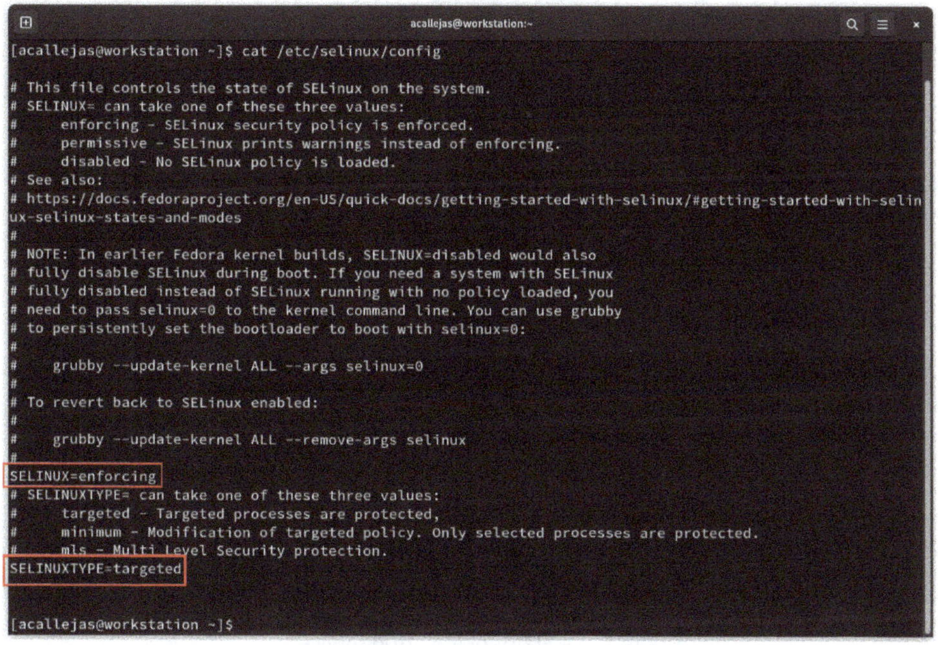

Figure 12.2 – SELinux config file

During execution, for testing, the SELinux mode could change. But upon *rebooting* the system, it will again take the mode configured in the configuration file to set it. Use the `getenforce` command to find out the mode SELinux is running in and the `setenforce` command to change the mode, as the `root` user:

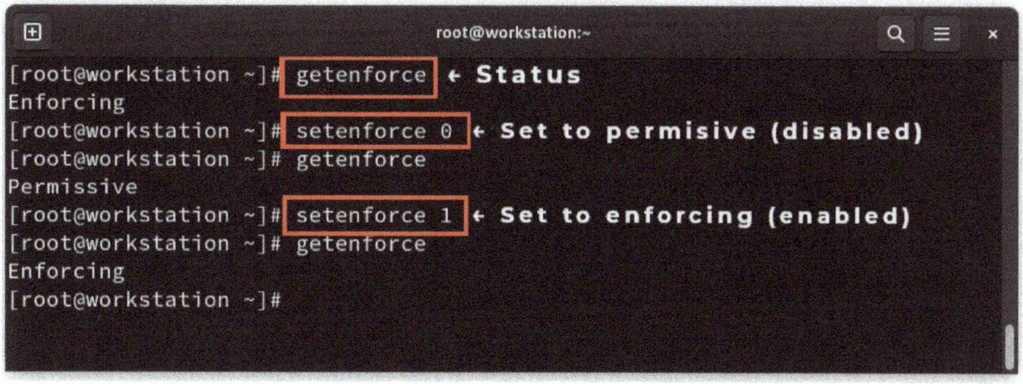

Figure 12.3 – Changing the SELinux run mode

Now, let us see how SELinux works.

So, how does SELinux work?

Linux was born in the early days of the operating system's usefulness. It's used as the main operating system running a web server.

The Apache web server (httpd) is not insecure, but its *access range* is very wide so it is very important to secure it.

So, let's start with this example to understand how SELinux works. Follow the subsequent steps:

1. Verify that the httpd service is installed and active on the system:

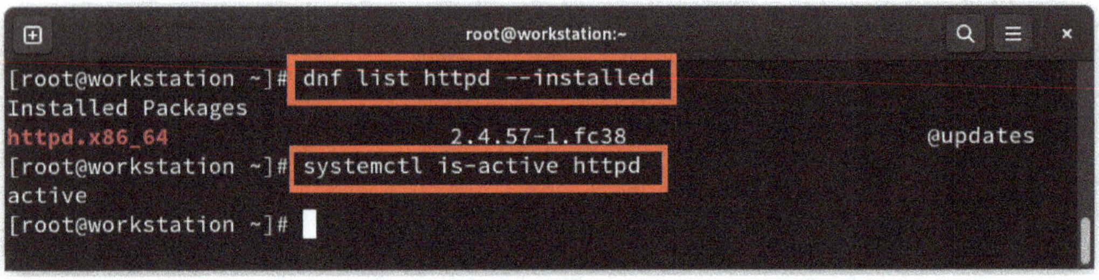

Figure 12.4 – Status of the httpd service

2. If not, use the dnf and systemctl commands to perform this:

    ```
    # dnf install httpd
    # systemctl enable --now httpd
    ```

    The httpd service runs a binary file to start. This file launches from /usr/sbin/.

3. The Linux kernel integrates an option, in most commands, to know the SELinux context type. Use the ls command with the -Z (or –context) option to identify the SELinux context type of the binary file:

    ```
    # ls -Z /usr/sbin/httpd
    system_u:object_r:httpd_exec_t:s0 /usr/sbin/httpd
    ```

    The context type of the binary file is httpd_exec_t.

4. The configuration files for the httpd service are found in /etc/httpd. Let's see what context type they have:

    ```
    # ls -dZ /etc/httpd/
    system_u:object_r:httpd_config_t:s0 /etc/httpd/
    ```

    The context type of the configuration files is httpd_config_t.

5. The logs of the `httpd` service are found in `/var/log/httpd`. Find their context type using the following:

    ```
    # ls -dZ /var/log/httpd
    system_u:object_r:httpd_log_t:s0 /var/log/httpd
    ```

    The context type of the logs is `httpd_log_t`.

6. The content type directory of the `httpd` service is found in `/var/www/html`. Find their context using the following:

    ```
    # ls -dZ /var/www/html
    system_u:object_r:httpd_sys_content_t:s0 /var/www/html
    ```

    The context type of the content directory is `httpd_sys_content_t`.

7. The unit file for the `httpd` service startup is found in `/usr/lib/systemd/system/`. Find its context type using the following:

    ```
    # ls -Z /usr/lib/systemd/system/httpd.service
    system_u:object_r:httpd_unit_file_t:s0 /usr/lib/systemd/system/
    httpd.service
    ```

    The context type of the unit file is `httpd_unit_file_t`.

8. Use the `ps` command to find the context type of the `httpd` service daemon while it is running:

    ```
    # ps auxfZ | grep httpd
    ```

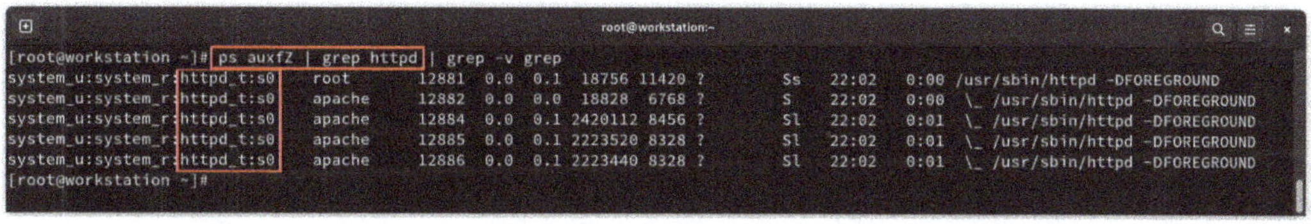

Figure 12.5 – Finding the context of the httpd daemon

The context type of the service daemon is `httpd_t`.

9. Use the `netstat` command to find the context type of the `httpd` service port while it is running:

    ```
    # netstat -tulpnZ | grep httpd
    ```

Figure 12.6 – Finding the context of the httpd port

The context type of the service port is `httpd_t`.

The preceding example can be summarized in the following table:

Type	Context type
Binary file	`httpd_exec_t`
Config files	`httpd_config_t`
Logs	`httpd_log_t`
Content directory	`httpd_sys_content_t`
Unit file	`httpd_unit_file_t`
Process	`httpd_t`
Port	`httpd_t or http_port_t`

Table 12.1 – The httpd service contexts

Note the relation of contexts; all belong to the `httpd_t` domain.

Thus, type enforcement is the concept under which it makes sense for a process running in the `httpd_t` context to interact with a file labeled as `httpd_sys_content_t`.

Let's see what context the `/etc/shadow` file has, where user passwords are stored:

```
# ls -Z /etc/shadow
system_u:object_r:shadow_t:s0 /etc/shadow
```

The context of the `/etc/shadow` file is `shadow_t`.

From a basic functional perspective, the web server (`httpd`) *reads and publishes* documents that live within it. Besides the file's proprietary permissions, security could enhance this through the SELinux policy. With proper proprietary permissions, there would be nothing to prevent the `httpd` service from publishing the file with user passwords.

With SELinux policies enabled, no matter what permission level the file has, the policy would *prevent* it from doing so.

Files with the `httpd_t` context type can only interact with files *under the same context type*. The password file belongs to a different context type than `httpd_t`; its context is `shadow_t`, thus their *interaction is denied*.

This is the most basic way SELinux works, and the way the policy works. It is not free of issues, but these are also limited by its nature.

Let's see how to determine SELinux errors.

How to troubleshoot SELinux issues

The popular belief is that it is very difficult to determine and fix SELinux issues. This stems from the fact that the *logs* get logged with the system audit. This log reading is not intuitive and, in fact, to the human eye is quite complex; but it isn't.

Carrying on with the example of the `httpd` web server, consider the following sequence of commands:

1. As the `root` user, create the `myfile` file:

    ```
    # touch myfile
    ```

2. Move the `myfile` file to the *web content directory*:

    ```
    # mv myfile /var/www/html/
    ```

3. Use the `curl` command to get the contents of the `myfile` file published by the web server:

    ```
    # curl http://localhost/myfile
    ```

4. Observe the output:

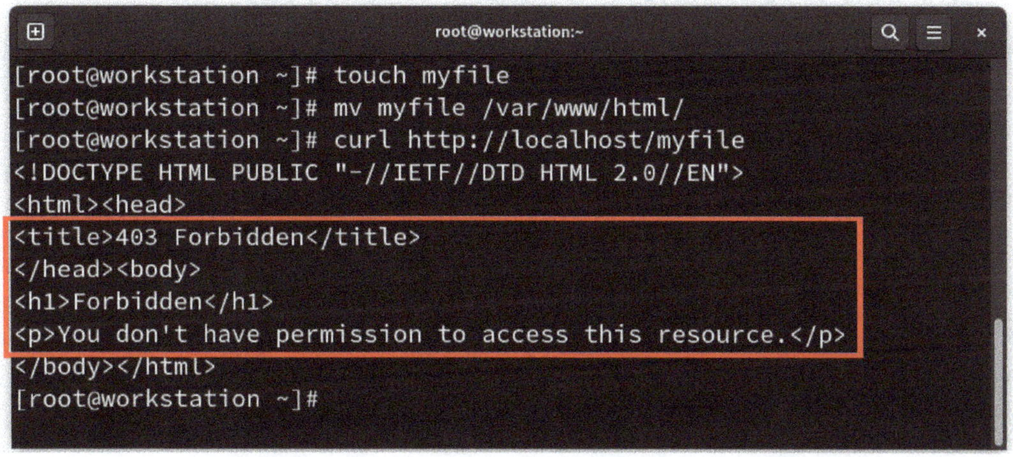

Figure 12.7 – Creating the myfile web file

5. Use the `grep` command to search for the `myfile` string in the *system audit log*:

    ```
    # grep myfile /var/log/audit/audit.log
    ...
    type=AVC msg=audit(1689045662.823:264): avc:  denied  { getattr
    } for  pid=1035 comm="httpd" path="/var/www/html/myfile"
    dev="vda3" ino=769948 scontext=system_u:system_r:httpd_t:s0
    tcontext=unconfined_u:object_r:admin_home_t:s0 tclass=file
    permissive=0
    ```

At first glance, it is not very easy to read, but let's analyze it in parts:

- `type=AVC`: **AVC Audit Events** generated by the *AVC subsystem* (**AVC** means **Access Vector Cache**) as a result of access denials, or where specific events have requested an `audit` message.

- `msg=audit(1689045662.823:264)`: The *timestamp* of the message in **Unix format** (epoch); use the `date` command to determine the time:

  ```
  # date -d @1689045662.823
  Mon Jul 10 09:21:02 PM CST 2023
  ```

- `avc: denied { getattr } for pid=1035`: The result of the `avc` audit event called `denied for pid 1035`

- `comm="httpd"`: The `httpd` command

- `path="/var/www/html/myfile"`: The `var/www/html/myfile` file path

- `dev="vda3"`: The `vda3` device

- `ino=769948`: Inode identifier

- `scontext=system_u:system_r:`**`httpd_t`**`:s0`: *Source* context

- `tcontext=unconfined_u:object_r:`**`admin_home_t`**`:s0`: Target context

- `tclass=file`: Target class is a file

- `permissive=0`: SELinux permissive mode disabled

Then, the audit message reads as follows:

At the described timestamp, an AVC event resulted as denied for pid 1035 *of the* httpd *command on the* /var/www/html/myfile *file, located on the device and the described inode. The source context type is* httpd_t *and the target context type is* admin_home_t. *The permissive mode is set as disabled.*

This indicates that it is an error of the SELinux contexts since they do not correspond and cannot interact with each other. That is, the web server is not allowed to read that file, as indicated by the output of the `curl` command.

At first, it looked very complicated, but when analyzing the log, the error stands out at a glance.

This is the most common error with SELinux, about contexts that *cannot interact* and whose access is *denied*.

What is SELinux trying to tell me?

Let's analyze each of them and their solutions or workarounds.

Labeling

As we observed, every process and object in the system has a *label* associated with it. If files are not labeled in the right context, access may be denied. Or, if *alternate or custom paths* get used for confined domains, SELinux needs to know about it.

Let's use the following illustrative example.

Labeling issue: The files in /srv/myweb are not labeled correctly and the web server cannot access them.

In this particular case, a *custom path* to the web server's content directory appears to be used. To assign the correct label, there are two ways:

- If you know the correct label, use the semanage command to assign it to the policy:

    ```
    # semanage fcontext -a -t httpd_sys_content_t '/srv/myweb(/.*)?'
    ```

    The semanage command applies the httpd_sys_content_t label to the entire contents of the /srv/myweb directory and inherits it to the new files created in it. This means the (/.*)? characters appear at the end of the command.

- If you don't know the correct label, but know a file with the correct label, use the semanage command to assign it:

    ```
    # semanage fcontext -a -e /srv/myweb /var/www
    ```

    With the -e option of the semanage command, assign the label with reference to another known file with the correct label.

In both cases, to restore the context from the policy, use the restorecon command:

```
# restorecon -vR /srv/myweb
```

Using the example from the previous section, let's solve the issue.

Labeling issue: If a file moves, instead of copying it, it keeps its original context.

To fix this, use the chcon command to change the context:

- Change the context to the correct label:

    ```
    # chcon -t httpd_system_content_t /var/www/html/myfile
    ```

- Change the context with a reference label:

    ```
    # chcon --reference /var/www/html/ /var/www/html/myfile
    ```

In the same way as before, for both cases, to restore the context from the policy, use the `restorecon` command:

```
# restorecon -vR /var/www/html
```

As shown, the main cause of error with SELinux is in the labeling. To correct the context, change the file context with the `chcon` command. This is the easiest way to fix it.

If there is a custom path, it is necessary to inform SELinux that an alternate directory to the policy is going to be used. To change the policy, use the `semanage` command.

To save context changes in the policy, use the `restorecon` command.

When there is a customization that modifies the policy, this falls into the second case of SELinux failures. If the standard usage of a task changes, then SELinux must be informed.

Let's look at these cases.

SELinux needs to know

Following the web server configuration, in the case of using a port other than the standard port (80) – for example, 8585 – let's start by finding out the *port label*. Use the `semanage` command to ask the policy about the configured label:

```
# semanage port --list | grep -w 80
http_port_t    tcp      80, 81, 443, 488, 8008, 8009, 8443, 9000
```

The context type of the `httpd` port is `httpd_port_t`.

Then, use the `semanage` command to add the 8585 port to the `httpd` policy:

```
# semanage port -a -t http_port_t -p tcp 8585
```

Besides these custom configurations, SELinux also offers to change pre-loaded configurations in the policy, turning them on and off.

These configurations, known as *Booleans*, allow parts of SELinux policies to get modified at runtime without the need to rewrite the policy.

For example, if we want to allow the web server to send mail with the `sendmail` service, *turn on* the Boolean with the `setsebool` command:

```
# setsebool -P httpd_can_sendmail 1
```

With the -P option, the Boolean change persists on system restart.

To see all Booleans, use the `getsebool` command with the -a option:

```
# getsebool -a
```

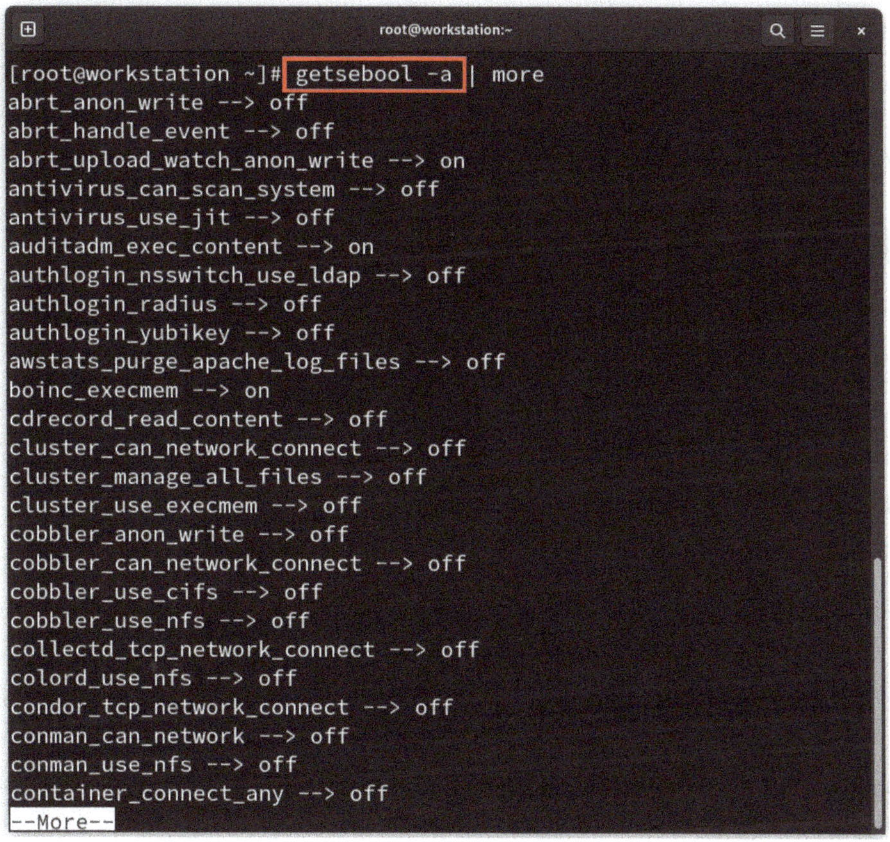

Figure 12.8 – SELinux Booleans

To review the Boolean description, use the `semanage boolean` command with the `-l` option:

```
# semanage boolean -l
```

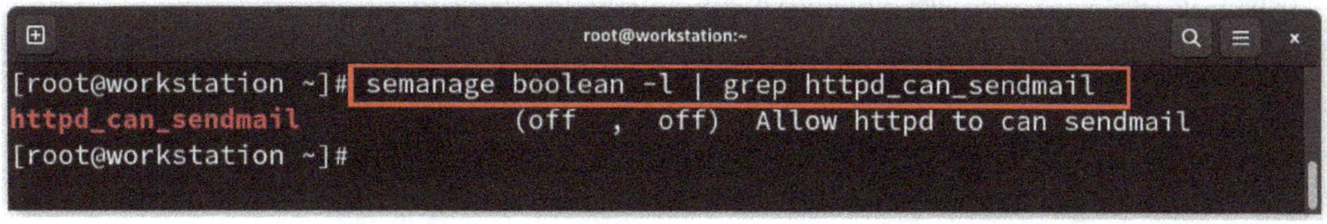

Figure 12.9 – Reviewing the Boolean description

These two cases, incorrect labeling and custom configuration, are the most common causes of errors with SELinux.

There are two other cases that, although not as common, could happen.

Let's look at the first one.

Policy bugs

In some events, the policy might not work when the behavior fails to meet expectations, as in the following cases:

- Configurations
- Redirection of stdout
- Filtered file descriptors
- Executable memory
- Libraries built wrongly
- Unusual paths in the code

There is a high likelihood that the policy or application has bugs. These bugs or behavioral flaws should be reported to the developers to get them fixed.

This is an unusual situation as developers pay close attention to SELinux policies , but do not rule out the possibility of it happening.

A less common situation is that the system might be *compromised*, and the behavior of the policies changes to grant the escape of information or an intrusion.

Let's look at this last case of failure with SELinux.

Hack attack

There is a risk of a hack attack if the current tools *don't do a good job* of differentiating contexts, or if you detect the case where *confined domains* attempt to do the following:

- Load kernel modules
- Turn off SELinux enforcing mode
- Write to `etc_t/shadow_t`
- Change firewall rules

If this happens, then be careful, because the system could become compromised and your information could be in danger.

Hacker attacks are not that common, but rest assured that hackers know how to use SELinux. Don't trust, and follow your instinct. If you notice *unexpected behavior* and it is not related to the other SELinux failures, there is a possibility that your system might be hacked.

Take it *seriously*, and *thoroughly* inspect your system.

You never know when you might be a target for security attacks.

Summary

In this chapter, we gave an overview of the use of SELinux and differentiated the types of access control: *discretionary* and *mandatory*. SELinux, as a mandatory access control could help us to harden the security of our systems.

The use of SELinux is considered very complex, but we gave several examples that simplify how it works. SELinux is a *labeling system*.

We learned how to read the error logs with SELinux and found that there are only *four* scenarios where SELinux could fail, as looked at their solutions. The most common failures are with labels or when using custom configurations for services.

Also, policies could have errors and they should be reported to their developers.

In a less common case, we analyzed that the change of behavior of the policies could be due to an *attack* on our system.

In the next chapter, we will take an in-depth look at how to virtualize complete systems or take them to their smallest expression using containers.

Further reading

To learn more about the topics covered in this chapter, you can visit the following links:

- *A sysadmin's guide to SELinux: 42 answers to the big questions*: `https://opensource.com/article/18/7/sysadmin-guide-selinux`

- *A sysadmin's handy cheat sheet for SELinux*: `https://opensource.com/article/18/8/cheat-sheet-selinux`

- *SELinux troubleshooting and pitfalls*: `https://www.redhat.com/sysadmin/selinux-troubleshooting`

13

Virtualization and Containers

Going back to the 1990s, most companies had physical servers and IT stacks from a single vendor that did not allow *legacy applications* to run on another vendor's hardware. This led to large, multi-service server environments that were very complex to manage.

As companies upgraded their IT environments with less expensive servers, operating systems, and applications from a variety of vendors, they began to underutilize physical hardware. Each server could only run one specific task from one vendor.

Virtualization was the natural solution to two problems: companies could partition their servers and run legacy applications on multiple types and versions of operating systems and servers began to be used more efficiently, reducing the costs associated with purchasing, installation, cooling, and maintenance.

The next step was the containerization of these services. **Containerization** is a form of virtualization. The goal of virtualization is to run multiple instances of the operating system on a single server, while containerization runs a single instance of the operating system, with multiple user spaces to isolate the processes from each other and provide the service.

In this chapter, we will take a brief tour of *virtualization* and *containerization* by covering the following main topics:

- Virtualization with QEMU, KVM, and `libvirt`
- Using GNOME Boxes
- Discovering OCI containers with Podman

Technical requirements

To complete the topics mentioned in this chapter, you must install the packages indicated in each section. In each section, you will find instructions for the different types of installation for each package as required.

Virtualization with QEMU, KVM, and libvirt

Fedora Linux comes with native support for virtualization extensions. This support is provided by **Kernel-based Virtual Machine** (**KVM**) and is available as a *kernel module*. **QEMU/KVM** in combination with the **Libvirt management toolkit** is the standard virtualization method in Fedora Linux.

Quick Emulator (**QEMU**) is a full system emulator that works together with KVM and allows you to create virtual machines with hardware and peripherals.

Finally, `libvirt` is the API layer and allows you to manage the infrastructure – that is, create and run virtual machines. It includes a local virtual network that enables secure communication between virtual guest systems with each other and with the host. libvirt's default configuration also allows *NAT access* to the public network, which is useful for virtual machines or containers that don't have direct access to the public interface.

The following figure illustrates the QEMU/KVM architecture with `libvirt`:

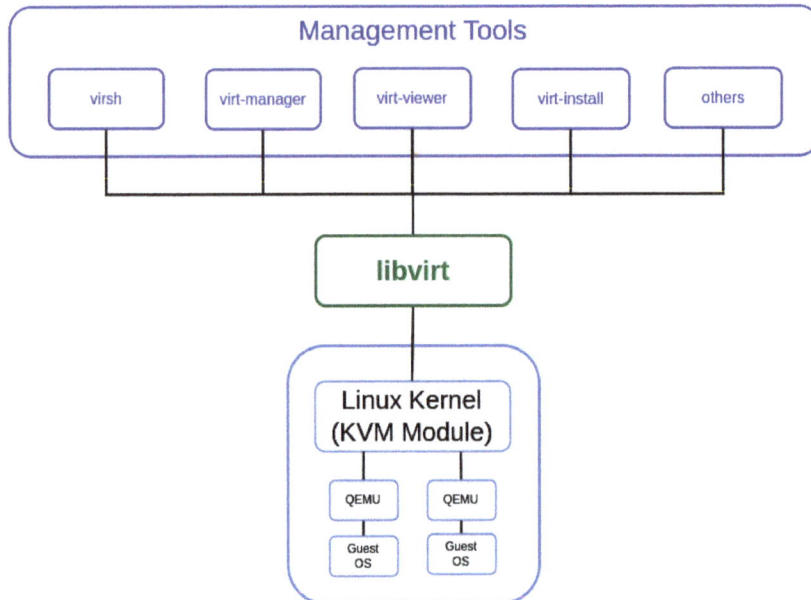

Figure 13.1 – The QEMU/KVM architecture

Let's take a brief look at the management tools.

Management tools

`libvirt` is a C toolkit that interacts with the virtualization capabilities of Fedora Linux. The main package includes the `libvirtd` server for exporting virtualization support.

The basic management tools are as follows:

- `virsh`: This is the main interface for managing `virsh` guest domains. The program can *create*, *pause*, and *shutdown* domains. It also *lists* the current domains and their status.

- `Virt-manager`: This is a desktop tool for managing virtual machines. It provides *life cycle control* of current virtual machines (startup/shutdown, pause/resume, and suspend/restore), provisions new virtual machines and various types of storage, manages virtual networks, gives access to the graphical console of virtual machines, and generates performance statistics locally or remotely:

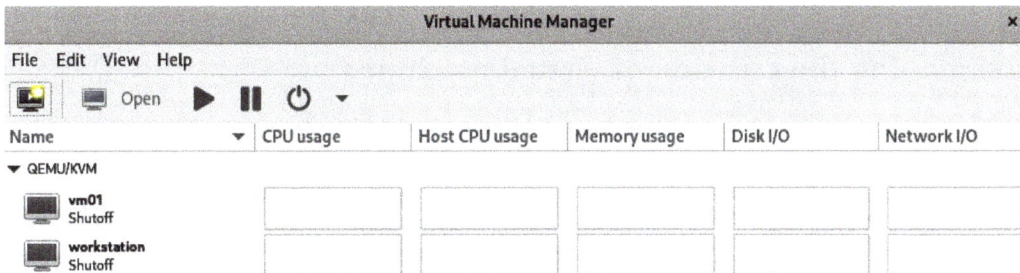

Figure 13.2 – Virtual Machine Manager

- `virt-viewer`: This is a minimal tool for displaying the graphical console of a virtual machine. It accesses the console using the VNC or SPICE protocol. Refer to the virtual guest based on its *name*, *ID*, or *UUID*. If the guest is not running yet, the viewer could wait until it starts before attempting to connect to the console. The viewer could connect to remote hosts to look up console information, as well as connect to the remote console using the same network transport.

- `virt-install`: This is a command-line tool for creating new KVM, Xen, or Linux container guests using the `libvirt` hypervisor management library. The `virt-install` tool supports graphical installations that use VNC or SPICE protocols, as well as text mode installations via serial console. The guest could be configured to use one or more virtual disks, network interfaces, audio devices, and physical USB or PCI devices, among others.

The installation media could include local **ISOs** or **CDROMs**, or a *distribution installation tree* hosted remotely via **HTTP**, **FTP**, or in a local directory. In the case of the installation tree, virt-install obtains the minimum files necessary to start the installation process, allowing the guest to get the rest of the operating system distribution as needed. PXE booting and importing an existing disk image (thus skipping the installation phase) are also supported.

With the proper command-line arguments, virt-install can run completely unattended, with the guest "booting" itself. This allows for easy automation of the guest installation.

Using virt-install capabilities enables you to streamline the process of creating virtual machines, minimizing the installation time. Let's learn how to perform this procedure.

Streamlining the creation of virtual machines

QEMU uses the qcow file format for disk image files. It stands for *QEMU Copy On Write*. The qcow format uses a disk storage optimization strategy that delays the allocation of storage until it is needed. Files within the qcow format could contain a variety of disk images that are generally associated with specific guest operating systems. There are three versions of the format: qcow, qcow2, and qcow3.

At the time of writing, the vast majority of distributions, including Fedora Linux, offer a *cloud-ready* downloadable version. One of the available options is the qcow2 image disk format.

OpenStack, an *open standard cloud computing platform*, provides a web page that references cloud images for many distributions and operating systems (which you'll find in the next example).

Using the virt-customize command-line tool, you can modify the downloadable disk image to import it as a *ready-to-use* virtual machine.

Follow these steps to create a virtual machine in a short time with these three tools:

1. Before starting, verify that your workstation runs virtualization-enabled from the **BIOS/UEFI**.

> **Note**
>
> This process depends on the manufacturer of your workstation. Please refer to the manufacturer's documentation to confirm that they have virtualization capability enabled in the BIOS/UEFI.

2. Confirm that the processor of your workstation has the flags that support virtualization:

    ```
    $ sudo grep -E 'svm|vmx' /proc/cpuinfo
    ```

3. Use the sudo command to install the packages required for virtualization:

    *   qemu-kvm
    *   virt-manager

- `virt-viewer`
- `guestfs-tools`
- `virt-install`
- `genisoimage`:

  ```
  $ sudo dnf install qemu-kvm virt-manager virt-viewer guestfs-
  tools virt-install genisoimage
  ```

4. Use your browser to navigate to `https://docs.openstack.org/image-guide/obtain-images.html` and download the `qcow2` disk image of the chosen distribution/operating system:

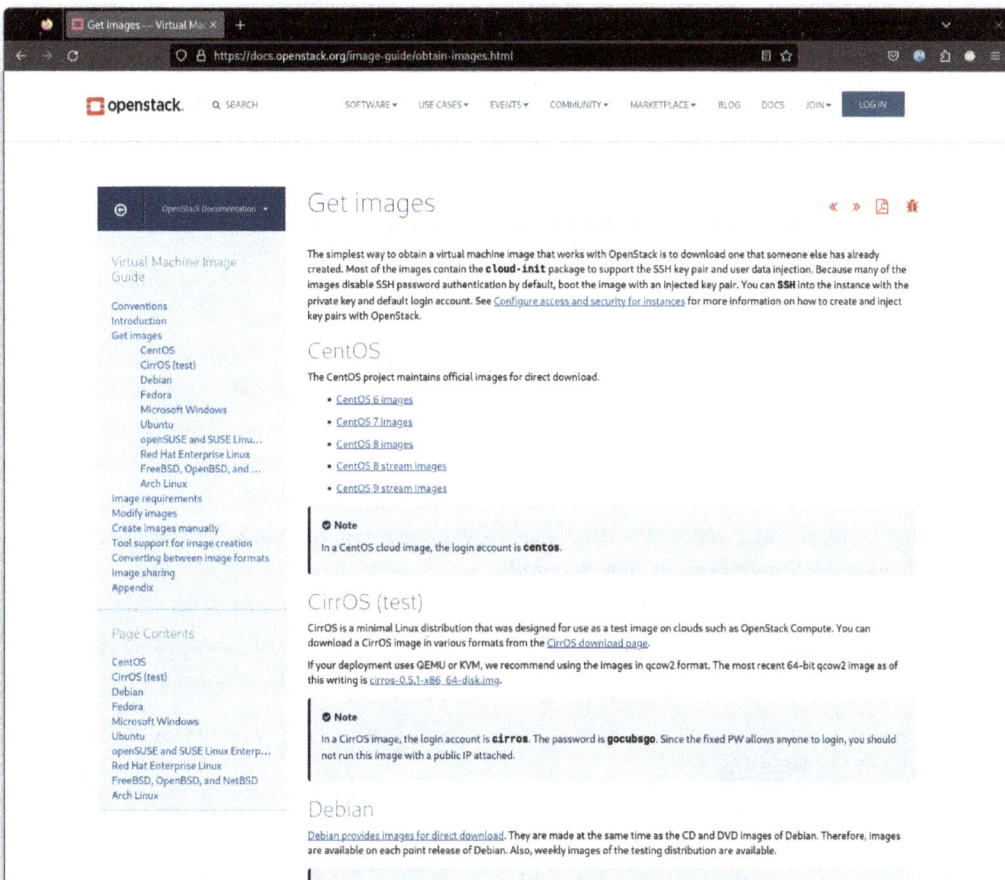

Figure 13.3 – OpenStack – Get images

5. For this example, download the Fedora Linux image. Use your browser to navigate to `https://fedoraproject.org/cloud/download/`:

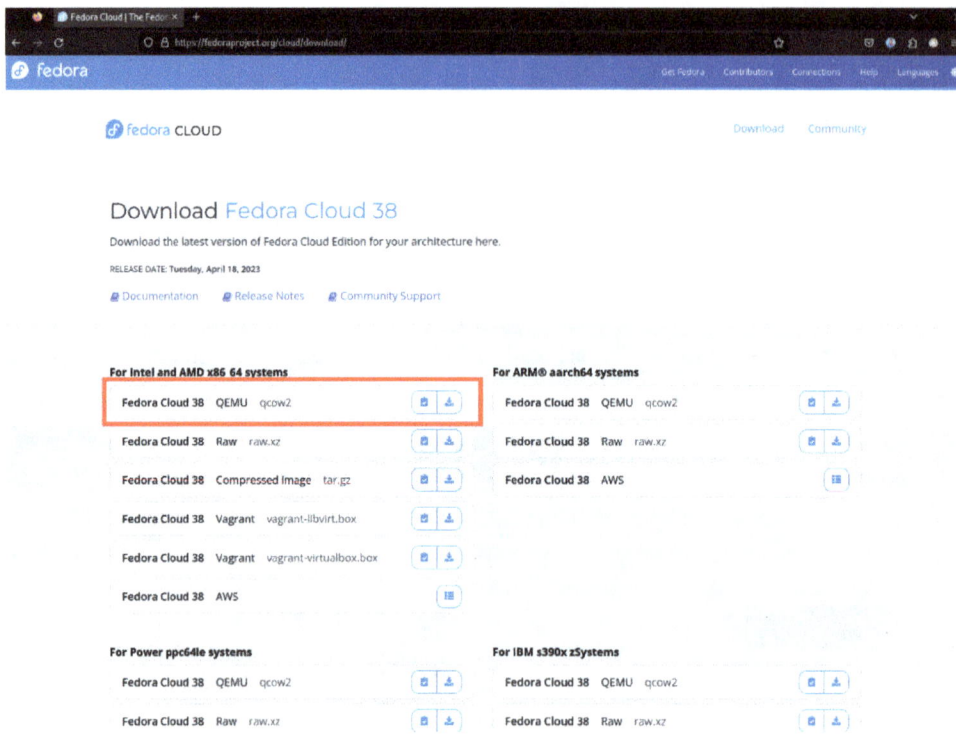

Figure 13.4 – The Fedora Cloud download page

Download the qcow2 image for x86_64 architectures.

> **Note**
>
> Each image requires about 400 MB of disk space. Ensure that you have enough storage space to store them and let them grow as they get used.

6. Move the downloaded qcow2 image to the **KVM** working directory in /var/lib/libvirt/images:

```
$ sudo mv Fedora-Cloud-Base-38-1.6.x86_64.qcow2 /var/lib/libvirt/images/
```

> **Note**
>
> A best practice is to copy the qcow2 image with the virtual machine name instead of moving it. Reuse the original downloaded image to create many virtual machines:
>
> ```
> $ sudo cp Fedora-Cloud-Base-38-1.6.x86_64.qcow2 /var/lib/libvirt/images/vmtest01.qcow2
> ```

7. Use the `virt-customize` command to modify the downloaded image:

```
$ sudo virt-customize \
-a /var/lib/libvirt/images/vmtest01.qcow2 \
--hostname vmtest01.packt.lab \
--root-password password:rootpw \
--ssh-inject 'root:file:labkey.pub' \
--uninstall cloud-init \
--selinux-relabel
```

Let's look at each of the options that we used in detail:

- `virt-customize` modifies the guest or disk image in place. The guest must power off to modify the disk image. There's no need to run `virt-customize` as `root` user. In this case, use the `sudo` command since there are no access rights to the path where this image resides.

- `-a` indicates the path of the disk to customize.

- `--hostname` sets the virtual machine hostname.

- `--root-password` sets the new `root` password, which in this case is `rootpw`.

- `--ssh-inject` allows you to inject an SSH key to some user. In this case, this is `labkey` for the `root` user.

To generate the SSH key, use the `ssh-keygen` command:

```
$ ssh-keygen -t ecdsa -b 521 -f labkey
```

> **Note**
>
> For more information on the `ssh-keygen` command, refer to the command manual: `man ssh-keygen`.

- `--uninstall` allows us to uninstall the software contained by default in the downloaded image.

cloud-init is a suite that helps initialize an image for use in OpenStack. In this case, it is not necessary since a basic functional level of customization works best here.

> **Note**
>
> If the `cloud-init` package is not uninstalled, the VM will take a long time to boot as it waits for the parameters for initialization with `cloud-init scripts`.

- Since it is a Fedora Linux image, the SELinux contexts must *relabel* with the `--selinux-relabel` option as several files must be changed or removed:

```
[acallejas@workstation ~]$
[acallejas@workstation ~]$ sudo virt-customize -a /var/lib/libvirt/images/vmtest01.qcow2 --hostname
vmtest01.packt.lab --root-password password:rootpw --ssh-inject 'root:file:labkey.pub' --uninstall
cloud-init --selinux-relabel
[   0.0] Examining the guest ...
[   8.8] Setting a random seed
[   8.8] Setting the machine ID in /etc/machine-id
[   8.8] Setting the hostname: vmtest01.packt.lab
[   8.8] SSH key inject: root
[   9.5] Uninstalling packages: cloud-init
[  16.6] Setting passwords
[  17.2] SELinux relabelling
[  27.4] Finishing off
[acallejas@workstation ~]$
```

Figure 13.5 – Customizing the qcow2 image

Now that we've finished customizing, let's import the disk image as a new virtual machine.

8. To import the disk image as a new virtual machine, use the `virt-install` command:

```
$ sudo virt-install \
--name vmtest01 \
--memory 1024 \
--vcpus 1 \
--disk /var/lib/libvirt/images/vmtest01.qcow2 \
--import \
--osinfo fedora38 \
--noautoconsole
```

Let's look at each of the options we used in detail:

- `virt-install` is the command-line tool for creating new VMs.

- `--name` sets the name of the new guest VM instance. The name must remain *unique* among all guests known to the hypervisor on the connection, including those not currently active.

- `--memory` indicates the memory to allocate for the guest in MiB.

- `--vcpus` indicates the number of `vcpus` to configure for the guest.

- `-disk` specifies the device to use as storage for the guest. In this case, this is the path to the disk image.

- `--import` indicates that the disk image gets imported as a new VM building a guest around this disk image.

- --osinfo optimizes the guest configuration for a specific operating system version or distribution. In this case, fedora38 is indicated.

> **Note**
>
> To find the list of supported operating system name values, use the virt-install command – that is, virt-install --osinfo list.

- --noautoconsole specifies not to try to connect to the guest console automatically:

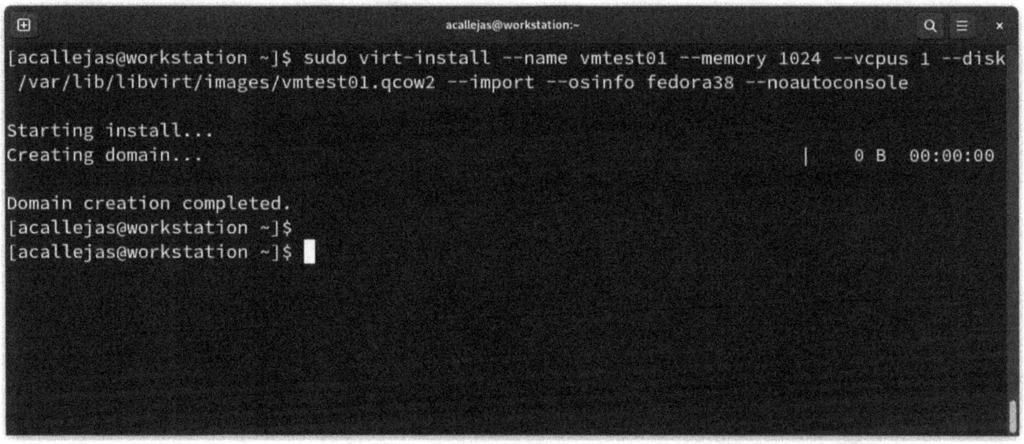

```
[acallejas@workstation ~]$ sudo virt-install --name vmtest01 --memory 1024 --vcpus 1 --disk
 /var/lib/libvirt/images/vmtest01.qcow2 --import --osinfo fedora38 --noautoconsole

Starting install...
Creating domain...                                                |    0 B  00:00:00

Domain creation completed.
[acallejas@workstation ~]$
[acallejas@workstation ~]$
```

Figure 13.6 – Creating a new virtual machine

9. Verify the status of the created virtual machine:

   ```
   $ sudo virsh list
   ```

   Here's the output:

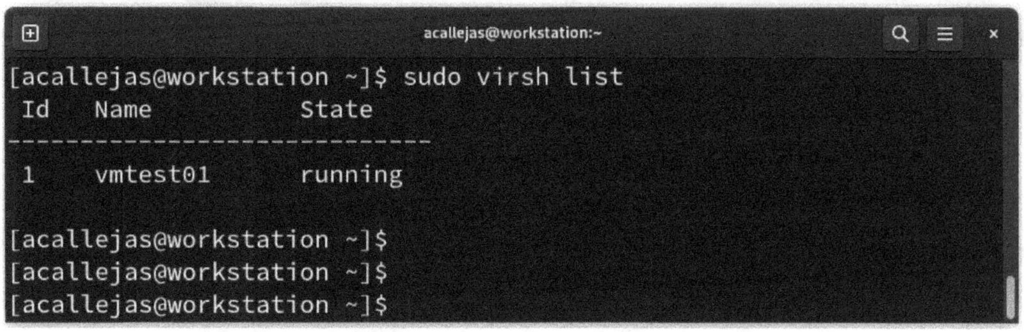

```
[acallejas@workstation ~]$ sudo virsh list
 Id   Name         State
----------------------------
 1    vmtest01     running

[acallejas@workstation ~]$
[acallejas@workstation ~]$
[acallejas@workstation ~]$
```

Figure 13.7 – Verifying the new virtual machine's status

Now, let's connect to the virtual machine via SSH.

10. Use the `virsh` command to find the IP address that was assigned by the virtualization **DHCP** service:

```
$ sudo virsh domifaddr vmtest01
```

Here's the output:

```
[acallejas@workstation ~]$ sudo virsh domifaddr vmtest01
 Name       MAC address         Protocol     Address
--------------------------------------------------------------------------
 vnet1      52:54:00:ee:64:de   ipv4         192.168.124.225/24

[acallejas@workstation ~]$
[acallejas@workstation ~]$
[acallejas@workstation ~]$
```

Figure 13.8 – Finding the VM's IP address

11. Use the `ssh` command and the SSH key to access the virtual machine:

```
$ ssh -i labkey root@192.168.124.225
```

You will get the following output:

```
[acallejas@workstation ~]$ ssh -i labkey root@192.168.124.225
The authenticity of host '192.168.124.225 (192.168.124.225)' can't be established.
ED25519 key fingerprint is SHA256:UrZ6JMxeZcmuHtvfRi6Op7UqJpTAdYV5ofENs9pmlFA.
This key is not known by any other names
Are you sure you want to continue connecting (yes/no/[fingerprint])? yes
Warning: Permanently added '192.168.124.225' (ED25519) to the list of known hosts.
X11 forwarding request failed on channel 0
[root@vmtest01 ~]#
```

Figure 13.9 – Accessing the VM

With that, you can get a working virtual machine up and running in a short time. Mastering these commands speeds up this task.

Before moving on to containerization, which is virtualization in miniature form, let's look at the tool that GNOME includes as part of its desktop suite.

Using GNOME Boxes

GNOME Boxes is an application of the GNOME desktop environment that's used to access remote or virtual systems. Boxes uses the QEMU, KVM, and Libvirt virtualization technologies.

Besides the virtualization extensions seen in the previous section, Boxes requires at least *20 GB of storage space* and *500 MB of RAM* to allocate to virtual machines. GNOME recommends at least 8 GB of RAM and 20 GB of storage on the workstation to run Boxes efficiently. Boxes assigns resources to virtual machines *automatically* and *dynamically* based on the vendor's recommendations.

Let's review the process of creating a virtual machine with **Boxes**:

1. To access Boxes, open *Activities Overview* and type Boxes:

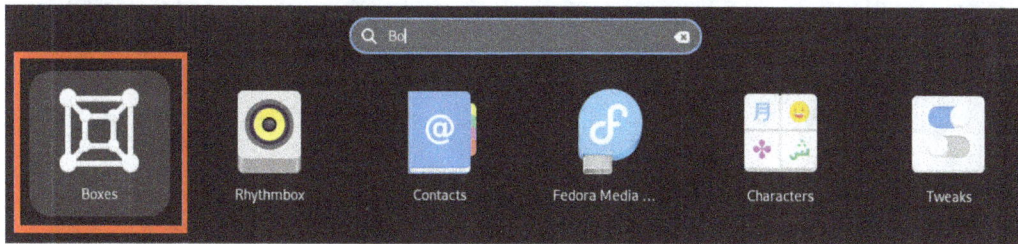

Figure 13.10 – GNOME Boxes via Activities Overview

2. The main Boxes window will appear. To create a new virtual machine, click on the *plus* (+) button in the top-left corner:

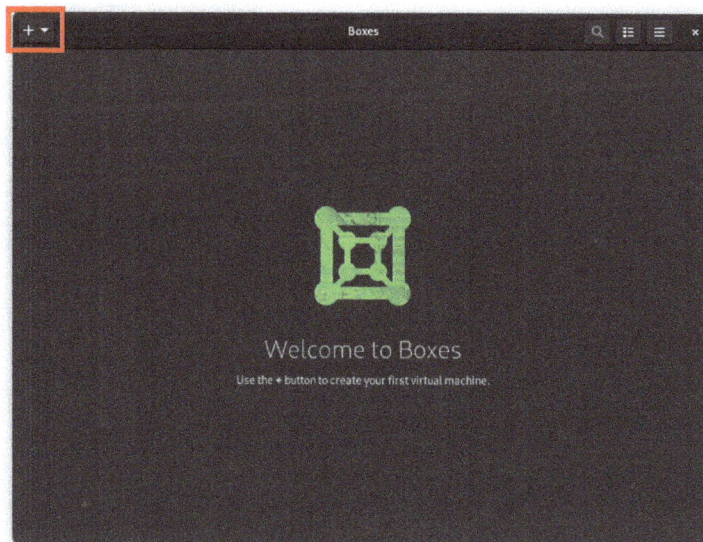

Figure 13.11 – GNOME Boxes main window

3.   Boxes offers two options for creating a new virtual machine:

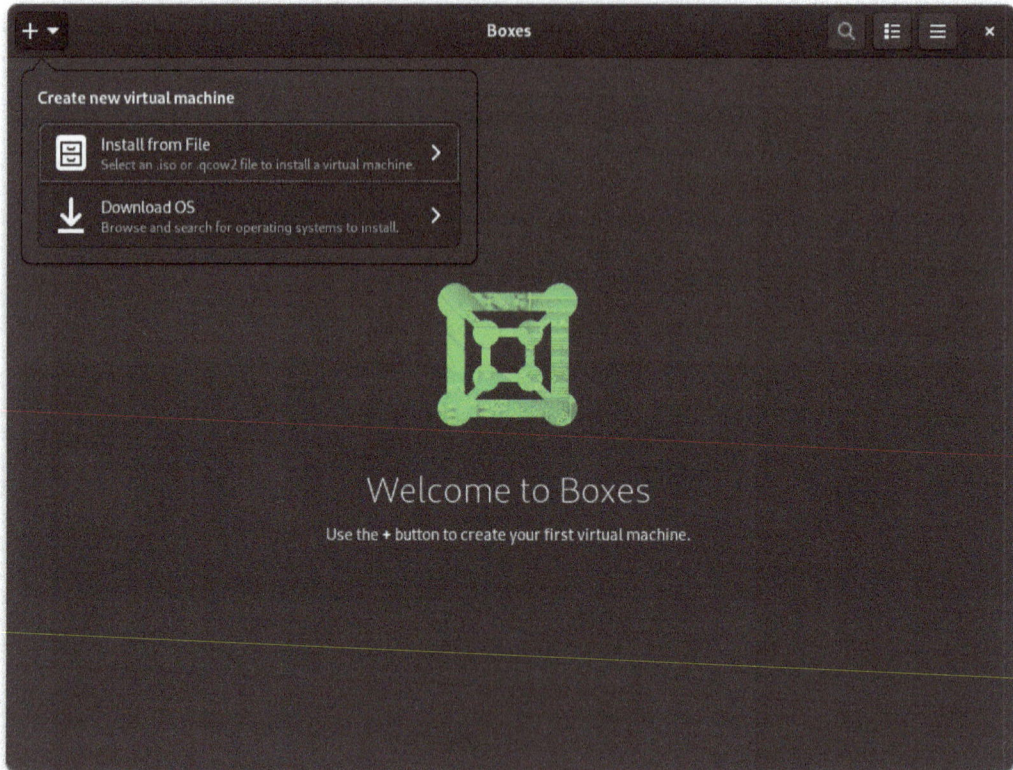

Figure 13.12 – Creating a new virtual machine with Boxes

They are as follows:

- **Install from File**: When using this option, you must state the location of the **ISO** image of the operating system to install in the new virtual machine

- **Download OS**: This option selects an operating system version or distribution and downloads the corresponding image for installation in the new virtual machine:

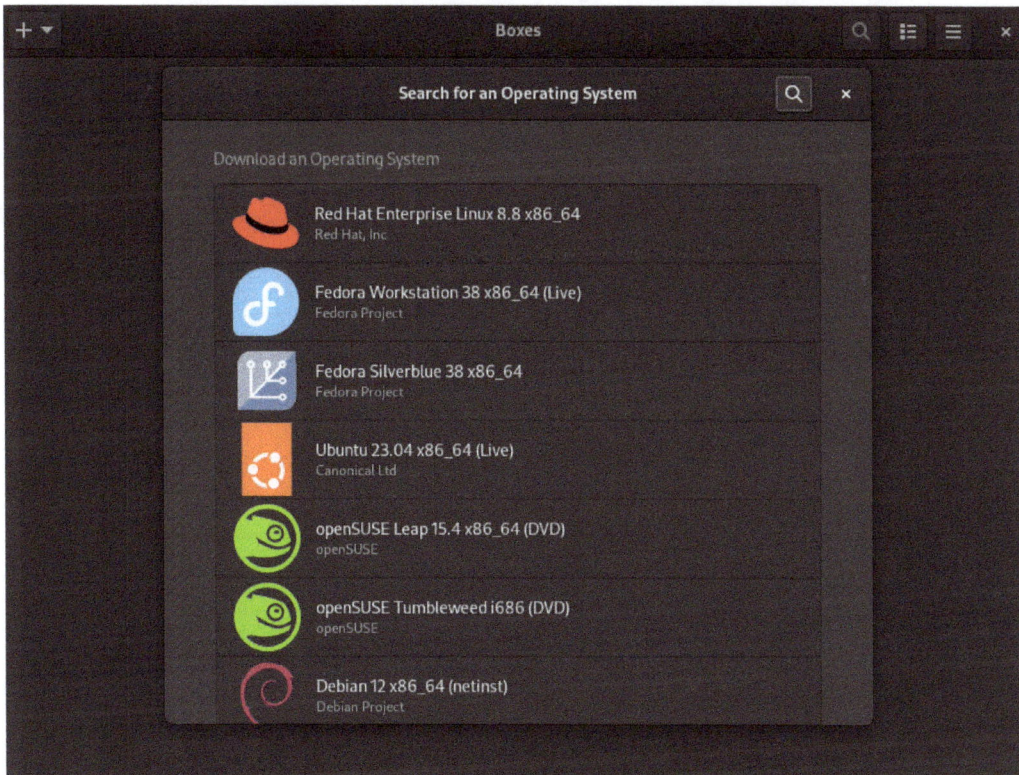

Figure 13.13 – Selecting an operating system image

For this example, let's download the ISO image by ourselves.

4. Use your browser to navigate to `https://fedoraproject.org/workstation/download/`:

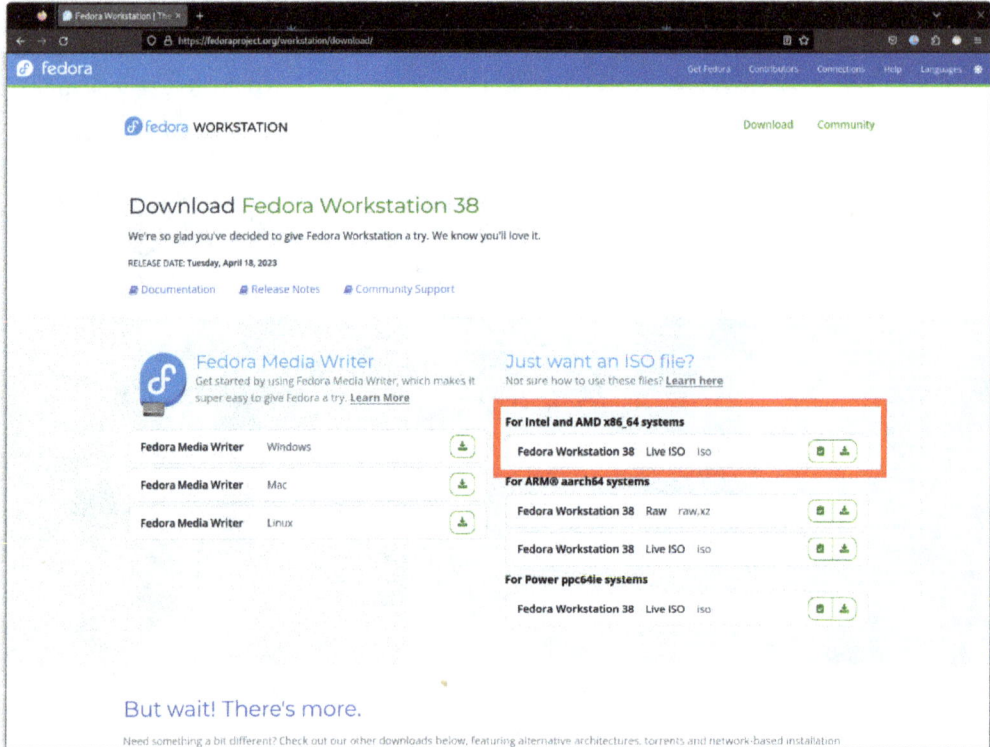

Figure 13.14 – Fedora Workstation download page

Download the **ISO** image for `x86_64` architectures.

5. In **Boxes,** click on the *plus* sign (+) and select the **Install from File** option. Navigate to the location of the downloaded **ISO** image and click the **Open** button:

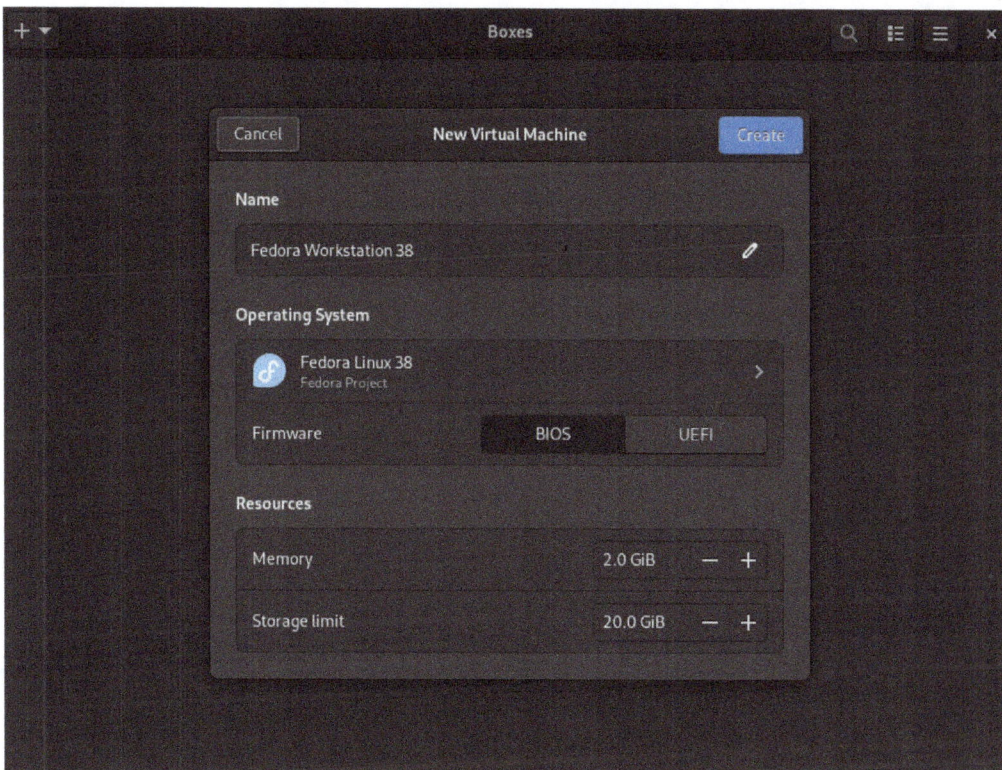

Figure 13.15 – Creating a new virtual machine

Boxes will display the virtual machine creation options. Use the default options and click the **Create** button.

6. The installation of the downloaded image – in this case, Fedora Workstation – starts on a bare-metal machine:

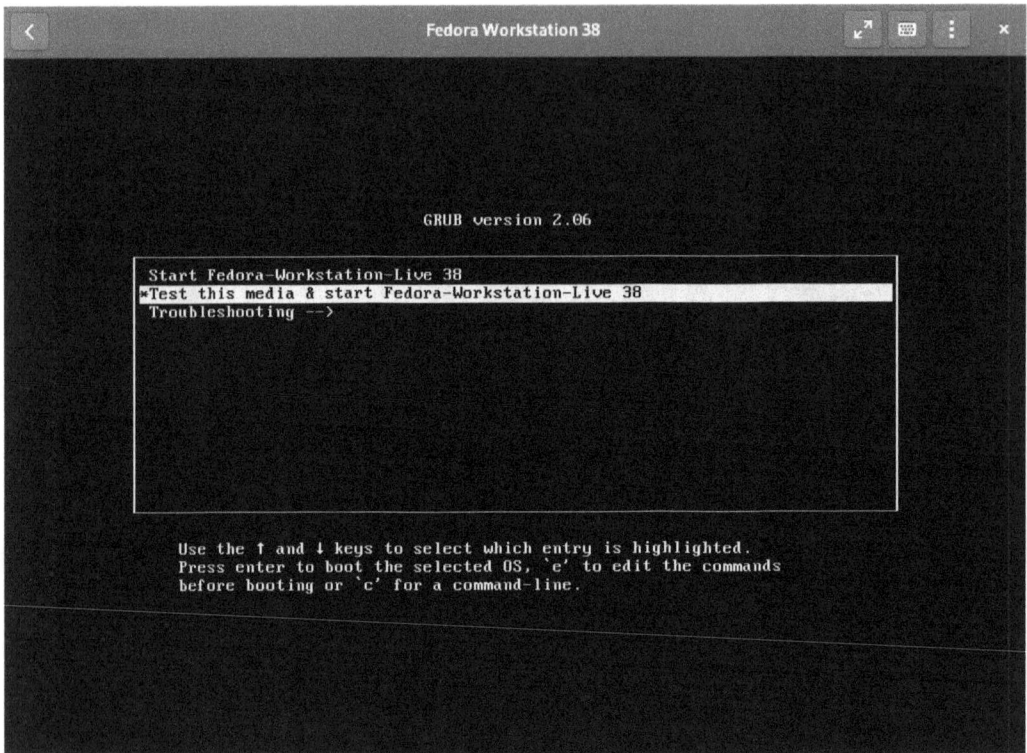

Figure 13.16 – Fedora Workstation live image

7. In the Fedora Workstation installation window, click the **Install Fedora** button and continue installing the operating system:

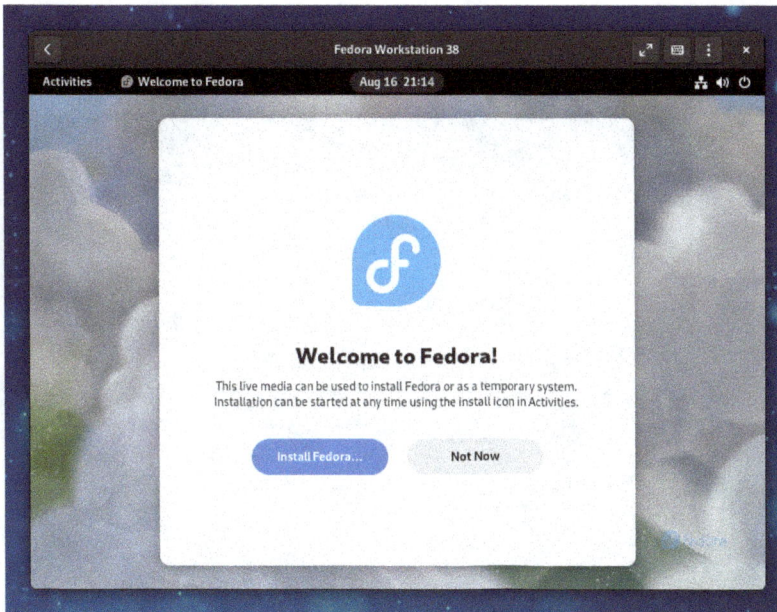

Figure 13.17 – Fedora Linux installation window

8. Once the installation has finished, click on the **Finish installation** button and restart the virtual machine:

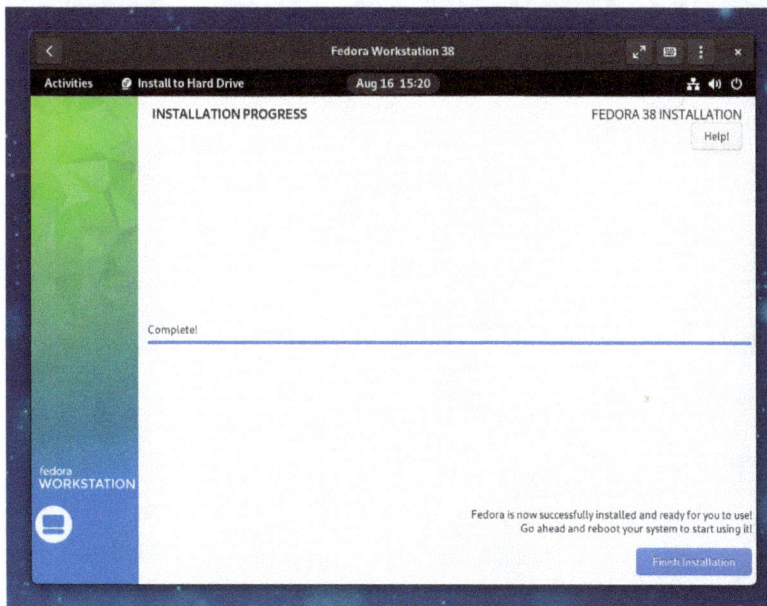

Figure 13.18 – Finishing virtual machine installation

Upon restarting the virtual machine, it will appear in the main **Boxes** window:

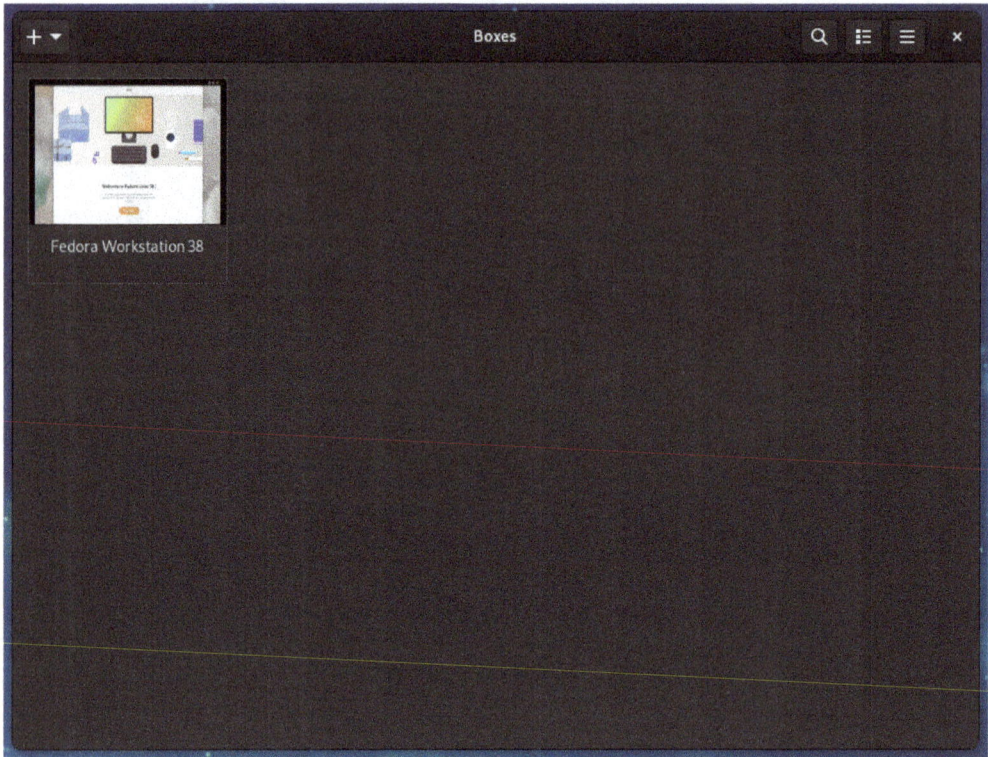

Figure 13.19 – The Boxes main window

9. Click on the virtual machine icon to access it:

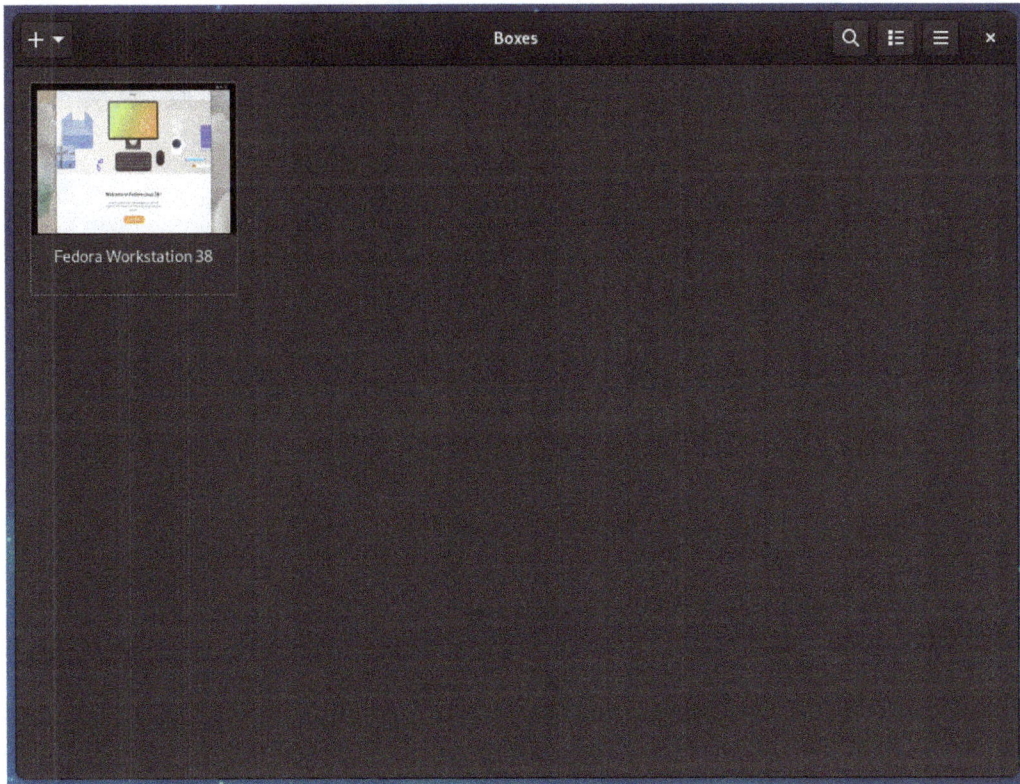

Figure 13.20 – Accessing the virtual machine

The virtual machine window takes up the space of the main **Boxes** window and allows us to use it graphically, as a remote session:

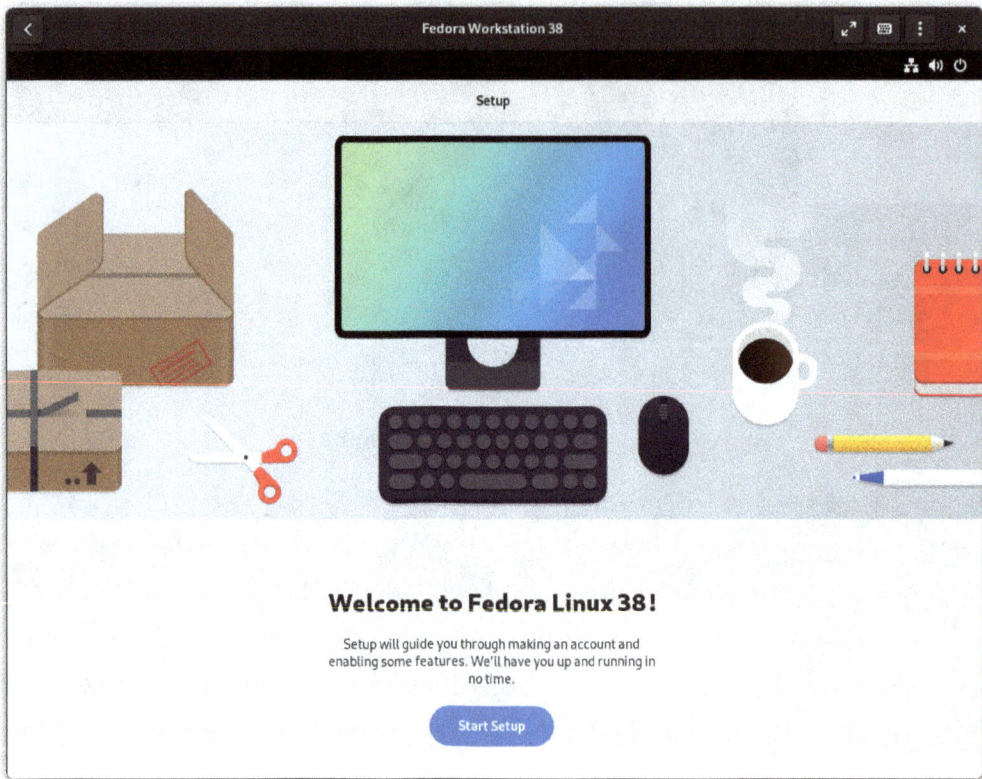

Figure 13.21 – Fedora Workstation virtual machine

Now, use the virtual machine for the tasks assigned to it.

If the virtual machine gets turned off, it will appear in the main window, as shown in the following figure:

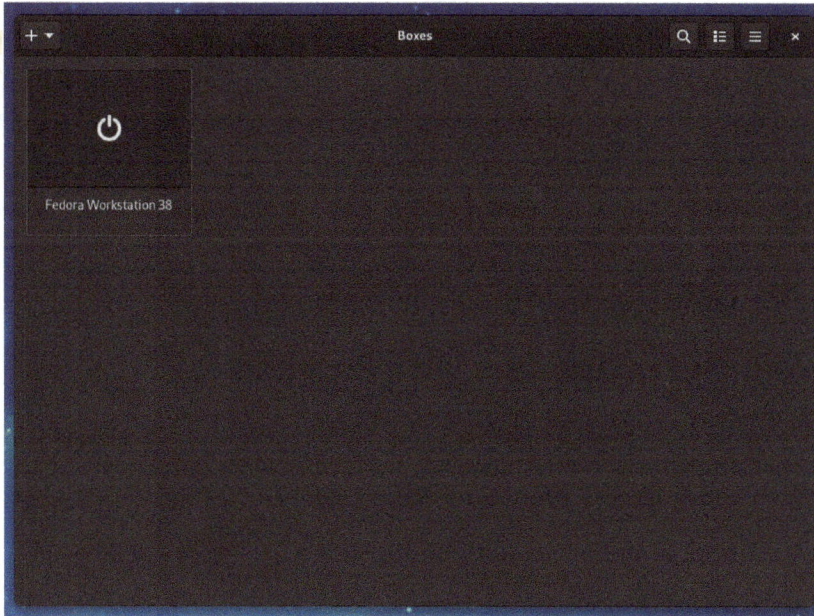

Figure 13.22 – The virtual machine turned off in Boxes

10. Right-click on the virtual machine icon to access the administration options:

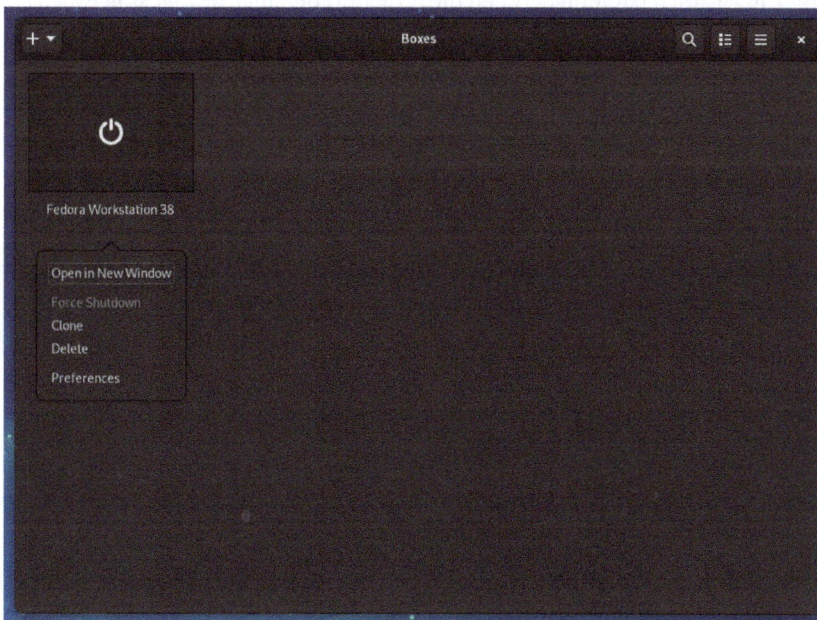

Figure 13.23 – Virtual machine management options

11. To turn on the virtual machine, double-click its icon.

GNOME Boxes is a simple application for accessing and managing virtual machines. It does not provide *granular management* and *automation facilities* of `virsh`, but it is a good tool to become familiar with the use of virtual machines.

A more granular method, with less creation time and better optimization of host resources, is to use containers.

Now, let's learn how Fedora Linux implements the use of open containers.

Discovering OCI containers with Podman

A Linux container, roughly speaking, works like the virtualization process, where we import a *pre-built image* of an operating system and create a virtual machine from it. In the case of containers, the image only packages the *programs and their minimal dependencies* needed for the operation of an application.

A container is a set of one or more processes that stand isolated from the rest of the system.

The kernel provides the following main components:

- `namespaces` to ensure process isolation
- `cgroups` to control system resources
- `SELinux` to ensure separation between the host and container, as well as between containers

The administration interface interacts with the kernel components and provides tools for *building and managing* containers. All the files needed to run a container come from an image.

Container images live in an external repository called a **registry**. To create a container, download the registry image and generate a runnable copy of the application on the host. These processes require a runtime and the image needs to be in a specific format to run.

The Linux Foundation sponsors the **Open Container Initiative** (**OCI**) project with the purpose of creating open industry standards around container formats and runtimes.

The OCI currently contains three specifications:

- The **Runtime Specification** (`runtime-spec`). This specifies how to run a filesystem bundle that is unpacked on disk.
- The **Image Specification** (`image-spec`). This provides interoperable tools for building, transporting, and preparing a container image for running.
- The **Distribution Specification** (`distribution-spec`). This defines an API protocol to ease and standardize content distribution.

An OCI implementation would download an OCI image and then unpack that image into an OCI runtime filesystem bundle.

Fedora Linux implements **Podman** for OCI container management.

Podman relies on an *OCI-compliant container runtime* (runc, crun, runv, and so on) to interact with the operating system and create the running containers via the command line:

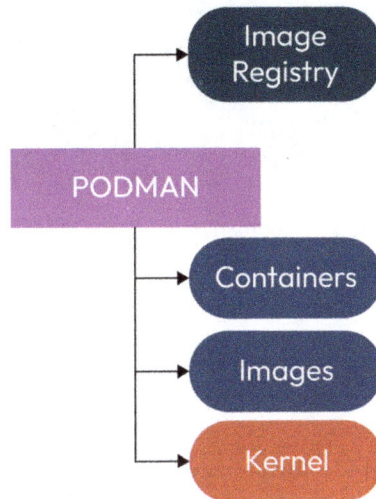

Figure 13.24 – Podman interaction

Containers controlled with Podman can be run by root or an *unprivileged user*. Podman manages the entire container ecosystem, including pods, containers, container images, and container volumes, using the libpod library.

To run containers as a non-root user, you must have some considerations about the resources you use:

- The container images get stored in the user's home directory ($HOME/.local/share/containers/storage/) instead of /var/lib/containers
- Due to not having root privileges, these rules must be followed:
  - No capability to access a port less than 1024
  - Storage must live on a local filesystem

Let's start by installing the utility.

Installing Podman requires administrator privileges. As the root user, run the dnf command:

```
# dnf install podman
```

Now, let's create an example container to exemplify the scope of the utility as a *non-root user*:

1. Verify rootless configuration:

    ```
    $ podman unshare cat /proc/self/uid_map
    ```

    You should see the following output:

Figure 13.25 – Podman rootless configuration

2. Create a base container. Use the podman pull command to download the image:

    ```
    $ podman pull ubi9/ubi
    ```

> **Note**
>
> The Red Hat **Universal Base Image** (**UBI**) enables you to build, share, and collaborate with containerized applications.

Here's the output:

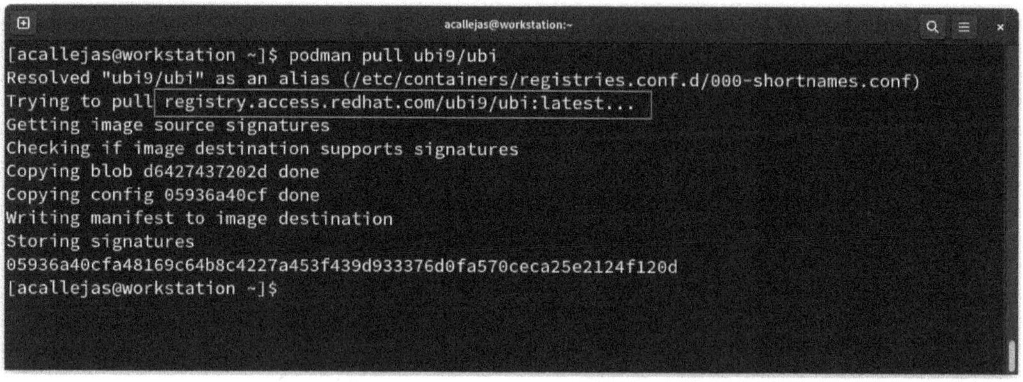

Figure 13.26 – Obtaining the container image

After the download is complete, verify and inspect the image.

3. Use the `podman images` command to list the downloaded images:

    ```
    $ podman images
    ```

Here's the output:

Figure 13.27 – Listing container images

Use `image ID` to inspect it.

4. Inspecting the downloaded image provides us with information on the creation and use of the image, besides the available variables to use on it. Use the `podman inspect` command with the name of the image or its ID:

    ```
    $ podman inspect 05936a40cfa4
    ```

You will see the following output:

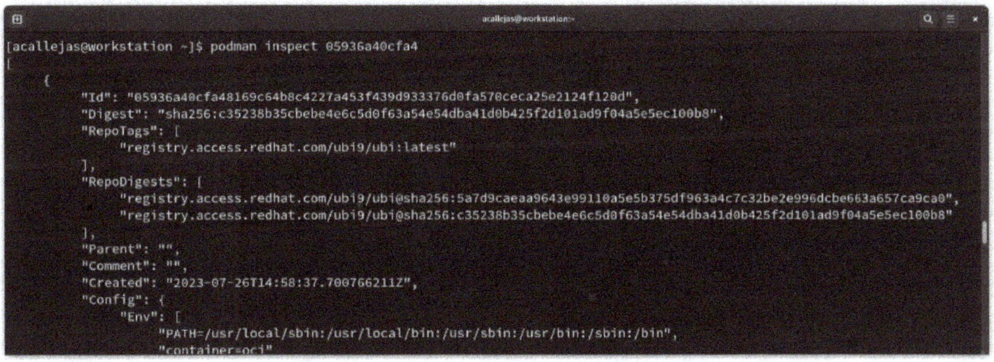

Figure 13.28 – Inspecting the UBI image

Now, let's create a container from the downloaded image.

5. Run a container of the UBI image to display the operating system version:

    ```
    $ podman run ubi9/ubi cat /etc/os-release
    ```

Here's the output:

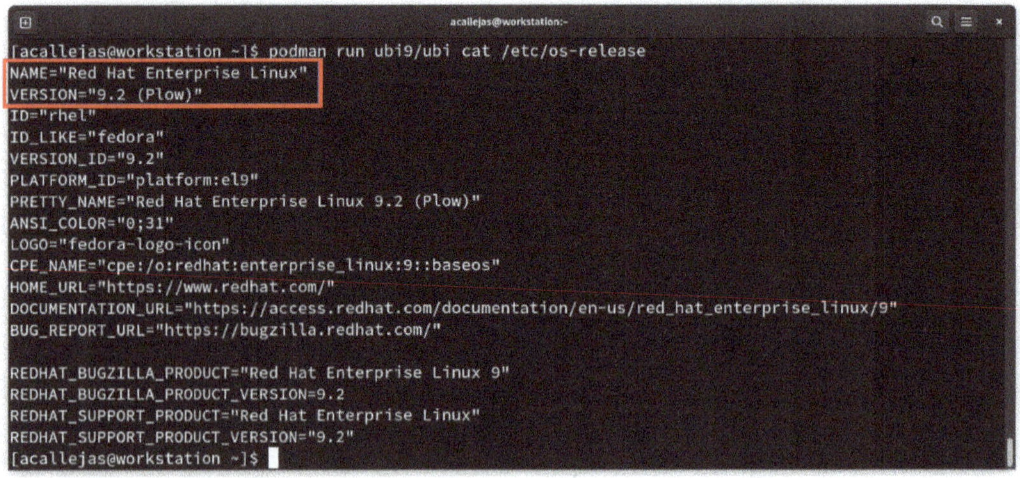

Figure 13.29 – Running a container

The container is a base image of RHEL9 that's running on Fedora Linux.

Now, let's create an example of a containerized service. Follow these steps:

1. Use your browser to navigate to `https://registry.fedoraproject.org/`:

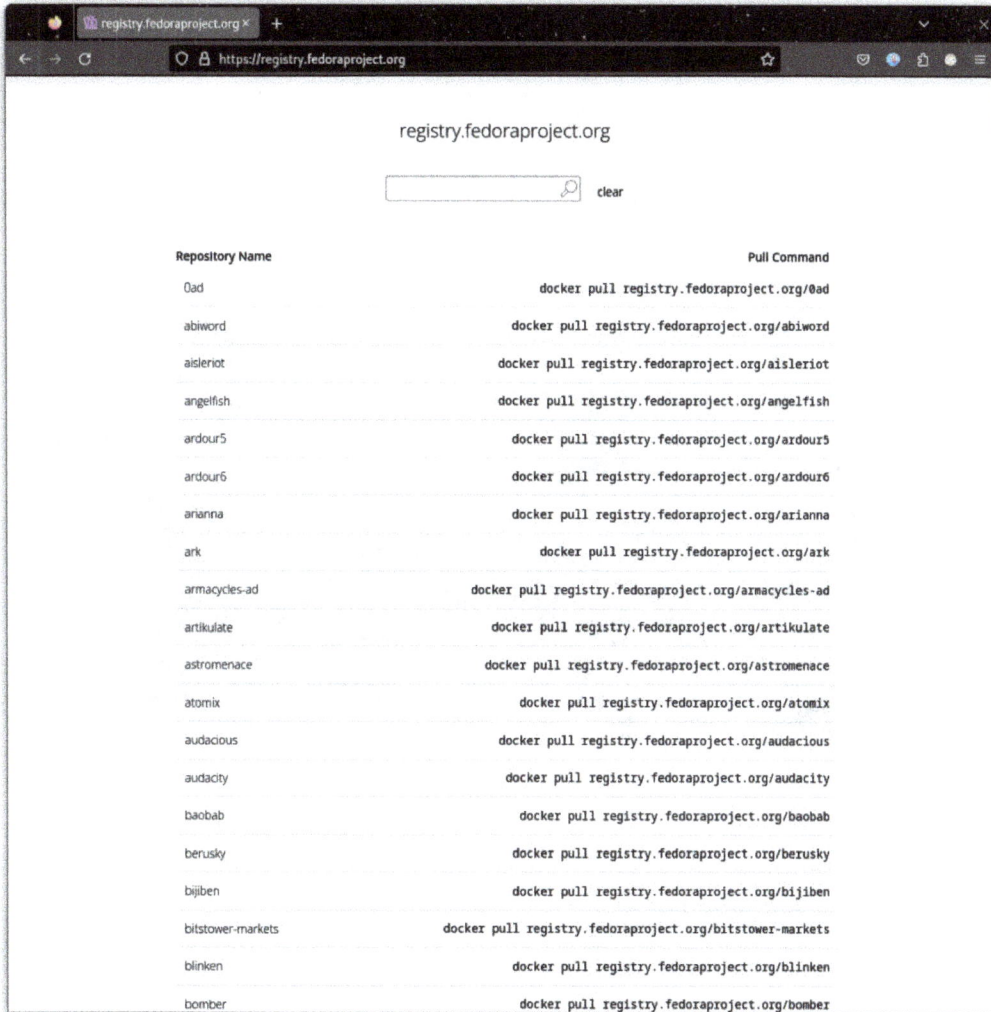

Figure 13.30 – Fedora Project container image registry

2. Find the latest *web server image* (`httpd`) and copy its `pull` command:

    `docker pull registry.fedoraproject.org/f29/httpd`

> **Note**
>
> Change the `pull` command so that it uses `podman` instead of `docker`.

3. Download the container image and verify it:

    ```
    $ podman pull registry.fedoraproject.org/f29/httpd
    $ podman images
    ```

    You should get the following output:

```
[acallejas@workstation ~]$ podman pull registry.fedoraproject.org/f29/httpd
Trying to pull registry.fedoraproject.org/f29/httpd:latest...
Getting image source signatures
Copying blob d77ff9f653ce done
Copying blob 7692efc5f81c done
Copying blob aaf5ad2e1aa3 done
Copying config 25c76f9dcd done
Writing manifest to image destination
25c76f9dcdb5f512fe2d41587bbae84c25adf36126f46fba2ad6bad2ab1afabc
[acallejas@workstation ~]$ podman images
REPOSITORY                              TAG       IMAGE ID       CREATED       SIZE
registry.access.redhat.com/ubi9/ubi     latest    05936a40cfa4   3 weeks ago   217 MB
registry.fedoraproject.org/f29/httpd    latest    25c76f9dcdb5   4 years ago   482 MB
[acallejas@workstation ~]$
```

Figure 13.31 – Getting the httpd image

4. Test run the container for the `httpd` image:

    ```
    $ podman run httpd
    ```

Here's the output:

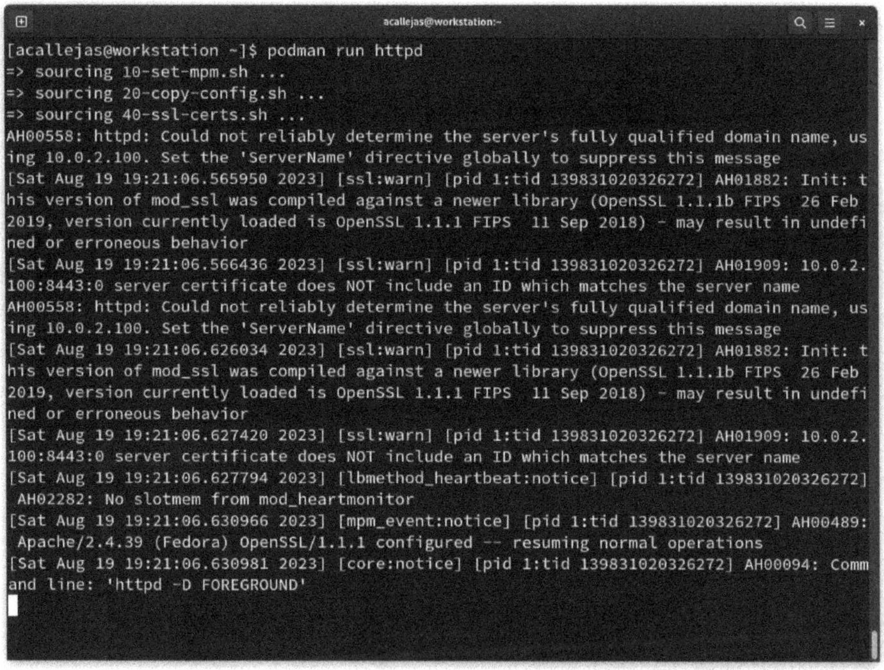

Figure 13.32 – Running the httpd image container

Running the httpd image container in this way inhibits the use of the Terminal. Let's run it with a custom name and in the background.

5. Run the httpd image container as myapache and in the background. Use the --name and -d options with the podman run command:

```
$ podman run --name myapache -d httpd
```

Verify the container's status with the podman ps command:

```
$ podman ps
```

You should see the following output:

Figure 13.33 – Running the container and verifying its status

Inspect the running container to find information you can use to access the service.

6. Use the `podman inspect` command:

```
$ podman inspect myapache | grep IPAddress
$ podman inspect myapache | grep expose-service
```

You should see the following:

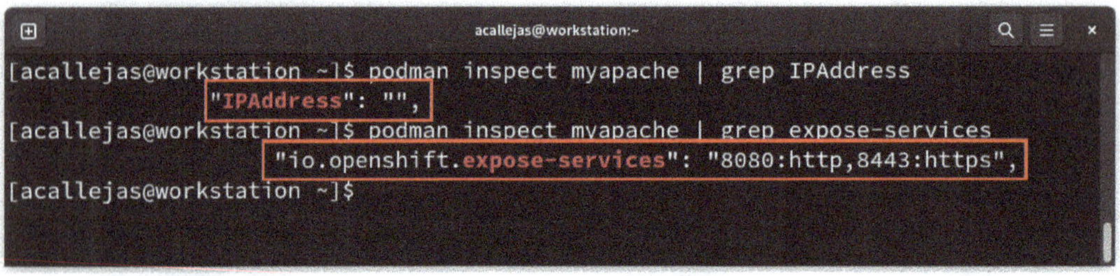

Figure 13.34 – Looking for access to the containerized service

The containerized service has no `IPAddress` assigned to it but opens ports `8080` and `8443`. Check the logs for more information.

7. Use the `podman logs` command to review the logs:

```
$ podman logs myapache
```

Here's the output:

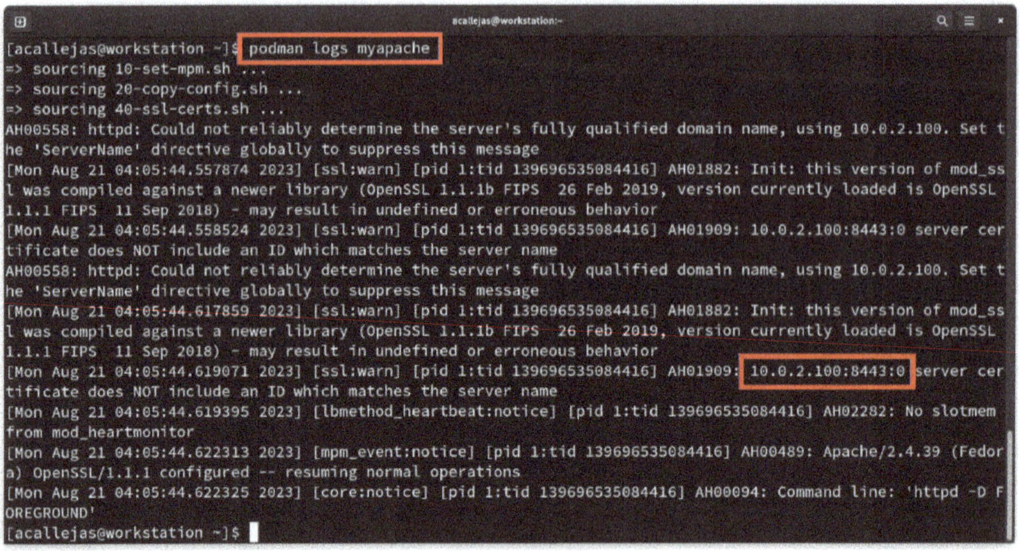

Figure 13.35 – Reviewing service logs

In the logs of the containerized service, find the IP address that opens port 8443. Verify access to the service with this information.

8. Verify access to the containerized service. Use the following `curl` command:

```
$ curl 10.0.2.100:8443
```

Here's the output:

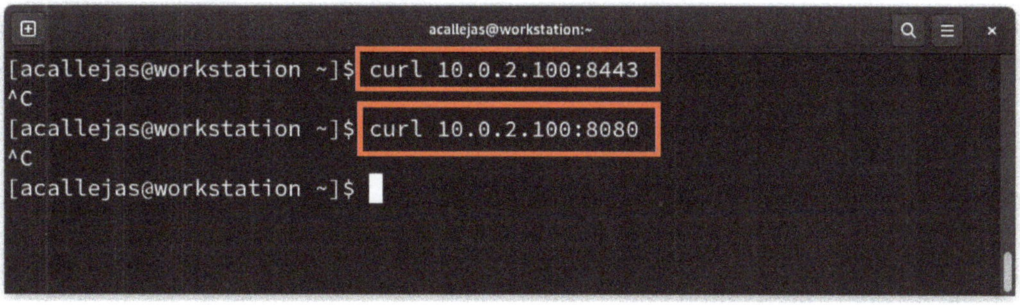

Figure 13.36 – Verifying access to the web service

The service fails to answer on port 8443 or 8080.

This is due to the container port not referring to a host port. Delete the container and recreate it with the reference to a local port.

9. Remove the container. First, use the `stop` option to interrupt the container run and then the `rm` option to delete the container with the `podman` command:

```
$ podman stop myapache
$ podman rm myapache
```

You should see the following output:

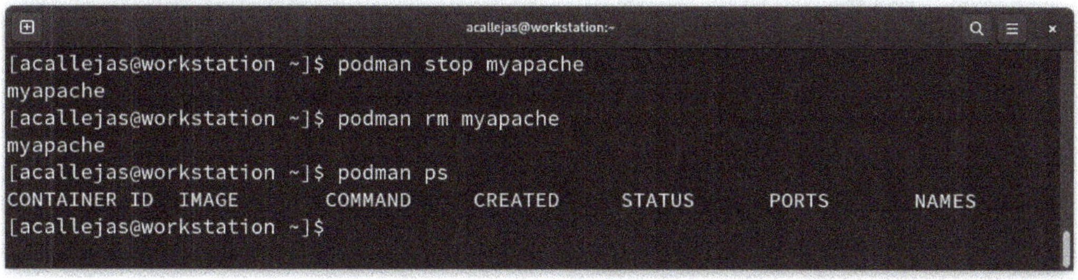

Figure 13.37 – Removing the container

Verify that the `myapache` container is not running anymore. Use the `podman ps` command to do so.

10. Recreate the myapache container by mapping the container's port, 8080, to local port 8080. Add the -p option to the podman run command that we ran in *step 4*:

```
$ podman run --name myapache -d -p 8080:8080 httpd
```

Here's the output:

Figure 13.38 – Mapping the container port to the local port

11. Use the podman ps command to confirm that the port was mapped correctly.

12. Test the service again but on local port 8080:

```
$ curl localhost:8080
```

You should see the following output:

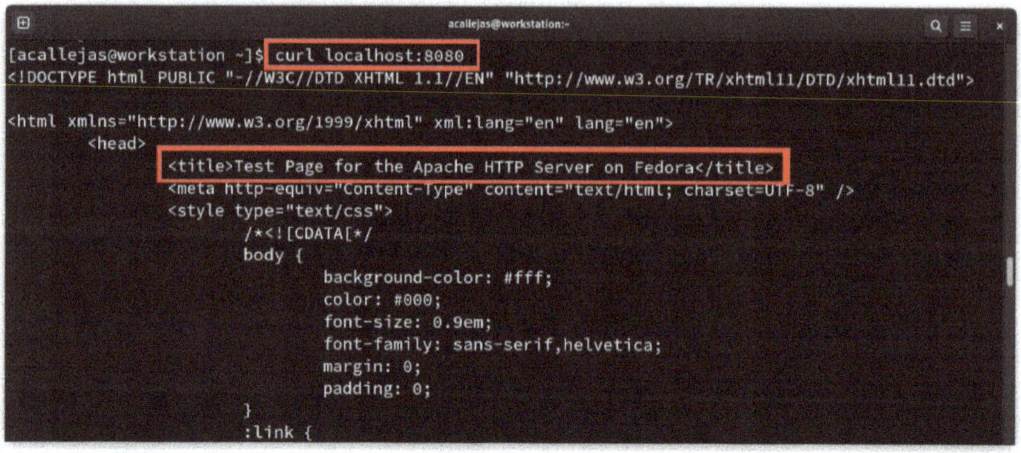

Figure 13.39 – Testing service access

Now that the service is accessible, it shows the Apache test page.

An application that always runs on a single host accesses local disk storage to get the information it needs while running. These storage volumes remain both *logically* and *physically* persistent. Containerized dynamic and elastic deployments separate the logical and physical states of application storage.

A containerized application could be *logically resident but physically transient* due to the redistribution and scaling capabilities inherent in OCI technologies.

If a container resides on a host, but that container stops working, the container manager could start a new instance on another host. The application may need some data available when it is running; this is known as logical persistence. Since container information is ephemeral by default, the storage is physically transient.

In containerized storage in general, the trend is to integrate *persistent storage* with *ephemeral containers* as best as possible.

Now, let's learn how to add persistent storage to our containerized service. Follow these steps:

1. Stop and remove the `myapache` container:

    ```
    $ podman stop myapache
    $ podman rm myapache
    ```

2. In the user's home directory, create the working directory for persistent storage of the myapache container:

    ```
    $ mkdir -p ~/containers/myapache/var/www/html
    ```

    Now, let's create a custom home page for our service.

3. Create the `index.html` file inside the persistent storage directory we created for the myapache container:

    ```
    $ echo "Hello from myapache container!" > ~/containers/myapache/
    var/www/html/index.html
    ```

4. Regenerate the myapache container with the `-v` option to add persistent storage as a volume of the myapache container.

5. Run the container again with the option to attach the volume mentioned previously. As with the port, the local directory must be mapped to the container directory. In this case, since it deals with files, add the `-Z` option to apply the SELinux policy from the container directory to the local directory:

    ```
    $ podman run --name myapache -d -p 8080:8080 -v ~/containers/
    myapache/var/www/html:/var/www/html:Z httpd
    ```

6. Verify that the container is running, as well as that you have access to the service:

Figure 13.40 – Testing the container with persistent storage

Now, our web service has persistent storage. This can be managed locally or independently of the container instance(s) running with the content.

This service could manage itself as a container and give this management to `systemd` as part of the system. Let's learn how set up self-management.

Using the same `myapache` container from the previous example, follow these steps:

1. Stop and remove the `myapache` container:

    ```
    $ podman stop myapache
    $ podman rm myapache
    ```

2. To make the `myapache` container self-managed, add a command that determines the health of the container. In our case, we will use the `curl` command from the previous example. Use the `--health-cmd` and `--health-interval` options to define them in the container:

    ```
    $ podman run --name myapache -d -p 8080:8080 -v ~/containers/
    myapache/var/www/html:/var/www/html:Z --health-cmd="curl
    localhost:8080 || exit 1" --health-interval=0 httpd
    ```

    Here's the output:

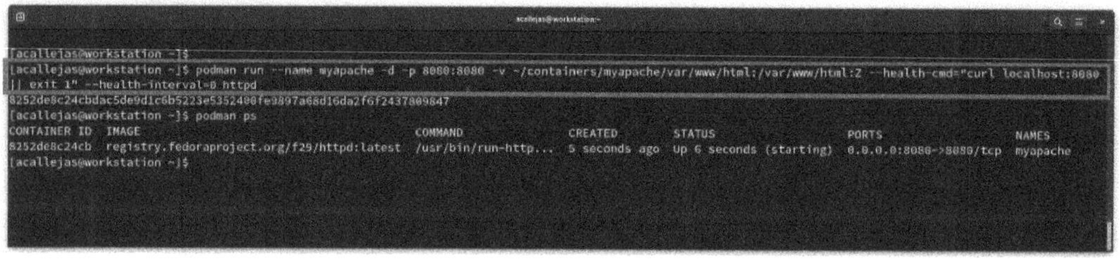

Figure 13.41 – Making the container self-managed

    Verify the creation of the container. Then, use the `podman ps` command.

3. To check the health of the container, run the `podman healthcheck run` command:

    ```
    $ podman healthcheck run myapache
    ```

    Here's the output:

Figure 13.42 – Reviewing the health of the container

4. The output of the preceding command should return nothing. Run an `echo` command on the special variable, `$?`, to get the output of the command:

    ```
    $ echo $?
    ```

    If it is equal to zero (0), the command ran *successfully*, which means that the health of the container is good.

Thus, the `myapache` container indicates when it is working correctly – that is, it is self-managing. This management could delegate to the operating system as part of one of its services. For this, `systemd` must be set up to support services that are started from the user session. Follow these steps:

1. As `root`, enable user lingering by running the `loginctl` command:

    ```
    # loginctl enable-linger acallejas
    ```

2. Create a directory to host the containerized services and change to that directory:

    ```
    $ mkdir -p ~/.config/systemd/containerized-services
    $ cd ~/.config/systemd/containerized-services
    ```

3. Build the configuration files for `systemd` using the `podman generate` command:

    ```
    podman generate systemd --name myapache --files
    ```

    Here's the output:

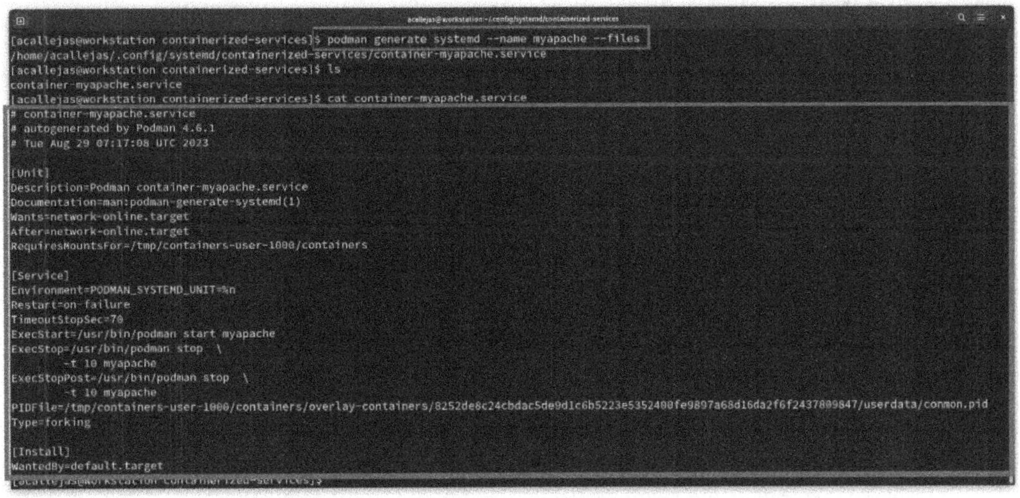

Figure 13.43 – Containerized service configuration file

The preceding command creates the `container-myapache.service` unit file with the configuration for `systemd` to manage.

4. Reload the user's daemons by running the following `systemctl` command:

```
$ systemctl --user daemon-reload
```

5. Enable the user's containerized service by running the following `systemctl` command:

```
$ systemctl --user enable --now ~/.config/systemd/containerized-services/container-myapache.service
```

6. Verify the status of the containerized service by running the following `systemctl` command:

```
$ systemctl --user status container-myapache
```

You should see the following output:

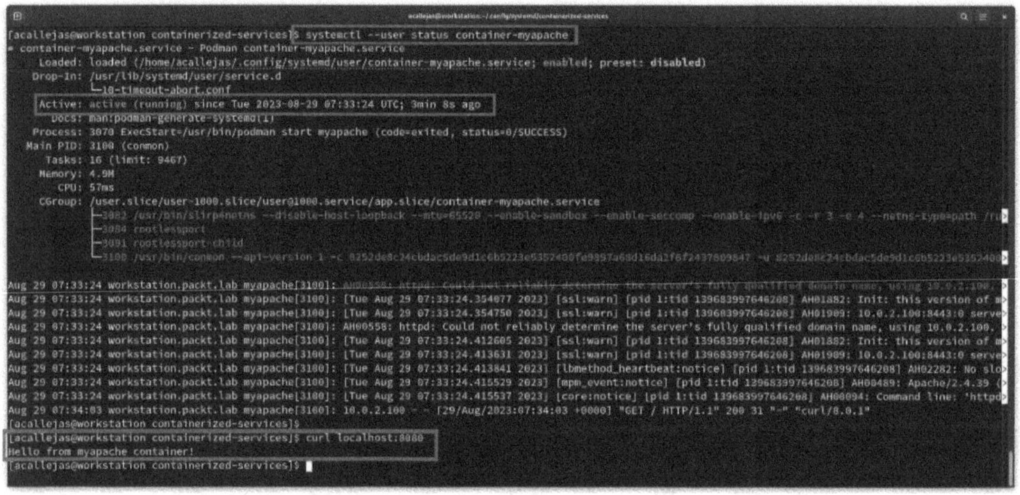

Figure 13.44 – Verifying the containerized service

Finally, verify that the containerized service continues to operate. Use the `curl` command we used previously.

With that, we've learned how to use OCI containers, from their simple use to creating a containerized service that's managed by the operating system.

Fedora Linux implements the use of OCI containers as a way to ease service management. With this bouquet of possibilities, depending on the workload, we can choose a virtual machine, either created with a cloud-based image or created with its installation image traditionally. Alternatively, we can use containers if we only need to deploy a simple service such as `myapache`.

I hope these options can help you improve the performance of your day-to-day tasks as a Linux system administrator.

Summary

In this chapter, we provided a quick overview of the methods for creating a virtual machine. In my opinion, the easiest and fastest way is to rely on the use of pre-built cloud images. In a couple of steps, and with enough practice, we can have them working in a matter of minutes.

Besides that, we used Gnome Boxes as a traditional method of creating virtual machines with an installation image. This method is a bit slower but allows us to customize the guest operating system installation.

Next, we looked at services, where we learned how to use OCI containers implemented by Fedora Linux. This is a simple option for creating containerized services because it gives us the power to customize them so that they meet our needs. For example, we can use them for persistent storage, self-management, or even to delegate a containerized service as a system service managed by `systemd`.

All these tools make up an arsenal that could ease the performance of a Linux system administrator's day-to-day tasks. As we mentioned in *Chapter 10*, "*a good system administrator backs up, automates, and studies in their spare time.*"

Congratulations on making it to the end of this book! I hope you found it useful.

Further reading

To learn more about the topics covered in this chapter, you can visit the following link:

- *Build a lab in 5 minutes with three simple commands*: `https://www.redhat.com/sysadmin/build-lab-quickly`

Index

‹packt›

Packtpub.com

Subscribe to our online digital library for full access to over 7,000 books and videos, as well as industry leading tools to help you plan your personal development and advance your career. For more information, please visit our website.

Why subscribe?

- Spend less time learning and more time coding with practical eBooks and Videos from over 4,000 industry professionals

- Improve your learning with Skill Plans built especially for you

- Get a free eBook or video every month

- Fully searchable for easy access to vital information

- Copy and paste, print, and bookmark content

Did you know that Packt offers eBook versions of every book published, with PDF and ePub files available? You can upgrade to the eBook version at packtpub.com and as a print book customer, you are entitled to a discount on the eBook copy. Get in touch with us at customercare@packtpub.com for more details.

At www.packtpub.com, you can also read a collection of free technical articles, sign up for a range of free newsletters, and receive exclusive discounts and offers on Packt books and eBooks.

Other Books You May Enjoy

If you enjoyed this book, you may be interested in these other books by Packt:

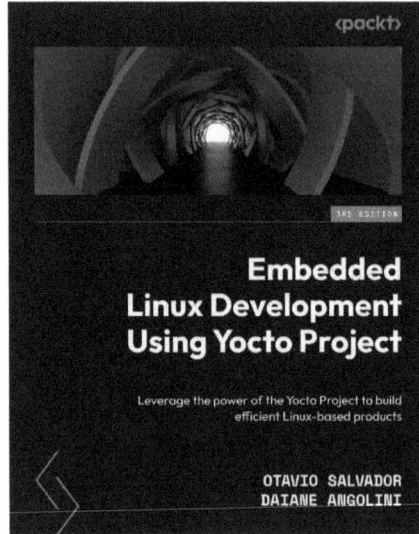

Embedded Linux Development Using Yocto Project - Third Edition

Otavio Salvador, Daiane Angolini

ISBN: 978-1-80461-506-5

- Get to grips with Poky workflows
- Configure and prepare the Poky build environment
- Explore the latest version of Yocto Project through examples
- Configure a build server and customize images using Toaster
- Generate images and fit packages into created images using BitBake
- Support the development process by setting up and using Package feeds
- Debug Yocto Project by configuring Poky
- Build and boot image for BeagleBone Black, RaspberryPi 4, and VisionFive via SD cards
- Explore the use of QEMU to speed up the development cycle using emulation

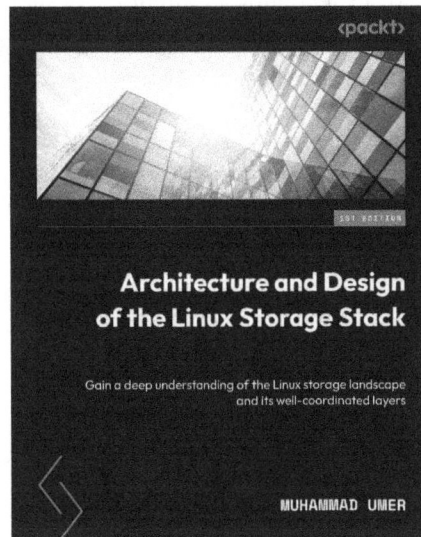

Architecture and Design of the Linux Storage Stack

Muhammad Umer

ISBN: 978-1-83763-996-0

- Understand the role of the virtual filesystem
- Explore the different flavors of Linux filesystems and their key concepts
- Manage I/O operations to and from block devices using the block layer
- Deep dive into the Small Computer System Interface (SCSI) subsystem and the layout of physical devices
- Gauge I/O performance at each layer of the storage stack
- Discover the best storage practices

Packt is searching for authors like you

If you're interested in becoming an author for Packt, please visit `authors.packtpub.com` and apply today. We have worked with thousands of developers and tech professionals, just like you, to help them share their insight with the global tech community. You can make a general application, apply for a specific hot topic that we are recruiting an author for, or submit your own idea.

Share Your Thoughts

Now you've finished *Fedora Linux System Administration*, we'd love to hear your thoughts! Scan the QR code below to go straight to the Amazon review page for this book and share your feedback or leave a review on the site that you purchased it from.

`https://packt.link/r/1804618403`

Your review is important to us and the tech community and will help us make sure we're delivering excellent quality content.

Download a free PDF copy of this book

Thanks for purchasing this book!

Do you like to read on the go but are unable to carry your print books everywhere? Is your eBook purchase not compatible with the device of your choice?

Don't worry, now with every Packt book you get a DRM-free PDF version of that book at no cost.

Read anywhere, any place, on any device. Search, copy, and paste code from your favorite technical books directly into your application.

The perks don't stop there, you can get exclusive access to discounts, newsletters, and great free content in your inbox daily

Follow these simple steps to get the benefits:

1. Scan the QR code or visit the link below

https://packt.link/free-ebook/978-1-80461-840-0

2. Submit your proof of purchase
3. That's it! We'll send your free PDF and other benefits to your email directly

www.ingramcontent.com/pod-product-compliance
Lightning Source LLC
Chambersburg PA
CBHW072006230326
41598CB00082B/6796